AN ANNOTATED

SECONDARY BIBLIOGRAPHY SERIES

ON ENGLISH LITERATURE

IN TRANSITION

1880–1920

HELMUT E. GERBER

GENERAL EDITOR

W. SOMERSET MAUGHAM

JOSEPH CONRAD

THOMAS HARDY

E. M. FORSTER

JOHN GALSWORTHY

GEORGE GISSING

D. H. LAWRENCE

H. G. WELLS

WALTER PATER

G. B. SHAW

THE CONTRIBUTORS

RICHARD B. BIZOT
University of North Florida

FRANCIS L. NYE
University of Minnesota

LAWRENCE SCHRIEBER
Elgin, Illinois

SAMUEL WRIGHT
Colchester, Essex, England

Walter Pater

AN
ANNOTATED
BIBLIOGRAPHY
OF WRITINGS
ABOUT HIM

COMPILED AND EDITED BY

FRANKLIN E. COURT

NORTHERN ILLINOIS UNIVERSITY PRESS
DE KALB, ILLINOIS

Franklin E. Court is an associate professor of English at Northern Illinois University, DeKalb.

Library of Congress Cataloging in Publication Data

Court, Franklin E   1939–
    Walter Pater, an annotated bibliography of writings about him.

    (An Annotated secondary bibliography series on English literature in transition, 1880–1920)
    Includes indexes.
    1. Pater, Walter Horatio, 1839–1894—Bibliography.
I. Title.   II. Series: Annotated secondary bibliography series on English literature in transition, 1880–1920.
Z8664.C68   [PR5136] 016.824'8   78-56125
ISBN 0-87580-072-6

Preface

This volume includes a representative body of criticism on Walter Pater from 1871 through 1973. Included in it are abstracts of critical articles, critical books, reviews of primary works, general appreciations and reminiscences, biographies, scattered references in books and articles, significant letters to editors, chapters in books, introductions to editions of Pater's works, satirical caricatures, critical notes, and certain prefixed notices and prefaces. Doctoral dissertations that are known have been listed, in most instances without any accompanying commentary; master's theses have not been included. Dissertations that have been published subsequently as books are annotated under the title and date of publication.

Some of the items contained here may seem trivial; but the majority, it is hoped, will provide something of solid value for scholars interested in Pater or in any of the many subjects that this bibliography has turned up along the way. I have kept the editorial comments on the works abstracted to a minimum and have tried to avoid completely passing judgment on their quality. The volume is as comprehensive and complete as is realistically possible, though it lays no claim to covering everything that has been written through 1973 on Pater. Omitted purposely are many minute one- or two-line references that say nothing substantive about Pater or simply quote in passing from his works.

A few leads could not be verified; some were verified but could not be located. If the work did exist but cannot be found, that fact is noted in the abstract or the entry. My hope is that the ones not located will eventually be found and included in future supplements. The languages represented here are many, but the list is incomplete. Some foreign language items, such as works in Japanese, were inaccessible or misdated and impossible to find. The Japanese items listed in Rennosuke Ueki's "A Revaluation of Walter Pater," in KWANSEI GAKUIN UNIVERSITY ANNUAL STUDIES, XIV (Nov 1964), 33–48, came to my attention too late to be included here. I also suspect that there may exist a substantial number of works on Pater in the holdings of Eastern European libraries, works that were also inaccessible to us. I do feel confident, however, that most of the substantive items on Pater that are available in the United States and Britain have been included.

Most of the entries listed here have never appeared in any single secondary bibliography on Pater. Much of the initial working bibliography was drawn, however, from Germain d'Hangest's WALTER PATER: L'HOMME ET L'OEUVRE; John Sparrow's bibliography on Pater in NEW CAMBRIDGE BIBLIOGRAPHY OF ENGLISH LITERATURE; Edward S. Lauterbach and W. Eugene Davis's THE TRANSITIONAL AGE: BRITISH LITERATURE, 1880–1920; and the section on Pater in BIBLIOGRAPHY OF MODERN AUTHORS by C. A. and H. W. Stonehill. I also found helpful Lawrence Evans's chapter on Pater in VICTORIAN PROSE: A GUIDE TO RESEARCH and Samuel Wright's A BIBLIOGRAPHY OF THE WRITINGS OF WALTER H. PATER.

All of the entries are listed under the date of first publication. Whenever possible, information on reprints and later revisions or translations has also been included. Omitted from the book are all reviews of secondary works and most editions of letters. With the exception of a few select letters written by people close to Pater that provide important biographical information or by prominent literary figures who acknowledge his impact on various phases of their art, the many general displays of appreciation for him or his works that appeared in letters, particularly from student friends and admirers, have not been included.

ACKNOWLEDGMENTS

The contributors to this volume are listed opposite the title page. Without their generous assistance this work would still be far from completion. The time they have put into the project can never be sufficiently compensated, for work of this nature is seldom adequately rewarded. The work includes numerous hours of reading and abstracting, time-consuming and sometimes futile searches for items, and the additional burden of keeping up with correspondence related to the project. I am sincerely indebted to them.

I would also like to acknowledge the assistance of John Conlon (University of Massachusetts, Boston) who kindly agreed to abstract a series of items on very short notice. Other colleagues who have contributed along the way are Helmut Gerber (Arizona State University), Bernard Richards (Brasenose College, Oxford), and Dale Kramer (University of Illinois). Thanks are also extended to Mary Elizabeth O'Connor Chandler, James K. Chandler, George Craven, and Robert Langbaum (University of Virginia) for help with specific research problems, and to J. Gill Holland (Davidson College), John Haggstrom (University of Minnesota), Gustaaf van Cromphout (Northern Illinois University), Lev Soudek (Northern Illinois University), and Dale L. Clifford (University of North Florida) for generous assistance with translations. Other translators who have earned a debt of gratitude are Rebecca M. Bizot, James H. Gilmore, and Noreen Smith. I would also like to acknowledge the assistance of Maryse You, Chantal Eveillard, and Paul Mornet for help with many French items; Nora Teklenburg for help with the German; Cristina Michelassi and Leandro Toboga for abstracting Italian items; Irene Carr for help with the Spanish; and John T. Paek for his assistance with Japanese.

Many graduate students, student assistants, friends, and family members also contributed their time and effort. Grateful thanks are extended especially to the following: Jaimy Slifka, for her relentless search for newspaper items; G. Randall Colville, Jonel L. Aller, and Nadine N. Morrison, for leg-work and typing; James E. Alderman, Jr., for thorough and intelligent research assistance; Richard B. Bizot, Jr., and John E. Bizot, for proofreading; and Linda Schlafer and Pat Laing for help with the indexes.

One would hardly get a project of this magnitude beyond the works-at-hand stage without the aid of dedicated, knowledgeable librarians and well-equipped libraries. My contributors and I are indebted to the personnel of the Interlibrary Loan Division, University of Minnesota Library, and particularly Erika Flink and Gertrude Battel; also to Robert P. Jones, III, Associate University Librarian, University of North Florida Library; and to Sam T. Huang and Myrtie Podschwit of the Interlibrary Loan Office of the Swen Parson Library, Northern Illinois University. I would also like to acknowledge the gracious assistance of the library personnel at the University of Illinois, Urbana; Memorial Library, University of Wisconsin; the Newberry Library, Chicago; the Chicago Public Library; the British Museum; the British Museum Newspaper Library; and the University of London.

I am grateful to the English Department at Northern Illinois University for recommending me for a sabbatical leave to work on the volume in London; the Northern Illinois University Graduate School, particularly Associate Dean Jon D. Miller and the members of the Graduate School Fund Review Committee, for two generous research grants in support of the project. Thanks are also extended to the Department of Language and Literature, University of North Florida, for material assistance.

Finally, I would like to acknowledge the assistance as translator and abstracter of Abigail Loomis, the graduate research assistant who became so interested in the project that she married the editor.

FRANKLIN E. COURT

Contents

NOTE ON ENTRY STYLE

Titles of Pater's works appear in italic type; titles of his stories, in roman capitals and lower case with quotation marks. Titles of books by other authors, collections of stories and letters edited by other writers, and names of periodicals and newspapers appear in capitals and small capitals. The translations appearing in parentheses are confined to meanings of the phrases; however, it should be noted that the titles of translations are seldom literal ones.

Walter Pater

AN ANNOTATED BIBLIOGRAPHY
OF WRITINGS ABOUT HIM

A Checklist

I. ESSAYS, REVIEWS, PORTRAITS[1]

"Coleridge's Writings," WESTMINSTER REVIEW, 1866; partially rptd with revisions and omissions as "Coleridge" in APPRECIATIONS: WITH AN ESSAY ON STYLE, 1889. A section which was omitted from APPRECIATIONS was printed as "Coleridge the Theologian" in SKETCHES AND REVIEWS, NY, 1919.

"Winckelmann," WESTMINSTER REVIEW, 1867; rptd in STUDIES IN THE HISTORY OF THE RENAISSANCE, 1873.

"Poems by William Morris," WESTMINSTER REVIEW, 1868; partially rptd as "Conclusion" to STUDIES IN THE HISTORY OF THE RENAISSANCE, 1873; another portion of this essay was rev and rptd as "Aesthetic Poetry" in APPRECIATIONS: WITH AN ESSAY ON STYLE, 1889, but was omitted from second and later eds.

"Notes on Leonardo da Vinci," FORTNIGHTLY REVIEW, 1869; rptd as "Lionardo da Vinci," in STUDIES IN THE HISTORY OF THE RENAISSANCE, 1873; generally rptd as "Leonardo da Vinci."

"A Fragment on Sandro Botticelli," FORTNIGHTLY REVIEW, 1870; rptd as "Sandro Botticelli" in STUDIES IN THE HISTORY OF THE RENAISSANCE, 1873.

"Pico della Mirandula," FORTNIGHTLY REVIEW, 1871; rptd as "Pico della Mirandola" in the 1877 ed of THE RENAISSANCE.

"The Poetry of Michelangelo," FORTNIGHTLY REVIEW, 1871.

"Children in Italian and English Design," THE ACADEMY, 1872.

"Aucassin and Nicolette," STUDIES IN THE HISTORY OF THE RENAISSANCE, 1873; rev and included with an account of a thirteenth-century story, "Li Amitiez de Ami et Amile," as "Two Early French Stories" in 1877 ed of THE RENAISSANCE.

---

[1]Reprints that involve a change of title are noted in the entries.

"Luca della Robbia," STUDIES IN THE HISTORY OF THE RENAISSANCE, 1873.

"Joachim du Bellay," STUDIES IN THE HISTORY OF THE RENAISSANCE, 1873.

"Preface," STUDIES IN THE HISTORY OF THE RENAISSANCE, 1873.

"A Fragment on MEASURE FOR MEASURE," FORTNIGHTLY REVIEW, 1874; rptd as "Measure for Measure" in APPRECIATIONS: WITH AN ESSAY ON STYLE, 1889.

"On Wordsworth," FORTNIGHTLY REVIEW, 1874; rev and rptd as "Wordsworth" in APPRECIATIONS: WITH AN ESSAY ON STYLE, 1889.

"The Myth of Demeter and Persephone," FORTNIGHTLY REVIEW, 1876.

"Romanticism," MACMILLAN'S MAGAZINE, 1876; rptd as "Postscript" in APPRECIATIONS: WITH AN ESSAY ON STYLE, 1889.

"A Study of Dionysus I. The Spiritual Form of Fire and Dew," FORTNIGHTLY REVIEW, 1876.

"The School of Giorgione," FORTNIGHTLY REVIEW, 1877.

"Imaginary Portraits 1. The Child in the House," MACMILLAN'S MAGAZINE, 1878; rptd generally as "The Child in the House."

"The Character of the Humourist: Charles Lamb, "FORTNIGHTLY REVIEW, 1878; rptd as "Charles Lamb" in APPRECIATIONS: WITH AN ESSAY ON STYLE, 1889.

"The Marbles of Aegina," FORTNIGHTLY REVIEW, 1880.

"Samuel Taylor Coleridge," introductory essay to selection of Coleridge's poems in Volume IV of THE ENGLISH POETS: SELECTIONS, 1880; rptd with revisions as latter part of "Coleridge" in APPRECIATIONS: WITH AN ESSAY ON STYLE, 1889.

"Dante Gabriel Rossetti," introductory essay to selection of Rossetti's poems in Volume IV, second ed, of THE ENGLISH POETS: SELECTIONS, 1883.

"On 'Love's Labours Lost,' " MACMILLAN'S MAGAZINE, 1885.

"A Prince of Court Painters: *Extracts from an old French Journal,*" MACMILLAN'S MAGAZINE, 1885; rptd generally as "A Prince of Court Painters."

"Amiel's Journal: The 'Journal Intime' of Henri-Frédéric Amiel," THE GUARDIAN, 1886; rptd as "Amiel's 'Journal Intime' " in ESSAYS FROM THE "GUARDIAN," 1896.

"Denys l'Auxerrois," MACMILLAN'S MAGAZINE, 1886.

"Four Books for Students of English Literature," THE GUARDIAN, 1886; rptd as "English Literature" in ESSAYS FROM THE "GUARDIAN," 1896.

"M. Feuillet's 'La Morte,' " MACMILLAN'S MAGAZINE, 1886; rptd as "Feuillet's 'La Morte' " in APPRECIATIONS: WITH AN ESSAY ON STYLE, second ed, 1890.

"Sebastian van Storck," MACMILLAN'S MAGAZINE, 1886.

"Sir Thomas Browne," MACMILLAN'S MAGAZINE, 1886.

"Duke Carl of Rosenmold," MACMILLAN'S MAGAZINE, 1887.

"The Life and Letters of Flaubert," PALL MALL GAZETTE, 1888; rev and enlgd to become "Style," FORTNIGHTLY REVIEW, 1888.

"Robert Elsmere," THE GUARDIAN, 1888.

"Style," FORTNIGHTLY REVIEW, 1888; derived from "The Life and Letters of Flaubert," PALL MALL GAZETTE, 1888.

"The Bacchanals of Euripides," MACMILLAN'S MAGAZINE, 1889.

" 'The Complete Poetical Works of William Wordsworth' with an Introduction by John Morley," "The Recluse by William Wordsworth," "Selections from Wordsworth by William Knight and Other Members of the Wordsworth Society with Preface and Notes," ATHENAEUM, 1889; rptd THE GUARDIAN, 1889; rptd as "Wordsworth" in ESSAYS FROM THE "GUARDIAN," 1896.

"Giordano Bruno. Paris 1586," FORTNIGHTLY REVIEW, 1889; rptd as chap seven, "The Lower Pantheism" in GASTON DE LATOUR, 1896.

"Hippolytus Veiled. A Study from Euripides," MACMILLAN'S MAGAZINE, 1889.

"Shakespeare's English Kings," SCRIBNER'S MAGAZINE, 1889.

"Art Notes in North Italy," NEW REVIEW, 1890.

"On Viol and Flute," THE GUARDIAN, 1890; rptd as "Mr. Gosse's Poems" in ESSAYS FROM THE "GUARDIAN," 1896.

"Prosper Mérimée," FORTNIGHTLY REVIEW, 1890.

"Emerald Uthwart," NEW REVIEW, 1892.

"The Genius of Plato," CONTEMPORARY REVIEW, 1892.

"Raphael," FORTNIGHTLY REVIEW, 1892.

"Apollo in Picardy," HARPER'S NEW MONTHLY MAGAZINE, 1893.

"Some Great Churches in France: 1. Notre-Dame d'Amiens," NINETEENTH CENTURY, 1894; rptd as "Notre-Dame d'Amiens" in MISCELLANEOUS STUDIES: A SERIES OF ESSAYS, 1895.

"Some Great Churches in France: 2. Vézelay," NINETEENTH CENTURY, 1894; rptd as "Vézelay" in MISCELLANEOUS STUDIES: A SERIES OF ESSAYS, 1895.

"Diaphaneitè," MISCELLANEOUS STUDIES: A SERIES OF ESSAYS, 1895.

"Pascal," CONTEMPORARY REVIEW, 1895.

"Imaginary Portraits 2. An English Poet," FORTNIGHTLY REVIEW, 1931.

II. BOOK-LENGTH WORKS

Studies in the History of the Renaissance, 1873; rptd as *The Renaissance: Studies in Art and Poetry,* 1877.

Marius the Epicurean: His Sensations and Ideas. Two Volumes, 1885.

Imaginary Portraits, 1887.

Appreciations: With an Essay on Style, 1889.

Plato and Platonism: A Series of Lectures, 1893.

Greek Studies: A Series of Essays, 1895.

Miscellaneous Studies: A Series of Essays, 1895.

Essays from the "Guardian," 1896.

Gaston de Latour: An Unfinished Romance, 1896 (originally pub in MACMILLAN'S MAGAZINE, 1888).

III. UNPUBLISHED WORKS

"Gaudioso, the Second" [MS., Harvard University]
"Tibalt the Albigense" [MS., Harvard University]

IV. COLLECTED EDITIONS

Edition de Luxe, Lond and NY, 1900–1901. Contents:
    Volume   I—*The Renaissance: Studies in Art and Poetry*
                II—*Marius the Epicurean: His Sensations and Ideas, I*
                III—*Marius the Epicurean: His Sensations and Ideas, II*
                IV—*Imaginary Portraits* and *Gaston de Latour: An Unfinished Romance*
                V—*Appreciations: With an Essay on Style*
                VI—*Plato and Platonism: A Series of Lectures*
                VII—*Greek Studies: A Series of Essays*
                VIII—*Miscellaneous Studies: A Series of Essays*
                IX—*Essays from "The Guardian"*
New Library Edition, Lond and NY, 1910; rptd, NY, 1976. Contents:
    Volume   I—*The Renaissance: Studies in Art and Poetry*
                II—*Marius the Epicurean: His Sensations and Ideas, I*
                III—*Marius the Epicurean: His Sensations and Ideas, II*
                IV—*Imaginary Portraits*
                V—*Appreciations: With an Essay on Style*
                VI—*Plato and Platonism: A Series of Lectures*
                VII—*Greek Studies: A Series of Essays*
                VIII—*Miscellaneous Studies: A Series of Essays*
                IX—*Gaston de Latour. An Unfinished Romance*
                X—*Essays from "The Guardian"*

Introduction

The first convincing effort to place Pater in the context of literary history as a
serious writer of individual achievement appeared in the ACADEMY in 1898, four
years after his death. During his lifetime, critics tended to concentrate on his
moral character, or lack of it, and his subordinate position as a disciple to either
John Ruskin or Matthew Arnold or both. Appropriately, considering the extent of
criticism that has appeared in the past century linking Pater with Arnold, the first
critical reference to Pater recorded in this volume is Arnold's, who in 1871, while
commenting on Pater's "The Poetry of Michelangelo," published in THE
FORTNIGHTLY REVIEW, censured the young critic's judgment.

The extent of Matthew Arnold's and John Ruskin's influence on Pater has
been a consistently controversial issue. In 1896, Edward Everett Hale, Jr., was
one of the first to advise against confusing Pater's views on art with those of
Ruskin or Arnold. And as recently as 1967, Ian Fletcher, echoing advice he
originally offered in his 1959 study of Pater, reiterated his warning against
undervaluing Pater by judging him primarily in relation to Arnold and Arnoldian
culture. Doing so, he suggested, overlooks Pater's importance as a forerunner of
Yeats, Pound, Joyce, and others.

But it was the author of that article in the ACADEMY in 1898 who boldly
urged, in spite of the general consensus, that Pater must be viewed in the context
of a new literary tradition, for he had painstakingly worked out a "creed as large
and austere as that of Carlyle himself." More to the point, the critic noted that
Pater was responsible for setting the tone in prose for a great change that became
apparent in the spirit of English literature around 1870.

Locating Pater's place in the development of both late Victorian and early
modern art and literature has been a major concern of Pater scholars. By 1901, the
publication date of Hale's edition of SELECTIONS, Pater had become a subject for
serious literary study. In 1903, Ferris Greenslet published the first book-length
study, followed in 1906 by A. C. Benson's critical biography and in 1907 by
Thomas Wright's controversial two-volume biography. Frank Harris, in 1906,
felt confident enough about Pater's reputation to assure the literary world that his
place in the history of English letters was secure. By the time the 1910 library
edition of his works appeared, he was viewed as either a decadent threat and

literary "aside" or a minor literary classic. By 1910 his reputation, though still highly controversial, was made.

Of all of his works the one that seems to have had the most impact over the years on his reputation as a critic and aesthetic theorist is *The Renaissance*. In 1873, when it originally appeared, it was summarily dismissed by many, including Mrs. Margaret Oliphant and W. J. Courthope, who reviewed it as the dangerous ramblings of a windy pagan dilletante; most other reviewers saw it, for better or worse, as part of an artistic tradition extending in a line from John Ruskin to the PRB to Swinburne. But after the turn of the century, criticism of *The Renaissance* took on additional dimension as more and more critics, George Saintsbury, A. R. Orage, and G. K. Chesterton, for instance, became aware of Pater's value as a stylist. Finally, in 1929, Norman Foerster concluded that *The Renaissance* was clearly a statement outlining and defending Impressionism. The value of *The Renaissance* as art as well as Pater's reputation, now tested for impressionistic propensities, seemed generally to wane through the 1930s, owing largely to T. S. Eliot's essay "Matthew Arnold and Pater." Following the line advocated earlier in the century by Irving Babbitt, Paul Elmer More, and the "New Humanists," Eliot faulted Pater for having abandoned religion to "the anarchy of feeling," a carefully shaded view of Pater's artistic merit that Eliot had revealed more acrimoniously earlier in 1920 in an essay in which he claimed that Pater appealed to feeble minds.

In 1938, in a PMLA article, Ruth Child argued that the "Preface" to *The Renaissance* had been misunderstood for too long and that Pater was not primarily an Impressionist or an advocate of impressionistic theories. In 1940, in THE AESTHETIC OF WALTER PATER, a pioneering work in Pater criticism, she continued the argument for a renewed look at his artistic and critical value, suggesting that his impressionistic tendencies had been exaggerated all along; in fact, if he advocated any single, dominant position at all it was that careful, objective critical analysis should yield the essence, the formula, of a given artist. She advanced the theory, reinforced more concisely later in 1969 in R. V. Johnson's AESTHETICISM, that Pater's outlook is morally stable because he deals with the timeless ethical problem of "how to live."

Criticism of *The Renaissance* since 1940 and the publication of Child's study has been characterized by an invigorating diffuseness. At the end of the Forties attention focused on the pedagogical value of individual essays in the book: the essay on Botticelli, for instance, was now acknowledged to have been largely responsible for the rediscovery of that painter in the nineteenth century. Pater's value as a scholar of Renaissance art, something earlier critics surprisingly neglected, was also scrutinized and his sources finally investigated. Sir Kenneth Clark argued, in the introduction to a 1961 edition of *The Renaissance,* that Pater probably did not read Jacob Burckhardt's CIVILISATION OF THE RENAISSANCE, a theory that remains controversial. Clark also noted that Pater probably did read Jules Michelet's HISTOIRE DE FRANCE (1835) and, most assuredly, Giorgio Vasari's LIVES. And he added that Pater's comments on fashion in the Giorgione

essay were strikingly similar, perhaps betraying an influence, to Baudelaire's in
UN PEINTRE DE LA VIE MODERNE.

Over the past forty years, critics have also uncovered reasonable cause to
argue that Pater's aesthetic-philosophical concepts developed in *The Renaissance*
and in subsequent works have their roots in the thought of Hume, Darwin, Hegel,
and Newman, as well as John Ruskin, Matthew Arnold, and others. The growing
complexity of the study of Pater's sources was first pointed up in book form in
1933 by Helen H. Young in THE WRITINGS OF WALTER PATER. A REFLECTION OF
BRITISH PHILOSOPHICAL OPINION FROM 1860 TO 1890, followed in 1966 by
Anthony Ward's WALTER PATER: THE IDEA IN NATURE, and in 1969 by David
DeLaura's challenging study, HEBREW AND HELLENE IN VICTORIAN ENGLAND:
NEWMAN, ARNOLD, AND PATER. Studies of the influence of Pater on the works
and theories of Wilde, Symons, George Moore, and Hopkins have consistently
appeared since the turn of the century, one of the most thorough being David A.
Downes's VICTORIAN PORTRAITS: HOPKINS AND PATER, published in 1965. The
extent of Pater's impact on many early modern writers has only recently been
measured and indicates that Pater has had a significant impact on contemporary
artists and contemporary artistic theory. In an essay entitled "Pater as Prophet"
Wendell Harris in 1964 discussed the effects produced by viewing many of
Pater's literary theories against the practices and theories of subsequent
twentieth-century writers, including Nabokov, Woolf, Hemingway, and Faulkner. In another essay published in 1964, Samuel F. Morse discussed at some
length what had only been alluded to by many up to that time, notably the
knowledge that the "Conclusion" to *The Renaissance* spoke directly to Wallace
Stevens, a contention that Harold Bloom and others since have applied to Yeats as
well, at least as it is related to both Yeats's and Stevens's romantic affirmation of
faith in the autonomy of art.

The influence of Pater's thought and techniques on Joyce's ULYSSES and the
character of Dedalus in A PORTRAIT OF THE ARTIST AS A YOUNG MAN has also
interested Joyce scholars, including Robert M. Scotto, who published an essay
in 1973 discussing the relationship between Pater's and Joyce's use of visions and
epiphanies. Recently, Hugo von Hofmannsthal's debt to Pater has received
considerable attention, particularly among continental European scholars. And
during the past thirty years, scholars have consistently linked Pater in critical
essays and books with Heine, Nietzsche, Baudelaire, Mallarmé, Malraux,
Proust, Pascal, Thomas Mann, the "New Criticism," Roger Fry, and Bernard
Berenson. Fry's conception of "visual music" is said to have been anticipated by
Pater's demand in *The Renaissance* that art be free of "mere intelligence." And
in 1960, Sylvia Sprigge, in her biography of Berenson, noted that *Marius the
Epicurean* was no less than Berenson's handbook for living.

Criticism of Pater's fiction has appeared with increased regularity during
the past few decades, but earlier studies, although fewer in number and much
broader in scope, did manage to keep *Marius* and, particularly, the shorter
portraits from obsolescence. Early reviews of *Marius* were generally guarded.

The ambiguous nature of the novel's religious focus engaged many critics and continues to be a subject for study, as attested to by the publication in 1965 of U. C. Knoepflmacher's RELIGIOUS HUMANISM AND THE VICTORIAN NOVEL: GEORGE ELIOT, WALTER PATER, AND SAMUEL BUTLER. There has also been significant disagreement over the years about the classification of *Marius*. One of the first to attempt to type it was J. C. Squire, who called it a confessional novel in 1929. In 1948, Richard Aldington classified it as a prose idyll. R. V. Osbourn in 1951 discussed it as a fictive autobiography paralleling events in Pater's own time. Frederick R. Karl in 1964 called it a prose epic; and both Avrom Fleishmann in 1971 and Curtis Dahl in 1973 discussed its value as an historical novel.

The shorter portraits received little attention, with the exception of occasional reviews and George Saintsbury's insistence that they were not suited to Pater's talents, until the decade of the 1920s when an increase of interest became apparent. Since then much of the criticism of Pater's fiction has dealt with the shorter works. In 1924 John Smith Harrison discussed Pater's reworking of the myths of Apollo and Dionysus in the portraits. His treatment of the mythic figures has prompted many critics, particularly since 1961 and the publication of R. T. Lenaghan's study of "Pattern in Pater's Fiction," to search for visibly structural patterns in the portraits and definitive character types. Louise M. Rosenblatt in 1962 called attention to the possibility of distinguishing a typical "Paterian hero" in the fiction, a hero of sensibility whose origins could be traced at least as far back as Sterne's Yorick. Since then, studies of mythic patterns and Pater's character types have abounded, with particular attention being paid to "The Child in the House," as exemplified by Jan B. Gordon's reading of the "Child" in 1968 as representing an earlier autobiographical version of *Marius* and Richard Bizot's reading of it in 1972 as a reflection of Pater's mental development from childhood to the late 1870s. Gerald C. Monsman in 1967 published PATER'S PORTRAITS: MYTHIC PATTERN IN THE FICTION OF WALTER PATER, the most ambitious study of mythic elements in the fiction in which he argues for the "Paterian hero" as a divine priest of Apollo.

Interest in Pater continues. If the number of items investigating his life and his works that have appeared since 1973, the cutoff date for this volume, is any indication of what critical response will be like in the last two decades of this century, then we can anticipate a continuous outpouring of criticism.

The Bibliography

1871

---

1 [Arnold, Matthew]. "A French Elijah," PALL MALL GAZETTE, 24
 Nov 1871, p. 10.
[Arnold writes, apropos of François Coppée's "Fais ce que Dois":] "First let us
remark the law—the beneficent law—which . . . connects bad poetry with false
moral sentiments. Good rhetoric may consist . . . with false moral sentiments, but
good poetry . . . never. The critic, in many respects so ingenious, who in the last
number of the FORTNIGHTLY REVIEW parallels M. Victor Hugo with Michael
Angelo, will do well to ponder this law, which is eternal." [WP was the critic.
"The Poetry of Michelangelo," FORTNIGHTLY REVIEW, X (Nov 1871), 559–70.]

1872

[No entries for this year.]

1873

---

2 Editor [John Morley]. "Mr. Pater's Essays," FORTNIGHTLY REVIEW,
 nsXIII (April 1873), 469–77; rptd in John Morley, NINETEENTH-
 CENTURY ESSAYS, selected with intro by Peter Stansky (Chicago and
 Lond: University of Chicago P, 1970), pp. 227–36.
Studies in the History of the Renaissance constitutes the most remarkable example
of a movement among younger critics "towards a fresh and inner criticism." Such
criticism, transcending "the futile hubbub" raised by "rival partisans in philos

11

ophy and philosophical theology," signals a "general stir of intellectual energy" in England. In a line with Ruskin, the Pre-Raphaelites, Swinburne, and Morris, WP (his face "averted from theology") raises "aesthetic interest to the throne lately filled by religion." This recent pagan movement is "a protest against the mechanical and graceless formalism of the modern era." WP's book is a wedge driven into "the prodigious block of our philistinism." An occasional "tinge of obscurity" does little to weaken WP's "clear, vigorous, and ordered thought." His writing is marked by "reserve," concreteness, a "subtle and penetrating suggestiveness," and an "abundance of intellectual ideas." WP is "an able and shrewd-witted man of wide culture and knowledge." [Morley tends to soften the severity of WP's Heraclitean premises and to blunt the force of the "Conclusion." E.g.: "Of course this neither is, nor is meant to be, a complete scheme for wise living and wise dying." In private correspondence Morley asked Frederic Harrison to "pardon my light dealing" with WP's "transgressions." EARLY LIFE AND LETTERS OF JOHN MORLEY, ed by F. W. Hirst. Two Volumes (Lond: Macmillan, 1927), I, 240.]

3 "Fine Arts," ATHENAEUM, No. 2383 (28 June 1873), 828–29.
[A short, generally appreciative review of Studies in the History of the Renaissance, more than half of which is devoted to quibbling about where and when the Renaissance began, flourished, and declined.]

4 [Oliphant, Margaret.] "New Books. XIV. Pater's History of the Renaissance," BLACKWOOD's EDINBURGH MAGAZINE, CXIV (Nov 1873), 604–9.
WP's "pretentious volume" is a "mixture of sense and nonsense, of real discrimination and downright want of understanding." WP is a windy dilettante, a failed Ruskin, whose "fantastic criticism" attributes to Botticelli the sentiments of "a delicate Oxford Don in the latter half of the nineteenth century." His misreading of Leonardo seems to reflect "some fundamental incompetence—some impotency of the mind and imagination." The "elegant materialism" of the "Conclusion" may be consistent with the rococo nature of the volume as a whole, but it is nonetheless "a pompous confession of faith," in "bad taste," and a sign of "the decay among us of all true and living art."

5 "Pater's Studies of the Renaissance," SATURDAY REVIEW (Lond), XXXVI (26 July 1873), 123–24.
WP's interest in the Renaissance and his "deification of passion" link him with Rossetti, Swinburne, Burne-Jones, and Sidney Colvin. His idea about a pre-Renaissance in the twelfth and thirteenth centuries is not to be taken seriously. WP's "tone of thought and style of ideas," though not his ideas per se, are Ruskinian. His prose is by turns "florid" and "sugary"; at its worst it is "a train of heated rapture rather than of cool criticism." [The sour tone of the review may reflect its author's disapproval of what he calls WP's "advanced creeds"—those expressed, e.g., in the "Conclusion."]

6 [Pattison, Mrs. Mark] [Lady Dilke.] "Contemporary Literature, Art," WESTMINSTER REVIEW, nsXLIII (April 1873), 639–41; p. 305 in American ed.

Studies in the History of the Renaissance has no value as history. WP studies individuals in isolation, without sufficient reference to their milieu. He perpetuates factual inaccuracies about Leonardo. Although WP's sensibility is fine and his style often radiant, the book's flaws destroy "much of the charm of a charming book, a book which shows a touch of real genius."

7 "Recent Literature," ATLANTIC MONTHLY, XXXII (Oct 1873), 496–98.

Neither WP's manner nor his thinking, in *Studies in the History of the Renaissance,* is like Ruskin's; yet he has acquired the "vice" ("which Mr. Ruskin invented") of practicing "attributive" rather than "interpretive" criticism. Much of what WP attributes to Leonardo reflects essentially his own emotional responses to *La Gioconda*. His main strength is "his clear perception of particular aspects and characteristics" of the Renaissance rather than his perception of the Renaissance as a whole (which tends to be vague).

8 R., H. *"Studies in the History of the Renaissance,"* PENN MONTHLY, IV (June 1873), 424–29.

In *Studies in the History of the Renaissance* WP writes "brilliantly" and "tenderly" about the great revival. Although he "may be wrong in his doctrine, and he certainly is often obscure and mannered in his expression," he is "a remarkable teacher." His interpretation of Leonardo is "acute" but incomplete; it fails to note the religious influence on Leonardo. The study of Pico della Mirandola is the "least satisfactory of the studies"; but "it is poor only by contrast" with the others, which are "charming," "clever," "poetic."

9 [Stillman, W. J.] "The Renaissance," NATION (NY), XVII (9 Oct 1873), 243–44.

Studies in the History of the Renaissance is "fascinating"; but it tells us more about WP than it does about the Renaissance. We must reject WP's dilettantish idea that art is relative. Art is based on principles that not only can but must be defined absolutely. WP makes the common mistake of applying the term *renaissance* to what was, in fact, the decay of art. "Art that looks back ceases to be art, and becomes artifice: a renaissance that is the renewal of dead forms is not a new birth, it is a galvanic resuscitation; and the modern sympathy (like Winckelman's) with the Renaissance so-called, is but a modern abhorrence of life and health, and fondness for death and artifice." WP's book is not unified; its essays must be taken individually on their merits. The essay on Winckelmann is a dilettante's perception of a dilettante; that on Pico Della Mirandola, however, is quite satisfactory. "Generally the essays on literary themes are better than those on artistic." Whatever its faults, the book's "power, individuality, and charm of style" make it worth acquiring.

10 Symonds, J[ohn] A[ddington]. "Art and Archaeology," ACADEMY, IV (15 March 1873), 103–5.

Rightly practised, aesthetic criticism is superior to dogmatic criticism. *Studies in the History of the Renaissance* is "a masterpiece of the choicest and most delicate aesthetic criticism." WP's subtle and original studies of Renaissance figures are generally successful, although his interpretations of Botticelli and Michelangelo are "somewhat over-refined." WP's style is "perfectly suited to his matter and the temper of his mind." [Symonds's quite different private opinion of WP's first book is revealed in THE LETTERS OF JOHN ADDINGTON SYMONDS, ed by Herbert M. Schueller and Robert L. Peters. Three Volumes (Detroit, Mich.: Wayne State UP, 1968), II, 273.]

1874

11 [Art. IV.—Modern Culture], QUARTERLY REVIEW, CXXXVII (Oct 1874), 389–415.

"Poetical prose. . .has made rapid advances in England." WP's criticism in *The Renaissance* is not criticism at all; it is "pure romance." Critics like WP and Symonds are examples of how rejecting "common sense in favour of private perceptions" can make one into a dupe "of quackery and imposture." [Review of *The Renaissance*. Review also incorporates critical estimate of Arnold's LITERATURE AND DOGMA, CULTURE AND ANARCHY, and ST. PAUL AND PROTESTANTISM and Carlyle's SARTOR RESARTUS.]

1875

[No entries for this year.]

1876

12 [Courthope, William John.] "Wordsworth and Gray," QUARTERLY REVIEW, CXLI (Jan 1876), 104–36, espec pp. 132–36; pp. 55–71, espec pp. 69–71 in American ed.

[Toward the end of a long essay that concludes, "we must reject the analytic spirit of Wordsworth, and revive the constructive spirit of Gray," WP is cited as "the most thoroughly representative critic that the romantic school has yet produced."]

The "Conclusion" of *Studies in the History of the Renaissance* exactly describes "that analytical process of the imagination which we have traced in the poems of Wordsworth." "Our sound and manly writers" (e.g., Milton, Addison, Byron, Scott) would have rejected "stuff like this" (i.e., the "Conclusion"). Yet poetry "written to meet this kind of taste" is current in "polite society." Such poetry (e.g., Swinburne's) seductively casts doubt on religion, weaves "a subtle casuistry about matters of morality," and deals with love not as "noble and chivalrous" but as "an epicene something between a physical impulse and an intellectual curiosity." "In common, we believe, with most Englishmen we repudiate the effeminate desires which Mr. Pater, the mouthpiece of our artistic 'culture,' would encourage in society." [The brunt of the essay's attack is reserved for Wordsworth.]

13 [Mallock, William Hurrell.] "The New Republic," BELGRAVIA (Lond), XIX (June–Dec 1876); rptd, anonymously, with revisions, as THE NEW REPUBLIC: OR CULTURE, FAITH, AND PHILOSOPHY IN AN ENGLISH COUNTRY HOUSE (Lond: Chatto & Windus, 1877); rptd (1878); [subsequent editions "By W. H. Mallock"] rptd with slight revision (Lond: Chatto & Windus; NY: Scribner, Welford, & Armstrong, 1878); rptd (Rochester, NY: G. W. Fitch, 1879); rptd (Lond: Chatto & Windus, 1879); (1880); (1881); (1884?); (1889); (1895); (1900); (1902); (1906); (1908); rptd (Lond: Michael Joseph, [1937]); the "new" edition of 1878 rptd with textual and explanatory notes, ed by J. Max Patrick (Gainesville: University of Florida P, 1950).

[Mallock's clever *roman à clef* has interest for WP scholars as a quasi-critical document. Mr. Rose, Mallock's caricature of WP, speaks of two topics: "self-indulgence and art." He raises his eyebrows "wearily"; his manner is "dreamy"; he murmurs in "a languid monotone." His relatively infrequent speeches in Books I and II contain references to "the weariness of creeds," to "life's choicer and subtler pleasures," and to literature's making "life intenser." Most of these early speeches are innocuous rhapsodies, but Mallock's caricature takes on a sharp edge at two points: first, when Rose muses about the aesthetic pleasure of witnessing a melodramatic suicide; second, when he is pointedly attentive to a curly-headed page boy. Rose does not appear in Books III and V, but he takes a central role in Book IV. Here he has an attentive audience, and he develops his ideas at some length. Sometimes he merely appears silly: "when I go to ugly houses, I often take a scrap of some artistic cretonne with me in my pocket as a kind of aesthetic smelling salts." Sometimes he is mildly scandalous: when he offers to buy a copy of CULTES SECRETS DES DAMES ROMAINES. Sometimes he is merely a dilettante: when he discusses the stage effects of ritualistic religious services. But at times he is treated with scarcely a trace of caricature: when he discusses the architecture of the capital of the imaginary New Republic. The Benjamin Jowett figure in the story (Dr. Jenkinson) is repeatedly irritated by, and antagonistic toward, Mr. Rose. At one point the Matthew Arnold figure (Mr. Luke) comes to Rose's defense against

Jenkinson. But Luke's final comment on Rose, said out of Rose's hearing, is condescending praise: "even poor Rose has really some right on his side."

Mallock's book has interest, not only for its frequently able parodies of WP's prose rhythms and for its presentation—even if distorted—of many of the young WP's leading ideas but also for its suggestive hints about WP's reputation in various literary quarters during the years immediately following the publication of *Studies in the History of the Renaissance*. This abstract is based on the 1877 ed.]

> **14** Saintsbury, George. "Modern English Prose," FORTNIGHTLY RE-VIEW, nsXIX (Feb 1876), 243–59, espec pp. 256–57; rptd in THE COLLECTED ESSAYS AND PAPERS OF GEORGE SAINTSBURY, 1875–1920 (Lond & Toronto: Dent & Sons; NY: Dutton, 1923), III, 62–87, espec pp. 82–83; rptd (Freeport, NY: Books for Libraries P; NY & Lond: Johnson Reprint, 1969); rptd in MISCELLANEOUS ESSAYS (Lond: Percival; NY: Scribner's, 1892), pp. 81–113, espec 107–9; rptd (Freeport, NY: Books for Libraries P, 1972).

English prose style has fallen on bad days. The harmful influences have been journalism, novel-writing, scientific study, and the democratic spirit. Even the best of our established modern prose stylists (viz., Ruskin, Arnold, and Froude) are not without limitations. Among younger writers, Swinburne shows promise. WP's *Studies in the History of the Renaissance* "sets the possibilities of modern English prose in the most favourable light, and gives the liveliest hope as to what may await us, if writers . . . should set themselves seriously to work to develop *pro virili* the prose resources of the English tongue." WP's prose is flawless; his mastery is "extraordinary."

1877

> **15** Lefroy, Edward Cracroft. MUSCULAR CHRISTIANITY (Oxford: Slatter & Rose, 1877).

[The published text of a lecture. Not seen. See John Addington Symonds's response to Lefroy in IN THE KEY OF BLUE AND OTHER PROSE ESSAYS (1893).]

> **16** "Notes and News," ACADEMY, XI (24 Feb 1877), 160.

[WP announced as one of four candidates for the Chair of Poetry at Oxford.] "Mr. Pater we hope to see some day in one of the Slade chairs of Fine Art."

1878

17 "Fine-Art Gossip," ATHENAEUM, No. 2658 (5 Oct 1878), 441.
[Announcement that WP's *The School of Giorgione, and Other Studies,* a sequel to *Studies in the History of the Renaissance,* is forthcoming from Macmillan's. The volume was never published. For an account of WP's decision to abort the volume, see LETTERS OF WALTER PATER, ed by Lawrence Evans (Oxford: Clarendon P, 1970), pp. 52–58 and *nn.*]

18 "Notes and News," ACADEMY, XIV (5 Oct 1878), 336.
[Announcement that WP's *The School of Giorgione, and Other Studies,* a sequel to *Studies in the History of the Renaissance,* is forthcoming from Macmillan's. The volume was never published.]

1879

[No entries for this year.]

1880

19 Quilter, Harry. "The New Renaissance; or the Gospel of Intensity," MACMILLAN'S MAGAZINE, XLII (Sept 1880), 391–400.
The original Pre-Raphaelite movement was a healthy attempt to introduce original-ity into art. But by the mid-fifties, Rossetti and other "Oxford men" had corrupted the original ideal. The men responsible for initiating the corruption are Swinburne, Burne-Jones, and WP. This debased "gospel of intensity" also represents a force for social change supported by such followers as William Morris. [For a commen-tary on Quilter's essay, see Lona Mosk Packer's article "William Michael Rossetti and the Quilter Controversy: 'The Gospel of Intensity,' " VICTORIAN STUDIES, VII (Dec 1963), 170–83.]

1881

20 "Mr. Cimabue Brown on the Defensive," BELGRAVIA (Lond), XLV (1881), 284–97.

[Written in the name of the prototype "aesthete," the figure of fun in a number of *Punch* drawings, this curious and interesting document manages both to parody the "aesthetic movement" and to defend it as a serious cultural phenomenon. While Ruskin, Rossetti, and Morris (among others) are referred to by name, WP is not. He seems, however, to have been the model for "Prigsby, . . . the celebrated Oxford aesthetic don who collects hawthorn-pattern porcelain, and supplies us all with good Greek words." Prigsby ("a fellow of St. Catherine's College, Oxford") is mentioned several times in the essay.]

1882

[No entries for this year.]

1883

21 Lee, Vernon [Violet Paget]. "The Responsibilities of Unbelief: A Conversation Between Three Rationalists," CONTEMPORARY REVIEW, XLIII (May 1883), 685–710; rptd in BALDWIN: BEING DIALOGUES ON VIEWS AND ASPIRATIONS (Bost: Roberts Bros, 1886); rptd (Freeport, NY: Books for Libraries P, 1972).
[Vere, one of the three participants in this imaginary conversation, may have been modelled in part on WP. His relativism, his alleged aestheticism, and his troubled unbelief are at least generally reminiscent of WP.]

22 Nicoll, Henry James. LANDMARKS OF ENGLISH LITERATURE (NY: Appleton, 1883); rptd (1888), pp. 440–41.
[Passing references to the publication of WP's *The Renaissance* and the critical reaction to it. Claims that discerning readers see much value in it.]

1884

23 Lee, Vernon [Violet Paget]. EUPHORION: BEING STUDIES OF THE ANTIQUE AND THE MEDIEVAL IN THE RENAISSANCE. Two Volumes (Lond: T. Fisher Unwin, 1884); rptd (Phila: Richard West, 1973); rptd (Folcroft, Pa: Folcroft Library Editions, 1974).

[No references to WP in the text of the book. Dedication: "To Walter Pater, in appreciation of that which, in expounding the beautiful things of the past, he has added to the beautiful things of the present."]

1885

24 Ellis, Havelock. "The Present Position of English Criticism," TIME (Lond), XIII, nsII (Dec 1885), 669–78, espec pp. 674–75; rptd in VIEWS AND REVIEWS: A SELECTION OF UNCOLLECTED ARTICLES, 1884–1932; FIRST AND SECOND SERIES (Bost: Houghton Mifflin; Lond: D. Harmsworth, 1932).

WP is a "true critic" but "not a critic of the first order," because his range is narrow and his criticism is too fixed into a "definite method." Still, WP's "ingenious and almost scientific" method allows him to be marvellously evocative within a narrow range. For him, "there is nothing so good in the world as the soft, spiritual aroma . . . that exhales" from Della Robbia, Mirandola, Botticelli, or du Bellay. If only WP "had not . . . seemed to swoon by the way over the subtle perfumes he had evoked, he might, one thinks, have gone far." [The essay is mainly concerned with Matthew Arnold's harmful influence on English criticism.]

25 Goodwin, Alfred. "Critical Notices: W. Pater, *Marius the Epicurean,*" MIND, X (July 1885), 442–47.

Marius the Epicurean is a continuation, an elaboration, of *The Renaissance* (especially of the essay on Winckelmann). The impression it leaves on the reader is "of hopelessness in regard to systems, mixed with a remarkable religiosity and belief in the individual desire to believe." [The bulk of this review consists of an effort to discover just what Marius and WP are looking for.]

26 Gray, J[ohn] M[iller]. "Literature," ACADEMY, XXVII (21 March 1885), 197–99.

Marius the Epicurean, WP's "most important and sustained work" to date, more than justifies its author's relative silence in recent years. WP's "The Child in the House" was an "initial sketch" for this "true and finished work of art." Although *Marius* does not go far enough in showing that "Epicureanism . . . can be no permanent dwelling-place of the human spirit," still its author goes further than he has before in detailing "the difficulties and weaknesses" of that philosophy. The book's style is flawless. [Well over half of this review consists of summary of or quotation from the novel.]

27 *"Marius the Epicurean,"* ATLANTIC MONTHLY, LVI (Aug 1885), 273–77.

Marius the Epicurean is a book that achieves perfection of a rarefied sort. It is subdued, delicate, subtle, refined—perhaps too refined. It is not particularly successful as a portrait of second-century Roman life.

28 *"Marius the Epicurean,"* PALL MALL GAZETTE, 18 March 1885, pp. 4–5.

Marius the Epicurean "defies classification." It has almost no story, yet "its five hundred pages . . . are far, very far, from being ill-filled." WP's "careful and long-matured scholarship" and his "mastery of English style" make it "a book to be read and re-read."

29 Powers, Horatio N. *"Marius the Epicurean,"* DIAL, VI (Aug 1885), 90–91.

This book is charming, graceful, delicate, profound, exquisite, powerful, instructive, etc.

30 [Sharp, William.] *"Marius the Epicurean,"* ATHENAEUM, No. 2992 (28 Feb 1885), 271–73.

Although WP is "the chief English exponent of the central doctrine of Epicurus," *Marius the Epicurean* is not simple propaganda on behalf of Epicureanism. It makes us view that philosophy seriously, though we are aware of its shortcomings. [Mainly summary of or quotations from *Marius*. There is relatively little direct praise of WP, but the tone throughout is favorable.]

31 Sharp, William. *"Marius the Epicurean. A Review,"* TIME (Lond), XII: nsI (March 1885), 341–54; partly rptd with slight revisions as *"Marius the Epicurean"* in PAPERS CRITICAL & REMINISCENT (Lond: Heinemann; NY: Duffield, 1912), pp. 229–40.

[Similar to Sharp's unsigned review of *Marius the Epicurean* in ATHENAEUM (q.v.) but with more praise of WP's prose. Virtually everything that is omitted from the 1912 reprint is plot summary or quotations from *Marius*.]

32 W[ard], M[ary] A[ugusta] [Mrs. Humphry Ward]. *"Marius the Epicurean,"* MACMILLAN'S MAGAZINE, LII (June 1885), 132–39.

Twelve years ago *The Renaissance* evoked both admiration and antipathy. In essays WP has published since then (e.g., "the masterly essay on Wordsworth"), he has revealed "a steadily widening and developing power." "The Child in the House" (1879) was an unsuccessful departure for WP; its clearly autobiographical content was not sufficiently disguised. *Marius the Epicurean* succeeds, however, where "The Child in the House" failed. It attains the distance and maintains the reserve that we English prefer in our autobiographical writings. Its style has a "subdued and measured charm"; its impressive learning is "deftly handled." The humaneness of its vision is "worthy of George Eliot." Perhaps it is most important as "a wonderfully delicate and faithful reflection of the workings of a real mind," namely WP's. Although its "fundamental argument is really the same" as that of WP's earlier book, *Marius* extends "the Epicurean principle of an aesthetic loss and gain not only to morals, but to religion." It is not, finally, an acceptable philosophy, because it demeans religion by ignoring whatever claim to truth religion may have. In this regard, Clough's honest doubt is preferable. Whatever reservations the reader may have, he will nonetheless cherish this book, "in which a poetical and meditative nature has poured out a wealth of imaginative reflection."

33 Wedgwood, Julia. "Fiction," CONTEMPORARY REVIEW, XLVII (May 1885), 750–51.

WP's attempt to translate nineteenth-century feelings into the terms of the age of Marcus Aurelius, while interesting and not inappropriate, is less than fully successful. *Marius the Epicurean* has "a peculiar charm," but its emphasis is "too purely intellectual" for a novel.

34 [Woodberry, George Edward.] "Ideal Aestheticism," NATION (NY), XLI (10 Sept 1885), 219–21; rptd with slight revisions as "Illustrations of Idealism. III. Mr. Pater on Ideal Aestheticism," in STUDIES IN LETTERS AND LIFE (Bost: Houghton Mifflin, 1890), pp. 98–112; rptd in MAKERS OF LITERATURE (NY & Lond: Macmillan, 1900); rptd (1901), pp. 171–85; and in STUDIES OF A LITTERATEUR (NY: Harcourt, 1921), pp. 3–21.

The title character of *Marius the Epicurean* embodies WP's vision of an ideal form of aesthetic morality. Marius represents a unification of forces that are Roman, southern, and "Catholic" (sensuous and aesthetic forces), with those that are Greek, northern, and "Protestant" (Puritan seriousness and austerity). His receptivity to beauty is so intense and so refined that it amounts to a moral sense. The book, however, is not convincing. We do not really see how this aesthetic morality works nor what good comes from it. Still, there is much in the book that is "profound," "original," and "wise." It bears serious attention.

1886

35 "Contemporary Literature. Belles Lettres," WESTMINSTER REVIEW, nsLXIX (Jan 1886), 594–95.

As an examination of the merits of ancient philosophies and Christianity "tinctured with a sort of select aestheticism," *Marius the Epicurean* is "dreary." The "very vivid and realistic pictures of Roman life, manners, and scenery . . . constitute the real charm of the book." Its style is elegant but at times affected.

36 "Literary Gossip," ATHENAEUM, No. 3050 (10 April 1886), 490.
[Notice that WP is now at work on a romance to be set in sixteenth-century France *(Gaston de Latour)*.]

37 [Repplier, Agnes.] *"Marius the Epicurean,"* CATHOLIC WORLD, XLIII (May 1886), 222–31.

Marius the Epicurean is a "spiritual autobiography," in which the philosophy of WP's *The Renaissance* reappears, but "greatly softened by the corrective hand of time." The sadness that permeates the book, of which WP seems unaware, is owing to Epicureanism's inevitable failure to satisfy our "unquenchable hope" for an afterlife. WP's treatment of early Christianity is "reverent." [Mostly summary of or quotation from the novel; praise for WP is hedged on sectarian grounds.]

1887

38 "Briefs on New Books," DIAL, VIII (Sept 1887), 102.
With the exception of "A Prince of Court Painters," which charms and is as "delicate and graceful" as one of Watteau's paintings, the remainder of *Imaginary Portraits* is made up of portraits that address the "intellect rather than the sympathies." "Denys l'Auxerrois" recalls Hawthorne's "Donatello" and his "Pearl" in SCARLET LETTER, for it too deals with a returning spirit.

39 "Contemporary Literature," WESTMINSTER REVIEW, nsLXII (July 1887), 515.
Imaginary Portraits is "pensive, dreamy, curiously unsubstantial."

40 *"Imaginary Portraits,"* SATURDAY REVIEW (Lond), LXIII (25 June 1887), 920–21.
The style of *Imaginary Portraits* represents an advance upon that of *Marius the Epicurean,* just as the style of *Marius* was an improvement over that of *The Renaissance.* WP's method in *Portraits* is "distinctly synthetic." It works by "gradually adding stroke to stroke, and producing, not so much a successive effect, as in narration, but a combined and total impression, as in drawing." Of the four portraits, the subjects of "A Prince of Court Painters" and "Denys l'Auxerrois" are more interesting than those of the other two. The portrait of Watteau "is a very excellent instance of real realism, instead of the stuff, alternately foul and glaring, which generally goes under that name." "Denys l'Auxerrois" is a skillful adaptation of various elements of the Dionysiac character.

41 Lyster, T. W. "Literature," ACADEMY, XXXI (18 June 1887), 423–24.
These beautiful *Imaginary Portraits,* primarily imaginative but implicitly critical, deal with unfulfilled aspirations, at four points in history, toward "liberty, light, the better part." [Mostly summary of and quotation from the book.]

42 "Pater's *Imaginary Portraits,* " CRITIC, nsVIII (24 Sept 1887), 149.
[Three paragraphs of superlatives for WP's style, thought, and narrative ability—broken only by the comment that "Sebastian Van Storck" evokes "an unpleasant sensation."]

43 [Pattison, Mrs. Mark] [Lady Dilke.] *"Imaginary Portraits*, by Walter Pater, M.A.,"* ATHENAEUM, No. 3113 (25 June 1887), 824–25. These evanescent portraits, like *Marius the Epicurean,* are "images of himself which Mr. Pater sees in the mirror of past days." They reflect "some of the most interesting currents of the thought of the [present] day."

44 Ritchie, D[avid] G[eorge]. "Critical Notices: B. Bosanquet, Hegel's Philosophy of Fine Art," MIND, XII (Oct 1887), 597–601, espec p. 600. WP's "Winckelmann" reveals Hegel's influence. [A one-sentence reference to WP in a five-page article.]

45 Symons, Arthur. "Walter Pater: *Imaginary Portraits,"* TIME (Lond), XVII (Aug 1887), 157–62. The development of WP's style can be traced from the "finished and perfect" style of *The Renaissance* ("the most beautiful book of prose in our literature") to the restrained, more ascetic style of *Marius the Epicurean* and *Imaginary Portraits.* What is really remarkable in his work "is the attention to, and perfection of, the *ensemble."* His works have logical, almost mathematical, precision. *Marius* may be too large to be constructed quite satisfactorily; but the *Portraits* are "quite flawless." "Denys l'Auxerrois," the finest of the portraits, is "a poem in prose." [This essay, extensively reworked, forms the basis for—roughly—the first third of Symons's essay on WP in STUDIES IN TWO LITERATURES (1897). The two essays are distinct enough to warrant separate annotation. This essay incorporates a wide range of comparisons to other artists: Lamb, Tennyson, Baudelaire, Browning, Gautier; in painting, Albert Moore and Meissonnier.]

46 "Two Roman Novels," EDINBURGH REVIEW, CLXV (Jan 1887), 248–67, espec pp. 248–55. *Marius the Epicurean* has almost no plot. Its style is "uniformly monotonous," and its argument is "not seldom . . . unintelligible." Still, it is "often very suggestive and not infrequently interesting." Marius's "healthy growth" toward Christianity is commendable.

47 [Wilde, Oscar.] "Mr. Pater's Imaginary Portraits," PALL MALL GAZETTE, 11 June 1887, pp. 2–3; rptd in Oscar Wilde, A CRITIC IN PALL MALL: BEING EXTRACTS FROM REVIEWS AND MISCELLANIES (Lond: Methuen, 1919), pp. 51–55; rptd in THE COMPLETE WORKS OF OSCAR WILDE, XII: CRITICISMS AND REVIEWS (Garden City, NY: Doubleday, Page, 1923), and THE WRITINGS OF OSCAR WILDE, XII: CRITICISMS AND REVIEWS (NY: Gabriel Wells, 1925), pp. 374–79; rptd in LITERARY CRITICISM OF OSCAR WILDE, ed by Stanley Weintraub (Lincoln: University of Nebraska P, 1968), pp. 57–60. *Imaginary Portraits,* "a singularly attractive book," consists of "a series of philosophic studies, in which the philosophy is tempered by personality." Denys l'Auxerrois "symbolizes the passion of the senses," Sebastian Van Storck "the philosophic passion," and Duke Carl of Rosenmold "the passion for the imaginative world of art." The portrait of Sebastian Van Storck is the most fascinating of the four: "charmingly drawn," a "subtle psychological study." In its rich imagery, "Denys l'Auxerrois" is "like a picture by Mantegna." The portrait of Watteau is "perhaps a little too fanciful." "Mr. Pater is an intellectual impressionist. He does not weary us with any definite doctrine, or seek to suit life to any formal creed. He is always looking for exquisite moments, and, when he has found them, he analyzes them with delicate and delightful art, and then passes on, often to the opposite pole of thought or feeling, knowing that every mood has its own quality and charm, and is justified by its mere existence. He has taken the sensationalism of Greek philosophy, and made it a new method of art criticism." His "curiously ascetic" style is "at times . . . almost too severe in its self-control . . . it is apt to become somewhat laborious. . . . And yet . . . what wonderful prose it is, with its subtle preferences, its fastidious purity, its rejection of what is common or ordinary! Mr. Pater has the true spirit of selection, the true tact of omission. If he be not among the greatest prose-writers of our literature he is at least our greatest artist in prose."

48 [Woodberry, George Edward.] *"Imaginary Portraits.* By Walter Pater," NATION (NY), XLV (28 July 1887), 78–79.
This book illustrates anew WP's "literary individuality" and the "extraordinary distinction" of his style. But it does not come up to the level of his best work, principally because of the uneven quality of the four portraits. "A Prince of Court Painters" is masterly, clearly the best of the four. The other three, lacking substance and point, tend to resemble the work of "Pater's feminine disciple, Vernon Lee."

1888

49 Bourget, Paul. ÉTUDES ET PORTRAITS. II: ÉTUDES ANGLAISES (Studies and Portraits. II: English Studies) (Paris: Alphonse Lemerre, 1888); (1899); rptd "Édition définitive" (Paris: Plon-Nourrit, 1906), pp. 293, 304.
[Flattering, passing references to WP in essays on Pre-Raphaelitism and English aestheticism. The former essay is dated August 1884, the latter 1885.] [In French.]

50 Bradford, Gamaliel, Jr. "Walter Pater," ANDOVER REVIEW, X (Aug 1888), 141–55.
Among WP's works, *The Renaissance* is the root, *Marius the Epicurean* the stem, and *Imaginary Portraits* the flower. This is the order in which they should be read. *The Renaissance* combines "delicate analysis and imaginative sensibility"; but, as

in all of WP's work, the delicacy and subtlety are "too fine-spun," too subjective, the work as a whole too inconclusive. *Marius,* though "not a novel" (having "no plot, no climax, and only one character") is "profound and thoughtful." Its faults are vagueness (the product of WP's subtlety) and a lack of power, vigor, distinctness. It contains marvelous descriptions, however; and its portrait of Marcus Aurelius is superb. Among the *Portraits,* "Duke Carl of Rosenmold" is the least successful; but "Denys l'Auxerrois" and "Sebastian Van Storck" are "perfect." They blend, in unity and harmony, WP's "critical insight and his imaginative sensibility."

51 Moore, George. CONFESSIONS OF A YOUNG MAN (Lond: Swan Sonnenschein, Lowrey, 1888); rptd [in French] in LA REVUE INDÉPEN-DANTE (March–Aug 1888); rptd (Paris: Nouvelle Libraire Parisienne, 1889); rptd (NY: Brentano's, 1901); rvd ed (Lond: T. W. Laurie, 1904); rptd (NY: Brentano's, 1907); rptd (Lond: Boni & Liveright, 1923); rptd (NY: Modern Library, 1925); rptd (Lond: Heinemann, 1928); rptd (Harmondsworth, Middlesex: Penguin Books, 1939); rptd (NY: Capricorn Books, 1959); rptd (Lond: Brown, Watson, 1961); rptd (St. Clair Shores, Mich: Scholarly P, 1971); rptd in variorum edition, ed by Susan Dick (Montreal: McGill-Queen's UP, 1972), pp. 37–38, 41, 42–44, 165–66. [This list of editions is selective. Dick's variorum edition supersedes all others; hence page numbers are cited for that edition only. Moore continually revised the book over a period of thirty-six years, yet the only changes related to WP are comments introduced in the prefaces to the editions of 1904 and 1917.]

My first reading of *Marius the Epicurean* was an awakening; it provided me with "a fourth vision of life." (The first three were provided by Shelley, Gautier, and Balzac.) I always associate *Marius* with MADEMOISELLE DE MAUPIN: both have "the same glad worship of the visible life, the same incurable belief that the beauty of material things is sufficient for all the needs of life." *Marius* proved to be more than a "precious and rare" emotional experience, however. It also taught me that English prose can rise to the level of art. [In the 1904 Preface, Moore reproduces a letter sent to him by WP, which had praised CONFESSIONS in guarded terms.] WP was "the last great English writer," whose *Imaginary Portraits* is "the most beautiful of all prose books." "I give you Pater's letter, for I wish you to read this book with reverence; never forget that Pater's admiration has made this book a sacred book. Never forget that." My opinion of WP now is the same as it was twenty years ago; it shall never change. [According to Dick, "This preface also appeared in DANA in November 1904." Moore includes the same letter from WP in the 1917 Preface, with different commentary.] WP's "rule of life [was] never to separate himself wholly from his art." In all of his waking hours he was composing. This led, though he was really "the most courteous of men," to his apparent coolness toward others. His mind was elsewhere, composing.

1889

52 *"Appreciations*. With an Essay on Style. By Walter Pater," NATION (NY), XLIX (26 Dec 1889), 524.

This collection of essays admirably displays WP's unique sensibility and his "vigorous and highly cultivated intelligence"—especially in the essays on individual authors. The ideas are seldom original, but WP's freshness of treatment makes them worthy of attention. WP's imaginative work is more important than his critical work; yet these essays present him in a "more friendly," a more accessible fashion than do his loftier works.

53 "Mr. Pater's Essays," SPECTATOR, LXIII (21 Dec 1889), 887–88.

WP's mannered style "has sometimes moved us to impatience"; but in *Appreciations* we have only occasionally had the impression that WP was less interested in expressing ideas than he was in impressing us with his writing. The annoyances are there—in the Gallic affectation of the volume's title; in a handful of precious paragraphs and foppish phrases; and especially in "Aesthetic Poetry" (in which WP, "without intending it, almost persuades the plain person to be a Philistine")—but for the most part these essays reveal WP's maturing as a writer. Compared with his earlier work, here "his diction [is] less exuberant" and "his criticism is riper, sounder, and more manly." [Praises "Shakespeare's English Kings," the essays on Rossetti, Wordsworth, Coleridge, Lamb, and Sir Thomas Browne, and especially "the short postcript on Classicism and Romanticism": "the best and most penetrating criticism in the volume."]

54 "Notes on Contemporary Work," CENTURY GUILD HOBBY HORSE, IV (Jan 1889), [unpaginated].

[Commends WP's essay "Style" in FORTNIGHTLY REVIEW.]

55 "Pater's New Essays," ATHENAEUM, No. 3242 (14 Dec 1889), 813–14.

Sixteen years ago, in *The Renaissance,* WP raised criticism to the level of a fine art. His "modulated prose . . . made the splendours of Mr. Ruskin seem exaggerated, . . . the neatness of Matthew Arnold . . . finikin, the orchestration of Carlyle . . . strident." *Appreciations,* WP's second volume of essays, lives up to the standard set by the first, though some changes are noticeable. "Mr. Pater's outlook is larger to-day than it was sixteen years ago"; and his style is emancipated, more natural, less sensuous, more controlled. As a critic, WP is generous and sympathetic, capable of divining the highest intention of the artist whose work he is studying.

56 Paul, C. Kegan. "On English Prose Style," CENTURY GUILD HOBBY HORSE, IV (Jan 1889), 11–26.

WP, Newman, Hardy, and Hesba Stretton reveal the perfection to which language can be brought. Newspapers are corrupting English style. [A lecture delivered in Lond at the Bedford College for Ladies on 10 Oct 1888.]

57 Watson, William. "*Appreciations*. By Walter Pater," ACADEMY, XXXVI (21 Dec 1889), 399–400.

The erstwhile tendency of WP's style toward "honeyed effeminacy" or "mere daintiness" (e.g., in "The Child in the House") is scarcely evident in *Appreciations*. Only "Aesthetic Poetry" strikes a "falsetto" note. The volume as a whole consolidates "its author's fame as one of the most catholic of living critics, and beyond rivalry the subtlest artist in contemporary English prose."

1890

58 A. "New Publications. *Appreciations, with an Essay on Style*," CATHOLIC WORLD, L (Feb 1890), 704–6.

Appreciations is delightful, though "not always easy reading." WP reveals his affinity for "the school of modern aestheticism" in his sympathetic understanding of Morris and Rossetti, in his "devotion to art for art's sake," in his concern for form, in his "sense for the weird and the bizarre," and in his "anxiety to leave all beaten paths and explore new fields of thought and construct new forms of expression."

59 Bainton, George (ed). THE ART OF AUTHORSHIP (NY: Appleton; Lond: J. Clarke, 1890), pp. 229, 292–94; rptd (NY: Appleton, 1891); (1898).

[Conventional praise for WP, introducing a statement attributed to him. The volume is composed of such statements, solicited from a wide variety of writers. WP cites Tennyson and Browning as influences, and calls Newman "our greatest master of prose."]

60 Courthope, William John. "Noticeable Books. 2. *Appreciations*," NINETEENTH CENTURY, XXVII (April 1890), 658–62.

The operative principle of WP's criticism is sympathy. "In his fine perception of the motives of his authors, and in his delicate description of their styles, his *Appreciations* are all that can be desired." The defect of his method is that he does not judge; "he seems to me to flinch from the severe application of critical law." Too many modern writers (e.g., Wordsworth, Coleridge, Lamb, Flaubert, WP) overvalue contemplation, meditation, "being" rather than "doing." The greatest artists (e.g., Homer, Virgil, Shakespeare, Milton, Dante, Addison) understand the importance of action, understand that "Doing, to a greater extent than Being, lies at the foundation of their art."

61 Earle, John. ENGLISH PROSE: ITS ELEMENTS, HISTORY, AND USAGE (Lond: Smith, Elder, 1890); rptd (Lond: Smith, Elder; NY: Putnam's Sons, 1891), pp. 284–85, 337, 349–50, 367–68, 496–97.

"The Latin cast of diction . . . in our day . . . is most ably represented by the artistic pen of Mr. Walter Pater." [Quotes WP several times; conducts a running argument with WP's tendency to make "style" and "diction" synonymous.]

62 "Mr. Pater's Minor Essays," ATLANTIC MONTHLY, LXV (March 1890), 424–27.

[Commends, but does not emulate, WP's "economy in the use of words."]

63 [Oliphant, Margaret.] "The Old Saloon. XXI," BLACKWOOD'S EDINBURGH MAGAZINE, CXLVII (Jan 1890), 131–51, espec pp. 140–45.

WP is an esoteric, overly subtle, wordy purveyor of "learned nonsense." The "elegant Don" is a precious nit-picker, a "refiner of refined gold." "Nothing but a slowly growing climax of intellectual overproduction, and the artificiality of art could have brought him into being." [Review of *Appreciations*. Grudgingly acknowledges some merit in the essays on Wordsworth, Browne, and Shakespeare.]

64 [Pain, Barry Eric Odell.] "The Sincerest Form of Flattery. IV. Of Mr. Walter Pater. Marius at Sloane Street," CORNHILL MAGAZINE, nsXV (Oct 1890), 374–75; rptd in LIVING AGE, CLXXXVII (15 Nov 1890), 411–12; rptd in Barry Pain, PLAYTHINGS AND PARODIES (NY: Cassell, 1892), pp. 21–24.

[A brief parody; amusing fluff. Others parodied on adjoining pages: Kipling, Ruskin, Blackmore, Tolstoy.]

65 "Pater's *Appreciations*," CRITIC, nsXIII (8 Feb 1890), 61–62.

WP's new book "continues the excellent and delicate critical work which has made of his *Renaissance* a classic and of *Marius the Epicurean* a delight. He is one of the daintiest word artists of the day."

66 Richards, C. A. L. "Pater's *Appreciations*," DIAL, XI (June 1890), 37–38.

Appreciations is a disappointment. WP's "style, once so apt and choice and dainty, has become entangled and intricate." It is artificial and over-elaborate, the language "Latinized," the construction "clumsy with contortion."

67 Symonds, John Addington. "Is Music the Type or Measure of All Art?" in ESSAYS SPECULATIVE AND SUGGESTIVE (Lond: Chapman & Hall, 1890), II, 181–96; rptd in one volume (NY: Scribner's Sons, 1894); rptd (1907); rptd (Lond: Smith, Elder; NY: Scribner's Sons, 1907), pp. 335–44; rptd from first ed in two volumes (NY: AMS P, 1970).

In "The School of Giorgione" WP advocates "the opinion that art has a sphere independent of intellectual or ethical intention . . . with lucidity, singular charm of style, and characteristic reserve." But he undervalues the intellectual and spiritual qualities of art; he overvalues its sensuous qualities. Therefore, he fixes upon music as the ideal art. Popular critics, on the other hand (e.g., Matthew Arnold), who tend to overvalue art's intellectual and moral qualities, identify poetry as the ideal art. Both views are "partial and one-sided." "Considered as paradoxes," WP's ideas "have real value"; they serve as correctives to a tendency to over-intellectualize art. Considered in and of themselves, however, they "contradict the utterances of the greatest craftsmen in the several arts": those, e.g., of Milton, Sidney, Shelley, Goethe, Rossetti, Michelangelo, and Beethoven.

68 Wilde, Oscar. "Mr. Pater's Last Volume," SPEAKER, I (22 March 1890), 319–20; rptd as "Mr. Pater's *Appreciations*" in Wilde, A CRITIC IN PALL MALL: BEING EXTRACTS FROM REVIEWS AND MISCELLANIES (Lond: Methuen, 1919), pp. 187–94; rptd in THE COMPLETE WORKS OF OSCAR WILDE, XII: CRITICISMS AND REVIEWS (Garden City, NY: Doubleday, Page, 1923), and THE WRITINGS OF OSCAR WILDE, XII: CRITICISMS AND REVIEWS (NY: Gabriel Wells, 1925), pp. 471–80; rptd in LITERARY CRITICISM OF OSCAR WILDE, ed by Stanley Weintraub (Lincoln: University of Nebraska P, 1968), pp. 61–66; rptd in CRITICS OF THE 'NINETIES, ed by Derek Stanford (Lond: John Baker; NY: Roy Publishers, 1970), pp. 82–87.

WP's "beautiful and suggestive essays on the Renaissance" taught me "what a wonderful self-conscious art the art of English prose-writing really is, or may be made to be. Carlyle's stormy rhetoric, Ruskin's winged and passionate eloquence, had seemed to me to spring from enthusiasm rather than from art. . . . But Mr. Pater's essays became to me 'the golden book of spirit and sense, the holy writ of beauty.' They are still this to me." His new book, *Appreciations,* "is an exquisite collection of exquisite essays, of delicately wrought works of art." Over the years, "the architecture of the style" has become "richer and more complex, the epithet more precise and intellectual." "If imaginative prose be really the special art of this century, Mr. Pater must rank amongst our century's most characteristic artists. In certain things he stands almost alone. The age has produced wonderful prose styles, turbid with individualism, and violent with excess of rhetoric. But in Mr. Pater, as in Cardinal Newman, we find the union of personality with perfection. He has no rival in his own sphere, and he has escaped disciples. And this, not because he has not been imitated, but because in art so fine as his there is something that, in its essence, is inimitable." [On individual essays: "Style" is "perhaps the most interesting, and certainly the least successful" (because too abstract); the essay on Wordsworth is the "finest."]

69 Wilde, Oscar. "The True Function and Value of Criticism; With Some Remarks on the Importance of Doing Nothing: A Dialogue," NINETEENTH CENTURY, XXVIII (July and Sept 1890), 123–47, 435–59, espec pp. 131, 144, 448–49; rptd as "The Critic as Artist," in INTENTIONS (NY: Dodd, Mead, 1894); rptd (Portland, Maine: T. B. Mosher, 1904);

rptd (NY: Brentano's, 1905); rptd as INTENCIONES, trans by Paulo Barreto (Rio de Janeiro: Livraria Imperio, 1957); rptd in Volume VI, THE WRITINGS OF OSCAR WILDE (Lond & NY: A. R. Keller, 1907); in Volume VIII, THE FIRST COLLECTED EDITION OF THE WORKS OF OSCAR WILDE (Lond: Methuen, 1908); rptd (Lond: Dawsons; NY: Barnes & Noble, 1969); in Volume X, THE WORKS OF OSCAR WILDE (NY: Lamb Publishing, 1909); rptd (NY: AMS P, 1972); rptd in Volume IV, THE COMPLETE WORKS OF OSCAR WILDE (NY: Bigelow, Brown, 1921); rptd in INTENTIONS AND OTHER WRITINGS (Garden City, NY: Doubleday, 1961); rptd in INTENTIONS AND THE SOUL OF MAN (Lond: Dawsons, 1969).

One laments the increasing tendency of literature to appeal more to the eye than to the ear. "Even the work of Mr. Pater, who is, on the whole, the most perfect master of English prose now active amongst us, is often far more like a piece of mosaic than a passage in music." The highest criticism is creative. "Who . . . cares whether Mr. Pater has put into the portrait of Monna Lisa something that Lionardo never dreamed of." Whenever I pass that painting in the Louvre, I murmur to myself WP's imaginative reflections upon it. "And so the picture becomes more wonderful to us than it really is, and reveals to us a secret of which, in truth, it knows nothing."

Each of WP's *Imaginary Portraits* "presents to us, under the fanciful guise of fiction, some fine and exquisite piece of criticism, one on the painter Watteau, another on the philosophy of Spinoza." [All references to WP in this dialogue are spoken by "Gilbert," the Wilde persona. Besides the overt references to WP, scattered throughout the essay are echoes and sometimes (unintentional?) caricatures of his ideas and language. For example (on pp. 447–48), "The aesthetic critic, constant only to the principle of beauty in all things, will ever be looking for fresh impressions, winning from the various schools the secret of their charm. . . . "]

1891

70 [Barry, William Francis.] "Neo-Paganism," QUARTERLY REVIEW, CLXXII (April 1891), 273–304; rptd in HERALDS OF REVOLT, STUDIES IN MODERN LITERATURE AND DOGMA (Lond: Hodder & Stoughton, 1904), pp. 271–308.

[A long, learned, and usually judicious argument against "Neo-Paganism": the merely sensuous—and ultimately decadent—tendency of a partial Hellenism. Singled out for strongest attack are Leconte de Lisle, Baudelaire, and (especially) Jean Richepin. English "Neo-Paganism," as exemplified in Arnold, Swinburne, Symonds, and WP, is perceived as relatively unthreatening. "The thoughtful and languorous prose of Mr. Pater" is quoted throughout the essay; and toward its end several of the precepts of the "Conclusion" of *The Renaissance* are flatly denied. (E.g.: " 'To maintain' sensuous 'ecstasy,' if we could, which is impossible, would *not* be 'success in life.' ") But the tone toward WP is consistently respectful. He is viewed more as an observer than a practitioner of "Neo-Paganism." His "delicate sense of the becoming would shrink from contact with" such an "unabashed and ferocious cynic" as Richepin.]

> **71** Yeats, W[illiam] B[utler]. "The Celt in Ireland," PILOT (Boston), 12 Sept 1891, p. 1; rptd as "A Ballad Singer," in LETTERS TO THE NEW ISLAND, ed by Horace Reynolds (Cambridge, Mass: Harvard UP, 1934); (1970), pp. 137–42; rptd (Oxford: Oxford UP, 1970).

"I am . . . writing out on the lawn of an old Irish thatched farmhouse. . . . To talk of books at all on this green clover spotted grass seems sadly out of keeping, unless, indeed, it be some dreamy romance like *Marius the Epicurean,* whose golden sentences, laden as with sleepy sunlight, I have been reading slowly and fitfully since morning. . . . the doctrines I have just been studying in Pater's jewelled paragraphs—the Platonic theory of spiritual beings having their abode in all things without and within us, and thus uniting all things, as by a living ladder of souls, with God Himself—have some relation to those very matters of Irish thought that bring me to Ireland just now."

1892

> **72** Bosanquet, Bernard. A HISTORY OF AESTHETIC (Lond: Swan Sonnenschein; NY: Macmillan, 1892), pp. xiii, 122, 123, 126–27, 129, 239, 464; rptd in *The Renaissance* (Lond: Allen & Unwin, 1904); (1917); (1922); (1934); (1956); rptd (NY: Macmillan, 1934); rptd (NY: Meridian Books, 1957); rptd (Cleveland: World Publishers, 1957); (1961).

WP correctly identifies second- and thirteenth-century foreshadowings of the Renaissance. His "delightful" essay on Winckelmann in *The Renaissance* may keep that important writer's name alive.

> **73** LeGallienne, Richard. "Walter Pater: *Marius the Epicurean*—Third Edition Revised," in RETROSPECTIVE REVIEWS: A LITERARY LOG (Lond: John Lane; NY: Dodd, Mead, 1896), I, 174–81; rptd in *Marius the Epicurean. His Sensations and Ideas* (Portland, Maine: T. B. Mosher, 1900), II, 201–9. [This review of *Marius,* 3rd ed rvd, was apparently first published in Oct 1892. Its place of publication has not been determined, however.]

"Perhaps no book since SARTOR RESARTUS has been read with such a sense of awakening" as *Marius the Epicurean.* And indeed *Marius* may be seen as a needed corrective to SARTOR, with its "sublime factory gospel of work. For the imperative

'Do!' of Carlyle it substitutes the gentle pleading 'Be!' 'Be ye perfect!' " The revisions that WP made for this edition "bear almost painful witness" to his sometimes "maiden-like fastidiousness." There are countless changes of punctuation, a number of changes of chapter headings (some of them improvements, some not), and not a few changes of wording (which are "vexacious," because unnecessary). The substance of *Marius,* however, is unchanged; it remains "one of the most convincing expressions of the inherent priesthood of man."

1893

74 "Books. *Plato and Platonism,*" SPECTATOR, LXX (1 April 1893), 422–23.
Plato and Platonism is "a very fine and delicate" work of scholarship. WP's reading of Plato is excellent in most respects, though we disagree with his view that the Platonic ideas represent "a kind of abstract Polytheism," and "we think that Mr. Pater sympathizes a little more with Plato as an unsatisfied searcher after truth than he does with Plato as a spiritual moralist of the highest rank." "One of the best characteristics of Mr. Pater's book is that he translates . . . Plato's theory, with the greatest freedom and vivacity, into its true modern equivalents."

75 Campbell, Lewis. "Pater's *Plato and Platonism,*" CLASSICAL REVIEW, VII (June 1893), 263–66.
Plato and Platonism, the "last and largest of Mr. Pater's 'Appreciations,' " is "a brilliant critical essay" as well as a "symphony in prose." WP's range of learning, which he draws upon for illustration and analogy, is dazzling. "Mr. Pater is essentially a poet"; his "refined aesthetic sensitiveness is blended with a quiet intensity of religious feeling." As an "Essayist," rather than a "mere interpreter," WP may be forgiven a number of "trivial flaws": discrepancies, oversights, and errors of translation. He underestimates "the Puritanism of the *Republic*"; he places more emphasis on Beauty (as opposed to Goodness and Truth) than Plato himself does. *Plato and Platonism* is not the last word on the subject; indeed, it has relatively few original ideas. "But it is not the less a solid gain to possess this bright and genial exposition of truths which we have long potently believed."

76 "Contemporary Literature. Philosophy and Theology," WESTMINSTER REVIEW, nsLXXXIII (April 1893), 447–48.
Plato and Platonism is lucid and charming, "far from dry and formal, though . . . sufficiently systematic." WP effectively translates Plato's ideas into modern equivalents.

77 Dodgson, Campbell. "Literature: *Plato and Platonism,*" ACADEMY, XLIII (15 April 1893), 317–18.

In *Plato and Platonism* WP emphasizes the attractions of a " 'dry,' Dorian beauty, chastened severe." WP's prose is "quiet and austere mainly, matching the Dorian mode." [More concerned with Plato than with WP.]

78 Ellis, E[dwin] J[ohn]. *"Plato and Platonism,"* BOOKMAN (Lond), III (March 1893), 186–87.

Plato and Platonism brings to life "the personalities of the different platonic and pre-platonic philosophers"—as if "described from the standpoint of a sympathetic biographer." "Platonism is shown as though it were a thing of yesterday—a sort of Oxford Movement." WP is vivid without being merely fanciful. The style is "loose and wandering"; "nevertheless, the book is full of a stimulating charm."

79 [Johnson, Lionel.] "Reviews. The Spirit of Plato," SPEAKER (Lond), VIII (28 Oct 1893), 469–70; rptd as part of "Mr. Pater upon Plato," POST LIMINIUM: ESSAYS AND CRITICAL PAPERS BY LIONEL JOHNSON, ed by Thomas Whittemore (Lond: Elkin Mathews, 1911), pp. 1–10; rptd (NY: Kennerley, 1912); 1912 ed rptd in facsimile (Freeport, NY: Books for Libraries P, 1968). [The POST LIMINIUM essay supposedly consists of two reviews written by Johnson. One is the review cited above; the other is said by Whittemore to have appeared in the WESTMINSTER GAZETTE for 2 March 1893, but no review of WP's *Plato and Platonism* was found for that date. The WESTMINSTER GAZETTE review has not been located.]

Plato and Platonism is a scholarly book, but not of the dry, conventional sort. It is also a work of the imagination. WP wrote these lectures for Oxford undergraduates. "How excellent a thing for them," and for the readers of this book, "that they should have their Plato at least presented to them, vitalised for them, by a writer who to an admirable erudition joins just that intuitive sympathy which recreates, reanimates, the great things of a world gone by!" WP's "sense of the values of words" distinguishes his reading of Plato. The book reveals a depth of humanity in a writer "whose name is sometimes taken in vain by lovers of an absolutely heartless art."

80 "Literature. *Plato and Platonism,"* CRITIC, nsXX (1 July 1893), 1–2.

Plato and Platonism is a "remarkable," a "delightful," even an "inspiring," book: "a successful attempt to set forth the spirit of the Greek philosopher." Its plan is "orderly and logical." WP demonstrates "very clear insight and a subtle understanding; . . . both sympathy and breadth of view." His style, however, while "rich, sensuous, and musical, . . . is anything but a good style." It is too musical, too baroque, to be easily read.

81 "Logroller" [Richard LeGallienne]. STAR, 23 Feb 1893, p. 2; rptd as "Walter Pater: *Plato and Platonism,"* in RETROSPECTIVE REVIEWS: A LITERARY LOG (Lond: John Lane; NY: Dodd, Mead, 1896), I, 224–29.

Even the appearance and feel of WP's books are imbued with "that gracious union of the austere and the sensuous so characteristic of Mr. Pater's writing." This altogether beautiful book is doubly charming because it retains evidence that these essays were originally lectures. We hear the sound of WP's voice; and "this intimate accent" is "curiously seductive."

82 Mabie, Hamilton W. "The Dialogues of Plato as Literature," OUT-LOOK (NY), XLVIII (9 Sept 1893), 465–66.

The value of *Plato and Platonism* "is not that of philosophical interpretation, but of reproduction of the atmosphere and background of the Platonic thought." The focus is literary rather than philosophical. [Reviews *Plato and Platonism* and Jowett's translation of THE DIALOGUES OF PLATO; deals with WP's book favorably but briefly. Plato's eminence as a literary artist and Jowett's skill as a translator receive most of the attention.] Compared with Jowett's book, WP's is "lighter but very interesting."

83 [McDaniels, J. H.] "Pater's *Plato and Platonism*," NATION (NY), LVII (30 Nov 1893), 413–14.

"To Mr. Pater, in an eminent degree, philosophy is a spirit to live with, not a piece of property to lay upon one's shelf; and his learning, which is the growth of leisurely acquisition pursued *con amore*, he uses as an instrument—as a spell to evoke the figures of the past and make them live to our duller eyesight and imagination." [Favorable review of *Plato and Platonism*; mostly summary.]

84 McLaughlin, Edward T. LITERARY CRITICISM FOR STUDENTS (NY: Holt, 1893), p. 203.

WP's own writing is occasionally too studied; but what he has to say here about style is nonetheless worth attending to. [Pp. 204–10: excerpts from WP's "Style"; p. 235: study notes for the reader regarding "Style."]

85 "New Books. *Plato and Platonism*," MIND, II (April 1893), 251.

Plato and Platonism "is delightful reading throughout." [Brief, largely favorable notice; mostly descriptive.]

86 *"Plato and Platonism,"* ATHENAEUM, No. 3412 (18 March 1893), 339–40.

In *Plato and Platonism*, the virtues of WP's style and manner are effectively turned to an uncharacteristically "technical and scholastic subject." It is a literary rather than a philosophical study. WP's enthusiasm for the austere, Dorian temper is perhaps surprising, but it is welcome.

87 Shorey, Paul. *"Plato and Platonism,"* DIAL, XIV (April 1893), 211–14.

Plato and Platonism "is the first true and correctly proportioned presentation of Platonism that has been given to the general reader." WP "has brought Plato into intelligible relation to the life and thought of his time, has clearly apprehended the chief elements of his complex personality, the distinctive note of his genius, and so has interpreted the work from within."

88 Stevenson, Robert Louis. [Interview], THE CHRISTCHURCH, NEW ZEALAND PRESS, 24 April 1893, [not seen].
[A notice of the interview was published in J. C. Furnas, VOYAGE TO WINDWARD: THE LIFE OF ROBERT LOUIS STEVENSON (1951). Stevenson is supposed to recall the impressions that *The Renaissance* made on him at the time of its publication.]

89 Symonds, John Addington. "Edward Cracroft Lefroy," in IN THE KEY OF BLUE AND OTHER PROSE ESSAYS (Lond: E. Mathews & J. Lane, 1893), pp. 87ff, espec 92–94; rptd (NY: Macmillan, 1896); rptd (NY: AMS P, 1970). [A shorter version of this essay, containing no reference to WP, appeared under the same title in NEW REVIEW, VI (1892), 341–52; rptd in LIVING AGE, CXCIII (23 April 1892), 250–55.]
[Quotes at length from, without directly responding to, Edward Cracroft Lefroy's attack upon "pseudo-Hellenism" in "Muscular Christianity." According to Symonds, the attack "is mainly directed against Mr. Pater and myself, and to some extent also against Matthew Arnold." The most interesting phrase he quotes is "Pater-paganism and Symonds-sophistry."]

90 Symonds, John Addington. "The Lyrism of the English Romantic Drama," in IN THE KEY OF BLUE AND OTHER PROSE ESSAYS (Lond: E. Mathews & J. Lane; NY: Macmillan, 1893); rptd (1896), pp. 241–64, espec 253; 1893 Lond ed rptd in facsimile (NY: AMS P, 1970).
WP has noted, "with his usual felicity of phrase," an example (in MEASURE FOR MEASURE) of the English romantic dramatists' habit of condensing the essence of a play into a song.

91 Symons, Arthur. "The Decadent Movement in Literature," HARPER'S NEW MONTHLY MAGAZINE, LXXXVII (Nov 1893), 858–67; rptd in DRAMATIS PERSONAE (Indianapolis: Bobbs-Merrill, 1923).
WP's "prose is the most beautiful English prose which is now being written." His "reticence" sets his style apart from the floridness of a Goncourt; "but how far away from the classic ideals of style is this style in which words have their color, their music, their perfume, in which there is 'some strangeness in the proportion' of every beauty!" *The Renaissance* "raised criticism almost to the act of creation." *Marius the Epicurean* and *Imaginary Portraits* exhibit "that morbid subtlety of analysis, that morbid curiosity of form," characteristic of the decadent movement. In WP's small *oeuvre* "there is not a page that is not perfectly finished, with a conscious art of perfection. In its minute elaboration it can be compared only with goldsmith's work—so fine, so delicate is the handling of so delicate, so precious a material." [This influential essay deals primarily with French literature: the Goncourts, Verlaine, Mallarmé, Maeterlinck, Huysmans, etc. Symons cites WP and Henley as English analogues, pp. 866–67.]

92 "Talk About New Books. 4.—*Plato and Platonism*," CATHOLIC WORLD, LVII (April 1893), 139.
[Brief, favorable, but inconsequential notice.]

1894

93 B[ussell], F[rederick] W[illiam]. "Walter Pater," OXFORD MAGAZINE, XIII (17 Oct 1894), 7–8; "From a sermon preached in Brasenose College Chapel on Sunday last"; rptd as pamphlet, IN MEMORIAM W.H.P., signed "F.W.B." ([Oxford: Horace Hart, 1894]).
WP led an "ascetic and simple life." "The entire interest of his later years was religious; not as some would put it, ecclesiastical." He was responsible in university affairs. He was tolerant, modest, accessible, polite, hospitable. [This solemn tribute, by a close friend, emphasizes WP's "child-like simplicity." It aims to correct the "false impressions" about WP the man "which certain passages of his books" may have fostered.]

94 Carpenter, Edward. HOMOGENIC LOVE, AND ITS PLACE IN A FREE SOCIETY (Manchester: Labour Press Society, 1894), pp. 9–10; rptd as DIE HOMOGENE LIEBE UND DEREN BEDEUTUNG IN DER FREIEN GESELLSCHAFT, trans by H. B. Fischer (Leipzig: M. Spohr, 1895); rptd as "The Homogenic Attachment," in THE INTERMEDIATE SEX (Lond: Swan Sonnenschein, 1908); 2nd ed (1909), pp. 39–82, espec 45, 47; rptd in SEXUAL HERETICS: MALE HOMOSEXUALITY IN ENGLISH LITERATURE FROM 1850 TO 1900, ed by Brian Reade (Lond: Routledge & Kegan Paul, 1970), pp. 324–46, espec 327–28.
[An early "gay lib" document. Cites in passing WP's "Winckelmann" and "the interesting story of Amis and Amile (thirteenth century), unearthed by Mr. W. Pater from the BIBLIOTHECA ELZEVIRIANA."]

95 C[otton], J. S. "Obituary. Walter Pater," ACADEMY, XLVI (11 Aug 1894), 102.
The "youthful ardour" of WP's early Cyrenaicism "was redeemed by the philosophic simplicity of his mature years." [Primarily a factual account of WP's life and career, with conventional praise of "his sense of duty," etc.]

96 "The Crier." "The City of Books," PALL MALL BUDGET, 12 July 1894, p. 13.
"The Child in the House" is one of the "loveliest things Mr. Pater has written, full of his own incommunicable dignity and sweetness." [The occasion for the comment was the publication of a limited edition of 250 copies of "The Child in the House" by Mr. Daniel at Oxford.]

97 Dyer, Louis. "Walter Pater. Oxford, August 1, 1894," NATION (NY), LIX (23 Aug 1894), 137–39.
[A sympathetic, unoriginal account of WP's life and career; repeatedly quotes from WP's writings in portraying WP. Contains a number of factual inaccuracies: "Coleridge's Writings" is misdated; *The Renaissance* is mistitled, etc.]

98 Gosse, Edmund. "Walter Pater: A Portrait," CONTEMPORARY RE-VIEW, LXVI (Dec 1894), 795–810; rptd in LIVING AGE, CCIV (19 Jan 1895), 151–63; and ECLECTIC MAGAZINE, CXXIV (1895), 103ff; rptd with minor revision in CRITICAL KIT-KATS (Lond: Heinemann; NY: Dodd, Mead, 1896), pp. 241–71; rptd (NY: Scribner's Sons, 1914); rptd in SELECTED ESSAYS, by various authors (Lond: Heinemann, 1928), pp. 25–58; rptd (Freeport, NY: Books for Libraries P, 1968).

Accounts of WP's life, at the time of his death, were filled with inaccuracies. This essay, written with "the encouragement and help of the surviving members of his family," attempts to set the record straight. [Pp. 796–805 comprise a detailed account of WP's ancestry and life; in pp. 802–5 Gosse speaks from his personal acquaintance with WP.] "When I had known him first he was a pagan, without any guide but that of the personal conscience; years brought gradually with them a greater and greater longing for the supporting solace of a creed. His talk, his habits, became more and more theological, and it is my private conviction that, had he lived a few years longer, he would have taken orders and a small college living in the country." [Pp. 805–7 describe WP's method of composition and attempt to assess his style. Pp. 807–10 attempt to define (and through numerous anecdotes, to illustrate) WP's personality and temperament.] "The perennial conflict in his members, between his exquisite instinct for corporeal beauty on the one hand and his tendency to ecclesiastical symbol and theological dogma on the other, is the secret, I think, of what made the character of Pater so difficult for others to elucidate, in some measure also so painful and confusing for himself. He was not all for Apollo, nor all for Christ, but each deity swayed in him, and neither had that perfect homage that brings peace behind it." [Partisan, and not without error itself.]

99 Hammond, W[illia]m. "Reviews of Books: *Plato and Platonism,*" PHILOSOPHICAL REVIEW (Boston), III (1894), 77–81.

In *Plato and Platonism,* WP comes to Plato "as an art lover"; his treatment of Plato's aesthetics is valuable. This is not WP's most readable book, however, partly because the book has "an academical air," partly because WP's translations from the Dialogues are disappointing. [A conventional review, largely favorable.]

100 Johnson, Lionel. "The Work of Mr. Pater," FORTNIGHTLY REVIEW, LXII: nsLVI (Sept 1894), 352–67; and ECLECTIC MAGAZINE, CXXIII (1894), 504ff; rptd in POST LIMINIUM: ESSAYS AND CRITICAL PAPERS BY LIONEL JOHNSON, ed by Thomas Whittemore (Lond: Elkin Mathews, 1911), pp. 19–42; rptd (NY: Mitchell Kennerly, 1912); rptd (Freeport, NY: Books for Libraries P, 1968).

WP's devotion to the service of art was austere, passionate, and self-disciplined. His "reverent study of things rare and fine" has about it an "air of tranquillity and serene accomplishment." In the perception of beauty he was a kind of mystic. "The perpetual wondering joy in the messages brought by beautiful things, through their visible forms, was a kind of worship to him." Certainly he was no dilettante. In his work there is "no dreamy toying with rich and strange expressions," "no languorous playing with things of beauty, in a kind of opiate dream." The "living energy of his scholarship" was too vital, his "piercing power of vision" too exacting for that.

> **101** LeGallienne, Richard. "Walter Pater: died July 30, 1894," in RETROSPECTIVE REVIEWS: A LITERARY LOG (Lond: John Lane; NY: Dodd, Mead, 1896), II, 136–41. [This essay was apparently first published in Aug 1894. Its place of publication has not been determined, however.]

WP is a writer "destined to rank as a classic along with Sir Thomas Browne and Charles Lamb." He is "one of those writer's writers": not widely read by the general public, but influential "at second or perhaps tenth hand." "Some found his teaching enervating and his criticism thin." Some found his style "mannered and very sugary." Some thought him not "manly." Granted that his doctrines were sometimes half-truths. Granted that he was subjective, even idiosyncratic. Still, his writings contain "considerable spiritual and intellectual significance"; and above all they are beautiful. He "is to be regarded first and foremost as an artist." As a study of spiritual development, abounding in "subtle psychological observations," *Marius the Epicurean* "stands alone." Moreover, "for sheer beauty, glamour, fragrance . . . where in English literature is there a book like it?" WP rivalled Matthew Arnold's "comprehensiveness of appreciation," though he was not Arnold's equal as a critic. He was less of the mainstream than Arnold. "Arnold was all for the 'moral idea' in literature; Pater was, broadly speaking, for the *l'art pour l'art* conception of it."

> **102** "Mr. Walter Pater," SATURDAY REVIEW (Lond), LXXVIII (4 Aug 1894), 118–19.

WP's style lacks "readiness and flexibility"; it borders on the precious; it bears "the blemish of mannerism"; "his Muse is not only daintily, but too tightly, shod." But WP's work also stands as "a perpetual protest against the slipshod, the *banal*." WP's interests were narrow, tending (especially early in his career) toward the bizarre and (one of his favorite words) the "strange." Despite his limitations, however, he was "absolutely unique" and "perfectly original." Moreover, he was a sound and serious scholar. "His criticism never left us where it found us; it was rich in ideas which we might accept or reject, but which compelled us to think."

> **103** "A Note on Walter Pater. By One Who Knew Him," BOOKMAN (Lond), VI (Sept 1894), 173–75.

WP was retiring and reserved. Though not "self-absorbed," he "had lost touch with the world early in life, and was always striving to regain that contact." He was methodical and precise; he prized exactitude. Not a forceful man, he influenced students subtly and for the good. His private life was uneventful, without scandal. "He had no leanings to the madness which marks much of the Decadence."

104 "Obituary. Mr. Walter Pater," TIMES (Lond), 31 July 1894, p. 10.
WP was a learned scholar and a serious stylist, though some have found his style
too "opulent and luscious." He was an influential teacher, though his influence on
"youthful minds of a particular caste" was perhaps not always "wholesome."

105 "The Obituary Record. Walter Pater," NEW YORK TIMES, 1 Aug
1894, p. 5.
WP was a writer of high and noble purpose; "the soul of humanity is revealed" in
his work. He was "an excellent scholar," but "his gracefulness veiled his solemnity." His style faultlessly reproduced his impressions, and these impressions are
"inimitable." He was not widely popular, but "his admirers . . . worshipped him."

106 O'Hagan, Archibald [Hugo von Hofmannsthal]. "Walter Pater,"
DIE ZEIT (Vienna), 17 Nov 1894, pp. 104–5; rptd with minor revisions in
Hofmannsthal, GESAMMELTE WERKE IN EINZELAUSGABEN, PROSA I
(Complete Works in a Single Edition, Prose I) (Frankfort: S. Fischer,
1950), II, 235–40; rptd (1956), II, 202–6.
The Renaissance reveals WP's greatness as a critic, even though some of his flights
of interpretive fancy are overextended. WP brings us in contact with a strange
world and makes us feel in harmony with it. When one understands his symbolism,
one understands the soul of his work. There is something unhealthy in his
Imaginary Portraits. He makes an ideal of the aesthetic way of life, but it is as
dangerous as opium. *Marius the Epicurean* is scholarly but lifeless; its characters
are not convincing human beings. It is the work of a naive person whose view of
what life is like is narrow. [Misidentifies *Portraits* as WP's second book and
Marius as his third.] [In German.]

107 *"Plato and Platonism.* By Walter Pater," POPULAR SCIENCE
MONTHLY, XLV (May 1894), 132.
[A brief review, which sketchily summarizes and scarcely evaluates WP's book.]

108 Sharp, William. "Some Personal Reminiscences of Walter Pater,"
ATLANTIC MONTHLY, LXXIV (Dec 1894), 801–14; rptd as "Personal
Reminiscences of Walter Pater," in PAPERS CRITICAL & REMINISCENT, ed
by Mrs. William Sharp (Lond: Heinemann; NY: Duffield, 1912), pp.
187–228.
"There are few more autobiographical writers" than WP, though his works contain
little direct autobiography. His books amount to a biography of his "inner life."
The reason for his "extreme interest in all youthful, unconventional, or unusual
life was that Pater himself had never been joyously young, and that he lacked the
inborn need as well as the physical energy for adventurous life." WP's "ideals of
conduct were Spartan rather than . . . Epicurean"; he prized austerity in thought
and expression, and in life itself. "He was a thinker first, and a rare and distinguished stylist by virtue of his thought." [Sharp depicts, through anecdote, the

private WP. He attacks the stereotyped view of WP and makes him seem human, though eccentric.]

109 S., T. B. "Mr. Walter Pater," ATHENAEUM, No. 3484 (4 Aug 1894), 161–62.

WP "formed an ideal of life and art for himself, and pursued it with conscientious devotion." He was a distinguished and original scholar and writer, and a conscientious teacher, though he was not always fortunate in his disciples. [Contains a conventional account of WP's life and a conventional appraisal of his career and reputation. Mistakenly claims that WP wrote "Winckelmann" at age seventeen.]

110 S[tickney], J[oseph] T[rumbull]. "Book Notices. *Plato and Platonism,*" HARVARD MONTHLY, XVIII (May 1894), 134–36.

Plato and Platonism is "startlingly incomplete. It contents itself with vague sketches here and there of the great mind it purports to study." Still, WP's "belabored style insinuates itself" with a "strange fascination." The book "is a somewhat deformed *Marius, the Epicurean";* but WP's style, more mannered than ever, is seductively beautiful.

111 Titchener, E. B. "Walter Horatio Pater," BOOK REVIEWS, II (Oct 1894), 201–5.

[Recollections of WP by "one of the scant half-dozen Brasenose undergraduates" who heard WP's lectures on Plato and Platonism in their original form. Interesting for its account of how WP was perceived by an intelligent undergraduate: with awe, as "the incarnation of Art."]

112 "Walter Pater. By an Undergraduate," PALL MALL GAZETTE, 2 Aug 1894, p. 3.

[Trivial recollections by a student of WP's. Recalls his "patriarchal manner" and "playful conservatism."]

113 "Walter Pater," CRITIC, nsXXII (11 Aug 1894), 93–94.

[Unimportant obituary, containing standard praise. Consists mainly of an extended quotation from an article previously published in THE PALL MALL BUDGET.]

114 "Walter Pater," DIAL, XVII (16 Aug 1894), 84–85.

"Since the deaths of Matthew Arnold and Cardinal Newman, at least, Pater has been the greatest of English prose-writers." [Brief obit.]

115 Waugh, Arthur. "London Letter," CRITIC, XXV (1 Sept 1894), 145–46.

WP's "scattered writings" will be collected by Mr. Shadwell. There is talk as well about a memoir of WP, consisting of a series of appreciations by various friends.

1895

116 [Barry, William Francis.] "Latter-Day Pagans," QUARTERLY RE-
VIEW, CLXXXII (July 1895), 31–58, espec pp. 31–32, 42–43, 46–58;
and LIVING AGE, CCVI (21 Sept 1895), 707–25; rptd in HERALDS OF
REVOLT: STUDIES IN MODERN LITERATURE AND DOGMA (Lond: Hodder
& Stoughton, 1904), pp. 309–42.

The lives and careers of John Addington Symonds and WP illustrate and embody
the "aesthetic movement which has been with us these thirty years" and the
influence of which is so much to be lamented. Symonds was "a self-absorbed
dilettante." Marius the Epicurean, whom we assume to be WP in disguise, is a sort
of nobler, wiser, happier Symonds. WP's earliest writings advocated "a doctrine
fatal to men": a self-indulgent philosophy of sensation. *Marius the Epicurean*
seems to be a recantation. Its hero is "self-discipline personified." Similarly, in
Greek Studies and *Plato and Platonism,* WP "has turned completely round."

Latter-day paganism is a decadent humanism. It is, "like the Renaissance, which,
on a limited scale, it has striven to imitate," a "false Platonism." Its devotees, such
as Symonds and WP, have been willing to "sacrifice the Good to the Beautiful,"
willing to sacrifice substance for form. Although Symonds and WP (the greater of
these "two distinguished writers") managed to extricate themselves from a
poisonous dilettantism, "still it is melancholy to remember how many have
followed them along slippery paths, not turning back when they turned, but going
on . . . towards the great deep." [Written in a kind of latter-day Carlylese.]

117 Beerbohm, Max. "Be It Cosiness," PAGEANT (Lond), I (Dec 1895
[dated 1896]), 230–35; rptd as "Diminuendo," in THE WORKS OF MAX
BEERBOHM (Lond: John Lane, 1896); rptd (1921); (1923), pp. 129–38;
rptd (NY: Scribner's Sons, 1896), pp. 153–65; rtpd (Lond: Heinemann,
1922); rptd (NY: Dodd, Mead, 1922); rptd in WORKS AND MORE (Lond:
John Lane, [1930]); rptd in THE INCOMPARABLE MAX (Lond:
Heinemann; NY: Dodd, Mead, 1962), pp. 59–66; rptd in AESTHETES AND
DECADENTS OF THE 1890's: AN ANTHOLOGY OF BRITISH POETRY AND
PROSE, ed by Karl Beckson (NY: Vintage, 1966), pp. 67–73.

When I was a freshman at Oxford in 1890, my tutor "laughed when I said that I
wished to attend the lectures of Mr. Walter Pater." And I was more than a little
disappointed when I first saw that "small, thick, rock-faced man." I had never
admired WP's style; he treated English "as a dead language." But I had been
fascinated by *Marius the Epicurean*, "mainly as a tale of adventure"; and I went up
to Oxford with expectations modelled on "the coming of Marius to Rome." I was
bitterly disillusioned, for Oxford "had lost its charm and its tradition." Then I
realized that "abandonment of one's self to life," as WP counseled, was "impos-

sible for to-day." So I have decided to shun all but intellectual " 'sensations,' 'pulsations,' and 'exquisite moments.' " "I shall contemplate the world" without being of it. "I shall write no more. Already I feel myself to be a trifle outmoded. I belong to the Beardsley period."

118 Brown, Horatio [Robert] F[orbes]. JOHN ADDINGTON SYMONDS: A BIOGRAPHY COMPILED FROM HIS PAPERS AND CORRESPONDENCE (Lond: John C. Nimmo; NY: Scribner's Sons, 1895), II, 246, 321; rptd, One Volume (Lond: 1903).

[Quotes from two of Symonds's letters which criticize WP's style as having "a peculiarly disagreeable effect upon my nerves—like the presence of a civet cat" (1885). "I tried Pater's *Appreciations* to-day, and found myself wandering about among the 'precious' sentences, just as though I had lost myself in a sugar-cane plantation" (1890).]

119 Dodgson, Campbell. "Literature. Greek Studies," ACADEMY, XLVII (16 March 1895), 229–30.

WP's studies of Greek life, literature, and art are seductively beautiful, filled with strange and evocative allusions. Some of his interpretations may be questionable, but the charm of his "intensely personal" manner more than compensates for any such flaws.

120 Escott, T[homas] H[ay] S[weet]. "Some Oxford Memories of the Prae-Aesthetic Age," NATIONAL REVIEW (Lond), XXIV (Oct 1895), 232–44.

In the early 1860s WP was "a most painstaking, sympathetic, and impressive teacher." "His life . . . was tranquil, his manner shy." His later development into the "high priest of the 'Renaissance' " cannot be accounted for in terms of the Oxford of those days. [Although WP is referred to on almost every page, there is remarkably little about him.]

121 G[osse], E[dmund]. "Pater, Walter Horatio," DICTIONARY OF NATIONAL BIOGRAPHY, ed by Sidney Lee (Lond: Smith, Elder; NY: Macmillan, 1885–1901), XLIV; reissued (Lond: Smith, Elder, 1908–9), XV, 458–60; rptd (Lond: Oxford University, 1921–22); (1937); (1949–50).

[Primarily a factual account of WP's life; unreliable on bibliographical matters. Contains some interesting commentary on WP. The biographical sections are culled from Gosse's 1894 essay on WP in the CONTEMPORARY REVIEW, q.v.] *Marius the Epicurean*, "an apology for the highest epicureanism," was both WP's most important work and the most admirable product of "modern humanism." "His books are singularly independent of influences from without; they closely resemble one another, and have little relation to the rest of contemporary literature."

122 Hale, Edward E[verett], Jr. "The New Books. Walter Pater's Last Volume," DIAL, XIX (16 Nov 1895), 279–81.

Over the course of his publishing career, WP's style changed considerably, and so did his thinking. His style grew less trenchant, more modulated, more exacting, more complex. It is difficult to generalize about changes in his thought; but certainly *Marius the Epicurean,* while consistent with *The Renaissance,* is markedly different from it in tone and temper. WP probably did not reject so much as simply leave behind his earlier thinking. His later work, particularly, "tends to make one believe that he was himself advancing from the ground on which he had once felt secure, advancing cautiously, slowly"—though toward what is never very clear.

123 Lang, Andrew. "Mr. Pater's *Greek Studies,*" ILLUSTRATED LONDON NEWS, CVI (9 March 1895), 299.

WP's book is not history, nor is it comparative mythology. He gives an idealized, "a prettified picture of Greek faith and custom." He ignores the "ruffianly element of Sparta." He takes us not to Greece but to "a Hellas of dreams," of romance. WP's province is art, not science. His book "is full of pretty and even poetic ideas," but it is uninteresting to anyone who wants facts. [Lang cheerfully acknowledges both that he is unsuited to review this book and that he has reviewed it unfairly.]

124 "Literature. *Greek Studies: A Series of Essays,*" ATHENAEUM, No. 3513 (23 Feb 1895), 244–45.

Printed together for the first time, these essays ("studies" is a word "somewhat too heavy for these delicate meditations") constitute a unified, "a harmonious and satisfying," volume. "Pater's life was one continuous study of beauty . . . ; and if his interpretations of a myth or a sculpture seem far-fetched," it should be added that his special imaginative skills lead to insights far beyond the reach of a mere researcher. WP may not have been a master stylist, but he had a gift for suiting words to thought. He is "Ruskin without his rhetoric."

125 "Literature. *Miscellaneous Studies: A Series of Essays,*" ATHENAEUM, No. 3554 (7 Dec 1895), 783.

WP's literary executor, Mr. Shadwell, has exercised tact in this selection from among WP's minor works. The previously unpublished "Diaphaneitè" is interesting for its prefiguration of WP's mature style and thought. The essays are of uneven value, but the volume is a welcome one.

126 M., A. "New Books. Mr. Pater's *Miscellaneous Studies,*" BOOKMAN (Lond), IX (Nov 1895), 58.

This "representative collection" of WP's writings reflects the range of his interests. "Diaphaneitè" is as interesting as it is remarkable ("Was his mind ever crude, that he could produce this at twenty-four?"). The "Imaginary Portraits" represent the weakest part of the volume, for they show the least of WP's individuality. They tend toward "the merely pretty." "It is in his criticism that his highest imaginative qualities are revealed, where he is lightest, brightest, and also most profound."

127 [McDaniels, J. H.] "Pater's *Greek Studies,*" NATION (NY), LX (13 June 1895), 464–65.

Greek Studies reveals "the precision of the scholar without pedantry, the taste of the artist without technicality." [Concludes with a brief survey of WP's career; favorable to WP throughout.]

128 "Mr. Pater's *Miscellaneous Studies,*" SPECTATOR, LXXV (28 Dec 1895), 937–38.

This volume reminds us of WP's recurring concerns (e.g., his "half-sensuous, half-aesthetic theories of religion"), of his strengths (e.g., his "keen perception of beauty"), and of his weaknesses (e.g., his "over-loaded," mannered, and "somewhat artificial" style). While "Diaphaneitè" shows but "slight traces of his more mature writings," its "wistful desire for perfection" contains "the germ of that nature that is fully pictured in *Marius the Epicurean.*"

129 [Preface to WP's] "Pascal," THE CONTEMPORARY REVIEW, LXVII (Feb 1895), 168–81.

[The preface included by the eds notes that there is good reason to believe that WP "would not have greatly extended" this essay on Pascal. WP was at work on the essay when he died. The essay, the editors add, "is printed here, with as close adherence to his text as possible, from his scored and tormented original MS."]

130 Ramsay, W. M. "New Books. *Greek Studies,*" BOOKMAN (Lond), VIII (April 1895), 18.

The most important essays in *Greek Studies* are those on Greek mythology and religion. The view WP presents is "luminous and impressive—though perhaps one-sided." It needs to be supplemented with the views of Lang and Fraser. The essays on Greek art are less valuable. WP has depended for his information too much on the work of Overbeck.

131 "Reviews. Mr. Pater's *Greek Studies,*" SATURDAY REVIEW (Lond), LXXIX (9 Feb 1895), 191.

Greek Studies demonstrates that WP "added something of the poet to the critic." He had "some of the poet's unifying power" and "some of the poet's delight in a chastened richness of details." This volume is "a reconstruction of genius." WP's style, however, is too unvarying, too controlled.

132 Shadwell, Charles L. "Preface," *Greek Studies: A Series of Essays,* by Walter Pater (Lond & NY: Macmillan, 1895); rptd (1911), v–ix; rptd (Oxford; Blackwell; NY: Johnson Reprint, 1967); (1973).

WP perceived an "essential unity" in the many-sided Greek character. The essays on Greek sculpture are part of a series that, had WP lived, he intended to expand into a separate volume. Fragments of the other essays he intended to write are among his papers. WP's "distinction does not lie in his literary grace alone, . . . but in the depth and seriousness of his studies" as well. [Gives publishing histories of the essays collected in *Greek Studies.*]

133 Shadwell, Charles L. "Preface," *Miscellaneous Studies: A Series of Essays,* by Walter Pater (Lond & NY: Macmillan, 1895); rptd (1910), v–xii; rptd (Oxford: Blackwell; NY: Johnson Reprint, 1967); (1973).
Miscellaneous Studies has no unifying principle. If WP had lived, he would have revised some of the essays. [Contains an incomplete list of WP's published writings.]

134 [Sharp, William?]. *"Greek Studies,"* REALM, I (25 Jan 1895), 417–19.
"Unity is pre-eminently the characteristic" of WP's work. His method of composition was subordinate to the "law of organic development." All that is most restrained in WP's style can be found in this volume. [The author includes a passage on style that he claims was written by WP in a letter to him. He also notes that "The Bacchanals of Euripides" was probably contemporaneous with WP's "Study of Dionysus" and his essay on Demeter and Persephone (1876) but was certainly written by 1878 though not published until 1889. Germain d'Hangest (WALTER PATER: L'HOMME ET L'OEUVRE, 1961) identifies Sharp as the author.]

135 Verrall, A[rthur] W[oollgar]. "Pater's *Greek Studies,"* CLASSICAL REVIEW, IX (May 1895), 225–28.
WP misinterprets Euripides. Especially questionable is his view that in the BACCHAE Euripides recants his earlier views.

1896

136 "Books and Authors. Walter Pater's Last Essays," OUTLOOK (NY), LIII (25 Jan 1896), 160.
WP, Matthew Arnold, and Ruskin were the three "great critics of our time." WP shared with the other two an interest "in art, not for itself alone, but in its relation to life." Indeed, WP's "real interest in actual life," his "feeling for concrete humanity," surpassed that of the other two. Arnold's view of "literature as a sort of guide to conduct" was "largely intellectual." Ruskin saw "all art as didactic." "But Pater always sought for the actual people who had produced any artistic thing; he always strove to see the artist behind and in his work." This is particularly evident in his later work, as *Miscellaneous Studies* reveals. His early interest in art's capacity "to give the highest quality to the passing moment" gave way to an interest in the "moral quality" of style, "the formative power of good style." And WP's own style underwent significant change. His later writing works by "suggestion, . . . conjecture, . . . approximation," rather than by "clear, direct statements." His later style is colloquial and "very human"; he speaks "to the reader as a friend to a friend."

45

137 Dodgson, Campbell. *"Miscellaneous Studies,"* ACADEMY, XLIX (8 Feb 1896), 110–12.

"Apollo in Picardy" is "a fantastic but beautiful story, told in Pater's lightest manner." The other two imaginary portraits in *Miscellaneous Studies* are "somewhat morbid and gloomy." "Diaphaneitè" is "severely abstract" and obscure. [There are brief assessments of the other contents of the volume.]

138 *"Gaston de Latour,"* CRITIC, nsXXVI (5 Dec 1896), 359.

Gaston de Latour "is a book to be read three times—once for its deep and searching thought, once for the poignant beauty of the pictures which pass before us, and once again for the music of the style." Its publication softens, while it underscores, our regret at WP's untimely death. [Mainly plot summary.]

139 *"Gaston de Latour: An Unfinished Romance,"* ATHENAEUM, No. 3599 (17 Oct 1896), 518–19.

Gaston de Latour, if completed, would have shown how the skepticism of a Montaigne "might be subdued and overcome by the spirit" of Christianity. This much can be inferred from the book's obvious similarities to *Marius the Epicurean.* What we actually have, however, is but "a fine fragment, or, rather, a collection of fine fragments." The treatment of Montaigne "is an excellent example of Pater's exquisite power of seizing the essential thought of a philosophy, and rendering it again in picturesque phrase and discriminating epithet." WP's style is at its best in this volume: "easier and less elaborate" than ever before.

140 Hale, Edward E[verett]., Jr. "The Work of Walter Pater," BOOK REVIEWS, IV (July 1896), 69–73.

Seen in retrospect, *The Renaissance* does not provide an accurate version of WP's ideas. In the later 1870s he began to modify his views. "The School of Giorgione" is "a last consideration of art for art's sake." *Marius the Epicurean* both epitomizes his earlier work and suggests the direction of his later work. *The Renaissance* saw art "as a solace in the presence of almost impending death"; *Marius* saw art as "the means of conceiving a reasonable and noble life." WP became increasingly aware of art's potential as "a moulding, a formative force in life." Finally, in *Plato and Platonism,* WP emphasized the refining, disciplining, chastening effect that art could have on life. He resembled Ruskin and Arnold in thinking of art as an element in life; but his notion of art as discipline should not be confused with Ruskin's conception of art as a moral force or with Arnold's conception of art as an intellectual force.

141 Jacobus, Russell P. "The Blessedness of Egoism. Maurice Barrès and Walter Pater. Part First," FORTNIGHTLY REVIEW, nsLIX (Jan, March 1896), 40–57, 384–96.

WP and Barrès are examples of the modern hedonist, a kind of egoist. WP was the born aesthete. "He possessed probably the most thorough aesthetic culture of his time"; and he possessed it innately. Barrès, on the other hand, had to achieve the aesthetic view; he "was driven to egoism by his morbid sensitiveness." He had more passion and irony than WP; but he lacked WP's serenity, his "evenly-sustained gravity," and his urbanity. WP was "a Keats in prose . . . a Keats with health, maturity, and a placid indifference to passion." His secret was a rare "conjunction of wonderfully delicate sensibilities with abundant vitality, perpetual well-being." Sometimes, when his work is purely analytical, his writing becomes "strangely contorted, intricate, obscure." Then, rather than suggesting Keats, "he frequently suggests Mr. Herbert Spencer." And occasionally his work has "a touch of foppery and affectation." At its best, however, his criticism has "a wonderful breadth"; it reveals "the most delicate taste, and the keenest sensibilities of our time. Never . . . has a more admirable genius been devoted to aesthetic criticism." "He brought aesthetic hedonism to its perfect type."

142 Lee, Vernon [Violet Paget]. RENAISSANCE FANCIES AND STUDIES (NY: Putnam's Sons; Lond: Smith, Elder, 1896), pp. 255–60; rptd (Lond: John Lane, 1909), pp. 255–60.

WP "began as an aesthete, and ended as a moralist." *The Renaissance,* despite its technical excellence, left readers with "a sense of caducity and barrenness." It contained, however, the germ of WP's mature thought. WP's "inborn affinity for refined wholesomeness" led him eventually to articulate, "in the midst of aesthetical anarchy, . . . and with subtle and solemn efficacy, the old Platonic and Goethian doctrine of the affinity between artistic beauty and human worthiness." His "spiritual evolution" parallels "that of his own Marius." He became an exponent "of art, not for art's sake, but . . . for the sake of life—art as one of the harmonious functions of existence."

143 LeGallienne, Richard. PROSE FANCIES: SECOND SERIES (Chicago: Herbert S. Stone; Lond: John Lane, 1896), pp. 166–69; rptd (Chicago: 1897); rptd (NY: Duffield, 1906).

WP's Sebastian van Storck illustrates an unfortunately common modern type: a temperament "hypnotised by the Infinite."

144 M., A. "Mr. Pater's *Gaston de Latour,*" BOOKMAN (Lond), XI (Nov 1896), 41–42.

WP makes the past real to us, in *Gaston de Latour,* not by obvious or crude means but by gentle hints and suggestions. His method is true as well as artful. The development of the title character's soul is fascinating. The portraits of Ronsard, Montaigne, and Bruno are "finished." The style is WP's "own style at its best, which had every quality save vivacity."

145 Mosher, Thomas B. [Introduction to WP's] "Joachim du Bellay: A Renaissance Study," BIBELOT, II (1896), [301–2].

To WP was given "a clairvoyant sense of the imperial Past."

146 Mosher, Thomas B. "Note," "Preface," *Essays from the Guardian by Walter Pater* (Portland, Maine: Pvtly Ptd, 1896), pp. [v]–vii, xi–xii.

WP contributed nine articles to the GUARDIAN. The Rothenstein portrait "is here given for the first time." In ATHENAEUM, 12 June 1897, eleven of WP's uncollected articles are cited by an anonymous reviewer.

147 "Mr. Pater's *Miscellaneous Studies,*" SATURDAY REVIEW (Lond), LXXXII (1 Aug 1896), 107–9.

The faults of WP's style should be seen as the necessary result of "the peculiar subtlety with which he apprehended and expressed things." His style is exactly "expressive of the peculiar cast of his mind" and thus meets the truest test of style. More than any other critic of human life, WP possessed "the power of disengaging the rare, the peculiar quality, of this or that work of art, this or that personality, this or that circumstance or occasion: no one ever approached human life with a keener sense of the subtlety of its colours, its lights and shadows, its complexity, its evasiveness." [Only nominally a review of *Miscellaneous Studies.*]

148 "The New Art-Criticism," QUARTERLY REVIEW, CLXXXIV (Oct 1896), 454–79, espec pp. 454, 462.

The Renaissance studies of WP, "a man . . . remarkable for his attainments and culture," were weakened by his ignorance of "the writings of Morelli and his followers." WP's essay on Botticelli contributed to interest in that painter. [Two sentences on WP in a twenty-six page essay.]

149 "Pater's *Greek Studies,*" SPECTATOR, LXXVI (20 June 1896), 876–77.

Greek Studies shows WP "at his best as a writer. He was first and last an aesthetic critic of a high order. And his characteristic and peculiar merit is that he can deal subtly with things that are in their nature subtle and elusive; that he can interpret the mystical, or the suggestive, or the symbolical without losing himself or his reader in the merely vague." His self-conscious, experimental style has its pros and cons; but it is well-suited to do what he does here. The studies of Dionysus and Demeter and Persephone represent "a brilliant effort to revivify and recreate" old myths "for the modern reader." WP works "imaginatively, not with the cold handling of modern science." "Hippolytus Veiled," however, is "over-fanciful and unduly romantic . . . ; it is not so much a study of Euripides' play as a set of variations on the same theme."

150 "Pater's Last Essays," NATION (NY), LXII (9 April 1896), 291–93.
WP was at his best in the criticism of art (he was "a far safer and less whimsical guide than Mr. Ruskin"). His literary criticism is always interesting; but one feels that WP was never so consumed by his subject as when he wrote about art (e.g., in his early Renaissance essays—his best work). When he was less caught up with his subject, he became too self-conscious; his style became too artificial and contrived. "Apollo in Picardy," for example, is but "a pretty bit of moonshine" (though it does "demonstrate that prose is not necessarily prosaic"). All in all, *Miscellaneous Studies* is a welcome collection; its essays "are so many codicils to his studies in art or in literature." The clearly autobiographical "The Child in the

House" is "unique and indispensable": "it sums up all the peculiarities of his style and manner, as well as of his temperament."

151 "Pater's Unfinished Romance," SATURDAY REVIEW (Lond), LXXXII (17 Oct 1896), 421.

Gaston de Latour is "a chain of remarkably ingenious and subtle essays" on Renaissance France. It exhibits WP's characteristic method of portraiture: starting with "a single fact or condition, and then cautiously, almost furtively," constructing a likeness based as much on imaginative as on scholarly insight. In *Gaston,* more than in any of his other works, "the pictorial quality" of WP's fancy is seen to advantage.

152 Saintsbury, George. A HISTORY OF NINETEENTH CENTURY LITERATURE (1780–1895) (Lond & NY: Macmillan, 1896), pp. 398–401.

WP's "exceedingly refined and carefully guarded Hedonism" represented an "advance" on Arnold and a "heretical deviation" from Ruskin. His controversial style, at its best in *The Renaissance,* was "a distinct and remarkable experiment . . . in English prose." *Marius the Epicurean* was easily the best of his later books; *Imaginary Portraits* was an effort in a form not suited to his talents.

153 Saintsbury, George. "Walter H. Pater," in ENGLISH PROSE SELECTIONS, ed by Henry Craik (Lond & NY: Macmillan, 1896), V, 747–50.

WP was a master, unparalleled in his time, of the "architecture of the sentence." As prose stylist he is "worthy, not indeed of an unqualified, but of a decided admiration." His style is at its best in *The Renaissance, Marius the Epicurean,* and some parts of *Appreciations,* the style of *Imaginary Portraits* is "extremely unequal, and sometimes even slipshod."

154 Shadwell, Charles L. "Preface," *Gaston de Latour: An Unfinished Romance.* By Walter Pater (Lond & NY: Macmillan, 1896, 1910), v–vii; rptd (Oxford: Blackwell; NY: Johnson Reprint, 1967); (1973).

Gaston de Latour, "if completed, would have been a parallel study of character to *Marius the Epicurean:* the scene shifted to another age of transition, when the old fabric of belief was breaking up, and when the problem of man's destiny and his relations to the unseen was undergoing a new solution." One surmises that WP "deliberately abandoned" the book because he was "dissatisfied with the framework which he had begun." Of WP's writings, "nothing more remains . . . in a shape sufficiently finished for publication." [With notes on the text of the book.]

155 Symons, Arthur. "A Literary Causerie on Edmund de Goncourt," SAVOY, No. 5 (1896), p. 87.

WP is the only English writer who has ever handled language in the spirit of the Goncourts. He frequently referred to MADAME GERVAISIS, to L'ART DU XVIII SIÈCLE, and to CHÉRIE. He found the last book "immodest." Goncourt regretted not being able to read WP because of his ignorance of English.

156 "Talk about New Books," CATHOLIC WORLD, LXIV (Dec 1896), 406–15, espec pp. 407–8.

Some of the "essays" in *Gaston de Latour* are "amazingly beautiful," but too often the style is "labyrinthine." [Review of *Gaston.*]

157 "The Theology of Walter Pater," BRITISH WEEKLY, XXI (31 Dec 1896), 197–98; rptd in CHRISTIAN LITERATURE, XVI (1897), 406–12.

Essays from "The Guardian" enables us to understand WP's final "theological position." In the essays on ROBERT ELSMERE and Amiel, for example, is "proof" that WP was a "professed believer in Christ." [With additional comments on Clough and Balzac.]

158 Wyzewa, Teodor de. ÉCRIVAINS ÉTRANGERS (Foreign Authors) (Paris: Perrin, 1896), "Walter Pater et James Anthony Froude" (Walter Pater and James Anthony Froude), pp. 131–82, espec 131–63; "La Renaissance du Roman Historique en Angleterre" (The Renaissance of the Historical Novel in England), dated Jan 1890, pp. 164–82; "Deux Morts: Pater et Froude" (Two Deaths: Pater and Froude), dated Jan 1895, pp. 135, 136, 150–173, 175.

WP and J. H. Shorthouse succeeded Scott, Kingsley, Thackeray et al., as English historical novelists. [The first part of this essay is actually devoted to WP's *Marius the Epicurean* and Joseph Henry Shorthouse's JOHN INGLESANT; Froude is not mentioned. Summarizes the plot of *Marius;* compares *Marius* with Shorthouse's JOHN INGLESANT; gives a brief account, largely drawn from Gosse, of WP's life; makes conventionally appreciative remarks *passim* about the quality of WP's style and the value of his work.] [In French.]

159 Zangwill, I[srael]. "Pater and Prose," in WITHOUT PREJUDICE (NY: Century; Lond: T. Fisher Unwin, 1896), pp. 207–19.

Wilde, during his trial, cited WP as his master, with the effect that WP has been, so to speak, tried in English court and found guilty by association. It is entirely unfair, even libelous, that his name should be linked with those of his inferiors. His "one-sided disciples" never really understood WP, nor tried to. It can be charged against WP that he was too aloof from the world, that he was excessively serious (and humorless). But perhaps he would not have done his work if he had been less aloof or less serious. At any rate, this "great writer" deserves better than to be associated in the public mind with "the empty-headed acolytes of the aesthetic." [Wilde's name does not appear in the essay, though he is quoted and clearly alluded to.]

1897

160 Addleshaw, Stanley. "Walter Pater," GENTLEMAN'S MAGAZINE, CCLXXXII (March 1897), 227–51.

WP's "ideas, from being purely Pagan in the *Renaissance,* became in the greatest and most thoughtful of his books, *Marius the Epicurean,* actually Christian." *Studies in the History of the Renaissance* appeared in 1869 [*sic*], in "a time of singular ugliness." Its "Conclusion" appealed to those "who were repelled by the teaching of Carlyle." But as a guide to the conduct of life it was false and dangerous. *Marius the Epicurean* tempered the "excessive individuality" of WP's earlier book with "a sense of responsibility." [Distorts WP's position in *Marius,* ignoring the ambiguity of its ending.]

161 "Books and Authors: *Gaston de Latour,*" OUTLOOK (NY), LV (27 March 1897), 853.

The parts of *Gaston de Latour* are pleasing, but the book does not constitute a "single whole." WP seems not to have thought out the character of Gaston: he is "shadowy"; his development is traced vaguely or merely hinted at. WP probably abandoned the book because he lacked a "constructive imagination" and because he had not "secreted material enough for the task." The fragments, however, taken simply as such, are delightful. The subject is "well suited to the soft casuistries and the subtle refinements" of WP. In its weaknesses and in its strengths, it is "very representative of the man who wrote it"—and thus it is "a singularly appropriate final volume to his complete works."

162 "Comment on Recent Books of Fiction," ATLANTIC MONTHLY, LXXIX (May 1897), 711–12.

WP's *Marius the Epicurean* was a work of "delicate research and literary distinction." It is ironic that "the Neo-pagan" should have depicted the influence of Christianity so winningly. "No modern writer of them all has shed so mild and full a light as he on the evolution of Christian ritual." *Gaston de Latour* is an "exquisite" fragment in the same manner. WP's "style is here at its very best."

163 *"Essays from the* Guardian *by Walter Pater,"* ATHENAEUM, No. 3633 (12 June 1897), 769–70.

[A favorable review. The reviewer lists eleven uncollected reviews written by WP, "probably unknown to many students of his work." All of the titles now appear in Samuel Wright's WALTER H. PATER: A BIBLIOGRAPHY, 1975.]

164 Gosse, Edmund. A SHORT HISTORY OF MODERN ENGLISH LITERATURE (NY: Appleton, 1897); rptd (Lond: Heinemann; NY: Appleton, 1898), 383–84.

WP was "the most original and the most philosophical" of a group of writers who quickened the spirit of English literary criticism. Although he was "almost obscure" at the time of his death, his fame and influence "have been rising by leaps and bounds" since then. Until lately it was "desirable to demand attention" for the high qualities of his prose. Now it seems necessary to offer the counter-thought: that there is "something heavy, almost pulpy, in his soft magnificence of style": and it should not "be ignorantly imitated." Although WP's mind "underwent an austere metamorphosis in advancing years," he exercised his greatest influence through the "elevated hedonism of his youth."

165 Hale, Edward E[verett], Jr. "A Last Volume from Walter Pater,"
DIAL, XXII (1 Feb 1897), 85–87.

In the later 1880s WP spoke with less assurance than he had at the outset of his career. He became less of a critic, "more of a seeker, a speculator." Perhaps because he found himself in such an age, he set both *Marius the Epicurean* and *Gaston de Latour* in ages of transition. *Marius,* twelve years after *The Renaissance,* represented an advance on it. But *Gaston,* only three years after *Marius,* represented no advance. Perhaps WP abandoned it because he had not found "a further answer."

Action almost never takes place in WP's fiction; it takes place offstage and is reported after the fact, often without explanation. "It seems almost impossible for him to conceive directly of anybody really doing anything." Perhaps, in his own life, he was "waiting for some intervention" (such as that which takes place in his fiction). But after *The Renaissance,* "assurance . . . never came again."

166 Johnson, Lionel. "A Note Upon Mr. Pater," ACADEMY, LI (16 Jan 1897), 78–79; rptd as "Mr. Pater's Humour," POST LIMINIUM: ESSAYS AND CRITICAL PAPERS BY LIONEL JOHNSON, ed by Thomas Whittemore (Lond: Elkin Mathews, 1911), pp. 11–14; rptd (NY: Mitchell Kennerly, 1912); rptd (Freeport, NY: Books for Libraries P, 1968).

Too many of WP's readers have been intimidated by his scholarly seriousness and have missed "the wise laughter rippling so pleasantly beneath the studied phrases." They have seen him as "ceaselessly . . . pontificating; stiff and stately in his jewelled vestments; moving with serious and slow exactitude through the ritual of his style." "Let us have done with the fabled Mr. Pater of a strict and strait solemnity." Let us recognize his "rich humanity," his "quiet mirth," his "peaceful irony." There is humour in WP, "in profluent abundance," as there is "in Plato and in Berkeley." [Peripherally a review of *Essays from "The Guardian."*]

167 [McDaniels, J. H.] "Pater's Unfinished Romance," NATION (NY), LXIV (4 March 1897), 166–67.

As in *Marius the Epicurean,* in *Gaston de Latour,* WP is "the historian of sensations and ideas, not of actions, and passions, and hairbreadth escapes." But in this later philosophical romance, WP seems to have lost, along the way, the thread of his hero's personal experiences. Perhaps that is why he abandoned it. Each chapter of *Gaston,* however, is a self-contained vignette (and thus the book is well worth having). The chapter on Montaigne is a "classic": "a nearly perfect miniature of a singular and fascinating personality" (though WP somewhat over-emphasizes the "negative and sceptical" aspect of Montaigne's thinking). To the end of his career, WP retained, "fresh and pure and true," his openness and responsiveness to beauty. Moreover, "he bridged in a Platonic manner the passage from the beautiful to the good," showing how a "refined epicureanism . . . may ally itself in the end with morality." His "counsel of perfection," though it may seem esoteric or elitist, is really "a doctrine that . . . needs preaching to a gross and materialized democracy like ours."

168 Mosher, Thomas B. [Introduction to] "Sandro Botticelli, Luca della Robbia, Two Renaissance Studies by Walter Pater," BIBELOT, III (1897), [283–84].

"The man in the street knows nothing" of WP's major works, "yet . . . these books will influence his children's children."

169 "Mr. Pater's Last Work," SPECTATOR, LXXVIII (30 Jan 1897, Supplement), 144.

While we deeply regret WP's failure to finish *Gaston de Latour*, it remains "a noble fragment." In it "we have Mr. Pater's prose at its best" (all the better, perhaps, because WP—who was frequently guilty "of trying to write too well"— did not subject it to further revisions). WP's narratives have a pale, dreamy beauty, but they are "scarcely . . . vivacious." They are at their best in "short moments of inspired expression"; and this book abounds in such moments.

170 Nencioni, Enrico. "Pater, *Appreciations*," in SAGGI CRITICI DI LETTERATURA INGLESE (Critical Studies in English Literature) (Firenze: Successori de Monnier, 1897), pp. 415–18; rptd (1910).

WP is to criticism what Rossetti was to poetry: a refined, aristocratic dilettante. Writers are either dilettantes or pessimists these days; WP was one of the most elite and exquisite representatives of the former category. Sometimes WP's tone is too much that of the oracle, so that one could say of him what was said of Giacobino: "He carries his head like the Holy Sacrament." Some of the writing in *Appreciations* seems too subtly meditated, too meticulously conscientious. Certain of his pages, like certain sonnets of Rossetti, are filled with a mystic vapor. Still, the essays of this volume are among the most beautiful and perfect of modern English prose. The essay on Wordsworth is the most beautiful, right, and suggestive on the great contemplative poet. It surpasses those of Palgrave, Rossetti, Arnold, and Scherer; in fineness and profundity it ranks with what Coleridge says of the lyrical ballads in BIOGRAPHIA LITERARIA. [In Italian.]

171 Raleigh, Walter [Alexander]. STYLE (Lond: Edward Arnold, 1897), pp. 116–17; rptd (1898); (1918); (1929).

[In his discussion of style, Raleigh agrees with WP that a characteristic of style is " 'soul,' " which gives to words "the stamp of an individual mind and character."]

172 Symons, Arthur. "Walter Pater," STUDIES IN TWO LITERATURES (Lond: Leonard Smithers, 1897), pp. 169–85; trans by Georges Khnopff and rptd as "Introduction," PORTRAITS IMAGINAIRES (Paris: Société du Mercure de France, 1899), pp. 11–35; rptd with slight revision in STUDIES IN PROSE AND VERSE (Lond: Dent, 1904), pp. 63–76. [Approximately the first third of this essay is based upon Symons's essay on WP in TIME (1887).]

WP's charmingly unconventional personality ("at once shy and complex, languid and ascetic, sensuous and spiritual") "found for its expression an absolutely personal and absolutely novel style, which was the most carefully and curiously beautiful of all English styles." In *The Renaissance* "prose seemed to have conquered a new province." The style of *Marius the Epicurean* strikes "a graver note," has "a severer kind of beauty." Of all WP's works, the style of *Imaginary Portraits* is "the ripest, the most varied and flawless." WP's "modulated prose" made Ruskin seem "gaudy," Matthew Arnold "mincing," and Carlyle "strident." WP's criticism was itself "fine art." It combined "exact and profound scholarship," "inexorable logic," and "mathematical precision" with a creative (and generous) faculty that enabled him to divine the perfection which other artists—his subjects—only partially achieved. He taught us to be sympathetic to "some of the subtler aspects of art"; and in this he "did much to rescue us from the dangerous moralities, the uncritical enthusiasms and prejudices, of Ruskin." His taste, uniquely among art critics, was "flawless." [Contains thoughtful appraisals of a number of specific works.]

173 Wyzewa, Teodor de. "Romans Anglais. II. Le Roman Posthume de Walter Pater: *Gaston de Latour*" (English Novels. II. Walter Pater's Posthumous Novel: *Gaston de Latour*), ÉCRIVAINS ÉTRANGERS, Deuxième Série (Foreign Authors, Second Series) (Paris: Perrin, 1897), pp. 248–68.

Gaston de Latour is incontestably the most beautiful of WP's books. Had he finished it, it would have been the most beautiful of philosophical novels. While its subject makes it, of all of WP's works, the one most interesting to French readers, it is the most untranslatable of his works (because the language is the most perfect of all his works). Unlike Marius, Gaston had to define his faith precisely: to choose, finally, between Calvin and Ignatius. To end the novel, WP would have had to make Gaston choose Protestantism or return to Catholicism. [In French.]

1898

---

174 Buchan, John. BRASENOSE COLLEGE (Lond: F. E. Robinson, 1898), pp. 84, 137–42.

WP's rooms "were the gathering-place of much of the best wit and culture in

England; and over a small body of undergraduates he exercised a profound influence." The college is full of his memory: for some time he acted as Dean and Tutor of the college, though he "always shrank from the responsibility of any University office." While he was an acting member of the governing body, the Cain and Abel statue was sold for old lead. WP was quite upset, for apparently he believed it to be an original by Giovanni da Bologna. His dinners were famous, usually given in the company of his friend, Dr. F. W. Bussell. He once remarked to the present Bishop of London, " 'I do not know what your object is. At present the undergraduate is a child of nature; you want to turn him into a turnip, rob him of all his grace, and plant him out in rows.' " Swinburne was often his guest. WP wrote the letterpress for Rothenstein's portrait of Bussell in OXFORD CHARACTERS. At Oxford, a whole mythology of WP stories evolved. "No man felt more keenly the problems of his age."

> **175** Eno, Henry Lane. "Walter Pater. An Appreciation," CITIZEN (Philadelphia), III (Jan 1898), 248–50.

"As Wordsworth's is a transcendental note, that of Nature, and Browning's a dramatic theme, that of the Soul, Pater's motive is aesthetic, that of an Epicurean ascesis, or an ascetic Epicureanism."

> **176** Grant Duff, Sir Mountstuart E. NOTES FROM A DIARY, 1873–1881 (Lond: John Murray, 1898), I, 29, 60, 118. [NOTES FROM A DIARY was published in seven installments of two volumes each between 1896 and 1905.]

[An off-hand reference to *The Renaissance* (1873); a remark that WP was not an engaging conversationalist (1874); and mention of lunching with WP (1875). Other references to WP in volumes published in 1901, 1904, and 1905.]

> **177** Mosher, Thomas B. [Introduction to] "The Poetry of Michelangelo by Walter Pater," BIBELOT, IV (1898), [123–24].

[Appreciative comments.]

> **178** Mosher, Thomas B. [Introduction to] "The School of Giorgione," BIBELOT, IV (1898), [281–82].

[General appreciation. Contains quotations from William Sharp's description of WP in ATLANTIC MONTHLY, Dec 1894, q.v.]

> **179** P. "Reputations Reconsidered. II.—Walter Pater," ACADEMY, LIII (1 Jan 1898), 13–14.

About 1870, "a great change became apparent in the spirit of English literature." Writer-moralists, such as Carlyle and Tennyson, gave way to younger writers who abjured the roles of prophet or teacher. Morris and Swinburne in poetry, WP in prose, set the tone for this movement. WP "was the first great Englishman to preach the gospel of art for art's sake." The movement included real talents, though they were "not, indeed, of the very highest rank." (This seems to be the case, generally, in reactions which follow moral movements in literature.

PARADISE LOST was succeeded merely by Restoration drama. The reaction to IN MEMORIAM, THE FRENCH REVOLUTION, and ADAM BEDE "has flowered into no achievement of the highest class, and is ending in something like paralysis.") The movement "has failed to produce any book of the first importance." In WP's case, the failure may be attributed to several causes. His attempt to make language convey a precision of meaning that it cannot convey led to "over-bookishness and super-refinement and preciosity." WP exalted art too highly. His work lacks vitality because he took nothing from life itself. The largest imaginations and the greatest interpreters of human experience (e.g., Scott, Fielding, Shakespeare) are fed on more than books alone. WP's work, while "brilliantly successful" within its limits, is narrow and rigid. "He has no humour. . . . With nine-tenths of the pursuits of mankind he is out of touch." He is "cold and austere"; and his work can never appeal to more than a small minority of readers. On WP's behalf it should be added that his work is immeasurably superior to that of his imitators. They have been almost uniformly small-minded, under-talented, and superficial. They have produced distorted caricatures of his beliefs, which, worked out painstakingly over a lifetime, constitute "a creed as large and austere as that of Carlyle himself." WP was intellectually honest; his imitators were not. Whatever his faults, he was "certainly a great writer, one of the first of his day." His vivid imagination gave the best of his writings an unsurpassed pictorial quality. His disciples have only aped his "hothouse mannerisms." They have scarcely been touched by the impressive and valuable side of his work. [The first thoroughgoing effort to "place" Pater in the context of literary history.]

1899

180 Beerbohm, Max. "A Cloud of Pinafores," MORE (NY & Lond: John Lane, 1899); rptd (1907); (1921); rptd (Lond: Heinemann; NY: Dodd, Mead, 1922), pp. 189–200; rptd in WORKS AND MORE (Lond: John Lane, [1930]); rptd in THE INCOMPARABLE MAX (Lond: Heinemann; NY: Dodd, Mead, 1962).
[Facetious reference to WP's "The Child in the House": it is making a comeback now that "children are in vogue."]

181 Beerbohm, Max. "Madame Tussaud's," MORE (NY & Lond: John Lane, 1899); rptd (1907); (1921); rptd (Lond: Heinemann; NY: Dodd, Mead, 1922), pp. 41–47; rptd in WORKS AND MORE (Lond: John Lane, [1930]).
[Quotes WP on statuary; describes the sentence quoted as "pregnant (if rather uncouth)."]

182 [Burroughs, John.] "Some Tendencies of Prose Style," EDIN-BURGH REVIEW, CXC (Oct 1899), 356–76, espec pp. 372–73.
WP's style is unnatural: elaborate, studied, affected. His vocabulary "became the mark of a sect, and had the misfortune to be made ridiculous." Stevenson's stylistic eccentricities stem from "an extremely vigorous personality"; but "a sickly air pervades" WP's pages. Yeats's prose, though influenced by WP's, is "more natural and spontaneous."

183 Burroughs, John. "The Vital Touch in Literature," ATLANTIC MONTHLY, LXXXIII (March 1899), 399–406, espec p. 403; rptd as "Style and the Man" in LITERARY VALUES AND OTHER PAPERS (Bost & NY: Houghton Mifflin, 1902), pp. 52–79, espec 69–70; rptd (Lond: Gay & Bird, 1903); rptd (Bost & NY: 1904).
"Arnold's style is better than Walter Pater's, because it is easier to follow . . . not so conscious of itself . . . not so obviously studied." WP sacrificed "ease, simplicity, flexibility, transparency" for "the perfumed, the academic, the highly wrought."

184 F [James Edward Freeman?]. "In Pater's Rooms," SPEAKER, 26 Aug 1899, pp. 207–8.
["Stray memories" by one, who, when "a mere freshman," had known WP slightly.]

185 Mosher, Thomas B. [Introduction to] "Demeter and Persephone: Three Translations," BIBELOT, V (1899), [178–79]
[Appreciative comment.]

186 Mosher, Thomas B. [Introduction to] "Two Appreciations: I. Aesthetic Poetry, II. Dante Gabriel Rossetti," BIBELOT, V (1899), [299–300].
WP's essay on Morris's poetry is "the most subtly interpretive of all judgments upon his poetry."

1900

187 Gates, Lewis. "Impressionism and Appreciation," STUDIES AND APPRECIATIONS (NY: Macmillan, 1900); rptd (Freeport, NY: Books for Libraries P, 1970), pp. 205–34.
Instead of looking to Arnold, the modern impressionist, in his search for precept and example, in his pursuit of disinterestedness, looks to WP, who "more than all other English critics, has illustrated what appreciative criticism may accomplish." But impressionism is neither WP's nor Arnold's invention.

188 J[ohnson, Lionel]. "For a Little Clan," ACADEMY, LVIII (13 Oct 1900), 314–15; rptd, with three sentences omitted, as "Notes on Walter Pater. III.—Mr. Pater and His Public," POST LIMINIUM: ESSAYS AND CRITICAL PAPERS BY LIONEL JOHNSON, ed by Thomas Whittemore (Lond: Elkin Mathews, 1911), pp. 14–19; rptd (NY: Mitchell Kennerly, 1912); rptd (Freeport, NY: Books for Libraries P, 1968).

WP's monk-like devotion to "the laws of his literary conscience," which prized an "ultimate precision" of language and a "perfect correspondence between conception and expression," kept his total production (and his audience) small. He was no mere "artificer in words," however. He had much to say; indeed, such faults as there are in his writing result from "a too great compression of meaning," rather than from a superfluity of words. [A disciple's paean, occasioned by the forthcoming *édition de luxe* of WP's *Works.*]

189 Malley, Rev. A. D. "Walter Pater: A Study," CATHOLIC WORLD, LXX (Feb 1900), 602–9.

WP's hedonism and skepticism, though expressed beautifully, are decadent: "too refined to be vigorous or healthy." His quasi-Catholic "devotional tendency . . . is only superficial." *Marius the Epicurean* is a masterpiece, yet its philosophy is that of vacant "worldliness, moral triviality."

190 Mosher, Thomas B. [Introduction to] "Leonardo da Vinci," BIBELOT, VI (1900), [33–34].

Swinburne initiated "that Aesthetic school which was shortly to culminate in Pater's criticism."

191 Reedy, William Marion. "Foreword. A Golden Book," in *Marius the Epicurean,* by Walter Pater (Portland, Maine: T. B. Mosher, 1900), I, ix–xxvi.

WP has made the definitive statement, for the modern world, about "true Epicureanism" (which, far from being "a philosophy of sensuality," is but the doctrine of "a sane enjoyment of the senses"). *Marius the Epicurean* "is a Bible of the true religion of the higher sensuousness," which develops "eventually into a tender and an exalted spirituality."

192 Reedy, William Marion. "The Quiet Life," ST. LOUIS MIRROR, 23 Aug 1900, p. 1.

A great event for the thinking, considerate, quiet man will occur when Macmillan publishes the *édition de luxe* of the works of WP.

1901

193 Bourdillon, F. W. "Mr. Pater's *Essays from The Guardian*," ATHENAEUM, No. 3857 (28 Sept 1901), 416.

Symons, as one of WP's friends who first collected and reprinted WP's contributions to the *Guardian,* is himself one of those indirectly responsible for its publication now for general sale. [Letter to the editor; the second of five on this subject.]

194 Bourdillon, F. W. "Mr. Pater's *Essays from The Guardian*," ATHENAEUM, No. 3859 (12 Oct 1901), 493.

In his original letter (21 Sept), Symons seemed to include himself among the friends of WP for whom the 1896 *Essays from "The Guardian"* was printed. [Letter to the editor; the last of five on the subject.]

195 Grant Duff, Sir Mountstuart E. NOTES FROM A DIARY, 1889–1891 (Lond: John Murray, 1901), I, 169–70, 182; II, 73–74. [NOTES FROM A DIARY was published in seven installments of two volumes each between 1896 and 1905.]

[A reference to WP making small talk about his recent travels in Italy—Henry James was present (1889); mention of *Appreciations* (1889); an account of a conversation with WP on many topics (1891). Other references to WP in volumes published in 1898, 1904, and 1905.]

196 Hale, Edward Everett, Jr. SELECTIONS FROM WALTER PATER (NY: Holt, 1901), "Preface," pp. iii–v; "Introduction," pp. ix–lxxii; "Chronology," pp. lxxiii–lxxiv; "Bibliography," pp. lxxv–lxxvi; and "Notes," pp. 219–68.

[Hale's 70-page "Introduction" is an ambitious and largely successful essay. Its main purpose is to trace the important lines of development in WP's thought, using *The Renaissance* (especially its "Conclusion") as point of reference.] WP is important not for his early views, brilliantly stated though they were, but for the thought that matured slowly over the course of his career. Gradually, his tone and his method of inquiry changed; emphasis changed; his manner of expression became less definite (as he became more a seeker, less the purveyor of a doctrine); his interest centered more and more on ethical concerns; his sense of values gravitated toward ascesis, or discipline. [Hale also has informative things to say about WP in relation to Pre-Raphaelitism and the Aesthetic movement and about WP's reputation during his lifetime. The "Notes" are remarkable almost entirely for their length. They are addressed to the student who might be using this collection of essays and seldom get beyond the level of identifying people, places, and terms; translating foreign phrases; identifying variant wordings and sources of ideas and quotations; and so on. Of conceivable interest to the present day reader are Hale's cross-referencing of WP's ideas, as they appear in various works, and his occasional comparisons of WP to his contemporaries (especially Ruskin).]

197 Kauffman, M. "Art. VII—Humanism and Christianity," QUAR-
TERLY REVIEW, nsCXCII (April 1901), 458–81.

Modern humanism, in contrast to earlier stages of humanism, is not antagonistic to religion; indeed, it attempts "to effect a reconciliation of the moral and religious ideas of the age with the love of the beautiful in nature and man." WP is "the accredited representative" of modern humanism. His life, his thought, and even his style reflect "the character of the humanistic movement." [An important essay. Apart from the last four pages, it is as much a study of WP as it is of "Humanism and Christianity," though, since WP is taken as the best and most complete example, as well as propounder, of modern humanism, the two are scarcely distinguishable. Contains sensible readings of *The Renaissance, Greek Studies, Imaginary Portraits, Marius the Epicurean,* and *Gaston de Latour,* stressing their semi-autobiographical nature. Contrasts the lives of WP and J. A. Symonds and the styles of WP and Ruskin.]

198 M[acPherson]., E. F. "LXXIV," in BRASENOSE ALE: A COLLEC-
TION OF VERSES ANNUALLY PRESENTED ON SHROVE TUESDAY, BY THE
BUTLER OF BRASENOSE COLLEGE, OXFORD, Rvd with Additions (1878–
1889) (Oxford: Clarendon P, 1901), pp. 295–98, espec 297; originally pub
(Bost & Lincolnshire: Robert Roberts, 1878). [Ed of 1878 does not
contain 1885 poem with lines on WP.]

[Four of the 90 lines of the poem for 1885 refer to WP: "For our 'father' (Mr. W. H. Pater.—Ed.) of aesthetes is soon, as we hear/ (Inspired beyond doubt by this wonderful beer),/ To teach us the graces in art and in 'natur,'/ And how to live up to a lily or 'tater.' " These undergraduate verses, abounding in references to crew and football, suggest what an incongruous figure WP must have cut at Brasenose College.]

199 Mountain, William. "Walter Pater," POET-LORE, XIII (April 1901),
275–81.

[An unintentionally hilarious distillation of rhapsodies about WP (e.g., WP "deliberately turned his back on the dark, and set his face ever towards the light"). Mountain's labors produce a critical mole-hill.]

200 "Mr. Pater's First Impressions," ACADEMY, LX (29 Oct 1901),
356–57.

Essays from "The Guardian" admittedly contains slight work, but it is worth having because WP, as a reviewer, was a master of his craft.

201 Newman, Ernest. "Walter Pater on Music," in STUDIES IN MUSIC,
BY VARIOUS AUTHORS, REPRINTED FROM 'THE MUSICIAN,' ed by Robin
Grey (Lond: Simpkin, Marshall, Hamilton, Kent, 1901), pp. 292–301.

WP's idea that in music matter and form are unified (making music the highest of the arts) is based on a misconception of music. Unlike the other arts, music makes "no direct reference to actual life." Hence it is capable of conveying only "vague and generalised emotion." Like Wagner, WP "was more susceptible to vague than to specialised artistic emotion." His elevation of music to the ideal art simply reflects his own taste and preference. [See reply by J. F. R. in "Walter Pater on Music," SATURDAY REVIEW (Lond), CIII (7 Dec 1901), 712–13.]

202 R., J. F. "Walter Pater on Music," SATURDAY REVIEW (Lond), CIII (7 Dec 1901), 712–13.
Ernest Newman's essay, "Walter Pater on Music," demolishes WP's attempt to theorize about music; but the effort was scarcely worth making. As a writer, WP was inept. He stuttered and stumbled; he had no "sense of the rhythm of . . . language"; he "lacked all sense of idiom." For awhile people thought of him as a stylist; but "we can now see that Pater had no style, that whatever else he might be, he was not an artist in words." His thoughts, moreover, whether on music, or the other arts, or life itself, are "farcical." His desire "to keep the flame of the spirit burning with a 'hard, gem-like flame' was a monstrous desire." And WP failed "ignominiously" even to do that. Throughout his writings "you find not only depression, a slow, smouldering fire, but an innate love of depression, and low fires."

203 "Some Recent Books," CONTEMPORARY REVIEW, LXXX (Oct 1901), 603.
Essays from "The Guardian" reprints essays "much too precious to be entombed in newspaper files." [Brief, favorable attention to "English Literature," "Robert Elsmere," and "Mr. Gosse's Poems."]

204 Stott, David. "Mr. Pater's *Essays from The Guardian,*" ATHENAEUM, No. 3857 (28 Sept 1901), 416.
The publication of *Essays from "The Guardian"* ignores Shadwell's (WP's literary executor) statement in the "Preface" to *Gaston de Latour:* that nothing else of WP's uncollected writings was finished enough for publication. [Letter to the editor; the third of five on this subject.]

205 Symons, Arthur. "Mr. Pater's *Essays from the Guardian,*" ATHENAEUM, No. 3856 (21 Sept 1901), 384; No. 3858 (5 Oct 1901), 453.
Publication of *Essays from "The Guardian"* in an edition uniform with the *édition de luxe* of WP's works was a mistake. These are mere reviews, "done without the least attempt to make literature." WP "would never have consented" to their publication for mass distribution. In 1896, these reviews were published in a limited edition for friends of WP; but that was an entirely different matter. [Letter to the editor; the first of five on this subject: see Bourdillon (twice), Stott, and Symons's second letter (below). Symons here notes that WP contributed reviews not only to THE GUARDIAN but also to ATHENAEUM, PALL MALL GAZETTE, BOOKMAN, DAILY CHRONICLE, NINETEENTH CENTURY, and MACMILLAN'S MAG-

AZINE. In his second letter, Symons avows that he had "nothing to do" with the privately printed collection of *Essays from "The Guardian."*]

1902

206 Beerbohm, Max. "A Needed Noun," ACADEMY AND "LITERATURE," LXI (8 Feb 1902), 149–50; rptd in A PEEP INTO THE PAST AND OTHER PROSE PIECES, ed by Rupert Hart-Davis (Brattleboro, Vt: S. Greene, 1972), pp. 31–36.
[Cites WP: 1) on the difficulty of writing prose, 2) as a writer of beautiful prose, and 3) together with Ruskin, Stevenson, and Newman, as one of the nineteenth-century masters of prose.]

207 Burroughs, John. LITERARY VALUES AND OTHER PAPERS (Bost & NY: Houghton Mifflin, 1902), p. 189.
"The lust of mere style" pervades WP's work. The workmanship is "faultless"; "yet the best qualities of style—freshness, naturalness, simplicity—are not here." [In essay titled "Mere Literature."]

208 Dowden, Edward. "Walter Pater," ATLANTIC MONTHLY, XC (July 1902), 112–23; NEW LIBERAL REVIEW, July 1902, pp. 777–94; rptd in ESSAYS MODERN AND ELIZABETHAN (Lond: Dent; NY: Dutton, 1910), pp. 1–25; rptd (Freeport, NY: Books for Libraries P, 1970).
WP sought for truth "with the eye, and with the imagination penetrating its way through things visible." Ideas meant little to him "apart from their concrete embodiment." Even in *The Renaissance,* he was a seeker not merely for pleasure "but [for] fullness and vividness of life." The "Conclusion" of *The Renaissance,* far from being WP's "ultimate confession of faith," was in fact "a prologue." In *Marius the Epicurean,* and elsewhere, he sought to reconcile his essentially skeptical intellectual scheme with an inherited moral scheme. In *Marius* he subordinated the "doctrine of the perpetual flux" (and the ethic appropriate to it) into "a larger, really a more liberal view of things." *Plato and Platonism* shows most fully the tendency of his mind "away from the brilliantly colored, versatile, centrifugal Ionian temper of his earliest days toward the simpler, graver, more strictly ordered, more athletic Dorian spirit." [An account of WP's life and thought, emphasizing the development of thought which accompanied "that endless dialogue with self which constituted his life." The markedly Pateresque quality of the prose occasionally verges on unintentional parody.]

209 Garnett, Richard. "Pater's *Essays from 'The Guardian,'* " BOOK-MAN (Lond), XXII (April 1902), 29.
The republication of *Essays from "The Guardian,"* while not "a literary event of

great moment," is scarcely a cause (as some have said) for regret. The essays on ROBERT ELSMERE and Amiel reveal WP's "instinctive preference of picturesqueness to verity" ("the hedonism of Mr. Pater's early writings in clerical garb"). Overall, the importance of this collection is slight; but it does give us a sense of the workaday writer and "proof that he was not always in full dress."

210 H., F. E. "Pater's Philosophy of Life," MACMILLAN'S MAGAZINE, XXXIX (Jan 1902), 193–98.

Marius the Epicurean and *Gaston de Latour* are WP's "children"; their title characters have inherited the strengths, and especially the weaknesses, of their progenitor. WP was "far removed from the healthy human type." Certainly he was not a modern man, but a sort of "medieval survival." Placing beauty above truth, he lacked the "robustness" of "saner thinkers." In Marius too "there is something lacking on the human side." He is undeveloped spiritually and stunted emotionally. He is incapable of effective action or decision. Passive, "shadowy, unreal, visionary, ineffectual": he "illustrates the extreme academic attitude, which is a paralyzing one." Gaston and Marius alike are "wilfully short-sighted," shunning the sight of anything unpleasant, even "sin itself." They cannot see life steadily and whole, though to begin with they are merely spectators on life. Gaston is "a feebler edition of Marius, himself painted in none too brilliant colours." *Gaston's* narrative stagnates; the book should have been a series of essays. If *Gaston* is a failure, however, *Marius* (for all its main character's inherited weaknesses) is a success. Its theme is interesting; WP's imaginative conception of that theme is brilliant; and his execution is first-rate. In "these days of crudity and hurry," of "over civilisation," "its stateliness and distinction of style" are "a needed antidote." Moreover, it can teach us much, by negative inference, about how to live our lives (Marius fails so completely to live his).

211 "Pater, Walter Horatio," NEW AMERICAN SUPPLEMENT . . . ENCYCLOPAEDIA BRITANNICA, 10th ed (NY: Werner, 1902), XXVIII, 361.
[Brief biographical notice, with conventional praise of WP.]

212 Saintsbury, George. A HISTORY OF CRITICISM AND LITERARY TASTE IN EUROPE FROM THE EARLIEST TEXTS TO THE PRESENT DAY (Edinburgh & Lond: Blackwood, 1900–4, 1949); rptd (Lond: Blackwood; NY: Dodd, Mead, 1906), III, 120, 183*n*, 326*n*, 451, 544–52; rptd in A HISTORY OF ENGLISH CRITICISM: BEING THE ENGLISH CHAPTERS OF "A HISTORY OF CRITICISM AND LITERARY TASTE IN EUROPE" (Edinburgh & Lond: Blackwood, 1911); rptd (1930); rptd (NY: Humanities P, 1961); rptd (Edinburgh & Lond: Blackwood, 1962).

WP "was the most important English critic of the last generation of the nineteenth century." He was to his generation what Coleridge and Arnold were to theirs, though he was "somewhat less than either of his forerunners." He was superior to them in "faculty of expression" and equal to them in "fineness of appreciation"; but, by virtue of his "ecletic and composite character," he was not their equal in originality. He was "more of a transmitter than a kindler of the torch." As an advocate, and a superb practitioner, of impressionistic criticism, WP participated in the highest form of modern criticism. [Saintsbury himself was an advocate of impressionistic criticism, which he contrasted with "the antecedent rule-system." He acknowledges that, in his later work, WP "became rather more of a preceptist and less of an impressionist"; but he insists that the spirit of impressionism can be found in nearly all of WP's work.]

213 Schölermann, Wilhelm. "Einführung" (Introduction), DIE RENAISSANCE: STUDIEN IN KUNST UND POESIE *(The Renaissance: Studies in Art and Poetry)* (Leipzig: Diederichs, 1902), pp. v–viii.

[Schölermann claims that this is the first translation into German of WP's *Renaissance*. He briefly compares Ruskin's and WP's artistic motives and styles and comments on WP's debt to French literature.] [In German.]

1903

214 Beerbohm, Max. "An Aesthetic Book," SATURDAY REVIEW (Lond), XCVI (19 Sept 1903), 360–61; rptd in AROUND THEATRES (Lond: Heinemann, 1924); (NY: Knopf, 1930), I, 349–53.

PLAYS, ACTING AND MUSIC, by Arthur Symons, exhibits "the Pateresque manner." Conscious imitation reveals itself in "his frequent 'Well!' for the resumption of an argument," in his muffled sense of humor, and in a multiplicity of commas. Imitation aside, Symons is simply a lot like WP: "sensitive, fastidious, ever-ruminating," one for whom "art matters more than life, and form in art more than meaning." "Emerald Uthwart" illustrates WP's "horror and ignorance of the hurly-burly." Unable to look at life closely or directly, "the impression he transmits" is not vivid and is neither bracing nor filling.

215 Beerbohm, Max. "The Critic as Pariah," SATURDAY REVIEW (Lond), XCVI (31 Oct 1903), 543; rptd in AROUND THEATRES (Lond: Heinemann, 1924); rptd (NY: Knopf, 1930), I, 371–74.

"Temperamental" (as opposed to "academic") critics, such as WP and Anatole France, "have a way of smiling to themselves and talking under their breath. They might be nicknamed 'the Hornerists' of literature. You need no more exact description of Pater or France than that he sits in a corner, eating a Christmas pie, and puts in his thumb, and pulls out a plum, and says 'What a good boy am I!' "

216 [Beerbohm,] Max. "The Invariable Badness of Amateur Acting," SATURDAY REVIEW (Lond), XCV (24 Jan 1903), 105–6; [part II of this essay (31 Jan 1903), 138–39, contains no reference to WP]; rptd in AROUND THEATRES (Lond: Heinemann, 1924); rptd (NY: Knopf, 1930), I, 305–7.

WP was "essentially an amateur" prose writer, not a professional. He wrote for himself, to please himself, at his own rate. This is the source of the exquisiteness of his work. If he had had to write for a living, the exquisiteness would have been lost. "Pater was a great man in a small way, and professionalism would have been fatal to him."

217 [Walter Pater,] CHAMBER'S CYCLOPEDIA OF ENGLISH LITERATURE. Three Volumes (Lond & Edinburgh: W. & R. Chambers, 1903), III, 607–8.

Marius the Epicurean, WP's "principal legacy to the world," depicts the Epicureanism "of the nineteenth-century Englishman who had drunk from the wells of Oxford, had studied Goethe and Ruskin, and had essayed an even higher synthesis of culture and beauty and the spiritual life." "*Marius* was a spiritual maieutic" to many of WP's younger contemporaries. [Contains brief biographical sketch.]

218 Gosse, Edmund. ENGLISH LITERATURE: AN ILLUSTRATED RECORD (Lond & NY: Macmillan, 1903), III (FROM MILTON TO JOHNSON), p. 187; IV (FROM THE AGE OF JOHNSON TO THE AGE OF TENNYSON), pp. 358–60.

WP's early interest in philosophy was "supplanted by a study of the aesthetic principles underlying the pleasure we receive from art and literature." Though affectionate and playful in private, he was withdrawn and shy by nature— "essentially self-absorbed and unrelated to the common life which passed around him." [Mainly a biographical sketch; reproduces a page of the "Pascal" manuscript.]

219 Greenslet, Ferris. WALTER PATER (NY: McClure, Phillips, 1903); rptd (Lond: Heinemann, 1904); rptd (Bost & NY: Houghton Mifflin, 1911); rptd (NY: Haskell House, 1974).

WP's literary criticism is in the tradition of Sainte-Beuve; his prose is less Attic than that of Newman and Arnold, less Asiatic than that of De Quincey; his idealism is less exuberant and doctrinaire than that of Shelley or Sidney. Compared with Arnold, he has a keener sensibility; his scholarship is better, and his interests are more esoteric. Although WP's "work as a whole lacks energy, speed, carrying power," *Marius the Epicurean* is distinguished by "richness of the scholarship, . . . power of the interpretive imagination, . . . suave and seductive grace of style." *Plato and Platonism* "is perhaps the most thoroughly satisfactory of all his works." In WP there is a "slowly ripening growth" and progress "from scepticism to . . . idealism . . . from virtual paganism toward practical Christianity." [The first book-length study of WP. It is brief (under 20,000 words); one-fifth of it consists of quotations, either from WP or from his critics; its biographical sections rehash previously published accounts of WP's life. But Greenslet does make some effort to "place" WP with regard to other writers.]

220 Hutton, Edward. "Walter Pater," MONTHLY REVIEW, XII (Sept 1903), 142–55; and LIVING AGE, CCXXXIX (24 Oct 1903), 242–50.

In an age of barbarous English prose, WP stood out, easily surpassing "all his contemporaries in the use of words." He was less a thinker than "an artist in thought." *The Renaissance* is his richest book, *Imaginary Portraits* both the simplest and the most imaginative. *Marius the Epicurean* is unique in English literature: scholarly, profoundly charming, and above all exquisitely written. In many ways, no doubt, writers such as Scott, Thackeray, Dickens, and Meredith were greater than WP; "but in the actual genius of writing, in the generalship, the art of words, they are not his peers." Compared with the delicacy, the fineness, of WP's criticism, that of Arnold "appears almost obvious, almost common."

221 Hutton, Laurence. LITERARY LANDMARKS OF OXFORD (NY: Scribner's, 1903), pp. 56–57, 215.

After graduation from Queens, WP lost some of his shyness and "moved more freely among the men of his own world." As a fellow of Brasenose, he associated chiefly with the PRB. He is said to have had a sense of fun "as playful as that of a child."

1904

222 Barrows, Eleanor. "Walter Pater in Perspective," DIAL, XXXVI (1 March 1904), 140–42.

WP may be compared to Botticelli. They share "a union of philosophic and artistic susceptibilities," an awareness of life's brevity, a "belief in the relativity of truth," and a "subjective temperament." Their work shares the charm of a distinct personality expressing itself through form and style. Ten years after his death, WP seems "like a courteous gentleman of the old school": a rather delightful, if unemphatic, "old-fashioned gentleman."

223 Beerbohm, Max. "An Actress, and a Playwright," SATURDAY REVIEW (Lond), XCVIII (9 July 1904), 42–43; rptd as "Sarah" in AROUND THEATRES (Lond: Heinemann, 1924); (NY: Knopf, 1930), II, 424–27.

Queen Victoria in old age used to remind me, and now Sarah Bernhardt reminds me, of WP's description of Mona Lisa ("Hers is the head . . . " etc.).

224 Benson, Arthur C[hristopher]. ROSSETTI (Lond & NY: Macmillan, 1904), pp. 41, 82, 107, 142, 151.

[Several incidental references to WP. Takes polite issue at two points with WP's essay on Rossetti.]

225 Bronner, Milton. "Some Notes About Pater," LAMP, XXVIII (April 1904), 252–55.

The similarities between Flaubert and WP, in their lives and works alike, and the influence of Flaubert on WP have never been sufficiently acknowledged by WP's commentators. WP's "off-hand reviews contributed to the magazines," unreprinted and now hard to locate, may reveal more of their author than his more formal, more famous, and more self-conscious essays. [Review of Greenslet's WALTER PATER; contains comment as well on the criticism and reminiscences of Edmund Gosse, Lionel Johnson, William Sharp, and Israel Zangwill.]

226 [Creighton, Louise.] LIFE AND LETTERS OF MANDELL CREIGHTON ... BY HIS WIFE (Lond: Longmans, Green, 1904); rptd (1905), I, 46, 93–94, 128; II, 111–12.

"Pater is the only man [among modern pagans] who carries out his [William Morris's] views in the least. In him you feel the ideal of beauty absolutely dominates, and all that does not come under its influence is to him external. You will find him worth a study in that matter." [From a letter of May 1871. Another letter—to Edmund Gosse, November 1894—relates several anecdotes about WP, including the one about the student named "Sanctuary."]

227 Grant Duff, Sir Mountstuart E. NOTES FROM A DIARY, 1892–95 (Lond: John Murray, 1904), I, 81, 115, 134. [NOTES FROM A DIARY was published in seven installments of two volumes each between 1896 and 1905.]

[Recalls WP conversing on the subject of incense (1892); mentions a meeting with WP (1892); says that WP said he "planned a theological work in three divisions, the first to be called *Hebrew and Hellene,* the second *The Genius of Christ,* and the third *The Poetry of Anglicanism*" (1892). Other references to WP in volumes published in 1898, 1901, and 1905.]

228 [McDaniels, J. H.] "Walter Pater," NATION (NY), LXXIX (20 Oct 1904), 318–20.

WP's philosophy of life, especially after he had worked out its moral implications (e.g., in *Marius the Epicurean*), "is perfectly rational and intelligible." No better example of WP's mature ideal could be found than Gladstone. [Ostensibly a review of Greenslet's WALTER PATER; actually—except for the reference to Gladstone—a fairly conventional account of WP's life and thought.]

229 Moore, George. "Avowals: Walter Pater, Being the Sixth of a New Series of 'Confessions of a Young Man,'" LIPPINCOTT'S MONTHLY MAGAZINE, LXXIII (Feb 1904), 168–78; rptd with revisions as "Avowals. VI. Walter Pater," PALL MALL MAGAZINE, XXXIII (Aug 1904), 527–33.

If *The Renaissance* is a spring morning, *Imaginary Portraits* is a summer afternoon. The former ("the only example in literature of a man coming before the public in the perfect accomplishment of his genius") has more "sting," is more intense; the latter has "a vaster beatitude," is more harmonious. WP's style was "the perfect expression" of his mind, accurately reflecting its "wistful uncertainties" and its slow unwinding.

WP was "a very ugly" and an abnormally shy man. He wore a mask, controlling his appearance, speech, and gestures to hide the fact that "his life was a weariness." "In his letters the social mask dropped a little; perhaps it was only in literature that Pater became human." Eventually "this grave, impenetrable man began to seem to me a little ridiculous," though I never ceased to respect his work or his literary judgment. [These two essays, of about equal length, may be considered jointly. Although between the two there are many differences in wording and in the arrangement of ideas, relatively little of the substance of either is not to be found in the other. Not so with the sections on WP in the 1919 AVOWALS (q.v.). Although Moore goes back over much of the same ground there, he moves at a much more leisurely pace; besides, he adds a good deal of new material. The 1919 version (chaps 10 and 11 and part of chap 9) is not only about twice as long as the 1904 "Avowals;" it is different enough in substance to be treated as a separate entry.]

230 Symons, Arthur. "An Artist in Attitudes: Oscar Wilde," STUDIES IN PROSE AND VERSE (Lond: Dent, 1904), pp. 124–28.
One of the many souls which Wilde made for himself was "after the fashion on Pater." His prose style is sometimes "a bewildering echo" of WP. [Symons's prose style in this essay, as elsewhere, also echoes WP; here no doubt consciously.]

1905

---

231 Dilke, Sir Charles W[entworth]. "Memoir," in THE BOOK OF THE SPIRITUAL LIFE, by the late Lady Dilke (Lond: John Murray; NY: Dutton, 1905), pp. 29–31, 34, 74, 90.
Mrs. Pattison's severe review of *The Renaissance* did not prevent her from becoming WP's friend in later years. [Quotes from a letter in which Mrs. Pattison, later Lady Dilke, recalls a conversation with WP: "He looks for an accession of strength to the Roman Catholic Church, and thinks that if it would abandon its folly in political and social intrigue, and take up the attitude of a purely spiritual power, it would be, if not the best thing that could happen, at any rate better than the selfish vulgarity of the finite aims and ends which stand in place of an ideal in most lives now. He has changed a great deal . . . for the better, and is a stronger man." Plus several incidental references to WP.]

232 Durham, James. MARIUS THE EPICUREAN AND JOHN INGLESANT. TWO BOOKS: A RELIGIOUS STUDY OF THEM (Lond: Hatchards, 1905).

Marius proves that it is "by nature we live, and through that nature our religion, if we care to have any, comes." Marius and John Inglesant have similar characters; they both seek truth. But the result that religion had on each was different. [The work is a sixteen-page pamphlet.]

233 Foster, Alfred E. Manning. "Walter Pater, Humanist," THE SENSI-TIVE, AND OTHER PIECES (Lond: George Allen, 1905), pp. 99–110.
WP, as a teacher, is neglected. He is much more than a mere "stylist." He did not believe in "art for art's sake," nor did he believe in the supremacy of form. His style follows his thought. WP sympathizes with all things; he reveals the temperament of the "true humanist."

234 Grant Duff, Sir Mountstuart E. NOTES FROM A DIARY, 1896 to January 23, 1901 (Lond: John Murray, 1905), I, 52. [NOTES FROM A DIARY was published in seven installments of two volumes each between 1896 and 1905.]
[Regrets that WP never finished his "proposed article on the poetry of Anglicanism." Other references to WP in volumes published in 1898, 1901, and 1904.]

235 Wilde, Oscar. DE PROFUNDIS (Lond: Methuen, 1905), pp. 45, 67–68; (NY & Lond: Putnam's Sons, 1905); rptd (1909); rptd (NY: Modern Library, 1926); rptd as Volume XIII of THE WRITINGS OF OSCAR WILDE (Lond & NY: A. R. Keller, 1907); as Volume XI of THE FIRST COLLECTED EDITION OF THE WORKS OF OSCAR WILDE, 1908–1922 (Lond: Methuen, 1908), rptd (Lond. Dawsons of Pall Mall, NY. Barnes & Noble, 1969); rptd (NY: AMS P, 1972); as Volume VIII of THE WORKS OF OSCAR WILDE (NY: Lamb, 1909); rptd (Berlin: S. Fischer, 1914); as Volume VIII of THE COMPLETE WORKS OF OSCAR WILDE (NY: Bigelow, Brown, 1921); as Volume XI of THE COMPLETE WORKS OF OSCAR WILDE (Garden City, NY: Doubleday, Page, 1923); rptd (NY: Philosophical Library, 1950); (1960); rptd for the first time in its complete form as a letter "To Lord Alfred Douglas" (written Jan–March 1897), in THE LETTERS OF OSCAR WILDE, ed by Rupert Hart-Davis (NY: Harcourt, Brace & World, 1962), pp. 423–511 (pp. 430, 471, 476 on WP); rptd with notes by Rupert Hart-Davis (NY: Avon Books, 1964); rptd (NY: Vintage Books, 1964); rptd as DE PROFUNDIS AND OTHER WRITINGS (Harmondsworth, Middlesex: Penguin, 1973). [A selective list of editions. The references to WP, pp. 471, 476 of LETTERS are substantially, though not exactly, the same as those in the earlier versions. That on p. 430 of LETTERS had not seen print before 1962. See LETTERS, pp. 423–24n. for a history of the manuscript, typescript, and published versions of DE PROFUNDIS. The following annotation is based on the text in LETTERS.]
WP's "failure is to form habits" contains "a wonderful, a terrible truth." [Wilde is blaming Douglas for having exercised control over him; and, to a lesser extent, he

is blaming himself for falling into the habit of submitting to that control—in effect, for having forgotten WP's words.] "During my first term at Oxford" I read WP's *Renaissance*—"that book which has had such a strange influence over my life." "In *Marius the Epicurean* Pater seeks to reconcile the artistic life with the life of religion. . . . But Marius is little more than a spectator . . . and perhaps a little too much occupied with the comeliness of the vessels."

1906

236 Benson, A[rthur]. C[hristopher]. WALTER PATER (Lond & NY: Macmillan ["English Men of Letters" series], 1906); rptd (Lond: 1907); rptd (NY: 1911); (1916); (1917); rptd (Lond: 1921); rptd in facsimile (Detroit: Gale Research, 1968).

[Chap I, "Early Life": Brief genealogical outline. Sketchy account of WP's childhood. Attention to architecture at Queen's College and Brasenose College. General description of WP's style of living and manner of behavior, emphasizing reticence, simplicity, delicacy, and quiet. Chap II, "Early Writings": Emphasizes the autobiographical overtones of "Winckelmann." Considers (in very general terms) the possible effect on WP of Mallock's THE NEW REPUBLIC. Discusses (almost entirely without reference to particulars) the Jowett-WP relationship. Chap III, "Oxford Life": Chapter title misleading, since only about four (of twenty-nine) pages are devoted to WP's life at Oxford, his duties at BNC, etc. Rhapsodizes over the "charm" and "sweetness" of "The Child in the House." WP was temperamentally too different from Rossetti to be an effective critic of him, whereas the quality of his insight into Wordsworth is traceable to his natural sympathy with him (see "Rossetti" and "On Wordsworth").

Chap IV, *"Marius the Epicurean":* "Bears . . . a strong personal, almost autobiographical impress; but . . . essentially a learned book." The "workmanship" of *Marius* "is from first to last perfect." (Yet Benson criticizes, among other things, the "priggishness" of Cornelius and the "false atmosphere" in WP's account of the Mass.) Some general discussion of the "poetical" qualities of WP's prose. Chap V, "London Life": An analysis of the *Imaginary Portraits* (especially why this form suited WP's personality and talents). Includes readings of individual portraits, sufficiently attentive to their shortcomings (e.g., lack of dramatic situations) as well as their virtues. Chap VI, "Later Writings": *Gaston de Latour* is "a great unfinished canvas by a master of minute, imaginative, suggestive portraiture." "Style" has "immense" autobiographical value (WP's acknowledgement that art done in God's service is the highest art amounts to an open profession of faith). *Plato and Platonism* reveals that WP was "philosophically cultured" but not a philosopher, a "psychologist," who approached philosophy "through the effect of metaphysical ideas upon personality." Though a "beautiful" instance of WP in the role of educator, *Plato and Platonism* is not among his greatest books (e.g., those in which he provided "more intimate self-revelations" and "in which he uttered oracles"). "Pascal" is WP's "most deliberate utterance on ethical things. It reveals him . . . as a deep though unwilling sceptic; it shows a soul athirst yet unsatisfied."

Chap VII, "Personal Characteristics": Generalized personality sketch (e.g., "a fine simplicity of nature"). WP was shy, reclusive, yet pleasant in unchallenging circumstances. He deliberately shielded himself "against the roughness of the world" (maintaining an ironic posture as "a sort of fence" around himself). He was capable of kindness, courteousness, consideration, and sincerity—but not intimacy. Five pages on WP's religious position, emphasizing his later sympathy for, if not commitment to, traditional Christianity. As a stylist, WP was not lucid, but painstaking, utterly self-conscious.] [An unambitious, reasonably sound biography. Chapters II–VI consist largely of paraphrase of and quotation from WP's major writings, considered chronologically. Benson consistently assumes that WP's writings are semi-autobiographical. Chapters V and VI contain the most valuable criticism.]

> **237** Elton, Oliver. FREDERICK YORK POWELL: A LIFE. Two Volumes (Oxford: Clarendon P, 1906), I, 158–59, 422.

Powell introduced WP to Mallarmé, but they scarcely spoke to each other. WP once shuddered at the sight of Rodin's "The Man with the Broken Nose": it clashed with his "ideal of manly beauty."

> **238** Harris, Frank. "Walter Pater: The Pagan," JOHN BULL, 8 Sept 1906, pp. 329–30.

For A. C. Benson, the "beneficed champion of Mrs. Grundy," to write about WP, the pagan, is like asking Casanova "to write the life of St. Elizabeth of Hungary." Benson's biography of WP is verbose and misleading. WP was a pagan; he viewed Christianity as "a sort of moral leprosy with shining white scales." WP's heart was weak and his circulation poor; all of which explains much of his "self-restraint" that actually obscured "an inordinate desire." Had he been born with a strong heart, he might have been another Goethe. His place in the history of English letters is secure. "His influence was a liberating influence." He helped to lead us "out of the prison of Puritanism."

> **239** Hutton, John A[lexander]. "Walter Pater in *Marius the Epicurean*," in PILGRIMS IN THE REGION OF FAITH: AMIEL, TOLSTOY, PATER, NEWMAN (Edinburgh & Lond: Oliphant, Anderson & Ferrier, 1906), pp. 59–102; rptd (Cincinnati: Jennings & Graham; NY: Eaton & Mains, 1906).

WP ranks in "spiritual degree" and "sensitiveness" with Augustine, Dante, Bunyan, Goethe, Carlyle, Newman, and Tolstoy. His work "will always serve as a kind of confessional for those who . . . are aware of . . . a certain spirit of questioning in their religious faith." *Marius the Epicurean,* which traces "Pater's own spiritual career," "contains his most finished and deliberate message on the things of faith." It will have "a permanent place in the confessional literature of the soul." [Nearly three-fourths of the essay is devoted to plot summary of *Marius*.]

> **240** "Literature. WALTER PATER. By A. C. Benson," ATHENAEUM, No. 4101 (2 June 1906), 659–60.

"No one admired Pater more than Oscar Wilde, or learnt more from him, or understood him less." Other writers (Vernon Lee, D'Annunzio) were influenced by WP; they too lacked "his tact or instinct." WP suppressed the "Conclusion" of *The Renaissance* and "Aesthetic Poetry" because he saw that he had inadvertently spawned a flurry of "vague and feverish writing"—"precisely the kind of writing he himself most disliked."

WP's criticism of painting and poetry was "often wrong in detail" but "never in matters of general principle or essential feeling." WP's irony was not merely a mask; it often conveyed "a perfectly definite and well-aimed criticism" (as when he blandly asked, regarding Pierre Loti, "Isn't he rather like Charlotte M. Yonge?"). [A review of Benson's biography. The author of the review indicates that he had known WP. Benson's not knowing WP, he says, makes his portrait less vital than it could have been. Overall, however, the review is favorable. Follows an annotation of the reviewer's comments on WP; he says a good deal more about Benson's view of WP.]

> **241** Manson, Edward. "Recollections of Walter Pater," OXFORD MAGAZINE, XXV (7 Nov 1906), 60–61.

[Memoir by one whom WP had tutored, containing virtually nothing of interest. Reports an old rumor that WP had sat for Simeon Solomon's portrait of Judas Iscariot.]

> **242** Mosher, Thomas B. [Introduction to] "Charles Lamb: An Appreciation," BIBELOT, XII (1906), [217–18].

[Appreciative comments.]

> **243** Mosher, Thomas B. [Introduction to] "Giordano Bruno," BIBELOT, XII (1906), [311–13].

"It is evident" that WP "abandoned his earlier idea of completing *Gaston de Latour* when he had written and published in MACMILLAN'S MAGAZINE during the months of May to October, 1888, the five chapters which . . . contain portions of his most finished prose." [Swinburne's "Four Sonnets on Bruno" are placed after WP's essay for comparison.]

> **244** Saintsbury, George. "Walter Pater," BOOKMAN (Lond), XXX (Aug 1906), 165–70; rptd in PREFACES AND ESSAYS (Lond: Macmillan, 1933), pp. 345–60; rptd (Freeport, NY: Books for Libraries P, 1969); rptd (Westport, Conn.: Greenwood P, 1970); rptd (Folcroft, Pa: Folcroft P, 1971).

While "true Paterism" is "a highly respectable, as well as attractive creed," misinterpretations of what WP thought can do actual harm (e.g., if one patterns his life according to a misinterpretation). The ideal interpreter of WP would be an Oxford man, familiar with the intellectual climate at Oxford from the late 1850s to the early 1870s. This was a remarkable period at Oxford. It was a transitional period of ferment, of innovations; it was a period that tolerated the unconventional. "From the larger world outside came larger elements of fermentation" [Saintsbury lists these elements in an interesting paragraph, p. 166]. WP's "Neo-Cyrenaicism" should be understood as an attempt to encourage intelligent enjoyment of the "welter of interests and influences" which produced that complex and exciting period. The core of WP's work is found in *The Renaissance, Marius the Epicurean,* and *Appreciations.* The *Imaginary Portraits* "are interesting, but a little out of the author's true line." *Plato and Platonism, Greek Studies,* and *Miscellaneous Studies* "are valuable as side-lights chiefly."

> **245** Sherard, Robert Harborough. THE LIFE OF OSCAR WILDE (Lond: T. W. Laurie, 1906); rptd (NY: Dodd, Mead, 1928), pp. 308–11; rptd (Phila: Richard West, n.d.); rptd as OSCAR WILDE (Folcroft, Pa: Folcroft Library Editions, 1974).

WP's review of DORIAN GRAY is "finely written" but evasive; his comments on Wilde himself, quoted at length, are "more interesting."

> **246** Symons, Arthur. "Walter Pater," MONTHLY REVIEW (Lond), XXIV (Sept 1906), 14–24; rptd in FIGURES OF SEVERAL CENTURIES (Lond: Constable, 1916), pp. 316–35; rptd with slight revisions as "Introduction," *The Renaissance,* ed by Arthur Symons (NY: Boni & Liveright, 1919); also rptd as "Introduction" to *The Renaissance* (NY: Random House, n.d.), pp. xi–xxiv.

WP was, as Mallarmé said, "le prosateur ouvrage par excellence de ce temps." His strangeness, subtlety of temperament, and delicacy of form made him truly unique. In his work "thought moves to music." His style is indeed the man himself: harmonious; slow and deliberate in movement; settled in repose; timid, yet scrutinizing; mannered, yet personal; urbane; and painfully conscientious. All of WP's work is confessional, "the *vraie vérité* (as he was fond of saying) about the world in which he lived." He was not a hedonist but accepted quietly and with discrimination all that was "beautiful, active, or illuminating in every moment." In his older years, he added a stoic sense of duty to his earlier doctrine of pleasure. [Symons notes that although they had corresponded earlier, he did not meet WP until WP was nearly fifty. He admits that what Browning was to him in verse, WP was in prose. He made prose "a fine art." WP was instrumental in getting Symons's first volume of verse published. Symons notes also that WP hated all forms of extravagance and whatever seemed morbid or sordid. WP never would have liked Verlaine, Symons conjectures. He valued poets like Rossetti and Dante for their concreteness, but saw little value in Coleridge's "Kubla Khan." Symons includes a letter of 8 Jan 1888 from WP and notes that he had received over the years from fifty to sixty letters from WP (only twenty-eight addressed to Symons are included in Evans's ed of WP's LETTERS, 1970). Symons notes further that WP had a distaste for writing letters; reviews sometimes took him a year to finish; and lecturing was a trial for him.

WP was familiar enough with Baudelaire to know that he loved cats. WP owned a copy of M. Bourget's ESSAIS DE PSYCHOLOGIE CONTEMPORAINE with its essay on Baudelaire. "The Child in the House" was meant to be the first chapter of a prose romance that would reveal, like AURORA LEIGH, the "poetry of modern life." Because he always planned to go on with the romance, he purposely never reprinted "Child" in *Imaginary Portraits*. Symons also suggests that "The Prince of Court Painters" was most certainly influenced by WP's work on Goncourt's essay and the "Life of Watteau" by Count de Caylus in L'ART DU XVIII SIÈCLE (FIRST SERIES). WP also had planned to do a portrait of a burgomaster based on Moroni's PORTRAIT OF A TAILOR in the National Gallery and another one set in the time of the Albigensian persecution. Symons claims that WP never mentioned Ruskin to him but felt his influence; he did speak with admiration of De Quincey, of Flaubert, of Stendhal, and of Zola; the Goncourts, he both admired and disliked.]

1907

247 "The Aesthetic Outlook: Walter Pater," EDINBURGH REVIEW, CCVI (July 1907), 23–49.

All of WP's criticism, whether of life or art or thought, took as its chief aim the perception of the beautiful. His point of view was not that of the man of religion, the moralist, the scientist, or the contemplative; yet to his search for beauty he brought "the reverence of a pilgrim, the patience of a scholar, the zeal of an explorer . . . and the devotion of the votary of a faith." His "susceptibility to things beautiful" is joined to a susceptibility to "things sorrowful." Both in *Greek Studies* and in the imaginary portraits "Denys l'Auxerrois" and "Apollo in Picardy" this dual attraction drew his attention to "the dying god" (Dionysus) and "the deity of sorrow" (Demeter). WP's best art criticism deals with "the emotional expression of art." All other interests in art were subordinate to his interests in its expressiveness, the "intimate impress of an 'indwelling soul.' " This is evident in many of his Renaissance studies, but less so in his studies of figures more nearly his contemporaries (Coleridge, Wordsworth, Lamb). These latter reveal less of his "critical creative talent" and are consequently below the level of his best criticism.

Marius the Epicurean and *Gaston de Latour* have, as their "sole end and purpose," the aesthetic apprehension of human lives. Their title characters are embodiments of thoughts and feelings, products of converging influences among which they are searchers. Their stories, like the best of WP's art criticism, illustrate his "dual susceptibility" to the beautiful and the sorrowful. WP was an ascetic stylist who avoided superlatives, overstatement, high coloration of any kind. He characteristically displayed "a reticence amounting to taciturnity," an "almost ostentatious reserve." His writing suffered from "occasional obscurity," not because of vague thinking but because of overly subtle thinking and "fastidiousness . . . in the choice of language."

248 Bowen, Edwin W. "Walter Pater," SEWANEE REVIEW, XV (Jan 1907), 271–84.
[An unoriginal overview of WP's life and work.]

249 Butler, Samuel. THE NOTE-BOOKS OF SAMUEL BUTLER, ed by H. F. Jones (NY: Dutton, 1907); rptd (Lond: Fifield, 1912); rptd (NY: Kennerly, 1914); rptd (NY: Dutton, 1917), p. 184; rptd (Lond: Cape, 1921); rptd with minor revisions in SAMUEL BUTLER'S NOTEBOOKS, ed by G. Keynes and Brian Hill (Lond: J. Cape, 1951), p. 280.
WP's style is "like the face of some old woman who has been to Madame Rachel and had herself enamelled. . . . the odour is cherry-blossom. Mr. Matthew Arnold's odour is as the faint sickliness of hawthorn."

250 Reedy, William Marion. "Introduction," *Gaston de Latour. An Unfinished Romance*. By Walter Pater (Portland, Maine: T. B. Mosher, 1907), pp. vii–xi.
Gaston is another Marius. [Speculates pointlessly on how WP might have ended *Gaston de Latour.*]

251 Saintsbury, George. THE LATER NINETEENTH CENTURY, Volume XII of PERIODS OF EUROPEAN LITERATURE, ed by George Saintsbury (Edinburgh & Lond: Blackwood; NY: Scribner's Sons, 1907), pp. 25, 165–68, 181, 370, 402; rptd (Folcroft, Pa: Folcroft Library Editions, 1970).
WP was "distinctly more academical" than Arnold or Ruskin; his range of interests was relatively narrow. Though his style was sometimes denounced as "effeminate," "no one has surpassed or equalled . . . the ambitious and successful refinement of his prose." The whole of his work "is associated with a peculiar ethical-aesthetic or aesthetic-ethic to which he sometimes gave the name of Neo-Cyrenaicism."

252 Wright, Thomas. "John Payne and Walter Pater," ACADEMY (Lond), LXXII (6 April 1907), 349.
[Wright replies to an attack on his LIFE OF WALTER PATER by Walter Phelps Dodge in ACADEMY (Lond), 30 March 1907. Wright claims that Burton's ARABIAN NIGHTS is plagiarized from John Payne's translation and from other important translations. His LIFE OF WALTER PATER, in contrast, was all original. WP's acquaintance with R. C. Jackson and his visits to St. Austin's priory "led him to

write *Marius."* The only contemporary who really understood WP as a writer was Lady Dilke. WP was more of a scholar than an art critic. Wright claims to "love the man (deploring, of course, the one lamentable stain on his life)."]

253 Wright, Thomas. THE LIFE OF WALTER PATER. Two Volumes (Lond: Everett; NY: Putnam, 1907); rptd (NY: Haskell House, 1969).

[Wright imparts virtually no sense of coherence to his account of WP's life. He assumes that every event that occurs in the life of every hero of every one of WP's imaginary portraits is directly autobiographical. Wright really has nothing of substance to add to the sparse information, already published at the time he wrote, about WP's childhood and youth. His account of the years 1855–1860, however, which draws heavily on the memories of J. R. McQueen, does add to our knowledge of WP's school and college years. The imbalance of the biography is perhaps best illustrated by the attention which Wright pays, respectively, to WP's sisters and to Richard C. Jackson. The sisters had refused to help Wright. In his biography their existence is scarcely acknowledged (though WP made his home with them for years); they are never mentioned by name. Jackson, on the other hand, who first made WP's acquaintance in 1877, is alluded to well over 200 times in volume II alone. (Most of the 50 illustrations in volume II are related, in one way or another, to Jackson). Wright's account of the last third of WP's life is heavily colored by the presence of Jackson. Jackson was apparently a wealthy collector, a dilettante, and a crank. The picture that emerges between Wright's lines is of a vain, affected man who had very little taste but who had enormous pretentions. His claim to being the model of Marius the Epicurean can be dismissed. Wright is totally uncritical in his acceptance of Jackson's version of his acquaintance with WP. Wright publishes dozens of statements which Jackson attributed to WP.

Wright's attitude toward WP is erratic. Fulsome praise of WP alternates with cutting gossip. Sometimes he goes out of his way to demean WP and his work. One example: there are dozens of references, mostly gratuitous, to WP's physical unattractiveness. (Wright seems to relish the subject.) On the subject of WP's apparent (though, it seems, latterly sublimated) homosexuality, Wright says nothing directly. He contents himself with sly nudges and an occasional innuendo. Usually he merely quotes and paraphrases, noting in passing the "fine passages" in WP's works. He gives little indication that he understands, or cares, what they are about. The biography is lopsided, patronizing, self-contradictory, alternately catty and unctuous. Unfortunately, it is practically all we have (at least in English). Benson's slim and sketchy study (1906) is generally reliable within its limits; but its limits are severe. So Wright, by default, is indispensable. His work does contain most of what is known about WP's life. For Wright's account of his sources for the bibliography and the difficulties he encountered from WP's sisters while writing it, see his AUTOBIOGRAPHY, 1936.]

1908

254 Dickinson, Thomas H., and Frederick W. Roe. NINETEENTH CEN-
TURY ENGLISH PROSE: CRITICAL ESSAYS (NY: American Book Co.,
1908), pp. 338–41.
WP's "Leonardo da Vinci" is the best essay in his best book. All of WP's work,
even his fiction, is static. It is the "art of design," resembling painting and
sculpture, in this respect, more than drama. WP was "an etcher and not a
narrator." Among the disadvantages of WP's style are its "lack of warmth and
spontaneity." Its two main qualities, however, are exactitude in language and
mystery. The "curiosity" he perceives in Leonardo "was Pater's also." His
"marvelous" style is "rich in mystery" (rather than obscure); it is "sinuous, lithe,
and complex but never tortuous and turbid." [Reprints the Leonardo essay, pp.
341–68.]

255 Orton, W. Aylott. "Walter Pater," WESTMINSTER REVIEW, CLXX
(Nov 1908), 536–41.
Fascinated by the theme of gods in exile, WP was himself a sort of pagan in modern
times. His "sensuous intelligence" enabled him to translate psychology into
"terms of sense" and to induce "a desired mood or temper in the mind of his
reader" by "using purely sensual impressions." *Marius the Epicurean* "is the
completest manifestation in our language" of a "subjective interpretation of
nature." WP's "masterly subjectivity" makes "On Wordsworth" the "most
luminous of all his critical writings."

WP is profoundly skeptical. "There is no Providence conveniently lurking in the
background" of his *Imaginary Portraits*. Melancholy, never explicit, is implicit in
all his work. Even in his later years, when his interest in "matters of religion"
increased, he had too much "intellectual candour and integrity" to return "to
principles of so different a nature from those which his own temperament forced
upon him." His was "the pagan temper, spiritually isolated in an age and environment so uncongenial."

1909

256 Bradley, A. C. "Poetry for Poetry's Sake," in OXFORD LECTURES
ON POETRY (Lond: Macmillan, 1909), pp. [3]–34; rptd (1911); (1923);
(1950); rptd in THE PROBLEMS OF AESTHETICS: A BOOK OF READINGS
(NY: Rinehart, 1953), pp. 562–77; rptd (Lond: Macmillan; NY: St.
Martin's P, 1955).
"What is the gist of Pater's teaching about style, if it is not that in the end the one

virtue of style is truth or adequacy; that the word, phrase, sentence, should express perfectly the writer's perception, feeling, image, or thought."

257 Buchan, John. "Nine Brasenose Worthies," in BRASENOSE COLLEGE QUATERCENTENARY MONOGRAPHS (Oxford: Clarendon P, 1909), II, Part II (XIV:2A), 23–30.

The "landmarks" of WP's career "were all in the intellect." From his writings "we can piece together some record of his development." The "Conclusion" of *The Renaissance* marks the culmination of the first stage, in which *aesthesis* outweighed *theoria*. *Marius the Epicurean* exemplifies the second stage, in which he began to dwell more on *theoria*. In *Plato and Platonism,* representative of the third stage, "*Theoria* is beginning to oust *Aesthesis* altogether." Having "dallied" with art for art's sake, he eventually approached art for righteousness' sake. WP was "a true humanist in the old and right sense of the word." He was also a naturalist, whose mission was "to proclaim the beauty of all natural things." He was not, strictly speaking, a philosopher, "for he does not seek explanation or unity. . . . his tendency is always to individualism in thought—to disintegrate and to individualize." His works are "studies, not in the philosophy, but in the art, of life."

WP "was as little like Mr. Rose in THE NEW REPUBLIC as he was like John Calvin." As for Wright's biography, that "volume of gossip can only be described as an outrage." [Also contains biographical and anecdotal information, of no particular significance, and a discussion of WP's style.]

258 Cecil, Algernon. "Walter Pater," in SIX OXFORD THINKERS (Lond: John Murray, 1909), pp. 214–51.

WP was a descendant of the Oxford movement. He was a disciple of Ruskin who broke with his master in valuing art for its own sake. *The Renaissance* contained exquisite criticism, but it held "a certain unwholesome fascination" for "the Oxford aesthetes." Those who were fascinated by the gem-like flame were playing with fire. *Marius the Epicurean,* though scholarly, subtle, original, and deeply thought, "was not true. It depicted not life, but a pale reflection of it." It was "a magnificent success," but it has not "moved one single mind of first-rate eminence."

259 Dawson, William J., and Coningsby W. Dawson. THE GREAT ENGLISH ESSAYISTS (NY & Lond: Harper & Bros., 1909), p. 269.

WP's love of beauty moved him to "passionate moments, when his page grows lyric." [Quotes, pp. 290–93, an excerpt from the "Conclusion" to *The Renaissance,* under the heading "Philosophy of Life"—in a section of the volume titled, "Impassioned Prose."]

260 Huneker, James. "From an Ivory Tower," in EGOISTS: A BOOK OF SUPERMEN (NY: Scribner's Sons, 1909); rptd (NY: Scribner's Sons, 1925), pp. 304–16.

[Draws heavily on previously published accounts of WP's life and work: those of

Gosse, Sharp, Moore, Symons, Benson, etc. Compares and contrasts WP, rather glibly, with Paul Bourget, Ruskin, Stevenson, Mallarmé, De Quincey, Herbert Spencer, Maurice Barrès, Leslie Stephen, Anatole France, Keats, and—especially—Flaubert and Newman. Speaks at length about WP's style; e.g.: "he will always be a writer for writers, . . . [he is] the composer of a polyphonic prose-music that recalls the performance of harmonious adagio within the sonorous spaces of a Gothic cathedral, through the windows of which filters alien daylight."]

261 Kellner, Leon. DIE ENGLISCHE LITERATUR IM ZEITALTER DER KÖNIGIN VITTORIA (English Literature in the Time of Queen Victoria) (Leipzig: Tauchnitz, 1909), pp. 8, 329n, 383n, 464n, 511-17.
Marius the Epicurean characterizes modern man completely. [Contains commonplaces about WP's critical premises and practices. Riddled with errors of fact and interpretation.] [In German.]

262 Madan, Falconer. "Brief Annals of the College with a List of Books Relating to it," in BRASENOSE COLLEGE QUATERCENTENARY MONOGRAPHS (Oxford: Clarendon P, 1909), I (VII), 9, 25.
[Records WP's election to a fellowship in 1864; the preceding entry is: "1854. Installation of gas lighting." Bibliographical description of F. W. Bussell's pamphlet, "In Memoriam W. H. P."]

263 M[osher]., T[homas]. B[ird]. "Preface," *The Child in the House*. By Walter Pater (Portland, Maine: T. B. Mosher, 1909), pp. ix-xix.
[Consists almost entirely of quotes from A. C. Benson, Edmund Gosse, and Arthur Symons. Gives publishing history.]

264 Ross, Robert. "Mr. Benson's Pater," MASQUES AND PHASES (Lond: Humphreys, 1909), pp. 125-34.
"When good mediocrities die" in England, they "run a very fair chance of burial in Westminster Abbey." Benson's book on WP is a masterpiece. *Marius the Epicurean* is a failure by WP's own standards. Its scheme is similar to that of JOHN INGLESANT, but its characters are lifeless. WP is "an aside in literature," an ornament.

265 Waddington, Samuel. CHAPTERS OF MY LIFE: AN AUTOBIOGRAPHY (Lond: Chapman & Hall, 1909), pp. 3, 35-37.
[Inconsequential reminiscences by one who was "never personally acquainted" with WP, but who remembers him slightly from his Brasenose College days, and who once received a letter from WP (which appears in facsimile). Recalls WP in his mid-twenties as being "by no means plain or ill-featured" (this *contra* Wright).]

266 Ward, T. Humphry. "Reminiscences: Brasenose, 1864-1872," in BRASENOSE COLLEGE QUATERCENTENARY MONOGRAPHS (Oxford: Clarendon P, 1909), II, Part II (XIV:2C), 74-75, 77.

[Recollections of WP in 1866–67, by one of WP's earliest students.] WP's lectures presupposed more knowledge than we had, but for me they were "an extraordinary stimulus." WP's "teaching was immensely fruitful," both in the originality of his view of life and in his insistence on clear thinking and writing. [Recalls long walks and "a delightful month" with WP during vacation.]

1910

---

267 [Bailey, John Cann.] "A Modern Platonist," TIMES LITERARY SUPPLEMENT (Lond), 1 Sept 1910, pp. 305–6; rptd in Bailey, POETS AND POETRY: BEING ARTICLES REPRINTED FROM THE LITERARY SUPPLEMENT OF "THE TIMES" (Oxford: Clarendon P, 1911), pp. 187–94.

In contrast to the clamorous, partisan (and intolerant) voices of Ruskin, Carlyle, and Macauley, the voice of WP was a "critical, questioning" voice: analytical but sympathetic, open to the world of ideas on all sides. "The old notion that Pater was an epicurean and a hedonist may be supposed now to be finally dismissed." He was essentially a Platonist, in both the visionary and the inquiring senses of that term. His "controlling desire" ("everywhere evident") was for unity. He "felt his way along, through hesitations and scruples, to a unity for which no serious effort of the human spirit could be an object either of scorn or of dread or of denunciation. He was the high priest of the artistic world of his day; but he was also a Puritan": an ascetic in the spirit of Sparta and of Plato.

268 Browning, Oscar. MEMORIES OF SIXTY YEARS AT ETON [,] CAMBRIDGE AND ELSEWHERE (Lond & NY: John Lane, 1910), pp. 106–7, 182, 272, 289.

My ten-year friendship with WP (we were "very intimate") revealed him "as one of the kindest men I had ever known." WP was also a "very intimate" friend of Simeon Solomon.

269 Laurent, Raymond. ÉTUDES ANGLAISES (English Studies), with "Introduction" by R. J. E. Tiddy (Paris: Bernard Grasset, 1910), pp. 21, 38, 47–48, 51, 73, 77, 82, 96, 106n., 109, 141–258, 262–64, 267–68, 273n, 274–75, 277, 279, 285–86, 298, 304n, 308, 310, 312.

WP's *Greek Studies* does not include as many foreign elements as did his *Renaissance*. He now seems to turn almost exclusively to the Greek authors. WP attempts to resolve the problem of art when he speaks of the role of the imagination in Greek sculpture. Nature is important, but there is an unconscious symbolism beyond any work of art which reaches the deeper parts of our being because it suggests dormant associations. WP reminds us that aesthetics played an important part in the formation of the best religious legends.

"The Child in the House" is a suite of impressions from childhood with two vague characters: one is destiny; the other is a heart facing life. The child benefits from the world but then he learns about suffering and unfulfilled desire. He understands suffering but he cannot conceive death. Marius (*Marius the Epicurean*) is the "child" matured; he tries to realize his dreams. The novel is, essentially, the story of a search for freedom. The novel's conflict deals with the triumph of individualism over repression. In the *Imaginary Portraits,* WP does not put his characters into contact with exterior circumstances. They deal mainly with problems of conscience; their conflicts are internal. The success of *Marius* is due to the reader's finding in it sensations which he has felt before. But Marius is a toy in the hands of nature; without the messages that nature gives him, he could not live.

WP has a legitimate place in English psychology. He followed the example of Mill, Spencer, Hartley, and Bain by writing monographs instead of theoretical tracts. He shows that paradise is within the self and is discovered through innocence. WP's imaginary portraits are poetic in character. In *Plato and Platonism,* he tries to reconstruct Plato's life. Nothing about WP's work is revolutionary. WP was one of many writers who were involved in the nineteenth century with the revival of interest in Italy. [In French.]

> **270** Lee, Sidney. THE FRENCH RENAISSANCE IN ENGLAND (Oxford: Clarendon P; NY: Scribner's Sons, 1910), pp. ix, 199.

WP's *The Renaissance* and *Gaston de Latour* "defined with rare insight the aesthetic quality of French literature in the sixteenth century."

> **271** "The Oxford Spirit," OUTLOOK (NY), XCVI (19 Nov 1910), 621–23.

WP's work is "saturated with the Oxford atmosphere." WP was a "little master" rather than a great writer. His style was sometimes eloquent and elegant, sometimes involved and heavy. His work "lacks fiber and manliness of tone"; but he "was always serious, nearly always charming, at times penetrating and luminous." [Primarily deals with the educational atmosphere of Oxford.]

> **272** Sharp, Elizabeth A. WILLIAM SHARP: A MEMOIR COMPILED BY HIS WIFE ELIZABETH (NY: Duffield; Lond: Heinemann, 1910), pp. 67, 69–72, 119–20; rptd, Two Volumes (1912).

[William Sharp intended to rewrite his study of Rossetti with a dedication to WP. In it he writes to WP that of all that has been written about Rossetti " 'nothing shows more essential insight . . . than the essay by yourself included in . . . *Appreciations.' "* Sharp recalls having discussed Rossetti with WP at Oxford and the rightness of WP's observations on Rossetti's genius. Mrs. Sharp recalls a meeting at their house between WP, Alfred Austin, and Theodore Watts-Dunton, with reference to WP's fear of snakes (cf. *Marius the Epicurean*), and relates an anecdote about WP's declining to row because he was afraid to trust himself to a "townsman." Letters from WP to Sharp appear on pp. 67–68, 69, 73, 99–100, 104–5, 116, 133.]

273 Tiddy, R. J. E. "Introduction," ÉTUDES ANGLAISES (English Studies), by Raymond Laurent (Paris: Bernard Grasset, 1910), pp. ii–vi, viii–ix.
[A summary of Laurent's commentary on WP, q.v.]

274 Walker, Hugh. THE LITERATURE OF THE VICTORIAN ERA (Cambridge: Cambridge UP, 1910), pp. 977–78, 1019–23; rptd (New Delhi: S. Chand, 1964).
WP's work bears "unmistakably the marks of decadence." In its wide range of topics, it "illustrates the complexity of the age." It is "critical rather than creative." All of WP's work is autobiographical; "there is nothing in the least degree objective in his work." His influence on the aesthetic movement ranks behind only that of Ruskin and Rossetti.

275 "Walter Pater," SPECTATOR, CIV (25 June 1910), 1075–76.
WP is already a minor classic. Now that the aesthetic school, with which his name was rather inappropriately linked, has disappeared, we may see his real value more clearly. He was a serious scholar and thinker. His collected works reveal significant development in his ideas. His style, for all its faults, has unique attractions; it will assure his enduring reputation.

276 Whiting, Lilian. LOUISE CHANDLER MOULTON: POET AND FRIEND (Bost: Little, Brown, 1910), pp. 147, 237.
1889 [?]—had lunch at WP's and met M. Gabriel Sarrazin, the French critic; talked of de Maupassant. [Letter to WP on p. 237.]

1911

277 "The Alleged Corrupting Influence of Walter Pater," CURRENT LITERATURE, LI (Aug 1911), 213–15.
[This article contains a summary of the debate on WP's worth initiated by Paul Elmer More in 1911 in his review of the library edition of WP's works (NATION [NY] and EVENING POST [NY]) and carried in an abstract that appeared in CURRENT LITERATURE, L (June 1911). More attacks WP. In reply, the author of this article suggests that WP is a brilliant interpreter of the artistic life. The real question is not whether WP is demoralizing but whether art is demoralizing. WP represents the artistic life; does, therefore, a constant preoccupation with artistic ends corrupt one? The author notes that More has been answered by James Huneker in the NY SUN, 11 June 1911 (q.v.). Huneker is said to have made a case for WP as a moralist whose theories bear a remarkable similarity to those of

William James and Henri Bergson, a " 'pragmatism poetically transfigured.' " WP, viewed as a humanist instead of " 'the verbal virtuoso, is getting more distinct with the years.' " In the St. Louis Mirror, 22 June 1911 (q.v.), J. L. Hervey argues that WP's influence was inspiring. WP judged Wilde's Dorian Gray in terms of the "Conclusion" to *The Renaissance* and found him remiss, his soul corrupted. Wilde himself may be judged by WP's "Conclusion." WP is not to be held responsible for Wilde's life, as More claims, for Wilde was " 'congenitally unbalanced.' " But " *'ascesis* . . . temperance . . . was Pater's motto.' " WP sought truth, Hervey claims, not only beauty, and his works are therefore sacerdotal.]

278 Bendz, Ernst. Some Stray Notes on the Personality and Writings of Oscar Wilde (Gothenburg: Wettergren & Kerber, 1911) [not seen.]

[Supposedly touches upon the close intellectual relationship between Wilde and WP, a thesis expanded in detail in "Notes on the Literary Relationship between Walter Pater and Oscar Wilde" in Neuphilologische Mitteilungen, 1912.]

279 Burchard, Russell D. "The Writings of Pater," Evening Post (NY), 21 April 1911, p. 8.

[In this letter to the editor, Burchard agrees with Paul Elmer More's evaluation of WP's philosophy in Nation (NY) (q.v.) and in Evening Post (NY), 1911. Burchard questions More's statement that WP acknowledged Rossetti as one of his teachers. Burchard can find no biographical support for this claim. He also suggests that a basic difference between WP and Rossetti as thinkers is that Rossetti's work reflects a concern with substance, the "life of the body," while WP's work reflects a concern for the "shadow," "the life of the spirit." Burchard also maintains that it is doing WP an injustice to hold him "responsible for anything that Oscar Wilde stands for." The fact that WP omitted the "Conclusion" from the second edition of *The Renaissance* suggests that he was very much aware of and wanted to avoid its possible misinterpretation by some of his followers.]

280 Christian, Israel. "Pater's Philosophy," Evening Post (NY), 27 April 1911, p. 8.

[This letter to the editor is in response to an earlier article on WP by Paul Elmer More in 1911 in Nation (NY) (q.v.) and Evening Post (NY). Christian is critical of More's emphasis on WP "as the Aristippus of Oxford, the direct inheritor and expounder of the Epicureanism of the ancient Cyrenaics, and thus the god-father of the detestable tribe of modern decadents" rather than as "the *parfait prosateur,* the author of exquisite and hauntingly melodious prose." Christian does not specifically dispute More's "philosophical disquisitions," since he feels he is "not sufficiently skilled in the art of dialectic juggling of high-sounding and sonorous, grandiloquent phrases and periods to reach a final conclusion as to the soundness or weakness of Pater, the philosopher," but he does take issue with More's overly simplistic dismissal of *Marius the Epicurean* as a misrepresentation of Christianity. Christian cites several passages from the novel that he feels demonstrate that WP is a master stylist and that *Marius* is a delight.]

281 Harris, Frank. "Walter Pater," ACADEMY, LXXXI (28 Oct 1911), 530–31.

WP may hold a place in English literature because of "his one page description of Leonardo's Mona Lisa. At any rate . . . his prose is assuredly finer and rarer than the faded, colourless picture." WP talked freely on art and literature but said little of himself; "it was difficult to get to know him well." He belonged "by nature to the Fraternity of the Faithless." "Decorum" was WP's gospel, his "rule of life." Yet his writing was often "sensuous, bold." WP takes great delight in the Bacchante revel in "Denys l'Auxerrois"; he is "all in the mad revel." But why is he so rigid? Why in him do we see "the lava-crust of self-restraint"? The answer is that his heart was weak. [Harris says that he thought he found WP's "confession" in "Denys l'Auxerrois," in the artist-spirit who is a lover of strange souls. Partly derived from Harris's "Walter Pater: The Pagan," JOHN BULL, 8 Sept 1906, pp. 329–30.]

282 Hervey, J. L. "Pater, Plato, and Paul More," ST. LOUIS MIRROR, 25 May 1911, pp. 4–7.

WP's influence was inspiring. Paul Elmer More, who has been known for his respectable scholarship of WP's work, has weakened his own credibility by his hateful assault on WP's works. More provides insufficient references to both WP's and Plato's actual texts. He his misinterpreted WP. [This article was written in response to More's attack on WP in his review (1911) of the library ed of WP's works for the NEW YORK EVENING POST and NATION (NY) (q.v.).]

283 Hervey, J. L. "Wilde and Pater," ST. LOUIS MIRROR, 22 June 1911, pp. 4–7.

WP judged Wilde's hero in DORIAN GRAY by the "Conclusion" to *The Renaissance* and found him remiss. Wilde himself may also be judged by this "Conclusion." His life was "a most lamentable catastrophe," but WP is not to be held responsible for it. Wilde was "congenitally unbalanced" and fell willingly and joyously into the depths. But "*ascesis . . . temperance*" was always WP's motto. WP's works are sacerdotal; Wilde's are like fine, strong wine.

284 [Huneker, James.] "Pater Reread," SUN (NY), 11 June 1911, Sec. 1, p. 8.

In spite of charges that WP is an immoral hedonist, his writings, which can be described as "a pragmatism poetically transfigured," justify classifying him as a moralist. He is always "earnest" in essentials. He distills from art and literature a " 'quickened sense of life.' " He does not overburden his writing with direct didactic messages; he "is both ardent and sceptical" in his "role as spectator in the game of life." WP cannot be described as the originator of any school of thought; his work does not revolve around "the simple, great idea" that gives a school its foundation. Rather his originality lies in his style, which is the "result of accretions and subtle rejections; the tact of omission as he put the phrase." WP is largely a romantic. His critical method involves discovering what an artist sought to express in a work and then determining the means by which that artist sought to express it. While WP's art does not extend to the realm of the sublime as does that of Dante or Goethe or Beethoven, his work does stand "the test of rereading, because he wrote beautifully of beautiful things."

285 "Is Walter Pater Demoralizing?" CURRENT LITERATURE, L (June 1911), 667–68.
[Article is largely a resumé of Paul More's review (1911) of the 1910 Macmillan library edition of WP's works. More claims that WP perverted reality and confused the moral sense, a perversion exemplified in the character of his disciple, Oscar Wilde. WP's description of Lacedaemonian life in *Plato and Platonism* is fantasized history; the Spartans were not aesthetes but warriors. In *Marius the Epicurean,* WP betrays Christianity; *The Renaissance* is an extension of his own ego. "No one, Mr. More admits, has seen more clearly than Pater that virtue is not acquired by a rebound from excess, but is the exquisite flower of the habit of moderation." Article adds that William Marion Reedy in the ST. LOUIS MIRROR endorses More's judgment but that Russell D. Burchard, writing in the EVENING POST (NY) claims that WP should not be held responsible for the excesses of his followers. Burchard, however, does agree with More's evaluation of WP's work. The article also mentions that Israel Christian (EVENING POST) reproaches More for not seeing the value in WP's prose, particularly in *Marius.*]

286 More, Paul Elmer. "Walter Pater," NATION (NY), XCII (13 April 1911), 365–68; rptd as "A New Edition of Pater," EVENING POST (NY), 15 April 1911, Sec. 3, pp. 2–3; rptd with slight changes in THE DRIFT OF ROMANTICISM (Bost & NY: Houghton Mifflin, 1913), pp. 83–115.
In the last analysis, WP represents something "false and dangerous." Although his style reflects a remarkable talent, he did not have a critical mind, lacking discrimination and certainty. The true critic's first concern must be the work itself, not his impressions of the work. At times, WP's interpretations are weakened by preconceived ideas. He disregards objective truth. In *Plato and Platonism,* although it is meticulously written, he falsifies the reality that was Plato's Greece. The Spartans were warriors, not aesthetes. He also inverts Plato's teachings: "to undergo philosophical discipline for the purpose of adding zest to sensuous pleasure . . . to make truth the servant of beauty, and goodness the servant of the body, is . . . the contrary of everything that Plato believed and held sacred." *Marius the Epicurean* misrepresents the age of Marcus Aurelius. WP's depiction of Christianity bears little resemblance to the faith embraced by St. Paul or St. Augustine, a militant faith preparing for world conquest, not a languorous faith characterized by bucolic settings and graceful women playing in the lilies. *The Renaissance* changes "the tone, the energy, the *ethos,*" of the Renaissance. WP seems never to deal with "facts" but with emotions. He undermines truth; history is only an extension of his own ego. For better or worse, all of his works stem fundamentally from a single,

self-oriented vision of the world. His outside sources are Goethe, Winckelmann, Ruskin, Rossetti, Plato, and the Bible; Oxford was his inspiration. From them he learned "the worship of beauty," a romantic ideal reinforced by a life lacking in vitality and isolated from the real interests of mankind. "Paterism might . . . be defined as the quintessential spirit of Oxford emptied of the wholesome intrusions of the world." But WP also teaches us to practice self-discipline and moderation, to sharpen our senses by a "certain chastity of use." That lesson, his followers, particularly Wilde, never understood. WP's philosophy of life is unacceptable.

287 Murdoch, W. G. Blaikie. THE RENAISSANCE OF THE NINETIES (Lond: Alexander Morning, 1911), pp. 63–67, 68, 80.
WP "incited the young writers to delicacy." Symons, more than anyone else, felt WP's influence. The art of the Nineties is full of WP's philosophy.

288 Reedy, William Marion. "The Cult of Pater," ST. LOUIS MIRROR, 20 April 1911, p. 3.
WP's writing is morbid affectation moving in the direction of hedonism. He perverts Plato. His doctrine is as "vicious" as that of Oscar Wilde. Paul Elmer More, the man responsible for exposing WP's hedonism and perversion, is to be applauded. [Reedy is referring to More's attack on WP in his review of the library edition in 1911 in NATION (NY) (q.v.) and in the NEW YORK EVENING POST. More's charges were answered the same year by Russell D. Burchard and Israel Christian in the NEW YORK EVENING POST (q.v.), J. L. Hervey in the ST. LOUIS MIRROR (q.v.), and James Huneker in the NEW YORK SUN (q.v.).]

289 Shanks, Lewis Piaget. "Walter Pater," DIAL, L (16 April 1911), 289–92.
There is a definite lack of biographical studies of WP. The clearest biographical portrait of him is implied in his collected works, particularly in *The Renaissance,* which "exhibits most clearly what one might term the fundamental contradiction of his temperament." Behind nearly every portrait in this book is seen "the figure of the author." In these essays he reveals himself to be a "modern romanticist" who has a solid background in the classics but who is attracted by "the force of his imagination" to the Renaissance. *The Renaissance* reflects "Romanticism tempered by the study of philosophy—a poet corrected by the discipline of an intellectual ideal!" In WP's writings occasional "exaggerations of delicacy" are the defects that are due to his "sensitiveness of temperament," which is essential to the romantic nature. The rewards of this same romantic attitude are "warmth, fervor, the force of a personal appeal." In later works, such as *Marius the Epicurean,* WP learned to temper his fundamental romanticism with classical restraint, to trim away the excesses in his prose. In *Marius* is found another side of Pater's nature, "the child who loved to play 'church' in his tender years, the deeply religious boy of the school-days at Cambridge." The novel also reflects WP's ability both as scholar and as poet, as well as his "sense of the picturesque." The portraits in *Imaginary Portraits* and *Appreciations* have, as portraits, "a certain

unreality, despite the fact that Pater himself sat for most of them." Most of the characters in these essays are "dream-figures." WP's essay "Style" and his "Postscript" to *Appreciations* "constitute the most valuable part of his studies in English letters." But the true significance of *Appreciations* "lies in its slightness of texture, its inequality to the rest of his published work."

> **290** Wa[ugh]., A[rthur]. "Pater, Walter Horatio," ENCYCLOPAEDIA BRITANNICA, 11th ed (NY: Encyclopaedia Britannica, 1911), XX, 910–11.

"Those who can sympathize with a nervous idealism" (most fully stated in *Marius the Epicurean*) will find WP inspiring. [Primarily biographical.]

1912

> **291** Babbitt, Irving. MASTERS OF MODERN FRENCH CRITICISM (NY: Houghton Mifflin, 1912), pp. 118, 155, 321, 322, 323, 350; (Lond: Constable, 1913); rptd (NY: Houghton Mifflin, 1923); (1926); (1928); (1930); rptd (NY: Farrar, Strauss, 1963), intro by Milton Hindus, pp. 118, 155, 321, 322, 323, 350.

If Sainte-Beuve can be called an aesthetic humanist, then WP is a humanistic aesthete. WP is often compared with Anatole France, but France's prose has more "purity of contour." WP was not as voluptuous as France and reacted to Hugo in a way France never could. But both WP and France reveal an "epicurean relaxation" combined with "a great suavity." Both are comely decadents. Unlike France's obvious influence in France, WP's influence in England is doubtful. WP's description of the *Mona Lisa* is perhaps the best example of a critic in English baring his soul for his public before a masterpiece. There is a constant note of appreciation found in WP that is not found in France.

> **292** Bendz, Ernst. "Notes on the Literary Relationship between Walter Pater and Oscar Wilde," NEUPHILOGISCHE MITTEILUNGEN (Helsingfors), XIV (May–June 1912), 91–127; rptd with revisions as Chap I in THE INFLUENCE OF PATER AND MATTHEW ARNOLD IN THE PROSE WRITINGS OF OSCAR WILDE (Gothenburg: Wettergren & Kerber, 1914), pp. 21–64.

Prior to writing INTENTIONS, Wilde saturated his mind with WP's *The Renaissance*. "No other book has left so many or so various traces in his prose-works." In his first series of ESSAYS AND LECTURES, published posthumously, Wilde cleverly adapts WP's work "in a manner we are unable to designate by any more courteous term than plagiarism." In INTENTIONS (1891), he plagiarizes less glaringly; in THE SOUL OF MAN (1891), considerably less; in DE PROFUNDIS, hardly at all, though at times it vaguely resembles WP's *Marius the Epicurean*. [The remainder of the study is primarily a collection of comparative passages with commentary.]

293 Fehr, Bernard. "Der ästhetische Impressionismus von Walter Pater," (The Aesthetic Impressionism of Walter Pater). STREIFZÜGE DURCH DIE NEUESTE LITERATUR (Encountering Modern Literature) (Strasbourg: K. J. Trübner, 1912) pp. 81–86.

WP does not advocate any one philosophy of life. He desires to capture impressions of the world in the solid tower of his ego. He was influenced by Novalis's theory of the ideal ego, but he gave the theory new direction. With him, the theory became more aesthetic; desire is no longer gratified by action but by inner excitement—by beauty. WP only gives us the sensation that the art object creates in him. He is indeed an impressionist rather than a philosopher. He recognizes the eternal commutation in the presence of the outside world, the defectiveness of all systems, and, as the only constancy, the beauty which is the origin of his impressions. [In German.]

294 Kelman, John. AMONG FAMOUS BOOKS (Lond, NY, Toronto: Hodder & Stoughton, 1912), pp. 38–62; rptd (Freeport, NY: Books for Libraries P, 1968), pp. 38–62.

No study of Marcus Aurelius and his age has been done which conveys "a more intimate and familiar conception of that remarkable period and man" than WP's *Marius the Epicurean*. WP's religious background as a child and his companions at Oxford are important sources for a basic dualism in WP's spirit: "the dominion both of a high spiritual rationalism, and of the beauty of flesh and the charm of the earth." WP's style is distinctive and contains no traceable borrowing from other writers. Although it is at times somewhat affected and labored, it is still an adequate expression of his mind and reflects his continuous search for the unique word. Fundamental to both his style and his humanistic thought is WP's love of beauty. His sensitivity to beauty and his meticulous search for the most articulate way to express it set the stage for a central conflict in his works between the tendencies of idealism and those of paganism. A particular manifestation of this general conflict is found in the conflict between Christianity and Hellenism. WP's attempt to reconcile these two doctrines is the central theme of *Marius*. Reconciliation is ultimately achieved by Marius, whose spiritual development involves three stages: a developing awareness of the human conscience; the growth of his "consciousness of an unseen companion," which is synonymous with "the untranslated and indeed the unexamined Christian doctrine of God"; and the development of the idea of "the city of God, which for him assumes the shape of a perfected and purified Rome, the concrete embodiment of the ideals of life and character." In *Marius* WP's attempt to find a reconciliation is successful, for while many aspects of the world's beauty belong to paganism, they "are purified from all elements that would make them pagan in the lower sense, and under our eyes they free themselves for spiritual flights which find their resting-place at last and become at once intelligible and permanent in the faith of Jesus Christ."

295 Kennedy, J. M. ENGLISH LITERATURE 1880–1905 (Lond: Stephen Swift, 1912; Bost: Small, Maynard, 1913), pp. 28–58.

Many late nineteenth-century writers continually displayed romantic influences while yet revealing a classical awareness. Five men stand out: Oscar Wilde, John Davidson, Arthur Symons, George Gissing, and WP. Never at any time did WP advance extravagant claims in his own behalf. He was shy and retiring; he was never able to speak a foreign language; and the music of words was beyond him. Although intellectual excitement appealed to him, WP was not attracted by physical excitement. He never undertook to reinterpret nature for the benefit of mankind—the artist's "highest task." Instead, he concentrated on one point or one characteristic, as *The Renaissance* clearly demonstrates. The real WP emerges in the essay on Leonardo, however. The famous "La Giocanda" passage reveals that WP was in his element indeed when he could concentrate his efforts on a solitary human production. As this passage makes clear, WP believed that one need not find in a work exactly what the artist intended. For WP criticism is also creation; he proves Wilde's theory that at times criticism may even be more difficult than creation. Winckelmann also had some things in common with WP, although Winckelmann had a "much broader mind." In the essay on Winckelmann, WP is obviously attempting to explain his own religious position when he describes Winckelmann's desire to escape from the "crabbed Protestantism" of Germany. WP's work was carried to its logical conclusion by Wilde. Wilde meditated with greater profundity upon WP's theories and developed them to an extent that WP had never dreamed of.

WP began as a metaphysician absorbed in the doctrines of the neo-Platonists. Significantly, his first major essay was on Coleridge as a philosopher. It was Thomas Hill Green who familiarized WP with Hegel's works. In his twenties, WP came across Jahn's LIFE OF WINCKELMANN; the book influenced his thinking, eventually enabling him to find Goethe too passionate and Ruskin too idealistic. Although in his early years WP believed that he had little to do with Christianity, its influence clung to him through his reading of Hegel and his intense study of Plato. He also looked with favor upon Kant and Mill. Eventually, he began to be muddled because he hoped to reconcile art and metaphysics; he was never able to make up his mind between one or the other. He mistakenly advises combining the qualities of romanticism and classicism. WP never had a clear understanding of his own canons of aesthetic criticism. He was not very creative and consequently felt attracted to the decadent period of the Roman Empire—the period described in *Marius the Epicurean*.

296 Le Gallienne, Richard. "On Re-reading Walter Pater," NORTH AMERICAN REVIEW, CXCV (Feb 1912), 214–24; rptd in VANISHING ROADS, AND OTHER ESSAYS (NY & Lond: Putnam, 1915).

WP was a "master of the literature of meditation." His books reveal that he was a fastidious Puritan. Those who see WP as a hedonist have not read him, for he is primarily a beautiful stylist—a teacher and an artist.

297 "Richard Le Gallienne's Tribute to Walter Pater," CURRENT LITERATURE, LII (March 1912), 349–50.

[This article is a resumé of Le Gallienne's "On Re-reading Walter Pater," which appeared in NORTH AMERICAN REVIEW, CXCV (Feb 1912), 214–24.]

298 Saintsbury, George. A HISTORY OF ENGLISH PROSE RHYTHM (Lond: Macmillan, 1912), pp. 420–26; rptd (1922); rptd (Bloomington: Indiana UP, 1965).

WP's style reflects a deliberate and decorative blending of Ruskin and Newman. But unlike Ruskin's, WP's prose emits a tone of "quietism," of rest. One of WP's "greatest anxieties" was the care of the paragraph; he preferred to "drop off" at the end, gliding with "a new sort of modified *aposiopesis.*" [Saintsbury scans two paragraphs from the "Leonardo da Vinci" essay.] Most of the feet are trisyllabic, disyllabic, or monosyllabic; the tone is quiet throughout; and the paragraphs end with a gliding "muffled arrest." The meter is more intricate than Ruskin's or Kingsley's, and subtler than Gibbon's. WP's prose method was meticulous, but from *Gaston de Latour* onwards his style reveals an increasing array of weaknesses.

299 Wedmore, Sir Frederick. "Walter Pater," MEMORIES (Lond: Methuen, [1912]), pp. 156–65.

[Wedmore disagrees with Frank Harris's unflattering portrait of WP in ACADEMY, 1911. He claims that WP appeared "as the High Priest of an artistic religion." He also claims that Symonds talked to him of WP and of the mark made by "the volume of Essays that had just appeared" (*The Renaissance*). Symonds also spoke of the "mark that Pater himself had made at Oxford."]

1913

300 Bock, Eduard Jakob. OSCAR WILDE'S PERSÖNLICHE UND FRÜHSTE LITERARISCHE BEZIEHUNGEN ZU WALTER PATER (Oscar Wilde's Personal and Earliest Literary Connection with Walter Pater) (Bonn: Peter Hanstein, 1913). Published dissertation, Bonn, 1913. [This work constitutes the major portion of the first two chapters of Bock's WALTER PATER'S EINFLUSS AUF OSCAR WILDE (Bonn: Peter Hanstein, 1913), q.v.]

[In German.]

301 Bock, Eduard J[akob]. WALTER PATER'S EINFLUSS AUF OSCAR WILDE (Walter Pater's Influence on Oscar Wilde), Volume VIII of BONNER STUDIEN ZUR ENGLISHEN PHILOLOGIE (Bonn: Peter Hanstein, 1913); derived in part from Bock's OSCAR WILDE'S PERSÖNLICHE UND FRÜHSTE LITERARISCHE BEZIEHUNGEN ZU WALTER PATER (Bonn: Peter Hanstein, 1913). Published dissertation, Bonn, 1913.

When Wilde went to Oxford, he was fascinated by many Victorian poets and also by Milton, Dante, Mazzini, Heine, Goethe, and the French symbolists. WP's

Renaissance also had a major influence on him; evidence for this contention is revealed in DE PROFUNDIS. WP, however, was aware of a distance between them that excluded any intimate confidence even in the period of their best understandings. WP's influence on Wilde can be traced, therefore, from the year 1874. During the early years of his career, Wilde seems to have read everything that WP published. Wilde characterizes the English Renaissance with the same expressions that WP used to describe the Italian Renaissance of the fifteenth century. Wilde's "far too literal" adoptions from other writers come to an end with the "Lecture to Art Students" (1883). At this time there is an obvious change in Wilde's mode of presentation; he develops a more independent style. WP's essay on Wordsworth influenced Wilde's flirtation with Platonism, an interest that is abandoned in DORIAN GRAY. The novel reveals that Wilde is free from aesthetic hedonism and has returned to his earlier interest in Cyrenaicism. WP was also largely responsible for Wilde's characteristic "formalism." [In German.]

> **302** Chesterton, G. K. THE VICTORIAN AGE IN LITERATURE (Lond: Williams & Norgate; NY: Holt, 1913), pp. 69–71; rptd (Lond: Geoffrey Cumberlage, 1946); (1955); rptd (Lond & NY: Oxford UP, 1961); rptd with "Foreword" by Alvan Ryan (Notre Dame, Ind: University of Notre Dame P, 1962); rptd (Lond & NY: Oxford UP, 1966).

WP's works reflect the influence of Ruskin's art criticism in that their "moral tone" is "strictly and splendidly Pagan." Like Newman and Ruskin, WP is a "careful and graceful stylist" and a serious thinker, but, unlike these two writers, WP never digresses from the central focus of his works, which is "the point where all the keenest emotions meet. . . . The only objection to being where all the keenest emotions meet is that you feel none of them."

In his reflections on the *Mona Lisa* in "Leonardo da Vinci," WP is partially successful in his attempt to do what many of the aesthetes tried to do: "to see Paganism *through* Christianity." He is only partially successful, however, because the underlying philosophy of such an attempt is "false."

> **303** Huneker, James, "Pater Re-Read," in THE PATHOS OF DISTANCE. A BOOK OF A THOUSAND AND ONE MOMENTS (Lond: T. W. Laurie, 1913); (NY: Scribner, 1913), pp. 279–85.

WP is an extremely moral writer unfairly attacked by many "mock puritanical" critics. The "Aristippean flux and reflux of his ideas" recall the theories of William James and Henri Bergson. The "Conclusion" to *The Renaissance* is in tune with "modern notions of the plastic universe." WP is a humanist who is never didactic; he plays "the role of spectator in the game of life." His prose style is African or Alexandrian—musical and "never strongly affirmative." He had the critical temper of Arnold, though both are indebted to Sainte-Beuve. But WP does not have the wit and the ethical bias of Arnold. He "wrote beautifully of beautiful things." [This selection is written as a response to the publication of the library edition of WP's works.]

304 Jackson, Holbrook. THE EIGHTEEN NINETIES: A REVIEW OF ART AND IDEAS AT THE CLOSE OF THE CENTURY (Lond: Richards, 1913), pp. 31, 70, 162, 167; (NY: Kennerly, 1913); rptd (Lond: Grant Richards, 1922); rptd (NY: Knopf, 1922); rptd (Lond: Cape, 1927); rptd (Harmondsworth, Middlesex: Penguin, 1939); (1950); rptd (Berkeley Heights, NJ: Oriole P, 1964); rptd (NY: Capricorn, 1966), intro by Karl Beckson, pp. 28, 34, 38, 59–61, 74, 87, 135, 140.

Wilde's art bridged the distance between Whistler's "uncompromising artistic sufficiency" and WP's "art-culture." Decadence began in England with WP's *The Renaissance,* though that is not in itself a decadent work, and ended with Wilde's DORIAN GRAY and Beardsley's UNDER THE HILL. But passages in WP read like invitations, intended or not, to decadence. Wilde eventually shed a large part of the influence of WP between 1885 to 1890, choosing to retain only that which suited his purpose. He looked more to France during those years.

WP's chapter "White Nights" in *Marius the Epicurean* was named with full cognizance of the color white as a conventional symbol for innocence. White, in fact, was the color that dominated the period, not yellow, as many suspect.

305 Mobbs, Robert. ÉTUDE COMPARÉE DES JUGEMENTS, DE MME. HUMPHRY WARD, DE MATTHEW ARNOLD ET DE WALTER PATER SUR LE "JOURNAL INTIME" DE H. F. AMIEL (Comparative Study of the Judgments of Mrs. Humphry Ward, Matthew Arnold and Walter Pater on H. F. Amiel's JOURNAL INTIME) (Geneva: Imprimerie Atar, 1913). Published dissertation, University of Geneva, 1913.

The greatness of Mrs. Humphrey Ward's translation of H. F. Amiel's intimate journal is reflected in WP's favorable review of her translation in *Essays from the "Guardian."* Mrs. Ward's introductory essay provided WP and Arnold with the opportunity to express their professional opinion of Amiel. While bowing to Amiel's incomparable merit in dealing in his fragmentary manner with literary and ethnic questions, both Arnold and WP feel that Amiel missed his calling. WP had temperamental affinities with Amiel that should have made him more indulgent, but he, like Arnold, felt that Amiel had disappointed them in that he never wrote that monumental work he mentioned in his journal. Both tried to explain this failure.

Amiel and WP possessed two conflicting desires: an attraction to the metaphysical and philosophical and an attraction toward types of beauty that are clarified and precise. Yet for WP the first tendency took a back seat to the second, whereas for Amiel it was the opposite. WP also had his period of enthusiasm for Hegel and Schelling, particularly while working on his essay on Coleridge. But from the time WP developed an interest in Winckelmann, his spirit passed from an abstract world to a concrete one oriented towards the criticism of art and literature. But he did not lose all interest in philosophy; rather, he relegated it to the rank of collaborator. As is evident in the Winckelmann essay, WP freed himself from the tyranny of metaphysics. WP moved toward Attic clarity and precision; Amiel, on the other hand, moved deeper into Hegelian obscurities and cosmogonic and Buddhist musings.

While Arnold condemns Amiel's philosophic speculations as being futile, WP recalls the strong attraction they once had for him and sympathizes more than Arnold could. Arnold and WP fail to grasp completely the philosophical, psychological, and dramatic scope of Amiel's JOURNAL; it is precisely in the range of his vision that the work's value lies.

Neither Arnold nor WP could benefit from a far-reaching culture because they were removed from it by the traditional atmosphere of Oxford, unlike Amiel who was influenced by the spirit of free inquiry prevalent in university life in Geneva. Neither can grasp Amiel's background or his milieu. They view Amiel from afar; they are too closely aligned with the spirit of Oxford. [In French.]

> **306** Olivero, Federico. "*Marius the Epicurean* e gli *Imaginary Portraits* di Walter Pater" (*Marius the Epicurean* and the *Imaginary Portraits* of Walter Pater), SAGGI DI LETTERATURA INGLESE (Bari: Laterza, 1913), pp. 337–99.

WP's fiction reveals a distinction in type between the sorrow and frustration that comes from unattainable dreams as found in the character of Denys in "Denys l'Auxerrois" and Duke Carl of "Duke Carl of Rosenmold" and the eagerness for truth and light that is found in Marius and Sebastian van Storck. WP in his portraits reminds one of Huysman and the Goncourts; his interest in the spirit of the artist figure recalls Ruskin. His technique also resembles that of Watteau, whom he appropriately celebrates in "A Prince of Court Painters." "Denys l'Auxerrois" is in the tradition of romance that includes Hawthorne's THE MARBLE FAUN and THE SCARLET LETTER. WP's works, like those of Poe, Hawthorne, and Novalis, treat the unreal, the alien forces and strangeness of life. WP's characters do not belong to reality but live in an atmosphere of their own, one that surrounds them with a changing aura; they breathe an air too ardent and subtle to be vital. [In Italian.]

> **307** Orage, A. R. [Walter Pater,] NEW AGE, XIII (12 June 1913), 177.

WP "never had an idea in his life. In consequence he spent the whole of his energy in concealing the fact in his style. On his style he spent enormous pains, as he knew he would live by that or nothing."

> **308** Ransome, Arthur. "Walter Pater," PORTRAITS AND SPECULATIONS (Lond: Macmillan, 1913), pp. 131–59.

WP read Ruskin at nineteen, but it is difficult to recognize Ruskin's influence in WP's works. WP is a fitting illustration of how a personality can obliterate ideas. The presence of WP in everything he writes suggests the Nietzschean demand for placing the personal element in the development of a theory before the theory itself. WP seems to foreshadow Nietzsche in many of his works. Before THE BIRTH OF TRAGEDY was ever written, WP had discussed the Apollonian and Dionysian as the fundamentally opposed artistic tendencies. WP was also at one with Nietzsche in his conception of the relative nature of truth. Like Nietzsche, he viewed the influence of the "ideal," the "absolute," in Western thought as a basic evil. WP also traces the insanity of the European mind, as Nietzsche might have traced it, through the Neo-Platonists, Spinoza, Descartes, Malebranche, Leibnitz, and Berkeley. He shared Nietzsche's dislike of dialectic.

In *Plato and Platonism,* WP engages in portraiture, not exposition. The portraits of Heraclitus, Parmenides, and Pythagoras are "inset" in the volume "like the vignettes that encircle the central picture in those old engraved frontispieces" and suggest paragraphs of Nietzsche's EARLY GREEK PHILOSOPHY. Although he resembles Nietzsche, WP is remembered by many as the writer who brought to England the stylistic creed of Flaubert. When WP talks of "soul" in literature, he means the potential, suggestive element in the language of literature. His theories of style are an outgrowth of Symbolist theory. But WP's mistake is to try to appeal to the eye as well as to the ear in his writings. "Ear should be the sole dictator and eye the ear's obedient servant." Although he exerted great care in the construction of his essays, he was too insistent on detail. In his portraits, he often reduces entire complex personalities to the expression of a single mood. But the creation of the mood was, of course, what he aimed at. His criticism is personal and highly aesthetic. He criticizes works of art by attempting to reproduce the mood that the work inspires in him.

> **309** Thomas, Edward. WALTER PATER: A CRITICAL STUDY (Lond: Martin Secker, 1913); rptd (Folcroft, Pa: The Folcroft P, 1970).

WP is a legend, a mythical Oxford don said to have excused the lighting of bonfires in the college quadrangle because the glare enhanced the beauty of St. Mary's spire. The legend may have developed out of the need to create a god who would seem worthy of *The Renaissance,* the essay on "Style," and *Marius the Epicurean.*

The originals for many of WP's settings come from his childhood remembrances. Before leaving school at nineteen, he read the first four published volumes of Ruskin's MODERN PAINTERS. Ruskin was an obvious influence on the young WP. Little is known of his reading during his early college years. In 1863 he joined the Old Mortality Society. In 1869 he fell under the influence of Goethe and Winckelmann. As a young man he accepted the theory of the relative spirit. In 1869, he also met the Pre-Raphaelites. Mallock's caricature of him in THE NEW REPUBLIC and Mr. Jackson's (the supposed original of Marius) recollections probably led him to omit the "Conclusion" to the second edition of *The Renaissance.* He would not read Stevenson or Kipling because he was afraid of being "submerged by them."

Apart from what he reveals in his works, WP leaves little to be discovered. He was the "aesthetic critic" realized in the flesh. There is no reason to believe that he disapproved of the values of the middle-class, though he would not recommend them. He was always the spectator of life advocating that the love of art for its own sake had most to offer in life. He was mystified by youth, coming to this position through Winckelmann, the ancient Greeks, and sculpture. In the spirit of youth, he envisioned a "moral sexlessness."

As a stylist, he is artificially stiff and obscure, often expressing himself through images and colors rather than sounds. His style mirrors his own shy and reticent personality. But he is always admirably eclectic, ignoring the commonplace and dull. His "Hellenism" and his defense of the "life of culture" are indebted to Goethe. In his religious preferences, he leans toward ancient Greece, where religious sensuousness existed without the feeling of shame that hinders it in the Christian world. He wrote the lectures that comprise *Greek Studies* for an actual audience; his design was to teach those approaching an intensive study of Greek thought, a motive that accounts for differences in style in this volume.

Marius was purposely not called a novel because its chief merit is independent of fiction. WP was ill at ease when writing narrative. His studies of Marcus Aurelius, Apuleius, and Lucian in *Marius* "will some day be separated from their inessential context and printed together." The philosophy that touches WP most clearly in *Marius* is Cyrenaicism—the theory that life is the end of life. *Marius* has many grammatical errors, dangerous in a writer like WP, who provides little that guides his readers. In many of his imaginary portraits, he combines successfully his roles as critic and artist. He liked the amorous but could not handle sex in his works, nor could he use the word *dung*. The influence of Arnold is obvious in the Wordsworth essay, but unlike Arnold and Ruskin, WP willingly disregards the business of the world.

1914

310 Brooks, Van Wyck. JOHN ADDINGTON SYMONDS. A BIOGRAPHI- CAL STUDY (Lond: G. Richards; NY: Kennerley, 1914), pp. 90–92; rptd (NY: B W Huebsch, 1924)

WP gave the first volume of Symonds's THE RENAISSANCE IN ITALY (1875) a very favorable review. The only fault WP found with the work was the absence of " 'reserve in many turns of expression.' " In spite of this enthusiastic review, these fellow-Platonists were not the best of friends. In conversation WP habitually referred to Symonds as " 'poor Symonds.' " Symonds found that WP's style had " 'a peculiarly disagreeable effect' " on his nerves, an effect that was " 'like the presence of a civet-cat.' " He was particularly irritated by WP's style in *Appreciations*.

311 Chew, Samuel C. "Pater's Quotations," NATION (NY), XCIX (1 Oct 1914), 404–5.

WP's free use of quotations from various authors is in accord with his theory that criticism is a creative art. His use of quotations frequently involves "transposing, omitting, rearranging, misascribing, and in a few cases even apparently substituting his own for somebody else's ideas." He frequently alters the passages he borrows from other sources so as to remove "didacticism and over-frankness of expression" from the source in order "to produce a finer [artistic] effect" in the style of the passage.

1915

312 Harris, Frank. "Walter Pater," in CONTEMPORARY PORTRAITS. SECOND SERIES (NY: Kennerly, 1915); rptd (Lond: Methuen, 1915–24) pub as part of four-volume ed; (NY: Frank Harris, 1919), pp. 203–26.
[Harris argues that although WP is a great writer, Gautier, who has a similar mental outlook, is greater. Harris claims that he met WP in person "again and again" before he got to know him well and that there was a noticeable contrast between WP the person and his writings. His house and his sisters represent to Harris the "decorous dullness" to which WP fled in order to live out his fantasy of fuller life in creative art. Harris recalls a word-for-word dialogue about his works that he had with WP. WP consistently repeated his ideas to himself and then wrote them down on a slip of paper that he carried about with him. WP, while in the company of Wilde, seemed to come alive and spoke more freely. Wilde is said to have told Harris that WP spoke more openly at Oxford before he was caricatured by Mallock. Wilde saw WP as his "great friend." Harris also recounts word for word the conversation at a dinner that he gave for WP, Wilde, and Arnold at which they all debated the question of prose style. Harris recalls that WP was afraid he would harm his own reputation by defending Wilde's DORIAN GRAY when it appeared in 1890 in LIPPINCOTT'S MAGAZINE, so he waited until a year and a half later to review it and praise it. He felt the review was his "duty," Harris claims. WP had a devastating fear of public opinion and conflict of any kind. WP is said to have disliked the idolatry afforded Shakespeare. He hated Puritanism but lacked the vitality and courage of Gautier and so could really do nothing against it. Harris registers his dislike of Benson's attempt in the "1911" biography (Harris's date is wrong; Benson's biography appeared in 1906) to make WP out a devout Christian. He calls the claim a "disgraceful perversion of truth." Throughout the essay, Harris hints at WP's "mainly mental" homosexuality.]

313 Mason, Eugene. "Walter Pater and Some Phases of Development," A BOOK OF PREFERENCES IN LITERATURE (Lond: J. G. Wilson, 1915), pp. 167–93.
The present generation gives less thought to WP's works than did their fathers. But a cheaper edition is needed. WP's reputation will return. He ranks with Shakespeare, Lamb, and Newman as a prosaist; but as a novelist, he was unsuccessful.

Marius the Epicurean is really a volume of autobiographical essays recording the progress of a soul. Many of his friends believed that had he lived a few years longer, "he would have taken Orders, and a small college living in the country."

> **314** Powys, John Cowper. "Walter Pater," VISIONS AND REVISIONS: A BOOK OF LITERARY DEVOTIONS (NY: G. Arnold Shaw; Lond: William Rider & Son, 1915), pp. 227–37.

WP's greatness as a critic lies in the combination of imagination with "that rare, unusual, divine gift of limitless Reverence for the Human Senses." He is at the same time a precise scholar and a "Protean Wizard" with the ability to enter fully into the spirit of Christian mythology as well as that of Hellenic and German philosophy. He undermines metaphysics by approaching metaphysical systems as artistic fabrications. "Walter Pater's magnetic spell is never more wonder-working than when he deals with the *materials* which artists use. And most of all with *words*. . . . " Three of his essays may be singled out as "most characteristic of certain recurrent moods": "Denys l'Auxerrois," which treats the "legend of the exiled god"; "A Prince of Court Painters," which reflects WP's own "passion for things faded and withdrawn," and the essay on Leonardo with its memorable passage on the *Mona Lisa*. What finally makes WP "so great, so wise, so salutary a writer" is the wisdom of his hedonism.

> **315** Ralli, Augustus. "Pater the Humanist," NORTH AMERICAN REVIEW, CCI (Feb 1915), 217–22; rptd in CRITIQUES (Lond: Longmans, Green, 1927), pp. 137–44; rptd (Freeport, NY: Books for Libraries P, 1966).

In the twentieth century, where there is an increasing emphasis on materialism and the pragmatic, WP's writing is "a voice crying in the wilderness," for WP "stood for the humanities, as opposed to the utilities and the expediencies." As his life attests, WP desired "a state of mind rather than a motive for beneficent action." His was the "academic or disinterested type of mind" that "sought inspiration from the past, among those ages where the outer life has some correspondence with the inner vision." The emotions which emanate from his exploration of the past are "genuine, but they give light without warmth," for in his writings "emotion is generated by the movement of the intellect." Yet while WP's writings seem to be impersonal and "detached from experience," they are often just the reverse, for they are "a kind of disguised autobiography" in which WP is unconsciously self-analytic.

1916

> **316** Fehr, Bernhard. "Walter Paters Beschreibung der Mona Lisa und Théophile Gautiers romantischer Orientalismus" (Walter Pater's De-

scription of the Mona Lisa and Théophile Gautier's Romantic Orientalism), ARCHIV FÜR DAS STUDIUM DER NEUREN SPRACHEN UND LITERATUREN, CXXXV (1916), 80–102.

WP's description of the *Mona Lisa* in the essay "Leonardo da Vinci" is his most impressive piece of writing. Though the possible influences upon his description of the *Mona Lisa* are many, the most significant one is Théophile Gautier's romantic orientalism. The vitalizing effect of dream images upon reality is admittedly an old concept that appealed to many Romantics, but Gautier gave it an artistically unique and extremely refined form in his novel MADEMOISELLE DE MAUPIN (1834). Moreover, many of Gautier's poems are created "visions." WP did not borrow actual motifs from Gautier, but instead he adopted Gautier's method of creating motifs in a quite particular way—through life-giving vision, through the power of empathy which results in the individual's "multiplicity," through a series of affinities pervading and uniting not only the realm of the spirit but also material forms. Gautier himself was in this respect strongly influenced by oriental, more particularly, Persian poetry. [In German.]

317 Fehr, B. "Walter Pater und Hegel" (Walter Pater and Hegel), ENGLISCHE STUDIEN, L (1916), 300–308.

WP was considerably influenced by German writers such as Goethe, Novalis, and Fichte. Hegel's influence on him was also significant in at least four areas. WP's essay on Winckelmann in *The Renaissance* reveals how carefully he had read Hegel's three volume ÄSTHETIK. Several passages from this work were taken over and developed further by WP in the Winckelmann essay. More important, however, is the fact that WP completely adopted Hegel's view of the historical evolution of the arts and of artistic modes. Like Hegel, he pictures a development from "symbolic" through "classical" to "romantic" art—a development that parallels and expresses an historical evolution of the spirit. The characteristics that Hegel attributes to symbolic, classical, and romantic art are also found in WP's works. All this does not mean, however, that WP simply plagiarized Hegel. He actually made Hegel's key ideas truly his own, and in his re-expression of them he often added sensuous beauty to Hegel's rather colorless formulae and provided distinct examples that effectively illustrate Hegel's extremely abstract theories. [In German.]

318 Harris, Frank. OSCAR WILDE. HIS LIFE AND CONFESSIONS. Two Volumes (NY: Frank Harris, 1916), pp. 48–49, 123–24, 560; rptd (1918); rptd in one volume (NY: Covici-Friede, 1930), pp. 31, 33, 36, 53, 86, 458; rptd (Garden City, NY: 1932); rptd as OSCAR WILDE (Lond: Constable, 1938); rptd with intro by L. Blair (East Lansing, Mich: Michigan State UP, 1959); rptd with note by L. Blair (NY: Dell, 1960), pp. 39–40, 41, 56, 84; rptd (Lond: Panther Books, 1965).

[Harris claims that Wilde told him that WP had written some of the greatest prose in all literature and that WP was responsible for his "full growth." Wilde looked upon WP as a sympathetic older brother and found him a poor talker but an admirable listener. Harris recounts the fantastic story that Wilde, during a discourse on "the exquisite ideals of the new paganism," suddenly found WP on his knees before him kissing his hand. Harris cautions the reader, however, that Wilde told the story more than ten years after it was supposed to have happened. Wilde, of course, was not alive to refute the story that Harris himself may have fabricated. Harris also agrees with the hypothesis advocated by E. Bendz in THE INFLUENCE OF PATER AND MATTHEW ARNOLD IN THE PROSE-WRITINGS OF OSCAR WILDE (1914), originally published as "Notes on the Literary Relationship between Walter Pater and Oscar Wilde" (1912), that many of Wilde's lectures were little more than elementary paraphrases of WP and Arnold with, however, titles borrowed from Whistler.]

319 Symons, Arthur. "Some Browning Reminiscences," NORTH AMERICAN REVIEW, CCIV (Oct 1916), 602.
[Symons sent a copy of his INTRODUCTION TO THE STUDY OF BROWNING to WP. WP thanked him and invited him to call.]

320 Walker, Hugh. "Critical and Miscellaneous Prose: John Ruskin and Others," CAMBRIDGE HISTORY OF ENGLISH LITERATURE, Volume XIV, ed by A. W. Ward and A. R. Waller (Cambridge: Cambridge UP, 1916), 158–59; ed and with additions by George Sampson (1941).
WP is singularly different from Ruskin: WP retires into artistic seclusion; Ruskin remained unconquerably optimistic. WP teaches that "the love of art for art's sake is the highest form of wisdom." Oscar Wilde's development follows logically from such a philosophy. WP as an essayist illustrates the theory that if the aim of life is to make each moment as exquisite as possible, then the aim of the essayist should be to make each sentence an end in itself. The result is a beautiful but overlabored style. WP's Epicureanism fails because no single form of pleasure should represent all forms of pleasure. WP, nevertheless, represents "the aesthetic movement in its most earnest phase." As a stylist, WP seeks a renewed refinement, a movement away from the colloquial, informal quality of most mid-century prosaists, Ruskin and Newman particularly.

1917

321 Gosse, Sir Edmund. THE LIFE OF ALGERNON CHARLES SWINBURNE (Lond & NY: Macmillan, 1917), pp. 39, 202; rptd (Lond: Heinemann; NY: G. Wells, 1927).
Swinburne, in 1871, escaped regularly from Balliol to visit WP, with whom he remained intimate for a short time. WP entertained him.

322 Jackson, William Walrond. INGRAM BYWATER. THE MEMOIR OF AN OXFORD SCHOLAR 1840–1914. (Oxford: Oxford UP, 1917), pp. 8–12, 77–80, 196–97.

WP and the members of the Old Mortality Society held the highest place among Ingram Bywater's friends. He and WP were undergraduates together. Bywater claims that WP came to Oxford with the intention of seeking Holy Orders and was extremely attracted to Catholicism. In a draft of a letter to Dr. H. Diels, Berlin, Bywater writes that if WP "had come across a really great Catholic like Cardinal Newman he would have satisfied his emotional and aesthetic nature." As it was, WP "devoured" Carlyle, Ruskin, Browning, J. S. Mill, Berkeley, and Hume. He learned enough German to read Hegel's PHÄNOMOLOGIE DES GEISTES during one vacation; Bywater guesses at the date 1862. All of this reading came during WP's period of intellectual *Sturm und Drang,* the end of which is marked by the essay on Coleridge, published anonymously. As a critic WP was "a literary impressionist," Bywater claims, and adds the strong conviction that he was led to it by his reading of Sainte-Beuve. The publication of *The Renaissance* provoked a storm of criticism at Oxford. The "Conclusion" had in substance been published earlier in WP's review of William Morris's EARTHLY PARADISE [WESTMINSTER REVIEW, 1868]. Dr. Mackarness, Bishop of Oxford, delivered his "Charge to the Clergy of the Diocese" shortly afterwards in the Cathedral of Christ Church; he fastened on certain passages in *The Renaissance* as exemplary of dangers that Oxford tutors, free of clerical restrictions, might transmit to their pupils. As a friend of WP's, Bywater was exposed to much suspicion at the time.

> **323** Proesler, Hans. WALTER PATER UND SEIN VERHÄLTNIS ZUR DEUTSCHEN LITERATUR (Walter Pater and his Relationship to German Literature) (Freiburg im Breisgau: Buchdruckerei der Freiburger Werkstätten für Plakate und Kalender, 1917). Published master's thesis, University of Freiburg, 1917.

WP was interested primarily in the cultures of classical antiquity and the Renaissance. But inside his sphere of influence, the reader misses any sense of continuous historical correlation and a strictly systematic treatment of special problems. He was a scientific dilettante with distinct artistic traits.

WP visited Germany. Goethe was the German author who exercised the most intense influence on him. But WP read many other German poets and philosophers. He was particularly interested in the German mystics of the Middle Ages. Historically, his interest moved directly from the Middle Ages to the German reformation and Luther. WP saw his antipodes in Lessing and Hegel. It is amazing, however, that he had no relation at all with Herder. WP devoted a special essay to Winckelmann in which he tried to save Winckelmann from artistic oblivion. Heine also exercised an influence on WP, but only as a romanticist and not as a politician. WP did not consider "romantic" an historical period; for him it was a certain characteristic temperament. Kant, Hegel, and Schelling were the most important German philosophers to influence WP. From philosophy WP did not expect absolute or transcendental standards but only the possibility and direction to understand life in its endless multiformity and in the fullness of its contradictions. His most profound sympathy was with the retained opinions of

Socrates and Montaigne. Probably, in the final analysis, German philosophy was essentially alien to him, for his personal assumptions and objectives had quite a different nature. [In German.]

324 Sherman, Stuart Pratt. "The Aesthetic Idealism of Henry James," NATION (NY), CIV (April 1917), 393–99; rptd in ON CONTEMPORARY LITERATURE (NY: Holt, 1917), pp. 226–55; and in THE QUESTION OF HENRY JAMES, ed by F. W. Dupee (NY: Holt, 1945), pp. 70–91.

To James, as to WP, his "closest English analogue," things are either beautiful or ugly instead of either good or evil. The "Conclusion" to *The Renaissance* and *Plato and Platonism* provide sound insight into James's own "philosophy." *Marius the Epicurean* and *Imaginary Portraits* provide interesting parallels with James's work, and WP's essay on "Style" can be read as an accurate statement of James's literary ideals. One might also compare WP's Gioconda passage in "Leonardo da Vinci" with James's description of a telegraph operator in IN THE CAGE.

325 Sholl, Anna McClure. "Walter Pater [with selections]," THE WARNER LIBRARY (NY: Knickerbocker P, 1917), XIX, 11157–60; rptd in THE COLUMBIA UNIVERSITY COURSE IN LITERATURE BASED ON THE WORLD'S BEST LITERATURE (NY: Columbia UP, 1928–29), XV; rptd (Freeport, NY: Books for Libraries P, 1969), XV, 207–9.

WP is an artist-critic; he looks at life with the discrimination of the poet, not the scientist. The Spartan ideal of temperance is for him "the governing principle" In life and art. He is a creator who gives to tradition the appeal of an immediate and fresh revelation. He moved, early in his life, from the influence of Ruskin and Rossetti to the influence of Winckelmann and Goethe. Enamoured of ancient Greek ideals, he could not always reconcile the conditions of nineteenth-century life with ancient Greece. His works are characterized best by the Greek ideal, his "hunger for perfection." This "hunger" is reflected in the extreme polish, the elaborate form, and the verbal nicety of his prose style.

1918

326 Michaud, Régis. "Un Païen Mystique: Walter Pater" (A Pagan Mystic: Walter Pater), MYSTIQUES ET RÉALISTES ANGLO-SAXONS (Paris: Colin, 1918), pp. 51–74.

WP's hypersensitivity to suffering made him an aesthete instead of a saint. In Canterbury, his religion was aestheticism. It is also in Canterbury that he conciliated two antiquities: the Christian and the pagan, the Middle Ages and the Renaissance. In ritualistic Oxford, he became a "mystical pagan." The subjective element in his works, a reflection of his personality, is the unifying element. In his prose, WP aimed at fusing two different sensibilities: again, the Middle Ages and the Renaissance; or it may be viewed as an attempt to fuse the north and the south—Germany with Italy, as in "Duke Carl of Rosenmold," or religion with humanism, as in *Gaston de Latour*. This Anglo-Saxon nostalgia for the southern countries is embodied again in WP as it had been in Byron, Keats, Shelley, Rossetti, Morris, and Ruskin. *Marius the Epicurean,* the synthesis of his philosophy and aesthetics, establishes Christianity on an Epicurean basis. WP's passion for beauty is essentially but one manifestation of the Christian desire for perfection. [In French.]

1919

---

327 Moore, George. AVOWALS (Lond: pvtly ptd; NY: Boni & Liveright, 1919), pp. 177–81, 185–212; rptd (Lond: Heinemann, 1924); rptd (NY: Horace Liveright, 1928); rptd (Lond: Heinemann, 1936). [Portions of this material appeared in 1904 in Moore's article on WP in LIPPINCOTT'S MONTHLY. Material varies in the different editions.]
[Speaking of *Marius the Epicurean,* Moore says that WP has "raised the English Language from the dead." Moore claims that he identifies somewhat with the Marius character. He reports that Henry James, when speaking of *Marius,* said he found WP's treatment of the pagan and Christian unusual: his point was "that we cannot admire opposites equally."

Moore recounts his many visits to WP's home in London. He refers to the *Mona Lisa* passage in "Leonardo da Vinci" as "flagrant sentimentality." Moore notes that WP admired the paintings of Burne-Jones. WP liked the "Protestant convention"; he admired the traditional. Moore includes a copy of WP's letter on Moore's CONFESSIONS OF A YOUNG MAN. Moore claims here to have wearied of WP eventually and comments on his puzzled response to WP's review of MODERN PAINTERS in the DAILY CHRONICLE (1893).]

328 Mordell, Albert. "Foreword," SKETCHES AND REVIEWS BY WALTER PATER (NY: Boni & Liveright, 1919), pp. v–vi; rptd (Freeport, NY: Books for Libraries P, 1969).
WP aided the reputation of those writers he reviewed: Fabre, Symonds, George Moore, Arthur Symons, and Oscar Wilde.

329 Wright, Thomas. THE LIFE OF JOHN PAYNE (Lond: Unwin, 1919), pp. 168, 172–73.
John Payne "despised Pater just as he despised Fitzgerald. He had no patience with 'niggling writers' and workers in mosaic." When Payne compared WP and Schopenhauer, he found WP to be the inferior, for " 'Schopenhauer says in a few

words what Pater takes a whole book to say.' " Payne had the opportunity to make more critical comments on WP after reading Thomas Wright's LIFE OF PATER (1907). He noted that WP's analysis of Du Bellay's active principle, the poet's ability to portray his most intimate mood, is " 'shallow characterization,' " for that ability is " 'the active virtue of *every lyrical* poet.' " Payne also conjectured that WP's familiarity with Du Bellay's writing was probably limited to a reading of "Winnower's Song" as " 'quoted in Sainte Beuve's well-known TABLEAU DE LA POÉSIE FRANÇAISE AU SEIZIÈME SIÈCLE.' " Thus the impression that WP thought of Du Bellay as " 'the poet of one poem' " is accurate, for WP had " 'not really studied the subject' " he was writing about.

Payne was also critical of WP's method in "Apollo in Picardy." Payne felt that to some extent WP was a " 'sciolist.' " He thought that although WP " 'had a genuine love for delicate perfection . . . he was too lazy to go into the tremendous work of making himself perfect in any way—of getting to the foundation of the whole thing.' " Payne did, however, approve of WP's treatment of Plato: " 'he had a genuine sense of the magic of Plato.' "

1920

330 Eliot, T. S. "Brief Treatise on the Criticism of Poetry," CHAPBOOK, II (March 1920), 1–10.
Etiolated criticism such as WP produces appeals "to minds so enfeebled or so lazy as to be afraid of approaching a genuine work of art face to face." Sainte-Beuve writes a type of philosophical-historical criticism; he is less interested in art than he is in man's moral condition. His work is certainly of much greater importance than either WP's or Anatole France's. The critic of poetry must be a poet himself.

331 Elton, Oliver. "Walter Pater: And Other Critics," in A SURVEY OF ENGLISH LITERATURE 1780–1880. Four Volumes (Lond: Edward Arnold; NY: Macmillan, 1920), III, 279–92; see also, I, 347; II, 37, 232, 331, 373; III, 6, 64, 91, 92, 143, 208, 237, 256, 266, 277, 293, 294, 365, 427n; IV, 20, 82, 311, 365, 371, 372n; rptd, Two Volumes (1928); [volumes I and II are reissues of Elton's SURVEY OF ENGLISH LITERATURE 1780–1830 (1912).]
WP is "our greatest critic since Coleridge." He proclaims his cult but always rises "well above it, so that it does not do him much harm." For WP, prose is a fine art. It is worthwhile to compare for style Landor's representation "in the high Epicurean style" of Montaigne with WP's more finished and subtle *Gaston de Latour.*

WP's and Wilde's doctrine of aesthetic pleasure differs from that of Hazlitt and his contemporaries in that the former doctrine extends "the range of feeling from which that pleasure can be drawn," and it associates "the idea of artistic pleasure, with that of its solitary (or coterie) enjoyment, and also with a studious, somewhat fingering calculation of it." [Summary analysis of most of WP's major works.]

332 James, Henry. LETTERS. Two Volumes, ed by Percy Lubbock (NY: Scribner's, 1920), I, 221–22.

[In a letter to Edmund Gosse, dated 13 Dec 1894, James comments on Gosse's study of WP (CONTEMPORARY REVIEW, 1894). He suggests that the study is informing on WP's personal history but that WP still remains "curiously negative and faintly-grey." James notes that WP has had and will have "the most exquisite literary fortune: i.e., to have taken it out all, wholly, exclusively, with the pen (the style, the genius,) and absolutely not at all with the person." Of WP's position in literature he writes: "He reminds me, in the disturbed midnight of our actual literature, of one of those lucent matchboxes which you place, on going to bed, near the candle, to show you, in the darkness, where you can strike a light: he shines in the uneasy gloom—vaguely, and has a phosphorescence, not a flame. But I quite agree with you that he is not of the little day—but of the longer time."]

333 Kirk, Richard C. "A Sentence by Walter Pater," JOURNAL OF ENGLISH AND GERMANIC PHILOLOGY, XIX (July 1920), 365–76.

In general WP's sentences are descriptive; that is, their "ideas are dissociated from all others and are organically or inseparably related." Thus a typical sentence of WP "presents a group of organically related—and not merely associated—ideas." The reader's focus is completely on those ideas presented to him: "the facts or ideas so presented are concrete: they are not 'class concepts.' " In general WP's descriptive sentences contain modifiers; they lack stress and they are "unassertive." In the following descriptive sentence from "The Child in the House"—"At the next turning came the closet which held on its deep shelves the best china"— the use of modifiers "brings to mind only the ideas named by its terms" and "dissociates" the particular ideas of this sentence from any similar, associative ideas. The sentence presents the ideas as equal and complementary parts of an organic whole. The object of the sentence is "conceived to exist in a 'timeless moment.' " The lack of stress in the sentence produces a continuous and measured movement, a modulated rhythm. The lack of stress also signals that the sentence is "unassertive"; it is "addressed to the unquestioning reader." The total effect of WP's use of modifiers and the lack of stress in his descriptive sentences are described in a passage from his essay on "Style": " 'The term is right, and has its essential beauty, when it becomes, in a manner, what it signifies, as with the names of simple sensations.' "

334 Mallock, W. H. MEMOIRS OF LIFE AND LITERATURE (Lond: Chapman & Hall, 1920), p. 65.

[Mallock claims to have based THE NEW REPUBLIC on Plato's REPUBLIC, the SATYRICON, and the novels of Thomas Love Peacock. The essential characters in the book, including WP, were drawn with an attempt at "fidelity of portraiture."]

335 Mitchell, F. L. "Walter Pater: A Study in Temperament," BOOK-
MAN'S JOURNAL AND PRINT COLLECTOR, 5 March 1920, p. 367.
WP seems an anachronism in this age of variety. Although not very successful as a
tutor, he took great pains with the few students and the small audience that admired
him. Paterism was a cult in the Eighties and Nineties. WP worshipped the scholar
as a culture hero. "It was the scholar alone who stood, quiet and receptive, at the
spot where the greatest number of vital forces . . . united. . . . It is the scholar alone
who . . . has the freedom of the ages." As a critic of art and an aesthetic
philosopher, WP stood on Ruskin's shoulders. His influence on the "aesthetic
movement" was second only to that of Ruskin and Rossetti.

336 Muddiman, Bernard. THE MEN OF THE NINETIES (Lond: Henry
Danielson, 1920), pp. 5, 48, 52, 57, 101, 104, 108, 109, 135.
Most of the writers of the Nineties failed to heed WP's urging in *Marius the
Epicurean* that " 'life in modern London' " provides "stuff sufficient" on which
"the fresh imagination of a youth" can build his "palace of art" and instead
followed Wilde's Dorian Gray. Lionel Johnson's "cloistral mysticism" owes much
to WP, whose influence he came under while at Oxford. His prose style is as
allusive as WP's, often imitating directly WP's "murmured obituaries." Impressionism, which "disseminated like a perfume" from WP's works, greatly stirred
the men who followed him.

337 Shafer, Robert. "Walter Pater Redivivus," OPEN COURT, XXXIV
(April 1920), 217–31; rptd as "Walter Pater," in PROGRESS AND SCIENCE.
ESSAYS IN CRITICISM (New Haven: Yale UP; Lond: Oxford UP, 1923),
pp. 194–218.
WP's reputation has waned, but his voice still speaks to us. His lasting vitality is
mainly the result of two distinct qualities: his fastidiousness and his ability to
combine thought and action. The idea that one welcomes experience of the outside
world simply for its own sake, a notion fundamental to WP's canon, is fully
explained in *Marius the Epicurean*. WP emphasizes in this romance the
resemblances between the age of Marcus Aurelius and the last few decades of the
nineteenth century. In spite of his capacity for feeling and sentiment, Marius
possesses an independent intelligence. He finds "truth" in the words of Aristippus
of Cyrene, who advocated interpreting life in terms of immediate certainties. He
wished to teach men "how to live." Aristippus' "truth" would today be linked
directly with the theory of the subjectivity of knowledge.

WP interpreted the concept of beauty in Epicurean terms or in terms directly
related to the utilitarian concept of pleasure. He did not, like John Stuart Mill,
however, differentiate between the quantitative and the qualitative nature of what
is beautiful or pleasurable. WP asserts that although the pleasures derived from the
arts are most satisfying, nevertheless each person must prove for himself through
"impartial experiment what sensations yield him the greatest amount of pleasure."
By the time WP wrote *Marius* he had realized to his dismay that "the creed of

sensation" nullified morals and religion. Marius is made therefore to conform, on the grounds of good taste alone, to the morality of the times. Marius finds Christianity aesthetically satisfying. But his attraction to Christianity is inconsistent, a point that underscores WP's own tenuous hold upon the development of Marius's character. One might conclude that although WP was not entirely unresponsive to the teachings of the Christian religion, he was unconvinced.

The grounds for WP's position are to be found in his own temperament. Like Ruskin, Morris, and Rossetti, he had a profound desire to save the artistic and the spiritual. But unlike them, he tried to go further by linking his position with the intellectual currents of the day; his objective was "to save and find some valid sanction for the rewards and fruits of culture on the terms imposed by scientific naturalism." The relationship, as odd as it may appear, between WP's position and the philosophy of Auguste Comte and Herbert Spencer is clear. Not only were WP's college lectures "Comtean," as Mrs. Humphry Ward noted, but also he was impressed with the empirical method of analysis. Historic Christianity and all other traditional forms of religion were rendered invalid under such analysis.

1921

338 Brie, Friedrich. AESTHETISCHE WELTANSCHAUUNG IN DER LITERATUR DES 19. JAHRHUNDERTS (The Aesthetic World View in Nineteenth Century Literature) (Freiburg im Breisgau: Boltze, 1921), pp. 67–70.

Aesthetic theory towards the end of the century was divided between the moralism of Ruskin and the aesthetic-epicureanism of WP. Montaigne was WP's prose master. He learned much from the French. [In German.]

339 Egan, Rose Frances. "The Genesis of the Theory of 'Art for Art's Sake' in Germany and in England," SMITH COLLEGE STUDIES IN MODERN LANGUAGES, II, No. 4 (July 1921) and V, No. 3 (Apr 1924), 1–33.

The roots of the "art for art's sake" movement are found in German aesthetic philosophy from Kant to Friedrich Schlegel to Schelling. The doctrines of the "autonomy of the artist, of the validity of the artistic conscience within its own sphere, and of the necessity of originality or peculiarity in a work of art" that both Flaubert and WP advocated are formulated in the works of earlier German philosophers. Schlegel's argument for the artist's need being above his creation gave philosophical countenance to the "art for art's sake" belief that although art bears an intimate relationship to the immediate mood of the artist, it need not be indicative of any permanent mood.

340 Hind, C. Lewis. "Walter Pater," AUTHORS AND I (NY & Lond: John Lane, 1921), pp. 239–245; rptd (Freeport, NY: Books for Libraries P, 1968).

[Hind reminisces about his impressions of WP based on a rather uneventful encounter with him at a dinner party and on reading about him in George Moore's AVOWALS.] WP's "gift to the world . . . lies in his withdrawal, in his communication of something beyond and above the insistent Present, something hidden yet revealed to initiates." WP's *Essays from the "Guardian"* and his "Sketches and Reviews" which deal only with the present do not represent the real WP. They are merely WP's "dinner-table, polite manner," his attempt " 'to do his bit' in modern literary life."

341 Jackson, W[illiam]. W[alrond]. "The Rev. C. H. Daniel, D. D., An Appreciation," in THE DANIEL PRESS: MEMORIALS OF C. H. O. DANIEL WITH A BIBLIOGRAPHY OF THE PRESS, 1845–1919 (Oxford: Printed on the Daniel P in the Bodleian Library, 1921), pp. 85–86, 113–14, 133, 149.

Daniel knew WP well but was hardly influenced by him. [Lines from a letter from WP are quoted, pp. 85–86; contains collation and appreciative comment on 1894 publication of "The Child in the House" by Daniel P.]

342 Lucas, St. John. "Walter Pater and the Army," BLACKWOOD'S MAGAZINE, CCIX (March 1921), 405–8.

WP is the last writer one would expect to depict the military life. His portrait of Emerald Uthwart, for part of his short life a soldier, may have been drawn as a type of challenge to his temperament. Emerald bears a strong resemblance to Marius: ascetic, self-controlled, intelligent, susceptible to form and to the romantic. In spite of the care with which WP has drawn this highly specialized character, "one would (if sufficiently large) have been sorely tempted to fall upon him and beat him." In drawing him, WP reveals his interest in the Spartan ideal—"soldier-like obedience." But Emerald is no young Greek; he is more like a prig, suffering from a lack of humor and stuffed with ideas. WP lacked sufficient dramatic sense to be able to create believable people. Most of WP's fictional heroes are made to endure some overwhelming tragedy, providing an outlet for his unusually morbid imagination. The extent of his morbidity may be seen in the grim postscript to Emerald's portrait marred by the excessive use of gruesome detail. But in spite of weaknesses, the portrait remains a singular contribution to military literature.

343 Marshall, Donald Worth. "Walter Pater: Some of His Imaginary Portraits," POET-LORE, XXXII (Autumn 1921), 431–40.

WP should be considered neither as "one of the wildest of aesthetes" nor as one of the coldest of stylists; rather he should be remembered as the author of the *Imaginary Portraits,* those "delicate, creative character studies" which are delightful blends of the short story and the literary essay. WP's particular strength as an essayist comes from "a certain delicately personal viewpoint and interest in his work" which permeates much of his writing. It is in the portraits that there is the clearest and best expression of his personality, of which the most powerful quality is tranquillity. Six of the portraits can be placed in categories. "Sebastian van Storck" and "Duke Carl of Rosenmold" constitute one group in which WP's primary interest is intellectual. In the first portrait WP deals with the destructive impact which results from the misinterpretation of a philosophical theory; in the second, he explores the attempts of an individual to bring about an intellectual awakening in his country. "Denys l'Auxerrois" and "Apollo in Picardy," which make up the second category of WP's portraits, "are expressions of a very quaint and charming fancy, growing, however, from a knowledge and love of the Greek myth and the French town." The third category is made up of the essays "Emerald Uthwart" and "The Child in the House." These essays are "alike in their comparative freedom from the purely intellectual, which is replaced in them by a more sustained character interest and narrative quality." In all six essays, the characters are living, novel characters whose inner as well as external selves are portrayed. And permeating all of these portraits is WP's warm, personal interest and personality. [One of the earliest attempts to discern some type of pattern in the imaginary portraits.]

1922

344 Ainslie, Douglas. ADVENTURES SOCIAL AND LITERARY (Lond: Unwin, 1922), pp. 95, 267–69.
[Author recalls his friendship with WP. He claims that though WP and Renan probably never met, they had much in common. He relates several anecdotes.]

345 Butler, Alfred Joshua. "Preface," AMARANTH AND ASPHODEL: POEMS FROM THE GREEK ANTHOLOGY (Oxford: Blackwell, 1922), pp. ix–xii.
[Butler says he treasures his letter (p. x) from WP.]

346 Harris, Frank. MY LIFE AND LOVES (Paris: pvtly ptd, 1922); rptd (NY: Frank Harris, 1925); (1927); rptd (Paris: Obelisk P, [1934]); (1945); rptd (Lond: Richards P, 1952); rptd (Lond: Elek Books, 1958); rptd (Paris: Obelisk P, 1960); rptd (San Luis Obispo, Calif: Century 21, 1962); rptd (NY: Grove P, 1963), pp. 12, 408, 416, 628, 686, 688, 887; rptd (Lond: W. H. Allen, 1964); rptd (Lond: New English Library, 1966); rptd (NY: Grove P, 1966); rptd (Lond: Transworld Publishers, 1966).
[Harris writes of having dined with Wilde, George Meredith, and WP. The discussion got around to the age of sex-awakening, which WP is said to have put at about thirteen or fourteen. Harris recounts that at a lecture given by WP, the

audience could not hear him and shouted for him to speak up. Harris regarded WP highly as a prose stylist; "there is hardly a finer passage in English literature than Pater's page of the Mona Lisa," Harris claims.]

347 Shuster, George N. "Ruskin, Pater, and the Pre-Raphaelites," THE CATHOLIC SPIRIT IN MODERN ENGLISH LITERATURE (NY: Macmillan, 1922); rptd (Freeport, NY: Books for Libraries P, 1967), pp. 166–86.

The "Catholic Spirit," a preoccupation with Europe's past in nineteenth-century England may be said to have begun with Ruskin. The aesthetic movement was dependent on Ruskin. WP, in particular, "took dictation" from Ruskin "rather obediently." WP's critical opinions are even more important today than Arnold's because he seems more modern. His intellect was centripetal, while that of many of his famous contemporaries (e.g., Carlyle, Arnold, and Newman) was centrifugal. The essence of his inner-directed thought is based on his deeply religious instinct. His attempts to reconcile Christianity and paganism by viewing the former as a "natural outcropping" of the latter reflect his love of beauty and his love of the sensuous and physically graceful. In "Leonardo da Vinci," "The School of Giorgione," as well as many of the other essays in *The Renaissance, Greek Studies,* and *Marius the Epicurean,* he tries to make Christianity "earthly and enjoyable rather than supernatural and troublesome." His conclusion in *Marius* argues that while Catholicism is not acceptable as truth, it is more acceptable than paganism as beauty. Christianity can "cure the inner malady of nature with a supernatural remedy"—this in contrast to the naturalistic philosophies popular during his time that are unable to cope with evil because they are too simplistic. WP was a natural pagan. What spoiled his understanding of Christianity was his view of the Catholic mass as a tableau instead of a drama. This centripetal pull, this immobile and stagnant vision of life, is reflected throughout his imaginary portraits. If he had been able to feel the "reality of God," he would indeed have become a mystic. Of all of his disciples, none is more noble than Lionel Johnson, who was admitted into the Church but "whose soul was given to the priesthood of art." The religious peace that WP sought in vain came so easily to Johnson. [Shuster summarily dismisses Wilde and the other aesthetes as being diseased by the intoxicating degradation of feverish Paris. The Pre Raphaelites were saved by their mystic fervor, although Dante Rossetti lacked intellectual conviction.]

348 Yeats, William Butler. "The Tragic Generation," in THE TREM-BLING OF THE VEIL (Lond: T. Werner Laurie, 1922); rptd in AUTOBIOG-RAPHIES: REVERIES OVER CHILDHOOD AND YOUTH, THE TREMBLING OF THE VEIL (Lond: Macmillan, 1926); THE AUTOBIOGRAPHY OF WILLIAM BUTLER YEATS: CONSISTING OF REVERIES OVER CHILDHOOD AND YOUTH, THE TREMBLING OF THE VEIL, DRAMATIS PERSONAE (NY: Macmillan, 1938); AUTOBIOGRAPHIES (Lond: Macmillan, 1955); and rptd as THE AUTOBIOGRAPHY OF WILLIAM BUTLER YEATS (NY: Macmillan, 1965), pp. 201–2, 214.

The Rhymers found Rossetti "a subconscious influence, and perhaps the most powerful of all" on their philosophy, but they "looked consciously to Pater." Though *Marius the Epicurean* still exemplifies the greatest prose in modern English, it may have been responsible for the many personal disasters among WP's admirers. Perhaps his influence made the Rhymers claim the whole tradition of literature as their authority. [Yeats acknowledges that whatever Villiers de L'Isle Adam had not shaped in ROSA ALCHEMICA was shaped by WP.]

1923

349 Bartlett, Randolph. "A Note on Sensations," in LONDON NIGHTS, by Arthur Symons (Bost: John W. Luce, 1923), pp. xi–xv.
The Cyrenaicism of *Marius the Epicurean* was a complete expression of the spirit of the Nineties, but WP was merely a forerunner, not the controlling genius of the period.

350 Buchan, John, and Edith Morley. "The End of the Century," in A HISTORY OF ENGLISH LITERATURE (NY: Nelson, 1923); rptd (1925); (1927); pp. 569–71; (1929); (1932); (1938).
WP was, after Arnold, "the greatest purely critical influence in later Victorian literature." [A brief historical summary of WP and his works.]

351 Duthuit, Georges. LE ROSE ET LE NOIR. DE WALTER PATER Á OSCAR WILDE (The Pink and the Black: From Walter Pater to Oscar Wilde) (Paris: La Rennaissance du Livre, 1923).
From his early religious education to Oxford, WP dwelt literally in the world of tangible beauty and symbolically in the monastery of New Kent Road in Walworth where his friend Richard C. Jackson used to "romanize." His *The Renaissance* made him the theoretician of the new school of art that revived English painting, which was dying for want of a doctrine free from metaphysics or embarrassing ethics. By ensuring the triumph of form and celebrating the individual, WP marks the starting point of the aesthetic movement. Because of the confusion between art and life, to the profit of art, aesthetic pleasure was limited to erotic, visual satisfaction and was largely responsible for the excesses of the aesthetes. WP's works were reserved for a restricted circle and were not read by the magistrate, the colonel, or the merchant. When the aesthetic movement became associated with excess, WP withdrew. His convictions grew less certain as the movement increased. Eventually, he turned from it and embraced Christianity. The "rose" period therefore turned to the "black" period. He even dressed in black like a churchman. Though WP is still an influence on literature and art, Wilde has been forgotten. But the movement has not yet died. It has become a national institution, and the time will come when the directors of museums, the historians of art,

philosophers, and professors will plead Wilde's cause. "The martyr will be beatified." [For a critical reaction to Duthuit's study, see Edmond Jaloux's "Walter Pater," LES NOUVELLES LITTÉRAIRES, 8 Sept 1923, p. 2.] [In French.]

352 "An Eccentric Recluse: Mr. Jackson and Walter Pater," TIMES (Lond), 30 July 1923, p. 8.
Richard C. Jackson was found dead holding a partly eaten orange in his hand. Jackson and WP were frequent visitors to the very ornate services held at St. Austin's Priory. Jackson's claim to be the original of Marius was "quite unknown" until the publication of Wright's biography in 1907. He was "inaccurate in matters of fact, believing just what he wanted to believe."

353 Jaloux, Edmond. "Walter Pater," LES NOUVELLES LITTÉRAIRES, 8 Sept 1923, p. 2.
Georges Duthuit's LE ROSE ET LE NOIR (1923) is an improper and ill-disposed study. Possessing a sounder knowledge of later nineteenth-century England, Raymond Laurent [ÉTUDES ANGLAISES (Paris: Grasset, 1910), pp. 139–258] nearly grasped WP's genius in his study. George Moore misunderstood the very essence of WP's genius. WP's mystery is the mystery of those writers whose thought takes its nourishment not from life but from thought itself. WP manages to make perceptible the abstract world of ideas and reveries. He evokes life without ever showing it. In *Marius the Epicurean,* what strikes WP is the moral beauty of his hero. He is the first to write so tenderly about the spiritual life. [In French.]

354 Nevinson, Henry W. CHANGES AND CHANCES (Lond: Nisbet, 1923), pp. 83–84.
WP looked "like a good statue of Buddha." His lecture was taken from the Wordsworth essay in *Appreciations.* When he finished, he left at once, "probably with a sense of failure." [The occasion for the description was a lecture that WP gave at Toynbee Hall that Nevinson attended. The date was 23 Nov 1890.]

355 "The Original of Marius the Epicurean," CURRENT OPINION, LXXV (Dec 1923), 692.
[This article contains a brief biographical sketch of Richard Charles Jackson, the man who was "best known as the esthete who inspired the central figure of Walter Pater's masterpiece, *Marius the Epicurean.*"]

356 Paget, Violet [Vernon Lee]. THE HANDLING OF WORDS AND OTHER STUDIES IN LITERARY PSYCHOLOGY (Lond: John Lane, 1923); rptd (Lincoln: University of Nebraska P, 1968), intro by Royal A. Gettmann, pp. 39, 62.
As a stylist, WP seems "to pass as in trance through the steps of an argument and awake only at its conclusion." He nears R. L. Stevenson in his ability to note the emotion felt in himself by the perception of the object rather than to attempt to reproduce the object's "impression." WP and Stevenson reveal in two completely different modes of work the perfect fusion of style and content.

357 "Rich Hermit's Romance," WEEKLY DISPATCH, 12 Aug 1923, p. 7. R. C. Jackson was the original of WP's Marius the Epicurean. [Obit note on Jackson.]

358 Trevelyan, Janet Penrose. THE LIFE OF MRS. HUMPHRY WARD (Lond: Constable; NY: Dodd, Mead, 1923), pp. 27–28, 99.
One of the members of "that small but gifted community" which Mrs. Humphry Ward moved in while at Oxford was WP, who "revolutionized the taste of Oxford with his Morris papers and blue china, shocked the Oxford world with his paganizing tendencies and would, besides, keep his sisters laughing the whole evening, when they were quite alone, with his spontaneous fun."

1924

359 Cazamian, Louis, and Emile Legouis. HISTOIRE DE LA LITTÉRATURE ANGLAISE (Paris: Hachette, 1924); rptd (1925); (1929); (1946); (1965); trans as A HISTORY OF ENGLISH LITERATURE, Volume II by Louis Cazamian; trans as MODERN TIMES (1660–1932) by W. D. Mac Innes (NY: Dent, 1926–27); rptd (NY: Macmillan, 1929); (1935), pp. 1310–14; rptd (NY: Dent, 1937); rptd (NY: Macmillan, 1938); (1944); rptd (NY: Dent, 1945); (1954); (1971).
WP writes in the type of "impressionism which Hazlitt and Lamb had brilliantly illustrated." [General historical survey and appreciation of WP's works.] [In French.]

360 Cazamian, Madeleine L. "Walter Pater: *La Renaissance.* Traduction française par F. Roger-Cornaz. Payot, 1917; *Platon et le Platonisme.* Traduction de l'anglais par le Dr. S. Jankélévitch. Payot, 1923,"LA REVUE ANGLO-AMERICAINE, I (1924), 443–45.
The last few years have witnessed an increasing interest in the works of WP. Accordingly, two of his major works have been translated into French. [Review of the translations.] [In French.]

361 Cox, E. H. M. (ed). THE LIBRARY OF EDMUND GOSSE (Lond: Dulav, 1924), p. 196.
[Contains a letter to Gosse from WP and Gosse's note on the ms. of WP's "Pascal," which was given to him by WP's sisters: "This MS. was given to me to be deciphered, and from my collation it was published in the CONTEMPORARY REVIEW."]

362 Escott, T. H. S. "Walter Pater and Other Memories," BOOKMAN'S JOURNAL AND PRINT COLLECTOR, X (July 1924), 109–11.
Gilbert and Sullivan had a personal meeting with WP at the home of Alfred

Rothschild, the first Lord Rothschild's brother. As teacher, writer, and critic, WP was largely the creation of his own Oxford College; "more especially of the most variously accomplished and learned of its tutors . . . the Rev. W. W. Capes, whose lectures and whose conversations were the opening of a new world to the Kentish-bred youth when he came up from King's School." From Capes, WP learned the value of Edgar Quinet, "the energising teacher of the school." In the year of his death, 1894, WP spoke of passing the remainder of his days in the country and giving up his rooms at Brasenose.

363 Fernandez, Ramon. "*Marius l'Epicurien; Platon,* par Walter Pa-
ter; LE ROSE ET LE NOIR, par Georges Duthuit" (*Marius the Epicurean,
Plato,* by Walter Pater; THE PINK AND THE BLACK, by Georges Duthuit),
LA NOUVELLE REVUE FRANÇAISE, CXXV (1 Feb 1924), 247–51; rptd in
MESSAGES (Paris: Gallimard, 1926), pp. 210–16; trans by Montgomery
Belgion (NY: Harcourt, Brace, 1927), pp. 287–95.

WP's style, aligning and building the elements of an idea within the frame of language, is the most analytical style in existence. WP is like a goldsmith polishing his sentence, producing a "meticulous cleaning of his impression and his idea." His style reflects a "delicious modulation of the intellect." But such perfection comports disadvantages: thought becomes monopolized by style. A difference must be established between the critic and the aesthete. For the critic, thought must free itself from style. The aesthete's concept of "life in beauty" implies a false conception of experience and life, and so of intelligence itself. As a critic, WP is successful, but when he passes from artistic thought to life, he fails. [In French.]

364 Golzio, Vincenzo. "La Critica di Walter Pater e il Misticismo
romantico" (The Criticism of Walter Pater and Romantic Mysticism), LA
CULTURA, III (15 July 1924), 417–22.

The term "romantic mysticism" best describes WP's philosophical inclination. The term is synonymous with WP's own definition of "aesthetics" (i.e., defining art as man's return to his primal origins, a unification of one's spirit with nature's forces). Imagination or fantasy is the supreme faculty since it transcends reason and reality. Intuition and dream become man's motive forces. There is a definite link between WP's "romantic mysticism" and neo-Platonism; both conceive of beauty as something outside of man's phenomenal experience, as something embodying eternal "ideas." The highest art must be music, since it leaves itself completely open to fantasy or dream. Poets must concern themselves with the unknown and inexpressible, but words have limitations and cannot express what music can induce.

WP's "romantic mysticism" can also be linked with symbolism, particularly Baudelaire's concept of nature and the symbolists' reverence for music as the supreme art. Da Vinci is valued by WP not for his art works per se, but for their essential quality of "romantic mysticism." The face of the Gioconda embodies the inexpressible. It fascinates while it repels; it has something perverse and so enigmatic about it that it embodies all of man's countless experiences. WP was also strongly influenced by Hegel's aesthetics. He obviously derived much from his study of Winckelmann. [In Italian.]

365 Harrison, John Smith. "Pater, Heine, and the Old Gods of Greece," PUBLICATIONS OF THE MODERN LANGUAGE ASSOCIATION, XXXIX (Sept 1924), 655–86.

Much of WP's works reflect his debt to Teutonic thought, particularly to the works of Goethe, Hegel, Winckelmann, and Heine. To the latter WP is indebted for an idea that pervades much of his work: that "at the advent of Christianity the old gods of Greece were not destroyed but exiled and driven from their thrones into distant places, where they lived in disguise, often in the form of devils or evil spirits." This theme of pagan gods playing a role in the new religion may have been originally suggested to WP in his reading of Heine's "The Gods in Exile" or of Théophile Gautier's GUIDE DE L'AMATEUR AU MUSÉE DU LOUVRE SUIVI DE LA VIE ET LES OEUVRES DE QUELQUES PEINTRES. The theme of pagan traditions surviving in Christian times forms the background for WP's *The Renaissance,* particularly in the study of Pico della Mirandola. The theme is especially appropriate in this study because WP characterizes Pico "as one of the gods returned from pagan times" whose writings attempted to reconcile Christian and pagan traditions. This perception of the beauty and power of the mythological stories of pagan religion and the attempts to reconcile paganism with Christianity are seen by WP as the key to understanding the Renaissance. They are also keys to understanding WP's writings. WP's studies of the myth of Dionysus, particularly in "Denys l'Auxerrois," are not merely works of scholarship in which historical data is accumulated; they are also artistic attempts to present concretely through imaginary portraits "the spirit or formula of an age." In the imaginary portrait of Denys l'Auxerrois, WP has reworked the "idea of the reappearance of old pagan gods" into a Christian tradition. Thus Denys and his life embody "the essential traits of the Greek god Dionysus and the outstanding incidents of his romantic history." In the portrait of Denys, there are three ways in which "old Greek conceptions reappear": (1) in certain aspects of the portrait the imaginary character himself is the pagan god "with many of the old god's powers and properties"; (2) at times the old Greek legend is "retold with human characters taking the part of the divine prototypes and with purely human incidents in the place of their supernatural equivalents"; and (3) at times "certain objects, places and one particular person associated with the old god in the original stories about him" are used in the new adaptation of the myth. These three techniques for incorporating pagan tradition into a Christian background are also found in WP's reworking of the myth of Apollo in "Apollo in Picardy." In this version of the legend of Apollo, WP sets forth Apollyon as "a blend of romantic and classical conceptions." To this characterization, he adds a medieval association: Apollyon as a devil, "at least in the thought of the people of his time."

366 Moore, George. CONVERSATIONS IN EBURY STREET (Lond: Heinemann; NY: Boni & Liveright, 1924), pp. 68, 81, 108, 226–27, 264; rptd (Lond: Chatto & Windus, 1969).
[Freeman, in a conversation with Moore, argues that R. L. Stevenson seems to be more highly esteemed than he deserves, "getting a great deal that was due to Pater." *Marius the Epicurean* is saved from drifting "into the novel" by WP's genius, and his *Imaginary Portraits* are no less true to his genius, "suave and punctilious." Later, while speaking with Aubry, Moore claims that the music of English prose style is always recognizable to those with the ears to hear. The language unites opposites: Morris and Meredith, Stevenson and WP. "The English tune is heard in both, but how differently."]

367 Quinn, John. LIBRARY OF JOHN QUINN: PART FOUR (NY: Anderson Galleries, 1924), pp. 743–46.
[Work contains a short biographical sketch of WP; claims that WP had an early inclination toward Unitarianism. A thirty-four item catalogue of editions written by and about WP follows the sketch.]

368 Smith, Paul Jordan. ON STRANGE ALTARS (NY: Boni, 1924), pp. 236–61.
WP turned to Plato for inspiration and to Heraclitus, Pythagoras, and Epicurus for thought. His power lies in his subtle imagination, which can "take us out beneath pomegranate trees with swarthy maidens, whose bands of pearls are contrasted with the ruby tips of their breasts." He had a religious reverence for the world of sense. Little wonder that the advocates of "muscular Christianity" feared him.

369 Snell, Ada L. F. "Introduction," SELECTIONS FROM WALTER PATER (Bost: Houghton Mifflin, 1924), pp. vii–xviii.
Above all else WP was an interested critic curious particularly about technique and the details of form and substance. The philosophical aspect of art held his attention, stimulated undoubtedly by his interest in certain aspects of the Pre-Raphaelite movement. WP gave himself to the old problem of what makes a work of art enduring. Two clearly perceived qualities that he advocated and practiced himself are intellect and sense perception—"resulting, on the one hand, in restraint and form; on the other, in grace and imagination." In WP's eyes, a house is most important in the nourishment of the aesthetic temper; just how important it is can be measured in Marius's ancestral home, White Nights, and the impact it had on Marius's development. The house image also appears as a significant force for development in *Gaston de Latour* in the old chateau with an irregular ground plan; and again in "Emerald Uthwart" in Chase Lodge, a soft, green, and fragrant place. The school described in "Emerald Uthwart" is King's School, Canterbury, a gray place that WP attended at age fourteen and that he always associated with rigorous discipline. WP was a devoted student of Ruskin and Goethe, and he read well into the works of Sainte-Beuve and Flaubert. In 1869 he became associated with the

Pre-Raphaelites, numbering among his friends such men as Burne-Jones, Rossetti, and Swinburne. WP maintains throughout his works that the successful artist is also a scholar; through his "fine and sensitive scholarship . . . his impressions are sorted and disciplined into form." For WP the harmony of form and substance is the central requirement for all good art, good government, and effective, vital living—but the emphasis, particularly in life-style, is clearly on form.

1925

370 Burdett, Osbert. THE BEARDSLEY PERIOD (Lond: John Lane, 1925), pp. 32–34, 52, 54–55, 154–57, 162, 170, 191, 193, 201, 206, 221–22, 265–66.

WP's personal response to the ugliness and disillusionment of his age and its consequent unnatural and self-conscious obsession with beauty was to retreat behind a mask and to seek in art that which is universally beautiful and that which reflects man's changing moods. *The Renaissance* gave the age's preoccupation with beauty the status of "an epicurean philosophy." Its innovative, "recondite" style also appealed to an age in which many of the newspapers and books did "no more than reflect the illiteracy of the masses." In WP's essays "Aesthetic Poetry," "Rossetti," and the "Postscript" to *Appreciations* can be found characteristics that are useful in considering the poetry and to some extent the prose of the *fin de siècle*. Although Arthur Symons greatly admired the writings of WP, their works are different in that WP emphasized style, whereas Symons emphasized subject matter.

371 Duclaux, Mary. "Souvenirs sur Walter Pater" (Memories of Walter Pater), LA REVUE DE PARIS, 15 Jan 1925, pp. 339–58.

Biographical details such as the imaginary relatives the isolated Paters invented for themselves and which foreshadowed the subjective world of the later imaginary portraits provide hints of WP's personality and of the meaning of his works. Physical details, also, such as his moustache, which contrasted with his soft and meditative aspect, symbolize the vision he had of himself as a "military monk," a champion of beauty. Without repudiating his ideal of beauty, without deserting his dream of faith, he hoped to discover a rule and a discipline for his contemporaries. [In French.]

372 Harrison, Jane Ellen. REMINISCENCES OF A STUDENT'S LIFE (Lond: Hogarth P, 1925), p. 46; rptd (1926).

[In these reminiscences, Miss Harrison recalls being a welcome guest at the house of WP and his sisters. She remembers thinking of WP as "a soft, kind cat; he purred so persuasively that I lost the sense of what he was saying." She remembers that Henry James was also a frequent guest at WP's.]

373 Le Gallienne, Richard. THE ROMANTIC '90S (Garden City, NY: Doubleday, Page, 1925); rptd (Lond & NY: Putnam, 1926), pp. 74–91; rptd with intro by H. Montgomery Hyde (Lond: Putnam, 1951).
[Le Gallienne reminisces about WP, whose *The Renaissance* established him as the founder of the Aesthetic movement. Several anecdotes about WP were told to Le Gallienne by Oscar Wilde, who popularized but also "vulgarized . . . the gospel of beauty and 'ecstasy' " that WP taught.]

374 Murry, J. Middleton. "Morality Again," PENCILLINGS (NY: T. Seltzer, 1925), pp. 119–27.
WP, although regarded by the recent generation as the prophet of art for art's sake, was perfectly clear on the subject of morality. He is too frequently misread. He clearly distinguishes in literature between "qualities of mind," finding expression in structure and language, and "qualities of soul" that render the work favorable to some, unfavorable to others. The "quality of soul" must be judged by moral standards; the "comeliness" that we seek in literature is quite different from the quality of mind that is found in a work's artistic merit.

375 Richards, I. A. PRINCIPLES OF LITERARY CRITICISM (Lond: Kegan Paul, Trench, Trubner, 1925), pp. 72, 132, 255, 270; (NY: Harcourt, Brace, 1925); rptd (Lond: Routledge & Kegan Paul, 1959); rptd (NY: Harcourt, Brace, 1959); (1961).
The belief for some thirty years that "the values of art are unique, or capable of being considered in isolation from all others" is due in part to the influence of WP, Whistler, and their disciples. WP's epilogue to *The Renaissance* "is the *locus classicus*" of the recent "insistence upon the quality of the momentary *consciousness* which the arts occasion." The passages on the importance of truth in WP's "Essay on Style" are prime examples of "unmistakable confusion between value and communicative efficacy." WP's belief that in order to get to the truth in literature one must eliminate all " 'surplusage' " is a belief that makes "excessive demands upon the artist," for surplusage is detrimental only if it interferes with the reader's response to the work. If it does not, surplusage may even improve the work by providing it with "extra solidity."

376 Sillard, P. A. "Some Aspects of Walter Pater," CATHOLIC WORLD, CXXII (Oct 1925), 61–65.
WP's writings, unlike those of most writers of the nineteenth century, particularly Arnold, Newman, and Ruskin, have no didactic, utilitarian interests to promote. WP's life and work were solely devoted to art. His works and the type of men he chose to do portraits of provide insights into the type of man WP was. The value of his works lies in their creation of "an atmosphere of refinement, of culture, in which we are enabled 'to withdraw the thoughts from the mere machinery of life.' " His works teach the reader to make the most of the present moment "wherein is 'the essence of classical feeling.' " WP's later works reflect an essential spirituality; he had "the essential grasp of Christianity . . . [which] saved

him from falling into the sea of unbelief" that was so common in the nineteenth century. His style is characterized by a "wealth of significance with economy of phrase."

> **377** Weygandt, Cornelius. A CENTURY OF THE ENGLISH NOVEL (NY: Century, 1925), pp. 6, 26, 255, 331, 344–46; rptd (Freeport, NY: Books for Libraries P, 1968).

"Mr. Rose" in Mallock's THE NEW REPUBLIC (1877) was the first glimpse of WP the novelist for many novel readers. Few at the time knew his work well enough to recognize the parody. But by 1885 when *Marius the Epicurean* was published, it was common knowledge that he was the apostle of a cult of beauty-worshippers satirized by Mallock. Both *Marius* and *Gaston de Latour* are less novels and more like "a series of essays devoted to the study of an era." In both works, the characterization of the heroes fails. "Pater knew little of life. . . . its humdrum and ugly details offended him." His future reputation may depend less on his own works than on the writers who felt his influence: e.g., George Moore, Vernon Lee, Arthur Symons, Sir Frederick Wedmore, Lionel Johnson, and George Santayana.

> **378** Williamson, George C. "Sir Frederick Wedmore," CERTAIN COMMENTS (Lond: Selwyn & Blount, 1925), pp. 13–19.

[Wedmore greatly admired WP "while feeling his limitations."]

1926

> **379** Andrews, C. E., and M. O. Percival. "Introduction," POETRY OF THE NINETIES (NY: Harcourt, Brace, 1926), pp. 16–17, 18, 19.

WP taught the young aesthetic poets to live intensely, to withdraw into the ivory tower, and to live only for the "moment." But his followers descended from that tower and brought their aestheticism into daily life. They left behind WP's "intellectual side"; their search for beauty was too often a search for sensations. WP's true disciple is Arthur Symons, who is equally as intellectual as he is responsive to sensations. But unlike WP, Symons refused to live in the ivory tower. His CREDO is his development in verse of WP's philosophy of life and art.

> **380** Crocker, L. "Voice Elements in Prose. An Examination of Pater and Emerson," QUARTERLY JOURNAL OF SPEECH EDUCATION (April 1926), pp. 168–75.

Forty-one out of forty-eight students preferred a reading from the conclusion to Emerson's "The American Scholar" to a reading from WP's conclusion to the essay on "Style." Emerson's lucidity won the day. WP's long, involved sentences made the thought hard to grasp when read aloud. But rhythm, i.e., the "voice element," is WP's stylistic forte, and by retaining as much rhythm as possible without resorting to poetry WP makes the sentence "stick in the consciousness."

The prose of WP and Emerson reads very much like free verse. Emerson wrote "The American Scholar" to be spoken; WP, however, intended only that his essay should be read. When read aloud, Emerson should therefore be more successful.

381 Lalou, René. PANORAMA DE LA LITTÉRATURE ANGLAISE CONTEMPORAINE (Panorama of Contemporary English Literature) (Paris: Kra, 1926), pp. 124–29.
The most important characteristic of WP's aesthetic theory is the way it defies arbitrary systematization. His only absolute truth is the individual; his impressionistic criticism that transposes into words individual artistic sensations is a "hymn to individualism." [In French.]

382 Mourey, Gabriel. "Marcel Proust, John Ruskin et Walter Pater," LE MONDE NOUVEAU, 15 Aug–15 Sept 1926, pp. 702–14; 15 Oct 1926, pp. 896–909.
Proust never mentioned WP's name, but he surely admired him. Similarities between *Marius the Epicurean* and À LA RECHERCHE DU TEMPS PERDU abound. Both deal with anxious, refined souls; Marius's anxiety, like that of Proust's hero, ever like Proust himself, is caused by his philosophical preoccupation. Marius builds his own world with remembrances and sensations. Both heroes also regret the time that has passed, and both choose to concentrate on the poetic aspects of everyday life. Both Proust and WP owed much to the influence of Ruskin. [In French.]

383 Staub, Friedrich. DAS IMAGINÄRE PORTRÄT WALTER PATERS (Walter Pater's Imaginary Portraits) (Zurich: Leemann, 1926). Published master's thesis, Zurich, 1926.
WP spent the best years of his life in a solitary, silent cell in Oxford; he had only one purpose—to gather and absorb mental impressions. The question of whether subject or object dominates one's outlook on life seemed senseless to him. He straddled a position between complete introversion and complete extraversion. His work is mainly a linguistic reflection or impression of artistic enjoyment. The external form that most of his work takes is the essay, which means for him a concentration of epic, dramatic, and lyric elements.

His imaginary portraits in characterization do not differ from his historical portraits. Only the method is different. Original criticism allows him to identify himself with an historical personage. In the imaginary portrait, he creates a character who has complete expression. But to be able to clothe this reflected image completely, an opponent must be created, accounting for the conflict in most of his portraits. "A Prince of Court Painters" is the only imaginary portrait that mentions the name of an historical personage, Antoine Watteau. This portrait is inferior to his original creations. The picture of Watteau that WP projects is not the creation of his imagination but is a result of exhaustive research. In "Denys l'Auxerrois" WP combines the characteristics of Dionysus and Apollo. Three different sources can be recognized in this portrait: WP's own personal impressions from his travel, the historical element of medieval France, and material that came to him from the Greek legends. "Sebastian van Storck" represents what WP calls "metaphysics." Next to Florian Deleal and Emerald Uthwart, Sebastian is the most inferior of WP's reflected images. Here, character and time are separated. WP has put all the immaterial elements in the character of Sebastian and all the material elements in the time period. WP seems to enjoy the drama of a pure, immaterial man in conflict with an environment that is highly materialistic. "Duke Carl of Rosenmold" is set in Heidelberg, Germany, in the eighteenth century. But WP suggests that Rosenmold is not only Heidelberg but also every other German city of the early eighteenth century. The "Duke Carl" portrait comes the nearest of all the imaginary portraits to the form of the essay. [In German.]

384 Stenberg, Theodore, "The Pater-Saintsbury Definition of Criticism," MODERN LANGUAGE NOTES, XLI (Dec 1926), 536.
Saintsbury is indebted to WP for his definition of criticism: " 'To feel the virtue of the poet, or the painter, to disengage it, to set it forth,—these are the three stages of the critic's duty.' " Although Saintsbury and WP are considered to be very modern in their theory of criticism, a similar definition of criticism is found in the writings of Alexander Gerard, which were written nearly a century and a half before Saintsbury's HISTORY OF CRITICISM.

385 Tuell, Anne Kimball. "Introduction," *Marius the Epicurean. His Sensations and Ideas* (NY: Macmillan, 1926), pp. vii–xix.
Like the crystal, the central symbol of "Diaphaneitè," WP also reflects many impressions, most of which were acquired from his vast learning. Of all of his works, *Marius the Epicurean* seems the most bookish, "a texture woven out of ravellings from all sorts of classic quotations." Students of WP will recognize WP himself in the person of Marius. "The death of the martyr *malgrè lui* . . . a frequent theme in fiction" may have been suggested by Newman's CALLISTA. The novel is above all a statement of WP's corrected Epicureanism stretched to include an affirmation of Christianity. His style "moves in curves," hardly what the modern reader has come to expect.

386 Welby, T. Earle. A STUDY OF SWINBURNE (Lond: Faber & Gwyer, 1926), pp. 187–88, 196, 222.
WP undoubtedly owed a debt to Swinburne's study of Leonardo da Vinci, done in 1864. In a letter from Swinburne to Morley, Swinburne refers to WP's "frank avowal of obligation."

1927

387 Chandler, Zilpha Emma. "An Analysis of the Stylistic Techniques of Addison, Johnson, Hazlitt, and Pater." Thesis, University of Iowa,

1927; pub as AN ANALYSIS OF THE STYLISTIC TECHNIQUE OF ADDISON, JOHNSON, HAZLITT, AND PATER (Iowa City: University of Iowa P, 1928), q.v. for abstract.

388 Fehr, Bernard. ENGLISCHE PROSA VON 1880 BIS ZUR GEGENWART (English Prose From 1880 until the Present) (Leipzig: B. G. Teubner, 1927), p. 97ff.

[The section on WP in this book includes a brief introduction in which Fehr states that in *The Renaissance,* particularly in the "Preface," WP lectures on how one can become an impressionistic or creative critic. The volume is also a reaction against Ruskin's claims for the appreciation of art on social terms. The lectures fascinated Wilde and were embodied in the flesh to some degree by Francis Thompson. Arthur Symons also greatly respected them, Fehr maintains. The chaotic state of of the aesthetic critic was noticeably characterized in 1925 by I. A. Richards in PRINCIPLES OF LITERARY CRITICISM. The remainder of the section on WP is the text in English of the "Preface" with Fehr's notes. He cites the works where Arnold specifically refers to the aim of criticism as "seeing the object as in itself it really is." He notes that WP was already, in 1873, affected by the metaphysics of Hegel's theory of aesthetics. He also records the source of the quote from Blake in the "Preface"; it is Blake's comment on Sir Joshua Reynold's DISCOURSES where he speaks of Albrecht Dürer; the quote may be found in THE WRITINGS OF WILLIAM BLAKE, ed by G. Keynes (1925), III, 27.] [In German.]

389 Hecht, Hans. "Walter Pater. Eine Würdigung" (Walter Pater. An Appreciation), DEUTSCHE VIERTELJAHRSSCHRIFT FUR LITERATURWIS-SENSCHAFT UND GEISTESGESCHICHTE, V (1927), 550–82.

A very strong autobiographical compulsion penetrates WP's writings, autobiographical in the sense of continuous self-confession of "sensations and ideas." The essay was the literary form he used best. His entire work can be viewed as an illumination of Platonic thought. He writes to recommend Platonic philosophy to his readers. [General biographical information and appreciative commentary.] [In German.]

390 Konody, P. G. "Introduction," SEBASTIAN VAN STORCK, with eight illustrations in colour by Alastair (Lond: John Lane; NY: Dodd, Mead, 1927), pp. 9–21.

This particular edition of WP's "Sebastian van Storck" is a *"tour de force,"* for "artist, writer and philosopher form here a kind of Holy Trinity, three in person, yet one in character." All three are "one with a unity almost of identity: Walter Pater was Sebastian van Storck himself, midway between the eternal 'no' and the eternal 'yes' of religion," and in Alastair's drawings can be seen "the same duality of temperament." WP characterizes van Storck as a "Dutch pantheist," a man who has a "touch of Catholicism in his Protestant soul." WP's portrait is so successful because as a "pagan" WP can present with detachment the two creeds that grip van Storck's mind. WP's "hero lives in philosophy rather than society," because for

WP thought was more important than action. Thus the heroic action at the end of the story seems almost anticlimactic, for "suddenly all the heroism of soul goes into the courage of heart." Unlike van Storck who, with all his philosophy, spent his life "in the very negation of all its huge possibilities," WP "followed his art with the true devotion of the craftsman." Although his style is at times " 'too austerely magnificent to be always persuasive,' " the " 'cumulative richness and sonorous depth of his language,' " harmonize effectively with his " 'deep and earnest philosophy of life.' " But of the two art forms, Alastair's illustrations are the most moving in their depiction of "the *flâneur,* the *penseur,* and the *sauveur,* those triple characteristics of Sebastian van Storck."

391 Lahey, G. F. "Walter Pater and the Catholic Church," MONTH, CXLIX (June 1927), pp. 542–45.
WP's life was restless. He was a seeker whose "quest brought him to the very heart and centre of the Catholic Church." He may have wished to enter the Church. He assisted at Mass and frequently visited the Carmelite church in Kensington.

392 Michaelson, Alexander [André Raffalovich]. "Oscar Wilde," BLACKFRIARS, VIII (Nov 1927), 694–702.
[Wilde and Raffalovich talked about Shakespeare after dinner at WP's.]

393 Preston, John Hyde. "Portrait of an Epicurean," VIRGINIA QUARTERLY REVIEW, III (Jan 1927), 99–110.
[Preston's brief, general philosophical and spiritual portrait of WP is based on "glimpses" of the "possible" WP suggested in some of his writings.]

394 Rawlinson, H. G. "Introduction," SELECTED ESSAYS (Lond: Macmillan, 1927), pp. vii–xviii.
WP's visits to Heidelberg enhanced his taste for German philosophy and literature. His religion remains a mystery. WP's criticism is "entirely impressionistic and subjective." He "differs lamentably from Ruskin" owing to his poor technical knowledge of art. He blunders; for example, he attributes work to da Vinci that is almost certainly not his. *The Renaissance* aroused criticism from a Victorian public that had not yet recovered from the shock of Swinburne's 1866 publication of POEMS AND BALLADS. WP has been identified with "Robert Langham" in ROBERT ELSMERE. His hedonism was purely intellectual. In many of his *Imaginary Portraits,* WP seems to want "to study the effects of the clash of the Pagan and the Christian ideals."

395 Smith, Logan Pearsall. "On Re-Reading Pater," TIMES LITERARY SUPPLEMENT (Lond), 3 Feb 1927, pp. 65–66; rptd in DIAL, LXXXIII (Sept 1927), 223–30; rptd in REPERUSALS AND RECOLLECTIONS (Lond: Constable, 1936); rptd (Freeport, NY: Books for Libraries P, 1968).
Rereading the works of WP, his early enthusiasts will discover that there is still much of value in these works which formulated "the beautiful, impracticable religion of their youth." WP was a euphuist who sought "to express with the most

scholarly exactness thought of the rarest quality, and to render with punctilious sincerity a beautiful and intense vision which was very personal to him." In much of his work, he attempted to express ideas and abstractions "in their concrete manifestation." This artistic formula was the product of his " 'sensuous love of the unseen.' " At the basis of his theory of subjective criticism was a belief in Cyrenaic philosophy which "taught him to live as much as possible in the present moment, the Ideal Now, and, above all, in those moments of experience in which the beauty and meaning of life seem to be mystically revealed."

396 "Winckelmann in Rome," TIMES LITERARY SUPPLEMENT (Lond), 15 Sept 1927, pp. 613–14.
[A biographical sketch of Winckelmann's years in Rome. Mentions WP's portrait of Winckelmann briefly.]

397 Wortham, H. E. OSCAR BROWNING (Lond: Constable, 1927), pp. 59, 60, 132, 150, 186, 262.
FitzJames Stephens, codifier of the Indian penal laws, in a note to Oscar Browning says that "though he does not wish to mention names, a man called Pater" was reported to have approved of Browning's loaning a copy of Gautier's MLLE. DE MAUPIN to Stephens's son. In his response to the story, WP informed Browning that he was "pained" and greatly disapproved of loaning the book to a young boy. WP was also overheard by "a lady" to say that he approved of another of Browning's student's [W. Graham] acquaintance with French novelists, finding it remarkable that a boy of his age should have literary taste geared to something more than the commonplace, such as Tennyson's poetry. During the years that *Marius the Epicurean* was being conceived and written, WP was on considerably intimate terms with Browning. *Marius* is the "epic of intellectual youth" and in "the 'pure and disinterested friendship of schoolmates,' " which is the central event of Marius's adolescence, one can detect more than traces of Oscar Browning's philosophy, and maybe of his influence." [WP appears to have been a source of support for Browning in his difficulties at Eton. While staying with WP at Oxford, Browning first met Oscar Wilde.]

1928

398 Chandler, Zilpha Emma. AN ANALYSIS OF THE STYLISTIC TECH-NIQUE OF ADDISON, JOHNSON, HAZLITT, AND PATER (Iowa City: University of Iowa P, 1928). Rvd master's thesis, University of Iowa, 1927.
Based on a passage of approximately fifteen-hundred words from WP's essay "Charles Lamb," one can conclude that WP's vocabulary seems more copious than either Addison's, Johnson's, or Hazlitt's. WP uses "comparatively few nouns . . . and no conspicuous number of sensory adjectives or of action verbs." His

vocabulary suggests an atmosphere of "quiet." He delights in lengthy phrases and is fastidious in his choice of words. [The major portion of the section on WP consists of an analysis of his use of figures of speech, idioms, sentence structure, grammar, and logic, etc. Most of Chandler's evidence is based on simple word-counting. Chandler's conclusion is that although WP sought for a quiet beauty in his prose, he is not a great prosaist.] "His style is seldom clear and never, in any sense, forceful." He does not create a feeling of "sympathy" or "good-will" in his readers.

399 Fernandez, Ramon. "Notes sur l'Esthétique de Proust" (Notes on the Aesthetic of Proust), LA NOUVELLE REVUE FRANÇAISE, XXXI (1928), 272–80.

The pages of the TEMPS RETROUVÉ which constitute an essay on style are comparable to WP's essay on "Style." These essays are separated by forty years, but they belong to the same spiritual period. They represent the same step in what might be called the conquest of the rights of art. But Proust worked from life itself; WP was an exile in the realm of culture and ideology. [In French.]

400 Hardy, Florence. THE EARLY YEARS OF THOMAS HARDY, 1840–91 (NY & Lond: Macmillan, 1928), pp. 236, 275, 278.

1886, summer: Hardy met WP " 'whose manner is that of one carrying weighty ideas without spilling them.' " 1888: WP called on the Hardys and told them a story of George III; on 14 July 1888 Hardy dined at WP's.

401 Isakovicsová-Weatherallová, M. "Cesty estetického myšleni u Waltera Patera" (The Ways of Aestheticism in Walter Pater's Thought), ČASOPSIS PRO MODERNI FILOLOGII (Prague), XV (1928–29), 257–65.

WP was French-oriented. His childhood perceptions must have been painful, for beauty and suffering seem to affect him most, although *Marius the Epicurean* does reflect a brighter side to WP's experience. Life is ritualistic rather than real for him. But the thought of home seems ever-present in his works. The early WP is attracted to Dionysius. In "Denys l'Auxerrois" Dionysian sacrifice penetrates cruelly into the bright figure of Dionysius. WP's critique of MEASURE FOR MEASURE combines his aesthetic perceptions with a sense of high moral deeds. The figure of the diaphanous being is found in all of his works. It is a spontaneous, naive, and intellectual figure.

Of all of the philosophical thinkers who influenced him, WP seems to share most with Montaigne. Like Montaigne, he is a skeptic who admires historical deeds inspired by ethical thinking. Montaigne taught WP the art of *"carpe diem."* But in *Marius* a yearning for the absolute is evident. Like *Marius,* WP was attracted to Christianity because of its authoritarianism. Marius's empathy enables him to balance pain with a great capacity for love.

WP loved historical periods in which people were able to feel and taste Promethean joy; he called these historical periods "Renaissance." His vision of history was highly impressionistic and subjective. He shared with Hegel the idea that the arts developed parallel with man's spiritual development. But he went beyond Hegel's limits. He stressed the potentiality of expression, interpreting the Romantic stage of development more concretely than Hegel. WP saw the development of art as the conquering of the inner man; the development is fluid. Christian art, for instance, was always there—it was included in early Greek art. When WP declares art to be autonomous in "The School of Giorgione," he frees himself from the influence of Hegel's ideology.

WP prepared the English-speaking world for the doctrine of art for art's sake. With Baudelaire, he sympathized with the literature of the Latin decadence, projecting its cultured beauty into the figure of Flavian in *Marius*. WP's works reveal two dominant inclinations: his French sympathies inclined him toward the formal aesthetics of art for art's sake, but his English philosophical tradition inclined him toward idealism. He identified himself artistically with Flaubert. Like Flaubert, he did with words what a musician does with tones; he molded thought into form. [In Czech.]

> **402** Lafourçade, Georges. LA JEUNESSE DE SWINBURNE (The Young Swinburne) (Strasbourg: Publication de la Faculté des Lettres, 1928), pp. 123–26, 165, 263.

Swinburne was hostile towards Oxford University. He knew WP rather well but never praised him. Unlike WP, Swinburne disliked Plato and Platonic morality. [In French.]

> **403** Mainsard, Joseph. "L'Esthétisme de Pater et de Wilde" (The Aestheticism of Pater and Wilde), ÉTUDES, 5 March 1928, pp. 525–52.

The doctrine of Heraclitus is a syllogism which developed into a philosophical theory with WP and a character type with Wilde. WP, recluse and prose artist, sees in art the manifestation of a nearly sacred reality, the expression of a living truth which the artist "represents." His Heraclitean philosophy of the moment requires the cultivation of the senses and of the mind. This voluptuous existence demands a life of asceticism. For Pater, hedonism is not to be confounded with Epicureanism. Marius's "pleasures" are experienced as "insight" that provides plenitude. WP's metaphysics are embodied in Wilde's life style. His life is itself an artistic work. Wilde proclaims the superiority of the contemplative over the active life. Art, superior to reality, cannot be immoral; but Dorian Gray is vanquished by morals since he dies tortured by remorse. As soon as aestheticism leaves the monkish cell that WP envisioned, it must come into conflict with society and conventional ethics. In prison, Wilde tries to be faithful to his philosophy. Dishonor and suffering are new, unknown quantities that add to the artistic work that was Wilde's life. [In French.]

> **404** Michaelson, Alexander [André Raffalovich]. "Giles and Miles and Isabeau," BLACKFRIARS, IX (Jan 1928), 18–29.

[WP gave Raffalovich copies of *Imaginary Portraits* and *Marius the Epicurean* when they appeared. Professor Keats warned him to avoid WP and J. A. Symonds, but he went ahead and made himself known to WP.]

405 Michaelson, Alexander [André Raffalovich]. "Walter Pater. In Memoriam," BLACKFRIARS, IX (Aug 1928), 463–71.

WP's *Rituale,* a white and violet volume, is now in the library of Blackfriars, Oxford. WP would have been pleased to know that his house in St. Giles is occupied by Dominicans. Few men have been kinder to young students "as they were" than WP. [Raffalovich notes that he was warned by Sidney Colvin to refrain from getting to know WP and John Addington Symonds. Michaelson records that "the semi-publicity of Symonds' case . . . is my excuse for this allusion. Could one imagine Pater figuring as case XZ of Havelock Ellis?"]

406 Nitchie, Elizabeth. THE CRITICISM OF LITERATURE (NY: Macmillan, 1928), pp. 107, 271.

WP, like most great critics, requires of literature a positive ethical value. The relation of literature to moral conduct is paramount in his philosophy.

407 Read, Herbert. ENGLISH PROSE STYLE (Lond: G. Bell; NY: Holt, 1928), pp. 24, 219–20.

One ascribes "enervation" to WP's prose style. His style is definitely his own; it has character and beauty. This "outer unity" must spring from an "inner unity." WP seems to have had "a self-consuming passion for style, an educated taste, an abnormal sensibility for the tonal value of words." Newman's stylistic aim was almost in direct contrast to WP's.

408 Scott-James, Rolfe Arnold. THE MAKING OF LITERATURE. SOME PRINCIPLES OF CRITICISM EXAMINED IN THE LIGHT OF ANCIENT AND MODERN THEORY (Lond: Secker & Warburg, 1928), pp. 294–315; rptd (NY: Holt, 1930); rptd (Lond: Secker & Warburg, 1956).

Much of WP's writing deals with the traditional aesthetic problems of the relationship between art and life and the distinction between art and morals. In his essay on Wordsworth, WP maintains that art has no didactic function and that it "is no longer the servant, but is to be the master; the highest morality will be to enable as much as possible of life to be lived in the spirit of the artist." Thus, for WP art is not a part of life; it is "the whole of life in so far as it is lived in the finer way of the spirit." In *Marius the Epicurean,* WP defines his critical approach to literature. Both Marius's spiritual development and WP's critical method involve discarding dogmatic, stereotyped modes of thinking, remaining open to "new opinions, new modes of expression," and constantly searching for beauty in all its varied forms. WP's critical approach does not begin with a priori principles; rather it seeks to discover the distinctive and unique qualities that make up and define a work of art.

WP's essay "Style" deals with another problem in literary criticism: the distinction between "the literature of fact" (science) and "the literature of the imaginative sense of fact" (art). In the former, one is concerned with an accurate "photographic 'imitation' of reality"; in the latter, the artist is concerned with an accurate transcription of his vision of reality.

409 Symons, A. J. A. "Introduction," AN ANTHOLOGY OF 'NINETIES' VERSE, ed by A. J. A. Symons (Lond: Elkin Matthews & Marrot, 1928), pp. xvii–xxi.

"In six explicit sentences" in the "Conclusion" to *The Renaissance* WP explained his own skepticism. His words became the "gospel" of the Nineties poets. Art was the solitary hope. The Nineties poets sought for new techniques through which to express new moods; all experience was to be "dragged into the net of literature." Their theory of art was "derived from Keats and Edgar Allan Poe" through WP and Baudelaire.

410 Winder, Blanche. "A Master of Aesthetic," SPECTATOR, CXLI (11 Aug 1928), pp. 185–86.

The initial response to reading "beautiful prose" such as that of WP is an "exquisite sense of wonder." After this initial response one begins the critical task of distilling from WP's writing that "quality of mind that has startled us into such delight." WP's portrait of Plato is also a portrait of WP. WP wrote as he thought. Plato wrote, "breaking visible colour, as it were, into the very texture of his work, and multiplying the glowing thread into 'large tapestried figures.' " For WP, as for Plato, abstract knowledge was "like knowledge of a person"; it was "something to *look* at."

Many of WP's insights and ideas are still relevant. His analysis of Socrates' teaching is of value to contemporary educational thought. His "attitude towards true pictorial achievement, springing from 'that quality which is quite independent of anything definitely poetical in the subject it accompanies' " is essentially the same as Clive Bell and Roger Fry's contemporary theory of " 'pure aesthetic reaction' to form and colour."

Marius the Epicurean seems to be WP's most important work, for in it is "the concentrated essence of his deepest, most intimate thought." WP "must have been very much like his own Marius—a 'nature composed of instincts almost physical, and of slowly accumulated intellectual judgments.' "

1929

411 Boas, Frederick S. "Critics and Criticism in the 'Seventies," THE EIGHTEEN-SEVENTIES, ed by Harley Granville-Barker (NY: Macmillan; Cambridge: Cambridge UP, 1929), pp. 204–6.

WP's *Renaissance* caused as much excitement at Oxford as Strachey's EMINENT

VICTORIANS has in our own time. Beneath the decorative surface of his essays is staunch "intellectual fibre."

412 Du Bos, Charles. LE DIALOGUE AVEC ANDRÉ GIDE (Dialogue with André Gide) (Paris: Au sans Pareil, 1929), pp. 95–104.

The "fervor of moments" is a recurrent theme in Gide's works. It animates LES NOURRITURES TERRESTRES, where the absolute is found in the moment itself. A parallel can be drawn between WP's "Conclusion" to *The Renaissance* and Gide's work. In both, an awareness of Heraclitus' doctrine of flux brings forth an insistence upon the absoluteness of the moment. This ethic of the moment refuses to give any significance to the role of memory. For Gide, time is the principal adversary. But for WP, the evolution from the "Conclusion" to *Marius the Epicurean* to *Plato and Platonism* reinstates the importance of memory. If in *Marius* the ethic of the moment becomes an ethic of sacrifice, it is because Marius himself is more and more aware that only the life of the memory can confer an identity to his being. But for Gide of the NOURRITURES TERRESTRES or L'IM-MORALISTE, reminiscences are only enemies. [In French.]

413 Durham, W. H. "Measure for Measure as Measure for Critics," ESSAYS IN CRITICISM: FIRST SERIES (Berkeley: University of California P [University of California Publications in English, I] 1929); rptd (Freeport, NY: Books for Libraries P, 1968), pp. 113–34.

WP's "exquisite" essay on MEASURE FOR MEASURE might mistakenly lead the reader into seeing the play as a preliminary study for *Marius the Epicurean*. Though WP saw the humor, sympathy, and study of character in it, all characteristic of Shakespeare's genius, he nevertheless projected many of his own fantasies onto the play.

414 Eliot, T. S. "Experiment in Criticism," TRADITION AND EXPERIMENT IN PRESENT-DAY LITERATURE: ADDRESSES DELIVERED AT THE CITY LITERARY INSTITUTE (Lond: City Literary Institute, 1929); rptd (NY: Haskell House, 1966), pp. 201–2.

In the sense intended by WP, the phrase "art for art's sake" means something quite different from the idea of "literature for literature's sake" as it was advocated up to the end of the eighteenth century. WP's "Conclusion" to *The Renaissance* makes clear that "art for art's sake" means no less "than art as a substitute for everything else, and as a purveyor of emotions and sensations which belong to life rather than to art." WP's doctrine would have been unintelligible to an earlier time when art and literature and philosophy were not substitutes for religion and morals but "special and limited adornments of life."

415 Foerster, Norman. "The Impressionists," BOOKMAN (NY), LXX (Dec 1929), 337–47.

"The vogue of impressionistic criticism in America in the twentieth century has been largely the result of revolt against the somewhat obtuse literary scholarship of the colleges and universities." Many young intellectuals reacted against the dominating tradition of historical study. The best critic is the one, like Coleridge, Lamb, and Hazlitt, who is keenly responsive to impressions and "contagious in his enthusiasm." These qualities appear later in Sainte-Beuve, Arnold, and WP, who drew much from Arnold but more from a romantic revival that developed in his time. WP stated clearly in the "Preface" and "Conclusion" to *The Renaissance* the creed of impressionism. Wilde and Symons followed, as impressionism triumphed in the last twenty years of the century. WP limits himself in the "Preface" to a defense of romantic theory; the "Conclusion" presents his theory of impressionistic criticism. In the "Preface" he maintains that knowing the impression is a preliminary step to sound criticism.

416 Frye, Prosser Hall. "Pater," VISIONS AND CHIMERAS (Bost: Marshall Jones Co., 1929); rptd (NY: Biblo and Tanner, 1966), pp. 225–49.

Except for the trouble with Jowett, WP's life was uneventful. He believed that style possessed its own "virtue." WP's essays appeal on a purely "sensational," nonintellectual plane. But WP completely misunderstood Flaubert on style. Flaubert calls for photographic realism; WP is an "illusionist" in contrast.

417 Grabowski, Zbigniew. WALTER PATER, ZYCIE, DZIELO, STYL (Walter Pater, Life, Works, Style) (Towarzystwo Przyjaciol Nauk: Poznan, 1929).

[Unable to locate.] [In Polish.]

418 Somervell, David Churchill. ENGLISH THOUGHT IN THE NINETEENTH CENTURY (Lond: Methuen, 1929); rptd (NY: David McKay, 1965), pp. 217–19.

WP best expresses the Victorian conception of "art for art's sake." He wrote for kindred spirits, in the style of a poet, and is much more of a stylistic specialist than either Ruskin, Morris, or Arnold. When WP wrote the passage on the death of Socrates in *Plato and Platonism,* he may well have been thinking of himself as another unintentional corrupter of youth. The aesthetic movement was openly hostile to Puritanism and aided the growing interest in Anglo-Catholic ritual. WP always felt drawn to the Catholic Church, particularly its ritual.

419 Souday, Paul. LA SOCIÉTÉ DES GRANDS ESPRITS (The Fellowship of Great Spirits) (Paris: Hazan, 1929), pp. 10–17, 85–93.

WP's *Plato and Platonism* proves that he is not a philosopher. He is instead an enemy of intellectualism, of concepts or abstractions. His sensitive and artistic mind rejoices in the concrete. For him, metaphysical propositions are not to be exhaustively studied but only enjoyed. He does not understand Plato's philosophy. He omits it completely from his study, preferring instead to treat Plato's role as a writer. In *The Renaissance* he falsely maintains that the reawakening of Greek and Latin tradition during the Renaissance was a result rather than a cause. He falsely separates one main current that informed the Renaissance into two different ones:

the return to the ancients and the return to nature. In "The School of Giorgione," his theory is disputable; poetry, not music, is the most perfect form of art. [In French.]

420 Squire, J. C. "Pater and Marius," *Marius the Epicurean. His Sensations and Ideas*. Two Volumes (Lond: Macmillan, 1929), I, vii–xxiii.

WP's themes were esoteric. He "was an aesthetic anchorite paying solitary and ceremonious devotions to the principle of Beauty." Ruskin was his aesthetic mentor. WP's nature was profoundly religious. He was an unconventional novelist. Marius (*Marius the Epicurean*) is but an "enchanting shadow" who never seems to exercise his will on life. The novel lacks a balanced development towards a climax. It must be regarded "as a miscellany with a thread." But it is the crown of WP's stylistic achievement. Much of the novel is autobiographical. Christianity must have been a revelation to Marius even if he did not profess his belief. WP added something to our appreciation of classical civilization. He created a pagan Rome that is "tender and sensitive." Marius arouses pity and affection. The novel is a confession to be compared with Augustine's CONFESSIONS. [The volumes contain plates in dry point drawn by Thomas Mackenzie.]

421 Welby, T. Earle. THE VICTORIAN ROMANTICS: 1850–1870 (Lond: Bodley Head, 1929), rptd (Hamden, Conn: Archon Books, 1966), pp. 5, 59, 76, 98, 133–35.

Simeon Solomon's "Bacchus" was admired by WP. Swinburne's "Cleopatra," the model for Wilde's poem "The Sphinx," gave WP some hints for his famous Gioconda passage. WP also modelled much of the style of his da Vinci essay on Swinburne's earlier essay on the drawings of old Florentine masters. Charles Lamb, Swinburne, Rossetti, and WP shared what might be called "a common language."

422 Wright, Cuthbert. "Out of Harm's Way: Some Notes on the Esthetic Movement of the 'Nineties," BOOKMAN (NY), LXX (Nov 1929), 234–43.

[Wright records how "with the humorless hero-worship of an undergraduate" he had reverenced WP. Prepared not to like Thomas Wright's biography of WP, he now turned to it and found far more than he had expected. With the exception of a limited number of revealing asides on WP by the author, this article is mainly a retelling of many of the stories and anecdotes about WP included in Wright's controversial biography. Among the more interesting asides are comments on WP's attraction to aestheticism and Roman Catholicism.] In Victorian England, to be an authentic artist was almost as bad as converting to Rome. *The Renaissance* was the textbook for the aesthetic confraternity "forsaking the lilies and languors" of conventional virtue to learn from Whistler to find beauty in a London fog. WP appeared, a theoretician far more seductive to his followers than ever was Ruskin. WP invented the phrase "creative criticism," and he likewise invented the aesthete. His message in *The Renaissance* was "we also serve who only stand and worship." His Marius [*Marius the Epicurean*] was a mixture of WP and Richard C. Jackson; Marius's story is set in the same Italian scene that Petronius uses in the SATYRICON. But Marius dies in the end as ignorant of Christianity "as he is of his real sex." Jackson and many of his generation were all WP's children. He alone "had produced this phenomenon: the uncreative esthete, the esthetic amateur."

1930

423 Cooper, Lane. THEORIES OF STYLE (NY & Lond: Macmillan, 1930), pp. xiv, 386–413, 450.
[Excerpts from some reviews of WP's essay "Style" are reprinted.]

424 Du Bos, Charles. "Sur *Marius l'Epicurean,* de Walter Pater" (On *Marius the Epicurean,* by Walter Pater), APPROXIMATIONS, 4th series (Paris: Corrêa, 1930), pp. 7–43; rptd 4th and 5th series (1948); rptd all 7 series (Paris: Fayard, 1965).
WP emphasized the religious importance of *Marius the Epicurean* in a letter in which he wrote of his obligation to finish this book because it set forth the conditions necessary for the religious spirit to exist in the modern age. The book cost WP a great deal of what was at times agonizing mental and physical effort. *Marius* is ostensibly an imaginary portrait, but essentially it is a spiritual portrait of WP himself.

It is difficult to classify *Marius* as a novel because it has a minimum number of the novel's characteristics, as Percy Lubbock points out in THE CRAFT OF FICTION. In *Marius* the dramatic elements are reduced to the barest minimum, while at the same time there is a maximum of subjectivity. All scenes are presented through the refractive voice of WP. Thus the external world has significance only as it reflects Marius's inner modification and development. Nor is the critical problem of classifying *Marius* resolved by calling it an historical novel. Certainly WP was able to use history with great sensitivity and accuracy, as seen in his subtle and complex characterizations of historical figures. But though there may be some objective value to WP's use of history, historical objectivity was clearly not his primary purpose. His basic purpose in writing *Marius* was subjective; the focus of the novel is on Marius.

The most important aspect of Marius's spiritual nature is his sense of seriousness. This seriousness is associated with natural grace. From childhood Marius believed that the body is the tabernacle of the soul and that one's surroundings are the tabernacle of one's entire being. Thus one's surroundings, as well as one's body, must be kept pure. In describing the young Marius, WP evokes Euripides' character, Ion, the young attendant of a Grecian temple. Marius's, as well as Ion's, entire life can be seen symbolically as a kind of dedication to the temple. For Marius there is no distinction between body and soul. Thus in *Marius* the term *epicurean* is used in a special sense which greatly differs from its more common usage. Unlike the original Epicureans, Marius's total orientation is not towards the pursuit of pleasure no matter how elevated that pleasure may be; rather Marius's total motivation is towards perfecting his inner life. Because Marius has a contemplative nature rather than an active one, the emphasis in his life is on being receptive to existing sensations rather than on actually creating new ones. As Marius matures he moves away from feeling to idea. This happens as Marius becomes more and more aware of a kind of universal or infinite memory which is so much greater than his own and to which his own being is attracted. Marius's life fluctuates between two poles: compassion, which is the key to one's devotion to Christianity, and the need for solitude. In solitude Marius participates in a continual dialogue with his other self. This double of himself is not a double in the psychological sense of the term. Rather this double is the model of an ideal, more like an older brother than a judge. Not only does this double provide a model of an ideal, but it also gives one access to the concept of God. In those moments of total harmony with his ideal model, Marius is in a state of ecstasy in which he feels himself to be in direct contact with God. The closer Marius is to his model, the closer he is to perfection. Clearly the evangelical call to its followers to seek perfection just as God is perfect is echoed in the themes of *Marius*. But the tragedy of both Marius and WP is that while they thought that the pursuit of perfection was the only thing of value in life, at the same time they did not dare to affirm totally the existence of that absolute and ultimate model of perfection, God. For them the pursuit of perfection was forced to become its own end. It is the pathetic paradox of such natures that their quest for self-perfection can only result in sacrifice. [In French.]

> **425** Eliot, T. S. "Arnold and Pater," BOOKMAN (NY), LXXII (Sept 1930), 1–7; rptd as "The Place of Pater" in THE EIGHTEEN-EIGHTIES, ed by W. de La Mare (Cambridge: Cambridge UP, 1930); rptd in SELECTED ESSAYS (Lond: Faber, 1932), pp. 393–405; rptd (1934); (1951); rptd (NY: Harcourt, Brace, 1960); (1967); rptd in part as "Walter Pater and *Marius the Epicurean*," POINTS OF VIEW (Lond: Faber, 1947), pp. 88–92; rptd in VICTORIAN LITERATURE: MODERN ESSAYS IN CRITICISM, ed by Austin Wright (NY: Oxford UP, 1961), pp. 238–47.

WP falls into a direct line of influence emanating from Carlyle, Ruskin, and Arnold. Arnold's insistence on sentiment as essential in matters of faith is adopted by WP. What results from this insistence is the replacement of religion with culture and consequently the abandonment of religion to "the anarchy of feeling." The danger is that the term *culture* may be interpreted as each man pleases—"so the gospel of Pater follows naturally upon the prophecy of Arnold." Both Arnold and WP are intellectual Epicureans. Ironically, Arnold is the forerunner of the new humanism, a doctrine that contrasts sharply with WP's aestheticism. "Arnold

Hellenizes and Hebraicizes in turns; it is something to Pater's credit to have Hellenized purely." *Marius the Epicurean* is an overrated book that has failed to exert any substantial influence on any of the great minds of the early twentieth century.

426 Farmer, Albert J. "Walter Pater (1839–1894) et l'Esthétisme" (Walter Pater [1839–1894] and Aestheticism), UNIVERSITÉ DE GRENO-BLE. LETTRES-DROIT. ANNALES, VII (1930), 212–53; rptd LE MOUVE-MENT ESTHÉTIQUE ET DECADENT EN ANGLETERRE (Paris: Champion, 1931), pp. 34–75; see also pp. 117, 125–26, 132, 135, 163–68, 185, 187, 206, 261, 267, 306.

WP is paradoxical. His work marks the starting point of the English "decadence," and yet his Epicureanism was always of superior merit. It seemed to attain the ideal of a passionate life in all the areas of action and thinking, but it discarded cheap pleasures, vulgar emotions. A spiritual discipline was necessary to WP. Misunderstood by the young aesthetes, ostracized by the academicians, WP nevertheless attempted to portray his own spiritual pilgrimage in *Marius the Epicurean*. The work lacks the qualities of the novel, but his readers were looking for a doctrine and not for a fiction. The evolution of Marius from Cyrenaicism to Stoicism to Christianity is WP's own evolution. The work is the story of his soul. The last part suggests not a conversion but a transition; the cult of beauty is not to be renounced. For WP, Christianity was a natural, logical prolongation of the cult of beauty. The "imaginary portraits" are a direct extension of *Marius*. Each portrait is the study of the adventures of a soul searching for the absolute. WP realizes the existence of an irreconcilable disagreement between beauty and the conditions of the outer world. The portraits are the counterparts of the "Conclusion" to *The Renaissance*. The analogies between *Gaston de Latour* and *Marius* are striking. WP studies the same problem, but the book was never finished. From the time of *Gaston,* WP's tone seems to be more tranquil. In fact, biographical details confirm the hypothesis that he possessed a quieter conscience during this later period in his life. In *Plato and Platonism,* he comes back to his original theories. In the fusion of the search for beauty and for a moral discipline, he once again reaffirms the need for a rule, a doctrine for his time.

WP's works viewed totally constitute a spiritual autobiography. This subjective attitude makes him a Romantic, but his Romanticism bears the stamp of his time. His malaise originates not just in his sensibility but especially in his intelligence. The feverish inspiration of *The Renaissance* disappears in his later works, where form becomes more important. In the essay on "Style" he advises a methodical approach to writing. He is also the first in English literature to recommend the study of Flaubert. If his doctrine of the cult of beauty always stands on a superior level, still his works did provide the seeds for the "decadence": his taste for artificiality; his taste for the bizarre which links him closely with Baudelaire; his morbid themes. [In French.]

427 Gilbert, Stuart. JAMES JOYCE'S ULYSSES (Lond: Faber & Faber; NY: Knopf, 1930); rptd (Lond: Faber & Faber, 1951); (1952), pp. 12, 34, 90, 91, 92, 301; rptd (NY: Vintage, 1952); rptd with revisions (NY: Knopf, 1952); rptd (NY: Vintage, 1955); rptd (Harmondsworth, Middlesex: Penguin Books, 1963); rptd DAS RÄTSEL ULYSSES, EINE STUDIE, (The Riddle of Ulysses, A Study), trans by Georg Goyert (Zurich: Rhein-Verlag, 1960).

To deepen the understanding of ULYSSES, one should read WP's *The Renaissance*. The style used by Joyce at the "Lying-in Hospital" episode in ULYSSES is in the manner of WP. In Joyce's essay on J. C. Mangan, published in the Dublin magazine, ST. STEPHEN'S, appears a passage that is obviously indebted to WP's famous Mona Lisa passage. Joyce's admiration for the painting in this passage is an echo of WP's admiration. Elsewhere in the essay are passages reminiscent of sections of WP's "Conclusion" to *The Renaissance*. WP's "exquisite moments" are identical to Joyce's "epiphanies." WP's influence on Joyce is also evident in STEPHEN HERO, the first fragmentary version of PORTRAIT OF THE ARTIST AS A YOUNG MAN. The picture given by Joyce of himself in his youth is similar to the picture of WP's young Marius [*Marius the Epicurean*].

428 Neel, Philippe. "Avant-Propos" (Foreword), *Portraits Imaginaires* [Imaginary Portraits] (Paris: Stock, Delamain & Boutelleau, 1930), pp. vii–xvii.
[Unable to locate in the U.S.]

429 Praz, Mario. LA CARNE, LA MORTE, E IL DIAVOLO NELLA LETTERATURA ROMANTICA (Flesh, Death, and the Devil in Romantic Literature) (Milan & Rome: Societa Editrice "La Cultura," 1930); trans by A. Davidson as THE ROMANTIC AGONY (Oxford: Oxford UP, 1933); rptd (Cleveland: Meridian, 1956), pp. xv, 3, 200, 213, 243–44, 247, 251, 276, 341–42, 400, 438, 454, 456, 458, 468, 472–74.

Wilde and WP vainly tried to resume some contact with the "real" world through religion, through a return to Christianity. WP was extremely interested in the type of fatal woman figure that develops in a tradition from Gautier and Swinburne. She is Swinburne's Faustine, the exotic, sinister, and "Medusean" beauty. WP owes his description of La Gioconda directly to Swinburne, less directly to Gautier and Flaubert. The passage describing La Gioconda also recalls lines from Swinburne's LAUS VENERIS. [For more on Swinburne's influence on WP's depiction of La Gioconda, see W. Gaunt's THE AESTHETIC ADVENTURER (1945).] WP's description of La Gioconda popularized the fatal woman to the point where it became fashionable in certain Parisian circles for women to copy the enigmatic smile.

Enrico Nencioni, the nineteenth-century Italian poet, admired WP's works, particularly his study of Giorgione, but in Nencioni's hands the themes of decadence become harmless and insipid. All of the "feminine souls" depicted in WP's portraits revive dominant motifs of the decadence: like Des Esseintes in Huysmans' À REBOURS, Duke Carl of Rosenmold is "a sensual dilletante"; the child in the house, Florian Deleal, is another of WP's many "exquisitely meditative youths"; "Denys l'Auxerrois" develops the theme of "beauty devastated by cruelty," another favorite of the decadents. WP's "Hippolytus Veiled" took from William of Malmesbury the story of a Roman nobleman who places a ring on the statue's finger; WP has Hippolytus place a ring given him by Phaedra on the finger of a statue of Diana. In *Marius the Epicurean,* WP chastened his decadent tendencies with "ascetical classicism, whose formula he had found in Winckelmann." His earlier "ideal" finds no satisfaction in history as his art develops, and he finally turns to writing imaginary portraits, to fantasy.

1931

430 Beyer, Arthur. WALTER PATERS BEZIEHUNGEN ZUR FRANZÖSISCHEN LITERATUR UND KULTUR (Walter Pater's Relationship to French Literature and Culture) (Halle: Niemeyer, 1931). Published dissertation, Göttingen, 1932.
[Beyer's work is divided into three parts. The first treats WP's borrowings from Flaubert, Gautier, and Sainte-Beuve. Beyer claims that in *The Renaissance,* particularly in the portraits of Du Bellay and Michelangelo, WP translated and borrowed many phrases literally from Sainte-Beuve. WP's idea of a twelfth-century Renaissance, presented in "Two Early French Stories" in *The Renaissance,* may well have come from his study of Michelet. The second part of the book deals with the influence of France in WP's fiction, particularly the influence of French landscape. *Gaston de Latour,* "Denys l'Auxerrois," and "Apollo in Picardy" are singled out as works that reveal WP's debt to France. The third part treats WP's use of French art. Beyer claims that WP drew from his knowledge of French churches and art particularly for his portrait of Watteau. In fact, WP may have been directly indebted to Viollet le Duc for his knowledge of French architecture. Listed in Lawrence F. McNamee's DISSERTATIONS IN ENGLISH AND AMERICAN LITERATURE (NY and Lond: Bowker, 1968). [In German.]

431 Burke, Kenneth. "Three Adepts of 'Pure' Literature," COUNTER-STATEMENT (NY: Harcourt, Brace, 1931); rptd (Los Altos, Calif: Hermes P, 1953), pp. 9–15.
WP skillfully adjusted his technique to aesthetic interests. A subject was valuable to WP when it provided possibilities for stylistic deftness. "He thought of a sentence as a happening." Ideology was used by him for its "flavor of beauty, rather than of argument." [The sixth chapter of *Gaston de Latour* is analyzed.]

432 Courtney, Janet E. AN OXFORD PORTRAIT GALLERY (Lond: Chapman & Hall, 1931), pp. 216, 226–38.
[Reminiscences of WP and his sister, Clara, while at Oxford.]

433 Farmer, Albert J. WALTER PATER AS A CRITIC OF ENGLISH LITERA-
TURE. A STUDY OF "APPRECIATIONS" (Grenoble: Didier & Richard,
1931). Rvd dissertation, University of Paris, 1931.

WP remains, as Saintsbury first noted in 1904 in HISTORY OF CRITICISM, the most
important critic of the last few decades of the nineteenth century. The whole of his
criticism is contained in *Appreciations* (1889) and *Essays from "The Guardian"*
(1896), the former including the most illustrative and informing essays. WP is the
most representative exponent of "the subjective method" of criticism in the
nineteenth century. He stands well apart from his predecessors (Coleridge, Hazlitt,
Lamb, DeQuincey, Carlyle, Macaulay, Arnold), all strong advocates of subjectivity in criticism, as "the first critic boldly to assert the rights of the individual
temperament in the appreciation of literature." For WP, the essential determinant
in criticism is based upon how vividly the critic "feels" the work he treats. The
measure of a work's value, its "virtue," depends on its power to produce "pleasurable sensations." No one genre or form must be exalted to the detriment of another;
all are equal.

WP advocates the improvement of one's existence through art, the "disinterested
love of beauty." He is an aesthete concerned with the quality of life. The "disinterested" exercise of the critical faculty is therefore the highest form of culture.
The ages are all equal, but individual genius always rises above the age. WP does
not turn from moral considerations; all of his essays "seek to convey some higher
truth of mind or soul." His critical vision is not the simple "impressionism" one
associates with a Lemaître, for he advocates the relationship between criticism and
an "innate idealism."

WP limits his study of Shakespeare to plays that are of secondary interest, because
he contends that the greatest works are not the most self-revealing. He always tries
to capture the man behind the work. His choice of plays in the Shakespeare essay
also reveals much about WP's own character. Likewise, his study of Coleridge
reflects his own obsessive interest in philosophy. He believed that Coleridge's
theory of art was weakened by his indifference to the process of logical construction employed by the artist and his preference for the intuitive. That Charles Lamb
and WP had similar natures is revealed in the depth and comprehension of the essay
on Lamb. Because Lamb loved the work of Sir Thomas Browne, WP's choice of
Browne for his next essay was perfectly logical. Earlier critics were interested in
Browne's work; WP was interested in Browne the man—his intellectual attitude,
particularly. The Browne essay marks the summit of WP's work. In his essays on
these famous prosaists, he argues for the ideal of form, a foreshadowing of the
coming essay on "Style."

Wordsworth's poetry illustrates the aesthetic method of criticism that WP champions in the "Preface" to *The Renaissance*. The similarities between the "Preface" and the "Wordsworth" essay are striking. WP and Arnold share a common
opinion of Wordsworth, but WP insists on the importance of the passionate

undercurrent in Wordsworth's poetry rather than the "healing power" celebrated by Arnold. WP probably provides a better appraisal of Wordsworth's greatness than Arnold. The "Coleridge" essay is a companion essay but is less successful. The figure of the poet in "Coleridge" is blurred and the argument unconvincing. WP unjustly plays down Coleridge's role in the romantic revival. But there is a personality clash: Coleridge supports notions of the "absolute"; Pater, the "relative." The "Rossetti" essay, written in 1883, defended Rossetti at a time when his reputation as a serious writer was highly questionable. WP delves far beneath the surface of Rossetti's verse and is one of the first critics to do so. Because he considers poetry as "the pure emanation of a temperament," in his essays on poets as poets WP is content to deal almost exclusively with their works rather than their lives. For WP, the poetic form of art is always spontaneous and highly personal.

In his essay on "Style" and in the "Postscript," WP sums up many of the points illustrated in the volume's literary portraits. Like DeQuincey and Arnold, WP argues for prose as a legitimate art form. He pulls together the tentative assertions of his predecessors and provides the strongest claim for prose as the greatest of literary arts. He prefers a style where the "classic" and the "romantic," the intellectual and the imaginative, are in perfect balance. Because he distinguishes "great art" as that in which the aim is lofty, he champions far more than a simple "art for art's sake" theory and seems to move closer to the position of Mallarmé and the symbolists. WP and R. L. Stevenson have much in common: both claim first importance for prose as an art form, although WP is more cautious in his claims than Stevenson. For WP, the writer must constantly seek a new medium appropriate to the times; he is the most "modern" of critics. In *Appreciations,* he offers the reader "the key to the mystery of artistic creation." By claiming that the most revealing criticism is always subjective criticism, he anticipates the new humanists.

434 MacColl, D. S. "A Batch of Memories. XII—Walter Pater," WEEK-END REVIEW, 12 Dec 1931, pp. 759–60.
For the most part, Oxford was "very little alive to the presence" of WP. On one occasion, WP referred to SALAMMÔ by Flaubert as a very wicked book. When *Plato and Platonism* appeared, WP asked to have it reviewed in the SPECTATOR. As late as 1893, he was still fearful of suspicion and disapproval. "The Pater of my Oxford years, 1881–84, was one doubtfully regarded by the authorities, in the light of what the 'aesthetes' had made of his doctrines." [Mainly assorted anecdotes.]

435 Ottley, May. "Introduction," "Imaginary Portraits. 2. An English Poet," FORTNIGHTLY REVIEW, CXXIX (April 1931), 433–35.
WP's fragmentary work found at his death was all hand-written on quarto-size white or bluish paper with carefully spaced lines and blanks left to be filled in later. The superb condition of the manuscripts attests to the neatness and order of WP's manner of writing, his "fidelity to detail." After WP's death, Dr. Shadwell and Sir Herbert Warren examined the manuscripts and decided what should be left unpub-

lished. It is time that the fragmentary portrait of "The English Poet," the story of an aspiring artist, be offered to WP's readers. [The editor acknowledges having omitted one or two "unessential passages" and bracketing imprecise words or phrases. At times the sense of the original manuscript is obscured by faulty grammar.]

436 Reid, Louis Arnaud. A STUDY IN AESTHETICS (Lond: Allen & Unwin; NY: Macmillan, 1931), pp. 13–28; rptd as "Artists, Critics, and Philosophers," in THE PROBLEMS OF AESTHETICS: A BOOK OF READINGS, ed by Eliseo Vivas and Murray Krieger (NY: Rinehart, 1953), pp. 19–30.

WP's point in *The Renaissance* is that beauty is an individual thing and defies definition. But WP constantly violates his own principles by talking "abstractly" about art; his generalizations, fortunately, are often illuminating.

437 Rosenblatt, Louise. L'IDÉE DE L'ART POUR L'ART DANS LA LITTÉRATURE ANGLAISE PENDANT LA PÉRIODE VICTORIENNE (The Concept of Art for Art's Sake in Victorian Literature) (Paris: Champion, 1931), pp. 169–205.

Matthew Arnold underlines the contacts between the critic and society; WP insists on the relations between the critic and the individual art work. He does not use his studies of the psychological or moral elements of the artist for a criticism of life. Art, in fact, has a superior morality, enabling a better appreciation of the diverse aspects of life. It represents the ideal of "being" rather than the ideal of "doing." But WP's position is paradoxical. His works can be characterized as an attempt to replace old moral, philosophical, and social values with aestheticism. He is no propagandist, no reformer; but his doctrine formed the ideological basis for a moral and aesthetic revolt. He attained the belief in "art for art's sake" through religious disillusionment rather than through rebellion against the moral and artistic narrow-mindedness of his time. In his essay on Mérimée, WP advocates that when a fundamental belief disappears, some vestiges, echoes, or reactions always remain and partly create a new intellectual atmosphere. Thus, the religious atmosphere becomes closely tied to the aesthetic experience. When WP lost faith, the perception of beauty was the only experience capable of offering him emotional joys analogous to those he formerly experienced through religious belief. In the cult of art, he found a derivative to his religious sensibility. His attitude toward art is therefore analogous to the religious mystic's attitude toward the supernatural. Reinforcing WP's aestheticism is his disdain for ethical and social theories advocated by Ruskin and Arnold. He was influenced more positively by Goethe's theory of art and by Winckelmann's life and personality. He was directly influenced by Hegel's AESTHETICS, from which he borrowed his "critical instruments" and the principle of the supreme importance of form in art. But he was no systematic follower of any philosophical system. He did not adopt the transcendental aspects of the German philosophers. The attitude of art for art's sake in

Swinburne's works and the Pre-Raphaelite tradition of beauty also influenced WP (a stronger influence than either Gautier's or Baudelaire's mystical conception of beauty). In the essay on "Style," WP applies the principle of the supreme importance of form to the practical problems of literature. WP also recognized Flaubert's attempts to achieve the perfect adaptation of form to thought. For WP, all schools, all genres are equally of value as long as each characterizes and expresses the personality that employs it. To the impassioned search for the perfect form, WP and the French aesthetes associate the conception of the artist as a disciplined worker, a craftsman who polishes his art indefinitely. In the last paragraph of the essay on "Style," WP no longer defends the extreme position of some aesthetes for whom the value of art depends entirely on the degree of perception found in the expression of the work. He distinguishes between "good art" and "great art." "Great art" is accomplished when the work increases man's happiness, ennobles him, enlarges his sympathies. All "good art" exists by virtue of the form, but "great art" depends on the impact the work has on the human soul. This progressive evolution toward a mystical and traditional point of view implies the conception of an aesthetic morality superior to conventional morality. The theory of "art for art's sake" is not abandoned but cannot be accepted as a final and complete philosophy of life. [In French.]

> **438** Rothenstein, Sir William. MEN AND MEMORIES, 1872–1900 (Lond: Faber & Faber; NY: Coward-McCann, 1931), pp. 124, 125, 138–39, 153, 155–57, 232, 242, 294, 316; rptd (NY: Tudor Publishing, 1937).

WP had a habit of assuming ignorance about subjects on which he was well informed; he was a master at eliciting indiscretions from his guests while at Oxford. He had no great regard for Whistler. He seems to have derived a certain "malicious enjoyment" out of entertaining the football and cricket players at Oxford and ignoring the young *précieux*. He worried over his appearance, asking Bussell, after having sat for Rothenstein's drawing, if he did indeed " 'look like a Barbary Ape.' "

> **439** Schaffer, Joel. "Walter Pater und sein Bildungsideal" (Walter Pater and his Ideal of Form). Unpublished dissertation, Vienna, 1931. [In German.]

> **440** Sechler, Robert Porter. "George Moore: A Disciple of Walter Pater." Unpublished dissertation, University of Pennsylvania, 1931.

> **441** Smith, Samuel Stephenson. THE CRAFT OF THE CRITIC (NY: Crowell, 1931), pp. 11, 20, 21, 44, 54, 59, 60, 61.

Havelock Ellis has the same feeling for paganism that WP had, but he treats the matter with more ease. But then Ellis found his way out of Victorian unfulfillment. The unique quality of *Marius the Epicurean* is found in WP's "wistful and elegiac presentation of the Roman spirit in its less known religious aspects." In his nostalgia for a past age, WP gives the reader a sense of Victorian unfulfillment. WP inlaid his words to achieve a cameo-like perfection. He learned the art of compression from the Latin writers.

442 Welby, Thomas Earle. "Walter Pater," in REVALUATIONS. STUDIES IN BIOGRAPHY, by Lascelles Abercrombie et al. (Oxford: Oxford UP, 1931); rptd in SECOND IMPRESSIONS, by T. Earle Welby (Lond: Methuen, 1933), pp. 49–53.

In his own fashion WP had some success in achieving a "correspondence between life and work." His attitude toward the outside world was a kind of "defensive ceremoniousness" that reflected his dislike for the abruptness with which life intrudes on man's dreams. In literature and in life he avoided everything that was not "to his purpose." In criticism he chose to ignore anything that did not satisfy his severe standard. He was like Landor in that he also achieved success through "elaborate rejection" and, like Landor, WP went a bit too far with this rejection. WP's later prose lost some of its charm because "dread of tawdriness" forced him "to be too sparing of the ornamentation, never insignificant, almost always structural, of which he was so exquisite a master." As to the origins of his prose, one can see striking similarities between WP's prose and Swinburne's essay on the drawing of Old Masters at Florence and Rossetti's "Hand and Soul."

As to WP's popular status today, it would appear that "people have wearied a little of the obvious Pater without going on to discover what is less evident and even more characteristic in his work." Many find that the "temper" necessary for reading WP is "unnatural, unwholesome, and . . . intolerable." Those who adopt the right approach to WP's writing find him to be "a kind of retreat, from which we return not only rested but rested by a grave and quietly strenuous exercise." Clearly WP is "an author to be approached only after initiation."

443 Wilson, Edmund. AXEL'S CASTLE. A STUDY IN THE IMAGINATIVE LITERATURE OF 1870–1930 (Lond & NY: Scribner's, 1931); rptd (1958); (1959); (1961), pp. 32–33, 258, 264, 269, 295; rptd (Lond: Collins, 1961).

WP had as profound an influence on English literature as Mallarmé had on French literature. However, his theory was rooted less "in the field of aesthetic theory than in that of the appreciation of life." In Yeats, WP's aestheticism is carried through to its consequences—a transportation of all that is human into the immortal world of fairyland. His conclusion to *The Renaissance* became the ideal, the philosophy of "the *fin de siècle* mind." In *Marius the Epicurean* WP gives voice to another doctrine of the *fin de siècle* generation, namely the "ideal of renunciation of the outside world for the experience of the imagination alone." Villiers de l'Isle Adam's protagonist, Axël, is the typical "super-dreamer" hero of the symbolist writers, and the character traits of this type of hero are found in WP's "contemplative, inactive Marius, [and] the exquisitely sensitive young men of his *Imaginary Portraits.*"

140

1932

444 Beach, Joseph Warren. THE TWENTIETH CENTURY NOVEL: STUDIES IN TECHNIQUE (NY: Appleton-Century-Crofts, 1932), pp. 51, 52, 88, 124, 207, 286.

WP deals primarily with the analysis of aesthetic impressions. He stands midway between the analysis of sensations and that of sentiments. Proust also deals extensively with aesthetic impressions. James Branch Cabell's THE CREAM OF THE JEST (1917) takes on the aspect of a treatise on WP's aesthetic way of life. The novelist Joseph Hergesheimer is prepossessed by the "Pateresque problem of finding words to render qualities."

445 Burgum, Edwin Berry. "Walter Pater and the Good Life," SEWANEE REVIEW, XL (July 1932), 276–93.

WP was Arnold's "disciple who accepted so sympathetically" Arnold's accounts of the Greek point of view that he neglected the corrective force of Arnold's Hebraism. In the "Preface" to *The Renaissance,* he extended Arnold's consideration of the best that has been thought and said in the world to all the arts. Even though WP ran contrary to Arnold on many points, he shared with Arnold the belief that art and religion offered a similar experience. WP better represents the spirit of his age than Arnold. He was more responsive to influences that bore directly on his own emotions. He lacked Arnold's interest in scientism. In *The Renaissance,* WP cut through the uncertainties of Victorian "art for art's sake" and discovered the "modern" theory of "significant form"; but eleven years later in the essay on "Style," he returned to the belief that literature is the greatest of all arts because it is the most formless and, therefore, the most conducive to exerting a moral influence. WP's mind had drifted toward humanism. In direct contrast to Arnold, who advised seeing the object as it really is, WP always saw whatever he wanted to see. He made Greeks out of all his figures in the portraits. The word *criticism* in his vocabulary was replaced by the word *appreciation,* suggesting that the most that a man can perceive accurately is his intuitions. He was at heart as sensual as Wilde, but the impulse toward the ascetic life and his continued interest in Christianity were so strong that he found Wilde and what he represented upsetting. If he had followed Arnold's advice to place himself in relation to one's age, he would have been a pagan. But by depicting other, earlier cultures, he sought escape in the past. And so "past and present . . . life and art, lost their distinctness and were transmuted into a new work of art, Pater's ideal of the good life." He saw in Greek myths clear examples of how poetry could be used to enhance religion. [Much of the essay deals with the author's conception of Greek life played off against WP's.]

446 Eaker, Jay G. "Walter Pater: A Study in Methods and Effects." Published dissertation, University of Iowa, 1932; pub as WALTER PATER:

A STUDY IN METHODS AND EFFECTS (Iowa City: University of Iowa P, 1933), q.v. for abstract. [Listed in Lawrence F. McNamee's DISSERTATIONS IN ENGLISH AND AMERICAN LITERATURE (NY and Lond: Bowker, 1968).]

447 Garvin, Katharine. "Walter Pater," in THE GREAT VICTORIANS, ed by H. J. and Hugh Massingham (Lond: Nicholson & Watson, 1932), pp. 381–94; rptd, Two Volumes (Harmondsworth, Middlesex: Penguin, 1937–38).

WP's life was "devoted to the preservation of beautiful experience." Although he loved nature, he chose to explore beauty as it is revealed through the human soul and through experience. Thus nature was important to WP only "as a manifold enricher of the human soul." The focus of WP's basic interest in human experience was the study of history. His character left the impression of being colourless and his writing supports a view of him as "a timid, effete personality, disturbed by high and right ideals," whose judgments were often "invalidated by the shallowness of his experience." His most interesting works, which represent his true contribution to literature, are his imaginary portraits. They function as confessional vehicles into which WP projected aspects of his own mind and supplied "qualities that he would like to have had as well as physical traits that were denied him."

A recurrent theme of lifelessness is found in WP's writing. Often there is a "synonymity of death with refinement" that is reflected in his "corpselike" style from which all that is "turbulent and accidental" has been purged. This preoccupation with lifelessness led WP to write about "the decadent aspects of civilization." He wrote about those periods in history "when the civilizing process had all but destroyed vigour, and when artificiality with its adorable elaborations more and more took the place of Nature."

WP's writing is weak; one example is found in his "incapacity" to understand women. His generalizations reflect his bias: Women can " 'perceive neither truth when they encounter it, nor beauty where it really exists.' " This prejudice detracted from the success of his characterizations of men who were involved with women, e.g., Sebastian van Storck.

WP's fascination with death is another dominant theme in his writing: an attraction evident in "Denys l'Auxerrois" and parts of *Greek Studies*. Yet in all of WP's "vacillation and morbidity shines a genuine passion for passion," which, as his writing clearly indicates, he was unable to realize. Only in his essay on "Aesthetic Poetry," which he suppressed for twenty years, is "a full blossoming of feeling" found. Here WP was able to state directly what he suggested elsewhere, namely that "the beauty he approved was an emotional one rooted in physical desire, and harmonious with the great body in nature." Clearly WP was a man who was torn by conflict, who longed for a "return to the life of the senses," but who also felt limited by the "gentility" of his age as well as by his "physical and psychological disabilities." Throughout his work there is a tension between the conflicting demands "of meekness and savagery, the primitive and civilized, ethics and beauty."

448 Glücksmann, Hedwig Luise. "Die Gegenüberstellung von Antike und Christentum bei Walter Horatio Pater" (The Antithesis between Antiquity and Christianity in Walter Horatio Pater), DIE GEGENÜBERSTELLUNG VON ANTIKE-CHRISTENTUM IN DER ENGLISCHEN LITERATUR DES 19. JAHRHUNDERTS [The Antithesis between Antiquity and Christianity in Nineteenth Century English Literature] (Hanover: Küster, 1932), pp. 42–73.

WP believed that a mixture of power and sweetness flowed into the Renaissance from classical antiquity and the middle ages. The power is represented in the tale of "Amis and Amile," the sweetness in "Aucassin and Nicolette." Winckelmann is proof to WP that the Hellenic tradition fulfills a vital requirement of the intellect. The Winckelmann essay summarizes and confirms the Renaissance spirit and also WP's own vision. WP is the antithesis to Swinburne, who totally jeopardized his artistic strength through a passionate attachment to life; WP, in contrast, is a spectator of life. WP's life takes its course from his years at Oxford. The tension between the sensual and spiritual characterized for Swinburne the temperament of the artist; WP, in contrast, envisioned no such conflict. But Swinburne's interpretation of literary history from the pagan standpoint influenced WP's mental conception of the Renaissance. The influence of Heine can be seen in WP's essay on Mirandola, in "Two Early French Stories," "Denys l'Auxerrois," and "Apollo in Picardy," and in WP's interpretation of the story of Abelard and Tannhäuser. *Marius the Epicurean* reveals WP's attempt to reconcile pagan sensuousness with the Christian spirit. [In German.]

449 Huneker, James. ESSAYS BY JAMES HUNEKER, intro by H. L. Mencken (NY: Scribner's, 1932), pp. 231, 234, 274, 374, 389, 390.

A profitable experience is to read WP's description of the Chartres Cathedral in *Gaston de Latour* after reading Huysmans's LA CATHÉDRALE. Huysmans "sees" more. [Huneker argues for the depth to which WP understood Watteau. The book contains many scattered references to WP, valuable mainly because it is Huneker who makes them.]

450 Molenda, Kitty. "Walter Pater und sein Verhältnis zur französischen Kritik der 18. Jahrhunderts" (Walter Pater's Relationship to Eighteenth Century French Critics). Unpublished dissertation, Vienna, 1932.

[In German.]

451 Newman, Bertram. "Walter Pater, A Revaluation," NINETEENTH CENTURY AND AFTER, CXI (May 1932), 633–40.

WP's inner life, which was devoted to art, was concealed "under a mask of the straitest conventionality" and self-restraint. Implicit in his character-study "Diaphaneitè," written when he was twenty-five, is the epilogue to *The*

Renaissance as well as a personal ideal to which he remained faithful throughout his life. His life and writing were devoted to "pure aesthetic appreciation," yet he avoided the potential danger "of passive and voluptuous sensation" because "the sensuousness of his temperament was controlled by . . . an intellect which demanded the keenest analysis of the elements which contributed to each mode of aesthetic pleasure." *Marius the Epicurean* is WP's attempt to apply his philosophy not only to art but "to the conduct of life itself: the hero was intended by his creator at any rate to represent Diaphaneitè in action." But this lengthy character-study is rather lifeless, for "Pater had no genius for creating character or conducting a narrative." WP "has most notably enriched English prose" in his essays on art, for he was more moved by art than by literature, and in these essays he expertly weaves "the borderland region which lies between images and thoughts." WP's *Imaginary Portraits* reflect "a wonderful command of atmosphere." His essay on "Style," which "must be nearly the last word that can be said on the subject," expresses his belief that style's "cardinal virtue must be that of expressiveness, of a strict adaption to its subject-matter." WP's style is "certainly expressive of himself." However, its deliberate, carefully calculated nature is achieved at the price of spontaneity. WP "has won a double immortality—as a critic where criticism is often creative, and as a writer who has revealed new capacities of subtlety and suggestiveness in English prose."

452 Ralli, Augustus. HISTORY OF SHAKESPEARIAN CRITICISM (Oxford: Oxford UP, 1932); rptd (NY: Humanities P, 1959), I, 486–88; II, 72–74.
WP's essays on MEASURE FOR MEASURE and LOVE'S LABOUR'S LOST are typical of his style as an aesthetic critic. They reveal a sustained interest in the "soul" of each character in the moments of self-analysis rather than in the outward development of the drama. WP provides a sound appreciation of the core of poetry that everything else in Shakespeare subserves. In his essay on "Shakespeare's English Kings," WP reveals more about himself than he does about Shakespeare. In this essay he strains to make much ado about the soliloquies of the historical heroes, but actually the speeches, less certainly in the case of Richard II than in those of Henry IV and Henry V, "rather illustrate the law of compensation, and could be uttered as well by those who have great powers as great place."

453 Stauffer, Donald A. "Monna Melancholia: A Study in Pater's Sources," SEWANEE REVIEW, XL (Jan–March 1932), pp. 89–93.
WP's essay on *La Gioconda* "has superseded" Leonardo da Vinci's painting and "rendered it unnecessary." The essay is inspired not by the original painting of the Mona Lisa which WP never saw but by an engraving of the painting, the sight of which WP transformed through his imagination into "a picture more memorable than reality." A careful comparison of WP's description and of the painting itself reveals that the more impassioned passages of the essay were inspired not by da Vinci's masterpiece but by Albrecht Dürer's painting *Melancholia*.

454 Symons, Arthur. A STUDY OF WALTER PATER (Lond: Sawyer,

1932); rptd (Folcroft, Pa: Folcroft P, 1969). [A large portion of this study of WP appeared earlier in 1916 in FIGURES OF SEVERAL CENTURIES.]
[Symons's study is a highly impressionistic response to WP, revealing as much about Symons as about WP but valuable for the comments that Symons provides on WP's interest in the French writers. Symons claims that WP never received the public recognition that he deserved. He concludes in his discussion of *The Renaissance* that WP would have been a great art critic if he had devoted himself exclusively to art criticism. WP is said to have corrected many of Ruskin's errors, bringing to art criticism a more tolerant attitude. Symons claims to have been surprised that WP's admiration for the Goncourts was tempered by dislike. He often read MADAME GERVAISAIS, Symons adds, and spoke approvingly of CHÉRIE. Symons claims that WP told him that when he was writing he read nothing that might interfere with his thought by introducing a new "current of emotion." Symons compares WP to Baudelaire, who also set out to "better nature," and *Marius the Epicurean* to Browning's SORDELLO. WP also shares with Baudelaire a fastidiousness as a creative critic. His essay on "Aesthetic Poetry" was "evidently written under the influence of Baudelaire," Symons adds, "whose prose, as he himself told me, he admired immensely." Symons claims that WP helped him get his first volume of poetry published and that he counseled Symons frequently. Symons believes that WP could never have liked the sordid works of Verlaine. He acknowledges in this study having received sixty letters from WP filled with advice and with information on work that he was doing. In 1889 WP was working toward another volume of *Imaginary Portraits*. "Hippolytus Veiled" was to be included, as well as a portrait based on Moroni's *Portrait of a Tailor,* another of a figure from the time of the Albigensian persecution, a "modern" study that Symons believes may have been "Emerald Uthwart," and "Apollo in Picardy." "The Child in the House" was intended to be the opening chapter of a romance on "modern life." He intended to finish the work but never did.]

455 Young, Helen Hawthorne. "Walter Pater, A Reflection of British Philosophical Opinion from 1860 to 1890." Published dissertation, Bryn Mawr College, 1932; pub as THE WRITINGS OF WALTER PATER: A REFLECTION OF BRITISH PHILOSOPHICAL OPINION FROM 1860 TO 1890 (Lancaster, Pa: Bryn Mawr UP, 1933), q.v. for abstract.
[Listed in Lawrence F. McNamee, DISSERTATIONS IN ENGLISH AND AMERICAN LITERATURE (NY and Lond: Bowker, 1968).]

1933

456 Arakawa, Tatsuhiko. (T. S. Eliot's Interpretation of Arnold and Pater), STUDIES IN ENGLISH LITERATURE (Tokyo), XIII (1933), 161–81.
In his interpretation of Arnold and WP, Eliot reveals an extraordinary depth of

understanding. His judgment of WP points out that while Pascal recognized the limitations of discontinuity in nature, spirit, and charity (*les trois ordres*), WP did not. WP ends up in confusion, treating contradictions as contradictions only. Pascal, on the other hand, as Eliot understood, saw greatness and tragedy in the contrarieties of life. WP settled down in his subjective, half-romantic domain. Arnold's desire to "see the object as in itself it really is" was achieved by neither him nor WP. They both were too subjective in their outlooks. Eliot accepts this tendency in the two and embraces their understanding of life, but he does not overlook the wisdom to be gained from contradictions. He does not deny simply for the sake of denial. Thus, he is in agreement with Pascal. [In Japanese.]

457 Eaker, J. G. WALTER PATER: A STUDY IN METHODS AND EFFECTS (Iowa City: University of Iowa P, 1933); rptd (Folcroft, Pa: Folcroft P, 1969). Rvd dissertation, University of Iowa, 1932.

WP's prose is a reaction to the didacticism found in much of the literature of his century. WP "accepted . . . the limitations defined by modern science and philosophy" and made it his objective to select from "the great body of art, literature, and philosophy those elements that offered him the highest quality of pleasure and to set them forth in a pleasing, artistic form for others." Perhaps his greatest contribution to English literature is found in his method and style.

In his two autobiographical sketches "The Child in the House" and "Emerald Uthwart," WP selects and idealizes details recollected from childhood, some of which might seem trivial, and weaves them together with the purpose of showing how they contributed to his spiritual awakening and development. In WP's "highest achievement," *Imaginary Portraits,* the method is similar, but in this work WP carefully selects details from art, mythology, or history, and through the imaginative process of idealization "he throws a character into a choice situation which 'lifts or glorifies' it," thereby revealing "the spiritual struggle" within the character's soul as well as within the age. In *Greek Studies,* "Pater's synthetic method" is again evident in his careful and limited selection of those details from "Greek art, poetry, and religious custom" which, after being tested against "responsive traits and touches in his own mind," are artistically combined to give a "unified impression" of those aspects of Greek culture "which Pater found paralleled in the modern mind."

The method in *Marius the Epicurean,* WP's "extended philosophical portrait," is similar to that found in his other works. In "an almost perfect union of matter and form," WP blends details selected from the history, art, literature, religion, and philosophy of second-century Rome with "the record of his own 'sensations and ideas' " in order to affirm his belief that there is still " 'a sort of religious phase possible for the modern mind.' " In his critical essays, particularly in *Appreciations* and *The Renaissance,* WP attempts to select those details from an artist's works which best express the essence of that artist's spirit.

458 Evans, Benjamin Ifor. ENGLISH POETRY IN THE LATER NINE-
TEENTH CENTURY (Lond: Methuen, 1933); rvd (1966), pp. 38, 155, 250,
257, 275, 393, 396, 397, 398, 399, 404, 408, 409, 416–17, 438, 444.
G. M. Hopkins's earlier poetry reveals the influence of WP. In 1885 appeared WP's
prose version of Apuleius' Cupid and Psyche myth and Robert Bridges's poetic
version, "Eros and Psyche." In many of his poems (e.g., "Panthea,"
"Humanitad," and "Helas"), Wilde versifies passages from WP's *The
Renaissance*. Dowson seems to fulfill through poetry the precepts taught by WP;
he records "moments of sensation to the utter exclusion of all moral and philosophical comment." In the best of his prose pieces, Lionel Johnson combined
WP's "sympathetic approach" with the terse rationalism of Samuel Johnson.

459 Field, Michael [pseud of Kathleen Bradley and Edith Cooper].
WORKS AND DAYS. FROM THE JOURNAL OF MICHAEL FIELD, ed by T. and
D. C. Sturge Moore (Lond: John Murray, 1933), pp. xi, 118–22, 135–37,
202, 260, 306.
[In these reminiscences, Misses Bradley and Cooper recall attending WP's lecture
on Prospér Mérimée at the London Institution. They noticed his apparent shyness
and his "sensitive" voice, which seemed to have "an audible capacity for suffering." WP's friends had further evidence of his shyness on the evening when he
gave his lecture at Toynbee Hall. Before the reading he went alone to a dark city
church for what he called " 'recueillement' " and stayed there for half an hour. Yet
the two women felt that behind WP's "courteous exterior" there was hidden "a
strong nature, not innocent of barbarism." They felt that there was a bit of
Mérimée and of Denys l'Auxerrois in WP. Oscar Wilde, who also attended the
lecture on Mérimée, was "visibly delighted to find that Mérimée regretted the
decay of assassination." On another occasion Wilde commented that WP was the
only man who could write prose in that century, as was proved by *Marius the
Epicurean*. He also was interested in WP's idea (developed in his essay on "Style")
that the scholarly conscience is male. Both Wilde and Miss Bradley agreed that
"the whole problem of life turns on pleasure" and that WP was accurate in his
portrait of the perfected hedonist as saint. The two women note that while WP
admired Oscar Wilde for having " 'a phrase for everything,' " he too was a master
of the "perfect 'mot.' " They recall one evening when WP was commenting on
boring performances of Greek drama. Mabel Robinson said that nevertheless she
was going to see THE FROGS, to which WP replied that then she should come to see
him, for he too was like a frog. The two women were delighted with WP's
comparison, for they agreed that he indeed resembled a "classic" frog of Aris-
tophanes. Miss Bradley and Miss Cooper deplored the fact that WP left his "Essay
on Aesthetic Poetry" out of *Appreciations* because it offended some "pious"
person: "he is getting hopelessly prudish in literature and defers to the moral
weakness of everybody."]

460 Maranini, Lorenza. PROUST: ARTE E CONOSCENZA (Proust: Art and Conscience) (Florence: Novissima Editrice, 1933), pp. 59, 67–69.

While WP considers style an instrument to express feelings, Proust considers style an instrument to form feelings. [In Italian.]

461 Read, Herbert. "George Saintsbury," SPECTATOR, CLI (22 Dec 1933), 938; rptd in Read's A COAT OF MANY COLOURS: OCCASIONAL ESSAYS (Lond: G. Routledge & Sons, 1945); rptd (1946), pp. 199–202; rptd with revisions (1956).

"At bottom Saintsbury's and Pater's attitude is the same attitude—the divorce of literature and art from everything that makes it significant."

462 Ri, Yoka. (Pater and Humanism), STUDIES IN ENGLISH LITERATURE (Tokyo), XIII (1933), 182–93.

The humanistic problems that we face today are not much different in substance from those faced by Arnold and WP a century ago. WP's artistic position in the nineteenth century is secure, but not as a critic in the strictest sense. For he lacked two important ingredients of the critic: first, he could not judge one historical movement or a single artist without distorting the reality; second, he stubbornly insisted on his own viewpoint. Irving Babbit reveals in his works on humanism that he could not have sympathised with the position advocated by WP on culture and the role of the artist. To Babbit, WP would be considered an "emotional naturalist." The notorious "Conclusion" to *The Renaissance* qualifies WP as an "emotional naturalist." For here is found WP's "doctrine of motion," which asserts that there can be no permanence in life. But there is considerable distance between the philosophy advocated in *The Renaissance* and that of his later works, particularly *Marius the Epicurean* and *Plato and Platonism*. Marius seems to fit into Babbit's humanism owing to Marius's development from Epicureanism to Stoicism to Christianity. As Paul Elmer More points out, however, it is questionable if Marius really ever embraces Christianity. Both Babbit and More make clear that WP has reduced intelligence to sensation. WP insisted that looking is more important than working. And the price of consistent looking is weariness. But in spite of limitations, WP's teaching emphasized the constant ordering of life. [In Japanese.]

463 Young, Helen Hawthorne. THE WRITINGS OF WALTER PATER. A REFLECTION OF BRITISH PHILOSOPHICAL OPINION FROM 1860 TO 1890 (Lancaster, Pa.: Bryn Mawr P, 1933); rptd (NY: Haskell House, 1965). Rvd dissertation, Bryn Mawr College, 1932.

More than any other writer of the period, WP reflects the opinions of his age. While at Oxford, he was close to historical scholars like Jowett and Bywater but never neglected the influential works of continental thinkers. His work falls into four periods: (1) from "Diaphaneitè" in 1864 to the second edition of *The Renaissance* in 1877—during this period his essays tend to mirror the opposing philosophical directions of the time; (2) from "The Child in the House" in 1877 to

Marius the Epicurean in 1885—the works written during this period introduce ideas that he explores more fully in (3) the works written from 1885 to 1889; (4) the essays from 1889 to his death in 1894, which deal mainly with supplementary material.

Each decade of the last thirty years of the century had a character of its own that is reflected in WP's works. In the early Sixties, his thought was directed by the influence of Mill and Mansel. By the end of the decade, he embraced the "liberal" line and, with the positivists, turned from theology and metaphysical speculation to empiricism. "In 1868, in the essay which became the 'Conclusion' to his *Studies in the Renaissance,* Pater wrote his version of Hume." *The Renaissance* is a reflection of WP the rationalist thinker analysing, decomposing, and defining characteristics and formulae by which he pinpoints the strength, the "virtue," of each of the figures he treats: e.g., for Da Vinci the "virtue" is an equal balance of curiosity and the desire for beauty; for Michelangelo it is "sweetness and strength"; for Botticelli, "sympathy" combined with a strong awareness of death, and so on. But between the time of his first essays and *Marius* in 1885, British philosophical thought had begun to shift from the positivism of Comte and the skepticism of Hume—who taught WP that nothing can be known by the mind but its own "impressions" or "sensations" (the message of the "Conclusion")—to German metaphysics, particularly to the theories of Hegel. T. H. Green advised closing one's Mill and Spencer and opening one's Kant and Hegel. WP concurred. During his later years, he became increasingly concerned with metaphysical problems; he is said to have taken sides in the controversy that surrounded the "Lambeth Judgment." And he took pleasure in church ritual, elaborate ritual. From the time of "The Child in the House" (1877) to *Marius* (1885), he developed the theme of retreat from wandering, the longing for home that appears in "The Child," "Charles Lamb" (1878), and "Bacchanals of Euripides" (1878). By the end of his life, as evidenced in *Plato and Platonism* (1893), he no longer identified with the "art for art's sake" movement. In the essay on "Style" (1888), he had conjectured that "soul" in style is most easily illustrated by religious writings; he had in mind Swedenborg. In *Plato and Platonism,* he expounded a theory of universals that emphasized " 'the accumulative capital of the whole experience of humanity.' " WP never really made up his mind on philosophical matters, retaining to the end the basically eclectic, open-ended character of his world-view. In his last essays he argued the position that one's philosophy of life is primarily an adumbration of one's temperament. His final word on philosophical concerns is "a plea for suspension of judgment."

1934

464 Brown, Leonard. "Arnold's Succession: 1850–1914," SEWANEE REVIEW, XLII (1934), 158–79.

T. S. Eliot, in his "Arnold and Pater" essay, suggests that the "art-for-art's-sake Decadents" are Arnold's successors. But there is far more in both Arnold and WP than latent decadence. To suggest that WP derives from Arnold is to forget De Quincey and WP's schooling in classical and medieval thought. Wilde is certainly not an heir to Arnold. WP ignored Arnold's desire to be needed by his society. Eliot "misunderstands his own literary heritage."

465 Burdett, Osbert. "Introduction," *Marius the Epicurean* (Lond: Dent; NY: Dutton, 1934), pp. vii–xiii.

WP was a semi-recluse who preferred dealing with life through the medium of art. After the publication of *The Renaissance* in 1873, he tried to enter London society. The essence of his contribution to a history of ideas is condensed in the "Conclusion" to *The Renaissance,* where he advocates a particular attitude toward life. The remainder of his essays in the volume are elusive. *Marius the Epicurean* has passages of elusiveness matching those of *The Renaissance.* The book "is not strictly a narrative but a series of essays in 'sensation and ideas,' strung upon a single, and intentionally not very individual, character." Marius is another of WP's many spectators of life. He lives in an age of alternatives: the second century A.D., when the old religion of Numa and the stoic philosophy of Marcus Aurelius are about to be replaced by Christianity. As a spectator, Marius has the opportunity to observe and weigh the benefits of each. The purpose of the novel is to set those alternatives before the reader. The work ends with a suspension of judgment typical of WP's temperament.

WP's imagination could also draw scenes of violence such as those found in "Denys l'Auxerrois" and "Apollo in Picardy." In the chapter entitled "Manly Exercises" in *Marius,* WP seems to delight in his description of the violence and bloodshed that characterized the Roman circus. Perhaps the mask he wore before the public hid a certain element of fanaticism that lurked in the hidden recesses of his nature. Add to this his willingness to indulge the escapades of the Oxford undergraduates, and it appears that at heart WP may have been a reckless prodigal who enjoyed vicariously the pranks of his unruly students.

WP has a definite place in the development of the Romantic movement as it progressed from Pre-Raphaelitism to late century aestheticism. The Epicurean creed, first manifested philosophically in *The Renaissance,* was applied to life in *Marius;* but because the book came to be valued more for its form than for its content, it failed to clarify the message of *The Renaissance,* as WP had intended. It remains, however, a monumental achievement in English prose-style.

150

466 Chapman, Walter. "Walter Horatio Pater's Contacts with the Religious Thought of the Nineteenth Century." Unpublished dissertation, Innsbruck, 1934.

467 Cunliffe, John W. LEADERS OF THE VICTORIAN REVOLUTION (NY: Appleton-Century, 1934), p. 300.

Kipling, at the beginning of his literary career, reacted against the forces of disintegration and decadence. "There was little inspiration for youth in the fashionable creed of disdainful estheticism and cloistered intellectualism" that WP advocated. WP was " 'a lover of words for their own sake.' " Kipling's enthusiasm "for strenuous exertion and heroic sacrifice was . . . a wholesome corrective."

468 Farnell, Lewis Richard. AN OXONIAN LOOKS BACK (Lond: Martin Hopkinson, 1934), pp. 76–77, 113.

WP "was the first to give . . . practical expression to the idea that Greek art was a fitting lecture-subject for a classical teacher." His lectures were characterized by daintiness and charm. But WP was not an authority on any kind of art, and his lectures were "wholly 'unscientific.' " WP was one of the best conversationalists at Oxford and gave charming dinner-parties "where his talk had the delicate aroma of his writings, but more ease and simplicity." WP thought that Tennyson generally excelled most of the other popular poets of the day and would probably outlive them. [In 1879, Farnell made WP's acquaintance.]

469 Richards, I. A. COLERIDGE ON IMAGINATION (Lond: Kegan Paul, Trench, Trubner, 1934); rptd (NY: Harcourt, 1935), pp. 38–42, 74; rptd (NY: Norton, 1950); rptd (Bloomington: Indiana UP, 1960); rptd (Lond: Routledge & Kegan Paul, 1962).

WP's view that true criticism deals with a " 'distinction . . . between higher and lower degrees of intensity in the poet's perception of his subject, and in his concentration of himself on his work' " is unsound. The statement is the beginning of a kind of "privileged position" of critical snobbism. In light of Coleridge's critical theories, it appears that WP's "is amateur's work, mere nugatory verbiage—empty, rootless and backgroundless postulation—unless we put into it just that very piece of patient laborious analysis that it pretends so airily to dismiss or surpass."

470 Van de Put, A. WALTER PATER AND THE ROSENMOLD PEDIGREE, Lingard Papers ns, No. 17 (Lond: Victoria & Albert Museum, 1934).

WP's Duke Carl of Rosenmold is "a dispenser of classicism . . . filtered through the Style Louis Quatorze." His descent, based on the particulars supplied by WP, is traced from the Emperor Charles V (d. 1558) to two Grand-Dukes of Rosenmold to Duke Carl. But WP had "an imperfect knowledge of historical fact" and grafted an imaginary figure upon a line of authentic descent. His portrait of Duke Carl has many historical incongruities that invite criticism: "the pseudo-historical details of Carl's infatuation for antiquity . . . , another is the anachronism of a grand-duke within the limits of the sixteenth century Empire," and a third is an "unenlightened" estimate of the career and descent of Charles V. [The author provides a detailed, highly complex discussion of the ancestry of Charles V.]

1935

471 Cazamian, Madeleine L. LE ROMAN ET LES IDÉES EN ANGLETERRE, Vol. II: L'ANTI-INTELLECTUALISME ET L'ESTHÉTISME (The Novel of Ideas in England, Vol. II: Anti-intellectualism and Aestheticism) (Paris: Les Belles Lettres, 1935), pp. 28–30, 31, 34, 39–44, 47, 49, 51–57, 119–49, 293–94, 299–300; rptd (1955).
WP's concept of art is opposed to the Christian idealism of Ruskin. His search for beauty produces an esoteric cult that has no concern for the relations between art and social life. To Ruskin's simplicity and purity is opposed WP's complexity, his search for the rare and the bizarre. He supports paganism. Like an Epicurean, he subordinates science to pleasure. Going back to the origins of thought, he shows the relation between the first atomic theories and the modern theories of Darwin and Hegel. His philosophic nihilism and his individualism stand between these two modern theories with a preference for the new idealism of Hegel, which allows a primordial role to sensations in art. Hegel's theory of beauty is in no way related to scientific aestheticism or Christian aestheticism. Art is superior to nature, which it does not imitate but transcends, and the independence of the artist from the physical reality is implicit in WP's works. Schopenhauer's theories led him to accord the first role to music in art. Implicit in Marius's [*Marius the Epicurean*] evolution is an attitude that anticipates the indefinite human future. His cult of virile beauty and violent passions, his cosmopolitanism, his accent on suggestion in art also make him the originator of all the varieties of "decadence" that flowered in the following decades. [In French.]

472 Cecchi, Emilio. *"Ritratti Immaginari* di Walter Pater"￼ (The Imaginary Portraits of Water Pater), SCRITTORI INGLESI E AMERICANI (Milan: Carabba, [1935]), pp. 74–79; rptd (1947); (1954).
[General appreciation with particular attention to WP's "The Prince of Court Painters," "Sebastian van Storck," and "Denys l'Auxerrois."] [In Italian.]

473 Child, Ruth C. "The Aesthetic of Walter Pater." Published dissertation, University of Michigan, 1935; pub as THE AESTHETIC OF WALTER PATER (NY: Macmillan, 1940), q.v. for abstract.

[Listed in Lawrence F. McNamee, DISSERTATIONS IN ENGLISH AND AMERICAN LITERATURE (NY and Lond: Bowker, 1968).]

474 Green, Z. E. "Pater's Unhappy Beginnings," ENGLISH JOURNAL, XXIV (May 1935), 421–22.
The beginnings of many of WP's essays are spoiled by excessive and monotonous definitions, classifications, and catalogues. Rather than let "innuendo or example" define and clarify his terms, WP was obsessed with clearing the way for what he had to say with unnecessarily long definitions.

475 Guerard, Albert. LITERATURE AND SOCIETY (Bost: Lothrop, Lee & Shepard, 1935), pp. 33, 107, 146, 259.
WP understood that the smile of the Mona Lisa symbolizes mysteries—"the sum total of the dreams of ten generations." The mysteries need never have even been in Leonardo's mind. WP's thought was too vital for him to be a mere "bookman."

476 Rosenblatt, Louise. "*Marius L'Epicurien* de Walter Pater et ses points de départ francais" (The French Origins of Walter Pater's *Marius the Epicurean*), REVUE DE LITTÉRATURE COMPARÉE (Jan–March 1935), pp. 97–106.
Many analogies can be drawn between WP's *Marius the Epicurean* and J. Lemaître's SÉRÉNUS. The similarities between the two protagonists, for example, are striking: they both search for an adequate philosophy amid the spiritual chaos of the Roman decadence; both sympathize with the Christian faith, and both die because of their emotional links with Christians. Yet differences can be noticed in the tone of the two works. WP's novel is more profound than Lemaître's, which is above all else a tale written to give pleasure. The final impression of irony in SÉRÉNUS is for different from the nostalgic tone of *Marius*. In spite of external differences, the two stories express the same dilemma: the incapacity of a religious temperament to believe. The confused chronologies of the works do not help to establish roles of influences. SÉRÉNUS, published two years before *Marius,* may have given WP a hint for the conclusion of his work, which ends in a deadlock. It could end neither with the hero's conversion nor with his complete repudiation of Christianity but only with his death. An inspiration that both WP and Lemaître had in common, however, was Ernest Renan's HISTOIRE DES ORIGINES DU CHRISTIANISME (1863–83), especially his works LES EVANQUILES and MARC-AURELE. Numerous analogies can be drawn: the Clémens-Sérénus analogies for Lemaître; the Marcus Aurelius-Marius analogies for WP. The theme of "piety without faith" that Lemaître owed to Renan is also the essential dilemma of WP's work. [In French.]

477 Sagmaster, Joseph. "Introduction," *Marius the Epicurean. His Sensations and Ideas* (Garden City, NY: Doubleday, Doran, 1935), pp. vii–xxxvii.

As a boy, WP was very devout and had planned to take orders in the Anglican Church, a decision that was strengthened by a meeting with John Keble. Ruskin's MODERN PAINTERS opened the whole world of art to him. By the time WP received his fellowship he had attained some distinction in Oxford and was elected to "The Old Mortality" in 1863. At one of the meetings he met Swinburne, "though he never came to know the poet intimately." In most of his critical essays, WP chose subjects in whom he believed he saw some resemblance to himself. When he first began to conceive the plan for *Marius the Epicurean* is not known, although it seems probable that he devoted the years 1879 to 1885 to it. He went to Rome in 1882 to gather material for it. *Marius,* an elaborate philosophical romance, was his most ambitious work. It is not, properly speaking, a novel: none of the characters is drawn fully. The theme is the moral self-education of Marius, and the four parts of the book define the stages of his development. In the first, he believes in the religion of his fathers, the religion of Numa. In the second, he accepts the teachings of Aristippus, the Cyrenaic, and becomes an Epicurean. In the third, he tests Epicureanism against Stoicism and Christianity. The final part reveals how far and in what manner Marius comes to accept Christianity. WP selected Rome during the Antonine Age because it was, like WP's own, an age of transition, religious transition, particularly. The spiritual progress of Marius bears a remarkable resemblance to WP's own. Marius comes to accept Christianity on trust, "though the faith it contains is still hedged about with doubt."

478 Squire, J. C. "Pater and Marius," in REFLECTIONS AND MEMORIES (Lond: Heinemann, 1935), pp. 175–210.

A common misconception is to view WP as an amoral critic who lived solely for art and the moment. But the doctrine of "art for art's sake" never totally satisfied him. He has as much in common with Ruskin as with Wilde, in fact occupying something of a middle position between them. He was concerned as much with ethics as with art. How people can read *Marius the Epicurean* as a statement in favor of art for art's sake is a puzzle. "No doctrine is examined in this book which has not a perennial appeal to some minds in some moods."

As a character, Marius is a shadow, a moral speculator, most of whose experiences occur by chance. What little dialogue there is in this novel is philosophic conversation; Marius is essentially the transmitter for these philosophical doubts and questions. Cornelius and Flavian are merely types, not individuals. The novel's construction is strange: when the ending comes, for example, it comes quite by accident; important characters are introduced and then drop out of sight. "We must regard the book as a miscellany with a thread: a religious 'revue' with an ancient Roman setting: a mixture of fiction, autobiography, aesthetic criticism, history, ethics, and metaphysics."

What is not clear is why WP chose to call his hero Marius the Epicurean. If he wants us to believe that Marius is an Epicurean, we must take his word for it. Perhaps the title is intended to suggest that Marius "can only be called an

Epicurean philosopher in so far as he was always an epicure in philosophies, and in so far as Christianity can be regarded as the crown and consummation of Epicureanism." Certainly Marius is never a pledged member of any specific philosophical school. He is instead "an Aeolian harp to both sensations and ideas." This book was not intended to be a novel in the first place; it is less a narrative than a series of essays on Marius's thoughts on life and, particularly, religion. WP skillfully places the chapter on Marius's self-communing immediately before another chapter in which Marius comes in contact with Christianity. The revelation is intense: Marius sees the light of joy in the eyes of the humble Christians. In the catacombs, he finds himself for the first time with people too happy to debate or question. He never does learn Christian doctrine; yet he is content to die a martyr to the Faith.

1936

479 Cattan, Lucien. ESSAI SUR WALTER PATER (Essay on Walter Pater) (Paris: Picart, 1936).

Before he went to Oxford, WP read Ruskin's MODERN PAINTERS, a hymn to the splendor and magnificence of artistic imagination. In 1858 the High Church movement was still popular. WP was one of its opponents; he thought it too dogmatic. He thought more highly of the Broad Church because it did not put so much emphasis on authority. Jowett encouraged WP to study the classics and German philosophy, particularly Hegel. Arnold also influenced the young WP, but in contrast to Arnold, WP thought it better to have a sound knowledge of both the world and the self. WP dreamed of a simpler aesthetic theory than that advocated by Ruskin, although Ruskin's influence on his thought is substantial. WP wanted the instantaneous pleasure of sensation; he was afraid that much contemporary art criticism would lead to a dangerous mysticism. Winckelmann was another important influence. Winckelmann, whose only love was beauty and whose sole teacher was Greece, became a model for WP. Through the study of his work, WP discovered Hellenism. WP learned that the world of Hellenism was a world of images. Winckelmann intuited Greece. WP also wanted a spontaneous approach to Greek culture, not an objective method of investigation. In his essay on Winckelmann, WP proposes a theory of Greek aesthetics. Classical revivalists have always had difficulty understanding that "Idealism" in Greece was only a tendency, an attitude; the Greek mind did not reject images. A classical interpretation of a statue of Athena is that it represents reason. But for WP a Greek idea is never separated from the past, from history and life. Hellenism has led to idealism, but we must not attempt to explain Hellenism through arguments about idealism. Greek culture emphasizes the balance between two tendencies: one to affirm the autonomy of reason and the other to take the past into account. WP understands these tendencies, and though he considers the first superior, he enjoys insisting upon the second. WP advocates a sensual understanding of Greek sculpture. He studies the origins of Greek art and concludes that one of its most telling and favorable aspects is that it left behind the archaic cult of nature associated with Oriental cultures.

WP attempted to compromise Goethe's and Winckelmann's positions on art. He wanted to be as comprehensive in his understanding as Goethe, but he discovered his limitations and restricted himself to aesthetics. He chose to live in seclusion. He accepted agnosticism. WP had no aptitude for philosophy; his concern is primarily with sensation and individual experience. But WP was more than an Epicurean, because he expected from "sensation" not merely enjoyment but inner ecstasy. Imaginative prose seems to be WP's favorite means of expression. Prose should tell us the truth, he suggests, but its truth is found basically in the impression it leaves. For WP, imaginative prose is superior to poetry. Style is a major concern; Flaubert is his master. The prosaist has to be disciplined; he must realize the natural limits of his freedom. WP discovers mysterious links between things (when looking at Greek statues, he evokes images from the Christian Middle Ages). A consequence of this method is that for him an essay starts like an analysis but becomes a literary creation. He maintains that the only function of art is to delight imagination through the senses. Art permits one to choose a world of beauty. WP does not propose his own aesthetic system; he borrows from Hegel. Following Hegel, WP puts architecture at the foundation of a historical hierarchy of art. In painting, one should attempt to discover an original means for handling form and color. Because of the sensual charm communicated through an adept handling of form and color, a painting is able to suggest deep spiritual meaning. Florentine painting is an example; it is mystical, primitive, and psychical. In his discussion of poetry, WP does not follow Hegel. For Hegel, poetry appeals to the mind only; for WP, it awakens the "imaginative reason" associated with sensual images. Music identifies form and matter. A fusion of form and matter should provide "imaginative reason."

WP's taste for French art is keen: he analyzes the work of Villon, la Pleiade, Gautier, and Flaubert and Provençal poetry. He also likes the periods in history posterior to classicism where the style is complicated. He likes the pre-classical periods: archaic Greece, the pre-Renaissance. During these times new artistic forms are born. He admires Wordsworth because he could feel a spiritual presence in nature. He is drawn to religion because it treats the human soul in an artistic manner. He is also drawn to youth, particularly to youth approaching adulthood harmoniously and youth which lasts and refuses to grow.

As a fictionist, WP succeeds with description and the creation of atmosphere, but he cannot make his characters "live." *Gaston de Latour* is superior to *Marius the Epicurean* because it is largely a series of pictures. Marius is a student who must learn how to think; he must learn discipline. Marius does not become a Christian;

156

God does not reward such a lazy attitude as Marius's. There is nothing in common between the love the Paterian hero gives to beautiful images and the love that God demands.

Platonism for WP is less a doctrine than it is a human creation. Platonism is to be explained by Socrates, but it is also better understood through a study of Heraclitus, Parmenides, and Pythagoras. WP attempts to explain Platonism through psychological analysis. Plato is a man with all the poetic qualities of his race. WP is fascinated by Plato's REPUBLIC even though he does not fully agree with Plato; the social reality of Plato's city appeals to him. Plato refused art that is not good for the city's welfare. WP is a man to be admired because he drew from his own nature all of its resources; he renewed interest in the philosophical novel and in philosophical criticism. But he should not be taken as a model, because he lost the sense of proportions. [In French.]

480 Fletcher, G. B. A. "A Textual Error in Pater," TIMES LITERARY SUPPLEMENT (Lond), 29 Aug 1936, p. 697.
The edition of "The Myth of Demeter and Persephone" found in the FORTNIGHTLY REVIEW in 1876 and in the 1895 edition of *Greek Studies* contains the sentence " 'you might think that the sea-wind flapped against the rocks.' " " 'Sea-wind' " should read " 'sea-weed.' " This error persists in the 1901 and 1910 editions of *Greek Studies*.

481 Guerard, Albert L. ART FOR ART'S SAKE (Bost: Lothrop, Lee, & Shepard, 1936); rptd (NY: Schocken Books, 1963), pp. xii–xiv, xviii, xx, xxi, xxii, xxiv, 20, 61, 63, 70, 88, 126–27, 131–32, 146, 217, 233, 349.
The fulfillment of the "art for art's sake" philosophy is "art for the sake of prestige." The careers of Mussolini and Hitler, therefore, are works of art. "Art for art's sake" has always been an elusive tendency, even in the works of WP and Baudelaire. WP's work retains its charm for its autobiographical gleanings. As a critic, WP is an impressionist who scoffs at systems. In his "Conclusion" to *The Renaissance* he does what he had warned against in the "Preface": he attempts a definition of art. It is not coincidence that WP's "breviary of Art for Art's sake should be entitled *The Renaissance*." The Renaissance is characterized by the "triumph of art" above religion and morality. WP borrowed his thesis for the essay on "Style" from Flaubert. WP is the link between Baudelaire and Oscar Wilde. Renan preached a "new Cyrenaicism" that makes WP seem tame in contrast. To retain his popularity, Wilde "borrowed ideas" from WP. The *Imaginary Portraits* are more real than many genuine likenesses.

482 Hone, Joseph. THE LIFE OF GEORGE MOORE (Lond: Victor Gollancz; NY: Macmillan, 1936), pp. 110, 112, 130, 139, 141, 183, 197, 222, 256, 257, 373, 374, 395, 446, 488, 489.
Although George Moore's enthusiasm for WP, the man, was dampened after several meetings with him because he sensed that behind WP's seemingly im-

penetrable mask was " 'a shy sentimental man, all powerful in the written word, impotent in life,' " his admiration for WP, " 'the last great English writer,' " continued to increase throughout his life. He noted that although WP's writing is somewhat monotonous and lacks humor, it reflects WP's remarkable ability to select " 'what was right' " and to omit " 'what was futile and frivolous.' " He enthusiastically praised WP's *Marius the Epicurean* as " 'the great atonement for all the bad novels which had been written in the English language.' " He admired the novel because it demonstrated "the beauty of 'mildness in life' " and made him realize that " 'by a certain avoidance of the willfully passionate and the surely ugly we may secure an aspect of life that is abiding and soul-sufficing.' " WP's critical comments on Moore's writing were important to Moore. In fact WP's two letters praising Moore's CONFESSIONS OF A YOUNG MAN, which were used in the prefaces to several editions of the work, gave the work "the character of a sacred book." Moore was also pleased by WP's review of MODERN PAINTING. Moore's unsuccessful novel, A MERE ACCIDENT, drew from WP "the comment that the object of violent acts was not very clear to him." In his account of WP's criticism of his novel, Moore suggested that WP may have "added that the object of art was to enable us to escape from the crude and violent."

483 O'Faoláin, Seán. "Pater and Moore," LONDON MERCURY, XXXIV (Aug 1936), 330–38.

Though WP would have hated it, his reputation is as a stylist. His subject matter and style reflect not only his own personal temperament but also the spirit of the age in which he lived. WP's emphasis is not on style as mere ornament. For WP "style is nothing because it is only a vehicle to matter"; yet style is at the same time everything, because it is only through style that an idea can exist. Thus for WP "a man's art is the affirmation of his life, its style is inseparable from its matter, in the sense that both, indivisible, are his acknowledged intimation of personality." According to WP, an exaggerated emphasis on style can lead to a self-consciousness and a "seriousness without a corresponding vigour" that are disastrous for writing. Such a misuse of style is found in the fiction of George Moore. Moore's writings also reflect another misunderstanding of WP's aesthetic theories, particularly those found in the "Conclusion" to *The Renaissance*. For in the hands of Moore and many of his contemporaries, WP's Epicureanism became "nothing but hedonism, and in that hedonistic search for rare moments all virtue [was] lost, all sense of what the moment possessed of deeper significance." Moore lacked WP's "transcendental turn of mind." Thus in Moore's writing, there is no evidence of WP's dichotomy between "the man interested in life . . . and the man interested in metaphysical views of life."

484 O'Sullivan, Vincent. ASPECTS OF WILDE (Lond: Constable, 1936), pp. 11–13.

Wilde thought WP too sensitive to criticism. [Author notes that H. D. Trail wrote an article entitled "Lamb—and Mint Sauce," which was intended to ridicule WP's essay on Lamb. WP was greatly disturbed.]

485 Wright, Thomas. THOMAS WRIGHT OF OLNEY: AN AUTOBIOGRA-
PHY (Lond: Herbert Jenkins, 1936), pp. 92–95, 119, 120–23, 124, 125.
[Wright notes that his biography of WP is founded largely on letters he borrowed
from John Rainier McQueen, the squire of Chailey, William Sharp, and other
intimate friends of WP. McQueen also gave him many of WP's unpublished
poems. All of the members of the Pater family that he contacted were helpful
except WP's two sisters. Wright was also helped in his task by W. K. W. Chafy,
another of WP's friends. Wright claims that WP during his lifetime and after "was
totally unhonoured in his own university." He notes that the opposition of the
sisters to his plan for the biography was aided by "several little-minded literary
men who . . . were in league with them." Gosse gave Wright as much help, from
memory, as he could. The LIFE was published on 14 Feb 1907. Several people tried
to keep the book from being published. Wright claims that A. C. Benson's
biography was an "unimportant booklet" with "crowds of mistakes." He recounts
an anecdote about WP passed on to him by E. Dugdale of Bembridge. He also
claims that Frank Harris lifted most of his material for his portrait of WP from his
biography. Wright includes a portion of a letter from W. K. W. Chafy on an
incident in WP's life while at King's School.]

486 Yeats, William Butler. "Introduction," THE OXFORD BOOK OF
MODERN VERSE, 1892–1935 (Oxford: Clarendon P, 1936), pp. viii, ix,
xxx.
Only by printing WP's *Mona Lisa* passage from *The Renaissance* in *vers libre* can
"its revolutionary importance" by demonstrated. WP gave to every sentence "a
separate page of manuscript, isolating and analysing its rhythm." He had the
uncritical admiration of the new generation of poets, and his *Mona Lisa* passage
dominated that generation, "a domination so great that all over Europe from that
day to this men shrink from Leonardo's masterpiece as from an over-flattered
woman." In his passage, WP may have foreshadowed a poetry or philosophy
where the individual counts for nothing, where the sitter for da Vinci's portrait has
no longer an individual soul; the idea reappears in the flux of Pound's CANTOS, the
flux of Turner's poetry, the flux of mind in Herbert Read's THE MUTATIONS OF THE
PHOENIX. [Yeats includes the famous description of the *Mona Lisa* as the first
selection in this book of modern verse.]

1937

487 Bush, Douglas. MYTHOLOGY AND THE ROMANTIC TRADITION IN
ENGLISH POETRY (Cambridge: Harvard UP, 1937); rptd (NY: Norton,
1963), pp. 135, 231–32, 300, 350, 397, 399, 402–3, 408, 415, 421–23,
447, 483, 506, 532–33.

Shelley's fascination with Medusa, the mingling of beauty with pain, looks ahead to WP's La Gioconda. WP, like Landor, lacks naturalness, spontaneity; Landor is "one of the lineal progenitors" of Wilde and WP. In William Morris's poetry, WP's exquisite moments are made explicit. But the distinction must always be cited between WP's own high, though vague, moral ideals and his misdirected influence. WP achieved a remarkable compromise between paganism and Christianity. He read himself into every character and period he treated. He mingled scholarship and fantasy freely, particularly when dealing with the Greek gods in a predominantly Christian setting, but he was always "in the garden of Epicurus, not Gethsemane." Michael Field's CALLIRRHOË: FAIR ROSAMUND (1884) recalls WP's "Study of Dionysus" (1876). Wilde's heroine in "The New Helen" is similar to Swinburne's Venus, WP's La Gioconda, and Lillie Langtry. Wilde completes, but perverts, the Hellenic gospel of Arnold and WP. T. Sturge Moore's "The Gazelles" could have started from WP's thoughts on progress destroying innocence in "Hippolytus Veiled."

> **488** Hopkins, Gerard Manley. THE NOTE-BOOKS AND PAPERS OF GERARD MANLEY HOPKINS, ed by Humphry House (Oxford: Oxford UP, 1937); rvd and enlgd in two parts as THE SERMONS AND DEVOTIONAL WRITINGS OF GERARD MANLEY HOPKINS, ed by Christopher Devlin, S.J. (Lond & NY: Oxford UP, 1959); and as THE JOURNALS AND PAPERS OF GERARD MANLEY HOPKINS, ed completed by Graham Storey (Lond & NY: Oxford UP, 1959), pp. 80, 133, 138, 167. [References to WP appear in THE JOURNALS.]

[Hopkins recounts occasions when he dined and walked with WP. On 31 May 1866, WP talked for two hours against Christianity.]

> **489** Praz, Mario. STORIA DELLA LETTERATURA INGLESE (History of English Literature) (Firenze: G. C. Sansoni, 1937), pp. 327, 347–49, 350, 352, 353, 372.

WP was much affected by the masterpieces of Italian Renaissance art that he saw during his stay in Ravenna in 1866. His principle that "all art constantly aspires towards the condition of music" influenced Angelo Conti and Gabriele D'Annunzio. Conti was particularly interested in WP's treatment of the Gioconda smile. WP's influence can be noted in Conti's essay on Giorgione. In D'Annunzio's novel, FUOCO, Daniele Glauro represents an Italian pupil of WP's. [In Italian.]

> **490** Venturi, Lionello. [Introduction], BOTTICELLI (Lond: Phaidon, 1937); rptd (1949), pp. 5–17.

[Passing references to WP's portrait of Botticelli in *The Renaissance*.] [In French.]

1938

491 Batho, Edith, and Bonamy Dobrée. THE VICTORIANS AND AFTER, 1830–1914, Volume IV of INTRODUCTION TO ENGLISH AND AMERICAN LITERATURE (Lond: Cresset; NY: McBride, 1938), pp. 40, 115–16, 200, 275, 333, 338, 341; rptd (NY: Dover, 1948); rptd (Lond: Cresset, 1950); rptd (NY: Dover, 1951); rptd (Lond: Cresset, 1962).

WP was "a moralist, in the direct line of descent from Arnold." It is now the fashion to abominate WP's prose.

492 Child, Ruth C. "Is Walter Pater an Impressionist Critic?" PUBLICATIONS OF THE MODERN LANGUAGE ASSOCIATION, LIII (Dec 1938), 1172–85; rptd as part of THE AESTHETIC OF WALTER PATER (NY: Macmillan, 1940).

There has been much critical discussion about the subjective nature of WP's criticism. It is true that certain parts of WP's works, such as passages in his essays on Leonardo da Vinci and Botticelli, are impressionistic in that they present WP's "own personal reactions to the work of art," thereby creating a new work of art rather than "a judgment or interpretation which will have value for others." But much of WP's criticism consists "of careful objective analysis rather than of personal reaction." For WP's main purpose in criticism is to discover the " 'formula,' " "the unique essence" of a given artist. Very often this search for an artist's "formula" involves a psychological analysis of that artist in order to find "the central quality of his temperament which of course [is] manifested" in his work. Often in his criticism, WP presents a biographical sketch of an artist in order to show the relationship of an artist's life to the development of his " 'active principle' " or artistic essence. WP's criticism frequently explores the historical milieu of an artist as background to his study. He was particularly interested in what an individual artist's work illustrated about "the great tendencies of human thought." But while WP felt that historical background was a necessary factor in understanding an artist and his work, he also felt that eventually the critic must move on to " 'what is unique in the individual genius which contrived after all, by force of will, to have its own masterful way with that environment.' " This theory is well illustrated in *Plato and Platonism*.

The "exaggerated emphasis which has been put on the subjective character of Pater's impressionism" is due in part to a misinterpretation of the "Preface" to *The Renaissance*. An analysis of the "Preface" as well as the "Conclusion" to *The Renaissance* and *Marius the Epicurean* suggests that while WP "believed that we can know nothing outside of our own impressions . . . at the same time he believed that criticism should have an objective aim, that of searching for the 'active principle,' the 'formula' of an artist's work." Thus like modern man, WP felt that while "no two people ever see things exactly alike, . . . the human faculties are sufficiently similar so that a fairly general agreement is arrived at by minds of a similar acuteness and degree of experience." Thus, such works as *The Renaissance* and *Appreciations* reflect a belief in "artistic standards of permanent validity," standards which can be known by most men due to "the fundamental similarity of human minds." These standards for WP were "perfection of form" and a concern for "a right scheme of human values."

493 Connolly, Cyril. ENEMIES OF PROMISE (Lond: G. Routledge, 1938); rptd (Bost: Little, Brown, 1939), rptd, rev ed (NY: Macmillan, 1948), pp. 18, 21, 37–38, 45, 218; rptd, rev ed (Lond: Routledge & Kegan Paul, 1949); rptd ENEMIES OF PROMISE AND OTHER ESSAYS (Garden City, NJ: Anchor, 1960).

WP and Henry James were the "last exponents of the Mandarin style." When at the height of their ability, "they wrote sentences which were able to express the subtlest inflexions of sensibility and meaning." Several passages in *The Renaissance* are examples of great passages of Mandarin writing at its best. But often James and WP were "prisoners of their style, committed to a tyranny of euphonious nothings." They were devotees of the long sentence and their allegiance to this form made them "force everything into its framework" even when this form was not particularly suited to their subject matter.

494 Fishman, Solomon. "Walter Pater and His Critics." Unpublished dissertation, University of California (Berkeley), 1938.

[Listed in Lawrence F. McNamee, DISSERTATIONS IN ENGLISH AND AMERICAN LITERATURE (NY and Lond: Bowker, 1968).]

495 Harrold, Charles Frederick, and William D. Templeman. "Introductory Survey," ENGLISH PROSE OF THE VICTORIAN ERA (NY: Oxford UP, 1938), pp. lxxv–lxxvii.

In order to understand WP, one must understand the concept of the separation of art from life. WP lost his faith in the ideals that characterize the Victorian world. WP turned to art, therefore, in order to find a "cloisteral refuge, from . . . the actual world." Many late-century artists saw in WP the rejection of systems, the modern conception of universal relativity, and the conviction that only "experience" provided satisfaction in a world of flux. Carlyle urged men to work and love God; WP urged them to withdraw from the confusion, to withdraw from action and achievement, and to seek truth in the aesthetic experience. In WP there is "no social gospel, no humanitarian passion, no concern with the problems of politics and the class struggle." WP represents the return at the end of the century to an older reliance on "*individual* salvation rather than on salvation through economic, political, or social organizations."

496 Manent, Maria. "Nota Preliminar" (Preliminary Note), in WAL-
TER PATER'S EL RENAIXEMENT (Walter Pater's *The Renaissance*), trans
by Maria Manent (Barcelona: Institució de les lletres Catalanes, 1938),
pp. [9]–12.

WP saw a positive relationship between life and art; Yeats, on the other hand,
envisioned an opposition, art as a refuge against life. WP was not a pure aesthete in
the same sense as Wilde; neither was he a mere hedonist. In *Marius the Epicurean*
he reveals his concern with the higher realities. Unlike Arnold, who divorced
reason and religion, WP walked the thin line between Epicureanism and faith. [In
Catalan.]

497 Powys, John Cowper. ENJOYMENT OF LITERATURE (NY: Simon &
Schuster, 1938), pp. 19, 38, 70, 72, 87, 108, 146, 148, 149–50, 168, 236,
331, 376, 424, 450, 490, 511.

WP's favorite book in the Bible was the Psalms, and WP is to be viewed as the most
sophisticated of all secular critics. The best introduction to Greek tragedy is his
Greek Studies. Keats, Nietzsche, and WP took the myth of Dionysus seriously. WP
was an expert on Montaigne; both he and Pascal saturated themselves in
Montaigne's philosophy. But WP assimilated Montaigne's attitude to his own.
WP's Montaigne, apart from his desparate act of faith, is as absolute a skeptic as
was Pascal. Devotees of WP or Henry James often feel they "can't read Dickens,"
because in Dickens one must put up with the bawdy and vulgar.

498 Shorey, Paul. PLATONISM ANCIENT AND MODERN (Berkeley: University of California P, 1938), pp. 16, 20, 197, 198, 233.

As WP and Emerson noted, Plato assimilated all the cultures of his age. WP
converts the loose, verbose, rhetorical Greek hexameters of Cleanthes' hymn to
Zeus in *Plato and Platonism* into the "likeness of an Old Testament psalm."

499 Smith, Logan Pearsall. UNFORGOTTEN YEARS (Lond: Constable,
1938); rptd (Bost: Little, Brown, 1939), pp. 191–94, 293.

[Smith records that he only knew WP from his books, but his voice, from "across a
whole world, as it were," reached him.] At the time, WP was held at no account in
Oxford (ca. 1888). In Balliol, the name of WP was mentioned with contempt. "To
maintain an ecstasy . . . was by no means the Balliol conception of triumphant
achievement." When WP published *Plato and Platonism,* Jowett modified the
severity of his earlier judgment.

1939

500 Baker, Ernest A. THE HISTORY OF THE ENGLISH NOVEL. Ten Volumes (Lond: H. F. & G. Witherby, 1939); rptd (NY: Barnes & Noble, 1950), ix, 117, 122, 164, 181, 190, 192, 204, 208, 209–13, 214, 215, 216, 217, 218, 219, 258, 331–32.

Joseph Henry Shorthouse's JOHN INGELSANT (1881) contrasts with WP's *Marius the Epicurean* (1885). The latter would make art a religion; the former makes religion into art. WP gave George Moore a prose standard, a fictional standard, and a standard for self-interpretation. When Moore's THE BROOK KERITH appeared, WP's *Marius* seemed its nearest parallel. The art of Henry James's final period is a development of WP's doctrine of " 'second intentions' " carried to the farthest extreme. At a time of turmoil and disillusionment, WP announced a panacea found in the aesthetic existence through making the act of living a form of art. *Marius* is the manual of the aesthetic existence; it suggests numerous transcendental possibilities for man. Maurice Henry Hewlett (1861–1923) was a romancer who dressed "semi-history in the garb of truth." His EARTHWORK OUT OF TUSCANY (1895), a series of Italian studies, reminds one of WP's *Imaginary Portraits*.

501 Clark, Kenneth. LEONARDO DA VINCI. AN ACCOUNT OF HIS DEVELOPMENT AS AN ARTIST (NY: Macmillan; Cambridge: Cambridge UP, 1939); rptd, rev ed (Baltimore: Penguin, 1959); (1961); (1963), pp. 17, 18, 24, 111, 112, 137.

WP's "beautiful essay" on Leonardo da Vinci is based, to a large extent, on work which Leonardo did not execute. This is due to the popular nineteenth-century interpretation of Leonardo da Vinci's works which erroneously attributed many paintings and drawings to him. However, WP's essay is still of value in that WP is concerned with "the Leonardesque" rather than with Leonardo. WP provides insight into how Leonardo's childhood on a Tuscan farm affected the growth of his imagination and his enduring preoccupation with organic life. WP's insight into one aspect of Leonardo's art, namely his interest in " 'beauty touched with strangeness' " is demonstrated in Leonardo's early painting of an angel in Verrocchio's *Baptism*. WP's description of the *Mona Lisa* as " 'beauty wrought out from within upon the flesh little cell by cell' " expresses most aptly the "real intention" of Leonardo's painting. WP also offers the best description of that "strange blend of mystery and tenderness, human and inhuman" which is found in Leonardo's *The Virgin and Child*.

502 Douglas, Lord A[lfred]. "Pater and Dorian Gray," TIMES LITERARY SUPPLEMENT (Lond), 12 Aug 1939, p. 479.

[Douglas states that "the cheap sneer" at Wilde's DORIAN GRAY in an article on WP in TIMES LITERARY SUPPLEMENT, 5 Aug 1939, would have caused WP "the greatest indignation and resentment." Douglas probably has in mind the anonymous article entitled "Walter Pater," in that issue of TLS; q.v.]

503 Elwin, Malcolm. OLD GODS FALLING (NY: Macmillan, 1939), pp. 61, 70–73, 216, 269, 307, 308, 383.

George Moore was inspired by *Marius the Epicurean* and admittedly enthusiastic about WP. But Moore was crushed when WP declined the offer to review A MERE ACCIDENT (1887). WP was the indirect source for CONFESSIONS OF A YOUNG MAN; as Moore declared, " 'having saturated myself with Pater, the passage to DeQuincey was easy.' " Moore never suspected until over thirty years after CONFESSIONS that WP was poking fun at him in the letter he wrote after receiving his copy of CONFESSIONS and that Moore paraded before the critics for years after. Maurice Hewlett (1861–1923), a notable Renaissance enthusiast and late "romantic" novelist, also came under the spell of WP. Mrs. Humphry Ward (1851–1920) was one of the celebrated personages in an Oxford society shocked by WP's " 'paganizing tendencies,' " his Morris wallpaper, and his blue china. WP praised her ROBERT ELSMERE (1888) in the GUARDIAN.

504 Gilbert, Katherine Everett, and Helmut Kuhn. A HISTORY OF ESTHETICS (Bloomington, Ind: Indiana UP, 1939); rptd with revisions (1953), pp. 485–88, 492, 496, 499, 500.

WP, like most members of the "art for art's sake" movement, was a disillusioned Romantic for whom beauty was supreme and absolute. WP "improvises nineteenth century Epicureanism." He also likes to compare literary style with metal works.

505 Hicks, Granville. FIGURES OF TRANSITION: A STUDY OF BRITISH LITERATURE AT THE END OF THE NINETEENTH CENTURY (NY: Macmillan, 1939), pp. 61–62, 219, 233, 247, 253, 268.

WP's philosophy, as reflected in the "Conclusion" to *The Renaissance,* is bleak and pessimistic. His disciples used this pessimism to shock the bourgeois. But to James Thomson such an attitude reflected the inability to confront "patent facts" of life. Thomson believed the universe indifferent to man's welfare. Unlike the aesthetes who followed WP, Thomson found absolutely nothing in life to attenuate the gloom.

Frank Harris's story that WP kissed Wilde's hand was a lie fabricated either by Harris or by Wilde. Wilde's hedonism was strengthened by what he learned from WP while at Oxford. It was consequently easy for Wilde to reject the social teachings of Ruskin and attend, instead, to Ruskin's writings on the beauty in literature and life. WP provided the perfect foundation for the philosophy of art that Wilde would develop. Another Oxford man influenced greatly by WP was Lionel Johnson. WP and J. A. Symonds were his mentors. WP had done more to condemn conventional Victorian morality than the Pre-Raphaelites. Accordingly, he remained a force in the Nineties among the young writers for whom the PRB was accorded "only appreciative sympathy."

506 "Memorabilia," NOTES AND QUERIES, CLXXVII (29 July 1939), 73.

[Note on the first centenary of the birth of WP.] WP now looks to us like an alien; "our problems are not his problems." His prose reveals "un-English cadences" but is charming; his scholarship was "somewhat slight."

507 Minchin, H. C. "Walter Horatio Pater," FORTNIGHTLY REVIEW, CXLVI (Aug 1939), 158–64.

The publication of *The Renaissance* (1873) caused a furor not only in the literary world but in the academic world of Oxford as well. Jowett, a professor at Balliol College, disapproved of WP's work, for it "seemed to advocate . . . that men should be taught to exist beautifully," a theory that seemed antithetical to the educational theories of Jowett. Although some critics find WP's style to be a bit " 'too precious,' " many of his passages are beautifully written, particularly those in which "he deals with subtle shades of thought and feeling, or looks at the past through the golden haze of memory." Although WP "never wrote a line in refutation of opponents," for he felt that it would destroy his " 'quietude of mind,' " his own spirit was not always "unruffled" as is seen in "Apollo in Picardy" and "Denys l'Auxerrois," which stir "turbid depths indeed." *Marius the Epicurean* is WP's "most considerable achievement." It does not succeed as a romance, for Marius is not a lifelike character and the plot is "incredibly" uneventful. Even if one views the work as "the history of a mind . . . the character does not seem to fit the exigencies of the situation which frames it." The true hero of the work is Marcus Aurelius, the philosophic emperor, whose characterization is realistic and thus "a triumphant success." WP's own religious experience was similar to that of Marius.

508 Olivero, Federico. IL PENSIERO RELIGIOSO ED ESTETICO DI WALTER PATER (The Religious and Aesthetic Thought of Walter Pater) (Torino: Societa Editrice Internazionale, 1939).

[The book has an unusually wide scope of reference. It attempts to locate WP's sources and the roots of his religious sensibility. Particular emphasis is placed on his interest in church liturgy and ritual, his treatment of the cultural forces of paganism and Christianity, his humanism, his attempts to "spiritualize" paganism, his obsession with suffering and death, and his use of Montaigne, Marcus Aurelius, and Apuleius. Art, for WP, is concluded to be the way through which he attains a meaningful Christian vision. He was a believer, though an austerely ascetic one.] [In Italian.]

509 Peel, J. H. B. "Pater and Perfection," POETRY REVIEW, XXX (May 1939), 181–83.

Although "it is imperative that persons of culture shall laugh at things Victorian . . . [because] the whole body of Victorian art, literature, and architecture cowers beneath the ghoulish shadow of the aspidistra," the works of WP are the exception to this rule. His fame, however, is presently at a low point due in part to "the persiflage of Wilde." Yet WP in his pursuit of beauty and perfection was very much aware of the dangers of such a pursuit, which might "if misinterpreted, lead other, lesser men into the primrose path of merely delectable dalliance." WP carefully avoided these pitfalls. However, his pursuit of perfection caused his prose to suffer "from a surfeit of academic pauses. . . . The perfection of his sentences is cloying, the smoothness of them deadly." Yet many pages "are neither exotic nor effete, but . . . shine with the gloss of valiant effort."

510 Trilling, Lionel. MATTHEW ARNOLD (Lond: Allen & Unwin, 1939); rptd (NY: Columbia UP, 1949); rptd (Cleveland: World Publishing, 1955), pp. 174, 286.

It is T. S. Eliot who claims that WP, Arthur Symons, J. A. Symonds, Leslie Stephen, and F. W. H. Myers all adopted the basic assumptions of Arnold's criticism. WP's praise of Mrs. Humphry Ward's (Arnold's niece) ROBERT ELSMERE is testimony to its literary quality.

511 Wainwright, Benjamin B. "A Centenary Query: Is Pater Outmoded?," ENGLISH JOURNAL, XXVIII (June 1939), 441–49.

WP's present lack of popularity is due in part to T. S. Eliot's essay on him in which he views WP as "the appalling issue of Matthew Arnold" and then dismisses him "because of his resolute undogmatism." A careful examination of WP's works reveals that he does not deserve such critical "doom." While it is true that WP's style lacks vigor, the frequently leveled charge that his writing is all style and no content is invalid. Nor does lack of vigor necessarily condemn WP's work, for vigor is not "an indispensable quality for the critic." WP's virtues as critic are "a flexibility of mind, a subtle insight into the special 'virtue' of an artist, and a willingness to listen to men who violated his most sacred beliefs." Unlike the "all-too-obvious tactics" of Matthew Arnold, WP's prose method is subtly persuasive. A selection of ideas from his writings reflects that he is indeed "a man of ideas as well as of expression." Eliot's attacks on WP's religious views and on his alleged allegiance to Wilde and the "art for art's sake" movement are also invalid.

512 "Walter Pater Born August 4, 1839. A Prose That Stands the Test of Time," TIMES LITERARY SUPPLEMENT (Lond), 5 Aug 1939, p. 466.

The critical response to WP's prose still varies between praise and condemnation. This varied response occurs because WP "did not impose his style: he spent all the vigour of his spirit in imposing his vision, intent on the sound workmanship of expression without thought of rhetoric." For WP, a writer's inner vision was "the kernel of style, as indeed of morality." Thus WP's works demand attentive participation from his readers. Often the rich and abstract nature of WP's subject-matter makes it difficult to present in concrete terms. "Yet, perhaps by virtue of his native austerity and clear-sightedness, there is always a core of concreteness in his writing." His prose "combine[s] a Latin definiteness with Northern thought." The chief characteristic of WP's style is "its scrupulous honesty, its faithfully authentic note." WP's inner vision, his individualism is "that of the humanist, a universal and generous eclecticism." From this humanism comes his ability to combine traditions of different cultures such as Greek and medieval traditions, to perceive the individual as "the whole universe, potentially a universe of amazing scope and variety," and to perceive the dualism inherent in many aspects of life, particularly in "Nature itself, in its relentless cruelty and ineffable loveliness." WP's temperament and personal life were not an "evasion of life" but a constant attempt to "enrich" it.

> **513** "Walter Pater," TIMES LITERARY SUPPLEMENT (Lond), 5 Aug 1939, p. 467.

[This article is a general summary of the points made in the centennial anniversary article in this same issue of TLS. The article attempts to clear up the more frequent misunderstandings about WP. It dismisses such myths as that WP was an aesthete of the same school as Oscar Wilde, that he was a "sentimental dabbler in religious sensations," and that he was a hedonist who cultivated the senses purely for the sake of physical pleasure. See Lord Alfred Douglas's reply to the observations on Wilde in "Pater and Dorian Gray," TIMES LITERARY SUPPLEMENT (Lond), 12 Aug 1939.]

> **514** Yvon, Paul. "Gustave Flaubert, Walter Pater et le probleme du style" (Gustave Flaubert, Walter Pater and the Problem of Style), L'IN-FLUENCE DE FLAUBERT EN ANGLETERRE (Flaubert's Influence in England) (Caen: Caron, 1939), pp. [4]–11.

WP himself acknowledged the influence of Flaubert in his work. With Flaubert he shared a longing for the past. WP was not so much attracted to Flaubert because of his picturesqueness or his realism as he was by his concern with aesthetics and his delicate but passionate descriptive style. WP never met Flaubert, but there are similarities in their personalities, although WP was never the leading figure of a school. While at Oxford, WP made daily translations from the works of Flaubert. From Flaubert he learned to stress the artist's point of view as a thing that mattered more than the description itself, a point WP advocated in his essay on "Style." He also admired the hard work and unceasing effort that he saw in the careful prose of Flaubert. [In French.]

1940

> **515** Boas, George. "The Mona Lisa in the History of Taste," JOURNAL OF THE HISTORY OF IDEAS, I (1940), 207–24; rptd in WINGLESS PEGASUS: A HANDBOOK FOR CRITICS (Baltimore: Johns Hopkins P, 1950), pp. 211–35.

Numerous references to the *Mona Lisa* appear throughout the eighteenth and nineteenth centuries, but no one, with the exception of Vasari, seems to have noticed anything mysterious about it until the early nineteenth century when the concept of the *femme fatale* seems to have come into vogue, emerging with Romanticism. "What Vasari was for the pre-nineteenth century critic, Theophile Gautier and Walter Pater became for their contemporaries and successors." Gautier's article on Leonardo with its description of the *Mona Lisa* as an eternal feminine first appeared in 1858 [see the 1863 publication of Gautier et al., LES DIEUX ET LES DEMI-DIEUX DE LA PEINTURE]. In 1869, WP describes the famous painting in his essay on Leonardo. Like Gautier, he envisions the figure as a symbol of metempsychosis. "From Gautier and Pater . . . runs a tradition which is the very opposite of that started by Vasari. . . . the Italian biographer and critic chiefly saw in the *Mona Lisa* a wonderful technical feat, the reproduction of a natural object[;] the French and English 'aesthetes' saw it as a hieroglyph which required . . . deciphering."

> **516** Brooks, Van Wyck. NEW ENGLAND: INDIAN SUMMER, 1865–1915 (NY: Dutton, 1940), pp. 165, 439, 442.

Bernard Berenson, the expert on Italian painting, was greatly influenced by WP. Berenson stood for hours before the *Mona Lisa*, repeating WP's passage on the painting to himself; eventually he perceived that the passage made no sense.

> **517** Child, Ruth C. THE AESTHETIC OF WALTER PATER (NY: Macmillan, 1940). Rvd dissertation, University of Michigan, 1935.

WP's work is remarkably stable, as if coming to us from another world. But his real stature as a critic and stylist is largely misunderstood and underrated because most moderns believe that art that does not treat social issues is of little significance. But WP deals with the timeless problem of "how to live"; he offers much to future generations.

Although an aesthete, WP had no share in aesthetic manifestations of revolt; he had a high code of morals and a wide ranging, though exotic, interest in all of the arts. His enthusiasm for Gautier, Flaubert, and Heine is apparent; and his interest in Goethe puts him in a tradition with Arnold. Certain tenets of his aestheticism need to be clarified: the first is his attitude toward the theory of art for art's sake, which is developed beyond a simple defense of the autonomy of art and embraces the theory of the ethical function of art (a realization he shared with Swinburne); the second is WP's defense of form, attainable only by a dedicated effort (in this concern, he reveals his strong relationship to the French aesthetes); the third is WP's insistence on the close association between art and life, that life must be lived in the spirit of art (here he parts company with his French predecessors)—the conception of life as art was distorted by WP's followers; the fourth concern deals with his criticism, which is less "aesthetic" and "impressionistic" than directed toward finding the "formula," the characteristic quality that distinguishes each work of art. [The four concerns listed above are treated respectively in the body of the book in four tightly argued chapters.]

518 Gutscher, Marianne. "Henry James und Walter Pater" (Henry James and Walter Pater). Unpublished dissertation, University of Vienna, 1940.
[In German.]

519 Maurer, Oscar, Jr. "William Morris and the Poetry of Escape," in NINETEENTH CENTURY STUDIES, ed by Herbert Davis, William C. De Vane, and R. C. Bald (Ithaca, NY: Cornell UP, 1940), pp. 247–76.
Because WP enthusiastically supported poetry of escape, it was identified with "art for art's sake." Morris did not, in his later years, agree with this extreme. WP is the critic "who represented the tendency toward 'escapism' also found in Morris's work."

1941

520 Allen, Gay Wilson, and Harry Hayden Clark. LITERARY CRITICISM: POPE TO CROCE (NY: American Book Co, 1941), pp. 524–25; rptd (Detroit: Wayne State UP, 1962).
WP "carried Ruskin's aestheticism to a height far removed from the moral purpose which Ruskin championed, he supplied a critical theory for the latter-day paganism which was springing up as a reaction against Victorianism," and the "Conclusion" to *The Renaissance* encouraged the development of art for art's sake. WP became in a sense a nineteenth-century Winckelmann, like that figure seeing antiquity through the eyes of his own age. In "The Child in the House," WP reveals the character traits that produced his aesthetics, his critical method, and the type of personality which is described in *Marius the Epicurean. Marius* reduces to a philosophy WP's cult of beauty and sense impressionism. WP is one of the best examples of an imaginative, impressionistic, and sympathetic critic, and in some ways he reminds one of "that supreme impressionist," Anatole France.

521 Arns, Karl. GRUNDRISS DER GESCHICHTE DER ENGLISCHEN LITERATUR VON 1832 BIS ZUR GEGENWART (Outline of the History of English Literature from 1832 to the Present) (Paderborn: Ferdinand Schöningh, 1941), pp. 14, 20, 35–36, 78, 81, 98, 101, 117, 178, 199, 221.
Condemned by his biographers and many of his critics and misunderstood by his students, WP is now considered to be one of the best prose writers of the nineteenth century. Maurice Hewlett's LITTLE NOVELS OF ITALY recalls WP. Oscar Wilde departed from John Ruskin's ethically founded aesthetic and coarsened WP's hedonism. In Germany, T. S. Eliot is as unknown as an upholder of culture as

Matthew Arnold or WP. In seeing art as "a personal re-thinking of life from end to end," George Moore was following his master, WP. [In German.]

522 Brooks, Van Wyck. "What Is Primary Literature?" YALE REVIEW, XXXI (Sept 1941), 25–37; rptd with revisions in OPINIONS OF OLIVER ALLSTON (NY: Dutton, 1941), pp. 211–27.

Though no two modern writers seem to have less in common than WP and Maxim Gorki, their definitions of great literature [see WP's "Style"] are similar. With WP, the beautiful was secondary to the good.

523 Havens, Raymond Dexter. THE MIND OF A POET, Volume I: A STUDY OF WORDSWORTH'S THOUGHT; Volume II: THE PRELUDE, A COMMENTARY (Baltimore: Johns Hopkins P, 1941); rptd (1942); (1951); (1962), p. 28, 29, 30, 68, 250, 293, 447–48, 562, 596, 604.

WP rightly observed in "Wordsworth" that the poet did not prefer scenes of pastoral life for their "passionless calm," but for "clearing the scene for . . . great exhibitions of emotion." WP wrote that Italy and Switzerland "had too potent a material life of their own to serve greatly [Wordsworth's] poetic purpose," and the same can be said for London. Though Books XII and XIII contain less real poetry than any other part of THE PRELUDE, WP rightly called them "those two lofty books."

524 Law, Helen H. "Pater's Use of Greek Quotations," PROCEEDINGS OF THE AMERICAN PHILOLOGICAL ASSOCIATION, LXXII (1941), xxxv–xxxvi.

[Abstract of a speech later worked into the article "Pater's Use of Greek Quotations," MODERN LANGUAGE NOTES, LVIII (Dec 1943), 575–85, q.v.]

525 Levin, Harry. JAMES JOYCE: A CRITICAL INTRODUCTION (Norfolk, Conn: New Directions, 1941), pp. 25, 49, 56.

Joyce's early essay on James Clarence Mangan employs the impressionistic standards of WP's *The Renaissance*. WP's influence on the thought of Stephen in A PORTRAIT OF THE ARTIST AS A YOUNG MAN is strong.

526 MacNeice, Louis. THE POETRY OF W. B. YEATS (Lond: Oxford UP, 1941), pp. 22–30, 33–34, 36–38, 57–58, 67, 76, 82, 84, 85, 93, 197, 199, 203, 233.

WP dropped Matthew Arnold's concept of "criticism of life" and believed that art was related to life only in a very rarefied form. Yeats's sacred books were *Marius the Epicurean* and Villiers de l'Isle-Adams's AXËL. For both WP and Arnold, philosophy was only scaffolding to help the artist build the "House Beautiful." The poets of the 1890s took their doctrine from WP and their models from the French Symbolists. Yeats's early cult of passion came from WP, though WP did not push his doctrine to its logical conclusion, sensual Epicureanism: in WP, what is valuable is "the relationship between a continually existent perceiving subject and a continuous and interdependent stream of objects." WP's aesthetic implies not merely passive receptivity but also deliberate selection; for WP, "aesthetic experience . . . implies interpretation." Yeats, like WP, insists that each experience is unique, but for Yeats experience and persons are manifestations of universal principles: Yeats "will not accept the world as a hailstorm of data which melt when they touch the ground." WP "supplied Yeats with a belief in the importance of passion, a belief in the importance of style, a distrust of the vulgar world, and a curious sort of aesthetic pantheism, a make-believe homage to material objects which professes to discount their materiality." In his early love poems Yeats seems to be seeking Marius's "ideal of a perfect imaginative love." WP influenced both the style and the content of James Joyce's early essay, "Homage to James Clarence Mangan" (1902). Villiers de l'Isle-Adam, like WP, hated science. WP implied that the stranger sensations were, the better. Yeats steadily moved away from the doctrines of WP and the aesthetes, eventually attacking WP's theory in "The School of Giorgione" that music is the highest type of all the arts and writing that "the ideal of culture expressed by Pater can only create feminine souls." In "The Decay of Lying," Oscar Wilde gave an epigrammatic exposition to the doctrines of WP. Beauty for the Nineties poets, as for WP, implies something in decline, tired, too good for this world, wan, world-weary. Yeats's story "Rosa Alchemica" shows the influence of WP. Both Yeats and George Moore considered *Marius* as the greatest example of English prose. Yeats's early prose was written under the influence of WP; sometimes his parentheses, like WP's, "beguile the reader from the point."

527 Matthiessen, F. O. "The Crooked Road," SOUTHERN REVIEW, VII (Winter 1941), 455–70; rptd in THE RESPONSIBILITIES OF THE CRITIC (NY: Oxford UP, 1952), pp. 25–40.

Nearly every prose expression which W. B. Yeats made of his doctrine that any deeply realized moment of life shares in the Universal Mind is closer to WP than to William Blake. James Joyce echoes WP in his early essay on James Clarence Mangan.

528 Mizener, Arthur. "The Romanticism of W. B. Yeats," SOUTHERN REVIEW, VII (Winter 1941), 601–23; rptd in THE PERMANENCE OF YEATS: SELECTED CRITICISM, ed by James Hall and Martin Steinmann (NY: Macmillan, 1950), pp. 140–62.

Yeats did not realize that the translators of the Bible and other seventeenth-century writers did not have the same self-conscious conception of style as WP. Yeats, like WP in *Marius the Epicurean,* makes an aesthetic use of the emotional appeal of religious materials. WP is closer to Matthew Arnold than to Sir Thomas Browne, and in fact, closer than Arnold would have been happy to believe possible.

529 Oman, Sir Charles. MEMORIES OF VICTORIAN OXFORD AND OF SOME EARLY YEARS (Lond: Methuen, 1941), pp. 209–10.

WP was regarded as a *poseur* at Oxford, not a leader of thought; "he talked in a precious style, and absorbed the conversation." [Oman admits that he met WP only once or twice. For a reply to Oman's observation, see Grundy, FIFTY-FIVE YEARS AT OXFORD (1945).]

530 Sampson, George. THE CONCISE CAMBRIDGE HISTORY OF ENGLISH LITERATURE (Cambridge: Cambridge UP, 1941); rptd (1961); rvd (1970), pp. 462, 844–45, 945.

[Abridges much of the entry by Hugh Walker in A. W. Ward and A. R. Waller, THE CAMBRIDGE HISTORY OF ENGLISH LITERATURE, Volume XIV (Cambridge: Cambridge UP, 1916), pp. 158–59, but adds]: The defect of WP's prose is not that it becomes a kind of poetry, but that it becomes a kind of science: every word is part of a formula. *Marius the Epicurean* is "sadly attractive, but leads to no conclusion of comfort. How could it? There was no comfort to offer, and Pater was too gravely sincere to offer delusions." His works "embody no faith and no exact knowledge of the Ruskinian kind." Like Wordsworth, WP was conscious of the weight of the world, but rather than seeking relief in nature, he sought it in man in a state of spiritual sensation, or in works in which man externalizes his inner apprehensions. It is difficult to believe that WP's public will ever be large.

531 Schoen, Max. "Aesthetic Experience in the Light of Current Psychology," JOURNAL OF AESTHETICS AND ART CRITICISM, I (Spring 1941), 23–33.

WP seems to be right in maintaining "that it is the sensuous element of art that is essentially artistic, from which follows his thesis that music, the most purely formal of the arts, is also the measure of all the arts."

532 Symons, A. J. A. "Wilde at Oxford," HORIZON (Lond), III (April 1941), 253–64; (May 1941), 336–48; rptd in ESSAYS AND BIOGRAPHIES, ed by Julian Symons (Lond: Cassell, 1969), pp. 145–69.

Though WP, like Matthew Arnold and John Ruskin, was in his own way a preacher, his doctrine was "an exaltation of personal experience above all restrictions, as the end of life." WP's answer to how one can get the most from life is "clear enough, and is hardly qualified by" his final words that art can best provide pleasure. A philosophy of "aesthetic indulgence" was not new in WP's time, but the "Conclusion" [*The Renaissance*] states it with extreme force and clarity. WP's dress was for the most part traditional: "only in his apple-green tie did he show any outward mark of the aesthetic enthusiast, the advocate of sensuous experience, the admirer of Winckelmann and his fiery homosexual friendships." It is doubtful that he ever "accepted the responsibility of physical love." W. H. Mallock's caricature of him in THE NEW REPUBLIC frightened WP, and he became "more self-enclosed than ever," sought only the company of "tried friends," withdrew the "Conclusion" from the second edition of *The Renaissance,* and did not publish a book for twelve years. The sonnet that "Mr. Rose" reads is a parody of one that Oscar Wilde had recently published.

533 Venturi, Lionello. "The Aesthetic Idea of Impressionism," JOURNAL OF AESTHETICS AND ART CRITICISM, I (Spring 1941), 34–45.

WP discovered a new creative impulse in Giorgione (see "The School of Giorgione") in that, rather than drawing on Christian or pagan subjects drawn from the Bible, mythology, or history, like his contemporary Florentines, Giorgione invented his own motifs, and subordinated them to his form and coloring. This is a technique which the Impressionists were later to use.

> **534** Warren, Austin. "Religio Poetae," SOUTHERN REVIEW, VII (Winter 1941), 624–38; rptd with revisions as "William Butler Yeats: The Religion of a Poet," RAGE FOR ORDER (Chicago: University of Chicago P, 1948); rptd (Ann Arbor: University of Michigan P, 1959); (1962), pp. 66–83; rptd in THE PERMANENCE OF YEATS: SELECTED CRITICISM, ed by James Hall and Martin Steinmann (NY: Macmillan, 1950), pp. 223–36.

The cry to God of Des Esseintes, in J.-K. Huysmans's À REBOURS, to have pity on the doubting Christian, the incredulous one who would like to believe, emanates mutedly from the pages of WP's *Marius the Epicurean*. Yeats's stories "Rosa Alchemica," "The Magi," and "The Tables of the Law" owe much to WP: they are told in the "incense-thick harmonies" of WP's *Imaginary Portraits,* and their solitary men recall the hero of "Sebastian Van Storck."

> **535** Wellek, René. "Literary History," LITERARY SCHOLARSHIP: ITS AIMS AND METHODS, ed by Norman Foerster, John G. McGalliard, René Wellek, Austin Warren, and Wilbur L. Schramm (Chapel Hill: University of North Carolina P, 1941), pp. 89–130; rptd with revisions in René Wellek and Austin Warren, THEORY OF LITERATURE (NY: Harcourt, Brace, 1942), pp. 263–82.

George Saintsbury's conception of criticism is close to WP's theory and practice of "appreciation."

> **536** Woods, Margaret L. "Oxford in the 'Seventies," FORTNIGHTLY REVIEW, CL (1941), 276–82.

[WP is only mentioned, but the author of the article (the daughter of G. G. Bradley, master of University College, Oxford, and later dean of Westminster) includes first-hand anecdotes of many of WP's Oxford contemporaries, including Andrew Lang, Mrs. Humphry Ward, Rhoda Broughton, Lewis Carroll, John Ruskin, and Oscar Wilde.]

1942

> **537** Carli, Enzo. MICHELANGELO (Bergamo: Instituto Italiano d'Arti Grafiche, 1942); rptd (1946); (1948), pp. 25–26.

The nude figures in the background of Michelangelo's *Doni tondo* have inspired several symbolic interpretations: some critics have seen them as models of heroic primordial humanity; WP saw them as "the sleepy-looking fauns of a Dionysiac revel"; Foratti saw them as a contrast between the vices and virtues, between the moral principles of paganism and Christianity; but they are angels or geniuses of youth, ready to render homage to the sacred meeting. [In Italian.]

538 Cramer, Maurice B. "Browning's Literary Reputation at Oxford 1855–1859," PUBLICATIONS OF THE MODERN LANGUAGE ASSOCIATION, LVII (1942), 232–40.

WP always praised Robert Browning's work, but he did not like Browning's later poetry. He particularly like PIPPA PASSES and MEN AND WOMEN. The passage on Browning in "Winckelmann" provides the clue to WP's admiration for a writer so different from himself: there he creates "something more like Pater and Pater's world than like Browning." WP's admiration for Browning is important, since he conveyed his enthusiasm to his disciples, William Sharp, Arthur Symons, and Oscar Wilde, who corresponded or conversed with WP on the subject of Browning.

539 Guérard, Albert, Jr. ROBERT BRIDGES: A STUDY OF TRADITION IN POETRY (Cambridge, Mass: Harvard UP, 1942), pp. 37, 77; rptd (NY: Russell & Russell, 1965).

Bridges's EROS AND PSYCHE appeared in the same year as WP's *Marius the Epicurean,* but he had not read WP's version of the Cupid and Psyche story in that novel. The doctrine that feeling is its own defense is important both to WP's aesthetic philosophy and to Rousseauistic naturalism.

540 Haines, Helen E. WHAT'S IN A NOVEL (NY: Columbia UP, 1942); rptd (1963), p. 63.

L. H. Myer's sequence-novel, THE ROOT AND THE FLOWER, has affinities with WP's *Marius the Epicurean.*

541 Kallen, Horace M. ART AND FREEDOM: A HISTORICAL AND BIO-GRAPHICAL INTERPRETATION OF THE RELATIONS BETWEEN THE IDEAS OF BEAUTY, USE AND FREEDOM IN WESTERN CIVILIZATION FROM THE GREEKS TO THE PRESENT DAY (NY: Duell, Sloan & Pearce, 1942); rptd (NY: Greenwood P, 1969), pp. 25, 532–39, 549, 551, 553, 555, 681.

John Ruskin could not accept the autonomy of art in WP's terms as the only salvation from the evils of the world. "Oscar Wilde reduced Pater's conception to an absurdity, making the liberty of art the contradiction of life, instead of the use of life to the ends of greater freedom and abundance." WP and James McNeill Whistler "developed with a parallel rhythm." To WP, as to Matthew Arnold, Goethe was the most perfect illustration of a harmonious, self-developing personality, but though Goethe was his early model, it "is Marius [*Marius the Epicurean*], not Goethe, who was finally the air-drawn figure of that which earthly Walter Pater aspired to become." The quality of WP's prose suggests that he lived in an emotional prison and that the freedom in art which he dreamed of was never realized. WP learned from the Germans the idea that art was the sensory expression of the idea, but sense was more significant to WP than it was to Hegel and the transcendentalists. For WP, a work of art's lesson, subject, or story was not what rendered it art, but rather its capability of enabling the beholder to burn with a hard, gemlike flame, and because art alone has this end, it is the purveyor of fulfillment and salvation. According to WP, the spirit of man can do without art in only one condition: that of the city itself as a work of art, as described in Plato's REPUBLIC. "Wilde was to Pater what Alcibiades was to Socrates, Petronius to Lucretius, or the Horatian hogs of Epicurus' sty to the ascetic men and women of Epicurus' garden."

> **542** Miles, Josephine. PATHETIC FALLACY IN THE NINETEENTH CEN-
> TURY: A STUDY OF A CHANGING RELATION BETWEEN OBJECT AND EMO-
> TION (Berkeley & Los Angeles: University of California P, 1942); rptd
> (NY: Octagon, 1965), pp. 265, 267, 270.

WP, in writing of the poetry of D. G. Rossetti, is aware of the new emphasis on feeling as connected with color, shape, and quality rather than with object. G. M. Hopkins, in practice, was more a student of John Ruskin than he was of WP.

> **543** Pick, John. GERARD MANLEY HOPKINS: PRIEST AND POET (Lond:
> Oxford UP, 1942), pp. 7–9, 11, 17, 55; rptd (1966).

A university notebook of Hopkins's, entitled "Essays for W. H. Pater," is extant, and Hopkins took notes on lectures that WP was giving on Greek philosophy. WP asked Hopkins to join him at Sidmouth during a summer vacation. Hopkins always retained affection for WP, and saw him often when, after he had become a Jesuit, he was at St. Aloysius' Church, Oxford. "However intellectualized and refined was [WP's] gospel of hedonism, at heart it preached beauty and pleasure as the goal of life." "Whenever Pater has anything good to say of religion, it is of religion as art." WP's view of asceticism was a mistaken one. WP, along with John Ruskin and Matthew Arnold, saw the futility of rationalism and turned to art. A few indications of Hopkins's leanings toward Catholicism are evident in the essays which he wrote for WP.

> **544** Praz, Mario. [Prefixed notice,] "Il Fanciullo Nella Casa" (The
> Child in the House), LETTERATURA (Jan–March 1942), [54].

[Here Praz calls attention to the similarities between Proust, Henry James, and WP.] [In Italian.]

> **545** Schoen, Max. "Walter Pater on the Place of Music among the
> Arts," JOURNAL OF AESTHETICS AND ART CRITICISM, II (Summer 1942),
> 12–23.

WP denies the value of universal aesthetic standards, but he nevertheless has implicitly "a theory of art, a universal formula for it, deny it though he may, which he uses as his standard for the critical evaluation of any one specific art work." He draws a distinction between the "feelingful" and the intellectual elements of aesthetic experience and indicates that the feelingful is aesthetically preeminent. When form (which belongs to the life of feeling) and matter present a single effect in a work of art, form is actually at the forefront, and matter sinks into the background. For WP, aesthetic feeling is abstract, not concrete, and he believes that each art owes its responsibility to its own particular sensuous material. If WP believes that a human product is expressive and that it lives, then it is a work of art. If it lives, it lives because the person lives in it, and this vitality is feelingful rather than intellectual. Music is the goal of the other arts because sound is most free of the intellectual elements, which art seeks to eliminate. Music rises above specific emotion, raising it from the practical to the aesthetic level, because its matter, feeling, is inseparable from its material, sound, and because when the feeling for music is for its material, that feeling is necessarily organized feeling, since music is organized sound.

546 Wellek, René, and Austin Warren. THEORY OF LITERATURE (NY: Harcourt, Brace, 1942); rptd with revisions (1955); (1962), pp. 3, 184, 253, 264.

Criticism like WP's description of the *Mona Lisa* in "Leonardo da Vinci" or the florid passages of John Addington Symonds or Arthur Symons are usually "needless duplication, or, at most, the translation of one work of art into another, usually inferior." It is not difficult to analyze the style of "mannered" writers like Thomas Carlyle, George Meredith, WP, or Henry James.

1913

---

547 Bowra, C. Maurice. THE HERITAGE OF SYMBOLISM (Lond: Macmillan, 1943); rptd (1951); (1954); (1959); rptd (NY: Schocken, 1961), pp. 3, 4, 13, 14, 184.

Symbolism is a mystical and theoretical form of English Aestheticism, whose apostles were WP and D. G. Rossetti. WP's aesthetic conclusions were more practical than theoretical. He "gave dignity and honour to the arts in an age which tended to misunderstand or to undervalue them." WP's "Sebastian Van Storck" contains the same sort of aesthetic withdrawal that is found in J.-K. Huysmans's À REBOURS and Villiers de l'Isle-Adam's AXËL. His "All art constantly aspires to the condition of music," in "The School of Giorgione" says "in his plainer English way what Mallarmé often said."

548 Coulton, G. G. FOURSCORE YEARS: AN AUTOBIOGRAPHY (Cambridge: Cambridge UP, 1943); (NY: Macmillan, 1944), p. 210.

[Coulton met WP in 1891 at a dinner at Hertford College, Oxford, and saw him again later the same evening. His impressions]: WP had a "heavy jaw and military moustache, strangely dissonant from preconceived ideas of the man who had written *Marius the Epicurean*. But that evening he talked like his books: not offensively like, but with a marked flavour of the same style." WP talked "at some length" about Abbé Prévost's MANON LESCAUT.

549 Hone, Joseph. W. B. YEATS, 1865–1939 (NY & Lond: Macmillan, 1943 [Lond ed misdated 1942]; rptd (Lond: Macmillan; NY: St. Martin's P, 1962), pp. 83, 111, 128, 136.

Lionel Johnson took from WP certain phrases that came to mean much to Yeats, like "hieratic," "marmorean," and "life should be a ritual." WP's was the only great prose in modern English for Yeats and the other members of the Rhymers' Club, and Yeats's THE SECRET ROSE is "Pater's style subdued to the matter of Villiers de l'Isle-Adam." It seemed to Yeats that Arthur Symons, more than anyone he knew, lived the temperate life recommended by WP. Yeats's story "Rosa Alchemica" is "Pater become uncanny."

550 Knickerbocker, Frances Wentworth. FREE MINDS: JOHN MORLEY AND HIS FRIENDS (Cambridge, Mass: Harvard UP, 1943); rptd (Westport, Conn: Greenwood P, 1970), pp. 106, 110, 179, 193–96, 209–10.

Morley, like WP, was at heart a moralist. "To set Morley's review of Pater's *Studies in the History of the Renaissance*" next to his attacks on Swinburne's POEMS AND BALLADS is to see "how far he had travelled in a few years along the way of imaginative insight." Morley felt that attention ought to be called to WP's *Renaissance* because it was likely to heighten public interest in good literature. Morley's review of that volume is one of the finest of his "synthetic" criticisms, and in it he anticipates T. S. Eliot's assessment of WP as a moralist. WP's "Wordsworth" is the most objective and sensitive Victorian essay on the poet, and in it he anticipates Matthew Arnold "in noting the 'perplexed mixture' of poetic and prosaic in Wordsworth."

551 Law, Helen H. "Pater's Use of Greek Quotations," MODERN LANGUAGE NOTES, LVIII (Dec 1943), 575–85; [derived from a speech, the abstract of which appeared in PROCEEDINGS OF THE AMERICAN PHILOLOGICAL ASSOCIATION (1941)].

Though WP's scholarship is usually taken for granted, it has on occasion been questioned, most notably by Thomas Wright and Samuel C. Chew. However, on checking over four hundred Greek references in WP with their sources, one reaches the conclusion that WP's Greek background was extensive, and that, despite a few slips and an occasional faulty memory, "in almost no passage can the essential accuracy of the translation be questioned," in contrast to Chew's opposite conclusion ["Pater's Quotations," NATION (NY), XCIX (1 Oct 1914)] on this matter.

552 Liptzin, Sol. "Heinrich Heine, Hellenist and Cultural Pessimist: A Late Victorian Legend," PHILOLOGICAL QUARTERLY, XXII (1943), 267–77 [sections on WP rptd in Liptzin, THE ENGLISH LEGEND OF HEINRICH HEINE (NY: Bloch, 1954), pp. 84, 93–94].

Heine's Hellenism influenced WP, Robert Buchanan, James Thomson, and A. C. Swinburne in the 1870s, and that influence can be seen in WP's writings from 1869 to 1893. The rehabilitation of the old gods was a passion with WP, as it had been with Pico della Mirandola and Heine. Heine's influence can be seen in "Denys l'Auxerrois," "Apollo in Picardy," and "Aucassin and Nicolette."

553 Montague, Clifford M. "Grub Street Fights (A History of Literary Feuds)," POET LORE, XLIX (1943), 25–40, 147–64, 248–65, 340–54.

Rossetti [D. G. or W. M.?] disliked WP immensely, and WP's opinion of Oscar Wilde was not high.

554 Peek, Katherine Mary. WORDSWORTH IN ENGLAND: STUDIES IN THE HISTORY OF HIS FAME (Bryn Mawr, Pa: Bryn Mawr College, 1943); rptd (NY: Octagon, 1969), pp. 52, 211–14, 216, 232, 233, 235, 238.

In his review of Wordsworth's THE EXCURSION in THE EXAMINER (1814), William Hazlitt "anticipates Pater's study of the almost elemental character of Wordsworth's genius, a character forever related to the country which has inspired him." WP's "Wordsworth" implicitly protests the tendency to praise the poet for his philosophical system, and this "emancipation of Wordsworth from the office of teacher" was continued by Matthew Arnold. Both WP and Arnold felt that Wordsworth's work was uneven, and WP's suggestion that his poetry would benefit from a selective anthology was actually carried out by Arnold. WP believed that Wordsworth's art approached the condition of music, and Arnold, in saying that at his best Wordsworth had no style, was saying approximately the same thing—in his greatest poetry form and substance merge. A. C. Swinburne made similar comments on Wordsworth's style. In "Wordsworth in the Tropics," Aldous Huxley develops WP's point that Wordsworth was the poet of nature in its modesty. George Saintsbury and A. C. Bradley, writing of Wordsworth in 1896 and 1903 respectively, return to the broader issues raised by WP on the subject.

555 Staebler, Warren. THE LIBERAL MIND OF JOHN MORLEY (Princeton: Princeton UP, 1943), pp. 42, 177–78, 183, 214.

WP's *The Renaissance* reassured Morely in two ways: it showed that a new school of English critics might arise who would combine "German thoroughness and historic sense with French acuteness and artistic arrangement," and that in spite of the preoccupation everywhere with science, manifestations of nonscientific intellectual activity could still be found. Morley especially admired the fact that WP linked art with real life. As a critic of literature, Morley never pretended to WP's subtlety.

556 Wagenknecht, Edward. CAVALCADE OF THE ENGLISH NOVEL FROM ELIZABETH TO GEORGE VI (NY: Holt, 1943); rptd (1954); (1965), pp. 507, 568, 569.

Marius the Epicurean is "one of the great spiritual autobiographies in the form of fiction." WP was one of the literary masters of the novelist Forrest Reid.

1944

557 Baldensperger, Fernand. "English 'Artistic Prose' and Its Debt to French Writers," MODERN LANGUAGE FORUM, XXIX (Dec 1944), 139–50.

With a few exceptions, there was a general lack of attention to prose style as an art in England until some writers, foremost among them WP, turned to French examples for inspiration. WP admired for stylistic reasons Honoré de Balzac, Prospér Mérimée, Théophile Gautier, and Gustave Flaubert. The portrait of the *Mona Lisa* in "Leonardo da Vinci" owes something to Flaubert's Helen in LA TENTATION DE SAINT-ANTOINE. George Moore's style was influenced more by Gautier than by WP.

558 Boas, George. "The Problem of Criticism," THE ENJOYMENT OF THE ARTS, ed by Max Schoen (NY: Philosophical Library, 1944); rptd (Freeport, NY: Books for Libraries P, 1971), pp. 300–328.

Until recent times the *Mona Lisa* has been universally admired, but in the sixteenth century it was admired for its fidelity to nature, while in the nineteenth, following Théophile Gautier and WP, it was seen as a symbol of "enigmatic womanhood"— but women were not considered to be enigmatic until the nineteenth century.

559 Brown, Calvin S., Jr. "The Poetic Use of Musical Forms," MUSICAL QUARTERLY, XXX (Jan 1944), 87–101.

Arthur Schopenhauer, in SCHRIFTEN ÜBER MUSIK, said "All arts constantly aspire towards the condition of music" before WP did, in "The School of Giorgione."

560 Coll., E, AEN, NAS. "Q and Pater," TIMES LITERARY SUPPLEMENT (Lond), 16 Dec 1944, p. 611.

[Having gone up to Oxford the year after Sir Arthur Quiller-Couch ("Q") left it, and having known WP "not only as a don," the author corrects some of the impressions of WP given in Quiller-Couch's MEMORIES AND OPINIONS (q.v.).] WP was not in the least like a soldier: he stooped, "he walked with short, tripping steps, with his head poked forward," and though he did have a large moustache, many, and perhaps most men did in those days. It is difficult to imagine WP sitting cross-legged on the floor, as Quiller-Couch describes him—his characteristic attitude was "sitting sideways, head on hand," on the window seat of his room in Brasenose. There may have been something oriental in his cheek-bones and eyes, "but to a youngster much more in the impression of profound wisdom and manifold experience."

561 Craig, Hardin. LITERARY STUDY AND THE SCHOLARLY PROFESSION (Seattle: University of Washington P, 1944); rptd (Freeport, NY: Books for Libraries P, 1969), p. 55.

The aesthetic point of view of WP and others in the late nineteenth century became popular in America, and their methods are still reflected in the curricula of American universities, though the historical approach is more widely practiced.

562 Ford, George H. KEATS AND THE VICTORIANS: A STUDY OF HIS INFLUENCE AND RISE TO FAME 1821–1895 (New Haven: Yale UP; London: H. Milford, Oxford UP, 1944); rptd (1945); rptd (Hamden, Conn: Archon, 1962), pp. 29, 101, 104, 115, 117, 143, 173–74.

Keats's "Nothing startles me beyond the moment" leads to the work of WP. D. G. Rossetti's position on poetics was stated by WP in 1868. When contrasting the different stages of Victorian thought, it is often useful to compare the attitudes of Thomas Carlyle, John Ruskin, and WP toward the same subject. "It is a strange gap in Pater's studies of romanticism that he has left us no essay on a poet [Keats] whose work would seem a model of the very beauties he sought in art," though from the scattered references to Keats in WP's work, it is clear that he admired him greatly. He valued Keats as "the complete exponent" of art for art's sake.

563 Gardner, W. H. GERARD MANLEY HOPKINS (1844–1889): A STUDY OF POETIC IDIOSYNCRASY IN RELATION TO POETIC TRADITION, Volume I (Lond: Secker & Warburg, 1944), pp. 5–9, 18, 151, 190.

WP's impact on Hopkins is certain but not clearly defined. Though no letters survive, they maintained a warm friendship for years. Hopkins's Platonic dialogue, ON THE ORIGIN OF BEAUTY, was possibly written for WP at Oxford and shows WP's influence. WP's intense feeling for Hellenic and Renaissance art and humanism would attract the aesthete but repel the Catholic in Hopkins. The doctrine of WP's "Conclusion" [*The Renaissance*] is opposed to the mature Hopkins's reconciliations of aesthetics and ethics. One of Hopkins's lecture notes of 1873–74, in which he says that meaning is essential to poetry only as an element necessary to support the shape which is contemplated for its own sake, is similar to a passage in WP's "The School of Giorgione." Hopkins's idea that beauty is enhanced by strangeness goes back to Bacon and Aristotle but is also found in WP's "The Poetry of Michelangelo." Hopkins illustrates as few English poets do WP's dictum in "The School of Giorgione" that "All art constantly aspires towards the condition of music." In "Style," WP, like Hopkins, stresses the full pleasure of artistic workmanship. To Keats, WP, and the aesthetes, Beauty was Truth; to Hopkins, it was two-fold: mortal beauty and immortal beauty. Hopkins's poetry often reminds one of WP's principle, *ex forti dulcedo* ("The Poetry of Michelangelo").

564 Ironside, Robin. "Walter Pater," CORNHILL, CLXI (May 1944), 66–78.

The appearance of remoteness in WP noticed by his acquaintances was probably due more to reserve than to indifference. Richard Jackson, whom Thomas Wright doubtfully claims as a great friend of WP's, was a "habitual romancer in the interest of his own greater glory as a scholar and patron of the arts." [A fair amount of information on Jackson is given.] In real life and in his writings WP wore a mask, but the mask is more transparent in the writings. He wanted ardor, rather than languor, to be perceived as the motive for his reticence, and in reading him "we may feel as he himself felt in reading Mérimée . . . that we have 'our hands on a serpent' or at least on a living force as hermetic and tortuous, but mysterious, rather than guileful." The *Imaginary Portraits* are remarkable for their historical intuition, "but their style lacks the comprehensive elaboration of the best essays of *The Renaissance* or of the discussions (as opposed to the narrative), in *Marius [the Epicurean]*." In general, there is an unfortunate separation of form and matter in most of WP's fiction. The matter of WP's writing has the same ambiguity as his style: "the beatings of his heart are encased in a hard, transparent envelope of thought, an intellectual armour that was a foil, if not positively a warrant, for the dark cluster of sympathies that he really needed to diffuse into the world." *The Renaissance* and *Greek Studies* are likely to endure because of WP's gift for eliciting the sensuous implications of works of art. He has been unjustly criticized for his scholarship. His fascination with "physical horrors" may have arisen partly because they served as a pretext for compassion.

565 Lalou, René. LA LITTÉRATURE ANGLAISE DES ORIGINES À NOS JOURS (English Literature from Its Origins to the Present) (Paris: Presses Universitaires de France, 1944), pp. 108–9; rptd (1947); (1957); (1960).
John Ruskin gradually subordinated aesthetics to a social philosophy, but WP restored autonomy to art, though he did not isolate art arbitrarily in order to draw from it a simple hedonism. In *Marius the Epicurean* WP hoped to combine ancient Roman and Christian civilizations in a synthesis analogous to the civilization he described in *The Renaissance*. His method is triumphant in *Imaginary Portraits*. WP and Walter Savage Landor were George Moore's masters. [In French.]

566 Lewis, D. B. Wyndham. RONSARD (Lond: Sheed & Ward, 1944), pp. 7, 24, 29, 37, 41, 91, 321–23, 333.
WP enunciated more clearly than his contemporaries the "essential Whig grievance against the Middle Ages"—that medieval man thought too much about God and not enough about himself. It is unfortunate that the best-known interpreter in English of Ronsard and the Pléiade should be WP. Without understanding Ronsard's Catholicism, one cannot understand Ronsard, as WP demonstrates. The portrait of Ronsard in *Gaston de Latour* redeems the impression that WP gives of him in "Joachim du Bellay"; in the latter, WP appreciates Ronsard's "sweetness," but WP's "old-maiderie" prevented a recognition of the poet's "stormy vigour." WP was attracted to the artistic products of a Catholicism that he despised, which led him to concentrate on Ronsard's "decorative grace" and to ignore his "swordmanship." But WP was "not the only eminent English critic to write foolishly of Pierre de Ronsard."

567 Matthiessen, F. O. HENRY JAMES: THE MAJOR PHASE (NY & Lond: Oxford UP, 1944); rptd (1946); (1963), pp. 41, 59.
James's portrait of Madame de Vionnet in THE AMBASSADORS recalls something

of the spell that WP evokes of the *Mona Lisa* in "Leonardo da Vinci," though James's character is more human than WP's. James could have subscribed to "much of Pater's famous exhortation for fullness of life, particularly to the sentence which urges that one's passion should yield 'this fruit of a quickened, multiplied consciousness.' " Susan Stringman's imagination, in THE WINGS OF THE DOVE, has been fed on WP and Maurice Maeterlinck.

568 [Morgan, Charles.] "Mary Duclaux," TIMES LITERARY SUPPLE-MENT (Lond), 22 April 1944, p. 195.

WP was among the visitors to the house of G. T. Robinson, the father of Mary Robinson Duclaux. WP "did not set out to write a judgment on the Renaissance, but, for his own generation, a reinterpretation of life in aesthetic terms."

569 Morgan, Charles. THE HOUSE OF MACMILLAN (1843–1943) (NY: Macmillan, 1944), pp. 58–59, 61, 104–6, 135.

[Book contains a copy of WP's letter from Brasenose dated 29 June 1872 introducing *The Renaissance* to Alexander Macmillan.] "Within two days" of receiving WP's letter, Macmillan accepted the book. WP cared much for the outward appearance of the book; he suggested that it should be bound " 'in paste-board with paper back and printed title.' " He wanted "covers of greyish blue and a paper back of olive green." Macmillan did not want "paper boards and labels." He claimed they were unpractical. WP finally gave in to Macmillan in a letter dated 13 Nov 1872 [text of letter included]. In Feb 1873, WP's *Renaissance* was "being bound in green cloth.

570 Peyre, Henri. WRITERS AND THEIR CRITICS: A STUDY OF MISUN-DERSTANDING (Ithaca, NY: Cornell UP, 1944), pp. 19, 47, 48, 52, 151, 193, 235, 275, 307; rptd as THE FAILURES OF CRITICISM (Ithaca, NY: Cornell UP, 1967).

The six keenest critical temperaments in the history of English criticism are Samuel Johnson, S. T. Coleridge, William Hazlitt, Matthew Arnold, WP, and T. S. Eliot. WP's *Appreciations* remains, "in spite of an overwrought style, one of the finest single volumes of criticism in English." He took little notice of contemporary literature and "erred most signally when he inserted a disappointing eulogy of a vulgar novel, Octave Feuillet's LA MORTE, in a series of studies on great masters." WP is second only to Hazlitt as the "truest critic in English": he "rightly knew that the primary task of a critic is to feel the world of shapes and colors and sounds, not to reason about it abstractly." The "Preface" to *The Renaissance*, even more than the "Conclusion," proposes, in his "too-languid prose, one of the most vigorous critical programs ever suggested to criticism: to feel the virtue of a writer, to disengage it, to set it forth."

571 Praz, Mario. "Introduzione" (Introduction), PATER, ed and trans by Mario Praz (Milan: Aldo Garzanti, 1944), pp. ix–xxv.

WP was a monk rather than a priest in the temple of Beauty, and if the young were converted to his faith, it was through the subtle fascination of his affable and shadowy personality rather than through direct preaching. Of his patron saints, Winckelmann and A. C. Swinburne cast suspicious shadows on his life, and it is impossible not to believe that his attraction for them was based on a similarity of unusual sensibilities. Cornelius, in *Marius the Epicurean*, is an Apollo disguised as a St. George. The key to Marius's attitude at the end of the novel lies in the ambiguity of the figures of the Madonna, Venus, and Judith in "Botticelli." All of WP's fictional characters either belong to periods of transition or are born out of their times; they find themselves in circumstances with which they are unfit to deal or wander in labyrinths of possibilities that disperse their energies. For WP, as for all the great Romantics, beauty was connected with decadence and death. *Marius* is as much about WP's own century as Tennyson's IDYLLS OF THE KING is. WP's thought, though showing a marvelous talent for exposition, as in *Plato and Platonism,* lacks originality, and WP was more a person learned in philosophy than he was a true philosopher. All his life WP had a nostalgia for the absolute, and science did not take the place of a faith he yearned for. As an art critic WP was unable to distinguish a true from a false attribution, but he excelled at intuiting things in painting like inspiration, taste, and manner, as, for example, in "The School of Giorgione." One finds echoes of WP in the Italian art critic Angelo Conti; and the character Daniele Glauro, in Gabriele d'Annunzio's IL FUOCO, is an Italian disciple of WP's. [In Italian.]

> **572** Praz, Mario. "Introduzione" (Introduction), *Ritratti Immaginari (Imaginary Portraits)*, by Walter Pater (Rome: Donatello de Luigi, 1944), pp. 9–22; rptd as "Ritratti immaginari di Walter Pater," in LA CASA DELLA FAMA (Milan: Ricciardi, 1952), pp. 328–37.

Imaginary Portraits is WP's crowning achievement and one of the most attractive works in European Romanticism. Like Robert Browning's DRAMATIS PERSONAE, the *Imaginary Portraits* are disguised autobiography. The genre of the imaginary portrait goes back to Ovid's HEROIDES. "A Prince of Court Painters," "Sebastian Van Storck," and "Duke Carl of Rosenmold" contain anachronisms, but WP was trying to present a historical atmosphere, not history. WP's prose is similar to the music of Richard Wagner. All of WP's characters belong to periods of transition, or are born out of their time, or find themselves involved in circumstances for which they are unfit, or are caught in labyrinths of possibilities that exhaust their energies. There are similar motifs and situations in many of WP's works of fiction, as, for example, a childhood in a jealously preserved traditional religious atmosphere or an exceptional protagonist who has a suspicious reputation. [In Italian.]

> **573** [Quiller-Couch, Sir Arthur.] MEMORIES AND OPINIONS: AN UN-FINISHED AUTOBIOGRAPHY BY Q, ed by S. C. Roberts (Cambridge: Cambridge UP, 1944); rptd (1945), p. 75.

In 1883–84, a literary club, "The Passionate Pilgrims," "used to hale [WP] from his rooms in Brasenose and plant him, amid our councils, upon a hearthrug with his back to the fire. There he would sit, cross-legged, with the light flickering over his baldish cranium, his moustaches pendulous in the shadow: a somewhat Oriental figure, oracular when his lips opened and he spoke, which was seldom."

574 Richardson, Dorothy. "Saintsbury and Art for Art's Sake in England," PUBLICATIONS OF THE MODERN LANGUAGE ASSOCIATION, LIX (1944), 243–60.

Though George Saintsbury espoused the principles of art for art's sake, he differed from WP, Théophile Gautier, and Gustave Flaubert in believing that form and idea could be separated. WP's classic statement of impressionistic criticism, in the "Preface" to *The Renaissance,* was always Saintsbury's ideal. WP and Saintsbury first met at the Oxford home of Mandell Creighton. Saintsbury believed that Oscar Wilde had gone beyond the "reasonable bounds" inherent in WP's "Conclusion."

575 Ruggles, Eleanor. GERARD MANLEY HOPKINS: A LIFE (NY: Norton, 1944); rptd (Port Washington, NY: Kennikat P, 1969), pp. 53, 179.

It is likely that Benjamin Jowett sent Hopkins to WP to be tutored. During his return to Oxford in 1878–79, Hopkins had little to do with the university, but he "did see something of Pater."

576 Temple, Ruth Z. "Some Notes on Anglo-French Literary Relations in the Late Nineteenth Century," COMPARATIVE LITERATURE NEWS-LETTER. II, No. 7 (April 1944), 3–6.

"Seeing Ronsard, du Bellay and the poet of AUCASSIN ET NICOLETTE through the same *fin de siècle* glasses [WP] turns their poetry into scenes by Corot."

577 Warren, Austin. "Instress of Inscape," KENYON REVIEW, VI (Summer 1944), 369–82; rptd in GERARD MANLEY HOPKINS, BY THE KENYON CRITICS (Norfolk, Conn: New Directions, 1945), pp. 72–88; rptd as "Gerard Manley Hopkins," in RAGE FOR ORDER (Chicago: University of Chicago P, 1948); rptd (Ann Arbor: University of Michigan P, 1959); (1962), pp. 52–65; rptd in HOPKINS: A COLLECTION OF CRITICAL ESSAYS, ed by Geoffrey Hartman (Englewood Cliffs, NJ: Prentice Hall, 1966), pp. 168–77.

WP was one of the real shapers of Hopkins's mind. "In the abstractionist academic world, Pater boldly defended the concrete—of the vital arts and music of perception, of the unique experience." Hopkins may have heard, in earlier versions, WP's lectures on Plato, "in which, with monstrous effrontery, the Doctrine of Ideas was praised as giving contextual interest to the concrete."

1945

578 Badger, Kingsbury. "Mark Pattison and the Victorian Scholar," MODERN LANGUAGE QUARTERLY, VI (Dec 1945), 423–47.
Pattison and WP often talked about books, but sometimes Pattison banned that subject; after one such occasion, WP remarked to Edmund Gosse that what Pattison apparently liked best was "romping with great girls in the gooseberry bushes."

579 Brégy, Katherine. "Conscience and the Critic," CATHOLIC WORLD, CLXI (July 1945), 325–28.
In the nineteenth century, perhaps in reaction to the savagery of previous critics, there developed a group of "delicate and profound" critics, like S. T. Coleridge, Charles Lamb, William Hazlitt, Matthew Arnold, and WP. "Now I have always believed there were quite valid reasons why . . . Catholic critics should be the best in the world. . . . Even an implicit or sympathetic sharing of Catholic thought adds to a man's critical stature, so that we find Pater pointing out that the ideal of a saint includes 'not rectitude of soul only, but fairness.' "

580 Buckley, Jerome Hamilton. WILLIAM ERNEST HENLEY: A STUDY IN THE "COUNTER-DECADENCE" OF THE 'NINETIES (Princeton: Princeton UP, 1945); rptd (NY: Octagon, 1971), pp. 78, 79, 117, 179.
The "non-literary" values of the paintings of James McNeill Whistler and the French Impressionists were valid and "exposed to ridicule" such purple passages as WP's description of the *Mona Lisa* in "Leonardo da Vinci." Technically, Henley's literary criticism is similar to WP's: each approached a work with the bias of an individualist, each evolved a highly personal style, and each sought the "distinctive trait" of the author under consideration. But WP sought a refuge from social conflict in art, while Henley was an activist. WP's "doctrine was destined, even in spite of its teacher, to inspire the literature of 'decadence.' The other served as a basis for Edwardian realism."

581 Gaunt, William. THE AESTHETIC ADVENTURE (NY: Harcourt, Brace; Lond: Cape, 1945), pp. 54–69, 87, 95, 121–22, 124–25, 135–37, 144–45, 180–81, 189, 197, 228, 242–43, 245, 253; rptd (Harmondsworth, Middlesex: Penguin, 1957); rptd (NY: Schocken, 1967).
WP greatly admired Simeon Solomon's painting of Bacchus, and in return Solomon asked to paint WP's portrait. Solomon became for WP the embodiment of art for art's sake. WP's early view of art was based on his study of the ancient Greeks and the modern French and Germans. WP "abstained from love as he had abstained from cricket, the better to enjoy contemplation." "There is no question but that an essay on Leonardo which Swinburne wrote in 1864 inspired the style and a celebrated passage of Pater's own later essay on the artist." WP's "spartan

care for form" and the fact that his essays served no moral end were new in English literature. Knowing nothing of visual art, WP's art criticism has little technical value. His idea that something evil or exotic that should be enjoyed lies at the heart of beauty may have come from Charles Baudelaire. WP lacked the "energetic and self-forgetful spirit" of the Pre-Raphaelites, with whom W. H. Mallock mistakenly connects him in the character of Mr. Rose in THE NEW REPUBLIC. Mr. Rose's views are so close to WP's that they seem to be quotations from him. WP was among the candidates whom W. H. Gilbert considered caricaturing in PATIENCE before he decided on Oscar Wilde. *Marius the Epicurean* is the confession of one who put art before faith. The two principal influences on George Moore's CONFESSIONS OF A YOUNG MAN were J.-K. Huysmans's À REBOURS and WP's *Marius*. WP was embarrassed by Wilde and bored by Moore. Late in life, WP came to see asceticism as a form of beauty. Roger Fry's insistence on the preeminence of form in the abstract is consistent with WP's belief (in "The School of Giorgione") that all arts aspire to the condition of music.

582 Grundy, George Beardoe. FIFTY-FIVE YEARS AT OXFORD: AN UNCONVENTIONAL AUTOBIOGRAPHY (Lond: Methuen, 1945), pp. 74–76, 78, 81.

[Impressions of WP, 1892–94.] Sir Charles Oman's observation [in MEMORIES OF VICTORIAN OXFORD (1941)] that WP's life was a pose is inaccurate: in reality, what seemed his mannerisms were an outward expression of the true nature of the man. WP felt that middle-aged dons playing field hockey was indelicate. WP was shocked by a blasphemous question asked of Canon Gore by an undergraduate. F. W. Bussell was WP's closest friend at Oxford. [For a response to Grundy's observations, see D. S. MacColl, "Victorians at Oxford," TIMES LITERARY SUPPLEMENT (Lond), 8 Dec 1945.]

583 Harrold, Charles Frederick. JOHN HENRY NEWMAN: AN EXPOSITORY AND CRITICAL STUDY OF HIS MIND, THOUGHT AND ART (Lond & NY: Longmans, Green, 1945); rptd (1946); rptd (Hamden, Conn: Archon, 1966), pp. 93, 257, 265, 348.

Newman's austere view of literary style allows no more room for unnecessary ornamentation than do the theories of Gustave Flaubert or WP. But Newman had nothing to say about the non-fictional prose works of either John Ruskin, Matthew Arnold, or WP.

584 Jennings, Richard. "Books in General," NEW STATESMAN AND NATION, nsXXIX, (17 Feb 1945), 111.

Arthur Symons was the "too faithful disciple" of WP, who was the first and worst influence on him. In his books, following WP, Symons attempted to be as little abstract as possible and saw life as a form of art. WP secured the publication of Symons's DAYS AND NIGHTS and reviewed it in a "rather jerky little essay." WP's advice to Symons to make prose rather than poetry his principal work may not have been sound.

585 Longaker, Mark. ENEST DOWSON (Philadelphia: University of
Pennsylvania P, 1945); rptd (1967), pp. 22, 61, 71, 88, 90.

Marius the Epicurean and WP's discussions of the utility of beauty for the full
cultivation of life were the chief influence on the Oxford undergraduates of the
Eighties who would become a part of the aesthetic movement. A line in Dowson's
poem "Extreme Unction" is drawn from a passage in *Marius*.

586 MacColl, D. S. "Victorians at Oxford," TIMES LITERARY SUP-
PLEMENT (Lond), 8 Dec 1945, p. 583.

G. B. Grundy's picture [in FIFTY-FIVE YEARS AT OXFORD: AN UNCONVENTIONAL
AUTOBIOGRAPHY (1945), q.v.] of "a rigidly conventional Walter Pater, Sunday-
dressed, may be exact enough as a defensive facet of that recluse."

587 May, J. Lewis. "Quis Desiderio—," JOHN HENRY NEWMAN:
CENTENARY ESSAYS, ed by Henry Tristram (Lond: Burns, Oates &
Washbourne, 1945), pp. 92–100.

Was WP, consciously or unconsciously, thinking of Newman in his description of
Fénelon [in "A Prince of Court Painters"]?

588 Pepper, Stephen C. THE BASIS OF CRITICISM IN THE ARTS (Cambridge, Mass: Harvard UP, 1945); rptd (1956), pp. 16, 39, 49, 67.

"The greatest critics . . . have made an effort to examine their tools and have done
something that amounted to showing their source of justification in one of the
relatively adequate world hypotheses. This is notably true of Coleridge and Pater."
The main line of mechanistic aesthetics and criticism—pleasure aesthetics—stems
from Thomas Hobbes and runs through John Locke and the associationists,
culminating in WP. The genius of mechanistic criticism is "a pervading sensuousness and fineness of sensuous discrimination," which WP exhibits to a high
degree.

589 Schirmer, Walter F. KURZE GESCHICHTE DER ENGLISCHEN
LITERATUR VON DEN ANFÄNGEN BIS ZUR GEGENWART (Short History of
English Literature from the Beginnings to the Present) (Halle/Saale: Max
Niemeyer, 1945), pp. 215, 217; rptd (Tübingen: Neomarius, 1949); rptd
(Tübingen: M. Niemeyer, 1964).

In *The Renaissance,* WP saw the work of art not in terms of form but as the
expression of a specific spiritual culture, and in the portraits of men in that volume
he delineated the contradictory coexistence in the same person of the thinker and
the sensualist. He had a preference for times of transition. *Imaginary Portraits* is
WP's most personal book. [In German.]

590 Spender, Stephen. "Introduction," BOTTICELLI (1444–1510)
(Lond: Faber & Faber, 1945); rptd (NY: Pitman, 1948), pp. 2–5, 24.

The admiration of A. C. Swinburne, D. G. Rossetti, John Ruskin, and WP for
Botticelli illuminates an aspect of Victorian England: "Botticelli's Virgins, and his
Venus, with their look of meditative sensuous wistfulness, gaze across the gulf of

five hundred years, and they respond to a thought in the minds of the late Victorians." Botticelli's paintings seem less quaint, archaic, and Greek to people today than they did to WP.

1946

591 Aldington, Richard. "Introduction," THE PORTABLE OSCAR WILDE (NY: Viking, 1946); rptd (1963), pp. 1–45.
Wilde took "too literally and was to apply too sensually, too coarsely, too self-ishly" the philosophy of the "Conclusion" [*The Renaissance*]. Bunthorne, in Gilbert and Sullivan's PATIENCE, was originally intended as a satire of WP but was "transferred hastily" to Wilde. Like WP, John Ruskin, and J. A. Symonds, Wilde believed that the purpose of criticism was to help people enjoy art.

592 Clark, Arthur Melville. STUDIES IN LITERARY MODES (Edinburgh & Lond: Oliver & Boyd, 1946); rptd (1958); rptd (Folcroft, Pa: Folcroft Library Eds, 1971), pp. 6, 27.
Later in the nineteenth century, the earlier taste for didactic historical novels changed, and the result was the historical novel, which presents the past for its own sake. *Marius the Epicurean* and *Gaston de Latour* are of this latter type.

593 Collingwood, R. G. THE IDEA OF HISTORY (Oxford: Clarendon P, 1946); rptd (1948); (1949); (1951); (1962); rptd (NY: Oxford UP, 1956), p. 88.
WP blundered in including a chapter on Winckelmann in *The Renaissance*, since Winckelmann differed from scholars who lived during the Renaissance in his approach to the past, in conceiving of a history of art as separate from biographies of artists.

594 Dédéyan, Charles. MONTAIGNE CHEZ SES AMIS ANGLO-SAXONS (Montaigne among His Anglo-Saxon Friends). Two Volumes (Paris: Boivin, [1946]), I, 201, 211, 297, 413–41, 445–46.
WP's doctrine is no doubt hedonistic, throwing aside all constraints and accepting only the rules of art, but it is less concerned with exhausting pleasures than with choosing the headiest, including the intoxication of knowledge. WP is interested in the psychology of his subjects, in laying bare their souls, sensibilities, and intelligence. For WP, the Montaignesque element in literature is the irresistible desire to reveal one's own personality, to let the reader get to know one. WP's method concentrates only on what interests him in his subject rather than on the entire subject. In *Gaston de Latour*, the central character's meeting with Montaigne represents WP's joyful discovery of the earlier writer's essays. WP was attracted by Montaigne's relativism and found in Montaigne's friendship for

Etienne de la Boétie a confirmation of his theory that one can be transported out of oneself through intensity. One can perceive WP's own personality in his treatment of Montaigne's essays in *Gaston,* a personality characterized by a contrast between outward serenity and a restless inner search to find himself and happiness. WP found in Montaigne an understanding of friendship and the cultivation of all our psychological possibilities. [Much of the discussion of WP consists of summary and paraphrase of portions of "Charles Lamb," "Sir Thomas Browne," "Pascal," *Plato and Platonism,* and *Gaston.*] [In French.]

595 Dobrée, Bonamy. ENGLISH ESSAYISTS (Lond: Collins, 1946), pp. 36–39.

WP was no "dreamy worshipper of beauty" but rather directed his readers to the increased vividness of life to be gained from being alert to beauty. He only indirectly urges action to make life better: though no overt reformer, what he said can have an appreciable effect on one's manner of living.

596 Du Bos, Charles. JOURNAL, 1921–1923 (Paris: Corrêa, 1946), pp. 19, 28, 116, 117, 161, 163, 164, 179, 180, 189, 193, 216, 229–30, 231, 233, 234, 236, 256, 260, 279, 280, 312, 351, 360, 362, 364, 380, 391, 398, 401.

WP profoundly noted that the principal unhappiness in Amiel's life came from what he considered as belonging to action and no longer to thought, and that in Amiel's JOURNAL INTIME "action" almost always refers to literary activity. WP "never had any idea of doing anything else than to distil in each page the fragrant essences of tranquil meditation." WP admirably felt and reproduced his impressions of Pontigny, Vézelay, and Auxerre. In order to produce his effects, WP employed indirect turns of phrase. Despite WP's wistfulness about Greece, he refused to deny that Christianity had brought an increase in spirituality—he may have regretted the passing of the physical harmony of the Greeks, but he never attributed a spirituality to them that they did not possess. [Second on a list of Du Bos's priorities: write an article on WP in Burgundy for LE GAULOIS. Entry for 22 Sept 1922: Du Bos sets a deadline of 4 Oct for finishing an article on WP in Burgundy. 25 Sept 1922: WP in a list of subjects to treat in future years.] *Marius the Epicurean* marks the point where the impossibility of ignoring suffering complltes and deepens the idea of the asceticism of beauty. The idea of the cult of beauty in WP can never be completely final because of the inevitable encounter with suffering, but whereas in others this encounter would cause them to discard their earlier aesthetic ideas, in WP it simply adds a burden to aesthetic sensations. [April 1923: Du Bos plans a book on WP for the following year. 24 April 1923: he plans to complete the book on WP by the end of the year. Edmund Gosse told Du Bos that he had the manuscript of WP's "Pascal," that he would show it to him, and that "that bounder Thomas Wright had blocked the way for a true biography of Pater."] WP, like Ralph W. Emerson, could keep, but not give. [In French.]

597 Ironside, Robin. "Aubrey Beardsley," HORIZON (Lond), XIV (Sept 1946), 190–202.
WP's *The Renaissance* was one of Beardsley's favorite books.

598 Kingsmill, Hugh [pseud of Hugh Kingsmill Lunn]. "Logan Pearsall Smith," NEW ENGLISH REVIEW, XII (May 1946), 473–74, 476; rptd in THE PROGRESS OF A BIOGRAPHER (Lond: Methuen, 1949), pp. 112–15.
Smith's early essays aim at a Paterian poetic prose, and WP was the greatest influence on his early years.

599 Lloyd Thomas, M. G. "Hopkins as Critic," ESSAYS AND STUDIES BY MEMBERS OF THE ENGLISH ASSOCIATION, XXXII (1946), 61–73.
[On a passage in G. M. Hopkins's NOTEBOOKS, dated 1880]: "The writing is the writing of an ex-pupil of Pater, but of a pupil who had so far outstripped the teacher that all which remains of their relationship is a reminder."

600 McCullough, Bruce. REPRESENTATIVE ENGLISH NOVELISTS: DEFOE TO CONRAD (NY & Lond: Harper Bros., 1946), pp. 119, 263, 264.
WP employed the historical novel to serve his aestheticism. *Marius the Epicurean* is an exception to the general practice of English novelists up to that time of paying little attention to artistry and workmanship.

601 Pearson, Hesketh. OSCAR WILDE: HIS LIFE AND WIT (NY: Harper & Bros, 1946), pp. 26–28, 38, 131, 171, 279; rptd as THE LIFE OF OSCAR WILDE (Lond: Methuen, 1946), rptd (1951); (1966); rptd (Harmondsworth, Middlesex: Penguin, 1960).
WP "was one of those timid, old-maidish scholarly recluses who, fearing even the uncertainties of matrimony, preach the gospel of living dangerously. In Germany he would have sung the glories of the sword and the superman. In England he hinted at forbidden fruit." The youth of Oxford felt that in the "Conclusion" [*The Renaissance*] one of their own professors was "actually telling them that it was their duty to run riot." Wilde is "still read with delight, while his masters in philosophy, Ruskin and Pater, are mainly studied in the places where dead languages are cherished."

602 Praz, Mario. "Prefazione" (Preface), WALTER PATER: IL RINASCIMENTO, (Walter Pater: *The Renaissance*), ed and trans by Mario Praz (Naples: Edizioni Scientifiche Italiane, 1946), pp. i–xiii.
WP falls into neither of Max Friedländer's categories of art critics: he is neither an academic critic nor a connoisseur, though he possessed the sensibility of the connoisseur. Despite the fact that some of the attributions that he used in "The School of Giorgione" are now known to be false, WP penetrated with incomparable subtlety the idyllic spirit of the "giorgionesque." Though the description of the *Mona Lisa* in "Leonardo da Vinci" is not authentic art criticism, one cannot say that many of the things which WP saw in her were not a part of Leonardo's world:

Leonardo had an ambiguous soul, and WP excelled at describing ambiguous souls. Several passages in the essays of *The Renaissance* anticipate passages in the imaginary portraits and *Marius the Epicurean*. A morbid interest in death and faded things pervades WP's writings. The merit of *The Renaissance* does not lie in its value as history or a new presentation of cultural values, but in the fact that it is a work of art in itself, an individual reaction by a unique sensibility to certain figures in the Renaissance. [In Italian.]

603 Praz, Mario. PROSPETTIVA DELLA LETTERATURA INGLESE DA CHAUCER A V. WOOLF (Prospect of English Literature from Chaucer to V. Woolf) (Milan: Bompiani, 1946), pp. 12, 33, 44, 45, 232, 815–39.
[Passing favorable references and a brief bio-bibliographical introduction to WP. Pp. 817–39 contain an Italian translation of Lionel Johnson's "The Work of Mr. Pater" (FORTNIGHTLY REVIEW, LXII [Sept 1894], 352–67, reprinted in Johnson's POST LIMINIUM [Lond: 1911]).] [In Italian.]

604 Roditi, Edouard. "Oscar Wilde's Poetry as Art History," POETRY, LXVII (March 1946), 322–38; absorbed in OSCAR WILDE (Norfolk, Conn: New Directions, 1947), pp. 21–39.
In Wilde's "Charmides" there is an idealized vision of antiquity that he shared with many nineteenth-century artists, including WP. Following WP's discovery of the "decadent beauties" of the PERVIGILIUM VENERIS, many Oxford undergraduates began to employ "almost Romanesque or Byzantine words" in their Latin compositions.

605 Sander, Ernst. "Nachwort" (Afterword), *Imaginäre Porträts (Imaginary Portraits)*, by Walter Pater, ed and trans by Ernst Sander (Hamburg: V. Schröder, 1946), pp. 239–61.
If WP had written nothing besides his essays, he would still hold an honorable and incontestable place in the history of ideas in his own and succeeding times, but in the *Imaginary Portraits* he reached the pinnacle of his greatness in creating a new art form. The philosophy of the "Conclusion" is a noble and passionate Epicureanism that was misunderstood by a later generation, and especially by Oscar Wilde: WP's ideal was fullness of life, not lust. "A Prince of Court Painters," "Denys l'Auxerrois," "Sebastian Van Storck," and "Duke Carl of Rosenmold" can be seen as the four movements of a sonata (Allegro lamentoso, Adagio, Scherzo, Allegro). [An enthusiastic general appreciation followed by a fairly long summary of WP's life.] [In German.]

606 Tillotson, Geoffrey. ENGLISH POETRY IN THE NINETEENTH CENTURY: THE FIGURE IN THE CARPET (Lond: Birkbeck College, University of London, 1946); rptd as "English Poetry in the Nineteenth Century," in CRITICISM AND THE NINETEENTH CENTURY (Lond: Athlone P, 1951); rptd (Hamden, Conn: Archon, 1967), pp. 188–228.

In the writings of Thomas Carlyle, John Henry Newman, John Ruskin, Matthew Arnold, George Eliot, and WP, much of the prose belongs as much to poetry as it does to the "prose of thinking," and in *Appreciations* WP saw that poetry was beginning its future as poetry in prose form. Though WP said that nineteenth-century verse was lawless, if one considers the best poetry of the period, it actually obeys the only law that counts—that the matter must be appropriately expressed. In speaking of the poetry of science in "Sir Thomas Browne," WP adapts phrases by Tennyson.

607 Tillotson, Geoffrey. "Pater, Mr. Rose, and the 'Conclusion' of *The Renaissance*," ESSAYS AND STUDIES BY MEMBERS OF THE ENGLISH ASSOCIATION, XXXII (1946), 44–60; rptd with revisions in CRITICISM AND THE NINETEENTH CENTURY (Lond: Athlone P, 1951); rptd (Hamden, Conn: Archon, 1967), pp. 124–46.

W. H. Mallock's claim, in a letter to Thomas Wright, that the satire of WP as "Mr. Rose" in THE NEW REPUBLIC "was meant to represent an attitude of mind rather than a man" is disingenuous: Mr. Rose is derived from WP the man and from the Pre-Raphaelites and hedonists, the type to which he was thought to belong. But once the reader realizes the identity of the individual satirized, that individual becomes "the helpless repository of everything said of the type," and WP "had to bear the full brunt of both the individual and the typical." When WP omitted the "Conclusion" from the second edition of *The Renaissance,* THE NEW REPUBLIC had already appeared in BELGRAVIA, and among those "young men" who WP felt might have been misled by the "Conclusion" were probably Oscar Wilde and Mallock himself. The revisions in the "Conclusion" as printed in the third edition of *The Renaissance,* however, are slighter in volume than in substance, though Mr. Rose could still have been derived from that version. There are flaws in the argument of the "Conclusion" which Mallock exploited. The "Conclusion" is to a certain extent the poignant confession of a man who exercised severe moral constraint "with great completeness in life, if not with a firm-minded completeness in [his] writings," and it must be read with certain revealing passages in "Winckelmann" and "The Child in the House" in mind. Like Matthew Arnold's CULTURE AND ANARCHY, *The Renaissance* was an attempt to make "the middle-class mind more lovely." Though Mallock and Wilde were misled by the "Conclusion," John Morley, in his review of *The Renaissance,* was not: he saw that WP was not recommending a complete scheme for life and understood WP better than as yet WP himself did. The "Conclusion" should be read with "Winckelmann," which offers a different remedy for the human condition: there, WP is content to deal with people as they are, "as people who, if they turn to literature at all for an interpretation of their daily lives, turn not to Greek literature but to novels." For WP the nineteenth century was the age of great novelists, unlike Arnold, "who expected a little too much of the Greeks and not enough of George Eliot."

1947

608 Baker, Joseph E. "Aesthetic Surface in the Novel," TROLLOPIAN, II (Sept 1947), 91–106.

In his "pseudo-novel," *Marius the Epicurean,* WP overstresses one difference between novel and drama by overdoing the scenic and social description, and he "has failed in handling an even more obvious difference, namely, that a novel should include narration of action as part of its own literary surface, whereas in a play the action is added by the actors."

609 Bonnerot, Louis. MATTHEW ARNOLD, POÈTE: ESSAI DE BIOGRAPHIE PSYCHOLOGIQUE (Matthew Arnold, Poet: Essay in Psychological Biography) (Paris: Didier, 1947), pp. 358–59, 464.

One is tempted to reproach Arnold for his lack of sympathy for Greek art and to oppose him to Goethe and WP, the latter of whom, in "Winckelmann," saw the Greek ideal reaching its highest expression in Greek art. But perhaps Arnold was more just than WP, who felt that conflict was necessary to relieve the ennui of perfection. Arnold tried to eliminate that discordance in himself, while WP welcomed it with "suspect" eagerness. Physical beauty was finally of secondary importance to the Greeks. In "The Scholar Gypsy" and "Thyrsis," Arnold achieved what WP in "The School of Giorgione" called "that modulated unison of landscape and persons." [In French.]

610 Carritt, E. F. AN INTRODUCTION TO AESTHETICS (Lond & NY: Hutchinson's University Library, [1947]); rptd (1949), pp. 45, 74, 96, 97, 110, 132.

What WP calls the addition of strangeness to beauty was the first idea associated with the word *romantic;* added later was the idea, articulated by WP, that that strangeness originates in the depths of the imagination.

611 Cazamian, Louis. SYMBOLISME ET POÉSIE: L'EXAMPLE ANGLAIS (Symbolism and Poetry: The English Example) (Neuchâtel: Éditions de la Baconnière, 1947), pp. 133, 140, 141.

The work of WP is a commentary on the secret cult of melancholy hinted at in John Keats's "Ode on Melancholy." The term *suggestive,* which was considered to be somewhat suspicious at the time, was often used by WP. From the time of Walter Savage Landor and Thomas De Quincey to John Ruskin, J. H. Shorthouse, and WP, a new kind of evocative and singing prose began to be written which, except for the absence of regular meter, is indistinguishable from poetry. [In French.]

612 Digeon, Aurélien. HISTOIRE ILLUSTRÉE DE LA LITTÉRATURE ANGLAISE (Illustrated History of English Literature) (Paris: Didier, 1947), pp. 368–70, 372.

In WP there is none of the dogmatism of Matthew Arnold or of the historical method of Hippolyte Taine. His stylistic care was fairly new in English literature, and that impeccable style is the chief merit of *Marius the Epicurean*. The historical veil that clothes WP's moral nihilism in *Marius* is fairly transparent. WP combined great liberty of thought with great prudence, apparently wanting to protect at all costs his existence as a pure intellectual, retired from the world. His influence, though negligible as far as the general public was concerned, was profound on his own generation and the next one. [In French.]

> **613** Eckhoff, Lorentz. "Den Estetiske Bevegelse" (The Aesthetic Movement), EDDA, XLVII (1947), 81–97.

The opposition to conventionality and materialism which characterizes *Imaginary Portraits* as well as the aesthetic movement in general is especially noteworthy in "Apollo in Picardy." Here the Christian milieu is subverted by a "peculiar atmosphere of satanic wildness and defiance." The skeptical attitude toward Christianity likewise typical of the movement is also evident in *Marius the Epicurean*. [In Norwegian.]

> **614** Gooch, G. P. "Historical Novels," ESSAYS BY DIVERS HANDS, nsXXIII (1947), 52–71.

If *Marius the Epicurean* is classified as a historical novel, it "must claim high rank," though it should probably be considered as a philosophical romance.

> **615** Haydn, Hiram. "The Last of the Romantics: An Introduction to the Symbolism of William Butler Yeats," SEWANEE REVIEW, LV (April–June 1947), 297–323.

In "The Body of the Father Christian Rosencrux" Yeats echoes both WP and William Blake.

> **616** Hough, Graham. "Books in General," NEW STATESMAN AND NATION, XXXIV (29 Nov 1947), 433.

Oxford exerted an unfortunately repressive influence on WP's writings: his reticence is generally the sort that results from not saying what one means. WP is philosophically sophisticated but not philosophically creative, and he is imaginatively creative in comparatively short flights, as in the imaginary portraits; in *Marius the Epicurean*, he has trouble filling the larger canvas. "His favorite cultural myth is the impact of a golden paganism on the foggy northern world." In his treatment of that theme in "Duke Carl of Rosenmold," for Duke Carl we may read WP of Brasenose, "cherishing a private religion of art in a world of mahogany-table diners-out, efficient administrators and industrious researchers." What WP intends to say in his use of that theme is that the Anglican public-school version of the classical world is not the only one, "that paganism implies passion and cruelty as well as the extension-lecture virtues"; but the shadow of Mrs. Humphry Ward lurked in the background: "there are the young men to be considered." In "A Prince of Court Painters" and "Sebastian Van Storck" WP excels in relating painting or a philosophical attitude to an emotional temperament or to a culture. He can write of people only by reflecting on their time, not by showing them in action, and thus his fiction is half criticism.

617 Logan, James Venable. WORDSWORTHIAN CRITICISM: A GUIDE AND BIBLIOGRAPHY (Columbus: Ohio State UP, 1947); rptd (1961), pp. 49, 52–53, 57, 60, 62, 63, 65, 169.

WP "treats with skill" several aspects of Wordsworth's poetry, but "the most remarkable thing" in WP's "Wordsworth" is "his apprehension of Wordsworth's doctrine of the presence of life in the objects of nature, of man as a part of nature, of the revival of the idea of the *anima mundi,*" and of Wordsworth's sincerity of feeling and diction.

618 Mulgan, John, and D. M. Davin. AN INTRODUCTION TO ENGLISH LITERATURE (Oxford: Clarendon P, 1947), pp. 136–37.

Sir Leslie Stephen and WP illustrate the distinction between the critic who is more interested in research, scholarship, and "its conservation of the fact," and the critic who attempts to assess "literary value as such." WP's prose is "both rich and subtle, musical, full of delicate shades, but always held in check by a firm classical sense."

619 Patmore, Derek. "Introduction," SELECTED WRITINGS OF WALTER PATER (Lond: Falcon P, 1947); rptd (1949), pp. 7–15.

All through his life, WP reacted against his own ugliness, and it is notable that the heroes of *Imaginary Portraits* are handsome. This detail is significant because many of his writings are autobiographical, and, his life being so uneventful, it is necessary to seek clues in his works to his complex character. As a youth, WP "longed to be a brilliant, handsome boy like the heroes he was to imagine in his writings, and he resented his own ugliness and lack of prowess in games." On the evidence of his works, he was unhappy at school. "Diaphaneitè" contains the first hints of WP's later style and philosophy. "Italy called forth all the sensuous and subtle qualities of his imagination and intellect." WP's prose in *The Renaissance* may be compared to D. G. Rossetti's poetry: "Here was criticism as a fine art, written in prose which the reader lingered over as over poetry, modulated prose which made the splendour of Ruskin seem gaudy, the neatness of Matthew Arnold a mincing neatness, and the brass sound strident in the orchestra of Carlyle." Whole passages in Oscar Wilde's THE PICTURE OF DORIAN GRAY recall WP's ideas and style. The hero of *Marius the Epicurean* is a projection of WP, but the novel is a "magnificent failure" because it lacks narrative skill and has inset passages which obstruct the story line. Several traits of WP are revealed in his writings: he had a Proustian preoccupation with the strange and unexpected aspects of life, there was a cruel streak in him, and he was fascinated with soldiers. No other writer wrote such fastidious and careful prose. In *Greek Studies* he shows a remarkable understanding of Greek art and the Greek character.

620 Praz, Mario. "Gli Interni di Proust" (Proust's Interiors), LET-
TERATURA (Florence) (Nov–Dec 1947), 61–71; rptd in LA CASA DELLA
FAMA (Milan: Ricciardi, 1952), pp. 267–83.
Marcel Proust's analysis of peculiar odors in some provincial rooms in DU CÔTÉ
DE CHEZ SWANN vies in subtlety with that masterpiece of interior description,
WP's "The Child in the House." [In Italian.]

621 Roditi, Edouard. OSCAR WILDE (Norfolk, Conn: New Directions,
1947), pp. 6, 18, 20, 23, 34, 53–54, 59, 69, 97, 176, 207–9, 214, 228;
[partly derived from Roditi's "Oscar Wilde's Poetry as Art History"
(1946)].
Most of WP's followers in criticism, "inspired by his tastes rather than by his few
principles," became either archaeologists or classical scholars, "or else rather
hedonistic or intellectually irresponsible decadents and impressionists." It was
only later in his career that Wilde understood what WP had meant when he told
Wilde that prose was more difficult to write than verse. WP's disciples in Victorian
England included not only the Decadents—even Mark Rutherford, a stern
moralist, was indebted to WP for some of his ideas. Wilde was a rare Aristotelian
among the many Platonists and Neo-Platonists of nineteenth-century aesthetics,
and rejected, on Aristotelian grounds, "Ruskin's confusion of ethics and aesthetics, and likewise saw the limitations of Pater, an 'intellectual impressionist'
who was doomed to be 'least successful' when his subject was abstract and
therefore more an artist than a thinker."

622 Roe, Frederick William. VICTORIAN PROSE (NY: Ronald P, 1947),
pp. xi, xxix, 567–69, 726–33.
WP was never in the truest sense an aesthete, "since for him as for Plato aesthetics,
basically and characteristically, was 'ever in close connection with ethics.' " But,
like the hero of *Gaston de Latour,* he had "a sober taste for delicate things," and he
saw art as a refuge from the vulgarity in the world. When he "expressed his views
in extreme and somewhat ambiguous language," as he did in the "Conclusion"
[*The Renaissance*], WP became the "hierophant of the aesthetes." Though the
appeal of his work will always be limited, and his reputation has had its "ebbs and
flows," "nothing in the field of letters seems more certain than that his place is now
secure among the prose masters of his time." For WP, truth was imaginative truth,
i.e., truth "expressed in sensuous forms, made beautiful by the artist. . . . Nothing
could be farther from a superficial or frivolous aestheticism." Aestheticism for
him was a serious matter, the concern of what he, S. T. Coleridge, and Matthew
Arnold regarded as "the highest faculty in man—imaginative reason." The in-
completeness of his aesthetics lies in the fact that he saw the end of life as
contemplation rather than action. To describe WP's criticism as "irresponsible
impressionism" is to misunderstand it. If his criticism does not seem to rely on
external standards, it is because he applies his standards implicitly. If his style is
sometimes languorous and cumbersome, he nevertheless wrote "distinguished
prose": though self-conscious, he is never insincere, and he "never permits his

manner to get the better of his theme." [Pp. 726–33 contain the texts, with annotations, of the "Preface," "Leonardo da Vinci," the "Conclusion," "Wordsworth," "Romanticism," "The Child in the House," and Chapter XVIII of *Marius the Epicurean.*]

623 Schirmer, Walter F. DER EINFLUSS DER DEUTSCHEN LITERATUR AUF DIE ENGLISCHE IM 19. JAHRHUNDERT (The Influence of German Literature on the English in the Nineteenth Century) (Halle/Saale: Max Niemeyer, 1947), pp. 119–20.

While Matthew Arnold sought to unite art and life in order that art might perfect life, for WP art and life were equally the material of life. WP's philosophy of life and art in the "Conclusion" really belongs to the period of the breakdown of Victorianism, when the influence of French literature replaced that of German on English literature. With the exception of Goethe, WP's knowledge of German literature does not seem to have been great. There is a relationship between Goethe's "original essence" (*Urwesen*) and WP's "spiritual form." [In German.]

624 Stoll, Elmer Edgar. "Critics at Cross-Purposes," JOURNAL OF ENGLISH LITERARY HISTORY, XIV (Dec 1947), 320–28.

Contrary to what Oscar Wilde (in "The Critic as Artist") and Padraic Colum (in his introduction to Volume XII of the 1923 edition of Wilde's works) seem to believe, WP was actually agreeing with Matthew Arnold on the matter of seeing the object as it really is (in the "Preface" to *The Renaissance*). There is no sign of "difference or dissent" in WP's discussion of the matter, and though he asks what the work of art is "to *me,*" the final step is still to know the object "as it really is."

625 Tindall, William York. FORCES IN MODERN BRITISH LITERATURE, 1885–1946 (NY: Knopf, 1947); rptd (Freeport, NY: Books for Libraries P, 1970), pp. 6, 8, 9, 10, 11, 12, 13, 14, 15, 16, 17, 18, 19, 20, 27, 154, 206, 213, 214, 216, 308, 378; rptd (NY: Vintage, 1956); (1960).

In the "Conclusion" [*The Renaissance*] WP "summarized his German, French, and English predecessors in a prose that was itself the best argument for the cause of art." Lord Henry Wotton's "New Hedonism" in Oscar Wilde's THE PICTURE OF DORIAN GRAY is a mixture of J.-K. Huysmans and WP. Under WP's "spell" George Moore "discovered the sentence, the paragraph, and finally, to Wilde's amusement, style." Ernest Dowson's poem "Non sum qualis eram bonae sub regno Cynarae" symbolizes the conflict between WP's ideal and reality. Lionel Johnson's "all but classical" verse represents WP's other side, his religious austerity. Arthur Symons's poetry owes almost as much to WP as to Baudelaire. W. B. Yeats's story "Rosa Alchemica" and his expository prose were influenced by WP. WP's critical forebears were William Hazlitt, Charles Baudelaire, and Immanuel Kant. Among WP's followers, Symons most closely approximated his method. Virginia Woolf's criticism is the climax of the tradition of WP, and in her fiction she gives a better sense of passing moments than WP. Though Henry James's ideas were similar to those of A. C. Swinburne and WP, he did not come into conflict with the middle class, since his treatment of their depravity was too subtle to offend. Arthur Machen's stories "unite the worlds of Pater and Huysmans." G. M. Hopkins combined WP and piety, and "made discordant concords of heaven and earth."

> **626** Woodring, Carl R. "W. H. Mallock: A Neglected Wit," MORE BOOKS, XXII (Sept 1947), 243–56.

WP, who is satirized as "Mr. Rose" in Mallock's THE NEW REPUBLIC, wished to work quietly and did not want the notoriety that Mallock and the aesthetes would bring him. He apparently did not realize that "his books were written in a more intimate tone than he cared to use in private conversation." Before T. S. Eliot, Mallock was aware of Matthew Arnold's influence on WP.

> **627** Zanco, Aurelio. STORIA DELLA LETTERATURA INGLESE, Vol. 2: DALLA RESTAURAZIONE AI GIORNI NOSTRI (History of English Literature, Vol. 2: From the Restoration to the Present) (Turin: Chiantore, 1947), pp. 482, 651, 711–25, 726, 729, 735, 736, 738, 739, 743, 751, 752; rptd (Turin: Loescher, 1958).

The sobriety of John Henry Newman's prose style influenced WP. There is nothing artificial or morbid in the writings of William Morris, unlike those of WP, or even more, of Oscar Wilde. WP saw an ideal portrait of himself in Winckelmann: both were converts to the religion of beauty. *Marius the Epicurean,* WP's masterpiece, is historically and archaeologically accurate and notable for its stylistic refinement, but in the final analysis it lacks vitality and is cold, the product more of meticulous workmanship than of inspired creativity. "Sebastian Van Storck" is fundamentally autobiographical in that one can recognize WP in the character of Sebastian. In "Denys l'Auxerrois" WP illustrates symbolically that a vein of paganism which was to emerge in the Renaissance lurked beneath the surface even in the Middle Ages. The characters that WP depicts in the *Imaginary Portraits* are obsessed with a need to find truth in beauty, a characteristic of WP himself. There is a profound analogy between *Marius* and *Gaston de Latour,* since in both WP describes the doubt of dissatisfied souls who finally arrive at new conceptions of life (implied in the case of the unfinished *Gaston*). WP's style finally fatigues the reader. The influence of WP's ideas is evident in Wilde's INTENTIONS and THE PICTURE OF DORIAN GRAY; Dorian is derived from certain figures in WP's works, like Duke Carl ["Duke Carl of Rosenmold"] and Flavian [*Marius the Epicurean*]. [In Italian.]

1948

> **628** Aldington, Richard. "Introduction," WALTER PATER: SELECTED WORKS (Lond: Heinemann; NY: Duell, Sloan & Pearce, 1948), pp. 1–27.

WP's purpose in *The Renaissance* was not to relate history but to reconstruct imaginatively a number of Renaissance personalities. In that volume, he repudiates the abstract approach to art of the Hegelians and the ethical views of John Ruskin. W. H. Mallock's THE NEW REPUBLIC "sums up extremely well the attitude of contemporary society towards Pater, aestheticism, and indeed any art and literature not subservient to religious, commercial and class interests." WP was neither a prose-poet nor a critic exclusively, but something between the two, with the critic predominating. Goethe was the greatest influence on his criticism. The suppressed poet in WP gradually developed essays into "imaginary portraits." "Like the men of the Renaissance, Pater wanted to make the best of both religious worlds, to run with the pagan hare and hunt with the Christian hounds." WP failed to recognize in Botticelli's madonnas a type of feminine beauty that still persists in Italy. He tended to put a good deal of himself into his historical portraits of Pico della Mirandola, Botticelli, and Watteau. His portraits are generally built around "documents" included in the piece, a picture, or a poem, or translations. He was a master at prose translation. "Demeter and Persephone" is based on a counterpoint of translated passages from the Homeric hymns, Theocritus' "Thalysia," Ovid's FASTI, and Claudian's "Rape of Persephone." *Marius the Epicurean* should be read as a prose idyll and an imaginary portrait rather than as a novel. In that work, WP was more interested in his own sensations and ideas than he was in Marius. The chapters of *Gaston de Latour* can be detached and read as separate essays. The most successful adaptation of WP's methods and attitudes is Rachel Annand Taylor's LEONARDO THE FLORENTINE. "To take subjects which the vulgar consider 'dry' and the highbrows vote 'academic,' and to invest them with new glamour, a wistful attractiveness, is part of Pater's achievement."

629 Berenson, Bernard. AESTHETICS AND HISTORY IN THE VISUAL ARTS (NY: Pantheon, 1948), pp. 105, 106, 194, 195; rptd as AESTHETICS AND HISTORY (Lond: Constable, 1950); rptd (1955); rptd (NY: Pantheon; NY: Doubleday, 1953); rptd (1954); (1965).
"I cannot sufficiently acknowledge my debt to Pater for what he wrote about Botticelli and Giorgione," yet when it came to individual pictures, WP was as ready to admire a Giorgionesque work or a product of Botticelli's workshop as he was an autograph painting.

630 Betjeman, John. "Introduction," THE EIGHTEEN-NINETIES, ed by Martin Secker (Lond: Richards P, 1948), pp. xi–xvi.
WP's dictum that art should have nothing to do with social consciousness, philosophy, morals, ethics, or laws of life is the equivalent in prose and verse of abstract painting.

631 Bhate, M. G. LITERATURE AND LITERARY CRITICISM (Bombay: Karnatak Publishing House, 1948), pp. 32, 100.
Impressionistic criticism "has a childlike quality of living completely in the present moment, without looking before and after," the quality cultivated by WP's

Marius [*Marius the Epicurean*]. In accepting the emotional content of poetry, Alfred Tennyson, the Pre-Raphaelites, WP, and the aesthetes are in a direct line from the Romantics.

> **632** Brown, Calvin S., Jr. MUSIC AND LITERATURE: A COMPARISON OF THE ARTS (Athens: University of Georgia P, 1948); rptd (1963), pp. 101, 194.

WP's dictum in "The School of Giorgione" that "all art constantly strives towards the condition of music" is theoretical rather than historical. Though form and substance are inseparable in music more than in any other art, the assumption of such an identity as the ultimate end of art is peculiar to the aesthetics of the romantics and their successors. Walt Whitman's "When Lilacs Last in the Dooryard Bloomed" approaches WP's goal of identity more closely than most literary works.

> **633** Cecil, David [Lord]. "Fin de Siècle," LISTENER, XXXIX (27 May 1948), 855–57; rptd with revisions in IDEAS AND BELIEFS OF THE VICTORIANS: AN HISTORIC REVALUATION OF THE VICTORIAN AGE, ed by BBC Third Programme (Lond: Sylvan P, 1949); rptd (NY: Dutton, 1966), pp. 365–71.

The "general view of life" of the aesthete is found in WP's "Conclusion" to *The Renaissance*. Two consequences of WP's doctrine are that it tends to make one contemplative rather than active and that one does not divide things according to moral categories. To Benjamin Jowett, WP's doctrines were morally irresponsible. The bohemian poets and artists of the Nineties tended to neglect self-discipline and to exaggerate the moral aspects of aestheticism, developing it in ways that would have shocked WP. Aestheticism influenced many later writers, like Virginia Woolf, though even she could not make aestheticism completely satisfying as a guide for living: since life contains much that is ugly, even if one could exclude the ugly, one cannot maintain continuously a proper receptivity to the beautiful. Moreover, aestheticism contains an unresolved discord: "It says on the one hand that life has no absolute significance, and on the other that beauty gives one a feeling of intense significance." Woolf seems finally to have realized this.

> **634** Cecil, David [Lord]. "Ideas and Beliefs of the Victorians: Writers and their Books," LISTENER, XXXIX (5 Feb 1948), 212–13; rptd as part of "Introducing the Ideas and Beliefs of the Victorians," IDEAS AND BELIEFS OF THE VICTORIANS: AN HISTORIC REVALUATION OF THE VICTORIAN AGE, ed by BBC Third Programme (Lond: Sylvan P, 1949); rptd (NY: Dutton, 1966), pp. 23–26.

Many modern writers, including Virginia Woolf and the Sitwell family, have developed WP's aesthetic point of view.

> **635** Chew, Samuel C. THE NINETEENTH CENTURY AND AFTER (1789– 1939), Bk IV of A LITERARY HISTORY OF ENGLAND, ed by Albert C.

Baugh (NY & Lond: Appleton-Century-Crofts, 1948); rptd (1967), pp. 1165, 1475–79, 1490, 1494, 1497, 1539; rptd (Lond: Routledge & Kegan Paul, 1967).

A comparison of WP's portrait of Montaigne in *Gaston de Latour* with Walter Savage Landor's imaginary conversation between Scaliger and Montaigne brings out interesting similarities and differences between WP and Landor; WP's *Imaginary Portraits* and "A Conversation Not Imaginary" in *Marius the Epicurean* also recalls Landor. Despite his insistence on moral values in art, John Ruskin, in seeking to make the social order comely, anticipated WP's advocacy of the comeliness of the individual life. In "The Child in the House," it is difficult to distinguish between the autobiographical and the imaginary. Though his later works exhibit compassion, there is no evidence that WP ever extended that compassion to social action. His two dominant temperamental traits were sensuous awareness and a realization of the brevity of life. There is a "troubling unwholesomeness" in all of WP's works; the "attraction exerted by mysterious iniquity" is most powerfully expressed in "Apollo in Picardy." In his later works there is "an increasing emphasis upon the beauty of order and upon the need to discipline the soul." WP is closer to Matthew Arnold than to Ruskin in his "fastidiousness," though he lacks Arnold's "superciliousness." The "Preface" to *The Renaissance* has been often misunderstood, but WP's impressionism did lead to "a confusion between the critical and creative processes," which in turn led him to falsifications of history. WP is less sensual and more profound than another impressionist critic, Anatole France. There are misinterpretations of evidence even in *Plato and Platonism*. Though his search for the "formula" of the subjects of his essays is suggestive, it leads to distortions, and in each case the quality he finds in his subjects is one possessed by WP himself. *Marius* and *Gaston* "are projections of Pater's inner life into other epochs, transitional as was his own." The picture of early Christianity in *Marius* is as historically fallacious as the description of Sparta in *Plato*. It is well that WP late in life did not try, as in his youth, to go into the clergy, since he remained until the end "a fastidious pragmatist"; it is thus no wonder that Marius's evolution toward Christianity was generally not noticed, "while the cult of Beauty gained new adherents," and that *Gaston* went unfinished. In WP's writings the manner is more important than the matter, and he "influenced no mind of absolutely first rank." Contemporary readers quickly noticed an "unlike likeness" between Joseph Henry Shorthouse's JOHN INGLESANT and *Marius*. WP's attitude toward George Moore's CONFESSIONS OF A YOUNG MAN was "somewhat condescending." In THE BROOK KERITH Moore is more cosmopolitan than WP, and his HÉLOÏSE AND ABÉLARD contains "exquisite little genre pieces" in the manner of WP's *Imaginary Portraits*.

636 Curtius, Ernst Robert. EUROPÄISCHE LITERATUR UND LATEINISCHES MITTELALTER (European Literature and the Latin Middle Ages) (Bern: A. Francke, 1948); rptd (1954); (1961), pp. 400, 401, 404; trans by Willard R. Trask as EUROPEAN LITERATURE AND THE LATIN

MIDDLE AGES (Princeton: Princeton UP, 1953); rptd (1967); rptd (Lond: Routledge & Kegan Paul; NY: Pantheon, 1953), pp. 396, 397, 400; rptd (NY: Harper, 1953); (1963).

WP's concept of a "House Beautiful" of creative minds, in the "Postcript" to *Appreciations*, is a landmark in literary criticism, since it replaces a standard of obedience to rules and imitation with a standard of creativity as a criterion for excellence in the arts. [In German.]

637 Du Bos, Charles. JOURNAL, 1924–25 (Paris: Corrêa, 1948), pp. 30, 31, 96, 119, 120, 122, 143, 146, 176, 182, 190, 192, 234, 256, 326, 361, 381.

In "Wordsworth," WP masterfully establishes the difference between those whose ideal is being and those whose ideal is doing. The importance of the memory is identical in Joseph Joubert and WP. Marius needs an "assistant" as a receptacle for the most perfect moments of his life. [In French.]

638 Ellmann, Richard. YEATS: THE MAN AND THE MASKS (NY: Macmillan, 1948); (Lond: Macmillan, 1949), pp. 71, 136, 145; rptd (NY: Dutton, 1958); rptd (Lond: Faber & Faber, 1961).

Marius eventually becomes a Christian "out of good taste as it were." The death of WP in 1894, and Lionel Johnson's work on a biography of him, prompted W. B. Yeats to unsuccessful efforts to imitate WP's prose rhythms.

639 Ferguson, Wallace K. THE RENAISSANCE IN HISTORICAL THOUGHT: FIVE CENTURIES OF INTERPRETATION (Cambridge, Mass: Houghton Mifflin, 1948), p. 239.

WP's *The Renaissance*, which "has achieved the permanent status of a minor classic," is the finest of the collections of critical essays on Italian Renaissance art published during the fifty years following the appearance of Jacob Burckhardt's CIVILIZATION OF THE RENAISSANCE IN ITALY (1860).

640 Freeman, William. THE LIFE OF LORD ALFRED DOUGLAS, SPOILT CHILD OF GENIUS (Lond: Herbert Joseph, 1948), pp. 66–67, 72, 79.

Douglas was introduced to WP, "that old-maidish dabbler in eroticism," by Oscar Wilde. Douglas tried to like WP, but aside from WP being no conversationalist, Douglas did not like his prose, which he considered "artificial and finicky." WP, along with A. C. Swinburne and James McNeill Whistler, was under consideration as a model for Bunthorne in Gilbert and Sullivan's PATIENCE.

641 Gere, John. "Catalogue," PRE-RAPHAELITE PAINTERS, ed by Robin Ironside (Lond: Phaidon, 1948), pp. 22–49.

Simeon Solomon's turning to classical subjects for his paintings in the late 1860s may have been influenced by his association with A. C. Swinburne and WP, and his prose-poem, "A Vision of Love Revealed in Sleep," must also owe something to that association.

642 Godfrey, F. M. "Rebirth of an Aesthetic Ideal; An Essay in Two Parts on Three Masters of Art Appreciation: Pater, Wilde and Fry," STUDIO, CXXXV (May, June 1948), 150–51, 182–85.

In a sense, WP as a writer is the equivalent of the Impressionist painters: he probes the artist's vision and observes how objects are dissipated into flickering impressions under the influence of one's reflection. "The impressions . . . like those of Monet or Pissaro are bound by the individual personality that gives them form." WP's belief in individual perfection was Greek and recalls the prayer of Phaedrus at the end of Plato's dialogue. WP's demand that art should be independent of "mere intelligence" and have no responsibility to its subject is ahead of its time and leads to Roger Fry's conception of "visual music." Fry's belief that art distills a new creation from visual sensations is reminiscent of WP's "feeling for spiritual line and colour." Wilde, like WP, wanted the artist to superimpose his own vision on life and nature.

643 Grassi, Luigi. "Walter Pater e il Rinascimento" (Walter Pater and the Renaissance), EMPORIUM (Bergamo), CVII (Jan 1948), 11–14.

For WP the correct attribution of a work of art is less important than the rapport established between the work and his own idea of it. In the description of the *Mona Lisa* in "Leonardo da Vinci" one finds a projection of WP's romantic and decadent sensibility, a new poetical synthesis which, though spiritually different from Leonardo's artistic vision, is inspired by it. The concept of all art aspiring to the condition of music in "The School of Giorgione" leads to a theory of pure form, free of content, which has become important in some forms of modern art. WP's romantic criticism is exactly the opposite of the positivistic criticism of Giovanni Morelli. [Much of this essay is a summary of some of the principal ideas in *The Renaissance*.] [In Italian.]

644 Hough, Graham. "Marius the Latitudinarian," CAMBRIDGE JOURNAL, I (April 1948), 409–28.

[This article and Hough's "A Study of Yeats," CAMBRIDGE JOURNAL (Feb 1949) constitute a major portion of Hough's observations on WP in THE LAST ROMANTICS (1949), q.v. for abstract.]

645 Huppé, Bernard F. "Walter Pater on Plato's Aesthetics," MODERN LANGUAGE QUARTERLY, IX (Sept 1948), 315–21.

"Plato's Aesthetics," the final chapter of *Plato and Platonism,* addresses itself to the problem of Plato's banishing art from his ideal city, but it avoids the issue. Plato's belief that the highest good consists in contemplating the Ideal contrasts with WP's belief that the love of beauty is the highest end. WP notes that Plato recognized that it is possible to love physical beauty for its own sake, but he fails to point out that Plato believed that it is wrong to love beauty as anything but a manifestation of the abstract, universal Beauty revealed in the beautiful object. The "implication that Plato is intellectually linked with the art for art's sake school is as fallacious as it is ingenious: art for art's sake gives art a final value directly contrary to Plato's mistrust of art." WP finds that Plato was even too aesthetic, fearing art because he realized that he was too susceptible to its influence. The problem that WP saw in Plato, of a man who appreciates art but distrusts it, was troubling because it reflected WP's own love of art and his doubt of its final value: like the hero of *Marius the Epicurean,* he "loved the moment but needed the assurance of the eternal." WP refused to see in Plato anything contrary to his own aestheticism, and this avoidance of an issue is a tendency typical of Victorian impressionism.

646 Jennings, Richard. "Books in General," NEW STATESMAN AND NATION, XXXVI (13 Nov 1948), 421.

Is there to be a revival of WP? *The Renaissance* offended many because, unlike John Ruskin, WP did not believe that art should teach. WP excelled at short studies rather than prolonged pieces. In *Marius the Epicurean,* "which cannot be called a novel," nothing suggests that the hero has "a 'soul naturally Christian,' in humility of mind, in fear of the world, in mystical submissiveness." The implicit theme of *Marius* no longer interests readers, since the fascination of WP's public for religious doubts has disappeared in the twentieth century. WP's sister told the author that WP himself had wanted the words *in te, Domine, speravi* placed on his grave. It is because WP never lectures to us that we still enjoy reading him: "if he cannot bring us dogmas he can give us peace of mind."

647 Joad, C. E. M. DECADENCE: A PHILOSOPHICAL INQUIRY (Lond: Faber & Faber, 1948); (NY: Philosophical Library, 1949), pp. 95–96, 99, 101, 117, 124.

The meaning most often attributed to "decadence" is that experience is valuable for its own sake, as defined in the "Conclusion" to *The Renaissance.* WP's concept of the significance of experience as such is endorsed by Virginia Woolf's essay on modern fiction and is voiced by Bruno Rontini in Aldous Huxley's TIME MUST HAVE A STOP. Even WP would probably agree that the experiences which are pleasurable to the sadistic commandant of a concentration camp are not objectively valuable and ought not to be promoted.

648 Lynd, Robert. "Beauty Culture," OBSERVER (Lond), 5 Sept 1948, p. 3.

Though WP's writings were a liberating influence in the last quarter of the nineteenth century, they are unlikely to make new converts if they are ever again widely read: "the conception of the perfect life as a continuous and successful pursuit of 'exquisite' moments was not likely to appeal for long to the moralist that lurks in every normal man." The "Conclusion" [*The Renaissance*] could easily be interpreted as a call to "lotus-eating egoism." WP's prose, at its best, is "almost tremulous with life, though it is the prose of an enchanter who is indifferent to many of the concerns of mankind." [Review of WP, SELECTED WORKS, ed by Richard Aldington.]

649 March, Harold. THE TWO WORLDS OF MARCEL PROUST (Philadelphia: University of Pennsylvania P, 1948), pp. 9, 93.

Proust appeared to be familiar enough with WP's work to include in his notes to the translation of Ruskin's THE BIBLE OF AMIENS (1904) references to WP.

650 Merle, Robert. OSCAR WILDE ([Paris]: Hachette, [1948]); also pub as OSCAR WILDE: APPRÉCIATION D'UNE OEUVRE ET D'UNE DESTINÉE (Oscar Wilde: Appreciation of a Work and a Destiny) (Rennes: Imprimeries réunies, 1948), pp. 31, 32, 33, 34, 41, 88, 101, 116, 131, 138, 155, 157, 159, 175, 198, 210–11, 214, 216, 218, 222, 232, 233, 238–43, 244, 245, 250, 253, 291, 297, 302, 305, 307, 318, 481.

In his youth Wilde admired James McNeill Whistler more than WP or John Ruskin. One finds in WP, Wilde, and André Gide the characteristic of availability (*disponibilité*) to impressions and circumstances that is typical of the state of mind of the introvert. Verbal echoes of the description of the *Mona Lisa* in "Leonardo da Vinci" are found in two of Wilde's poems, "Charmides" and "My Voice," and one also finds rhythmical echoes of WP in Wilde. The roots of Wilde's paganism are in John Keats, A. C. Swinburne, and WP. In "The Critic as Artist" Wilde applies to the genre of the dialogue remarks he had earlier applied to WP's style in "Mr. Pater's Last Volume" (SPEAKER, 22 March 1890). Like WP, Wilde wrote a beautiful description of the *Mona Lisa*. There is an echo of a passage from "Winckelmann" in Wilde's "The English Renaissance of Art." Wilde may have absorbed some of Hegel's ideas from WP. The influence of WP on Wilde's DE PROFUNDIS is negligible. WP was the greatest influence on Wilde's critical thought. Wilde's reaction on first reading *The Renaissance* was that of one who found his own traits already developed in the writings of an older man. More than certain biographical facts, more clearly than the masculine friendships of *Marius the Epicurean*, "Winckelmann," which is a veiled apology for homosexuality, allows one to guess at the same mystery in WP that in the case of Wilde did not remain a mystery until the end. Wilde codified the rules of impressionistic criticism, which WP never did. There is a liberty, richness, and grace in Wilde's style that neither Matthew Arnold nor WP possessed to the same degree. Wilde could not designate *The Renaissance* as the book that had influenced Dorian Gray without compromising WP. [In French.]

651 O'Connor, William Van. "The Poet As Esthetician," QUARTERLY REVIEW OF LITERATURE, IV (1948), 311–18.

Though a number of poets in the 1890s took some of the dicta of WP as an excuse for "license, self-indulgence and avoidance of conventional conduct," writers like Gustave Flaubert and Robert Bridges utilized the same or similar dicta in the cause of "restraint, personal integrity and discipline." With Flaubert, WP believed that mind and soul give significance to literary form, and his emphasis is similar to that of Henry Adams, "whose lifelong search was for definition, purpose, for meaning."

652 Osawa, Minoru. (Woolf and Pater), NEW ENGLISH AND AMERICAN LITERATURE (Japan), I (1948), 56–61.

Virginia Woolf's heroine in MRS. DALLOWAY is based on WP's conception of "art for art's sake." Although she rarely mentions WP in her critical essays, she does acknowledge in her autobiography that one of WP's sisters helped her translate some Greek. Her awareness of the musical quality and potential of prose is reminiscent of WP. She lived her life in a Pater-like environment. [In Japanese.]

653 Peyre, Henri. LES GÉNÉRATIONS LITTÉRAIRES (Literary Generations) (Paris: Boivin, 1948), pp. 13, 35, 146.

The word *Victorian* has come to be so associated with complacency and sanctimonious hypocrisy that it does not fit such writers as WP, George Meredith, A. C. Swinburne, and others. Because they happened to flourish in the last two decades of a century, authors like WP, George Gissing, Lafcadio Hearn, Francis Thompson, Arthur Symons, and many others have fallen victim to being classified as "fin de siècle" by critics, artists whose despair at having come too late in a century too old pushed them to premature deaths, alcoholism, homosexuality, or conversion to Catholicism. [In French.]

654 Pick, John. "Divergent Disciples of Walter Pater," THOUGHT, XXIII (March 1948), 114–28.

WP's influence on the writers of the Nineties was almost entirely based on his early writings, particularly the "Conclusion" [*The Renaissance*]: most of his disciples did not take into consideration the fact that WP's thought changed between the 1860s and the 1890s. WP's purpose in *Marius the Epicurean* was twofold: to show the inadequacy of the theories of *The Renaissance* and to lead Marius to the threshold of Christianity. Marius's passage through and beyond the Epicurean and Heraclitean philosophies is significant, since it is here that we find WP's criticism of his earlier beliefs and that the "Christian philosophy finally fulfills most completely all the needs of Marius." The point of including in the novel the translation from Apuleius of the Cupid and Psyche story is that it shows that WP has passed from art for art's sake to a position which sees art as an idealizing power. WP's distinction between good and great art in "Style" and his implication in *Plato and Platonism* that art has an ethical function also illustrates his departure from his earlier position. The disciples who were followers of the earlier WP only were Oscar Wilde, George Moore, Arthur Symons, and Ernest Dowson. Wilde's THE PICTURE OF DORIAN GRAY is a novelized form of the "Conclusion," and Moore's CONFESSIONS OF A YOUNG MAN reads the "Conclusion" into *Marius*. Lionel Johnson, who "attributed a large share in his own conversion to Roman Catholicism" to *Marius,* was the only disciple who "grew with" WP. [Pick is mistaken in the dates of both *The Renaissance* and *Marius* and quotes incorrectly and misleadingly from WP's remarks to Vernon Lee on *Marius.*]

655 Read, Herbert. "Authors Old and New (9): Walter Pater," WORLD REVIEW, Nov 1948, pp. 56–59.

WP is in more need of rehabilitation than any other nineteenth-century English writer. When he died in 1894, his reputation was established, and his influence was increasing, but then came the trial of Oscar Wilde, and WP's reputation, along with Wilde's, went into a decline, though there was no reason for involving WP with Wilde's downfall. WP had "an instinctive sympathy for the struggles and aspirations of the artists of his own time, and a readiness to listen to 'the note of revolt,' as he called it, whenever and wherever sounded." When he is at his stylistic best, "one is aware that our language is, perhaps for the first time, being used in the full measure of its music and meaning."

> **656** Srinivasa Iyengar, K. R. GERARD MANLEY HOPKINS: THE MAN AND THE POET (Calcutta: Oxford UP, 1948); rptd (Folcroft, Pa: Folcroft P, 1969), pp. 14, 188.

Hopkins's best achievement in creative criticism is the Platonic dialogue on the origin of beauty, which he probably wrote for WP's "perusal and correction" while at Oxford.

> **657** Thomson, J. A. K. THE CLASSICAL BACKGROUND OF ENGLISH LITERATURE (Lond: Allen & Unwin, 1948); rptd (1950); (1962), pp. 249, 256; rptd (NY: Collier, 1962).

WP is superior to both John Addington Symonds and John Ruskin in that he is not excessively wordy or florid. He was "qualified in every way" to judge both Greek art and Greek literature, and *Marius the Epicurean* and *Plato and Platonism* could only have been written by a scholar. His view of antiquity, however, seems to have been formed by Ruskin, the Pre-Raphaelites, and the French Romantics, rather than by his reading in Greek, since he gives the impression of seeing only those things in the Greeks which appeal to the aesthetic sensibilities. A. E. Housman's interpretation of the ancient world, though colored by his personality, is based on a more exact knowledge of ancient languages than that possessed by either WP or Matthew Arnold.

> **658** Wilde, Oscar. THE TRIALS OF OSCAR WILDE, ed by Montgomery Hyde (Lond: William Hodge, 1948); rptd (1949); (1952); rptd as THE THREE TRIALS OF OSCAR WILDE (NY: University Books, 1956), pp. 124, 157, 229; rptd with revisions as OSCAR WILDE: FAMOUS TRIALS, 7 (Baltimore: Penguin, 1962).

A passage in Wilde's THE PICTURE OF DORIAN GRAY was altered after WP told him that it was "liable to misconstruction."

1949

659 Bertocci, Angelo Philip. CHARLES DU BOS AND ENGLISH LITERA-
TURE: A CRITIC AND HIS ORIENTATION (NY: Columbia U, King's Crown
P, 1949), pp. 45–47, 51–99, 141, 146, 149, 157, 160, 161 and *n,* 204, 223,
224, 234, 235, 240, 251, 252, 254, 259.

For Du Bos, WP was an enchanter of the faithful and the already converted rather
than an interpreter. Du Bos sought to mediate WP's criticism to the wider audience
of the common reader. For both Du Bos and WP, criticism should extract the
"virtue" of a work of art, and both had a sense of the intemporality of art and
rejected a distinction between form and content. In "Pascal," WP makes much of
his subject's "malady." In his criticism of Watteau, Du Bos, like WP in "A Prince
of Court Painters," senses the emergence of the spiritual from the physical. There
is a conflict in WP on the plane of style between a genius for external, pictorial
representation and the need for "shaping from within." The artist's instinct in WP
kept him safely within the bounds of the plastic and prevented him from posing
questions that criticism cannot answer. Du Bos intended writing a book on WP
simultaneously in English and French, which his editors announced as WALTER
PATER OU L'ASCÈTE DE LA BEAUTÉ. In *Marius the Epicurean,* WP's epicureanism
is ascetic; physical perfection is an instrument of mental and moral perfection, and
no distinction between body and soul is countenanced. For both Du Bos and WP,
asceticism at least makes the flesh capable of spirit, if it does not actually
spiritualize it. For Marius, what the eye perceives as perfect beauty is also truth,
and for WP, spiritual insight can be gained through the senses. In *Marius,* love for
things, leading him to assign all things equal value, is at war with a tendency to
arrange values in a hierarchy. In WP, aesthetic intuition develops into the moral
sense, or may be one with it. The description of the Panathenaic frieze in
"Winckelmann" best illustrates WP's dreams of Hellenism, but he was aware of
the darker aspects of Greek life. WP's Hellenism is an attempt to cure the soul
through the senses. But even in *The Renaissance* WP cannot escape from a
brooding sense of moral responsibility and intimations of evil. "There is something in Pater half in love with beautiful death in wars not of one's own making."
According to Du Bos, the spiritual evolution of WP from the "Conclusion"
through *Marius* to *Plato and Platonism* is marked by the restoration of the memory
in the economy of existence. Marius's life vacillates between compassion and
solitude, but he values that solitude because only then is he not really alone, since
solitude provides the companionship of his "other self" [the "divine companion"]. Ecstasy, for Marius, is the possibility of the vision, the descent of God that
may one day occur.

660 Bowra, C. Maurice. THE ROMANTIC IMAGINATION (Cambridge,
Mass: Harvard UP, 1949); rptd (1957); rptd (Lond: Oxford UP, 1950);
(1961); rptd (NY: Oxford UP, 1961), pp. 220, 242.

D. G. Rossetti pursued the beautiful more vigorously and consistently than did John Ruskin or WP. WP's statement in "The School of Giorgione" that all art aspires to the condition of music is apposite to A. C. Swinburne's ATALANTA IN CALYDON. In poetry, WP valued the final effect more than intellectual or emotional content: meaning and emotion should be transcended in delight. WP's views on poetry and music are similar to Stéphane Mallarmé's, and Swinburne must have had analogous beliefs.

> **661** Bowra, C. M. "Walter Pater," SEWANEE REVIEW, LVII (Summer 1949), 378–400; rptd with revisions in INSPIRATION AND POETRY (Lond: Macmillan; NY: St. Martin's P, 1955); rptd (Folcroft, Pa: Folcroft P, 1969); rptd (Freeport, NY: Books for Libraries P, 1970), pp. 199–219.

Though WP was always to a certain extent "a friend of Circe, a devotee and a victim of magical things, an investigator, not entirely impartial or dispassionate, of strange, alluring regions in the mind," this element in his nature was always allied to "a powerful intellect which liked to probe problems until it found answers to them and was never content to believe that exciting experiences are in themselves enough." His very real appeal to his generation can be understood only in the context of the decay of religious belief and the rapid advance in industrialization: his early admirers sought in him "a gospel which would at once resist the onslaughts of the scientific spirit and forestall the menaces of a mechanized society." But WP was unwilling to fulfill their hopes because he was too uncertain of his ideas to form dogmas or creeds. On the contrary, he remained basically an empiricist in the tradition of David Hume and John Stuart Mill, denying absolute certainties. He was an exponent of Aestheticism in the sense that he hoped to restore vitality to an industrialized society through art and beauty, a hope shared in somewhat different forms by Friedrich Nietzsche and Stéphane Mallarmé. He was more of a critic than a creative artist, and his attempt to find the unique and essential truth about his subjects is valid as a method and succeeded well, for example, in "Wordsworth" and "Prosper Merimée," though in this respect "Raphael" is perhaps a failure. Though he owed much to scholarship and friends, WP's "greatest obligation was to this gift of living with some master's work until he really understood it and was able to distinguish what was essential in it from what was accidental." But he also related specifics to general principles of art and human nature, and sometimes his insights were prophetic, as, for example, his description of what might be called "pure poetry" in "Joachim du Bellay" and his observation that all art aspires to the condition of music in "The School of Giorgione." WP was a great critic because of the combination of his remarkable sensibility with an ability to relate single issues to general problems. Judging was alien to him because of his belief in the relativity of values and the unique character of every work of art. He has been accused of being too subjective, but even in the case of Coleridge, where there may be some basis for this criticism, he is at least partially correct. Poetic passages sometimes surface in WP's prose because the creative artist in him could not be stifled. Even in *Marius the Epicurean* and the imaginary portraits he is basically a critic, though their real interest lies in what they tell us of WP. The hero of "Emerald Uthwart" may represent what WP would have wished to be like; the pattern of a sensitive young man faced with difficult decisions and in conflict with society is present in *Marius* and the shorter portraits. Marius's search for spiritual certainty reflects WP's own search for a "final system of thought," and it is probable that WP, like Marius, never accepted Christianity "with his whole heart." The heroes of *Imaginary Portraits* and "Emerald Uthwart" are all to a certain extent ahead of their time, and WP transferred his own conflicts with his time to their situations. The morbidity sometimes found in his short fiction foreshadows the self-destructive element in the lives of men like Oscar Wilde, Lionel Johnson, and Ernest Dowson and is related to the fact that WP realized that society in general disapproved of his ideas and that "in the end a heavy price must be paid for them. . . . In a sense his imaginary portraits were his revenge on a society which misunderstood him." More profoundly, WP felt that the artist in his own time must to a certain extent be "a diseased creature" since, because of the artist's greater wisdom and sensibility, he must know in advance that society "would inevitably wound and harm him."

662 Cooke, John D., and Lionel Stevenson. ENGLISH LITERATURE OF THE VICTORIAN PERIOD (NY: Appleton-Century Crofts, 1949); rptd (NY: Russell & Russell, 1971), pp. 106, 340, 368, 401–2, 403–5.
WP fulfilled one of Matthew Arnold's ideals by reasserting Hellenism, but his emphasis on the ecstasy of artistic and intellectual experience was inconsistent with Arnold's belief in "high seriousness." WP admired John Ruskin and "had a vein of moral austerity," but younger critics used his theories to justify a divorce between art and morality. *Marius the Epicurean* is at the same time a work of fiction, a study of classical culture, and a declaration of WP's creed of beauty. Since it lacks a plot it cannot be called a novel; it is rather an imaginary biography or a veiled autobiography. WP's style is "full of melody, austere and at the same time highly ornamented."

663 Doughty, Oswald. A VICTORIAN ROMANTIC: DANTE GABRIEL ROSSETTI (Lond: Frederick Muller, 1949); rptd (Lond: Oxford UP, 1960); pub in U.S. as DANTE GABRIEL ROSSETTI, A VICTORIAN ROMANTIC (New Haven: Yale UP, 1949), pp. 615–16.
Though WP admired and admitted his indebtedness to Rossetti, the latter did not like WP: "Rossetti, meeting Pater, sensing his remoteness so different from his own remoteness, detecting his repressed, coldly contemplative spirit, 'disliked him extremely' if we may trust Watts."

664 Du Bos, Charles. JOURNAL, Vol. 3: 1926–1927 (Paris: Corrêa, 1949), pp. 25, 45, 101–4, 109, 126, 166, 181, 184, 195, 209, 278, 309, 360, 361.
Henry James, Gustave Flaubert, and WP were all afraid of life; WP refused to accept the brutal aspects of life. [Du Bos still intends to write a book on WP,

entitled WALTER PATER OU L'ASCÈTE DE LA BEAUTÉ. For 22 years, WP has been Du Bos's "divine assistant."] WP recoiled, horrified, when Oscar Wilde, with undeniable logic, put Paterian premises into action. "Je suis un homme pour qui le monde visible existe" ("I am a man for whom the visible world exists" [cf. *Plato and Platonism*]) is an adage of Théophile Gautier's. [In French.]

665 Gardner, W. H. GERARD MANLEY HOPKINS (1844–1889): A STUDY OF POETIC IDIOSYNCRASY IN RELATION TO POETIC TRADITION, Volume II (New Haven: Yale UP, 1949), pp. 15, 22, 31, 33, 81, 262, 271.
The influence of WP partly accounts for the fact that Hopkins's religious ideas were seldom divorced from aesthetic sensibility. In an essay written for WP, Hopkins discredits the Utilitarian view of morals. Hopkins's "Easter Communion" may be that " 'discipline wrapped up in a sonnet' which he did *not* propose to send to Pater with his best love." When, in December 1878, Hopkins was moved to St. Giles's, Oxford, for nine months, he saw WP again.

666 Hare, Humphrey. SWINBURNE: A BIOGRAPHICAL APPROACH (Lond: H. F. & G. Witherby, 1949); rptd (Port Washington, NY: Kennikat P, 1970), pp. 34, 86, 155–56, 175–76.
WP acknowledged that A. C. Swinburne's "Notes on Designs of the Old Masters at Florence" influenced *The Renaissance*. This influence can be seen in comparing WP's description of the *Mona Lisa* in "Leonardo da Vinci" with Swinburne's description of Michelangelo's studies of female heads in that essay. WP told Swinburne of the arrest of Simeon Solomon. Benjamin Jowett tried to "wean" Swinburne from WP "and such other influences as he considered subversive."

667 Highet, Gilbert. THE CLASSICAL TRADITION: GREEK AND ROMAN INFLUENCES ON WESTERN LITERATURE (NY: Oxford UP, 1949), rptd (1950); (1953); (1957); (1967); rptd (Oxford: Clarendon P, 1949); (1951), pp. 445, 446, 461, 464–65, 516, 525, 685.
Marius the Epicurean is a study of the process of Christian conversion through reflection rather than through passion or miracle and shows an understanding of the best in both paganism and Christianity. "And, instead of showing the great historical change from Greece and Rome to Christendom as a war . . . it makes us see the long interpenetration by which the highest elements of Greek and Roman spiritual life were taken up and transformed in Christianity."

668 Hodgkin, Robert H. SIX CENTURIES OF AN OXFORD COLLEGE: A HISTORY OF THE QUEEN'S COLLEGE, 1340–1940 (Oxford: Basil Blackwell, 1949), pp. 178–79, 197, 199.
William Thomson, provost of Queen's from 1855 to 1862, may be criticized for allowing such outstanding Queen's undergraduates as WP and Ingram Bywater to drift away to take fellowships after graduation at other colleges [in fact, WP was graduated from Queen's in December 1862, several months after Thomson had become archbishop of York]. In the 1850s WP and a friend had to move to another

table in Hall to avoid being "sconced" (i.e., fined in beer for talking of serious matters during meals). A. H. Sayce, who traveled with WP, was able to transfer from Brasenose to Queen's and receive a classical scholarship there on the advice of WP and Bywater.

> **669** Hough, Graham. "A Study of Yeats," CAMBRIDGE JOURNAL, II (Feb 1949), 259–78; (March 1949), 323–42.

[This article and Hough's "Marius the Latitudinarian," CAMBRIDGE JOURNAL (April 1948) constitute a major portion of Hough's observations on WP in THE LAST ROMANTICS (1949), q.v. for abstract.]

> **670** Hough, Graham. THE LAST ROMANTICS (Lond: Duckworth, 1949); rptd (Lond: Methuen; NY: Barnes & Noble, 1961), pp. xvi, xvii–xviii, 134–74, 196, 197, 227.

The ethical and social bias of Victorian culture began to produce within itself its own antithesis, though this did not develop into a real movement until after the publication of WP's *The Renaissance*. WP's "tone of hieratic solemnity on purely artistic matters which had not formerly been thought to require it" is a sympton of the tendency, beginning in the 1870s, to turn art into "the highest value, to assimilate aesthetic to religious experience." T. S. Eliot's main complaint against WP and Matthew Arnold seems to be that they tried to replace religion with culture; but while Arnold would retain traditional morality even after the theological basis for it had disappeared and was nostalgic for a lost age of faith, WP wanted to free the sensibilities to form new moral values and was reasonably content with metaphysical uncertainty, which he felt was intellectually honest. The "Conclusion" is somewhat cryptic because of WP's distaste for controversy and should be read with passages from his other works in mind; what he really intends in it is an attack on the idea of absolute truth and the substitution of a theory of development or emergence for that idea. The philosophy of the "Conclusion" sanctions almost any kind of conduct, which is exactly what WP intends: he has a great appreciation for the multitudinousness of the world, and "what is peculiar to his creed is not its sensationalism, but its unwillingness to sacrifice any of this variety." *Marius the Epicurean* is the most complete statement of WP's religious attitude; in it, the religious development of a cultivated agnostic in Antonine Rome represents a possible development of the same sort of sensibility in Victorian England. The religion of Marius's childhood seems to echo the "decorous, scrupulous Anglicanism" of WP's boyhood. Because the limitations in Cyrenaicism in *Marius* are defined, there are possibilities of development there that are not clear in the "Conclusion." Marius dies in uncertainty, comforted by Christian rites, but without being admitted into Christian society and with no assurance of the truth of Christian belief. He is drawn to Christianity not by ceremony but by "the sense of a community bound together in charity." WP was never a true believer, but what Dante would have called a trimmer. He was willing to sacrifice "scholarly completeness" for "unity of impression," as for example in *Plato and Platonism*, where he alters Plato's emphasis "for the sake of his own chosen picture of Plato's character." The canons of WP's criticism are a denial of dogmatism (he refuses to judge), the assumption that ethics is included in aesthetics ("moral goodness is a kind of beauty . . . and worthy of appreciation" as such), and the ideal of an art in which thought and the sensuous expression of it are fused (which he found in Greek art, the lyric, and music). The principal ingredients of the Paterian temperament are an attraction to domesticity and the fusion of beauty and pain in pity. In "Denys l'Auxerrois" and "Apollo in Picardy" he seems to be suggesting an "obscure alliance in the natural world between love and pain, something beyond the pleasure principle . . . a something which even Christian feeling finds it hard to assimilate." "Remembering too the continual evidences of homosexual feeling in Pater's life and writing, one almost inevitably begins to form a composite picture of a kind of temperament of more or less suppressed erotic fantasy, combined perhaps with the frustration or diversion of normal sexuality; a preoccupation with the periphery of religious experience; a tremulous sensitiveness to aesthetic impressions; a conscious pursuit of beauty; and the conscious cultivation of a precious or elaborate style, all play a major part." Many so-called judgments on WP's work are actually judgments of his "psycho-physical constitution." He tends to translate descriptions of physical things into sentiments. There is a constraint in WP's writing that differentiates it from John Ruskins's and Thomas De Quincey's, "as of a man determined on sincerity, yet afraid of saying too much." There is a mixture of WP and J.-K. Huysmans in Oscar Wilde's THE PICTURE OF DORIAN GRAY. W. B. Yeats "shows no disposition towards the aesthetic flirtations with the church that Marius the Epicurean had made fashionable" and was "hardly more satisfied" with the doctrine of the "Conclusion." [Many of the observations on WP first appeared in "Marius the Latitudinarian," CAMBRIDGE JOURNAL (1948) and "A Study of Yeats," CAMBRIDGE JOURNAL (1949).]

> **671** Izumii, Hisanosuke. "A Portrait of Walter Pater," URN (Japan), I (1949).

[Unable to locate.]

> **672** Mild-Ledoux, H. George. BRITISH AND AMERICAN LITERATURE THROUGH THE CENTURIES (Turin: G. B. Paravia, 1949), pp. 512, 547, 609.

While Samuel Richardson analyzed sentiment in his novels through letters and Thomas Love Peacock, Aldous Huxley, and George Meredith used dialogue, WP went to "another extreme" in reducing dialogue in *Marius the Epicurean* to a minimum and making the novel "almost an essay and a vehicle for discourse."

> **673** "Pater Preaches," TIMES LITERARY SUPPLEMENT (Lond), 16 April 1949, p. 249.

The times may be too preoccupied with simple animal needs to listen to WP. Ironically, WP now reads like a reformer who advocated a "civilizing moral purpose." If WP had not written at all, "the decadents would have found some prophet to justify unwholesomeness." Both he and Ruskin feared for the future of civilization. Both believed, with Newman, that the arts were "the instruments of education." [Article is largely a response to the publication of WP, SELECTED WORKS, ed by Richard Aldington (Lond: Heinemann, 1948).]

674 Redman, Ben Ray. "New Editions," SATURDAY REVIEW OF LITERATURE, XXXII (29 Jan 1949), 30.

WP was "a connoisseur and collector, whose art of living consisted in exposing himself to as many manifestations of beauty as possible, who colored the objects of his passionate contemplation with the hues of his own nature and imagination, and whose experience of beauty begat new beauties, as these experiences were lovingly recorded and related in studied, luminous, and polished prose." [Review, with three other books, of WP, SELECTED WORKS, ed by Richard Aldington.]

675 Smith, Grover. "T. S. Eliot's Lady of the Rocks," NOTES AND QUERIES, CXCIV (19 March 1949), 123–25.

In discussing, in "Leonardo da Vinci," Leonardo's portrayals of women in *Lady of the Balances, Lady of the Lake, Lady of the Rocks,* and *St. Anne,* WP "is more fanciful than exact. Leonardo probably did not paint the *Lady of the Balances* at all; the *Lady of the Lake* (unless it is the portrait of Ginevra de' Benci) I do not recognize. Pater, however, says *Madonna of the Lake*." WP [apparently unconsciously] noted the sybil-like qualities in Leonardo's women, linking them with rocks and water and connecting them with both salvation and damnation, and the latter duality extends into the poetry of Eliot.

676 Stokes, Adrian. ART AND SCIENCE: A STUDY OF ALBERTI, PIERO DELLA FRANCESCA AND GIORGIONE (Lond: Faber & Faber, 1949), pp. 37, 43.

WP justly considered the fusion of form and content in Giorgione to be unique in figurative art. The subtleties and intensities of Giorgione's imagination "elude any but Pater's words."

677 Tillyard, E. M. W. "Is a New History of Criticism Possible?" CAMBRIDGE JOURNAL, II (June 1949), 543–51; rptd in ESSAYS: LITERARY AND EDUCATIONAL (Lond. Chatto & Windus, NY: Barnes & Noble, 1962), pp. 154–64.

George Saintsbury was a disciple of WP, and when he wrote his history of criticism the prevailing critical trend was, following WP, to define what made a work different from all other works, what WP called a work's "virtue."

678 Wellek, René. "The Concept of 'Romanticism' in Literary History," COMPARATIVE LITERATURE, I (Winter, Spring 1949), 1–23, 147–72; rptd in CONCEPTS OF CRITICISM (New Haven: Yale UP, 1963), pp. 128–98.

The spread and final establishment of the term *Romantic* for English literature of the early nineteenth century is probably due to Alois Brandl and WP's "Romanticism" in *Appreciations* (1889). The nineteenth-century meaning of the term *realism* is turned upside down and becomes solipsism in the treatment of Proust and WP. The individual becomes the only "reality."

679 Woodcock, George. THE PARADOX OF OSCAR WILDE (Lond & NY: T. V. Boardman, 1949); rptd (1950), pp. 13–14, 15, 31, 42–57, 58, 66, 68, 72, 76, 116, 118, 128, 180, 208, 229, 232; rptd (NY: Macmillan, 1950).

Though John Pentland Mahaffy encouraged Wilde's love of Greek antiquity, his influence in that realm was not nearly so strong as WP's and John Ruskin's. *The Renaissance* is "a meticulously written work of self-conscious prose, a masterpiece of artificial writing in the best sense." There is nothing "intrinsically degenerate" in the "Conclusion." WP influenced Wilde stylistically and in his ethical views. Wilde's prose, except when he was writing dialogue, never attained the greatness of WP's because, unlike WP, he lacked restraint. WP may have occasionally written dully, but he never wrote carelessly or inaccurately. When WP reviewed THE PICTURE OF DORIAN GRAY, he may have begun by praising Wilde's essays in order to disassociate himself from the philosophy of the novel without appearing hostile, and he was careful to point out that Wilde's Epicureanism differed from his own. Despite this, "Wilde's doctrines of individualism and of the rightness of giving way to temptation were not wholly irrational conclusions" from the philosophy of the "Conclusion." WP also credited Wilde with a moral intention in DORIAN GRAY that Wilde might have repudiated. Wilde, like WP and the Renaissance humanists, believed that "the individual man was more important than moral laws and social usages, and that only through the experience of individuals could true knowledge be attained." The core of Wilde's theory of the function of the critic is based on WP. Though George Meredith and WP were more complete artists than Wilde, their influence has been limited, while Wilde's has been wide.

1950

680 Aldington, Richard. "Introduction," THE RELIGION OF BEAUTY: SELECTIONS FROM THE AESTHETES (Lond: Heinemann, 1950), pp. 1–45.

WP and John Addington Symonds revolted at about the same time against John Ruskin in expressing a view of the Renaissance radically different from his and in changing the moral climate of aestheticism. WP rightly attempted to destroy the verse of his youth; he is "a case of the aesthetic critic rising from the failure of a poet." English readers were initiated into Goethe's ideal of self-culture, which is "a transference of the Christian idea of individual salvation of the soul to the sphere of literature and art," by WP and Symonds, and it became an essential part of the aesthetic ideal. Though both WP and Ruskin found the contemporary world of politics and industry repulsive and put a high value on art, they were otherwise quite different. Ruskin is never mentioned in *The Renaissance,* but that book shows obliquely how wrong were Ruskin's ideas on the subject. WP, rather than Ruskin, introduced Botticelli to England. *Imaginary Portraits* and *Marius the Epicurean* should be read as essays. WP's popularity was at its height between 1894 and 1914. Oscar Wilde's dialogues are more readable than those of WP or Symonds, from which they derive. Rachel Annand Taylor's LEONARDO THE FLORENTINE concentrates what WP, Symonds, and Wilde said about the Renaissance and improves on them.

681 Baker, Joseph E. "Our New Hellenic Renaissance," THE REINTERPRETATION OF VICTORIAN LITERATURE, ed by Joseph E. Baker (Princeton: Princeton UP, 1950); rptd (NY: Russell & Russell, 1962), pp. 207–36.

Whereas the major English Romantic poets were classical critics, the more Romantic critics were prose writers: Edward Young, William Hazlitt, Charles Lamb, Thomas De Quincy, and WP. One can contrast WP's Romantic dictum in "Style" that the writer's aim is to transcribe not the fact but his sense of the fact with William Wordsworth's "avowed endeavor" to "look steadily at my subject." *Plato and Platonism* is written "in better prose than [is] usual" with WP, but "he got about as far away from Plato as one could get when he wrote that 'the *formula* of Plato's genius' is his 'sensuous love of the unseen.' " No Victorian Hellenist, with the exception of WP, has admired Sparta as much as the Germans, but WP was "fascinated by corpse-like 'beauty,' and ready to indulge himself in the contemplation of arrested decay wherever he could find it. In this he is close to the *fin de siècle* Byzantine revival.

682 Beach, Joseph Warren. "The Literature of the Nineteenth and the Early Twentieth Centuries, 1798 to the First World War," in A HISTORY OF ENGLISH LITERATURE, ed by Hardin Craig (NY: Oxford UP, 1950), pp. 539, 540–42, 561, 581, 592; rptd as ENGLISH LITERATURE OF THE 19TH AND THE EARLY 20TH CENTURIES, 1798 TO THE FIRST WORLD WAR (NY: Collier, 1962).

WP is "less shrill and contentious" than many of his Victorian predecessors: "the moral virtue appears in an attenuated form." In matters of religion, above all he was attracted to the symbolic correspondence between sacred history and the personal history of men. In THE NEW REPUBLIC W. H. Mallock "made a real point when he represented Mr. Rose as wishing to make the soul a musical instrument through culture." In the "Conclusion" [*The Renaissance*], which contains "more than a hint of attitudes not conformable to Christian and Victorian ethics," there are suggestions of philosophical materialism, solipsism, and Epicureanism. "As a man," WP "seems to have been nicely balanced between the masculine and the feminine disposition," and, except in the imagination, he was not subject to "the gross assaults of 'sin.' " His strong point is the discrimination of impressions, and beside him John Ruskin is "loud and bald." "Style" is the best essay on the subject in the language "if we have in mind the refinements of imaginative prose." *Plato and Platonism* is "first-rate." In WP the art for art's sake movement "appears in its most reasonable and distinguished form."

683 Booth, Bradford A. "Form and Technique in the Novel," THE REINTERPRETATION OF VICTORIAN LITERATURE, ed by Joseph E. Baker (Princeton: Princeton UP, 1950); rptd (NY: Russell & Russell, 1962), pp. 67–96.

In the prose of George Meredith there is a "studied rarity of language" reminiscent of WP and the prose poets. *Marius the Epicurean* anticipates twentieth-century subjectivity: "Influenced by the pre-Raphaelites, Pater rejected eighteenth-century rationalism and nineteenth-century materialism, fashioning a philosophy of subjective aesthetics that recalls Poe and the French Symbolists."

684 Brown, E. K. "Pater's *Appreciations:* A Bibliographical Note," MODERN LANGUAGE NOTES, LXV (April 1950), 247–49.

In the bibliographical note prefixed to WP's *Miscellaneous Studies,* Charles L. Shadwell describes three of the essays that appeared in the first edition of *Appreciations*—"Sir Thomas Browne," "Shakespeare's English Kings," and "Aesthetic Poetry"—as appearing there for the first time, and "Feuillet's 'La Morte' " appearing for the first time in the third edition of *Appreciations*. These indications are all incorrect: "Sir Thomas Browne" and "Feuillet's 'La Morte' " first appeared in MACMILLAN'S MAGAZINE, "Shakespeare's English Kings" first appeared in SCRIBNER'S MAGAZINE, and "Aesthetic Poetry," is the first part of "Poems by William Morris," which appeared in the WESTMINSTER REVIEW (the final portion of that early essay became the "Conclusion" to *The Renaissance*). WP's revisions are important only in the case of "Aesthetic Poetry," where they "indicate the distance Pater had travelled from the anti-religious position he had occupied in the late 1860's."

685 Buckley, Jerome Hamilton. "Pater and the Suppressed 'Conclusion,' " MODERN LANGUAGE NOTES, LXV (April 1950), 249–51.

One of the "young men" WP feared misleading when he omitted the "Conclusion" from the second edition of *The Renaissance* may have been W. H. Mallock, who had been satirizing WP as the effete "Mr. Rose" in his serialization of THE NEW REPUBLIC in 1876. Whatever his motivation in suppressing the "Conclusion," WP was "expressing a reluctance to subscribe to a thorough-going 'art for art's sake,' a diffidence which those who hail him as herald of the Aesthetic Movement have not succeeded in explaining."

686 D[avenport]., A[rnold]. "Some Notes on 'The Waste Land,' " NOTES AND QUERIES, CXCV (19 Aug 1950), 365–69.

"The Lady of the Rocks" in T. S. Eliot's "The Waste Land" recalls WP's description of the *Mona Lisa* in "Leonardo da Vinci," and in several other places Eliot's poem echoes WP's description.

687 Du Bos, Charles. JOURNAL, Vol. 4: 1928 (Paris: Corrêa, 1950), pp. 46, 180, 201–2.

[At an earlier period in his life, Du Bos sought intuitive truths that were a part of a secular mysticism in the sense that he, like WP, was a "secular cathedral." He plans to write a book on WP between October 1929 and February 1930.] [In French.]

688 Henn, T. R. THE LONELY TOWER: STUDIES IN THE POETRY OF W. B. YEATS (Lond: Methuen, 1950); rptd (NY: Pellegrini & Cudahy, 1952), pp. 27, 93, 98, 102, 105, 114, 199, 241, 251, 252; rptd with revisions (Lond: Methuen; NY: Barnes & Noble, 1965).

The prose of Yeats's THE TABLES OF THE LAW and THE ADORATION OF THE MAGI is derived from WP, who had taken it from Sir Thomas Browne. The fire and ice imagery of Yeats's "The Cold Heaven" may be a memory of WP's "The Poetry of Michelangelo." Around 1909, Yeats showed tendencies of developing a deliberate literary pose derived from WP, though his allegiance to WP was fading; but Yeats's ideal between 1915 and 1920 still owed something to WP's *The Renaissance.* The symbol of the chapel in Yeats's A VISION, with its links to creation and annunciation relics, may have been suggested by a passage in "The Poetry of Michelangelo." More important than the influence of painting on Yeats was the influence of art criticism, and particularly *The Renaissance.* The germ of Yeats's view of the passing away of Greek perfection is in WP's "Winckelmann," and WP's account of Pico della Mirandola is applicable to Yeats himself.

689 Patrick, J. Max (ed). THE NEW REPUBLIC, OR CULTURE, FAITH, AND PHILOSOPHY IN AN ENGLISH COUNTRY HOUSE, by W. H. Mallock (Gainesville: University of Florida P, 1950), pp. xvii–xviii, xxvi, 11, 21, 121, 123, 125–26, 127, 128, 129, 166, 167, 168, 170, 172, 173, 174, 175, 176, 177, 194, 210.

Mallock's "Mr. Rose" is mostly based on WP, but he also has characteristics of D. G. Rossetti and other Pre-Raphaelites. Mallock shows insight into the "dangerous implications" of WP's early writings. WP's love for the marginalia of worship and his scorn for the basis of that worship made him a perfect subject for satire. Mr. Rose, like WP in "Aesthetic Poetry" and other early essays, is "without moral standards, a decadent dilletante, a trifler in serious matters." WP lacked the "earnestness and selflessness of the Rossettis and their circle." "The Bacchanals of Euripides" exhibits morbidity. Mallock satirizes WP's stylistic "abuse of interpolation and length." WP's interpolation of foreign expressions into his sentences often obscures rather than clarifies his meaning.

690 Peters, Francis Edward, S.J. "Walter Pater's Lacedaemon," CLASSICAL BULLETIN, XXVII (Dec 1950), 16–17, 19.

WP's picture of Lacedaemon in *Plato and Platonism* is "a far cry from historic Sparta." One reason for this fact is that he used sources which tended to romanticize Sparta, like Plato, Plutarch, Pausanias, Xenophon, and K. O. Müller, rather than sources which took a more realistic view, like Tyrtaeus, Herodotus, Thucydides, and Aristotle. But his description of Lacedaemon is false also because he believed that means are ends and that moral values can be equated with aesthetic values. WP ignores the fact that the end of Spartan polity was military conquest and fails to distinguish between pre-classical Sparta, when considerable artistic ability was evident, and Sparta after 556 B.C., when the enforcement of discipline was carried out to the letter and art went into an eclipse.

691 Praz, Mario. "Museo dannunziano" (D'Annunzio Museum), LA NUOVA STAMPA (Turin), 18 April 1950, p. 3; pub simultaneously in IL TEMPO (Rome), 18 April 1950, p. 3; rptd in LA CASA DELLA FAMA: SAGGI DI LETTERATURA E D'ARTE (Milan: Ricciardi, 1952), pp. 284–87.

In "The School of Giorgione" WP based his interpretation of the giorgionesque spirit in painting on pseudo-Giorgiones, but he still penetrated into the idyllic quality of the giorgionesque with incomparable subtlety; neither Gabriele d'Annunzio nor Angelo Conti possessed such a talent. [In Italian.]

692 Praz, Mario. "Rivalutazione dei romantici" (Reevaluation of the Romantics), CRONACHE LETTERARIE ANGLOSASSONI (Rome: Edizioni di Storia e Letteratura, 1950), I, 123–28; originally pub in IL TEMPO, 31 Oct 1950.

In recommending, in MODERN PAINTERS, the cultivation of the senses, and particularly the visual faculties, to the highest point of accuracy and power, John Ruskin foreshadows the "Conclusion" to *The Renaissance*. Much of WP's style is in D. G. Rossetti's "Hand and Soul." [In Italian.]

693 Smith, Logan Pearsall. A PORTRAIT OF LOGAN PEARSALL SMITH DRAWN FROM HIS LETTERS AND DIARIES, ed by John Russell (Lond: Dropmore, 1950), pp. 50, 63, 64, 108.

[Remarks of an unnamed person in a diary entry for November 1889]: "Oh yes—I know Pater: one of the few who do. He hardly knows anyone in Oxford. Have you ever heard how he works? About 10 in the morning he goes to his desk, where he finds about a dozen cards—like visiting cards, but a little larger. His day's task is to write a sentence on each card. The next day he takes the twelve & works them into a paragraph." [July 1896]: According to Vernon Lee, WP was "a saint, an idealist in the true sense, the sense of choosing what was beautiful & charming & neglecting the rest." On his trips to Italy, always in August, his two sisters always complained of everything, but WP only remembered "what was beautiful & pleasant. . . . Then that day he spent at ———, where the idea of *Marius [the Epicurean]* came to him—what a horror it must have been, & yet how much he made of it! He would walk to all the museums, without cabs in the August heats, & yet he would not go to stay in a comfortable English country house, because he said he could not sleep in any bed save his own." Among modern writers, WP and Charles Lamb provide an ideal of what good English prose should be.

694 Stanford, Derek. "Wordsworth and his Nineteenth Century Critics: Introduction," TRIBUTE TO WORDSWORTH: A MISCELLANY OF OPINION FOR THE CENTENARY OF THE POET'S DEATH, ed by Muriel Spark and Derek Stanford (Lond & NY: Wingate, 1950); rptd (Port Washington, NY: Kennikat P, 1970), pp. 23–33.

WP's "Wordsworth," which in some ways prefigures the conclusions of Matthew Arnold's essay on the poet, concentrates on the aesthetic rather than the philo-sophical side of Wordsworth's poetry—"a fact of much significance." In advising the reader to go to Wordsworth for an increase in sensibility rather than philosophy, WP was reacting against the orthodox Wordsworthians. He reduces Wordsworth's landscape to a suggestive rather than a mystical universe, and "persuades us . . . to see in Wordsworth's verse not a spiritual but a subjective nature; a nature, saturated, so to speak, in anthropocentric colouring. . . . In Wordsworth, man and nature are of the same species." WP did much to develop the opinion that, whatever one thinks of his philosophy, Wordsworth must be reckoned a great poet. A. C. Swinburne's essay on Wordsworth follows in the track of WP and Arnold.

695 Tillotson, Geoffrey. "Arnold and Pater: Critics Historical, Aes-thetic and Otherwise," ESSAYS AND STUDIES BY MEMBERS OF THE EN-GLISH ASSOCIATION, nsIII (1950), 47–68; rptd as "Arnold and Pater: Critics Historical, Aesthetic and Unlabelled," in CRITICISM AND THE NINETEENTH CENTURY (Lond: Athlone P, 1951); rptd (Hamden, Conn: Archon, 1967), pp. 92–123.

Though Matthew Arnold professed himself a disinterested critic when he wrote that the endeavor of criticism is "to see the object as in itself it really is" [cf. "Preface" to *The Renaissance*], that kind of objectivity is impossible, and Arnold was anything but disinterested. And though WP sometimes appears to encourage historical criticism, neither he nor Arnold was an historical critic. This is seen in the case of WP by his refusal, in "Leonardo da Vinci," to approach the *Mona Lisa* with the same set of aesthetic principles that Vasari used: his description of the *Mona Lisa* "witnesses not so much to Leonardo but to the nineteenth-century idea of the fatal woman." When Arnold wrote of seeing the object as in itself it really is, he meant the object as seen by the common reader, as opposed to an idiosyncratic, personal estimate of the object; but for WP "the object as it really is lay in the privacy of the individual impression of it." One of the tenets of WP's "aesthetic" criticism is that the object concentrated on should be beautiful, but fortunately this was not always adhered to in practice. "Wordsworth" fails because the subject of that study "is made out as too exquisite, too tremulously sensitive, too freely passionate. . . . His Wordsworth was too much like Pater." WP's references to music "trespass beyond his knowledge."

696 Tindall, William York. JAMES JOYCE: HIS WAY OF INTERPRETING THE MODERN WORLD (NY & Lond: Scribner's, 1950); rptd (1966); rptd (NY: Grove; Lond: Evergreen: 1960), pp. 20, 85, 122.

The prose of Joyce's early essay on the poet Mangan is "Paterite," but Joyce differs from WP and Oscar Wilde in his emphasis on significant form. Joyce may have been introduced to Giordano Bruno through WP's essay on him.

697 Vines, Sherard. A HUNDRED YEARS OF ENGLISH LITERATURE (Lond: Duckworth, 1950), pp. 10, 48, 190, 209, 210, 214; rptd (NY: Collier, 1962).

"Not even Alfred de Musset has succeeded in truly defining the Romantic; and it may be doubtful whether Pater's Attic salt has arrested more than the tail feathers of this beautiful, effectual angel." Both D. G. Rossetti and WP, who owed something to him, proved that art is not always to conceal art. WP's objection to "surplusage" in *Appreciations* may in part account for the denudation of poetry in the early twentieth century, but his influence in the field of literary theory was supplanted by that of I. A. Richards. Lionel Johnson brought some of WP's word-consciousness within the scope of Irish poetry, and W. B. Yeats finally reduced his "terms of languor such as Rossetti and Pater bequeathed to the 'nineties."

698 Westland, Peter (ed). THE TEACH YOURSELF HISTORY OF ENGLISH LITERATURE, Volume VI (Lond: English Universities P, 1950), pp. 126–27.

WP has been called a refined sensualist because of his doctrine of art for art's sake, "which is a completely untrue belief for his theory meant only that art exists to give us our intensest and noblest pleasure, that it has its own ethical basis." WP's advocacy of aesthetic pleasure is "both a discipline and a happy study," but if long continued it becomes "enervating and tedious"—the "ultimate fate of 'art for art's sake.'"

699 Zink, Sidney. "The Moral Effect of Art," ETHICS, LX (July 1950), 261–74; rptd in THE PROBLEMS OF AESTHETICS: A BOOK OF READINGS, ed by Eliseo Vivas and Murray Krieger (NY: Rinehart, 1953), pp. 545–61.

Though both WP and John Dewey proposed making the experience of life into an experience of art, WP takes "art" more traditionally and narrowly than Dewey, who sees any satisfactory experience of life as a kind of work of art. Both see art as a fusion of contrary things which are usually separate, but for WP those two things are "form" and "matter," while for Dewey they are "means" and "end." WP "is so impressed with the refined delights of the aesthetic contemplation of individuals that to him nothing else seems greatly to matter," but life imposes moral demands which cannot be avoided. Unlike both WP and Dewey, Plato saw art and truth as opposed.

1951

700 Annan, Noel Gilroy. LESLIE STEPHEN: HIS THOUGHT AND CHAR-
ACTER IN RELATION TO HIS TIME (Lond: Macgibbon & Kee, 1951); rptd
(Cambridge, Mass: Harvard UP, 1952), pp. 106, 131, 133, 135, 194, 259.
Virginia Woolf studied Plato under WP's sister. Both WP and Mrs. Humphry Ward
believed that the scientific spirit made the visible world fairer and more desirable.
Though both Stephen and WP wrote on Sir Thomas Browne, Stephen's essay is
about Browne, while WP's "Sir Thomas Browne" is really about WP.

701 Bischoff, D. Anthony. "The Manuscripts of Gerard Manley Hop-
kins," THOUGHT, XXVI (Winter 1951–52), 551–80.
Among the Hopkins manuscripts at Campion Hall, Oxford, are several essays that
Hopkins wrote for WP.

702 Blackmur, R. P. "In the Hope of Straightening Things Out,"
KENYON REVIEW, XIII (Spring 1951), 303–14; rptd in THE LION AND THE
HONEYCOMB: ESSAYS IN SOLICITUDE AND CRITIQUE (NY: Harcourt,
Brace, 1955); rptd (1964), pp. 162–75.
T. S. Eliot's criticism is in "vital reaction" to Matthew Arnold and WP: "the fight
with, and use of, Matthew Arnold is life-long, the fight with Pater is more with his
'cause' than with his judgments and is more a foray than a war."

703 Borinski, Ludwig. ENGLISCHER GEIST IN DER GESCHICHTE SEINER
PROSA (The English Spirit in the History of its Prose) (Freiburg: Herder,
1951), pp. 189–90, 194.
Though WP, as a follower of Gustave Flaubert and other French writers, recommended a plain style, his own works, poor in ideas, often obscure because of
overlong periods, did nothing to forward this program. His style is not in the
English but in the French tradition. With WP, one finds for the first time in England
writing intended for a small esoteric circle. [In German.]

704 Brzenk, Eugene J. "The Fictional Technique of Walter Pater."
Unpublished dissertation, University of Iowa, 1951.
[Listed in Lawrence F. McNamee, DISSERTATIONS IN ENGLISH AND AMERICAN
LITERATURE (NY and Lond: Bowker, 1968).]

705 Buckley, Jerome Hamilton. THE VICTORIAN TEMPER (Cambridge,
Mass: Harvard UP, 1951), pp. 163, 176, 178–82, 183–84, 200, 216, 233;
rptd (NY: Vintage, n.d.).
Dante Gabriel Rossetti, like WP, viewed the drift toward aestheticism with ambivalence. In "The Child in the House" one may trace "not uncertainly much of
the overrefined delicacy, the aloofness, the introversion, the languor bordering on
neurasthenia, that helped stigmatize Pater himself as the arch-aesthete." Great art,

for WP, lifts the spirit above self by carrying the individual to a vantage point from which he can see the essential pattern of life. The Holland of "Sebastian van Storck" shows parallels with the prosperity of Victorian England; and the Rome of *Marius the Epicurean,* "threatened already with the coming of the barbarians," was a warning to modern empires. WP was more concerned with the climate of opinion and the temperament of the artist that go into a work of art than he was with the technical devices that produce a particular aesthetic effect. Every work of art was to him a means of communication. WP's aesthetic was, in the final analysis, ethical.

706 Church, Richard. THE GROWTH OF THE ENGLISH NOVEL (Lond: Methuen, 1951); rptd (1957); (1961); rptd (NY: Barnes & Noble, 1961), pp. 144, 171.

Marius the Epicurean is "a static study in which little happens except the ceaseless exfoliation of aesthetic mood in the few characters peopling the book." It fails as a novel, though it has "a certain monolithic splendour," and it points the way toward later novelists, such as Henry James, who were concerned with the "internal drama of the human spirit." In the 1880s, WP was "the deity of the moment, and it was thought *de rigueur* to write like him, every sentence revised a dozen times, in the search for the immaculate word."

707 Churchill, R. C. ENGLISH LITERATURE OF THE NINETEENTH CEN-TURY (Lond: University Tutorial P, 1951); rptd (Freeport, NY: Books for Libraries P, 1970), pp. 185–87, 231, 243, 244.

WP's prose is "exquisite, elaborate, languid, and—by comparison with Arnold's—feminine." The weakness of the case presented in *Marius the Epicu-rean* is that Marius is "converted or half-converted" to Christianity not by its truth or its power of sympathy but by its sensuous appeal and its liturgical solemnities, which are connected with both the religiosity of some of the Pre-Raphaelites and the conversion to Catholicism of some of the aesthetes of the Nineties.

708 Ervine, St. John. OSCAR WILDE: A PRESENT TIME APPRAISAL (Lond: Allen & Unwin, 1951); rptd (NY: Morrow, 1952), pp. 87, 91, 276–77.

As to Frank Harris's telling Wilde's anecdote about WP kissing his hand at Oxford: "We cannot be certain that this story is false or tell whether Wilde or Harris was the liar. Emotional aesthetes, like Habakkuk, are capable of all; and the queer Anglo-Dutchman may have behaved in that puerile manner." WP "struggled hard to avoid praising or dispraising" THE PICTURE OF DORIAN GRAY, but he "could not conceal his aversion from it."

709 Furnas, J. C. VOYAGE TO WINDWARD: THE LIFE OF ROBERT LOUIS STEVENSON (NY: William Sloane Associates, 1951); (Lond: Faber & Faber, 1952), pp. 32–33, 496.

WP's "informally graceful skill in the biographical essay" influenced Stevenson's early essays on François Villon and Charles d'Orléans. Stevenson recalled the impression that *The Renaissance* made on him in 1873 in an interview published in the Christchurch, New Zealand PRESS (24 April 1893).

710 Hamm, Victor M. THE PATTERN OF CRITICISM (Milwaukee: Bruce, 1951); rptd (1953); rptd with revisions (1960), pp. 4–6, 95, 172.

Probably the most distinguished and "metaphysically logical" of modern English exponents of impressionistic criticism is WP, who is both an articulate expositor of theory and a "brilliant practitioner of its technique." In the "Preface" to *The Renaissance* he is still something of an "objectivist," but he "must have become aware of the discrepancy between his earlier view of criticism as fidelity to the object and his experience with actual objects, for in the conclusion to the book he expresses a philosophy of utter relativism and change. . . . Obviously, not even impressions are, in the final analysis, more than accidents of sensory perceptions, of moods, of passing impulses and fancies." The impasse of impressionism is that it can never be criticism because it denies the validity of judgment. Prose as well as poetry can express affective states, as for example in the "highly wrought cadences" of WP and Virginia Woolf.

711 Lucas, F. L. LITERATURE AND PSYCHOLOGY (Lond: Cassell, 1951); rptd (Ann Arbor: University of Michigan P, 1957), pp. 96, 108, 130, 191, 236–43, 314.

WP is full of contradictions: an Epicurean and an ascetic, a hedonist and a moralist. But he reflects a "sickly unreality." The danger of WP's theories and of aestheticism generally is that it is unfruitful, unproductive. Literature loses its sense in sound when it aspires, as WP directed, to the condition of music. There are marked neurotic tendencies in his portraits, sadism in "Denys l'Auxerrois" and "Apollo in Picardy." WP also verges on necrophilia in some of his portraits. His prose, fittingly, is "corpse-like." He remains "a churchyard lily, a slightly inebriated swan, a bat flickering in the aisles of a twilit cathedral." His heir was Oscar Wilde.

712 Meaney, John W. "A Study in the Critical Method of Walter Pater." Unpublished dissertation, University of Texas (Austin), 1951.

[Listed in Lawrence F. McNamee, DISSERTATIONS IN ENGLISH AND AMERICAN LITERATURE (NY and Lond: Bowker, 1968).]

713 Michell, H. "Names Inscribed on Window Glasses," NOTES AND QUERIES, CXCVI (9 June 1951), 259.

[When he was an undergraduate at Queen's College, Oxford, fifty years before, the author heard that WP had scratched his name on his window pane there but that the pane had been removed. He inquires whether this story can be substantiated and whether the pane has been preserved.]

714 Neill, S. Diana. A SHORT HISTORY OF THE ENGLISH NOVEL (Lond & NY: Jarrolds, 1951); rptd (1952); (1954); rptd (NY: Macmillan, 1952), pp. 205, 239–42, 243, 246–47; rptd with revisions (NY: Collier, 1964).

Toward the end of the nineteenth century the novel came into its own as an art form through the serious efforts of writers like WP, Henry James, R. L. Stevenson, Joseph Conrad, and George Moore. WP cultivated an intense appreciation of the past, especially through its art. "In Pater the critic achieves his apotheosis." *Marius the Epicurean* is "written in a cool, marmoreal prose of quiet beauty," is "an artistically faultless expression of the noble philosophy of a dying culture," and inspired George Moore to write THE BROOK KERITH and HÉLOÏSE AND ABÉLARD. Compared with WP's style, that of Oscar Wilde in THE PICTURE OF DORIAN GRAY is "a little too rouged and bedizened."

715 Osbourn, R. V. *"Marius the Epicurean,"* ESSAYS IN CRITICISM, I (Oct 1951), 387–403.

The philosophical and religious stages through which Marius passes parallel WP's mental development. "The Child in the House" and "An English Poet" were WP's first attempts at disguised autobiography, preparatory to *Marius the Epicurean.* The novel is perfectly coherent, contrary to the opinion of T. S. Eliot, if one realizes that the historical setting is a disguise for a nineteenth-century autobiographical and philosophical progress and that its intention is to show the need for religion. Marius's early religion of Numa is equivalent to conventional Victorian religion, from which he passes to paganism, Cyrenaicism (in the description of which WP tries to correct misleading interpretations of his philosophy in *The Renaissance*), and Stoicism. All three of these philosophies founder because of their inability to deal adequately with death and lead to a rejection of philosophy in the dialogue of Lucian. The chapter entitled "The Martyrs," which shows Christians handling death successfully through religion, is the climax of the novel. The attraction of Christianity in *Marius* is not an attraction to ritual, but, among other things, to sympathy, as seen, for example, in the chapter "Sunt Lacrimae Rerum." The pattern of the novel has often been mistaken because it is presented in a low-keyed, non-didactic manner, which is also the technique of the later imaginary portraits. "Sebastian Van Storck," for example, similarly balances different points of view until the end, when the saving of the child "indirectly but conclusively" places WP's sympathy with "human relationships" as opposed to Sebastian's "Spinozistic" way of life.

716 Parkinson, Thomas. W. B. YEATS: SELF-CRITIC: A STUDY OF HIS EARLY VERSE (Berkeley & Los Angeles: University of California P, 1951); rptd (1971), pp. 2, 3, 5, 7, 76.

In Yeats's later verse, "Paterean aestheticism, theosophic, cabalistic, and hermetic philosophy, and aristocratic Irish nationalism" are unified. His poems of the period 1889–1901 have "style" in WP's sense of the term. WP's idea of style stresses personal qualities to the point of idiosyncrasy, and it was only through nationalism and the occult that Yeats escaped from this "Paterean cul-de-sac." By 1906 Yeats could quarrel with WP's conception of pure art.

717 Rau, Catherine. ART AND SOCIETY: A REINTERPRETATION OF PLATO (NY: Richard R. Smith, 1951), pp. 11, 12.

The "distorting medium" of art for art's sake caused scholars and critics, including WP, to misinterpret Plato. In *Plato and Platonism* WP attributes his own ideas to Plato, who expresses views "exactly contradictory" to WP's beliefs that the philosopher saw art as having no end beyond itself.

718 Sola Pinto, Vivian de. CRISIS IN ENGLISH POETRY, 1880–1940 (Lond: Hutchinson's University Library, 1951), pp. 15, 51, 61, 65, 68, 87; rptd (1965).

A passage in Thomas Hardy's preface to his second volume of poetry may be indebted to "Not the fruit of experience, but experience itself, is the end" in WP's "Conclusion" [*The Renaissance*]. John Henry Newman's influence on Gerard Manley Hopkins is greater than WP's or Benjamin Jowett's. Hopkins developed WP's teaching more successfully than did Oscar Wilde. In the language of "The Wreck of the Deutschland" Hopkins attempts the identification of matter and form that WP had prophesied in "The School of Giorgione." Lionel Johnson introduced William Butler Yeats to the writings of WP.

719 Tillotson, Geoffrey. "The Critic and His Material: On Critical Method," CRITICISM AND THE NINETEENTH CENTURY (Lond: Athlone P, 1951); rptd (Hamden, Conn: Archon, 1967), pp. 11–41.

WP, in speaking of works and their producers, sometimes makes them sound like his own and himself, in which case his criticism becomes autobiographical poetry and is criticism only of himself. A method of criticism employed by Thomas Carlyle, John Henry Newman, Matthew Arnold, and WP is to choose a significant detail that is an emblem of the whole.

720 Vardon, Bruce E. "Variant Readings in Walter Pater's *Studies in the History of the Renaissance*." Unpublished dissertation, University of Chicago, 1951.

[Listed in Lawrence F. McNamee, DISSERTATIONS IN ENGLISH AND AMERICAN LITERATURE (NY and Lond: Bowker, 1968).]

721 Vollrath, Wilhelm. VERSCHWIEGENES OXFORD: MATTHEW AR-NOLD, GOETHE UND WALTER PATER, FELLOW OF BRASENOSE (Discreet Oxford: Matthew Arnold, Goethe and Walter Pater, Fellow of Brasenose) (Heidelberg: Quelle & Meyer, 1951).

WP's unobtrusiveness is noteworthy. Arnold remembered WP by "unpopular names," but small-town gossip was inevitable in a place like Oxford. For Oxford, the implications of the illumination described in "Diaphaneitè" were incontestable: the desire to be changed, transformed in the religious sense. The "edge of light" in that essay is similar to the illumination in Paul's conversion on the road to Damascus. "Diaphaneitè" is not, however, a methodical and didactic essay but rather the monologue of a lonely person meditating on his fitness and aptitude for a calling. Its experimental form is reminiscent of poetry, and it is a fitting product of Oxford. WP did not wish to be a judge but rather an interpreter. In *Greek Studies* he feels that previous interpretations of Greek art have been too one-sided, neglecting the importance of the minor, household arts. Memory, even as a consecration of the unmentioned and unnoticed, is important in WP's works. The function of the imagination in scholarship, art, and history is of primary importance to him. "A Study of Dionysus" is an attempt to recover lost details of legend, religion, and art. The *Imaginary Portraits* are basically educational. The subject of "Sebastian Van Storck" is really what happens when Spinoza's philosophy is applied to life, and the subject of "Duke Carl of Rosenmold" is really Goethe. [In German.]

1952

722 Allott, Kenneth. "Pater and Arnold," ESSAYS IN CRITICISM, II (1952), 219–21.
Matthew Arnold's essay "Marcus Aurelius," which compares Antonine Rome to Victorian England, was probably the germ of *Marius the Epicurean*. Arnold's "On the Modern Element in Literature" reminded WP of that parallel, and W. W. Capes's THE ROMAN EMPIRE OF THE SECOND CENTURY provided WP with the details necessary to carry out Arnold's comparison.

> **723** Arnold, Matthew. THE NOTE-BOOKS OF MATTHEW ARNOLD, ed by Howard F. Lowry, Karl Young, and Waldo H. Dunn (Lond: Oxford UP, 1952), pp. 321, 341, 513, 515.

[Quotations and paraphrases from WP's "Winckelmann" (in the Note-Book for 1879) and "Wordsworth" (in the Note-Book for 1880).]

> **724** Batard, Yvonne. LES DESSINS DE SANDRO BOTTICELLI POUR LA DIVINE COMÉDIE (The Drawings of Sandro Botticelli for the DIVINE COMEDY) (Paris: Olivier Perrin, 1952), p. 17.

Commenting on Botticelli's Dante engravings of 1481, WP felt that Botticelli had forgotten the circumstances in which Dante "sees" the centaurs in Canto 12 of the INFERNO and that he had let his imagination wander in depicting little baby-faced animals of the grove, armed with toy bows and arrows. But WP was writing before the discovery of Botticelli's drawings of the same subject, and there the Minotaur is drawn with a vigor worthy of the ancients. No illustrator of Dante has penetrated so profoundly the sense of this canto as Botticelli. [In French.]

> **725** Bate, Walter Jackson (ed). CRITICISM: THE MAJOR TEXTS (NY: Harcourt, Brace & World, 1952); rptd, enlgd (NY: Harcourt, Brace,

Jovanovich, 1970), pp. 507–8, 564; pp. 507–8 rptd as "Walter Pater," in Walter Jackson Bate, PREFACES TO CRITICISM (Garden City, NY: Doubleday, 1959), pp. 193–96.

WP was the most distinguished representative of art for art's sake, though when he is read sympathetically he does not seem typical of the movement, since his "theoretical position is too moderate, too intelligently qualified." The "exquisite Epicureanism" of *The Renaissance* becomes more austere in his later works. Though they are not developed very far, his theoretical statements on art touch on "some of the more general ideals of both classical and romantic theory: the formative power of art to deepen our feeling and consciousness of life; the primary importance of the 'imaginative reason'—a term originally used by Arnold—in coalescing the activity of one's total mind; and the organic union of form and content." The "popular superstition" that Imagination and Fancy were first differentiated by eighteenth-century German aestheticians was probably first given currency by WP—the distinction is actually English in origin.

726 Baum, Paull Franklin. THE OTHER HARMONY OF PROSE (Durham, NC: Duke UP, 1952), pp. 41–42, 44, 61, 112, 115, 136–37, 138, 147–48, 151–68, 188–89, 190, 204, 224.

A phrase from the description of the *Mona Lisa* in "Leonardo da Vinci" illustrates the different possible readings of the same passage as regards syllabic duration. WP gave special attention to the rhythm of the paragraph. WP's writing is a modern representative of "numerous prose," but his effects and means may be sometimes too obvious for good art. A coda like shortening is a favorite device of WP's. A passage from "Leonardo" is a surprising example of an unsuccessful periodic sentence. Carlyle's description of Giotto's portrait of Dante is a sort of companion piece to WP's description of the *Mona Lisa*. Though WP's long sentences too often sacrifice sound for sense, his purple passages are masterpieces of their kind. A. C. Swinburne's "Notes on Designs of the Old Masters at Florence" inspired WP's *The Renaissance* in both matter and manner. WP has a "stained-glass style." George Meredith and James Joyce are stylistic successors of WP. WP almost deserves George Moore's quip that in his books the English language lies in state. WP copied certain tricks of Matthew Arnold's style, but not the rhythm. [Contains stylistic analyses of passages from "Botticelli," "The Poetry of Michelangelo," "Leonardo da Vinci," and "Style."]

727 Brion, Marcel. LÉONARD DE VINCI (Leonardo da Vinci) (Paris: Albin Michel, 1952); rptd (1963), p. 465.

In "Leonardo da Vinci," WP understood that Leonardo portrayed the eternal feminine in the *Mona Lisa* when he saw in the picture the sum total of feminine experiences through the centuries; he realized that Mona Lisa in the portrait had undergone a metamorphosis from the original model to something more vast and complex. [In French.]

728 Craster, Sir Edmund. HISTORY OF THE BODLEIAN LIBRARY, 1845–1945 (Oxford: Clarendon P, 1952), pp. 300–301.
The Bodleian contains the manuscript of WP's "Pascal" (MS. Don. d. 84).

729 Decker, Clarence R. THE VICTORIAN CONSCIENCE (NY: Twayne, 1952), pp. 102, 164, 167.
Like WP, Edmond and Jules de Goncourt are sensitive to the delicacies of literature, "though they are less scrupulous, more feverish, and are interested in a different kind of truth." George Moore's admiration for WP and R. L. Stevenson is one indication of how foreign naturalism really was to his nature.

730 Du Bos, Charles. "Walter Pater: Extraits d'un cours inédit" (Walter Pater: Extracts from an Unpublished Course), ÉTUDES ANGLAISES, V (May 1952), 117–21.
WP cherished the "shield of silence" that preserved him from the outer world. His work, his only means of communication, is a virtual, implicit confession, the "portrait of a soul." Each of his imaginary portraits has the value of an idealized autobiography. *Marius the Epicurean* is the spiritual portrait of the author. The "imaginary portrait" is practically a genre invented by WP, and it represents a second stage in his development, the sublimation of the thematic technique that formed *The Renaissance,* an original creation but one in which the point of departure was other works of art. In the "imaginary portraits," historical facts are only a background for spiritual situations. In "A Prince of Court Painters," the story is told refractively, through the diary of the sister of Jean-Baptiste Pater (whose last name, not surprisingly, is never mentioned), who is in love with Watteau. In the quiet simplicity of her provincial life, wondering if exciting success has brought happiness to Watteau, one is reminded of WP himself. [In French.]

731 Gaunt, William. VICTORIAN OLYMPUS (Lond: Cape; NY: Oxford UP, 1952), p. 132.
WP was among those who sat for the painter William Blake Richmond, who designed the tablet to WP's memory in the Brasenose College chapel.

732 Gosse, Edmund. [Letter], in Robert Ross, ROBERT ROSS, FRIEND OF FRIENDS, ed by Margery Ross (Lond: Cape, 1952), p. 315.
[Letter from Gosse to Ross, dated 20 Aug 1917, tells of A. C. Swinburne's abruptly leaving London in May 1873 to consult with WP and Ingram Bywater at Oxford on hearing of the Simeon Solomon scandal.]

733 Houghton, Walter E. "Walter Horatio Pater, 1839–1894," BRITISH LITERATURE FROM BLAKE TO THE PRESENT DAY, ed by Hazelton Spencer, Walter E. Houghton, and Herbert Barrows (Bost: Heath, 1952); rptd (1963), pp. 814–15.
Perhaps some of WP's "aloofness from the world of practical action and his delicate sense for distinctions of feeling" may be due to the early death of his father

and the feminine influence of his aunt, grandmother, and mother. Though WP and Matthew Arnold are the two major critics of the Victorian period, their differences are more striking than their similarities: while Arnold had the characteristic Victorian longing for certitude, WP's study of history led him to believe that nothing is true in an absolute sense and that everything is true in relation to its environment. In this sense, WP is closer to twentieth-century thought than Arnold. WP offered to his generation a new philosophy rather than a new criticism: "He was the architect, you might say, who built the Ivory Tower in which Morris was a visitor, and in which the aesthetes of the 90's, Wilde and Symons and the young Yeats, made their home." *The Renaissance* was a pioneer work in England. The critical rationale for WP's art for art's sake is contained in "The School of Giorgione," but one suspects that in claiming there that all art should aspire to the condition of music, WP "was simply trying to find critical grounds on which to exalt the kind of 'pure' poetry and painting which he wanted"; but still, his insistence on organic art (derived from Coleridge) was valid and much needed. In the "Preface" to *The Renaissance* he essentially demands that one look at a work of art as an organic whole and respond to it with "a unified sensibility," which is basically what T. S. Eliot and I. A. Richards have called for in the twentieth century.

734 Johnson, Robert Vincent. "Walter Pater as Critic: His Critical Practice Considered in Relation to His Theories of Life and Art." Published dissertation, University of Manchester, 1952; pub as WALTER PATER: A STUDY OF HIS CRITICAL OUTLOOK AND ACHIEVEMENT (Melbourne: Melbourne UP, 1961), q.v. for abstract.
[Listed in Lawrence F. McNamee, DISSERTATIONS IN ENGLISH AND AMERICAN LITERATURE (NY and Lond: Bowker, 1968).]

735 "Letters from Gosse and Benson," COLBY LIBRARY QUARTERLY, III (Nov 1952), 134–36.
Probably upon the announcement that A. C. Benson would write the English Men of Letters volume on WP, Violet Paget wrote to Benson, expressing interest in aesthetics and WP. In Benson's reply (16 July 1905), he writes: "I only knew Mr. Pater a very little, but I *seem*, by reading his books and talking to people who knew him and cared for him, to have come to know him, I won't say well, but perhaps as well as he could or would permit. . . . The only side I saw of Mr. Pater was a kind of weary courtesy, which seemed to desire to be sympathetic, to be prodigal of kindness, but to shrink from the effort of producing it; one felt that it was there in a sense; as though someone pointed to a heavy sack of gold and said—'you may carry that away if you will and can: it is yours; but I cannot rise and hand it to you!' "

736 Mendilow, A. A. TIME AND THE NOVEL (Lond & NY: Peter Nevill, 1952); rptd (NY: Humanities P, 1965); (1972), pp. 27, 49, 56, 88.
WP's dictum in "The School of Giorgione" that "all art constantly aspires towards

the condition of music" seems to be finding justification in fiction, as indicated by such titles as Thomas De Quincey's THE DREAM FUGUE, André Gide's TWO SYMPHONIES, and Aldous Huxley's POINT COUNTER POINT. Though WP, Robert Graves, and Baron Corvo all deal fictionally with the same period of history, they do so in different spirits.

737 Nejdefors-Frisk, Sonja. GEORGE MOORE'S NATURALISTIC PROSE (Upsala: A.-B. Lundequistska Bokhandeln [Upsala Irish Studies, III]; Cambridge, Mass: Harvard UP, 1952), pp. 23, 32–33, 34–35.

If one looks closely, one finds the voice of WP as well as that of Théophile Gautier in Moore's CONFESSIONS OF A YOUNG MAN; Moore found that they had similar or identical outlooks on life in their worship of beauty, their acceptance of the visible world, and their refusal of ascetic Christianity. Stylistically, WP appealed to Moore because of his mastery of shades of meaning and unexpected nuances.

738 Praz, Mario. LA CRISI DELL'EROE NEL ROMANZO VITTORIANO (The Crisis of the Hero in Victorian Fiction) (Florence: G. C. Sansoni, 1952), pp. 3, 28, 67, 350, 351, 352; trans by Angus Davidson as THE HERO IN ECLIPSE IN VICTORIAN FICTION (Lond & NY: Oxford UP, 1956); rptd (1969) pp. 1, 29, 71, 374, 376.

Charles Lamb seems to be a precursor of the Goncourts and WP in conjecturing on the evil beauty of Leonardo's women. In "The Child in the House," the manner in which WP dwells on place has acquired a spiritual quality, which represents a shift from George Eliot's minute observations of objects to "intimism," paralleling the transition in painting from the impassive realism of Caravaggio to the warm realism of Vermeer. In À LA RECHERCHE DU TEMPS PERDU, Marcel Proust's feeling toward the church at Combray, dear because of childhood associations, is reminiscent of "The Child in the House." [In Italian.]

739 Praz, Mario. "Leonardo in Inghilterra" (Leonardo in England), ULISSE (Rome), III (1952–53), 589–93.

WP's interpretation of Leonardo da Vinci was foreshadowed (in varying degrees) in England by William Beckford, Shelley, Charles Lamb, Thomas Griffiths Wainewright, and A. C. Swinburne; his interpretation influenced Oscar Wilde and Edward Dowden. [In Italian.]

740 Read, Herbert. "The Art of Art Criticism," LISTENER, XLVII (1 May, 15 May 1952), 714–16, 797, 799–800.

Interpretive, as opposed to descriptive, art criticism began with WP: "it consists in shifting the critical attention from the work of art as object, to the work of art as symbol: from the meaning of the work of art to its motive: in other words, the critic substitutes for description interpretation." WP's description of the *Birth of Venus* in "Botticelli" is not simply a description but an interpretation of its meaning as well and is "criticism raised in itself to an art." Today WP's method of criticism is not exceptional but unfashionable. The kind of art criticism written by WP, John

Ruskin, and Charles Baudelaire was concerned with pictorial motives—story and theme—but although there is often no story in modern abstract art, still the artist's symbols must be interpreted.

741 Reisdorff, Julius. "Die Ästhetische Idee in Walter Paters Kunstkritik" (The Aesthetic Concept in Walter Pater's Art Criticism). Unpublished dissertation, Bonn, 1952.
[Listed in Lawrence F. McNamee, DISSERTATIONS IN ENGLISH AND AMERICAN LITERATURE (NY and Lond: Bowker, 1968).] [In German.]

742 Ross, Robert. ROBERT ROSS, FRIEND OF FRIENDS: LETTERS TO ROBERT ROSS, ART CRITIC AND WRITER, TOGETHER WITH EXTRACTS FROM HIS PUBLISHED ARTICLES, ed by Margery Ross (Lond: Cape, 1952), p. 23.
[Excerpt from a lecture delivered by Ross at Liverpool in 1908]: "I remember that excellent third-rate writer, W. E. H. Lecky, making a speech at a dinner of the Authors' Society, in which he said that he was sorry to say there were no great writers alive, and no stylists to compare with those who had passed away. A few places off sat Walter Pater, George Meredith, and Mr. Austin Dobson. Tennyson, though not present at the banquet, was president of the Society, and Ruskin was still alive."

743 Sutherland, James R. THE ENGLISH CRITIC (Lond: University College, 1952), pp. 16–17.
Though in some ways characteristic of English criticism, WP is "too fastidious to be quite in the tradition, too amorous of the remote and the moribund, and never really happy with the kind of literature that teems with vulgar life."

1953

744 Abrams, M. H. THE MIRROR AND THE LAMP. ROMANTIC THEORY AND THE CRITICAL TRADITION (NY: Oxford UP, 1953), pp. 135–36, 224, 235, 259, 318; rptd (NY: Norton, 1958).
William Hazlitt's critical method prefigures the impressionistic method outlined in WP's "Preface" to *The Renaissance.* In "Coleridge," WP shrewdly points out that, since the laws of the inanimate world are fixed and given and operate unconsciously and without the possibility of choice, Coleridge's theory of organic artistic composition runs the danger of being reduced to artistic automatism. John Keble's idea that each personality has a "ruling taste or passion" goes back to the humours theory and the idea of the "ruling passion" and lives on in Sainte-Beuve's "faculté première," Matthew Arnold's "essential character," and WP's "personal formula." In "Style," WP's definition of literary truth as a personal sense of fact approximates the idea of truth as sincerity.

745 Blissett, William. "Pater and Eliot," UNIVERSITY OF TORONTO QUARTERLY, XXII (April 1953), 261–68.

T. S. Eliot views WP as a "horrible example" of what Matthew Arnold's view of culture and religion could degenerate into. But they share an interest in many of the same writers and reveal striking similarities in expression and use of imagery. Both refer to the SATYRICON, the PERVIGILIUM VENERIS, the ANIMULA; there are similarities between WP's description of the triumphal procession of Marcus Aurelius in *Marius the Epicurean* and Eliot's "Coriolan"; repeated references by both to the subjects of words and time are made; both seek to create a sense of the transcendence of time; both wrote essays on Pascal; both employ the image of the world as a hospital in which a cure comes from the church; Eliot's imagination, like WP's, is "deeply stirred by music"; the FOUR QUARTETS "consciously 'aspire to the condition of music' " (cf. "The School of Giorgione"). Eliot was probably attracted to the works of WP in his early years.

746 Crane, R. S. THE LANGUAGES OF CRITICISM AND THE STRUCTURE OF POETRY (Toronto: University of Toronto P, 1953); rptd (1957); (1964), pp. 92, 96.

WP sees form as internal and content, in the sense of the raw materials of experience, as external, unlike Louis Cazamian, Cleanth Brooks, René Wellek and Austin Warren, F. W. Bateson, and F. R. Leavis, each of whom has a different definition of form and content.

747 Crinò, Anna Maria. "Notizie sulla fama di Leonardo in Inghilterra" (Report on the Fame of Leonardo in England), LEONARDO NEL V. CENTENARIO DELLA SUA NASCITA, ed by Liceo Scientifico "Leonardo da Vinci" di Firenze (Florence: Tipografia Giuntina, 1953), pp. 61–76.

WP's "Leonardo da Vinci" is a very important article in the history of Leonardo's fame, although there are many pages in it on works no longer attributed to Leonardo. [In Italian.]

748 Doughty, Oswald. "Rossetti's Conception of the 'Poetic' in Poetry and Painting," ESSAYS BY DIVERS HANDS: BEING THE TRANSACTIONS OF THE ROYAL SOCIETY OF LITERATURE, nsXXVI (1953), 89–102.

Giorgione's *Concert Champêtre* served as a symbol of beauty, happiness, and peace for both A. C. Swinburne and WP, the idea for which they may have received from D. G. Rossetti. Rossetti's criticism of Marochetti's statue of Sappho may have influenced WP's description of the *Mona Lisa* in "Leonardo da Vinci."

749 Fletcher, Iain. "Introduction," THE COMPLETE POEMS OF LIONEL JOHNSON (Lond: Unicorn P, 1953), pp. xi–xliv.

The solution of the late nineteenth-century aesthetes' disgust with their time was to set their own private and inner world in opposition to their "disordered view of the public world": "It involved that relativity in religion and morals, that distillation of intellectual essences into tenuous sentiment—even the most intractably logical subject might be dissipated into pure feeling—so characteristic of all Pater's writing." The attitude of WP's Marius [*Marius the Epicurean*]—that religion has become "a matter largely of gracious sentiment"—typifies the attitude toward religion of many of the writers of the 1890s. WP was a student of spiritual evil, as witnessed, for example, in the themes of the scapegoat in "Denys l'Auxerrois" and the ambivalence of God in "Apollo in Picardy." WP was also preoccupied with the contrast between the monastic ideal and the life of the senses, often seen in a "beautiful ascetic youth," but he was never required to solve that dilemma. Lewis Hind, editor of THE ACADEMY, received Johnson's elegy on WP on 22 Sept 1902.

750 Fraser, G. S. THE MODERN WRITER AND HIS WORLD (Lond: Derek Verschoyle, 1953); rvd ed (Baltimore: Penguin Books; NY: Frederick A. Praeger, 1964), pp. 14, 102, 129, 193, 362–64.

WP understood that "full-blooded historicism implies the relativity of all values, including one's own." L. H. Myers's THE ROOT AND THE FLOWER recalls *Marius the Epicurean* more than any other work of English fiction; but Myers would have disapproved of WP's aestheticism. Wilde's THE SOUL OF MAN UNDER SOCIALISM draws on insights from Arnold, William Morris, and WP. As a literary critic, WP communicates the "sterile subjectivity of the *connoisseur.*" As T. S. Eliot points out, he was fundamentally as much of a moralist as any of the great Victorian " 'thinkers.' " His "refined hedonism" is "practicable morality for sheltered minorities." He consistently made writers over again in his own image. In Wilde and George Moore the cult degenerates into "gaudy self-display." The only first rate mind influenced by WP was Yeats. Saintsbury, though an aesthete like WP, had nothing of the Victorian moralist about him.

751 Gardner, W. H. "Introduction," POEMS AND PROSE OF GERARD MANLEY HOPKINS, ed by W. H. Gardner (Lond: Penguin, 1953); rptd (1954); (1960); (1966), pp. xiii–xxxvi.

WP's teaching and criticism were an important early influence on Hopkins. Early in 1868, WP introduced Hopkins to A. C. Swinburne and Simeon Solomon. Hopkins's theory of inscape probably owes something to WP, his Platonic dialogue ON THE ORIGIN OF BEAUTY may have been written for WP, and WP's influence can also be felt in some lecture notes on "Poetry and Verse" (1874).

752 Levinson, Ronald B. IN DEFENSE OF PLATO (Cambridge, Mass: Harvard UP, 1953); rptd (NY: Russell & Russell, 1970), pp. 4–5.

WP's version of Plato is "more secular though hardly less imposing" than Benjamin Jowett's. In *Plato and Platonism* "Plato appears essentially as the great seer of beauty, the true founder of that cult of harmonious living of which Pater himself was at once practitioner and priest."

753 Marlow, Louis [Louis U. Wilkinson]. SEVEN FRIENDS (Lond: Richards P, 1953), p. 67.

Llewelyn Powys's style shows the influence of WP, Charles Lamb, and Robert Burton.

754 Millhauser, Milton. "Walter Pater and the Flux," JOURNAL OF AESTHETICS AND ART CRITICISM, XI (March 1953), 214–23.

Much in WP is either idealized autobiography or an attempt to work out his own spiritual problems by embodying them in characters unlike himself. The heroes of "Sebastian Van Storck," "Emerald Uthwart," and *Marius the Epicurean* fall into the latter category, and those works resemble in technique, strangely enough, Émile Zola's experimental method. The circumstances of WP's childhood instilled in him an awareness of death and flux and a need for religion that he could never justify intellectually. In each of the *Imaginary Portraits,* "a person of marked singleness of character or purpose moves through a world to which he is more or less a spiritual alien, succeeding in life as he keeps that world at a distance, and coming to grief through its intrusion." There is an obvious parallel here with WP himself, as if he split his personality into fragments and placed each of them into a different hostile environment. The inconclusiveness of many of WP's works of fiction is due to his belief that life itself is meaningless and inconclusive. Though he acknowledged the flux, he protested against it and seemed to believe that the function of civilization was to establish fixed points in opposition to the flux, and thus his treatment of character tends to be static. His attempt to find a subject's "formula" is a corollary of this habit of mind.

755 Riewald, J. G. SIR MAX BEERBOHM, MAN AND WRITER: A CRITICAL ANALYSIS WITH A BRIEF LIFE AND A BIBLIOGRAPHY (The Hague: Martinus Nijhoff, 1953), pp. 4, 49, 50, 52, 71, 73, 113, 130, 175, 176, 178, 180, 181, 303, 328.

In "Diminuendo" (1895), Beerbohm turned his back on WP's philosophy of cultivating all kinds of sensations: henceforth his problem would be only to avoid those sensations that were not purely intellectual. His "A Defense of Cosmetics" is a parody of Oscar Wilde and a burlesque of WP. The hero of "James Pethel" is a kind of worldly WP. WP felt happier when criticizing life as revealed in a work of art than he did when dealing with life itself. Beerbohm felt that there was too much art in WP's style, though he found beauty in the descriptions of the madonnas in "Botticelli" and the *Mona Lisa* in "Leonardo da Vinci." On the relation between form and substance, Beerbohm agreed with WP rather than with Wilde. A manuscript notebook of Beerbohm's in the Columbia University Library contains quotations from or references to *Appreciations.*

756 Robinson, James K. "A Neglected Phase of the Aesthetic Movement: English Parnassianism," PUBLICATIONS OF THE MODERN LANGUAGE ASSOCIATION, LXVIII (Sept 1953), 733–54.

Théophile Gautier was the chief influence on the ideas of WP, as is particularly apparent in "Winckelmann," "Leonardo da Vinci," and "Wordsworth." *The Renaissance* is throughout "animated by aesthetic ideals derived to a considerable degree from *Pléiade* and *Parnassien* theory."

757 Rubinstein, Annette T. THE GREAT TRADITION IN ENGLISH LITER-
ATURE FROM SHAKESPEARE TO SHAW (NY: Citadel P, 1953); rptd (NY:
Russell & Russell, 1960); rptd (NY: Monthly Review P, 1969), pp. 848,
884; rptd (NY: Citadel Paperbacks, 1962).

WP's "cultivated hedonism" is developed in *Marius the Epicurean,* "which
served as bible for the comparatively small number that achieved decadence by
way of the universities, and the much larger number of those who admired it in
their salad days there." WP's younger followers had neither his material security,
his "timid or austere temperament," nor the "stable world" in which he had grown
up to make his "prudent aestheticism" a possibility for them: "It is only by an
unkind irony of fate that his dictum appears to have borne so much more fruit than
does most professorial advice."

758 Simeone, William E. "Leonardo and English Literature," THE
RESOURCES OF LEONARDO: PAPERS DELIVERED AT SOUTHERN ILLINOIS
UNIVERSITY, NOVEMBER 12TH–15TH, 1952, ed by George Kimball
Plochmann (Carbondale: Southern Illinois UP, 1953), p. 28 [abstract of a
speech].

Shelley, in his poem on Leonardo's *Medusa,* anticipates WP's discussion of the
picture. In "Leonardo da Vinci" WP examines Leonardo's genius as well as his art
and "brings to our attention not just the familiar fragments thrown off by an
over-wrought genius but also the magnitude of the volcanic mind from which they
all flow." John Addington Symonds and Lionel Johnson wrote of Leonardo in the
manner of WP.

759 Temple, Ruth Zabriskie. THE CRITIC'S ALCHEMY: A STUDY OF THE
INTRODUCTION OF FRENCH SYMBOLISM INTO ENGLAND (NY: Twayne,
1953); rptd (New Haven: College & University P, 1962), pp. 16, 17, 73,
82, 83, 86, 111, 112, 122, 123, 136, 154, 176, 177, 178, 211, 225, 232,
263, 270, 273, 281, 289.

Since WP had little to say about French poetry, his main contribution to the
acceptance of the French symbolists in England was the theory and method that he
passed on to A. C. Swinburne and Arthur Symons. Supplementing his theories
with those of Théophile Gautier and Charles Baudelaire, WP's followers asserted
that the critic's business is with art alone, divorced from considerations of utility or
morality. For John Crowe Ransom, Baudelaire, and WP, the critic owes a twofold
response to his material: "sensitivity (the experience of pleasure) and knowledge."
WP's critical ancestor is S. T. Coleridge, who believed that the end of poetry is
pleasure, that there should be a special relation between the parts and the whole in a
poem, and that the critic should isolate "specific symptoms" of poetic power, an
idea that anticipates WP's search for the "active principle" of a poet's work. WP
adapted for English purposes the impressionistic aspect of Sainte-Beuve's
criticism. In Swinburne's early critical essays, it is impossible to tell how much is
Gautier, Baudelaire, or WP. Symons seems to have tried to explain the work of

Edmond de Goncourt to WP and that of WP to Goncourt, and he believed WP to be the English equivalent in prose to Goncourt. Symons, following Gautier, Paul Verlaine, and WP, defined the literature of decadence as the literature of a beautiful disease. WP saw art through such a particularized temperament that all the works he described took on something of "its delicate melancholy and its strangeness." Implicit in the criticism of WP and Baudelaire is the idea that a work of art is a real object possessing qualities that may be apprehended or misapprehended. WP, like Symons, George Moore, and Swinburne, wrote for an artistic elite. Moore, like Oscar Wilde, followed WP and Gustave Flaubert "in evolving prose style as carefully wrought as verse." Though "aesthetic" and "impressionist" came to be used interchangeably in designating critics, "it is possible to subscribe to the doctrine of the autonomy of art, fundamental to Pater's and Baudelaire's theory, while deploring the excesses of the impressionist method in criticism. And it is possible for a critic to write impressionistically without embracing the doctrine of art for art's sake."

760 Welland, D. S. R. (ed). THE PRE-RAPHAELITES IN LITERATURE AND ART (Lond: George G. Harrap; NY: Barnes & Noble, 1953); rptd (Freeport, NY: Books for Libraries P, 1969), pp. 13, 31, 188, 203, 208.

Steeped in European literature and art, an authority on the Italian Renaissance, and a man of wide culture, WP was better equipped than Robert Buchanan to appreciate the poetry of D. G. Rossetti. Rossetti's prose study "Hand and Soul" anticipates in conception and method WP's imaginary portraits.

1954

761 Aldington, Richard. PINORMAN: PERSONAL RECOLLECTIONS OF NORMAN DOUGLAS, PINO ORIOLI AND CHARLES PRENTICE (Lond: Heinemann, 1954), pp. 27, 62, 88, 130.

Norman Douglas's prose is "classical," "as far from the finicky elegance of Walter Pater's writing as from banal neatness." When Charles Prentice was a student there, his dislike of C. L. Shadwell, the provost of Oriel College, Oxford, was so strong that it also included WP, Shadwell's friend, about whom Prentice "would not hear a word of praise." [According to a French writer referred to as J. S.,] the hedonism of Norman Douglas and Oscar Wilde derived from WP, who in turn picked it up from Théophile Gautier, and ultimately from Goethe.

762 Allen, Walter. THE ENGLISH NOVEL: A SHORT CRITICAL HISTORY (NY: Dutton, 1954), pp. 292, 333–34, 419.

A passage in Thomas Hardy's THE RETURN OF THE NATIVE is reminiscent of WP's *The Renaissance*. Virginia Woolf's attitude to experience, like WP's, is aesthetic.

763 Broad, Lewis. THE FRIENDSHIPS AND FOLLIES OF OSCAR WILDE (Lond: Hutchinson, 1954), pp. 38–39, 54, 55, 62, 65, 73, 93, 98; rptd (NY: Crowell, 1955); rptd as THE TRUTH ABOUT OSCAR WILDE (Tiptree, Essex: Arrow, 1957).

Though WP "was content in his monkish rooms to realize in thought the ecstasies and pulsating moments of his prose," unlike Wilde, who was not so detached about sensations, still WP and John Pentland Mahaffy made Wilde a pagan and a sensualist. Though WP's aesthetic pretensions were more considerable than Wilde's, he was outclassed as a personality: "The rather dreary, rather commonplace, rather insignificant don could not hold a sunflower to the flamboyant Wilde." WP's championing of THE PICTURE OF DORIAN GRAY did WP more harm than it did Wilde good.

764 Dale, E. Hilda. LA POÉSIE FRANÇAISE EN ANGLETERRE, 1850–1890: SA FORTUNE ET SON INFLUENCE (French Poetry in England, 1850–1890: Its Fortune and Its Influence) (Paris: Didier, 1954), pp. 8, 88–90, 94, 100.

WP's call for a life devoted to art in the "Conclusion" to *The Renaissance* seems less an artistic doctrine than an attitude toward life, which explains why he suppressed that essay in the second edition of *The Renaissance*. Though he calls for a fusion of matter and form in "The School of Giorgione," he departs from the doctrine that art should have no end besides itself even in that essay, in praising the moral and political poetry of Victor Hugo; and in "Style" he makes an even clearer break from that doctrine in distinguishing between good art and great art. In the latter essay he rejoins Matthew Arnold, for whom a divorce between art and life was impossible. But if the views of Arnold and WP are similar, their critical methods are different in that WP insists on interpreting rather than judging. Both critics followed French models. George Saintsbury followed WP in posing the principle of an adequate form in prose and poetry. [In French.]

765 Du Bos, Charles. JOURNAL, Vol. 5: 1929 (Paris: La Colombe, 1954), pp. 78, 100, 216, 223.

[Du Bos still plans to write a book on WP. Contains other minor references.] [In French.]

766 Eliot, George. THE GEORGE ELIOT LETTERS, ed by Gordon S. Haight. Seven Volumes (New Haven: Yale UP, 1954–55), V, 100, 455; VI, 406.

[In her journal for 27 May 1870, Eliot mentions WP's being present at the same dinner party as herself in Oxford. In a letter of 5 Nov 1873 to John Blackwood, she writes (in reference to Mrs. Oliphant's review of *The Renaissance* in BLACKWOOD'S, CXIV [Nov 1873], 607–8): "I agreed very warmly with the remarks made by your contributor this month on Mr. Pater's book, which seems to me quite poisonous in its false principles of criticism and false conceptions of life."]

767 Ellmann, Richard. THE IDENTITY OF YEATS (NY: Oxford UP, 1954); rptd (1964); rptd (Lond: Macmillan, 1954); rptd (Lond: Faber & Faber, 1964), pp. 132–33, 318.

In 1907, in some brief essays called DISCOVERIES, W. B. Yeats "went so far as to disagree" with WP and the French Symbolists that music was the type of all the arts. In saying that he who would write English vigorously must write it "like a learned language," Yeats unconsciously echoed WP.

768 Friederich, Werner P., and David Henry Malone. OUTLINE OF COMPARATIVE LITERATURE FROM DANTE ALIGHIERI TO EUGENE O'NEILL (Chapel Hill: University of North Carolina P, 1954); rptd (1962), pp. 189, 341, 366, 414, 415.

For WP and Matthew Arnold, a revival of classical antiquity seemed the best way of enriching Victorian literature. After the publication of Paul Heyse's DIE KINDER DER WELT, A. C. Swinburne's works, and *Marius the Epicurean,* "the air seemed filled with unrestrained sensualism." Charles Baudelaire was an influence on WP.

769 Hale, J. R. ENGLAND AND THE ITALIAN RENAISSANCE: THE GROWTH OF INTEREST IN ITS HISTORY AND ART (Lond: Faber & Faber, 1954), pp. 148, 194, 195; rptd with revisions (Lond: Arrow, 1963).

In *The Renaissance,* WP "invented" a "medieval Renaissance." Vernon Lee's two masters when she wrote EUPHORION were J. A. Symonds and WP: she "aped the purposeful delicacy" of WP's style and took the title of her book from *The Renaissance.*

770 Hardy, Barbara. "Pater, Walter Horatio," CASSELL'S ENCY-CLOPAEDIA OF WORLD LITERATURE, ed by S. H. Steinberg (NY: Funk & Wagnalls, 1954), pp. 1331–32; pub in England as CASSELL'S ENCY-CLOPAEDIA OF LITERATURE (Lond: Cassell, 1953).

When WP speaks of art for art's sake, art includes much of life. "As a critic he has his blindnesses: he respects historical criticism but sometimes forgets it; he recreates art in the image of his own vision; he writes oddly about Wordsworth and Coleridge. But his sensitive introspection and dual interest in form and matter (especially in literature) make him an influence as well as an eccentric."

771 Harris, Alan. "Oscar Wilde as Playwright: A Centenary Review," ADELPHI, XXX (1954), 212–40.

How short the distance is between the two poles of the Roman Catholic church and the doctrine of WP's "Conclusion" [*The Renaissance*] can be seen by the number of aesthetes who converted to Catholicism and, "up to a point," by WP's own development. Wilde's trip to Greece with his tutor, Mahaffy, is "sometimes credited with having turned the scale finally, or all but finally, in favor of *The Renaissance* rather than Rome." WP showed insight in perceiving that Wilde's criticism carried on the critical tradition of Matthew Arnold.

772 Hartman, Geoffrey. THE UNMEDIATED VISION: AN INTERPRETA-
TION OF WORDSWORTH, HOPKINS, RILKE, AND VALÉRY (New Haven:
Yale UP, 1954); rptd (NY: Harcourt, Brace & World, Harbinger Books,
1966), pp. 65–66, 188.

In "The Windhover" G. M. Hopkins is in revolt against both a "residual diction of
generality" and "the diction of sweetness which at the time of his writing was
uttering its swan-song in the work of Pater and the Pre-Raphaelites." WP's
awareness of physical beauty, though real, was "an ideal limited by Greek example
and too soon exhausted by the delicacy of a rose."

773 Holland, Vyvyan. SON OF OSCAR WILDE (NY: Dutton, 1954), pp.
17–18, 211–12; (Lond: Rupert Hart-Davis, 1954); rptd (Harmondsworth,
Middlesex: Penguin, 1957).

At Oxford Wilde fell under the "spell" of WP, an "obscure Fellow and Tutor of
Brasenose College" who "has been accused of being the most baneful influence
ever to be at Oxford." WP "preached that physical sensation is an end in itself, to
which it is noble to aspire." Neither John Ruskin nor WP can be accused of
decadence for admiring beauty for its own sake. [In a letter to William Ward, 19
July 1877 (quoted in full on pp. 211–12), Wilde mentions having promised to send
some of WP's articles to a Miss Fletcher whom he met in Rome and quotes in full a
letter from WP praising Wilde's article on the Grosvenor Gallery in the DUBLIN
UNIVERSITY MAGAZINE.]

774 Johnson, R. V. "Pater and the Victorian Anti-Romantics," ESSAYS
IN CRITICISM, IV (Jan 1954), 42–57.

The concept of "romantic" held by the anti-romantic Victorian critics, and particularly those who wrote in the QUARTERLY REVIEW, was exemplified in their own day
by the writings of WP, D. G. Rossetti, and A. C. Swinburne. They felt that these
contemporary "romantic" writers appealed too exclusively to a coterie culture, a
tendency the roots of which they detected in William Wordsworth and John Keats
and the manifestations of which they saw as "a lack of contact with the tastes and
interests of the educated public, a vague and often perverse sensuousness, a lack of
definite thought, an excessive preoccupation with superficial graces of form."
What the anti-romantic critics failed to realize was that, considering the social and
economic conditions of Victorian England, it was inevitable that highly educated
young men should turn to "self-culture" and the cultivation of a private sensibility,
since no other courses of life seemed to have any meaning. WP usually valued the
striking presentation of particular details in poetry. In "Style" he seems to see the
problem of communication as "involving merely the accommodation of objective
form to inner conception" and does not take communication with the reader into
account. In his view of literary sincerity, WP has something in common with some
later critics who are not "particularly appreciative" of him, like I. A. Richards.

775 Laver, James. OSCAR WILDE (Lond: Longmans, Green, 1954);
rptd with revisions (1956), pp. 9–10, 15, 17.

WP shared John Ruskin's passion for beauty, but he did not share Ruskin's social conscience, and WP had a stronger influence on Wilde than did Ruskin. WP "strove to cultivate an aesthetic sensibility sharpened almost to the point of neurosis." He made no effort to cultivate Wilde's acquaintance and is said to have disliked him. In THE PICTURE OF DORIAN GRAY, Lord Henry Wotton recommends to Dorian a life based on WP's doctrines.

> **776** Laver, James. VICTORIAN VISTA (Lond: Hulton P, 1954; Bost: Houghton Mifflin, 1955), pp. 241, 242.

Though the decadents of the Nineties evolved from the aestheticism of such figures from the Eighties as WP, Edward Burne-Jones, and William Morris, they added a new element: morbidity. The logical French perceived that art for art's sake inevitably becomes sensation for sensation's sake, but WP was very different from Charles Baudelaire: "In plain terms, Baudelaire knew what he was about, and Pater didn't. By comparison with the French ancestors of The Decadence, what a lot of innocently benevolent uncles the Englishmen seem!"

> **777** Main, William W. "Pater's 'Sebastian Van Storck,' " EXPLI-CATOR, XII (May 1954), item 44.

The end of "Sebastian Van Storck" illustrates the "Christian paradox of losing one's life in order to save it": Sebastian rejects his former selfish life and his doctrine of nihilism in an act of self-sacrifice. Furthermore, his dry intellectual pride is symbolically purged in the inundation. The piece is "basically a story of man's redemption told in the particular historical context of modern man's futile intellectual isolation in an alien world." Given the implications of the ending, the assumption that WP "separates art and life and takes refuge in aesthetics ought to be re-examined."

> **778** May, Merrill M. "Symbolic Theory and Practice in the Prose Fictions of Walter Pater." Unpublished dissertation, University of Chicago, 1954.

[Listed in Lawrence F. McNamee, DISSERTATIONS IN ENGLISH AND AMERICAN LITERATURE (NY and Lond: Bowker, 1968).]

> **779** Moore, Virginia. THE UNICORN: WILLIAM BUTLER YEATS' SEARCH FOR REALITY (NY: Macmillan, 1954), p. 39.

With the publication of THE WIND AMONG THE REEDS in 1899, Yeats repudiated WP's aestheticism.

> **780** Norwood, Gilbert. "The BACCHAE and its Riddle," ESSAYS ON EURIPIDEAN DRAMA (Lond: Cambridge UP; Berkeley & Los Angeles: University of California P; Toronto: University of Toronto P, 1954), pp. 52–73.

[On a linguistic crux in the BACCHAE]: In "The Bacchanals of Euripides," WP writes "Dionysus is seen stepping out from among the tottering masses of the mimic palace": "That (as usual with him) is exquisitely written—also (as too often with him) evasive: 'from among' suggests that the palace is down; 'tottering' suggests that it is not, as yet."

781 Ojala, Aatos. AESTHETICISM AND OSCAR WILDE. Two Volumes (SUOMALAISEN TIEDEAKATEMIAN TOIMITUKSIA [Helsinki], Ser B, XC:2, XCIII:2 [1954, 1955]); rptd (Folcroft, Pa: Folcroft Library Eds, 1971), I, 26, 43, 44–46, 97, 100–105, 112, 117–21, 136–37, 140, 154, 161, 176, 205, 215, 221; II, 17, 47–49, 99, 129, 135, 138, 144, 185, 196.

Living his solitary, ascetic life in his Oxford college, one could assign as a motto for WP's life what he said of AUCASSIN ET NICOLETTE: "Its subject is a great sorrow, yet it claims to be a thing of joy and refreshment." English decadence begins with the publication in 1873 of *The Renaissance*. WP's influence on Wilde is most palpable in the latter's early essays, "The English Renaissance of Art," "Lecture to Art Students," and "L'Envoi." WP gave Wilde's thought the initial impetus that eventually carried it beyond the limits that WP reached. From "The Critic as Artist" on, the ultimate goal of Wilde's thought is WP's ideal of the contemplative life. WP's style is "so elaborately and perfectly finished that all conscious pastiche in the dependent sense of the word" will inevitably mean a "deterioration." Certain words in Wilde's vocabulary have "a particularly clear Paterian ring about them."

782 Schwab, Arnold T. "Irish Author and American Critic: George Moore and James Huneker (Part One)," NINETEENTH-CENTURY FICTION, VIII (March 1954), 256–71.

Moore attempted "with increasing success, to achieve Pater's melodic line," and Huneker's indebtedness to WP is "well-attested" in STEEPLEJACK.

783 Singer, Irving. "The Aesthetics of 'Art for Art's Sake,' " JOURNAL OF AESTHETICS AND ART CRITICISM, XII (March 1954), 343–59.

In reaction to John Ruskin's belief that there was a correlation between "ethical nobility in a man's life" and "aesthetic nobility in his work," critics like WP "spent comparatively little time in the study of the artist's character but a great deal of time in the elucidation of what happened to themselves, as sensitive specialists, when they encountered his work." Though many of the adherents of art for art's sake were unaware that the concept was in reality ethical, A. C. Bradley and WP (in "Style" and "Wordsworth") recognized this aspect of the theory, and both rejected it.

784 Stanford, Derek. "Lionel Johnson As Critic," MONTH, nsXII (Aug 1954), 82–94.

The fact that Johnson recognized WP's humor removed him from the majority of WP's disciples.

785 Stanford, Derek. "Pater's Ideal Aesthetic Type," CAMBRIDGE JOURNAL, VII (May 1954), 488–94.

There are some remarks in "Diaphancitè" that set WP apart from the other great

Victorian critics: Thomas Carlyle, John Ruskin, and Matthew Arnold assumed that artist, connoisseur, and public were connected by common bonds and separated only by the kind and degree of knowledge they possessed, while WP believed that temperament rather than knowledge separated men. Since differences of temperament are more personal than differences of idea, WP's approach was necessarily more limited in its general appeal. The elements of WP's ideal in "Diaphaneitè" are "a personal poise and comeliness, an appreciative rather than an analytic mind, a sympathetic receptiveness and . . . a strain of divine discontent." In opposition to the more common view that ideas reveal truth, WP's belief in the relative spirit maintains that they reveal us to ourselves. Given his assumptions, WP could never expound a general system of aesthetics, or, like Ruskin and Arnold, "attempt (however inadequately) to implicate moral and aesthetic notions." One does not get from WP's criticism "an analysis of part from part, but an elucidation of the spirit of the whole."

786 Yeats, William Butler. THE LETTERS OF W. B. YEATS, ed by Allan Wade (Lond: Rupert Hart-Davis; NY: Macmillan, 1954), pp. 68, 237.
[In a letter of 5 Nov 1894 to J. B. Yeats, W. B. Yeats requests a copy of the FORTNIGHTLY REVIEW (Sept 1894) which contains Lionel Johnson's "The Work of Mr. Pater."]

1955

787 Bertocci, Angelo P. "French Criticism and the Pater Problem," BOSTON UNIVERSITY STUDIES IN ENGLISH, I (1955), 178–94.
[Primarily a survey of French criticism on WP by Ramon Fernandez, Charles Du Bos, Lucien Cattan, and Louise Rosenblatt, q.v.]

788 Brown, Malcolm. GEORGE MOORE: A RECONSIDERATION (Seattle: University of Washington P, 1955), pp. 48, 54, 59, 104, 106–11, 112–13, 122, 123–24, 158, 173, 192, 197, 202, 210, 213.
When Moore first read *Marius the Epicurean* in County Mayo in 1885, he found in it "a perfect likeness of his own predicament, surroundings, and emotions at Moore Hall." Compared to Théophile Gautier, WP was "more dainty, more profound, more lugubrious," yet their beliefs were essentially the same. WP "found aspect more precious than essence and the receptive powers superior to the reflective, anticipating thereby the extraordinary stress upon 'thisness' and 'inscape' which characterized so much of the poetry and criticism of the half century following his death." Though the styles of Moore and WP are similar, Moore's final style is not the style of *Marius:* Moore's is "superior in clarity, lacking Pater's mincing nervous need to pile qualification on qualification." Like Gautier, WP believed that religion and art were interchangeable. After switching his allegiance

from Émile Zola to WP, nine of the twelve novels that Moore wrote deal with WP's Christian-pagan dilemma. The fusion of sensuality and asceticism is behind WP's "high-church aestheticism." WP understood, unlike many readers, that Moore's work is misread unless its humor is perceived. WP seems to have "profoundly disturbed" Moore's creative impulse and to have confused his ability to judge his own work. The first of Moore's novels written under WP's influence was A MERE ACCIDENT, but WP found it too sensational. Moore's final novel, APHRODITE IN AULIS, succeeds "in recreating a believable pagan world, freed at last from Swinburne's sadism, Gautier's exotic taste, and Pater's effeminacy." Moore felt that WP's greatness lay in his intuition of feminine mentality.

> **789** Bullough, Geoffrey. "Changing Views of the Mind in English Poetry," PROCEEDINGS OF THE BRITISH ACADEMY, XLI (1955), 61–83; rptd (Lond: Oxford UP, 1956); rptd with revisions in MIRROR OF MINDS: CHANGING PSYCHOLOGICAL BELIEFS IN ENGLISH POETRY (Lond: Athlone P, 1962).

It is in the light of books like Henry Maudsley's PHYSIOLOGY AND PATHOLOGY OF MIND (1867), in which he argues that consciousness is a by-product of brain processes, that WP's "Conclusion" [*The Renaissance*] should be read. WP admired Hegel but rebelled against his idealism. He was attracted by Heraclitus' doctrine of fire and flux and Epicurus' atomism and his reduction of mind-content to sensations, and found parallels to Epicurus' thought in modern molecular theory and David Hume. WP's theory of the isolation of the individual personality came from Hume. In resolving all experiences into a series of moments, WP ignored "the constructive work of psychologists since Locke and Hartley." In the "Conclusion," WP was probably defying the altruism of John Stuart Mill's UTILITARIANISM. The extreme individualism of the "Conclusion," rather than WP's later qualification of it, influenced Oscar Wilde and other young men and "brought his teaching into disrepute." That essay was influential because it brought into focus a "current scepticism about absolutes, and agreed with a fashion for 'scientific subjectivity' and 'momentary effects' " brought over from France by Impressionism and art for art's sake.

> **790** Cecil, David [Lord]. WALTER PATER, THE SCHOLAR-ARTIST (Cambridge: Cambridge UP, 1955); rptd as "Walter Pater," THE FINE ART OF READING AND OTHER LITERARY STUDIES (Lond: Constable, 1957), pp. 203–21; (Indianapolis: Bobbs-Merrill, 1957), pp. 259–82.

Unlike most scholars who are also artists, the scholarly and the artistic are combined in WP's works: "Pater the lecturer on Plato is recognizably the same man as Pater the creator of *Marius the Epicurean*." WP wished to convey an intellectual vision of aesthetic experience, but he was a moralist as well: he was a critic of living as well as of art. He believed that criticism was useless if it did not help one to appreciate particular works of art. Rather than starting with a moral system and then judging art by how well it conforms to that system, WP started with aesthetic taste and judged moral precepts by how well they satisfied that taste.

As he grew older, WP shifted his viewpoint from the implicit unresolved discord expressed in *The Renaissance* that on the one hand, nothing in life has significance and on the other, beauty is significant. The importance that WP placed on beauty is in fact inconsistent with an untranscendental view of existence, and in *Marius* he expressed the possibility that the soul may return to another world at death. As time went on, his views moved slightly in the direction of Christianity. But Marius remains only half-converted because that is the most that WP could ever be. WP's two basic forms are the critical essay and the fictitious biography. In the former, the basic pattern is intellectual but heightened by aesthetic effects; in the latter, the basic pattern is aesthetic, but he is less interested in character or story than he is in the ideas for which his heroes stand. WP does more than simply enjoy the flavor of the subjects which he treats: he analyzes the flavor into its component parts. "No English critic is at once so sensitive and so hard-headed as Pater; so catholic and so acute." In his creative writing, however, the two strains combine less easily. His writing shows no sign of a sense of humor. The essays on English subjects in *Appreciations* are more successful than the essays of *The Renaissance* and *Greek Studies;* in the latter two, WP tried to identify himself with his subjects, but more often he identified his subjects with himself. "Like himself, Pater's sentences are a touch languid and spiritless, and they mirror all too accurately his nervous shrinking from conflict. Rather than commit himself in any way that might seem aggressive, he will hesitate, qualify, intersperse his statements with 'perhaps,' 'almost,' 'somewhat,' till the reader sometimes loses the thread of the argument altogether." His style is unsuitable for exposition or narrative. Like Henry James and James Joyce, he was sometimes so preoccupied with his own style that he forgot that the artist's first obligation is to communicate his meaning to his readers.

791 Du Bos, Charles. JOURNAL, Vol. 6: JANVIER 1930–JUILLET 1931 (Paris: La Colombe, 1955), pp. 80, 106–8, 114, 146–48.
[Before his conversion to Catholicism, Du Bos defined his individualism by WP and Marius. WP represents for Du Bos the natural meditation and contemplation that precede religon.] The difference between WP and Oscar Wilde as critics is that WP's criticism has to be seen as a natural result of his personality, produced in spite of himself, while Wilde's is deliberated. WP could only produce in a protected environment: if one had removed his Brasenose fellowship, he would have died silent. [In French.]

792 Eells, John Shepard, Jr. THE TOUCHSTONES OF MATTHEW ARNOLD (NY: Bookman Associates, 1955); rptd (New Haven: College and University P, 1963); rptd (NY: AMS P, 1971), pp. 23, 228, 231.
WP, "in characterizing subtle responses to works of art, commanded a felicity, a delicacy, an abstraction of phrase to which Arnold could never attain."

793 Gengaro, Maria Luisa. "Nota Leonardesca" (Note on Leonardo), PAIDEIA (Genoa), X (1955), 21–24.

The responsibility for the "romantic" interpretation of the *Mona Lisa* by WP (in "Leonardo da Vinci") and Théophile Gautier rests with Charles Baudelaire, who hinted at the painting's mystery in his poem "Les Phares" (LES FLEURS DU MAL, 1857). But Baudelaire's version of the painting is poetically closer to the truth, and the modern sculptor Francesco Messina's interpretation is critically closer to the truth than Gautier's or WP's. [In Italian.]

794 La Drière, James Craig. DIRECTIONS IN CONTEMPORARY CRITICISM AND LITERARY SCHOLARSHIP (Milwaukee: Bruce, 1955), pp. 37, 41, 71, 81.

T. S. Eliot's emphasis on analyzing "sensation," like much in his early criticism, is derived from WP or Arthur Symons rather than Aristotle. The profession of an analytical emphasis is perhaps the chief technical legacy left us by WP and the aesthetic critics. Looking "solely and steadfastly at the object" was revived and reaffirmed by Matthew Arnold and WP. The broader criticism of culture, rather than the criticism of literature, was the true concern of WP, Arnold, and Irving Babbitt.

795 Osborne, Harold. AESTHETICS AND CRITICISM (Lond: Routledge & Kegan Paul; NY: Philosophical Library, 1955), pp. 17, 29, 49, 100, 123, 165, 175, 176, 251, 308.

The importance of aligning the critic's emotional experience with the object of criticism was "very much in the mind" of WP, as for example in the "Preface" to *The Renaissance*, "though he never limited the function of criticism to describing that experience." Neither Matthew Arnold nor WP "eschewed judgement and evaluation in their criticism." Though WP repudiated attempts to define beauty in the abstract, he "had of course already assumed his own 'universal formula' of beauty—beauty, he was sure, was to be assessed by the degree and quality of the pleasure attending the impression which things made upon him."

796 St. John-Stevas, Norman. "The Victorian Conscience," LISTENER, LIII (24 March 1955), 517–19.

It was not until the publication in 1873 of WP's *The Renaissance* that autonomy was claimed for art. WP was widely attacked, since the Victorians recognized an enemy when they saw one. The real fury of the general public was not directed toward the "morality of art," however, until the publication of the writings of the French realists and naturalists, since, though both the aesthetes and the naturalists recognized no moral criterion for a work of art outside the work itself, the naturalists "strayed into the forbidden pastures of sex relationships."

797 Thomas, J. D. "Oscar Wilde's Pose and Poetry," RICE INSTITUTE PAMPHLET, XLII (Oct 1955), 32–52.

Wilde was exactly the sort of disciple WP dreaded having: "where Pater offered a balanced moral and artistic freedom, Oscar Wilde found the hagridden pleasures of a sybarite."

798 Ward, A. C. ILLUSTRATED HISTORY OF ENGLISH LITERATURE, Vol. III: BLAKE TO BERNARD SHAW (Lond & NY: Longmans, Green, 1955), pp. 241–42, 264, 266, 273, 281; rptd in Ward, ENGLISH LITERATURE: CHAUCER TO BERNARD SHAW (Lond & NY: Longmans, Green, 1958); rptd (NY: McKay, 1962).

Though *The Renaissance* was "intended to present innocuous 'studies in poetry and art,' " it "was thrust by certain of its readers into the role of an antinomian aesthetico-moral manifesto." As an art critic WP was a disciple of John Ruskin "who in clarity of perception and precision of statement excelled his master. . . . Like Ruskin's, Pater's writings on art consisted much less of formal criticism than of the translation of visual material into written language." Though this may be illegitimate from the point of view of aesthetics, it has made his description of the *Mona Lisa* in "Leonardo da Vinci" famous to many readers who have never seen the painting. The final version of the "Conclusion" is identical to the original version "in all but a few words which have no bearing on the whole." Though his followers carried the experimentation recommended in the "Conclusion" to "whatever paths life opened up," WP felt that art was the "appropriate mode of ingress to this intenser range of experience." Though WP recommended an economical manner of writing in "Style," his own practice did not always live up to this ideal; however, the style of *Marius the Epicurean* is "more austere than opulent." Spontaneity is rare in WP.

799 West, Paul. "Walter Pater and THE VOICES OF SILENCE," ADELPHI, XXXI (1955), 355–63.

The views on art in André Malraux's LES VOIX DU SILENCE are quite similar to those of WP. Both Malraux and WP believe that there is a permanent and continuous identity of man through the ages; both believe in a humanism founded on creative activity that should "replace theologies which are insufficiently religious"; both believe that life can be made tolerable through art.

800 Wild, Friedrich. "Zur Dichtungstheorie und Romanform der Viktorianer" (On the Poetic Theory and Fictional Form of the Victorians), ANGLO-AMERICANA: FESTSCHRIFT ZUM 70. GEBURTSTAG VON PROFESSOR DR. LEO HIBLER-LEBMANNSPORT, ed by Karl Brunner (WIENER BEITRÄGE ZUR ENGLISCHEN PHILOLOGIE, LXII [1955]), pp. 157–72.

WP expressed his world view in *Marius the Epicurean, Imaginary Portraits,* and related stories; his statements on Dante's style could apply to himself; his theory of impressions in the "Conclusion" [*The Renaissance*] is derived from David Hume. [In German.]

1956

801 Boas, F. S. "Some Oxford Memories, 1881–1886," ESSAYS AND STUDIES, nsIX (1956), 113–21.
[Two anecdotes on WP's nervousness before lecturing to "The Pilgrims" society and an Oxford University Extension summer meeting.]

802 Coombes, H. EDWARD THOMAS (Lond: Chatto & Windus, 1956); rptd (NY: Barnes & Noble, 1973), pp. 19, 23, 30, 120, 123–25.
Thomas's prose reveals the effects of having read Lamb, Wilde, and WP. Yet he finds much in WP "distasteful."

803 Edwards, Oliver. "Cras Amet," TIMES (Lond), 13 Dec 1956, p. 13.
No one knows who wrote PERVIGILIUM VENERIS. WP in *Marius the Epicurean* claims that Marius's friend, Flavian, wrote it after listening to young men singing the refrain of a popular song on "the sacred day in March when the 'Ship of Isis' was launched as a tribute to the Great Goddess, the patroness of sailors." They sang, "Cras amet qui nunquam amavit. Quique amavit cras amet." The words have baffled poets ever since. Efforts to unscramble them have been endless. WP, "alas, made no effort." He simply described the scene.

804 Hassall, Christopher. "Introduction," THE PROSE OF RUPERT BROOKE, ed by Christopher Hassall (Lond: Sidgwick & Jackson, 1956), pp. xix, xxxiv.
[Hassall refers to Brooke's parody of WP, entitled "From *Marius the Bank Clerk*," published in THE WESTMINSTER GAZETTE in 1907 as an example of one of Brooke's early prose attempts.]

805 Melchiori, Giorgio. THE TIGHTROPE WALKERS: STUDIES OF MANNERISMS IN MODERN ENGLISH LITERATURE (Lond: Routledge & Kegan Paul, 1956), pp. 12, 13, 19–20, 21, 23–25, 28–29, 51, 199, 267.
WP's style "prefigured an age of instability not yet existing in fact." WP is the link between Henry James and G. M. Hopkins. Hopkins appears to have written ON THE ORIGIN OF BEAUTY for WP; it contains much that Hopkins learned from him. WP helped Hopkins question Victorian artistic standards. James's debt to WP is by now an acknowledged fact. James also searches for beauty "caught in a moment and fixed and kept for endless contemplation." WP expresses his interest in Euphuism in *Marius the Epicurean;* by "Euphuism" he means a love of the word, an awareness of one's " 'forgotten duties towards language.' " Hopkins and James are euphuistic writers in WP's sense. They represent a "new" style for the age, a style that will "characterize the next half-century." Joyce in ULYSSES carries "to incredible lengths the precious formalism" of WP and of Wilde.

806 "The Scholar-Artist," TIMES LITERARY SUPPLEMENT (Lond), 3 Feb 1956, p. 69.

WP is not in fashion now; he is too well-informed to be popular. The verdict on him must be dual: censure for "a too-easy dilettantism," praise for his "exceptional ability to apprehend the connexions between different things." He lacked a stable basis in life, as is seen in his moving from skeptical aestheticism in *The Renaissance* to half-unwilling agnosticism in *Marius the Epicurean*. [Editorial comment on Lord David Cecil's Rede Lecture on WP (1955).]

1957

807 Fletcher, Iain. "Leda and St. Anne," LISTENER, LVII (21 Feb 1957), 305–7.

Yeats prints WP's description of the *Mona Lisa* in *vers libre* in the OXFORD BOOK OF MODERN VERSE because it has "revolutionary importance for him because the form—and the form is, intrinsically, the projection of a symbolic image—arises out of rhythm, in a way in which no mechanically imposed metrical form could hope to do." WP's image of the Gioconda is to Yeats "the seed of a new mythology" whose "aesthetic hypothesis" is "that the poetic image, or image symbol, has become disastrously disjoined from society." WP adumbrates the modern poetry of inscrutability and apocalypse (cf. "Leda and the Swan"). WP fuses two romantic traditions in his perception of the Gioconda: mystery (ideal beauty) and menace (*femme fatale*), paralleling his own inner conflict between Dionysian (subjective) and Apollonian (objective) impulses.

808 Frye, Northrop. ANATOMY OF CRITICISM: FOUR ESSAYS (Princeton: Princeton UP, 1957); rptd (1971), pp. 238, 267, 272.

Writers frequently called musical "in the sentimental sense" are usually most remote from actual music. The tendency to *opsis,* for instance, in WP, Ruskin, DeQuincey, and Morris "often includes a tendency to elaborate pictorial description and long decorative similes." "Associative rhythm" can be found in all writing. The Mona Lisa passage from WP's essay on da Vinci that Yeats rearranged for THE OXFORD BOOK OF MODERN VERSE illustrates the point.

809 Hafley, James. "Walter Pater's *Marius* and the Technique of Modern Fiction," MODERN FICTION STUDIES, III (Summer 1957), 99–109.

WP was "the first modern: the first author in whose work . . . we can find composed all of those characteristics which . . . illustrate what we mean by 'contemporary literature.' " He is a "new critic," not an impressionist; he treats the Joycean epiphany in "The School of Giorgione," the modern concern with mythic archetypes (Mona Lisa and "Apollo in Picardy"), Einsteinian relativism in the "Conclusion" to *The Renaissance,* Bergsonian time, and modern experiments with distance and dramatic intensity in *Marius the Epicurean. Marius* can be compared with Joyce's PORTRAIT OF THE ARTIST AS A YOUNG MAN; both examine the main character in the light of a particular aesthetic design. *Marius* also has similarities to the works of Proust, Virginia Woolf, Gide, and Lawrence. Marius is "the first modern character in fiction." The four divisions of the novel correspond to four "movements" in Marius's character as he progresses "from traditional values to skeptical intelligence to desperate rationalism to willed love." Marius's character develops progressively. [See Billie Andrew Inman's response, PHILOLOGICAL QUARTERLY, 1962.]

810 Highet, Gilbert. POETS IN A LANDSCAPE (NY: Knopf, 1957), p. 169.

WP's description of the Ambarvalia in *Marius the Epicurean* is based in part on an elegy of Tibullus.

811 Houghton, Walter E. THE VICTORIAN FRAME OF MIND, 1830–1870 (New Haven: Yale UP, 1957), pp. 14–19, 64, 107, 176–77, 280–81, 291, 338.

The turn toward the theory of the relativity of knowledge and the subjective character of thought is documented in the work of WP. In the opening paragraphs of his "Coleridge" essay (1866) and in the "Conclusion" to *The Renaissance* (1873), WP "revived the skepticism of Hume and reduced all knowledge to a series of 'impressions unstable, flickering, inconsistent.' " On the basis of such an approach, only the aesthetic life "of delicate perceptions and sensitive response" was important. But to turn from WP to Arnold is to turn toward the Victorian world-view. "For Arnold threw his whole weight against relativism." Arnold would fix standards by the authority of "Culture"; WP wholeheartedly denied absolutes. WP and Arnold "face each other across the gulf between two basic conceptions of the human mind that opened up between 1865 and 1875." What WP does share with Arnold as well as with Mill and Clough is a general sense of impatience with any one-sided and dogmatic opinions. WP believed that the end of life was not action but contemplation. "That is the pure aesthetic attitude. Some years earlier Matthew Arnold had felt its fascination, and had rejected it because he was a mid-Victorian." What WP does share with many Victorians is the conscious association of the family and home with security. For his child in the house, life at home with the family was a blessed time when doubt was unknown.

812 Kermode, Frank. ROMANTIC IMAGE (Lond: Routledge & Kegan Paul; NY: Macmillan, 1957), pp. 2, 3, 6, 11–12, 15, 17, 19–22, 29, 58, 62–66, 67, 100, 107, 114, 126, 131, 134, 137, 148.

The "epiphany" is Joyce's equivalent to WP's "vision." Arnold, and not WP, states the problem that best characterizes the nineteenth-century artist: the prophetic mind of the poet in conflict with the scientific mind. WP, in his life, "exhibits . . . the stigmata of isolation." Art for WP is the organ of morality. And he was well aware of the price of artistic specialization. In WP's "vision," spirit and matter are no longer separated, but fused. Music, more than any other art, resists the separation of matter and form. WP's *Mona Lisa* owes much to Rossetti. To Yeats, WP's "prose-poem," his description of the *Mona Lisa,* signalled the "revolt against Victorianism"; hence, Yeats called WP the first modern poet. Like the *Mona Lisa* , WP's "Child in the House" is also a dead face: "they are opposed . . . to what is fluid and abstract." "Emerald Uthwart" also treats the theme of death in life. Paradoxically, to WP, the dead face stands for "what is most 'vital' in art." WP provides early examples of the emblems that Yeats would later seek.

813 Rose, Edgar Smith. "James Gibbons Huneker: Critic of the Seven Arts," DISSERTATION ABSTRACTS, XVII (1957), 1343. Unpublished dissertation, Princeton University, 1955.
[Includes references to influence of WP on Huneker.]

814 Ryals, Clyde de L. "Decadence in British Literature before the *Fin de Siècle,"* DISSERTATION ABSTRACTS, XVII (1957), 3004. Unpublished dissertation, University of Pennsylvania, 1957.
WP is the "godfather" of decadence.

815 Watt, Ian. THE RISE OF THE NOVEL: STUDIES IN DEFOE, RICHARDSON, AND FIELDING (Lond: Chatto & Windus, 1957); rptd (Berkeley & Los Angeles: University of California P, 1962), p. 176.
The conflict between the need to adhere either to "the objective, social and public orientation of the classical world" or to "the subjective, individualist and private orientation" of the literature of the past two centuries is found in Hegel, Arnold, and Goethe. WP, in *Marius the Epicurean,* recognizes the conflict when he comments on the jealous restraint of the ancients, who do not give us " 'a glimpse of that interior self, which in many cases would have actually doubled the interest of their objective informations.' "

816 Wellek, René. "Walter Pater's Literary Theory and Criticism," VICTORIAN STUDIES, I (1957), 29–46; rptd with revisions in A HISTORY OF MODERN CRITICISM 1750–1950, IV (1965); rptd in BRITISH VICTORIAN LITERATURE: RECENT REVALUATIONS, ed by Shiv K. Kumar (NY: New York UP; Lond: University of London P, 1969), pp. 457–77.
The Mona Lisa passage in *The Renaissance* has become the stereotype for "creative criticism." But neither the Mona Lisa passage nor the "gemlike flame" passage is representative of WP's method or his philosophy. Actually, WP uses few other examples of this "metaphysical method of criticism." WP urges the critic to grasp the virtue, the quality which gives the work its individual excellence. The personal, impressionistic pleasure that one gets from a work is but the first step, "the prerequisite of criticism." The "virtue" or "formula" of a work, as WP calls it, is similar to Taine's "master faculty" or Croce's "dominant sentiment." WP's concept of the Renaissance is similar to Burckhardt's and Michelet's: "the age that

accomplishes the revelation of antiquity." His view of German romanticism reflects the influence of Heine and Madame de Staël. The pleasures that WP recommended are intellectual, not hedonistic. For WP, the best art is lyrical (cf. Poe, J. S. Mill, and Leopardi) and "sincere," i.e., faithful to the inner vision. As a stylist, he advocates a highly rhythmic, lyrical, and personal prose: "style *is* the man." In his essay on "Style," WP recants many of his earlier aesthetic claims. His later Hellenism is historical; it "sees Greece as a past stage of human culture that cannot be revived today." The ages are all in themselves equal; individual genius surpasses the age. But WP's works have not escaped the limitations of nineteenth-century history.

817 West, Paul. "Narrowed Humanism: Pater and Malraux," DALHOUSIE REVIEW, XXXVII (Autumn 1957), 278–84.
"The publication, in 1951, of André Malraux's LES VOIX DU SILENCE bestowed upon the public an up-to-date version of the views on art of Walter Pater." WP, like Malraux, "assembles parallel variations on a theme." The result is that he seems confused. Malraux strengthens WP's aesthetic position by displaying it in a more serious version. Malraux viewed all of pre-history and history as his province; WP's main concern was Europe. But they both proposed a concept of humanism based on human creativity, a humanism that is very likely to become a religion or to replace religions that are insufficiently religious. "Marius augurs the development of Malraux himself." For both WP and Malraux art is a religion founded in the spirit of defiance. Both are humanists who are forced "to narrow [their] faith."

1958

818 Brooks, Van Wyck. THE DREAM OF ARCADIA: AMERICAN WRITERS AND ARTISTS IN ITALY 1760–1915 (NY: Dutton, 1958), pp. 169, 246, 250, 253.
[Random comments on WP's influence on Henry James and Bernard Berenson.]

819 Brzenk, Eugene J. "Pater and Apuleius," COMPARATIVE LITERATURE, X (Winter 1958), 55–60.
WP's retelling of Apuleius' story of Cupid and Psyche reveals his understanding of the kind of material that could be used in fiction. It also illustrates some of his theories of language and style and demonstrates how his skill can make distinct from the original version as well as from William Adlington's 1566 version his own treatment of the myth. WP trimmed the original considerably; he left out the complaints of Psyche's jealous sister. WP also recast Venus from the rude and insulting "modish theatergoer" that Apuleius depicted into a much less offensive character. WP wanted to exclude the unseemly comic elements. He reproduced with fidelity the ornate description of the palace of Cupid, the scene with Venus

riding the waves, and her trip to Olympus in the dove-drawn chariot. He intensified the sensuous details through his " 'tact of omission' " and restored a "simple classic quality to a discursive . . . version of a Greek myth."

820 Brzenk, Eugene J. "The 'Epicureans' of Pater and Moore," VICTORIAN NEWSLETTER, No. 14 (Fall 1958), pp. 24–27.

Thomas Moore's now-forgotton novel THE EPICUREAN, which created quite a stir for its "supposed sensuousness" when it was first published in 1827, invites comparison with WP's *Marius the Epicurean* because of their similar titles and because Moore's book might have influenced WP's. Thematically, both novels are superficially similar; they both examine "a spiritual pilgrimage, a philosophical search for truth." WP's treatment of this theme of spiritual awakening, however, is far more detailed and interesting than Moore's. Moore's use of antiquity seems to reflect his love of the exotic; his novel most resembles Romantic historical fiction. WP's work does not fit into the pattern of the nineteenth-century historical novel; he does not use antiquity as background material; rather, he seeks "to recreate the intellectual and philosophical climate of Aurelian Rome" for the purpose of making a moral and ethical statement. While both novels reflect much scholarship, WP's novel, unlike Moore's, is not documented with copious footnotes. Moore concentrates on setting; WP, however, is primarily concerned with ideas, and he uses setting as a means for exploring common philosophical problems shared by sensitive, thinking individuals of both the Victorian and the ancient Roman ages. WP also departs from the techniques of the Romantic historical novelist in his omission of the dramatic presentation of scenes. The Romantic historical novelist exploits big scenes; WP focuses on the impact such scenes have on the minds of his characters. Moore's novel could only have had a negative influence on WP, for it is in no way experimental. WP's "concentration upon a stream of ideas, his use of translations as objective correlatives to recreate the intellectual atmosphere of a historical period, his impressionistic use of setting, and the abstract dimension of his characterization all indicate that he is on the verge of technical discoveries that later were fully developed by novelists like Henry James, Marcel Proust, and James Joyce."

821 Brzenk, Eugene J. "The Unique Fictional World of Walter Pater," NINETEENTH CENTURY FICTION, XIII (Dec 1958), 217–26.

Most critics have been content to deal with the external, autobiographical aspects of WP's fictional portraits. Most of the portraits do reflect the nostalgic attitude of romantic historical fiction but tend to establish similarities between the past and the present. WP seems intentionally to play down sensational scenes. He is preoccupied in all of the portraits "with revealing his protagonists' 'sensations and ideas' and showing the results of their inner experiences in some telling physical event or action." WP also tests various ethical points of view in his fiction. His settings are devised to aid the characterization, often through the "tact of omission." His characters resemble each other in temperament: all are sensitive, highly introspective observers of action. Each of the portraits, as Benson perceived, is based on the idea of intellectual or artistic revolt. Dialogue is rare; the portraits lack explicit narrative statement, the result of WP's highly refined style. WP anticipates changes in "the technique, forms, and subject matter of fiction."

822 Buckler, William E. "Introduction," PROSE OF THE VICTORIAN PERIOD (Bost: Houghton Mifflin, 1958), pp. xiv–xxvii.

WP's essay on "Style," as Saintsbury noted in 1904, is still the best piece written on the subject. WP admitted a distinction between the "laws" of prose and verse composition but warned against excluding from criticism the imaginative, poetic power of prose. True to the tradition of Wordsworth and DeQuincey, WP distinguishes between "literature of fact" and "literature of the imaginative sense of fact." Prose becomes "art" when the author appeals to the reader to catch his spirit. WP does invite, as he recognized, the dangerous "relegation of style" to the subjectivity of the individual; but, nevertheless, his criticism presents a long overdue defense of "the private element" in Victorian prose. Arnold in the "Preface" to POEMS, 1853, told the poet to prefer " 'action to everything else' "; WP told the prosaist to be "sincere" in his "apprehension of what is most real to him." Thus the writer should be able to avoid affectation or mere capricious subjectivity. Six questions are implicit in "Style": (1) Has the author grappled with "a full, rich, complex matter"? (2) Has he maintained a "balance between propriety and originality"? (3) Has he provided an "*intellectual* challenge" for the reader? (4) Has he provided a "*formal* challenge" for the reader? (5) Does his prose reveal "his own (or its own) unique personality"? (6) Is it devoted to " 'great ends' "? [Buckler suggests some approaches to the work of the major prosaists of the middle years in terms of WP's critical principles. He concludes that Newman, according to WP's standards, ranks highest stylistically.]

823 Chandler, Edmund. PATER ON STYLE: AN EXAMINATION OF THE ESSAY ON "STYLE" AND THE TEXTUAL HISTORY OF MARIUS THE EPICUREAN (Copenhagen: Rosenkilde & Bagger, 1958).

WP made many corrections and emendations to the second edition of *Marius the Epicurean,* which appeared in 1885. He also suppressed a sadistic passage describing a banquet where a favorite animal is burned alive. Considering the passage in question plus his seeming delight in the barbarism of the Roman games, WP must have had "an innate element of sadism" in his personality. The third edition, appearing in 1892, contained over six thousand textual variations from the earlier editions. It seems clear that the most extensive revision of *Marius* owed its inspiration to the essay on "Style," which appeared in FORTNIGHTLY REVIEW in 1888, reprinted in *Appreciations* (1889). For he applied many of the principles of the "Style" essay to his revision of *Marius.* [The book contains a close reading of "Style" and a discussion of the principles WP advocates in the essay, a textual history of *Marius,* a collative comparison and analysis of the first and third editions, and an examination of the novel's revisions in the light of the essay on "Style."]

824 Cox, R. G. "The Reviews and Magazines," FROM DICKENS TO HARDY. The Pelican Guide to English Literature, Volume VI, ed by Boris Ford (Baltimore: Penguin Books, 1958); rptd with revisions (1960), pp. 192, 193, 200.

Later contributors to the WESTMINSTER REVIEW were Frederic Harrison and WP. Under Morley's direction, the FORTNIGHTLY was a consistent supporter of WP, Swinburne, Morris, Rossetti, and the entire aesthetic movement.

825 Faber, Sir Geoffrey. JOWETT: A PORTRAIT WITH BACKGROUND (Cambridge: Harvard UP, 1958), pp. 376, 379–84.

Although WP was not one of Jowett's pupils, he was said by Edmund Gosse (DICTIONARY OF NATIONAL BIOGRAPHY, 1895) to have been coached by him. Gosse's and, later, Benson's claim that there was a "falling out" between WP and Jowett cannot be proven. "No evidence whatever is given—or . . . has ever been given—to support" Benson's "disagreeable statement" in his biography that Jowett, an " 'opportunist,' " was "an unscrupulous enemy" of WP. Benson also claims that WP was "amused" by Jowett's contriving sophistry. But Benson "quotes nothing" that WP said or wrote; he "cites no authority." If, as Benson claims, WP had Jowett in mind when he wrote in the review of ROBERT ELSMERE for the GUARDIAN that " 'we have little patience with those liberal clergy who dwell on nothing else than the difficulties of faith and the propriety of concession to the opposite force,' " then WP has misstated the position of the liberal clergy and of Jowett, who "sought to reconcile faith with reason." WP was a shallow thinker who was to the end fascinated with the trappings of religion.

826 Hulin, J. P. "Proust and Pater," TIMES LITERARY SUPPLEMENT (Lond), 18 July 1958, p. 409.

[Hulin, replying to Betty Miller's claim (TIMES LITERARY SUPPLEMENT, 25 April 1958, p. 2250) that the affinity between Proust and WP has been overlooked, cites G. Mourey's "Proust, Ruskin et Walter Pater," LE MONDE NOUVEAU (1926); Ramon Fernandez's "Notes sur l'Esthétique de Proust," NOUVELLE REVUE FRANÇAISE (1928); and chapters III and IV of Lorenza Moranini's PROUST: ARTE E CONOSCENZA (Florence, 1933) as examples of critics who have recognized the affinity. Hulin claims that Proust was probably introduced to WP by Paul Desjardins. Proust undoubtedly read *Appreciations* and *Miscellaneous Studies*. In his footnotes to his translation of Ruskin's THE BIBLE OF AMIENS, Proust specifically refers to WP's "Art Notes in North Italy," "Notre-Dame d'Amiens," and "Vézelay." Although there is no record that Proust ever read "The Child in the House," there is strong reason to believe that he must have known it. Hulin also claims that many aspects of the footnotes to Proust's translation of SESAME AND LILIES, by Ruskin, are reminiscent of WP's essay on "Style." Both Proust and WP are "expressionistic" prosaists. See also Mario Praz's response to Miller's letter in TIMES LITERARY SUPPLEMENT, 6 June 1958.]

827 Klingopulos, G. D. "Notes on the Victorian Scene," FROM DICK-ENS TO HARDY. The Pelican Guide to English Literature, Volume VI, ed by Boris Ford (Baltimore: Penguin Books, 1958); rptd with revisions (1960), pp. 51, 53.

WP was justified in seeing a connection between his own "stagnant spirituality" and Coleridge's religious discontent.

828 Klingopulos, G. D. "The Literary Scene," FROM DICKENS TO HARDY. The Pelican Guide to English Literature, Volume VI, ed by Boris Ford (Baltimore: Penguin Books, 1958); rptd with revisions (1960), pp. 66, 67, 68, 89–90, 114.

WP's "attempt to follow the French Parnassians would not appear so mistaken had he written as a poet, not as a critic and an Oxford don." But he deserved better than to be misused by Wilde. Only D. H. Lawrence transcends WP's "intellectual hesitations"; his novels actually show how " 'matter and spirit' " " 'play inextric-ably into each other' " to redeem life.

829 Madden, William A. "The Divided Tradition of English Crit-icism," PUBLICATIONS OF THE MODERN LANGUAGE ASSOCIATION, LXXIII (1958), 69–80.

Arnold's relationship to WP is to be found in his separation of romantic inspiration from Christian tradition. WP's vocabulary in his critical essays is frequently reminiscent of Arnold's, and passages in the essay on Coleridge read like echoes. But for WP, the aesthetic experience is a matter of individual not social salvation. Like Arnold, WP did not lose religion; he lost Christianity. Arnold's "call for a rationalistic and disinterested study of life" became for WP "the grounds for a radical cleavage between the poet and society."

830 Miller, Betty. "Proust and Pater," TIMES LITERARY SUPPLEMENT (Lond), 25 April 1958, p. 225.

The affinity between Proust and WP has been largely overlooked. "The Child in the House" recalls the early chapters of DU CÔTÉ DE CHEZ SWANN. [For critical responses to Miller's claim, see Mario Praz, TIMES LITERARY SUPPLEMENT (Lond), 6 June 1958, p. 313; and J. P. Hulin, TIMES LITERARY SUPPLEMENT (Lond), 18 July 1958, p. 409.]

831 Parkinson, Thomas. "Intimate and Impersonal: An Aspect of Modern Poetics," JOURNAL OF AESTHETICS AND ART CRITICISM, XVI (March 1958), 373–83.

The theory of poetry underlying the work of the writers of the Nineties is abstractable from WP's essay on "Style," particularly his stress on individuality.

832 Praz, Mario. "Proust and Pater," TIMES LITERARY SUPPLEMENT (Lond), 6 June 1958, p. 313.

[In his reply to Betty Miller's letter (TIMES LITERARY SUPPLEMENT, 25 April 1958,

p. 225), Praz claims that she had overlooked, in her assertion that the affinity between Proust and WP has been neglected, his notice prefixed to his Italian translation of "The Child in the House" in LETTERATURA, where he calls attention to the similarities between Proust and WP. See also J. P. Hulin's response to Miller's letter in TIMES LITERARY SUPPLEMENT, 18 July 1958.]

833 Rader, Melvin. "The Artist as Outsider," JOURNAL OF AESTHETICS AND ART CRITICISM, XVI (March 1958), 306–18.

WP exhibits symptoms of cultural estrangement. "We must . . . repudiate the extreme individualistic and isolationist theory of art that we have inherited from the nineteenth century."

834 Rodway, A. E. "The Last Phase," FROM DICKENS TO HARDY. The Pelican Guide to English Literature, Volume VI, ed by Boris Ford (Baltimore: Penguin Books, 1958); rptd with revisions (1960), pp. 387–88.

For the PRB, after Ruskin, the creation of art was a duty owed society; for the aesthetes, following WP, "it was a duty owed to oneself." WP's advice to maintain the ecstasy of discriminated moments was consistent with the lessons taught by the French Symbolists. His theory of art accorded with Gautier's doctrine of "art for art's sake" and with Whistler's claim for the superiority of art over nature; to John Bull, however, it was "a red rag."

835 Ryals, Clyde De L. "Toward a Definition of *Decadent* as Applied to British Literature of the Nineteenth Century," JOURNAL OF AESTHETICS AND ART CRITICISM, XVII (Sept 1958), 85–92.

"Decadence," as the culminating phase of romanticism, is the result of the "complete disintegration" of the "classical synthesis." WP defines romanticism as the blend of strangeness and beauty, a blend that also constitutes the basis of "decadence." Romanticism reveals a concern for social justice; "decadence," on the other hand, is entirely an expression of self (as in *Marius the Epicurean*). The Fatal Woman reaches its apotheosis in WP's description of La Gioconda in "Leonardo da Vinci." [For a reply to Ryals's article, see Robert L. Peters, "Toward an 'Un-Definition' of Decadent as Applied to British Literature of the Nineteenth Century," JOURNAL OF AESTHETICS AND ART CRITICISM, XVIII (Dec 1959), 258–64.]

836 Vandekieft, Ruth Marguerite. "The Nineteenth Century Reputation of Sir Thomas Browne," DISSERTATION ABSTRACTS, XVIII (1958), 2151. Unpublished dissertation, University of Michigan, 1957.

WP, an agnostic, was a perceptive critic of Browne.

837 West, Alick. "Walter Pater and Oscar Wilde," THE MOUNTAIN IN THE SUNLIGHT: STUDIES IN CONFLICT AND UNITY (Lond: Lawrence & Wishart, 1958), pp. 111–53.

The essays in *The Renaissance* are historical studies of great Renaissance artists and "are also a kind of imaginary living: Here he gives form to the pleasure that art has provided him." WP propogates "the weakness of German Idealist philosophy." He makes art abstract at a time when it was becoming "actual." He believed that the objective of the aesthetic life was aestheticism. He did not know that "with the growth of the socialist movement a new epoch was coming near when men would be able to create a more human world and to realize the vision of poets as never before." Art for art's sake was an obstacle to the achievement of this dream. But for WP art for art's sake meant art for life's sake. In *Marius the Epicurean,* for example, WP has Marius join the "forces of change" that have defied the authority of the existing ruling class. [The article attempts a Marxist justification for WP as an artist.]

838 West, Paul. "Pater and the Tribulations of Taste," UNIVERSITY OF TORONTO QUARTERLY, XXVII (July 1958), 424–32.
WP's achievement needs to be revalued in its entirety, free from tidy and damning catchwords. His mind was esemplastic; he worked "simultaneously in several different states of consciousness." He had a better sense of his age than Newman. *Marius the Epicurean,* as a novel, is flawed. WP identified too closely with his hero. But the novel should be examined against works like Rousseau's RÊVERIES or Bunyan's PILGRIM'S PROGRESS with which it has much in common. At the core of WP's philosophy is the belief that art makes life more pleasurable and therefore intensifies it; "and that since the purest form of pleasure furnishes an ethical impulse, art thus possesses . . . a moral function." WP retreated to Aurelian Rome to escape from the mental confusion of the times. WP's major contribution to letters is his explanation of the function of the aesthetic critic who must recreate the object contemplated in his criticism. John Addington Symonds imitates WP's style but makes himself ridiculous.

1959

839 Appleman, Philip. "Darwin, Pater, and a Critic in Criticism," in 1859: ENTERING AN AGE OF CRISIS, ed by Philip Appleman, William A. Madden, and Michael Wolff (Bloomington: Indiana UP, 1959), pp. 81–85; rptd in part in DARWIN: A NORTON CRITICAL EDITION, ed by Philip Appleman (NY: Norton, 1970), pp. 611–18.
According to Wright's biography of WP, WP discussed Darwin with his companions when he went up to Oxford in 1859. "Coleridge" (1866) is "clearly the work of a man impressed with the ORIGIN OF SPECIES." In *The Renaissance,* WP's own evolutionary, empirical view of art reappears. WP's statements on relativism mark the "starting point for all post-Darwinian criticism." It is unfair to limit WP's work with tags of "impression." He is also an historicist, "a student of process." WP was faced with the dilemma of choosing as his preference either impressionism or

historicism; both seemed of equal importance to him. In the end, he could not choose. His "indecision was a natural result of his Darwinian conditioning . . . and a saving grace" for his criticism.

840 Baines, Jocelyn. JOSEPH CONRAD: A CRITICAL BIOGRAPHY (Lond: Weidenfeld & Nicholson, 1959); (NY: McGraw-Hill, 1960), p. 188*n*.

In May of 1897, Conrad was sent a copy of *Marius the Epicurean*. In August of that year, he told Garnett that the preface to the NIGGER OF THE NARCISSUS was written. WP may have influenced the preface.

841 Baker, Joseph E. "Ivory Tower as Laboratory: Pater and Proust," ACCENT, XIX (Autumn 1959), 204–16.

It is often thought that WP conceived of the novel as a purely aesthetic form, but WP himself said that art may be devoted "to the glory of God" or to social purposes. Although both WP and Proust are detached from moral action, they both still see truth as a concern of art. They turn away from externals not to get away from reality but to inspire a new, fresh look at reality. For them, reality was not in physical objects but in the mind. The primary difference between WP and Proust was that WP was concerned with the present time, while Proust was concerned with the past, as in À LA RECHERCHE DU TEMPS PERDU.

842 Baym, Max I. "Three Moths and a Candle: A Study of the Impact of Pascal on Walter Pater, Henry Adams, and Wallace Stevens," COMPARATIVE LITERATURE: PROCEEDINGS OF THE SECOND CONGRESS OF THE INTERNATIONAL COMPARATIVE LITERATURE ASSOCIATION, Volume II, ed by Werner P. Friederich (Chapel Hill: University of North Carolina P, 1959), 336–48.

WP conducts the reader "from imagination as impassioned contemplation . . . to imagination attaining a 'blessedness' of vision," a vision similar to a piece of well-played music. But "the impassioned realization of experience might well be opposed to 'received morality'; i.e., the imperiousness of the one might well be matched against the imperiousness of the other. It is with this hazard in mind," that WP "brings together the names of Pascal and Montaigne." He notes correctly in his essay on Pascal that Pascal was moved by Montaigne's skepticism. WP, with Pascal in mind, attempts to define the differing functions of mind and soul in style.

843 Carr, Arthur J. "Introduction: Victorian Poetry and the Tradition," VICTORIAN POETRY: CLOUGH TO KIPLING (NY: Holt, Rinehart, Winston, 1959), pp. vii–xxi, 364.

In 1859, the "bench-mark" year in Victorian literature, WP was attracting the notice of Benjamin Jowett at Oxford, Swinburne was an undergraduate, and Arnold was professor of poetry. WP serves Mammon when he praises the "gem-like flame" as a symbol of "the concentrated impression of beauty in the work of art and in the artist's imagination." WP's aesthetic theory, explained in the "Conclusion" to *The Renaissance* is antithetical to Shelley's demand that poetry serve as the mediator between "experience" and "the fruit of experience." For WP the poet is not Prometheus but "a connoisseur of pulsations."

844 Eckhoff, Lorentz. THE AESTHETIC MOVEMENT IN ENGLISH LITERATURE (Oslo: University of Oslo P, 1959), pp. 17–19, 23.
Most writers of the late nineteenth century remained at a safe distance from the art for art's sake movement. WP's *Imaginary Portraits,* Stevenson's DR. JEKYLL AND MR. HYDE, and Wilde's PICTURE OF DORIAN GRAY tell tales "of a bitter and violent revolt on the part of the authors against a convention which constituted an intolerable and stifling position." All of WP's heroes in the *Imaginary Portraits* are in revolt against their age. [Book contains a brief analysis of "Apollo in Picardy" as an example of rebellious paganism, "satanic abandon," in conflict with conventional Christianity.]

845 Fletcher, Iain. WALTER PATER (Lond: Longmanns, Green, 1959).
Interest in WP's work has lately intensified. Generally, WP has come to be associated with an undisciplined impressionistic criticism and a few "uncharacteristic passages" of his works. But WP defies categorization. Much of his work is autobiographical. In "The Child in the House," he symbolizes home as "a Sanctuary from spiritual wandering." Many of his fictional characters return home to die fulfilled. Early in life, WP was heavily influenced by Comte. Though skeptical of religion, he desired, under the imposing influence of Keble, to take orders. All of his early writings reflect the spiritual uneasiness that characterized his restless age. His style was never in the mainstream of Oxford prose. Most of his later works supplement *Marius the Epicurean. Plato and Platonism* is one of the earliest statements in English for historical relativism. "*The Renaissance* was intended as a prolegomenon to a new age." For WP, the essence of the Renaissance was the impact of revived Greek values on the Middle Ages. WP discovered the importance of concentrating on "moments" of history from Burckhardt's CIVILIZATION OF THE RENAISSANCE (1860). But unlike Burckhardt, WP insisted on an historical continuity rather than distinct periods. WP extends Arnold's concern with literature to the other arts. WP, unlike Arnold, stresses Hellenism exclusively. WP argues for art but for a "specially conceived morality" rather than for art for its own sake. All of the heroes of the imaginary portraits are "destroyed by the age in which they live. . . . Portents of change, they are themselves unchanging." They reflect WP's own dilemma, his own sense of exile.

846 Fletcher, Ian. "Why Not Take Pater Seriously?" ESSAYS IN CRITICISM, IX (Oct 1959), 411–18.
Edmund Chandler says that T. S. Eliot fixed WP's image in 1930, and it has been "frozen by indifference" ever since. In terms of his religious feelings, WP moves from aestheticism to Christian humanism, reflecting a growing sympathy with the attitude that only Christianity among religions could "accomodate itself to progress." This development accounts for WP's "diminution of the ironies directed against historical Christianity in the first edition of *Marius the Epicurean.*"

[Review of Chandler's PATER ON STYLE (1958). Fletcher disagrees with Chandler on all of these points. In addition, he says that not all of WP's revisions enhance the unity of the individual works; old sentence structures are retained, the vocabulary remains cloudy, and removing "surplusage" occasionally leaves "an unfortunate effect of over-concision."]

847 Gordon, John D. "New in the Berg Collection: 1957–1958," BUL-LETIN OF THE NEW YORK PUBLIC LIBRARY, LXIII (March–April, 1959), 134–47, 205–15.

[Listing and brief description of an autograph letter, ms., and some presentation copies now in Berg collection sent originally to Violet Paget by WP.]

848 Gregory, Horace. THE WORLD OF JAMES MCNEILL WHISTLER (NY: Thomas Nelson, 1959), pp. 88, 96, 126, 217, 218, 235, 241; rptd (1961); rptd (NY: Books for Libraries P, 1969), pp. 88, 96, 126, 217, 218, 235, 241.

During Whistler's time, paintings were beginning to be compared to music. Fifteen years later, WP would provide a rationale for the comparison in "The School of Giorgione." To WP, Simeon Solomon looked like a "young Greek god." WP was Wilde's god. Sir William Eden was a follower of WP.

849 Iser, Wolfgang. "Walter Pater und T. S. Eliot. Der Übergang zur Modernität" (Walter Pater and T. S. Eliot. The Transition to Modernity), GERMANISCH-ROMANISCHE MONATSSCHRIFT, IX (Oct 1959), 391–408.

WP's works exerted a substantial influence on the literature of the end of the nineteenth century. His writings were viewed as a mirror for life at the turn of the century; he had discovered a new way of living—preached a new gospel. Eliot, like WP, was interested in the effectiveness of the "word." WP's "word" served the cause of reflecting subjective emotions; Eliot, however, doubted the ability of the singular word to produce so much. He chooses to use the "word" for experimentation and not to manifest any inner vision. [In German.]

850 Kronenberger, Louis. "Introduction," *The Renaissance: Studies in Art and Poetry* (NY: New American Library [Mentor], 1959), pp. vii–xi.

WP stands outside the Victorian world, like Lewis Carroll and Housman. The value of *The Renaissance* is not its theory but "the temperament it expressed" through its evocative and precise style.

851 Painter, George D. PROUST: THE EARLY YEARS (Lond: Chatto & Windus; Bost: Little, Brown, 1959), pp. 315, 327, 337; rptd in French (1966).

In 1897 Douglas Ainslie met Proust in a cafe; they argued about the artistic merits of Ruskin and WP. Ainslie is said to have quoted WP on Ruskin: " 'I can't believe Ruskin could see more in St. Mark's at Venice than I do!' " Proust probably read WP in translation, for he admitted to great difficulty with English.

852 Peckham, Morse. "Darwinism and Darwinisticism," VICTORIAN STUDIES, III (Sept 1959), 38–39; rptd in THE TRIUMPH OF ROMANTICISM (Columbia SC: University of South Carolina P, 1970), pp. 189–200.

WP's *Renaissance* is not logically structured; it is organized by recurring themes and by WP's revelation that all of the portraits reflect a similarity of pattern. This is Darwinian thinking. WP seems to be saying in the famous "burn with a hard, gemlike flame" passage that "the world cannot be known and that our modes of knowing and experiencing are instruments of the observer, not modes of comprehending metaphysical or even scientific truth." Darwin revealed earlier that the origin of species depended upon "the imperfect . . . adaptation of organism to environment."

853 Peters, Robert L. "Toward an 'Un-Definition' of Decadent as Applied to British Literature of the Nineteenth Century," JOURNAL OF AESTHETICS AND ART CRITICISM, XVIII (Dec 1959), 258–64.

Clyde De L. Ryals has failed "to see the diversity of the eighties and nineties; he has failed as well to detect the variety in some of the 'decadent' writers themselves," including WP. Ryals makes no allowances for WP's efforts "to dissociate himself from the aberrations of the Wilde group." WP is more properly an "aesthete" than a "decadent." [Article is a reply to Ryals, "Toward a Definition of *Decadent* as Applied to British Literature of the Nineteenth Century," JOURNAL OF AESTHETICS AND ART CRITICISM, XVII (Sept 1958), 85–92.]

854 Sudrann, Jean. "Victorian Compromise and Modern Revolution," JOURNAL OF ENGLISH LITERARY HISTORY, XXVI (Sept 1959), 425–44.

Marius the Epicurean lacks plot and character as Dickens and Thackeray understood those concepts. But it has a metaphorical center comprised of three images: the rose, death, and the dream of the heavenly city. "As these images develop, they become metaphoric and, in creating the very form of the narrative, make its meaning explicit." The contrasting symbols of the rose (life) and death are finally brought into harmony when Marius sees the "heavenly city," that is, the Christian community represented by Cecilia's house. Like a respectable Victorian, Marius is a typical product of progressivism and compromise. WP saw "the outlines of Victorian England in the decaying Roman Empire." In technique he is close to Joyce and Virginia Woolf. [See Billie Andrew Inman's response in PHILOLOGICAL QUARTERLY, 1962.]

855 Thorslev, Peter. "Pater and *Marius:* The Esthetic Stage," GRADUATE STUDENT OF ENGLISH, III (Fall 1959), 2–10.

Today, "estheticism" remains generally condemned. But there is a marked difference between the estheticism of Wilde and Whistler and the carefully reasoned estheticism of WP. He spread the influence of French symbolism, but he is also a modern "moral philosopher." He defends scientific relativism against the notion of absolute authority. He formulates the "existentialist dilemma: what we can know of truth does not teach us how to live." Our "values" must be self-created. In *Marius the Epicurean* he puts his esthetic creed to the test of life. Matthew Arnold wanted to protect moral absolutes; WP accepted the "skeptical consequences" of Victorian discoveries. T. S. Eliot in his essay on "Arnold and Pater" does both a disservice. *Marius* and *The Renaissance* are better understood in the light of Kierkegaard's discussion of the "esthetic stage" of life. WP must have understood the limitations of as well as the benefits to be gained by the esthetic creed.

1960

856 Behrman, S. N. PORTRAIT OF MAX: AN INTIMATE MEMOIR OF SIR MAX BEERBOHM (NY: Random House, 1960), pp. 55–56, 223.
Max Beerbohm could not draw WP because he could not caricature people unless he admired or liked them. He felt neither for WP. Reginald Turner, a favorite friend and a marvellous mimic, did entertaining impersonations of WP.

857 Buckley, Jerome H. TENNYSON: THE GROWTH OF A POET (Cambridge: Harvard UP, 1960); rptd (Bost: Houghton Mifflin, 1965), pp. 134, 244.
Tennyson's political verse seems to corroborate WP's conclusion in "Coleridge" that "good political poetry" can only be written "on motives which . . . have ceased to be open questions." In *Appreciations* (1889), published the same year as Tennyson's DEMETER AND OTHER POEMS, WP praises Tennyson's eclecticism, his scholarship. The DEMETER volume is an apt example supporting WP's claim.

858 Daiches, David. A CRITICAL HISTORY OF ENGLISH LITERATURE, Volume II (Lond: Secker & Warburg, 1960), 973, 986–90; rptd in four volumes (1968).
WP brooded "over the inner meaning of art." He advised seizing on "the shifting forms of experience at their moments of greatest intensity." In principle, WP's criticism was impressionistic. *Marius the Epicurean* is "hardly a novel in the accepted sense of the word." It is an extended study of the effect that art, religion, philosophy, and experience can have on one's sensibility. WP never seemed to be concerned with the world at large.

859 Duffey, Bernard. "The Religion of Pater's *Marius*," TEXAS STUDIES IN LITERATURE AND LANGUAGE, II (Spring 1960), 103–14.
Religiously, WP was a seeker. In imitation of Goethe, he burned his early Christian poems. When he began *Marius the Epicurean* in 1881, "he had in mind the irregular curve of his own religious and intellectual experience up to that time." The treatment of religion in *Marius* differs radically from the Arnoldian notion of

culture as religion. WP's novel has more in common with Hopkins's poetry, sharing "a feeling for nature as revelation, an emphasis on the paradox of sacrifice as redemption, and of participation in grace as the precedent reality, not of belief only, but of being itself." Marius sacrifices himself not out of religious conviction but for friendship. His religious sensibility lay more in good works than in testaments of faith. Christ's sacrificial death is viewed "as the ultimate model for Christian belief and action."

860 Garbáty, Thomas Jay. "An Appraisal of Arthur Symons by Pater and Mallarmé," NOTES AND QUERIES, VII (May 1960), 187–88.

Letters now in the Princeton University Library manuscript collection from both WP and Mallarmé to Symons reveal that he was equally indebted to both.

861 Hough, Graham. IMAGE AND EXPERIENCE (Lond: Duckworth, 1960), pp. 31, 76, 105, 180, 183, 185, 191, 192, 198, 201, 207.

Moore acknowledged that WP and Landor were his masters, but WP's "people do not converse." Instead, they only "reflect or make set speeches." Moore's people are vividly presented. WP's *Marius the Epicurean* has little in common with Gautier's MADEMOISELLE DE MAUPIN to which it is frequently compared. Gautier was an aesthetic sensualist; WP, a spiritual hedonist.

862 Iser, Wolfgang. WALTER PATER: DIE AUTONOMIE DES ÄSTHETIS-CHEN (Walter Pater: The Self-Reliance of Aestheticism) (Tübingen: M. Niemeyer, 1960).

WP teaches that one can transcend the world of flux through art, and he appeals to history and myth in an attempt to argue convincingly for the place of art as a transcending force. To that extent, WP is an historicist. *Marius the Epicurean* treats the dilemma of one man's attempt to remain uncommitted in life. Marius's desire for uncommittment becomes his only committment. He dies when his resolve weakens.

WP was the harbinger of a new philosophy that taught that life could be lived through art. His importance rests not so much in the propagation of the art for art's sake doctrine as in his revelation of the problems to be resolved: for example, the problem of how the final measurement of one's existence is related to the concept of the autonomy of art. He stands at the apex of a shifting tendency; he marks the transition between the end of the nineteenth-century literary tradition and the modern. His own character, because of this transitional position, is reflected in most of his works. This reflection is made possible by the aesthetic condition working from within in the structure of his works. WP discovered, in history and mythology, possibilities to legitimize claims of the autonomy of art. He questions how the limits of this legitimization can be known, and he sketches the problem of the place of the aesthetic existence in his fiction. In his works, WP shows how, through examples, the changeable qualities of aestheticism develop; his objective is to use this variableness in an attempt to define aestheticism. [In German.]

863 Keys, Thomas E. "Walter Pater's *Miscellaneous Studies,*" STECHERT-HAFNER BOOK NEWS, XV (Oct 1960), 17–19.
WP's works reveal a warm and tender personality. The best essay in *Miscellaneous Studies* is "Raphael." [The remainder of the article summarizes WP's life.]

864 Moers, Ellen. THE DANDY: BRUMMELL TO BEERBOHM (NY: Viking, 1960), pp. 300–301, 303, 320.
[Passing references to WP's influence on Wilde.]

865 Priestley, J. B. LITERATURE AND WESTERN MAN (NY: Harper & Row, 1960), pp. 215, 224.
WP was a "supreme taster" whose cautious awareness kept him from the ruin experienced by other aesthetes. As a fictionist, he wrote lifeless prose—"so many visits to an exquisite morgue."

866 Sprigge, Sylvia. BERENSON: A BIOGRAPHY (Bost: Houghton Mifflin, 1960), pp. 13, 34, 42, 44–56, 63, 73, 78, 82, 83, 90, 100, 106, 142, 146, 150, 169, 180, 197, 231, 233.
From George Eliot Bernard Berenson learned the value of the "art that conceals art." The idea later provided one of the keys to his understanding of WP. Charles Eliot Norton, who held the chair of History of Fine Art from 1873 to 1898 at Harvard, told Berenson that WP's *Renaissance* was a book " 'you can only read in your bathroom.' " But for Berenson, *The Renaissance* was a revelation. In STUDY FOR A SELF-PORTRAIT, he acknowledges his debt to WP and to having read *Marius the Epicurean, Imaginary Portraits,* "Emerald Uthwart," and "Demeter." Without some comprehension of *Marius,* one cannot fully appreciate Berenson's procedures. Berenson identifies with Marius's desire to acquire what higher education should impart. Berenson refers to WP's "moments" as the "itness" of life. Like Marius, Berenson believed that life was at its fullest in the morning in a new place. Berenson also felt an irresistible attraction for sacred places. He owed his introduction to early Florentine and Venetian art to *The Renaissance. Marius* was Berenson's handbook for living.

867 Starkie, Enid. FROM GAUTIER TO ELIOT: THE INFLUENCE OF FRANCE ON ENGLISH LITERATURE, 1851–1939 (Lond: Hutchinson, 1960), pp. 40–41, 51–57, 68, 101, 107–8, 192.
Swinburne and WP exercised the greatest influence in the development of art for art's sake in England. But WP, unlike Swinburne, was no rebel. He was attracted to the theories of Flaubert with whom he shares an affinity and from whom he borrows most. He wanted to do for English prose what Flaubert had done for French. WP seems not to have known much of Baudelaire's poetry. But he must have known Baudelaire's "aesthetic doctrine as expressed in his criticism, for he shares many of his ideas." He also drew his definition of beauty, expressed in the Michelangelo essay in *The Renaissance,* from Baudelaire. John Payne introduced WP to French poetry. WP advocated making one's life a perfect work of art with the

hope that knowledge may be gained. James Joyce transcribed passages from WP in his notebook for ULYSSES. WP is the only English author represented in Joyce's notebook.

868 Temple, Ruth Z. "The Ivory Tower as Lighthouse," EDWARDIANS AND LATE VICTORIANS (ENGLISH INSTITUTE ESSAYS, 1959), ed by Richard Ellmann (NY: Columbia UP, 1960), pp. 28–49.

WP is the definer of the aesthetic critic and of the impressionist method, but he is not given as much credit today as he deserves. He is difficult to grasp because of the inconsistent nature of his criticism. But in his brooding attraction to sickness and death, his preoccupation with significant moments of experiences, and his sense of the fundamental loneliness of man, he anticipates many of the dominant themes of modern fiction. His method of criticism is defined in *The Renaissance:* the ideal critic must have a temperament deeply touched by beautiful objects; he will distinguish and analyze the "virtue" in the work that produces a special "impression" of beauty. Once this essentially romantic critic isolates his image or "impression" of the work, he evokes that impression anew by means of his criticism. "Pater's criticism of a work might then be called the objective correlative of the original." The aesthetic critic is elevated, consequently, to the status of creator. His criticism is intended to induce his reader to rediscover or re-view the object of beauty. WP showed the way; the "new critic" of the twentieth century follows his light.

869 Turner, Paul. "Pater and Apuleius," VICTORIAN STUDIES, III (March 1960), 290–96.

The Victorians tended to emphasize the "superhuman, idealistic qualities" of classical translations and their "remoteness from ordinary life." WP's translation of the "Cupid and Psyche" myth attempts to make, in solid Victorian fashion, a grave classic out of "a pantomime type of fairy tale." His translation also reflects Victorian moral attitudes as he typically "improves" upon the tale. WP alters much of the vocabulary of Apuleius' tale to suit Victorian propriety. But he does eliminate much of Apuleius' "surplusage" and his absurd conceits. He also eliminates the humor of the tale and its realistic touches in the process. WP plays down Venus's savagery and her temper. In his hands, she becomes mere "plot machinery." WP is not always as "right" in his changes as Brzenk assumes. [Brzenk's study appears in COMPARATIVE LITERATURE, X (1958).]

870 Tuveson, Ernest Lee. THE IMAGINATION AS A MEANS OF GRACE: LOCKE AND THE AESTHETICS OF ROMANTICISM (Berkeley: University of California P, 1960), pp. 87–88, 95, 197.

"Not without reason" does WP appear to be "a descendant of Lockian philosophy" in the "Conclusion" to *The Renaissance,* where he maintains that all that we can really know are "impressions." WP pursues to a conclusion "a conception of reality as existing within the consciousness." He is a true aesthete because he was even able to absorb abstract thought into his aesthetic.

1961

871 Booth, Wayne C. THE RHETORIC OF FICTION (Chicago: University of Chicago P, 1961), pp. 29, 95.

WP's claim that "art constantly aspires towards the condition of music" would have puzzled Aristotle, but the idea has dominated discussions of artistic purity for the past century. Although WP never applied his musical theorem to fiction, "it has been adopted and extended by critics of fiction up to the present."

872 Clark, Kenneth. "Introduction," *The Renaissance* (NY: World; Lond: Collins Sons, 1961), pp. 11–26.

WP read Otto Jahn's biography of Winckelmann immediately upon its publication in 1866; that same year he wrote the essay on Winckelmann that would later be included in *The Renaissance*. Jahn's book had a profound effect on him. "Diaphaneitè" (1864) is autobiographical; specifically, as in the Winckelmann essay, it is a discussion of what WP wanted to become. The Winckelmann essay contains many of the conclusions and theories of art that underlie all the other essays in *The Renaissance*.

WP's reading on the Renaissance is unrecorded. "It seems clear that he had not read Burckhardt's CIVILIZATION OF THE RENAISSANCE which . . . was little known outside Basle till the later editions of the 1870's." Nor was he likely to have known Voigt's DIE WIEDERBELEBUNG DES CLASSISCHEN ALTERTHUMS (1859). He probably did read Michelet's HISTORY OF FRANCE (1835). Michelet first saw the spirit of the Renaissance reaching perfection in Leonardo da Vinci. WP also probably consulted Amoretti's monograph on da Vinci (1804) and certainly did read Vasari's LIVES OF THE ARTISTS for his portrait of da Vinci. "Even today . . . we cannot improve on" WP's characterization of da Vinci. WP does not treat Botticelli as well, speaking of him chiefly as an illustrator. His essay on Michelangelo's poetry must have been most difficult owing to the immense amount of available material. The Pico della Mirandola essay is, like his Winckelmann, a daydream realized. Pico's desire to fuse the Christian with the pagan was also WP's.

WP loved France far more than Italy. His portrait of Raphael does, however, describe "the realisation of antique ideas in the Renaissance more fully than any of the other essays." The Giorgione essay is undoubtedly the one that has been most theoretically influential. It contains his "most serious attempt to define his thoughts about the nature of art." Art, WP emphasizes, must obliterate the distinction between matter and form. That is what music does. In his rejection of system, WP "comes closer to Baudelaire than to any of his other predecessors." His comments on fashion in "The School of Giorgione" are similar to Baudelaire's in UN PEINTRE DE LA VIE MODERNE. Modern art has followed WP's prescription. To have had his famous analogy with music justified he would have had to wait for the work of Braque, Picasso, and Nicolas de Staël. WP, in *The Renaissance,* "first put forward the theoretical justification of abstract art." He certainly has had a significant influence on Marcel Proust and Bernard Berenson. WP also read Stendhal's HISTOIRE DE LA PEINTURE EN ITALIE, from which he learned of the disreputable nature of many Renaissance artists. WP's decision to withdraw the "Conclusion" was influenced by Ruskin's claims for the "moral" objective of art. The first part of the "Conclusion" presents WP's "perfectly correct understanding of idealistic philosophy." *The Renaissance* had "a determining influence" on Wilde, Proust, Yeats, F. H. Bradley, Roger Fry, and Berenson.

> **873** d'Hangest, Germain. WALTER PATER: L'HOMME ET L'OEUVRE (Walter Pater: The Man and His Works). Two Volumes (Paris: Librairie Marcel Didier, 1961).

[This is a valuable, lengthy, and, at times, inflated study of WP the man and his works. Volume I deals with his childhood, his years as a student at Oxford, the early works that formulated his aesthetic theory, the genesis of *The Renaissance,* and WP's conception of art. One entire chapter of Volume I is devoted to a study of the *Mona Lisa.* There are also chapters on the genesis of *Marius the Epicurean* and a lengthy analysis of the novel. Volume II deals at length with works written after *Marius.* The author's appreciation of WP is largely biographical: the man behind the work. The work includes a most extensive and helpful, though incomplete, bibliography of criticism to the mid-1950s. It is the most ambitious work on WP to have appeared to date and of indispensable value to scholars of WP and the period.] [In French.]

> **874** Evans, Lawrence Gove. "Some Letters of Walter Pater." Published dissertation, Harvard University, 1961; pub as LETTERS OF WALTER PATER (Oxford: Oxford UP, 1970), q.v. for abstract.

[Listed in Lawrence F. McNamee, DISSERTATIONS IN ENGLISH AND AMERICAN LITERATURE (NY and Lond: Bowker, 1968).]

> **875** Frean, Roland G. "Walter Pater's *Marius the Epicurean:* Notes and Commentary Preliminary to a Critical Edition." Unpublished dissertation, University of Toronto, 1961.

[Listed in Lawrence F. McNamee, DISSERTATIONS IN ENGLISH AND AMERICAN LITERATURE (NY and Lond: Bowker, 1968).]

> **876** Johnson, Robert Vincent. WALTER PATER: A STUDY OF HIS CRITICAL OUTLOOK AND ACHIEVEMENT. Australian Humanities Research Council Monograph, No. 6 (Melbourne: Melbourne UP, 1961); rvd dissertation, "Walter Pater as Critic: His Critical Practice Considered in Relation to His Theories of Life and Art," University of Manchester, 1952.

WP, as a critic of literature, lacks incisiveness; his aesthetic theory is based on the belief that the critic must be guided by his own impressions rather than by a general formula. In *Plato and Platonism,* he commends the historical method of criticism. Unlike Arnold, who was suspicious of historicism, WP enthusiastically supported it. The historical approach to criticism that attempts to judge a work in terms of the circumstances under which it was produced is responsible for blurring standards, Arnold contended. WP advocates, in contrast, the need to view the "everlasting picture of the world as a ceaseless flux." WP defends "the relative spirit." He maintains in *Plato* that we must try to understand Plato's doctrines as a response "to the life of his time." WP reduces "Hellenism" to aestheticism in the Winckelmann essay.

WP was antipathetic to transcendental theories and creeds. The conclusion to his essay on "Style" repudiates the extreme aesthetic position. The critic must be sincere, WP claims. But his own criticism is seriously limited in scope. In his art criticism, WP insists that "the artistic vision of his subject informs every detail of his presentation." He would have found most PRB painting impoverished and petty. But there is no reason to believe that WP thought all didactic art bad; he did believe that a dominant utilitarian trend in art was destructive. WP's critical method has many parallels. Swinburne's "Notes on Designs of the Old Masters in Florence" (1868) was one source for WP's famous Gioconda passage. Ruskin's comments on Botticelli's *Fortitude* in "Mornings in Florence" provide another influence. WP's interpretation of Botticelli was colored and limited by his own feelings about Botticelli. WP thought that Botticelli was second rate because of his extreme languor and melancholy. The Leonardo essay foreshadows much of the technique WP used later in *Marius the Epicurean* and *Imaginary Portraits.*

WP is "constantly aware of the intimate associations of form with matter." "The School of Giorgione" insists on it in painting; the essay on "Style," in literature. WP's literary criticism is most successful when he has some reservations about the subject, as in the Coleridge and the Sir Thomas Browne essays. In the Lamb essay, he is more vulnerable because of his close affinities with Lamb. This "sensitiveness to pathos" also occurs in his three essays on Shakespeare in *Appreciations.* The morbidity that WP finds in Rossetti keeps him from being totally supportive in his essay on Rossetti's art, although he does find much to admire. Rossetti's sincerity appeals to him. There are many similarities between WP and later critics: e.g., I. A. Richards and T. S. Eliot. Stereotyped impressions of WP must be discarded. [Johnson confines his study to essays in *The Renaissance* and *Appreciations.* He devotes separate chapters to WP's aesthetic theory, his art criticism, and his literary criticism.]

> **877** Knoepflmacher, U. C. "The Victorian Novel of Religious Humanism: A Study of George Eliot, Walter Pater, and Samuel Butler," DISSERTATION ABSTRACTS, XXII (1961), 2794. Published dissertation, Princeton University, 1961; pub as RELIGIOUS HUMANISM AND THE VICTORIAN NOVEL: GEORGE ELIOT, WALTER PATER, AND SAMUEL BUTLER (Princeton: Princeton UP, 1965), q.v. for abstract.

878 Lenaghan, R. T. "Pattern in Walter Pater's Fiction," STUDIES IN PHILOLOGY, LVIII (Jan 1961), 69–91.

WP's reading of Hegel may have been responsible for his tendency to organize by antithesis. WP may have written his imaginary portraits "with an eye to the implications of these Hegelian ideas for fiction," a pattern of "large-scale dialectical oscillations." The two gods Dionysus and Apollo may provide a pattern: WP sees in Apollo "the concentration of mortal achievement, an ideal human development"; in Dionysus, "the power of a massive vitality external to man . . . the promise of the continuity of life in nature." WP's fiction attempts to give form to these forces; hence, his many passages of sensuous description that attempt through imagery to give form to the forces. [The article provides a brief analysis of the imaginary portraits taken singly as they reflect the Apollonian-Dionysian duality.]

1962

879 Aivaz, David George. "A Study of Correspondences in the Writings of Walter Pater and Lewis Carroll." Unpublished dissertation, Harvard University, 1962.

[Listed in Lawrence F. McNamee, DISSERTATIONS IN ENGLISH AND AMERICAN LITERATURE (NY and Lond: Bowker, 1968).]

880 Charlesworth, Barbara. "Dark Passages: A Study of Decadence." Published dissertation, Radcliffe College, 1962; pub as DARK PASSAGES: THE DECADENT CONSCIOUSNESS IN VICTORIAN LITERATURE (Madison: University of Wisconsin P, 1965), q.v. for abstract.

[Includes a section on WP.]

881 Cierpial, Leo Joseph. "Degeneration and the Religion of Beauty: A Traditional Pattern in Coleridge's THE RIME OF THE ANCIENT MARINER, Pater's *The Renaissance*, Maugham's OF HUMAN BONDAGE, and Joyce's ULYSSES," DISSERTATION ABSTRACTS, XXIII (1962), 1361–62. Unpublished dissertation, Wayne State University, 1962.

882 Inman, Billie Jo Andrew. "Pater's Idea of Man," DISSERTATION ABSTRACTS, XXII (1962), 3665. Unpublished dissertation, University of Texas, 1961.

883 Inman, Billie Andrew. "The Organic Structure of *Marius the Epicurean*," PHILOLOGICAL QUARTERLY, XLI (April 1962), 475–91.

The structure of *Marius the Epicurean* is unified by "the concept in which pre-Victorian Wordsworthianism and post-Victorian Freudianism concur—that the child is father of the man." Marius's character is not "progressive," as Jean

Sudrann (JOURNAL OF ENGLISH LITERARY HISTORY, 1959) and James Hafley (MODERN FICTION STUDIES, 1957) contend; his character is in fact formed long before he reaches adulthood and is not significantly changed by any of the philosophies or experiences he encounters. As a child, he is a doubter drawn nevertheless to the mystery of religion. "The contemplative attitude, the aesthetic appreciation through sensory perception, the impulse toward self-sacrifice, the distinct feeling for places thought sacred, the occasional consciousness of divine presences, the sympathy, the scepticism, the penchant for idealizing love and home, the reverence for the body, and the yearning for perfection," all of which define his character, are ever present from childhood to his death. As a boy, Marius is as old as WP's Mona Lisa.

> **884** Knoepflmacher, U. C. "Pater's Religion of Sanity: *Plato and Platonism* as a Document of Victorian Unbelief," VICTORIAN STUDIES, VI (Dec 1962), 151–68.

Plato and Platonism is a "synthesis of all the assumptions that underlie his scattered essays and works of fiction." It is WP's final expression of his search for religious certainty in Greek thought, art, and mythology. In *Plato,* he questions how Greek paganism can be reconciled with Christianity, confronting the same philosophical systems that he examined earlier in *Marius the Epicurean.* Marius is exposed to a Graeco-Christian community, but the novel offers no reconciliation. Neither does *Plato and Platonism;* here WP traces traditions "only to efface them." The creed he tries to formulate in *Plato,* "the religion of sanity," is forever dependent on the individual's impressions.

> **885** Nathan, Leonard P. "W. B. Yeats's Experiments with an Influence," VICTORIAN STUDIES, VI (1962), 66–74; incorporated into THE TRAGIC DRAMA OF WILLIAM BUTLER YEATS: FIGURES IN A DANCE (NY: Columbia UP, 1965).

Yeats had the ability to discover what in WP's heterodox philosophy suited his needs. The hero, to Yeats, was one who totally dedicated himself to "the most intensely passionate life," a position advocated by WP, who believed that pure and intense feeling provided the basis for knowledge. WP's argument for the "lyrical effect" also reinforced Yeats's desire to write plays that would seek to attain the unity of the "single impression." But unlike Yeats, WP was "naturalistic in his assumptions about reality." ROSA ALCHEMICA embodies Yeats's reaction to WP's hedonism. Here he tests the response to reality of the "Paterian man," who fails because he has no concept of a view of man larger than that offered by other philosophical naturalists. In the drama, WP's position led to passivity; Yeats "went beyond" it.

> **886** Praz, Mario. "Due decadenti" (Two Decadents), IL TEMPO, 10 Aug 1962, p. 3.

[The two decadents are WP and Rossetti. Essay is partly a review of d'Hangest's

272

WALTER PATER: L'HOMME ET L'OEUVRE (1961); contains general observations on the place of WP in the age. WP was inspired by Rossetti.] [In Italian.]

887 Rosenblatt, Louise M. "The Genesis of Pater's *Marius the Epicurean*," COMPARATIVE LITERATURE, XIV (Summer 1962), 242–60.

Marius the Epicurean has "importance" for Virginia Woolf, Proust, and Joyce; there are many modern parallels for the ideological conflicts that appear in *Marius*. Arnold's "Marcus Aurelius" (1863), published originally in VICTORIA MAGAZINE, has been called by Kenneth Allott ("Pater and Arnold," 1952) the germ of the novel. But there is only a remote possibility that it influenced *Marius,* for WP did not begin serious work on *Marius* until approximately fifteen years later: "the hypothesis of a single influence operating *in vacuo* . . . for a decade and a half is somewhat oversimplified." WP was an eclectic writer and drew from many sources and intellectual traditions: Mill, Comte, Darwin, Spencer, Kant, Hegel, Goethe, and Spinoza. He may also have read the many contemporary articles and books that were being published at the time that treated Marcus Aurelius, an appealing figure to the late Victorians.

WP's account of Lemaitre's SÉRÉNUS in MACMILLAN'S (1887) reads like a plot summary of *Marius*. There are also many similarities between Séréna and WP's Cecilia and between Séréna and his Cornelius. Many of the incidents also recall scenes from Ernest Renan's LES ÉVANGILES (1877), published when WP was probably looking for a setting for *Marius,* and from Renan's MARC-AURÈLE (1881). It should be remembered that Arnold also was heavily influenced by Renan's style after 1859. [Article contains a brief list of contemporary British and foreign books and articles published during the years when WP was writing *Marius* that may have had an influence.]

888 Thorslev, Peter. THE BYRONIC HERO: TYPES AND PROTOTYPES (Minneapolis: University of Minnesota P, 1962), pp. 21, 91, 145.

The passionate and uncommitted "Hero of Sensibility" can be traced at least from Sterne's Yorick to Faust to Arnold's "Empedocles on Aetna," Clough's "Dipsychus," to WP's Marius (*Marius the Epicurean*), the "representative aesthete." Marius longs to find some certainty either in Apuleius' Neoplatonism, in stoicism, or in Christianity; but he finds none, since such a committment would mean "loss of self . . . or esthetic distance and moral detachment."

889 Watson, George. THE LITERARY CRITICS: A STUDY OF ENGLISH DESCRIPTIVE CRITICISM (Baltimore: Penguin Books, 1962), pp. 14, 134, 164–66, 167, 220.

"There is no Victorian literary aesthetic" before WP and Wilde; "no formal aesthetic of any kind after Coleridge until the work of I. A. Richards in the 1920's, and R. G. Collingwood's THE PRINCIPLES OF ART (1938)." WP and Wilde self-consciously attempted to denigrate the importance of meaning in criticism. Yet at the same time (late nineteenth and early twentieth centuries) the triumph of historical criticism was being heralded by George Saintsbury, Arthur Quiller-Couch, and Edmund Gosse. WP's criticisms are "fatally trivializing, and no good critic could afford to swallow them." The aesthetic movement, by belittling the study of origins of poetry, does to a minor degree foreshadow twentieth century "New Criticism."

1963

890 André, Robert. "Walter Pater et Marcel Proust" (Walter Pater and Marcel Proust), LA NOUVELLE REVUE FRANÇAISE, XXI (June 1963), 1082–89.

Proust's major preoccupation was not so much to try to revive the privileged moments of his childhood and adolescence as to try to withdraw his existence from time through the expedient of art. For WP, consciousness must become an aesthetic state; the work of art immobilizes the moment; the role of memory is reestablished. Within ourselves a duration occurs which reinforces for us the originality of the artistic vision. À LA RECHERCHE DU TEMPS PERDU is the story of the desire to link moments with reminiscences. If the moment is realized by visual sensation, the reminiscence becomes auditory. This passage from one sense to the other, this transposition of sense response, is produced, for instance, by music. WP believed that all art aspires to the condition of music, but his own attempts to transpose the senses failed. [In French.]

891 Bateson, F. W. "Work in Progress II: Renaissance Literature," ESSAYS IN CRITICISM, XIII (April 1963), 117–31.

WP's concept of "Renaissance" emphasized the "new forms of aesthetic activity [that] the classical revival . . . may or may not have stimulated." Eliot's "The Metaphysical Poets" (1921) is a "sophisticated version" of WP's *The Renaissance* "adjusted to an anti-Victorian view of English literary history." At the purely aesthetic level, Eliot's concept of Renaissance is not too different from WP's.

892 Fishman, Solomon. THE INTERPRETATION OF ART: ESSAYS ON THE ART CRITICISM OF JOHN RUSKIN, WALTER PATER, CLIVE BELL, ROGER FRY AND HERBERT READ (Berkeley: University of California P, 1963), pp. 1, 2, 4, 6, 7, 43–72, 76–78, 96, 108, 147, 150, 156.

WP "casts a vague image." His essays on Renaissance art and Greek sculpture are no longer viewed as reliable sources. His work on art is less important than Ruskin's. WP advocated the conviction, only latent in Ruskin, that art represents the highest form of life. But he never advocated the total autonomy of a work of art; rather he discussed aestheticism as a theory of how one should conduct his life. To that extent, WP was a moralist; he "placed aesthetics within the sphere of ethics." WP was always more interested in how one viewed a work of art than in the work itself. He is guilty of the "affective fallacy" in criticism; he records only his subjective impressions of subjects. The imaginary portraits fit his personality because he constantly viewed subjects as extensions of himself. He has an evident, overriding preference for the exotic with which he consistently associates artistic excellence. Only in the essay on "Style" does he reveal a truly "formalist" critical stance; here he subordinates the mimetic to a study of the "intrinsic" value of a work. His criticism "encompasses both of the dominant aesthetic approaches of our time—the expressionist and the formalist." He does not succeed, however, in achieving any satisfying synthesis.

893 Gottfried, Leon. MATTHEW ARNOLD AND THE ROMANTICS (Lincoln: University of Nebraska P, 1963), pp. 2, 44, 65, 216.
WP, in the face of modern problems, retreated; Arnold and George Eliot struggled to maintain a balance between accepting the new while preserving the valuable traditions. WP's essay on Wordsworth (1874) foreshadows Arnold's to some extent. Arnold also copied a sentence out of WP's *The Renaissance* that characterized the Romantic and the Hellenic spirits. Arnold believed that the Romantic artist dealt in falsehood.

894 Kissane, James. "Victorian Mythology," VICTORIAN STUDIES, VI (Sept 1963), 5–28.
WP and Ruskin focused on the fullest artistic embodiment of mythology rather than on the rudiments, as did many of their contemporaries. The notion that was commonly accepted was that myths were originally a kind of "nature poetry," a "faded metaphor," a corruption of history. In "A Study of Dionysus," WP views myth as a manifestation of the dreams of primitive peoples. Like Ruskin and Symonds, WP believes that myths develop "as a response to nature" growing finally into "a spiritual insight" with accompanying ethical implications. This pattern appears in WP's study of Dionysus; he taught that interpretation of myths should depend primarily on the imagination.

895 Knoepflmacher, U. C. "Historicism as Fiction: Motion and Rest in the Stories of Walter Pater," MODERN FICTION STUDIES, IX (Summer 1963), 139–48.
WP's "philosophico-historical fiction is a thin veneer both for his developmental and sensationalist theories and for his private search for 'diaphanous' models of the past." The portraits share a common theme: a lonely character's search for a meaningful atmosphere that is found in or, as often is the case, denied by the intellectual and physical environment. His fiction is static, "the fiction of an art-critic." His heroes belong to transitional historical periods; this historicism informs all of the portraits, each of which in turn illustrates the basic opposition between motion and rest, change and stoicism, as WP described it in *Plato and Platonism,* and the impossibility of ever harmoniously combining these opposed forces during any one given period of history. [Article is partially absorbed in Knoepflmacher's chapter on WP in RELIGIOUS HUMANISM AND THE VICTORIAN NOVEL: GEORGE ELIOT, WALTER PATER, AND SAMUEL BUTLER (1965).]

896 Lhombreaud, Roger. ARTHUR SYMONS: A CRITICAL BIOGRAPHY (Lond: Unicorn P, 1963), pp. 34, 37, 38–39, 41, 42, 43–44, 46, 48, 52, 53–54, 64, 94, 100, 111, 114, 180, 182, 187, 190, 195, 196, 220, 253, 255, 271, 291, 294, 295.

Symons appears, as a prosaist, to be WP's successor. He met WP at Oxford in 1889, but this meeting, contrary to what A. Farmer and Madelaine Cazamian claim in LE MOUVEMENT ESTHÉTIQUE ET DECADENT EN ANGLETERRE (Paris, 1931), p. 277, and LE ROMAN ET LES IDÉES EN ANGLETERRE (Paris, 1935), pp. 222–23, was not the first, for he had seen WP earlier at Oxford. WP possessed "the essence of decadence" for Symons. After WP and Verlaine died, Symons "awakened to an ideal more sober and more mature."

897 Malany, Richard Eugene. "The Fiction of Walter Pater: A Critical Analysis." Unpublished dissertation, Harvard University, 1963.

[Listed in Lawrence F. McNamee, DISSERTATIONS IN ENGLISH AND AMERICAN LITERATURE (NY and Lond: Bowker, 1968).]

898 Miller, J. Hillis. THE DISAPPEARANCE OF GOD: FIVE NINE-TEENTH-CENTURY WRITERS (Cambridge: Harvard UP, 1963); rptd (NY: Schocken Books, 1965), pp. 274–75.

"Hopkins' notion of the fixity of subjective consciousness within an evanescent flux of sensations recalls similar ideas in the writings of [WP]." With WP, the early Hopkins might have agreed that each mind is kept " 'a solitary prisoner' " in its " 'own dream of a world.' " His early poem "A Vision of Mermaids" dramatizes the tragic failure to escape Paterian phenomenalism. Unlike WP, however, Hopkins could not make a viable philosophy out of subjectivism.

899 Morra, Umberto. COLLOQUI CON BERENSON (Conversations with Berenson) (Italy: Aldo Garzanti Editore, 1963); trans by Florence Hammond as CONVERSATIONS WITH BERENSON (Bost: Houghton Mifflin, 1965), pp. 51, 119, 147, 157.

WP's prose is "an ornate and many-colored goblet." [Berenson comments on WP.] [In Italian.]

900 Packer, Lona Mosk. "William Michael Rossetti and the Quilter Controversy: 'The Gospel of Intensity,' " VICTORIAN STUDIES, VII (Dec 1963), 170–83.

WP's essays reached a large public. *The Renaissance* went through seven editions by the end of the century. Harry Quilter's concern for the corruption of art in 1880 ["The New Renaissance; or the Gospel of Intensity," MACMILLAN'S MAGAZINE, XLII (Sept 1880), 391–400] was well founded. Articles advocating the aesthetic "gospel of intensity" had been appearing from 1866 with regularity in FORTNIGHTLY REVIEW, MACMILLAN'S, and the WESTMINSTER REVIEW. Quilter certainly should have been familiar with those essays published by WP prior to 1880.

901 Schwab, Arnold T. JAMES GIBBONS HUNEKER: CRITIC OF THE SEVEN ARTS (Stanford: Stanford UP, 1963), p. 14.

Among prose writers, Huneker most admired WP. The "Conclusion" to *The Renaissance* "crystallized Huneker's worship of the present."

902 Stasny, John. "Doctor Johnson and Walter Pater on Stoicism: A Comparison of Views," WEST VIRGINIA PHILOLOGICAL PAPERS, XIV (1963), 18–25.

Johnson in RASSELAS and WP in *Marius the Epicurean* both examine Stoicism. Johnson rejects all but the solutions of Christian eschatology; Rasselas learns of the emptiness of Stoic doctrine. WP's Marius also rejects Stoicism but for less dogmatic reasons. WP's examination is much fairer.

903 West, Paul. "Pater's Cordial Canon," ENGLISH, XIV (Summer 1963), 185–88.

WP confuses art with morals and culture with religion. He also confuses himself with his subjects without giving the reader adequate direction through the maze. He plays a game of "pretend" with his readers, who want to believe he has something significant to say. But WP "has no idea of what is irrelevant." He smothers his ideas in ornate, glittering prose. He partitions his prose, "sleeping his nouns one above the other as in tiered bunks."

1964

904 Brzenk, Eugene J. "Introduction," *Imaginary Portraits* (NY: Harper & Row, 1964), pp. 1–15.

Most of WP's writings may be called imaginary portraits; WP thought of both *Marius the Epicurean* and his essays in *Greek Studies* as portraits. Personalities remained always the focus of his writings. "Walter Savage Landor's IMAGINARY CONVERSATIONS undoubtedly played a part in the genesis" of WP's imaginary portraits. WP hoped to achieve a transposition of art forms in his portraits; at certain times they do suggest paintings; at others, sculpture, tapestries, etchings, or porcelain. WP probably planned for a second volume of imaginary portraits that would have included "Gaudioso, the Second," "Tibalt the Albigense," "Apollo in Picardy," and "Emerald Uthwart." "The Child in the House" and "An English Poet" may have been intended by WP to be a prologue to a much larger work. *Marius* and *Gaston de Latour* were to be part of a trilogy, the third work of which was to be set in England at the end of the eighteenth century. The three English portraits ("Child in the House," "An English Poet," and "Emerald Uthwart") are possible sources or prototypes of this third part of the trilogy. Viewed together, the portraits anticipate the themes and techniques of Joyce, Proust, Henry James, and Virginia Woolf. His protagonists are anti-heroes "who are spectators of events."

Florian Deleal is an anti-hero: he is a highly introspective figure who remains throughout an observer of life; his one decisive act sums up his entire life. Emerald Uthwart is another of WP's "thwarted youths." Sebastian Van Storck, like most of the heroes of WP's fiction, cultivates detachment. Denys l'Auxerrois and Apollyon are dispossessed, isolated figures out of sympathy with their environment.

> **905** d'Hangest, Germain. "Un grand humaniste de la fin du dix-neuvième siècle: Walter Pater et la Grèce" (A Great Humanist at the End of the Nineteenth Century: Walter Pater and Greece), BULLETIN DE L'ASSOCIATION GUILLAUME BUDÉ, Supplement Lettres d'Humanité, XXIII (1964), 479–93.

WP's *Greek Studies* are stimulating but somewhat suspect, owing to his romanticism. For it forced him less to reconstruct in its exact dimensions an extinct universe than to give rise to an ideal, to communicate his poetic vision of one stage of the human spirit. In order to evoke the Greek spirit, WP turned to introspection. Remarkably learned but exalted by his visionary spirit, WP's archaeology thus reflects his own temperament. In *Greek Studies,* he associates himself almost exclusively with the romantic aspects of the Hellenic spirit, and he goes straight for those myths that are the most tormented, if not the most dismal. His supernatural mythic beings are always victims. They always emerge from tragedies with personalities that are profoundly changed. It is probably that in letting himself become obsessed thus by the currents of savagery and horror that appear in the Dionysian tradition, he was yielding to several unconscious obsessions. On the other hand, it seems that against his will the bacchanalian ecstacy, with its retinue of folly and crime, had all the value of a warning. It showed him to what mental ruination the unrestrained search for intense experiences in life could lead when they had no other criterion but intensity itself. It is perfectly understandable that after such a long study of Greek myths, WP would transpose them into many of his imaginary portraits. Of the nine imaginary portraits that he wrote, three deal directly with Greek myths. Greece, for WP, meant Hellenic antiquity—the golden age. His thoughts on Greece were always stimulated by his reading of Plato. He felt an affinity with Plato and with Greece. He saw in Plato what he desired for himself: a development leading from the pagan cult of experience and the impressions of the senses to analysis and asceticism, a development which through aesthetics bends towards ethics and which reconciles the beautiful with the good in an ideal no longer of passion but of moderation. [In French.]

> **906** d'Hangest, Germain. "Walter Pater. Critique Shakespearian" (Walter Pater. Critic of Shakespeare), ÉTUDES ANGLAISES, XVII (Oct–Dec 1964), 564–70.

In his essays on Shakespeare, WP tries to discover the dramatist's presence in the plays. His aim is to discover Shakespeare's genius, Shakespeare in the act of creating. In LOVE'S LABOUR'S LOST, WP concludes that the play's heightened, refined appeal provides for its real aesthetic value. In his essay "Shakespeare's English Kings" WP claims that the kings created by Shakespeare were in fact aesthetes, thrown into the whirl of a life for which they were not made. They imaginatively pursue their dream, their royal game. WP is at his best when interpreting aesthetic attitudes in Shakespeare. He always tries to capture the truly informing principle of the art work. That principle is no less than the link between the artist and the form he engenders. But WP's view is consistently impressionistic. As a critic of Shakespeare, he therefore does not rank among the best. [In French.]

907 Engleberg, Edward. THE VAST DESIGN: PATTERN IN W. B. YEATS'S AESTHETIC (Toronto: University of Toronto P, 1964), pp. xiv, xxiii, xxv–xxvi, 7, 9–11, 13, 25, 31, 69–72, 93–94, 101, 105, 106, 181, 184–90.

Yeats learned the rhythms for his early prose from Shelley, Arnold, Wilde, and WP. There is no evidence to prove how thoroughly Yeats read WP's *Greek Studies* and *Plato and Platonism,* but one must assume that he was familiar with these works. Yeats "parallels" WP; however, he does not "parrot him." "The Statues" (1938) simply gains in meaning when read with WP's conception of Greek art and philosophy as a backdrop. Yeats's earliest encounter with the Greek and Renaissance revival was probably from WP's *The Renaissance.* Yeats consistently paralleled the Renaissance with his own time. WP's contention that Hellenic sculpture was characterized by "restraint" was essential to Yeats's aesthetic scheme. In the first three chapters of *Plato and Platonism,* WP insists upon a philosophic balance between motion and rest that closely resembles Yeats's similar desire for balance between the conditions of stasis and flux.

908 Grosskurth, Phyllis. JOHN ADDINGTON SYMONDS: A BIOGRAPHY (Lond: Longmans, Green, 1964), pp. 56, 157–58, 162, 169, 172–73, 206, 224, 248, 252, 309–10, 326; rptd as THE WOEFUL VICTORIAN: A BIOGRAPHY OF JOHN ADDINGTON SYMONDS (NY: Holt, Rinehart, Winston, 1965).

Symonds's review of WP's *The Renaissance* (THE ACADEMY, 15 March 1873) was "inadvertently responsible for a subsequent association of their respective philosophies." But WP and Symonds were antagonists, at least from Symonds's point of view. He claimed that WP's view of life gave him the "creeps." He had no sympathy with WP's notion that art was "the only meaningful experience in life." Symonds, in 1876, campaigned for the professorship of poetry at Oxford; his earliest opposition was WP and F. T. Palgrave. WP's essay on "Style" was on Symonds's mind when he composed ESSAYS SPECULATIVE AND SUGGESTIVE (1890). Yet he is far more typical of the nineteenth century "than a narrow aesthete" like WP.

909 Harris, Wendell V. "Pater as Prophet," CRITICISM, VI (Fall 1964), 349–60.

Though WP cannot be held responsible for the "decadent" literature and life of the Ninetics, his theories of art and life "throw into perspective a surprising number of subsequent literary theories and practices": (1) "the evanescence, (2) complexity, and (3) aesthetic importance of the individual moment" emphasizing the singularity of one's experience (a theory that finds expression in Hemingway, Faulkner, Nabokov, Woolf, and Joyce, among others); (4) the self-conscious "complexity of mind" that is aware of the myriad forces that make us question freedom of the will; and (5) the aspiration of all art "towards the condition of music" (i.e., the attempt to reduce matter to form). Art's aspiration towards the condition of music is seen explicitly in the dependence on musical structure in T. S. Eliot's THE WASTELAND and the FOUR QUARTETS as well as in works by Joyce, Beckett, and Woolf.

910 Hassall, Christopher. RUPERT BROOKE: A BIOGRAPHY (NY: Harcourt, Brace & World, 1964), pp. 43, 63, 86, 90, 283.

Gautier's ideas become "art for art's sake" in the hands of WP. The young Rupert Brooke was attracted to the works of WP, particularly WP's treatment of Platonic thought.

911 Johnson, E. D. H. THE WORLD OF THE VICTORIANS: AN ANTHOLOGY OF POETRY AND PROSE (NY: Scribner's Sons, 1964), pp. 260–62, 317, 344, 404, 476.

Seeking to seize upon the ideal aspect of momentary experience and realize the cosmic order underlying the perpetual flux of matter and mind, WP gave full formulation to the theory of "art for art's sake" first advanced in England by Swinburne. As the aesthetic movement tended toward the Decadence, his doctrine of exquisite experience degenerated into the sensationalism of Wilde and the later aesthetes. [Also contains brief, factual introduction to selections from *The Renaissance*, "The Child in the House," (Johnson contrasts "The Child" with Darwin's AUTOBIOGRAPHY), and THE NEW REPUBLIC.]

912 Karl, Frederick R. AN AGE OF FICTION: THE NINETEENTH CENTURY BRITISH NOVEL (NY: Farrar, Strauss, Giroux, 1964), p. 274; rptd as A READER'S GUIDE TO THE NINETEENTH CENTURY BRITISH NOVEL (NY: Noonday P, 1964).

Marius the Epicurean is a prose epic. Following a pattern unlike that found in earlier novels of belief and doubt where the hero moves relentlessly towards unbelief, Marius devotes himself at the end to Christian ideals, a doctrine, in contrast to his earlier Epicureanism, that satisfies "the whole man."

913 Morse, Samuel F. "Wallace Stevens, Bergson, Pater," JOURNAL OF ENGLISH LITERARY HISTORY, XXXI (1964), 1–34.

Wallace Stevens's belief that we can " 'affect objects in nature, by projecting our moods, emotions, etc.' " squares with his interpretation of Bergson's theory of comedy and WP's theory of art. The "Conclusion" to *The Renaissance* spoke directly to Stevens, but he preferred to accept the world as it was. WP's ideal of "burning with a hard gem-like flame," though viewed as an absurdity to self-committed moderns, retained its appeal for Stevens. WP's influence is evident in Stevens's "The Comedian as the Letter 'C' " and "Tea at the Palaz of Hoon."

Stevens resembles Crispin, the poetic hero of "The Comedian as the Letter 'C.' " The apology that ends the poem echoes the last few paragraphs of WP's "Conclusion." Crispin's ambition was to achieve what WP and Bergson call the object of art: " 'immediate communion with things.' "

914 Poston, Lawrence Sanford, III. "Five Victorians on Italian Renaissance Culture: A Problem in Historical Perspectives," DISSERTATION ABSTRACTS, XXV (1964), 484. Unpublished dissertation, Princeton University, 1964.

[On Ruskin, Browning, Eliot, WP, and Symonds.]

915 Samuels, Ernest. HENRY ADAMS: THE MAJOR PHASE (Cambridge: Harvard UP, 1964), pp. 84, 265, 352, 425.

Henry Adams read *Marius the Epicurean* during a sea voyage to New York. The "disenchanted temper" of Marius "peculiarly chimed with his own." Berenson, who had taken up "the cult of beauty" where Ruskin and WP had left off, was also one of Adams's "acquisitions."

916 Schrickx, W. "On Giordano Bruno, Wilde and Yeats," ENGLISH STUDIES (Amsterdam), XLV (Supplement 1964), 257–64.

The revival of interest in Giordano Bruno can probably be dated from the publication of WP's essay on him in THE FORTNIGHTLY REVIEW (1889). In this essay, the parallels between the world soul and the soul of the artist are beautifully developed. WP's "account of Bruno is nothing but an unambiguous statement of the symbolist artist's position." One should compare WP's passage opening, "delighting in itself," with the stanza in Yeats's "Prayer for my Daughter" beginning, "Considering that, all hatred driven hence." Yeats had great praise for WP's prose style. It was York Powell who kept alive in the Nineties the interest in Bruno aroused earlier by WP.

917 Swann, Thomas B. ERNEST DOWSON (NY: Twayne [TEAS, 15], 1964), pp. 18, 19, 26, 98.

WP codified the aesthetic approach to life. The young Oxford undergraduates who read his works and listened to his lectures misunderstood his intentions. They began to seek experiences through questionable channels. Adrian Rome, the hero of Dowson's first novel of the same name, reveals artistic ideals that are highly reminiscent of WP's aesthetic pronouncements.

918 Uslenghi, Raffaella M. "Una Prospettiva di Unita nell'arte di George Moore" (A Perspective of Unity in the Art of George Moore), ENGLISH MISCELLANY, XV (1964), 213–58.

[Passing references to WP's influence on George Moore.] [In Italian.]

919 Vogeler, Martha Salmon. "The Religious Meaning of *Marius the Epicurean*," NINETEENTH CENTURY FICTION, XIX (Dec 1964), 287–99.

The religious significance of *Marius the Epicurean* may seem puzzling, for Marius dies without affirming his belief in Christianity. WP intentionally depicts "the struggle between faith and skepticism" in *Marius,* for he experienced it himself. He believed that doubts need not force one to dissociate himself entirely from religion, a position that he explains in "Amiel's JOURNAL INTIME" (1886) and his review of Mrs. Ward's ROBERT ELSMERE (1888). In keeping with the position expressed in these essays, Marius does not abandon the religious spirit. "His failure to consider himself a believer" is WP's "way of saying that the real difficulty of achieving religious faith lies in knowing what faith consists in." WP thought that too many of his contemporaries had a narrow conception of faith. Ironically, Marius dies a Christian in all but his own eyes.

920 Weintraub, Stanley. "Introduction," THE YELLOW BOOK: QUINTESSENCE OF THE NINETIES (Garden City, NY: Doubleday, 1964), pp. vii–xxv.

THE YELLOW BOOK appears "as a bridge between late Victorianism and the twentieth century, between the art-for-art's sake over-refinements" of Swinburne and WP "and the . . . more recent recognition of the social value of the literary artifact." [The publisher's announcement of THE YELLOW BOOK listed WP as one of its "expected" contributors.]

921 Wildi, Max. "Reappraisals of Walter Pater," ENGLISH STUDIES (Amsterdam), XLV (Supplement 1964), 243–48.

WP erected his "overdecorated House of Art" on a Pre-Raphaelite foundation. WP's work needs to be reappraised. But the "full rehabilitation will . . . scarcely come in our time with its almost exclusive preoccupation with committed art and its strong anti-individualistic tendencies." Contemporary post-Kierkegaardians must be repelled by WP's deep dislike of dogmatic choice. [Primarily a review of Wolfgang Iser's WALTER PATER: DIE AUTONOMIE DES ÄSTHETISCHEN (1960) and Germain d'Hangest's WALTER PATER: L'HOMME ET L'OEUVRE (1961).]

1965

922 Bloom, Harold. "Keats and the Embarrassments of Poetic Tradition," FROM SENSIBILITY TO ROMANTICISM: ESSAYS PRESENTED TO FREDERICK A. POTTLE, ed by F. W. Hilles and Harold Bloom (Oxford: Oxford UP, 1965), pp. 513–26; rptd in Harold Bloom, THE RINGERS IN THE TOWER: STUDIES IN ROMANTIC TRADITION (Chicago & Lond: University of Chicago P, 1971), pp. 131–42.

The intense self-consciousness of Keats's "Ode on Melancholy" and "The Fall of Hyperion" prefigures that of the "Conclusion" to *The Renaissance*. Yeats and Wallace Stevens are heirs of the Paterian tradition.

923 Campos, Christophe. THE VIEW OF FRANCE: FROM ARNOLD TO BLOOMSBURY (Oxford: Oxford UP, 1965), pp. 10, 17, 18, 35, 36, 61, 69, 90–105, 107, 139, 153, 155, 165, 175, 177, 187, 188, 212, 213, 219, 235, 238.

WP's *Renaissance* created in England "a new sort of francophily." His approach to France is based largely and "for the first time" on the history of art. Like Arnold, he based much of his understanding of French culture, particularly that of the sixteenth century, on Sainte-Beuve. Ancient Greek sensualism was revived in modern France. WP viewed France, positively, as a pagan country with its own kind of natural morality. The cultures of France and Greece and not Germany became his favorite subjects as his work matured. The Winckelmann essay contains the key to the study of *The Renaissance*. *Gaston de Latour,* his "biography of the French sixteenth century," confirms his conviction that France is strongly primitive. The *Imaginary Portraits* reveal his belief that "a fierce 'antinomian' spirit" lay beneath the surface of the French scene. The return of paganism to France is symbolized in Prosper Mérimée's story of the VENUS OF ILLE. But his view of France is "all effect." He unfortunately believed that people can be described and understood "in the same terms as the scenery in which they live."

924 Cecil, David [Lord]. MAX: A BIOGRAPHY (Bost: Houghton Mifflin, 1965), pp. 44, 47–49, 60, 65, 149, 373.

Max Beerbohm told his tutor, G. R. Scott, that he wanted to hear WP's lectures. Scott laughed. Beerbohm discovered he was right about WP's lectures; they were inaudible. Wilde influenced him far more than did WP. At the end of his copy of *The Renaissance,* Beerbohm inserted quotes from imaginary reviews, such as "at once a scourge and a purge" (WIGAN REMEMBRANCER).

925 Charlesworth, Barbara. DARK PASSAGES: THE DECADENT CONSCIOUSNESS IN VICTORIAN LITERATURE (Madison: University of Wisconsin P, 1965), pp. 36–52, 95, 119, 120, 122, and scattered references; rvd dissertation, "Dark Passage: A Study of Decadence," Radcliffe College, 1962.

WP was obsessed with the knowledge that time was ever moving past him, that he could not even take himself as a point of rest. He thought that whatever order might exist had its basis in the "moment of insight," the moment when "the flux was formed into a pattern within the consciousness of the observer." Marius (*Marius the Epicurean*) is WP's mask. The philosophy of flux of Heraclitus and Protagoras serves as WP's point of departure in the novel. Marius decides to rely exclusively on the senses; he puts aside abstract speculation and embraces Cyrenaicism. Here WP carries one of Locke's ideas to its logical conclusion—the notion of the mind keeping its own solitary dream of a world. To WP, memory is the finest hope, the best comfort. Like the young Marius, WP believed that art "by reincarnating the moment held in the memory, offered sufficient permanence." This is why clear form and definite outline are so important to WP; the object must be remembered clearly and wholly. WP believed with Rossetti and the French Symbolists that "the moment must be carved 'in ivory or in ebony.' " Three-quarters of *Marius* is taken up with demonstrating that the unrefined hedonism of Epicureanism is inadequate for happiness. Cyrenaicism fails because it does not permit the individual any knowledge beyond the "self": "no sense of an external order, either metaphysical or moral, save that of which he himself is aware in his happiest . . . moments." Near the conclusion, Marius is conscious only of the flux of events; he cannot believe in any absolute order; his vision is still completely personal. His position is that of "decadence." Happily, he is saved from decadence at the end by accepting the hypothesis, though unproven, of a transcendent reality. Only Lionel Johnson, of all of WP's followers, heeded the warning of *Marius*. Symons and Wilde were overawed by and lost to the message of the earlier work, *The Renaissance*. Its "Conclusion" is answered in the twentieth century by Martin Buber: Filling " 'each moment with experiencing and using' " causes it to cease burning. " 'He who lives with [the moment] alone is not a man.' " *Marius* illustrates WP's escape from the "decadent" theories of *The Renaissance;* most of WP's followers, however, were not as fortunate.

> **926** DeLaura, David J. "Pater and Eliot: The Origins of the 'Objective Correlative,' " MODERN LANGUAGE QUARTERLY, XXVI (Sept 1965), 426–31.

WP in "Sandro Botticelli" (*The Renaissance*) admires uniqueness; the usurping of sense data, " 'rejecting some and isolating others, and always combining them anew' "; and the infusion into an art work of sentiments "greater than any known issue [cause] of them explains." Eliot reverses WP's admiration, since he dislikes such romantic morbidity; but he retains, though transforming, WP's terms: "data" becomes " 'a set of objects, a situation, a chain of events' which in the case of Hamlet, are inadequate to embody 'a feeling which he cannot understand,' 'an emotion he cannot express in art.' " [Essay deals with "the psychological mechanism involved in the production of art which fails of an objective correlative" rather than with Eliot's formation, or borrowing, of the term itself.]

> **927** Downes, David Anthony. VICTORIAN PORTRAITS: HOPKINS AND PATER (NY: Bookman, 1965).

Hopkins and WP were friends. They both were greatly concerned with the problems facing modern man. WP's works reveal a process of religious development which "brought him to a new religious assent based upon his personal experience." The outline of his religious development is evident in *Marius the Epicurean*. The foundation of his religious belief was early Christian (Roman Catholic), though he had evident difficulty with Christian theology. [The book considers in some detail the significance of the friendship between WP and Hopkins, their critical philosophies (both espoused the "Humanistic goal of art—the soul of humanity and the glory of God"), and the patterns revealed in their lives and works which are responsible for their deep convictions. They both represent the "achievement of true holiness."]

928 Duffy, John. "From Essay to Portrait: Walter Pater after *The Renaissance,*" THOTH (Syracuse University), VI (1965), ii, 3–15.
WP's "aestheticism" was misunderstood by early twentieth-century critics as a defense of art for art's sake. But in the late Fifties and Sixties, criticism has dealt more with his fiction. To reappraise WP thoroughly requires a close examination of the work done after *The Renaissance.* Portraits in *The Renaissance* and *Appreciations* are flawed by WP's fixation with single aspects of the characters of the figures. From 1878 to his death in 1894, WP was preoccupied with fiction. A case can be made for the fictional qualities of *Plato and Platonism.* His essay on "Style" expresses clearly the aesthetic that governs his fictional portraits. [Article includes brief commentaries on "The Child in the House," *Marius the Epicurean,* "A Prince of Court Painters," "Sebastian Van Storck," "Denys l'Auxerrois," "Duke Carl of Rosenmold," *Gaston de Latour,* "Emerald Uthwart," and "Apollo in Picardy."]

929 Duffy, John Joseph. "Walter Pater: Studies Toward a Reappraisal," DISSERTATION ABSTRACTS, XXVI (1965), 1631. Unpublished dissertation, Syracuse University, 1965.

930 Gordon, John D. "Novels in Manuscript: An Exhibition from the Berg Collection," BULLETIN OF THE NEW YORK PUBLIC LIBRARY, LXIX (May 1965), 317–29, espec pp. 325–26.
[Brief biographical sketch of WP. Occasion was exhibition of ms. of *Gaston de Latour* from collection of Dr. A. A. Berg.]

931 Herendeen, Warren Richard. "The Aesthetic of Walter Pater: A Formulation," DISSERTATION ABSTRACTS, XXV (1965), 6593–94. Unpublished dissertation, University of Wisconsin, 1965.

932 Jullian, Phillipe. UN PRINCE 1900: ROBERT DE MONTESQUIOU (Paris: Phillipe Jullian, 1965); trans by John Haylock and Francis King as ROBERT DE MONTESQUIOU: FIN DE SIÈCLE PRINCE (Lond: Secker & Warburg, 1967); rptd as PRINCE OF AESTHETES: COUNT ROBERT DE MONTESQUIOU, 1885–1921 (NY: Viking, 1968), pp. 85, 86, 114, 123.
Robert de Montesquiou saw himself reflected in the heroes of WP's imaginary portraits. [In French.]

933 Killham, John. " 'Ineluctable Modality' in Joyce's ULYSSES," UNIVERSITY OF TORONTO QUARTERLY, XXXIV (April 1965), 269–89.
Stephen Dedalus in the opening of chapter three ("Proteus") of ULYSSES "pondering (as any young man would in 1904) the idealist position" which, in WP and Bradley, "could not but exacerbate his natural tendency to solipsism, recalls

Berkeley, smiles at Aristotle's happy unawareness of the subjective-objective distinction, and typically experiments with the idea by closing down the modality of sight . . . and trying what it is like to rely upon that of sound (and touch) alone." He is "inevitably" the victim of the tendency "to regard all things as inconstant modes" that WP discusses in the "Conclusion" to *The Renaissance*. WP here paves the way for Stephen's speech on his duty to repay the borrowed pound. Stephen's stroll by the sea in "Proteus" is also "intimately related" to the "Conclusion." This "Epicurean view of experience" is "intensely materialistic." Joyce had little sympathy with WP's hedonistic view of art. Stephen seeks the absolute, " 'the eternal affirmation of the spirit of man in literature.' " He wants to believe in the soul. WP's Cyrenaicism is crude. But ULYSSES dramatizes Stephen's "approaching recognition that experience itself, not the fruit of experience, is all."

> **934** Knoepflmacher, U. C. RELIGIOUS HUMANISM AND THE VICTORIAN NOVEL: GEORGE ELIOT, WALTER PATER, AND SAMUEL BUTLER (Princeton: Princeton UP, 1965); rvd dissertation, "The Victorian Novel of Religious Humanism: A Study of George Eliot, Walter Pater, and Samuel Butler," Princeton University, 1961; partially absorbs "Historicism as Fiction: Motion and Rest in the Stories of Walter Pater," MODERN FICTION STUDIES, 1963.

George Eliot considered WP's *The Renaissance* "quite poisonous in its false principles of criticism and false conceptions of life." WP has been erroneously identified with the tenets of the art for art's sake movement. His writings fall into two phases: the first begins with "Diaphaneitè" and ends with *The Renaissance;* the second spans the years from 1874 to 1894. Through his imaginary portraits WP tested out many of the assumptions that had gone into *The Renaissance*. These years of reappraisal led him to reject his earlier claim for a "universal pagan sentiment." After *Marius the Epicurean,* he wrote additional imaginary portraits in which he sought "to bridge the gap between his belief in the exclusive validity of the senses and his increasing awareness of the necessity for moral laws for which he could find no correlative in the visible world." *Plato and Platonism,* his last published volume, sums up his mature thoughts on this need for reconciliation. *Plato* is designed to check the irresponsibility and decadence that he associated with Plato's Athens; it is directed toward the undisciplined young followers who misinterpreted the "Conclusion" to *The Renaissance*. Like *Marius, Plato* is another of WP's efforts to make his position on morality and aesthetics clear. Most of WP's fictional characters are reiterations of the theme of an individual searching for the "influence" of a meaningful "environment." Most of his fiction is static, the fiction of an art critic. And all of his heroes belong to transitional historical periods. Each tale illustrates the opposition of motion to rest, the basic opposition that he would develop more fully in *Plato*.

> **935** Kronenberger, Louis (ed). "Johnson, Lionel Pigot," ATLANTIC BRIEF LIVES (Bost: Little, Brown, 1965), pp. 410–11.

All of Johnson's verse shows the influence of WP.

936 Kronenberger, Louis (ed). "Pater, Walter (Horatio)," ATLANTIC BRIEF LIVES (Bost: Little, Brown, 1965), p. 580.

WP's *The Renaissance* (1873) was viewed by aesthetes as a landmark of the aesthetic movement and became one of the most influential books of its day, especially for Oscar Wilde and George Moore. Through *Marius the Epicurean* (1885) WP was considered an apostle to the decadents of the Eighties and Nineties.

937 Kronenberger, Louis (ed). "Symons, Arthur," ATLANTIC BRIEF LIVES (Bost: Little, Brown, 1965), p. 759.

Symons's early poetry received praise from WP.

938 Lindeman, Ralph D. NORMAN DOUGLAS (NY: Twayne [TEAS, 19], 1965), pp. 55, 71, 85, 105, 159.

Reading Douglas's nature descriptions reminds one of WP's plea for life in the "Conclusion" to *The Renaissance*. [Douglas quotes WP in SIREN LAND (1911).]

939 Monsman, Gerald Cornelius. "Pater's Portraits: A Critical Analysis of the Fiction of Walter Horatio Pater," DISSERTATION ABSTRACTS, XXVI (1965), 3306. Published dissertation, Johns Hopkins University, 1965; pub as PATER'S PORTRAITS: MYTHIC PATTERN IN THE FICTION OF WALTER HORATIO PATER (Baltimore: Johns Hopkins P, 1967), q.v. for abstract.

940 Nathan, Leonard. THE TRAGIC DRAMA OF WILLIAM BUTLER YEATS: FIGURES IN A DANCE (NY: Columbia UP, 1965), pp. 42–50, 52, 54, 55, 60–61, 67, 71, 79, 87, 104, 105, 106, 110, 118, 122, 123–24, 172; derived from "W. B. Yeats's Experiments with an Influence," VICTORIAN STUDIES (1962).

WP and the French Symbolists influenced Yeats's "aestheticism." WP's works "had an impact on Yeats's work that did not cease even after the turn of the century." Central to this impact is WP's belief that human knowledge is rooted in human feeling. This contention reinforced Yeats's belief that the emotions and true vision were united and expressed in lyric poetry. Yeats tended to copy WP's prose style in THE SECRET ROSE, PER AMICA SILENTIA LUNAE, and THE AUTOBIOGRAPHY. Yeats paid close attention to WP's comments on the drama in "Shakespeare's English Kings." That he knew the essay well is made clear by his reliance on it in his essay "At Stratford-on-Avon" (1901). WP recommended drama that approached the " 'unity of lyrical effect, as if a song or ballad were still lying at the root of it.' " But Yeats, unlike WP, would decide that the essential element in serious drama was the "something" beyond human emotion. WP would not have agreed. Yeats's ROSA ALCHEMICA embodies his reaction to WP's hedonism. The story, like *Marius the Epicurean,* tests "the validity of the Paterian man's response" to reality and finds it wanting. But WP affirmed for Yeats that art should approach the purity of religious ritual.

941 Ohmann, Richard. "Methods in the Study of Victorian Style," VICTORIAN NEWSLETTER, No. 27 (Spring 1965), pp. 1–14.

Of thirty-three classes of basic sentences and transformations in a preliminary syntactic inventory of prose examples by six major Victorians (Arnold, Carlyle, Huxley, Newman, WP, Ruskin) and six eighteenth-century writers (Addison, Boswell, Burke, Defoe, Johnson, Shaftesbury), there are only three in which the two periods contrast exactly.

942 Peckham, Morse. ROMANTICISM: THE CULTURE OF THE NINETEENTH CENTURY (NY: Braziller, 1965), p. 257.

WP's "Sebastian Van Storck" shares "with Swinburne the nonfunctional and exquisite surface and the disturbing content; with Rimbaud the sustained metaphor, here historical rather than geographical; with Mallarmé the use of philosophy as a technique of withdrawal; and with Thomas Mann the use of diseases as a metaphor for alienation." The ending which seems sentimental at first is actually ironic.

943 Peters, Robert L. THE CROWNS OF APOLLO: SWINBURNE'S PRINCIPLES OF LITERATURE AND ART; A STUDY IN VICTORIAN CRITICISM AND AESTHETICS (Detroit: Wayne State UP, 1965), pp. 22, 24–25, 29, 51–52, 85, 93, 94, 101, 107, 138, 144, 146–47, 148, 154, 163, 168, 183, 185, 186.

Swinburne's formulas for art preceded WP's by at least seven years. Swinburne's critical stance insists on the critic's role as advocate and judge; WP, in contrast, delays judgments for the sake of minute discriminations and for capturing the single "virtue" of the work or the artist. The organic result of WP's "ideal of 'mind' " in writing is structurally discernable, WP claimed, in the word, the phrase, the sentence, and the paragraph. In his emphasis on technique and inner structure, WP moves beyond Swinburne and closer to twentieth-century thought. For WP the work of art is incomplete until it "engages a viewer, on whom it depends for its completion."

944 Roellinger, Francis X. "Intimations of Winckelmann in Pater's 'Diaphaneitè,' " ENGLISH LANGUAGE NOTES, II (June 1965), 277–82.

Certain parts of "Diaphaneitè" were used by WP in the later essay on Winckelmann in *The Renaissance*.

945 Scholes, Robert, and Richard M. Kain (eds). THE WORKSHOP OF DAEDALUS: JAMES JOYCE AND THE RAW MATERIALS FOR A PORTRAIT OF THE ARTIST AS A YOUNG MAN (Evanston: Northwestern UP, 1965), pp. xiii, 49, 165, 255–58.

Joyce put cadences from WP's prose and D'Annunzio's prose into Stephen Dedalus's speech and thought in A PORTRAIT OF THE ARTIST AS A YOUNG MAN. Dedalus's poem, "Villanelle of the Temptress," is built on the delicate balance between scholastic and humanistic ways of thought. The temptress may have been modelled on WP's Gioconda; Joyce was familiar with the passage and with WP's discussion of the balance between the scholastic and humanistic in the essay on Pico della Mirandola. [Eds include two passages from WP's essays on Giorgione and Leonardo da Vinci which they say "are relevant to Joyce's esthetic theory and his manner of presenting Stephen as a poet." Specifically, the eds have in mind Joyce's theory of "epiphany" and his theory of vocabulary and rhythm developed in the "Esthetic" section of his Trieste notebooks and used by him in describing Stephen's composition of the villanelle.]

946 Shuter, William Francis. "The Historical Piety of Walter Pater," DISSERTATION ABSTRACTS, XXVI (1965), 3352–53. Unpublished dissertation, University of Wisconsin, 1965.

947 Stanford, Derek (ed). POETS OF THE 'NINETIES (Lond: John Baker, 1965), pp. 17–45.

Yeats, intellectually, blames WP for the disaster of the young writers of the period. And WP's "dangerous doctrines" did approach the substitution of "sensation for wisdom." His teachings were dangerously subjective. From WP, the Nineties poets learned that life is flux (the "pathos of transcience") and that the individual is ultimately alone ("privately enclosed impressionism").

948 Tillotson, Geoffrey. "Walter Pater," in CRITICS WHO HAVE INFLU-ENCED TASTE, ed by A. P. Ryan (Lond: Geoffrey Bles, 1965), pp. 55–57.

Like Arnold, WP looked to literature to fulfill the need for culture. WP saw how the middle class could be enlisted in the service of art. He did not condescend but attempted to raise the reader to his level. Unlike Arnold, WP was not reluctant to read modern novels. He made it easier for Henry James to write THE ART OF FICTION. But he was too sensual at times for most middle-class readers.

1966

949 Alford, Norman William. "The Rhymers' Club (founded 1891): A Study of Its Activities and Their Significance," DISSERTATION AB-STRACTS, XXVII (1966), 451A. Unpublished dissertation, University of Texas, 1966.

[Includes references to WP's influence on the members of the Rhymers' Club.]

950 Beckson, Karl. "Introduction," AESTHETES AND DECADENTS OF THE 1890'S: AN ANTHOLOGY OF BRITISH POETRY AND PROSE, ed by Karl Beckson (NY: Random House, Vintage Books, 1966), pp. xxviii–xxxii.

Though the Aesthetes found in Keats and Rossetti examples of devotion to the ideal of beauty and in Swinburne a major source of the widened aesthetic sensibility, it was in *The Renaissance* that they discovered their "golden book"; its stress on the importance of intense experience and on the application of aesthetic standards to life "earned Pater a reputation as the foremost Aesthete of his day." Passages such as that on the *Mona Lisa* prompted Symons to describe the book as "heavy with the odour of tropical flowers" and Wilde to call it "the very flower of decadence"; but despite his use of the term "art for art's sake" in the "Conclusion," WP "was concerned with moral development through art," reportedly called Huysmans a "Beastly man," and in a letter to George Moore questioned the moral tone of his CONFESSIONS OF A YOUNG MAN. Among the members of the Rhymers' Club, whose philosophy, according to Yeats, was derived largely from WP, Lionel Johnson was the closest in temperament to WP himself, had as an Oxford undergraduate spent much time with him, and shared particularly his aesthetic approach to religion. Wilde, on the other hand, was WP's "most vocal and perhaps most unwelcome disciple"; WP disassociated himself from Wilde's amoral Epicureanism in his review of THE PICTURE OF DORIAN GRAY.

> **951** Bowra, C. M. MEMORIES 1898–1939 (Lond: Weidenfield & Nicholson, 1966), p. 119; rptd (Cambridge, Mass: Harvard UP, 1967).

F. F. Urquhart, known around Oxford as "Sligger," apparently provided a model for WP's Emerald Uthwart.

> **952** Buckley, Jerome Hamilton. THE TRIUMPH OF TIME: A STUDY OF THE VICTORIAN CONCEPTS OF TIME, HISTORY, PROGRESS, AND DECADENCE (Cambridge, Mass: Harvard UP, Belknap Press, 1966), pp. 8–9, 19, 81, 82, 89, 91, 96, 99, 100, 103–4, 113, 131–34, 135, 139–40, 145–46, 150, 170, 178.

WP was one of those Victorians who foreshadowed the Bergsonian sense of time as duration by expanding upon "Hume's concept of the self as function rather than substance, a concept which made the psychological life an incessant movement in time." His interest in the Renaissance was typical of the historical revivalism of the period, which often distorted the past; WP himself seemed to conclude that "the old masters had in some way anticipated a Paterian malaise." In describing the decadent splendor of imperial Rome in *Marius the Epicurean* WP was commenting upon the hollowness of Victorian materialism, and the Stoicism of Marcus Aurelius was likewise analogous to the pessimism of the late nineteenth century. In the essay on "Style" WP noted a decadent element in the eclecticism of Tennyson's poetry; in *Marius* he ascribed the same eclecticism to the typically decadent prose style of Flavian. *Marius, Imaginary Portraits,* and "The Child in the House" reflect the Victorian "autobiographical impulse" by which the self was rescued from time and given form and consistency by situating it in the fixity of the past: thus the importance to Marius of reminiscence and the significance of his returning to his childhood home before his death in an "effort to make peace with the past" and achieve "a final integration of spirit." Symons and Hopkins owed their concern for the intense moment to WP's emphasis on "the personal present"; but WP's hedonism was modified by a "respect for the public present." WP evidenced the same interest in modernity that he attributed to Marius. *The Renaissance* is more a study of the modern temper than it is art history. WP differed from Arnold in relying on art to provide modern man with a sense of freedom by means of intensified subjectivity rather than a new objectivity whereby he might rise above the diversity of the modern world. Hopkins's "That Nature is a Heraclitean Fire and of the comfort of the Resurrection" possibly derived from the "Conclusion" to *The Renaissance*. The "exquisite pauses in time" described in "The School of Giorgione" are related to Wordsworth's "spots of time" and Joyce's "epiphanies," examples of which Marius experiences, some having moral overtones but the most intense, the vision of Cornelius in armor, being something approaching apocalyptic illumination.

953 Crinkley, Richmond Dillard. "The Humanism of Walter Pater," DISSERTATION ABSTRACTS, XXVII (1966), 2527A. Published dissertation, University of Virginia, 1966; pub as WALTER PATER: HUMANIST (Lexington: University of Kentucky P, 1970), q.v. for abstract.

954 De Laura, David J. "Echoes of Butler, Browning, Conrad, and Pater in the Poetry of T. S. Eliot," ENGLISH LANGUAGE NOTES, III (March 1966), 211–21.
Though in his notes to "The Waste Land" Eliot glosses the lines "We think of the key, each in his prison / Thinking of the key, each confirms his prison" by a reference to the imprisonment of Dante's Ugolino and a quotation from F. H. Bradley's APPEARANCE AND REALITY on the solipsism of individual consciousness, they recall too the solipsism and the prison metaphor of the "Conclusion" to *The Renaissance,* well known to Eliot, in which WP describes "the individual in his isolation, each mind keeping as a solitary prisoner its own dream of a world."

955 DeLaura, David J. "Pater and Newman: The Road to the 'Nineties," VICTORIAN STUDIES, X (Sept 1966), [39]–69; rptd with revisions in HEBREW AND HELLENE IN VICTORIAN ENGLAND: NEWMAN, ARNOLD, AND PATER (Austin & Lond: University of Texas P, 1969), pp. [305]–44.
Newman had an important influence on WP as the most representative figure of the Oxonian school interested in developing a new literary humanism. WP himself had gone through different stages of religious commitment. At first an enthusiastic High Church ritualist, he became a skeptic and later discovered Newman; his notion of "elect souls" and of the purely aesthetic beauty of the old morality can be traced at least as far back as that discovery. But WP also found in the Calvinist tradition his notion of "the few" as opposed to "the many." He aligns himself squarely with Newman when he asserts that religious experience is very close to the aesthetic experience. His debt to Newman is consistently evident in *Marius the Epicurean*. Newman's works, particularly LOSS AND GAIN and GRAMMAR OF ASSENT, provide guides to a better understanding of the structure and complexity of *Marius,* containing ideas relevant to the understanding of each stage of Marius's conversion. Newman's famous "gentleman" in THE IDEA OF A UNIVERSITY and

WP's "Epicurean" also have similar features. But unlike Newman the believer, WP always stresses the subjective factor in religion and its aesthetic appeal. Newman also influenced WP's essay on "Style," *Plato and Platonism,* and *Essays from "The Guardian."* Newman is to be viewed as a "central figure in the later development of Pater's thought."

> **956** DeLaura, David J., "ROMOLA and the Origin of the Paterian View of Life," NINETEENTH CENTURY FICTION, XXI (Dec 1966), 225–33.

WP makes a highly favorable mention of George Eliot in his review of Mrs. Humphry Ward's ROBERT ELSMERE, and the especially high regard with which, according to Thomas Wright, he spoke of ROMOLA, particularly Piero di Cosimo's statement "The only passionate life is in form and color," suggests that a reading of the George Eliot novel may have been the impetus to the aesthetic vision of *The Renaissance.* WP would have found appealing the characterizations in ROMOLA of numerous historical figures of the Renaissance and would have identified too with the central motif of the conflict between Christian asceticism and pagan humanism. Most significant are WP's repeated references in *The Renaissance* to Savonarola, whom he had early envisioned in "Diaphaneitè" as approaching the ideal of a "colourless, unclassified purity of life." In "Winckelmann" he exemplifies, much as he does for Romola herself, a kind of selectively limited and intense culture; in "Pico della Mirandola" WP's mention of Savonarola's attending at Pico's death recalls George Eliot's treatment of the same event; and in "The Poetry of Michelangelo" WP relates Michelangelo's broad religious idealism to the reformative spirit of Savonarola. Thus Savonarola represents for WP, as he had for George Eliot, both the "higher life" of the soul and an important element in the Christian-pagan dialectic of the Renaissance. The influence of ROMOLA seems most marked, however, in *Marius the Epicurean.* Both are historical novels set amidst a conflict of Christian and pagan values that both reflects the contemporary intellectual milieu and provides the thematic center of each. Both are structured upon a series of intellectual and spiritual crises that culminate in an adherence to an ideal of human sympathy which owes something to, yet transcends, Christianity. But in the ethic of sympathy adopted in the end by both Romola and Marius there is a hollowness that reflects a lack of conviction on the part of George Eliot and WP themselves and which is responsible for the ultimate failure of both novels. [For a reply to DeLaura's article, see Donald L. Hill, "Pater's Debt to ROMOLA," NINETEENTH CENTURY FICTION, 1968.]

> **957** DeLaura, David J. "The 'Wordsworth' of Pater and Arnold: 'The Supreme Artistic View of Life,' " STUDIES IN ENGLISH LITERATURE, VI (Autumn 1966), 651–67.

The "aesthetic" view of life presented in *The Renaissance,* derived largely from Arnold's opinions on criticism, culture, and the "modern spirit," receives a more precise formulation in WP's "Wordsworth," the central argument of which derives again from Arnold, particularly from the "Sweetness and Light" section of CULTURE AND ANARCHY. While WP adheres to Arnold's advocacy in "Sweetness and Light" of a pursuit of "the things of the mind simply for their own sakes," a restatement of the ideal of "disinterestedness" put forth in "The Function of Criticism at the Present Time," and adopts the rhetoric and the religious air of CULTURE AND ANARCHY, he shows no concern for the social obligations attached to Arnold's conception of culture. WP's view of the perfected life as "a thing in which means and ends are identified" is misleading since the desired state of "impassioned contemplation" requires the eschewing of all practical means and ends and the attainment of a consciousness altogether beyond the bounds of practical life. WP sees the "aesthetic" life not in terms of the created object but in terms of the subjective vision of the artist or the art-observer, "beholding for the mere joy of beholding"; the aim of culture for WP is not, as it is for Arnold, to return the individual after a period of intellectual detachment, broadened and refreshed to the world, but to promote the joy of beholding for its own sake. WP's "Wordsworth," in attempting to redefine the Arnoldian ideal of culture, ends by simply reiterating the theory of self-culture advanced in *The Renaissance,* most notably in "Winckelmann," itself a revision of Arnold's concept of "disinterested-ness." Arnold's disinterested critic is reduced finally to the condition of the isolated aesthete of the "Conclusion." WP's contemplative aesthete is the opposite of Arnold's nineteenth-century man in "On the Modern Element in Literature," who views the confused spectacle of modern life for the ultimate purpose of interpreting it and thereby becoming "one of his age's intellectual deliverers." In turn, it appears that Arnold's own prefatory essay to Wordsworth's poems was written partly in adverse reaction to WP's "Wordsworth" and to certain of the *Renaissance* essays that give excessive attention to the formal while neglecting the moral concerns of art; on the positive side, WP's "Wordsworth" seems to have led Arnold in both his own Wordsworth essay and "The Study of Poetry" to making his furthest accomodation to poetic formalism and his most complete statements on the relationship between "poetic beauty and poetic truth."

958 Fleissner, Robert F. " 'Prufrock,' Pater, and RICHARD II: Retracing a Denial of Princeship," AMERICAN LITERATURE, XXXVIII (March 1966), 120–23.

Prufrock's "No! I am not Prince Hamlet, nor was meant to be" apparently echoes a statement by WP in "Shakespeare's English Kings": "No! Shakespeare's kings are not, nor are meant to be, great men. . . . " Prufrock's dual personality was probably suggested in part by WP's discussion of RICHARD II in the same essay. Eliot was well acquainted with WP's work, and Grover Smith, Jr., has demonstrated the influence of WP's description of the *Mona Lisa* on Eliot's poetry (NOTES AND QUERIES, 19 March 1949 [q.v.]). *The Renaissance* may have been the inspiration for the women who "come and go, / Talking of Michelangelo."

959 Guthke, Karl S. MODERN TRAGICOMEDY: AN INVESTIGATION INTO THE NATURE OF THE GENRE (NY: Random House, 1966), pp. 110–11.

"Impressionism found a strong appeal in that fusion of emotions which is the hallmark of tragicomedy." WP's opening paragraph in *Imaginary Portraits* (1887) sums up the tragicomic vision of life most gracefully: " 'a sort of comedy which shall be but tragedy seen from the other side.' " [Guthke's reference is to the first paragraph in "A Prince of Court Painters."]

> **960** Noël, Jean C. GEORGE MOORE: L'HOMME ET L'OEUVRE (1852–1933) (George Moore: The Man and His Works [1852–1933]) (Paris: Didier, 1966), pp. 62, 76, 117, 130, 132*n*, 134, 136, 143, 144, 157, 160, 164, 165, 169, 178, 191, 207, 226, 271, 288, 296, 297, 300, 301, 328, 372, 387, 400*n*, 408, 412, 424, 435, 441, 449, 466, 469, 528, 546, 548.

Although WP was an acknowledged influence on Moore, he and Moore disagreed on several points. Moore also was given to misquoting WP. Moore discovered WP through *Marius the Epicurean*. It is usually acknowledged that WP acted as a soothing influence on Moore to counterbalance others such as Hegel or Nietzsche. Moore's CONFESSIONS OF A YOUNG MAN is done largely in imitation of WP. WP's "Denys l'Auxerrois" may have been the model for Moore's HELOISE AND ABELARD. [In French.]

> **961** Rodgers, Paul C., Jr. "A Discourse-centered Rhetoric of the Paragraph," COLLEGE COMPOSITION AND COMMUNICATION, XVII (Feb 1966), 2–11.

The traditional conception of the paragraph as a group of sentences developing the single idea conveyed in the topic sentence is inadequate; having been arrived at deductively, it fails to account for the success of many paragraphs that are clearly effective despite their derivation from the norm. Representative of what Saintsbury called WP's "deliberate and successful architecture of the prose-paragraph" and subtle and various as it is in structure, WP's essay on "Style" provides an apt example of a sequence of effective though often nontraditional paragraphs. In it WP stresses "the necessity of *mind* in style" as determining the "architectural" quality of the work, and he must therefore have paragraphed it with special care. [Close paragraph-by-paragraph analysis.]

> **962** Schlesinger, Gabriella Pintus. "Walter Pater's *Renaissance* Essays: Attempts at Stability, Order, and General Criticism," DISSERTATION ABSTRACTS, XXVII (1966), 2509A. Unpublished dissertation, Yale University, 1966.

> **963** Wallace, Robert, [and the editors of Time-Life Books]. THE WORLD OF LEONARDO, 1452–1519 (NY: Time Incorporated [Time-Life Books], 1966), pp. 27, 126, 140.

WP's "beautiful and widely read" study of Leonardo discusses many paintings no longer attributed to him. The description of the *Mona Lisa* is unique in literature but factually limited.

> **964** Ward, Anthony. WALTER PATER: THE IDEA IN NATURE (Lond: Macgibbon & Kee, 1966).

WP's concerns typify the Nineties. Nostalgia is the dominant feeling in both his mind and his work. His thought must be related particularly to the works of Goethe and Hegel if it is to be understood. His mind resisted positivism from the outset. But his mind is incapable of solving the problems it confronts. "Comte . . . becomes very much like Hegel, Hegel merges into Darwin, and Goethe . . . reconciles opposites." WP had no choice but to defend the "relative spirit." His thought seems to be unfathomable at times because of his ambiguous diction. His main concern in most of his essays is with the theory of perpetual flux. WP approaches the concept of nature armed with Hegelian tools. He looks "for the 'sensuous semblance of the idea' in art." He avoids the notion that the physical world is man's product and the naturalistic belief that man's fate is always determined by his physical environment. He wants always to strike a balance between nature and man. His "attention to nature is always informed by . . . transcendental aspirations." For WP, the artist must approach the world unaffected and uninfluenced by existing orthodoxies; "yet he must reduce the world to, or contain the world within, some organising principle at the very moment when he is engaged in respecting and giving expression to, its multifarious detail." But WP can never sustain the "beatific vision" for long. His timidity kept him from becoming a strict disciple of Hegel. WP works out his own ideas in *The Renaissance* on other artist's creations. He attempts, for example, to find a modern myth in the passage on the *Mona Lisa*. She is viewed as the focus of modern complexities. His attempts to define the ideal art form in the Mona Lisa passage and in the Winckelmann essay are developed more fully in "A Study of Dionysus." WP moves deeper inward as his thoughts on art proceed. The art work gradually dissociates itself from the natural world and displays " 'an exaggerated inwardness.' " His emphasis on the "power" the artist exerts over nature increases. This progression is found in the "Leonardo da Vinci" essay and in the essays on Botticelli, Michelangelo, and "The School of Giorgione." Giorgione "is the artist who most exhibits 'intimate,' individual soul."

The hero's journey in *Marius the Epicurean* is purely intellectual. The novel treats the theme of nostalgia for childhood, the significance of the color white, sin, and dreaming. The style is largely euphuisitic, a style that WP defends. Marius's idealism is innate and operates against his flirtation with Cyrenaicism. Marius, throughout most of the novel, is detached from the immediate present and glimpses life from afar. While dying, Marius thinks of Christianity and feels a tinge of optimism. WP's prose style is based on the positing and attempted synthesis of dialectical situations. In *Plato and Platonism,* he "tries to formulate an artistic ideal to fit over the contemporary intellectual situation . . . he sees art as an activity which is an analogue of the *process* of his existence." In the end, he rejects the idea that truth can be attained intuitively, an ideal that his earlier lyrical essays are based upon.

1967

965 Busst, A. J. L. "The Image of the Androgyne in the Nineteenth Century," ROMANTIC MYTHOLOGIES, ed by Ian Fletcher (Lond: Routledge & Kegan Paul, 1967), pp. 51–52.

WP's interpretation of Leonardo's androgynous *Saint John the Baptist* helped establish the Decadent association of hermaphroditism with moral ambiguity.

966 Court, Franklin E. "Change and Suffering in Pater's Fictional Heroes," MODERN FICTION STUDIES, XIII (Winter 1967), 443–53.

Most of WP's fictional heroes suggest some form of intellectual or artistic revolt. Their dilemma can be viewed as symptomatic of WP's discontent with a society that had destroyed the classical heroic ideal. They are, by nature of their indefiniteness, symbols of man's timeless search for mystical perfection. During the search, each hero has a moral dilemma imposed upon him by his community; he must choose between a state of change (flux) and one of stagnation (stasis). Because he invariably chooses change, his community demands from him some form of suffering as compensation. Dionysus, the hero of WP's "Study of Dionysus" epitomizes this patterned development; he is the god and also the symbol of change; but, in addition, he is the victim, the symbol of suffering. [The remainder of the article is devoted to an analysis, based on the pattern of change and suffering, of "Denys l'Auxerrois," *Marius the Epicurean,* "Duke Carl of Rosenmold," *Gaston De Latour,* "Sebastian Van Storck," "Emerald Uthwart," and "Apollo in Picardy."]

967 Croft-Cooke, Rupert. FEASTING WITH PANTHERS: A NEW CONSIDERATION OF SOME LATE VICTORIAN WRITERS (Lond: W. H. Allen, 1967; NY: Holt, Rinehart & Winston, 1968), pp. viii, 3, 25, 43, 45, 55, 57, 58, 112, 118, 145, 163–90, 198, 237, 285–86, 292.

WP was known for his reticence, but his writing reveals "intense feelings" and "emotions that writhed out of sight." There are hints of snobbism in the "socially idealized" versions of his own childhood presented in "Emerald Uthwart" and "The Child in the House." Wright called him "the Caliban of Letters," but he and Rothenstein reported that though WP was self-conscious about his appearance, he surrounded himself at Oxford with handsome young men. Thus he belonged to the same group of "academic old queers" as William Cory and Oscar Browning. His extravagant praise of Wilde's writing probably indicates a personal affinity with him; the idea that he disapproved of Wilde's vulgarizing his philosophy is simply an exaggerated "piece of loose literary chit-chat." WP, in fact, had no philosophy; his writing is without substance, his criticism "flaccid," and *Marius the Epicurean* "a windy piece of fine writing." [Concentrates on the sexual overtones of WP's friendships, including those with Swinburne, Simeon Solomon, Richard Jackson, Veargett Maughan, and Walter Blackburn Harte.]

968 DeLaura, David J. " 'The Ache of Modernism' in Hardy's Later Novels," JOURNAL OF ENGLISH LITERARY HISTORY, XXIV (Sept 1967), 380–99.

Hardy's attempts in THE RETURN OF THE NATIVE, TESS OF THE D'URBERVILLES, and JUDE THE OBSCURE to present the ideal of an " 'Hellenic' view of life, which is also somehow 'natural,' " were inspired by Arnold and WP. RETURN reflects his having absorbed Arnold's and WP's views of the "modern condition." Eustacia Vye thus recalls WP's vision of the *Mona Lisa* as "the symbol of the modern idea," while Clym Yeobright embodies the malaise of "modern man" against which, in "Winckelmann," WP offered the corrective of "the Hellenic spirit." Both Hardy's and WP's modern man are oppressed by the awareness of the inexorable force of natural law.

969 Duffy, John J. "Walter Pater's Prose Style: An Essay in Theory and Analysis," STYLE, I (1967), 45–63.

Descriptions of WP's prose style as "musical" are inaccurate and misleading judged in terms of Northrop Frye's explanation of Aristotle's *melos* as depending, in prose, upon "a driving linear rhythm" that contributes to the forward development of the larger semantic structure. WP often tends instead toward *opsis*, the pictorial, this being most evident at those moments when he loses sight of the critical principles put forward in the "Preface" to *The Renaissance*, and fails to maintain the distinction between himself and the object of his criticism. In the passage on the *Mona Lisa* from "Leonardo da Vinci" the opsitic quality is revealed as much in sentence structure as in treatment of subject matter; the paragraph is an accumulation of qualifications and modifications that retard linear movement in an attempt at what Frye terms "simultaneous comprehension," which is achieved by turning about and revealing facet by facet what, in this case, is already contained in the first sentence. WP, however, focuses attention not on the object but away from it, toward "a set of wonderfully bizarre images" that are probably a projection of his own narcissism and not related convincingly to the painting. In contrast, the passage from the version of "Coleridge" published in *Appreciations* which argues the importance of philosophical detachment is rhythmically regular and demonstrates the basically linear movement associated with *melos;* this is in part the result of WP's maintaining here his own critical detachment. While the complex redundancy and hypnotic rhythm of the passage on the *Mona Lisa* prevents us from seeing "the object as in itself it really is," the linear structure and regular rhythm of the passage from "Coleridge" are integrally related to its clarity of prose meaning. WP's style is thus marked by two distinct characteristics, the melodic and the pictorial, the examination of which reveals something of WP the critic as well as WP the stylist. [Duffy supports his argument with a detailed analysis of the rhythmic structure of the two passages.]

970 Ellmann, Richard. EMINENT DOMAIN: YEATS AMONG WILDE, JOYCE, POUND, ELIOT, AND AUDEN (Oxford & NY: Oxford UP, 1967), pp. 13, 25, 61, 130.

Wilde impressed Yeats with his somewhat ironic overpraising of *The Renaissance;* though he admired WP, he felt his style wanting in vitality. WP, on the other hand, found Wilde's style too conversational. WP's impressionism lacked the solidity Yeats wanted in an aesthetic theory. In PERSONAE Pound was following WP's lead in attempting to "extend the self horizontally," while Yeats, in developing his theory of the mask, was moving vertically. [Yeats's idea, expressed in ON THE BOILER, of Greek sculpture as having provided the basis of all European culture derives from a similar idea in Wilde's "The Decay of Lying," which is taken in turn from WP's "Winckelmann."]

> **971** Ellmann, Richard. "The Critic as Artist as Wilde," WILDE AND THE NINETIES (Princeton: Princeton UP, 1966), pp. 1–21 [lecture opening the Princeton exhibition, 22 February 1966]; rptd in ENCOUNTER, XXIX (July 1967), 29–37; rptd in THE POET AS CRITIC, ed by F. P. W. McDowell (Evanston, Ill: Northwestern UP, 1967), pp. 44–59; rptd as "Introduction," in THE ARTIST AS CRITIC: CRITICAL WRITINGS OF OSCAR WILDE, ed by Richard Ellmann (NY: Random House, 1969), pp. ix–xxvii; rptd in Richard Ellmann, GOLDEN CODGERS: BIOGRAPHICAL SPECULATIONS (NY & Lond: Oxford UP, 1973), pp. 60–80.

WP's praise of Wilde's INTENTIONS as carrying on Arnold's critical work is a reminder not to forget WP himself. There are not two but three critical phases in the late nineteenth century, with WP transitional between Arnold and Wilde. In his preface to *The Renaissance* WP shifts Arnold's emphasis from the object of criticism to the critic's impressions of the object. Wilde is WP's disciple in INTENTIONS in that he not only draws examples from the "highly personal" criticism of WP and Ruskin but goes beyond them in his intention to free critics from subordination, to give them a larger share in the production of literature. WP's vocabulary shapes Wilde's "Helas." Yet WP complained of the tendency to moral drifting in DORIAN GRAY. Wilde could counter with another paraphrase of WP's "Conclusion" to *The Renaissance* that if it is wrong to drift, it is less wrong to drift gracefully.

> **972** Fletcher, Ian. "Bedford Park: Aesthete's Elysium?" ROMANTIC MYTHOLOGIES, ed by Ian Fletcher (Lond: Routledge & Kegan Paul, 1967), pp. 169–207.

The houses of Bedford Park reflect the concern of the aesthetes to grant, as WP did, equal value to "all periods, types, schools of taste." An early formulation of the doctrines of aestheticism appears in the first published version of "Winckelmann"; the "Conclusion" to *The Renaissance* helped give currency to the phrase "art for art's sake." WP was variously satirized as Basil Giorgione in George du Maurier's cartoons for PUNCH and as Gabriel Nash in James's THE TRAGIC MUSE.

> **973** Fletcher, Ian. "Foreword," ROMANTIC MYTHOLOGIES, ed by Ian Fletcher (Lond: Routledge & Kegan Paul, 1967), pp. vii–xiii.

The tendency to undervalue WP by judging him primarily in relation to Arnold and

Arnoldian culture while failing to consider his importance as a forerunner of Yeats, Pound, Joyce, and others is an indication of the danger in imposing a single tradition on the nineteenth century. WP created the atmosphere out of which was formed the sacramental imagery of Joyce, Wells, and Forster.

974 Gerber, Helmut E. "Introduction," p. xiii; "Walter Pater," pp. 19–20; "Arthur Symons," p. 35; "Max Beerbohm," p. 51; "George Moore," p. 457; "Bibliographies" ("Walter Pater"), pp. 501–2, in THE ENGLISH SHORT STORY IN TRANSITION, 1880–1920, ed by Helmut E. Gerber (NY: Pegasus, 1967).

The modern tendencies most notable in WP's work are the tension generated between skepticism and belief, the concern with individual temperament, and "the sense of isolation and the quest for identity" which were outgrowths of his childhood loneliness and were fostered by the reclusiveness of his adult life. During his years as an Oxford undergraduate, WP felt the various influences of Keble, Jowett, Ruskin, and Darwinian science; with the publication of *The Renaissance* he became in his turn a major influence on Wilde, Moore, and others of their generation. The essay on "Style" anticipates many principles of modern aesthetics. Historically, WP is a figure of Arnoldian stature transitional between Romanticism proper and aestheticism and between the literary theory of the late nineteenth century and that of Yeats and T. S. Eliot. [Introductions to the stories by Symons and Beerbohm make references in passing to the relationship of those writers to WP. Anthology includes a select bibliography of the works of WP and of biographical and critical writings about him.]

975 Hill, Charles G. "Walter Pater and the Gide-Du Bos Dialogue," REVUE DE LITTÉRATURE COMPARÉE, III (July–Sept 1967), 367–84.

In examining the nature of his friendship with André Gide, Charles Du Bos defined the spiritual-intellectual difference between himself and Gide in terms of the relationship of each to WP. In a 1925 lecture published in LE DIALOGUE AVEC ANDRÉ GIDE (1947), Du Bos identified the "ecstasy" of the "Conclusion" to *The Renaissance* with the "ferveur" of LES NOURRITURES TERRESTRES, both placing supreme value on the moment, while for Du Bos himself the essential WP was *Marius the Epicurean,* with its emphasis on memory and its importance in giving continuity to life. Further, in his "Lettre-Envoi" to the DIALOGUE, Du Bos quoted a passage from his 1923 lecture on *Marius* indicating his own need for carrying on, as Marius does, an internal colloquy, as with an ideal double of himself, by establishing accord with which he might gain access to "l'idée d'un Dieu"; this process, he implied, was one that Gide believed falsified one's true personality. Describing in his JOURNAL his own spiritual struggle, Du Bos applied to himself the terms "une cathédrale désaffectée" and "anima naturaliter christiana," which WP had applied to himself and to Marius respectively. It was partly his dialogue with Gide that prevented Du Bos's completing a projected full-length study of WP. Gide's discipleship to Wilde, who placed an active construction on the Paterian idea of "ecstasy," necessarily separated him from WP and Du Bos.

976 Holroyd, Michael. LYTTON STRACHEY: A CRITICAL BIOGRAPHY, Vol I: THE UNKNOWN YEARS (1880–1910) (Lond: Heinemann, 1967; NY: Holt, Rinehart & Winston, 1968), pp. 118, 133, 137.

Strachey read WP in his youth but found his writing "deathly" and "waxen" and lacking in substance. He preferred the more vital paganism of Swinburne to that of WP.

977 McKenzie, Gordon. THE LITERARY CHARACTER OF WALTER PATER (Berkeley: University of California P [University of California Publications/ English Studies: 32], 1967).

WP was physically weak and homely and had an aversion to physical activity. The diaphanous man, intensely alert to experience, was his ideal. He viewed personality as "the ultimate, important fact behind all experience"; he therefore drew philosophical ideas from wherever he pleased. He was a Christian and an aesthete at the same time. Unlike Arnold, WP had no nostalgia for the past. WP turned in his later years more and more to Christianity, particularly Catholicism. WP's subjects seem not to have much relation to each other. He is a fictionist, a student of culture, and a philosopher. His approach is primarily historical. He uses myths extensively to understand and elucidate primitive impressions. His mythic figures become "types"; to him, "a myth is comparable to a philosophy." It is also a form of poetry, replete with symbols and images. In his treatment of myths, WP keeps father figures in the background; mothers, on the other hand, are given greater importance as passionate, fiercely loving protectoresses. WP had a strong sense of change, historically and psychologically. WP attaches various meanings to the word *symbolism,* particularly in the myths he treats. In WP "associations are a formative part of the background of every artistic perception." WP was always a student of philosophy, rarely a creator of new ways of thinking. He believed that temperament dominated abstract thought. *Marius the Epicurean* is a study of the effects of various philosophies upon a young mind. He also believed that systems of thought must be understood in their historical context; ages, like individuals, have their "genius." His main philosophical concern was with the relationship between external objects and one's impressions. He also found "objective idealism" useful. For WP, Kant was the originator of ideas that destroyed traditional systems of thought. But WP disagreed with the idealistic concept of an absolute; his focus is on the principle of organic structure. "Idealism insists upon the need for understanding the past in terms of organic relations which change and evolve into meaningful cultural patterns." The ideas expressed in WP's treatment of philosophy and mythology "form the background for the sense of life his fiction conveys." The character revealed in his fiction is "the only one we can be sure of." The growth of a personality or of an impression is his favorite and most-often-used subject. [The author provides an analysis of "The Child in the House," "Emerald Uthwart," *Marius, Gaston de Latour,* "Apollo in Picardy," "Denys l'Auxerrois," "Sebastian van Storck," and "Duke Carl of Rosenmold," in that order.] WP presents the essential facts behind his method of criticism in the "Preface" to *The Renaissance*.

978 Marshall, William H. THE WORLD OF THE VICTORIAN NOVEL (South Brunswick & NY: A. S. Barnes; Lond: Thomas Yoseloff, 1967), pp. 381–404, 479.

Marius's dilemma in *Marius the Epicurean* is typical of the dilemma of the intellectual in Victorian England. He thrives on the tension between aspiration and fulfillment, between the continuity of the self and the flux of subjectivity. He finds paganism unfullfilling and becomes a questioner. At school, he becomes more detached from the world outside the self, and he is aware of the possibilities of developing a personality of his own. He shares his aesthetic experiences with Flavian. His knowledge of evil comes through the death of his friend, which also reveals to him the limitations of the pagan vision of the world. Assuming that life in this world required some kind of commitment, Marius found himself defending a position that had something to do with both the Epicurean and the Stoic philosophies. Marius finally refuses to follow Marcus Aurelius because Aurelius accepts the cruelty of human sacrifice. Marius finds another model in Cornelius, the Christian, and he postulates a God to account for his being alive. In Christianity, he sees how faith has overcome death by the notion of hope in an afterlife. Christianity appeals to his Epicureanism, for faith requires an emotional, sensual commitment. His moments of aesthetic bliss, experienced while attending the Mass, are followed by depressions and terrors that lead him to a position of sympathy with the rest of mankind. He dies, knowing that his life has been improved more through immediate experience with Christianity than through its transcendental nature. He takes the Eucharist and thus joins the whole of mankind in its hope for survival through sympathy.

979 Martin, Wallace. THE NEW AGE UNDER ORAGE: CHAPTERS IN CULTURAL HISTORY (Manchester: Manchester UP; NY: Barnes & Noble, 1967), pp. 163, 172, 248, 257ff.

Symons and WP found it "impossible to reconcile the realm of impersonal fact with the sensitive individual consciousness which constituted the only source of poetry." A. R. Orage, the editor of THE NEW AGE, believed that to write prose as if it were poetry, as WP did, was decadent: "the elevation of technique at the expense of content."

980 Mason, Mary Grimley. "The Imaginary Portraits of Walter Pater." Unpublished dissertation, Harvard University, 1967.

[Listed in Lawrence F. McNamee, DISSERTATIONS IN ENGLISH AND AMERICAN LITERATURE, SUPP I (NY & Lond: Bowker, 1968).]

981 Merton, Stephen. MARK RUTHERFORD (WILLIAM HALE WHITE) (NY: Twayne, [TEAS, 53], 1967), p. 109.

Charmides, the artist-hero of a story written by Cardew in Rutherford's

CATHARINE FURZE, resembles WP's Marius [*Marius the Epicurean*] in his life's being set in early-Christian Rome amid a conflict of Christian and pagan values and in his "heightened sense of beauty and his unconscious need for an all-embracing goal in life."

982 Monsman, Gerald Cornelius. PATER'S PORTRAITS: MYTHIC PATTERN IN THE FICTION OF WALTER PATER (Baltimore: Johns Hopkins UP, 1967); rvd dissertation, "Pater's Portraits: A Critical Analysis of the Fiction of Walter Horatio Pater," DISSERTATION ABSTRACTS, XXVI (1965), 3306.

WP's treatment of myth begins in *The Renaissance* with the theme of an artistic, cultural awakening that occurs when the universal and the particular are reconciled during the Renaissance period. The awakening is represented in WP's works by the figures of the two mythic brothers, Apollo and Dionysus, Apollo representing the universal and Dionysus, the revitalizing force which dies to make way for the new year. "Apollo is the embodiment of the spirit of humanity"; the Dionysian hero "is the divine consort of humanity, one who loves both the individual and all men supremely well." The "Paterian hero" is to be viewed as the divine priest of Apollo, for WP's heroes are all bearers of an awakening in each of their respective time periods. And like the Dionysian figure, the Paterian hero heralds the rebirth of intellectual vigor during that age. [This pattern is applied in detail to *The Renaissance,* the early portraits ("The Child in the House" and "An English Poet"), *Marius the Epicurean,* the collected *Imaginary Portraits, Gaston de Latour,* and the uncollected imaginary portraits ("Hippolytus Veiled," "Emerald Uthwart," "Apollo in Picardy," "Tibalt the Albigense," and "Gaudioso, the Second").] WP believed himself living in an age that was caught between fluid relativism and the "need for some normative aesthetic, religious, and metaphysical system of values." But WP believed that eventually the world of flux and change would be reconciled with the world of rest, "eternal rest, which is God."

983 Naremore, James. "Style as Meaning in A PORTRAIT OF THE ARTIST," JAMES JOYCE QUARTERLY, IV (Summer 1967), 331–42.

In Joyce's PORTRAIT OF THE ARTIST AS A YOUNG MAN style exists as meaning and suggests the ambience of character. The general characteristics of his style are those of the late Victorians and decadents; his notions about aesthetics are from WP. The style, by means of subtle parody, ironically suggests the limited, "dated" vision Stephen has of himself, a vision gathered from those who influenced him: the Pre-Raphaelites, WP, Poe, and the French Symbolists.

984 San Juan, Epifanio, Jr. THE ART OF OSCAR WILDE (Princeton: Princeton UP, 1967), pp. 13, 16, 49, 53, 62, 64, 69, 94–96, 103.

WP's approach to the problem of establishing a "permanent structure of truth" was "not to judge or act but to comprehend." He utilized culture to "refine and realize the essence of the soul" and was concerned with giving "absolute self-expression" to the subjects of his fictional "portraits." The doctrines of "exaltation of temperament" and "art's supremacy over nature" are based on his concept of flux. Wilde made use of WP's belief that the "relativity of values" justified the aesthetic approach to experience, and his criticism attempts, as do the *Imaginary Portraits,* to give sensuous form to the abstract and to trace the progress of the dialectic behind artistic or philosophic expression. [Summarizes Wilde's views on WP's criticism and refers briefly to WP's influence on and comments regarding THE PICTURE OF DORIAN GRAY.]

985 Stevenson, Lionel. "The Relativity of Truth in Victorian Fiction," VICTORIAN ESSAYS: A SYMPOSIUM, ed by Warren D. Anderson and Thomas D. Clareson (Kent, Ohio: Kent State UP, 1967), pp. 71–86.

[Stevenson quotes the passage from "Coleridge" in which WP defines the "faculty for truth" as "a power of distinguishing and fixing delicate and fugitive detail," sets it beside similar statements on the relativity of truth by Ruskin and Arnold, and uses all three as an introduction to his discussion of the effect of the new epistemology on the techniques of Victorian fiction.]

986 Weatherby, H. L. "Jude the Victorian," SOUTHERN HUMANITIES REVIEW, I (Spring 1967), 158–69.

Sue Bridehead in JUDE THE OBSCURE embodies the amoral sensationalism of WP and the late-Victorian aesthetes, seeking to burn with a "hard, gemlike flame" and to expand her "power of reception" as Marius did his.

1968

---

987 Bizot, Richard Byron. "Walter Pater's Argument with Himself: The Development of His Thought from 1866 to 1894," DISSERTATION ABSTRACTS INTERNATIONAL, XXVIII (1968), 3663A. Unpublished dissertation, University of Virginia, 1967.

988 Brooke, Rupert. THE LETTERS OF RUPERT BROOKE, ed by Geoffrey Keynes (Lond: Faber & Faber; NY: Harcourt, Brace & World, 1968), pp. 53, 55, 57, 161.

[Brooke adopted the "aesthetic" pose during his years at Rugby, wrote "a rhapsody in prose modelled on Pater's 'Leonardo,' " and praised the *Imaginary Portraits* and *Miscellaneous Studies.*]

989 Chapman, Raymond. THE VICTORIAN DEBATE: ENGLISH LITERATURE AND SOCIETY, 1832–1901 (NY: Basic Books, 1968), pp. 7, 237–39, 267.

WP helped encourage the late Victorian "aesthetic" craze and its playing down of the belief in the moral seriousness of art by advising the readers of *The Renaissance* "to shun no sensation that could lead to richer appreciation." He was nevertheless "a timid soul" and withdrew the "Conclusion" to *The Renaissance* for fear of misleading the young. *Marius the Epicurean* is "marred by a tendency to caution" and by stylistic mannerisms. WP's criticism, with its stress on form rather than subject, was more influential than is often supposed.

> **990** Cixous, Hélène. L'EXIL DE JAMES JOYCE, OU L'ART DU REMPLACEMENT (The Exile of James Joyce, or the Art of Replacement) (Paris: Éditions Bernard Grasset, 1968); trans by Sally A. J. Purcell as THE EXILE OF JAMES JOYCE (NY: David Lewis, 1972), pp. 432, 499, 607, 609–11, 625.

The "decadent prose" of WP, Wilde, and the French symbolists appealed to Joyce's taste for formal beauty, which he had found earlier in Catholicism; yet in describing the imaginative flights of Stephen Dedalus in PORTRAIT OF THE ARTIST AS A YOUNG MAN he parodies WP. Joyce's theory of the epiphany is prefigured in the "Conclusion" to *The Renaissance,* with its emphasis on seizing the significance of the passing moment, in WP's analysis of Leonardo's subjective vision of reality, and in his representation of the *Mona Lisa* as "a relative absolute" combining the unique and the universal. The moments of illumination that come to Stephen in PORTRAIT and STEPHEN HERO resemble those experienced by Marius; but the Joycean epiphany, while often described in the style of WP, arises characteristically out of the perception of the trivial or the vulgar and depends for its effect on the ironic contrast between aesthetic and practical experience. The poetry of CHAMBER MUSIC is informed by "the tradition of a Christianised Renaissance" popularized by WP. [In French.]

> **991** Cox, Catherine. "Pater's 'Apollo in Picardy' and Mann's DEATH IN VENICE," ANGLIA, LXXXVI (1968), 143–54.

The *Imaginary Portraits* are usually criticized for their weakness of plot and assumed to be excuses for mere word-painting. "Apollo in Picardy," which WP intended to include in a second collection of portraits, exhibits the most complicated plot found in any of his efforts in this genre; and while it too is faulty in execution, comparing it with Mann's DEATH IN VENICE, which develops a variation on the same theme of the "return of the gods," it helps to clarify WP's own intention. Both Prior Saint-Jean and Aschenbach are introduced as men of exemplary self-control, and each follows an austere intellectual occupation until he meets a youth with the Apollonian "attributes of music, sun, and great beauty," each of which represents a "mixed blessing." Though the musical qualities attributed to Tadzio and Apollyon are initially attractive, they are finally revealed as having disturbing pagan associations. The sun illuminates Tadzio's beauty and creates a "summer-in-winter" on Apollyon's arrival in Picardy, but it blinds Aschenbach to reason and produces a "solar storm" in the mind of Prior Saint-Jean. While the beauty of the two youths first inspires the men to formal perfection in their art, its necessary sensuousness entails "inevitable moral hazards." "Apollo in Picardy" reflects WP's concern with the relationship between the formal and the moral aspects of art; it is more than a reworking of Heine's THE

GODS IN EXILE, as suggested by John Smith Harrison (PUBLICATIONS OF THE MODERN LANGUAGE ASSOCIATION, 1924), and goes beyond the Nietzschean Apollonian/Dionysian dichotomy pointed out by R. T. Lenaghan (STUDIES IN PHILOLOGY, 1961).

992 Culler, A. Dwight. "The Darwinian Revolution and Literary Form," THE ART OF VICTORIAN PROSE, ed by George Levine and William Madden (NY, Lond & Toronto: Oxford UP, 1968), pp. 224–46; rptd in part in DARWIN: A NORTON CRITICAL EDITION, ed by Philip Appleman (NY: Norton, 1970), pp. 595–96.

By his reversal of the orthodox, theological view of the relationship between cause and effect in the adaptation of the living organism to its environment, Darwin created an intellectual climate that fostered such reactions to the Victorian system of accepted ideas as that represented by the aesthetic movement. In the "Conclusion" to *The Renaissance* WP aligns art with science in opposition to ethics, philosophy, and religion, which were ever attempting to burden with didactic content aesthetic forms and to anthropomorphize the structures of science. WP sees art as aspiring to transcend classification by genre, "the 'species' of the aesthetic world," and thus is concerned in *The Renaissance* primarily with "transitional figures" and "intermediate forms."

993 Duffy, J. J. "Conrad and Pater: Suggestive Echoes," CONRADIANA, I:i (Summer 1968), 45–47.

The echoes of WP in LORD JIM, the "Preface" to THE NIGGER OF THE "NARCISSUS," and CHANCE, though far from indicating any wholesale "conversion" of Conrad "to some kind of Paterism," nevertheless controvert T. S. Eliot's statement that WP failed to influence any first-rate mind beyond his own generation. Conrad was familiar with *Marius the Epicurean,* and although it is not known whether or not he read the *Imaginary Portraits,* "Sebastian van Storck" seems to have been one source for the character of Stein in LORD JIM. The conflict between Stein's vision of man as falling at birth into a dream as if into the sea and Marlow's materialistic belief in "the craft of the sea" corresponds to the conflict between Sebastian's desire to yield himself to the void and the practical concerns of his countrymen. The submissive attitude of the Moslem pilgrims of the *Patna* likewise is described in terms reminiscent of WP's description of the sea in "Sebastian." Conrad drew upon "The School of Giorgione" in formulating the symbolist aesthetic of the "Preface" to THE NIGGER OF THE "NARCISSUS." In CHANCE the character of Flora de Barral recalls WP's Mona Lisa, and the sea functions as in "Sebastian" and LORD JIM as both a material cause of death and a symbol of the immaterial.

994 Ellmann, Richard. "Overtures to Wilde's SALOMÉ," YEARBOOK OF COMPARATIVE AND GENERAL LITERATURE, XVII (1968), 17–28; rptd in TRI-QUARTERLY, XV (Spring 1969), 45–64 [lecture given at the School of Letters, Indiana University]; rptd as "Overtures to SALOMÉ," in

OSCAR WILDE: A COLLECTION OF CRITICAL ESSAYS, ed by Richard Ellmann (Englewood Cliffs, NJ: Prentice-Hall, 1969), pp. 73–91; rvd and enlgd as "Overtures to 'Salomé,' " in Richard Ellmann, GOLDEN CODGERS: BIOGRAPHICAL SPECULATIONS (NY & Lond: Oxford UP, 1973), pp. 39–59.

WP's *The Renaissance* does not mention Ruskin but uses him as an adversary, ends with a secular sermon exactly counter to Ruskin's in THE STONES OF VENICE, is Ruskin all inverted, and is all blend where Ruskin is all severance. For Wilde, Ruskin and WP came to stand heraldically, burning unicorn and uninflamed satyr, in front of two portals of his mental theater. He sometimes allowed them to battle, at other times tried to reconcile them. In THE PICTURE OF DORIAN GRAY, WP is enclosed in Lord Henry Wotton, and Basil Hallward has a little of Ruskin. While WP's side of Wilde's thought is routed, it is not deprived of fascination; and Hallward, at his closest to Ruskin, is killed too. In "The Soul of Man under Socialism" Wilde superimposes Ruskin's social ethic upon WP's "full expression of personality," fusing instead of destroying the two critics. In SALOMÉ a variety of Ruskinism lurks behind Iokanaan, and behind Salome's appetite for strange experiences lurks Paterism. THE IMPORTANCE OF BEING EARNEST demonstrates that Ruskin's earnestness and WP's paraded passionateness are not mutually exclusive for the artist but may, by wit, by weakness, by self-withholding, be artistically as well as tetrarchically compounded.

> **995** Fraser, G. S. LAWRENCE DURRELL: A CRITICAL STUDY (NY: Dutton, 1968), pp. 64–65, 81–82, 168.

WP's imitable, yielding, and feminine temperament and his liking for "purple panels" of prose find resonances in Durrell's THE BLACK BOOK. The novel's deliberately mannered prose lends itself to quantitative scansion; and the cadencing and manner of indirect and fantastic evocation recall passages of WP's "Leonardo da Vinci." Durrell goes beyond WP in deliberately disturbing conjunction or association of phrases and often counterpoints Paterian cadences with a deliberate choice of harsh or ugly words or images. Tempted by facile, "poetic" prose like WP's, Durrell pulls himself sharply up with a word or phrase willfully harsh, perhaps willfully disgusting. Like many of the novelists Durrell drew upon, WP could teach lessons about keeping narrative prose alive, lessons about texture. But neither WP nor any of the others Durrell studied is a great structural inventor.

> **996** Fraser, G. S. "Walter Pater: His Theory of Style, His Style in Practice, His Influence," THE ART OF VICTORIAN PROSE, ed by George Levine and William Madden (NY, Lond & Toronto: Oxford UP, 1968), pp. 201–23.

The essay "Style," suggestive and elusive as it is, remains, as Ian Fletcher suggests, the most coherent statement of WP's aesthetic *credo,* an argument in support of his own role as a "scholar-artist," the distinctive quality of whose work in prose is the result of a careful balance between attention to fact and "the imaginative sense of fact," the artist's peculiar vision of the world. WP's emphasis on stylistic restraint, precision of language, and removal of verbal surplusage as the only means to a truthful presentation of the individual vision are indications of his own most intimate concern as a writer and indexes to the importance of self-renunciation to the scheme of his aesthetics. His broad interpretation of Flaubert's doctrine of *le mot juste,* however, and his commending of Scott's ease of expression as altogether just to his artistic purpose, pointing as they do toward a less restrictive conception of good style as merely a matter of the appropriateness of means to ends, tend to undercut the significance of his own stylistic asceticism; there is thus an unresolved conflict in the essay between WP's idealization of himself as "scholar-artist" and the breadth of sensibility that otherwise characterizes his criticism. The attempt to equate finely wrought prose to music, in its striving toward fusion of form and matter, is logically weak but interesting as an indirect comment on the rhythmical possibilities of prose composition. WP may have felt that his own work, by virtue of the devotion he brought to it, contained something of the grand humanity he believes essential finally to all great art. In his NOTE-BOOKS Samuel Butler attacks the styles of both WP and Arnold as narcissistic and overly intent on charming the reader. Beerbohm, though parodying WP's mannerism in "Diminuendo" and comparing his style unfavorably to Thackeray's in "George IV," always respected the "couth solemnity" of WP's mind. Saintsbury's sensitive appreciation of WP's style and his recognition in A HISTORY OF ENGLISH PROSE RHYTHM of its distinctive rhythmic "quietism" seem to justify WP's view of himself as a highly disciplined "scholar-artist." While many of those influenced by WP were merely captivated by his verbal mannerism, others, such as Berenson and Santayana, shared his temperament more completely; Yeats, though unlike WP in temperament, helped substantiate his idea of the necessary tension between objective truth and the subjective vision of the artist.

997 Gettmann, Royal A. "Introduction," THE HANDLING OF WORDS AND OTHER STUDIES IN LITERARY PSYCHOLOGY, by Violet Paget [Vernon Lee] (Lincoln: University of Nebraska P, 1968), pp. vii–xviii.
In refining her conception of the nature of the aesthetic experience, Vernon Lee was undoubtedly influenced by WP's *Marius the Epicurean,* specifically his advice to love art "for its own sake."

998 Gettmann, Royal A. "Vernon Lee: Exponent of Aestheticism," PRAIRIE SCHOONER, X (Spring 1968), 47–55.
Although Wilde, "who cheapened everything he took from Pater," was popularly considered the heir to WP's aesthetics, "Vernon Lee was the only disciple that Walter Pater ever acknowledged." In refining her early sensational conception of the aesthetic experience "she was undoubtedly influenced by *Marius the Epicurean.*"

999 Gordon, Jan B. "The Beginning of Pater's Pilgrimage: A Reading of 'The Child in the House,' " TENNESSEE STUDIES IN LITERATURE, XIII (1968), 17–25.

Whether or not, as Mrs. Humphry Ward suggested, "The Child in the House" represents an attempt at an earlier, more plainly autobiographical version of *Marius the Epicurean,* many of the motifs and patterns used in the story are repeated in the novel. The beginning of "Child" is significant in the "penitential note" established when Florian helps to carry the burden of the old man he meets along the road and listens to his story as the wedding guest listens to the story of Coleridge's ancient mariner. In this way Florian is recalled to thoughts of his own past, in which the house of his childhood, the quiet home environment, is identified with the impressionable passivity of the child's mind. Florian develops a keen sensitivity to suffering, primarily through contact with the animals that are his childhood companions. The realization that he himself has caused the suffering of the caged starling brings him to believe in "a mechanistic epistemology" associated with the image of the bird's nest, which he uses to define the process of "brain-building." Florian's entry into the outside world is expressed in terms of his encounter with the blossoming hawthorn beyond the garden gate and is related to WP's use of flower symbolism to "punctuate the stages of mental growth" of Marius. At this point Florian's "sensationalist epistemology" begins to give way to "the realization that sensation is a transitory phase of our experience, that death is the inevitable result of Epicureanism, as it is of any other philosophy." Florian's development has striking parallels with that of Marius: both live with widowed mothers, are strongly attached to their childhood homes, become acutely aware of suffering early in life, and are moved by the death of a loved one toward the acceptance of "a transcendental religion." Finally, Florian's return to the childhood house to free the pet bird and Marius's recollection, after parting with Marcus Aurelius, of "the markers along the way of his own earthly pilgrimage" both function as curative memories of the past that free them to accept "a more theologically-rooted philosophy."

> **1000** Gordon, Jan B. "The Imaginary Portraits: Walter Pater's Aesthetic Pilgrimage," UNIVERSITY REVIEW, XXXV (1968), 29–39.

WP's imaginary portraits are based on the pattern of an aesthetic pilgrimage designed to find the relationship between life and art. This pattern is particularly evident in "The Child in the House," "Emerald Uthwart," and "Sebastian Van Storck." The hero of each story initially is over-protected and desires only self-preservation. But as the narrative progresses, he experiences beauty and suffering, and his previous personality is overwhelmed. Finally, each must accept the loss of self for the sake of art. In "Diaphaneitè," WP tells us that not only the saint but also the artist aspires to a greater simplicity to escape random sensationalism. The symbol of their achievement is the bisexual beauty of the Greek statue.

> **1001** Haight, Gordon S. GEORGE ELIOT: A BIOGRAPHY (NY & Oxford: Oxford UP, 1968), pp. 428, 464, 494.

George Eliot met WP on her first visit to Oxford in 1870 and eventually conceived an aversion for him. She agreed with R. C. Jebb that WP misrepresented the great artworks discussed in *The Renaissance*. One of her admirers, Edith Simcox, wrote EPISODES IN THE LIVES OF MEN, WOMEN, AND LOVERS, "a collection of sketches not unlike Pater's *Imaginary Portraits*."

1002 Harris, Wendell V. "John Lane's Keynotes Series and the Fiction of the 1890's," PUBLICATIONS OF THE MODERN LANGUAGE ASSOCIATION, LXXXIII (Oct 1968), 1407–13.

[Calls attention briefly to echoes of WP in Stanley Makower's THE MIRROR OF MUSIC and Francis Adams's A CHILD OF THE AGE and mentions WP's influence on the prose style of the period.]

1003 Hidden, Norman. "Walter Pater: Aesthetic Standards or Impressionism?" UNISA ENGLISH STUDIES, II (1968), 13–18.

Those contemporary critics of WP who took exception to the appreciative, impressionistic method of his criticism were concerned primarily with his failure to move beyond the limits of individual sensibility toward the establishment of objective critical standards. But while WP's stated aim in *The Renaissance* was to convey his own particular experience of the given work of art, those qualities of the works that hold the most consistent claim to his appreciation may be seen as falling under the heading of two large principles, sweetness and strength, the realization of either being, each in its own way, productive of pleasure. Though each artist has his own "virtue," a sweetness or a strength peculiar to himself and expressive of a unique temperament, the work of art must also reveal something of the universal, "the type in the individual." In *Appreciations* WP's emphasis shifts away from pleasure towards truth as his supreme critical principle, though his concern is not so much with fact as with the artist's "sense of fact," as determined again by the artist's personality and the pleasure he derives from his own particular ordering of reality. Highly conscious technique becomes for WP a species of artistic truth, and "mind" and "soul" become the guiding principles of *Appreciations* as sweetness and strength had been those of *The Renaissance*. Finally matter takes the place of form in WP's mind as the true measure of greatness in art. [Uses as examples of contemporary reaction to WP's impressionism and lack of clear aesthetic standards a review of *Imaginary Portraits* in SATURDAY REVIEW (25 June 1887), W. J. Courthope's review of *Appreciations* in NINETEENTH CENTURY (April 1890), W. J. Stillman's review of *The Renaissance* in NATION (NY) (9 Oct 1873), and an article by Gamaliel Bradford, Jr., from ANDOVER REVIEW (Aug 1888).

1004 Hill, Donald L. "Pater's Debt to ROMOLA," NINETEENTH CENTURY FICTION, XXII (1968), 361–77.

There is insufficient evidence to support David DeLaura's argument (NINETEENTH CENTURY FICTION, 1966) that ROMOLA had any appreciable influence either on the thematic development of the essays in *The Renaissance* or on the overall conception of *Marius the Epicurean*. WP's repeated references to Savonarola in *The Renaissance*, while significant in what they indicate of his characteristic mythologizing of historical figures, do not, as DeLaura suggests, indicate clearly any debt to the George Eliot novel. Though not, as DeLaura believes, "reverential," WP's mention of George Eliot in his review of ROBERT ELSMERE is plainly favorable; two comments on her in conversation, however, reported by Thomas Wright and A. C. Benson, are critical of the lack of diversity among her characters. Again, WP's recalling in conversation with William Sharp in 1884 the words of George Eliot's Piero di Cosimo, "The only passionate life is in form and color," is no indication that he remembered the line, as DeLaura suggests, from an initial reading of ROMOLA when it first appeared serially in 1862–63; nor does the single phrase adequately sum up the thematic complexity of *The Renaissance,* which was necessarily the product of a variety of experiences and associations. While in "Diaphaneitè," in which WP makes his only direct written reference to ROMOLA, Savonarola is to some degree an aspirant toward WP's ideal diaphanous character type, WP's approval of him is clearly qualified; and the essay indicates no undue interest in the novel. In "Winckelmann," as DeLaura says, WP makes of Savonarola an example, like Winckelmann himself, of intense culture achieved through selection and renunciation; but WP does not intend, as DeLaura believes, for Savonarola, in his "absolute sincerity" and consequent absence of critical power, to stand beside Winckelmann as an initiator of "a new organ for the human spirit." Though the three references to Savonarola in "Pico della Mirandola," two of which DeLaura fails to note, do seem to indicate that WP had in mind certain events recounted in ROMOLA, they neither evidence any particular sympathy for Savonarola nor argue strongly for any "influence" of ROMOLA on the essay. Of the four references to Savonarola in "The Poetry of Michelangelo," the first three, which DeLaura cites, merely reinforce the image of Savonarola as reformer and idealist presented earlier in "Diaphaneitè" and "Winckelmann"; the fourth, however, styles him, significantly, as the last great adherent to what WP perceived to be the dignifying Florentine tradition of preoccupation with death. Three further references to Savonarola, one in the essay on Leonardo and two in the essay on Botticelli, add little to the understanding of WP's conception of his character. All told, WP's references to Savonarola reflect an indifferent mixture of admiration and distaste; they do not indicate any significant debt to ROMOLA. Finally, it is clear from what WP writes in his review of John Addington Symonds's THE RENAISSANCE IN ITALY (1875) of the Renaissance spirit and of the relationship to it, though noted only briefly, of the spirit of Savonarola, that while he could admire Savonarola's heroic character, he placed him apart from the true humanistic tradition, the delineation of which was the central concern of his own study of the Renaissance.

1005 Johnson, R. V. "Aesthetic Traits in Charles Lamb," SOUTHERN REVIEW, III (1968), 151–58.

Swinburne and Arthur Symons wrote admiringly of Lamb, but only WP among the writers of the "aesthetic" and "decadent" persuasions saw Lamb as exemplifying "the principle of art for its own sake" in prose as fully as Keats had in verse. Lamb fulfills WP's ideal of the artist by an innocence of "mere abstract theories," which makes him highly receptive to sensuous experience. WP's distrust of "hard and abstract moralities" with their tendency to narrow the range of sensibility finds a parallel in Lamb's attack on the "Caledonian" mentality and in Keats's comments on the intellect of Charles Dilke and the morality of the Scots Kirk. Though in his defense of Restoration comedy, Lamb, anticipating Wilde and the Wildean aesthetes, sets art in opposition to life, he tends himself to treat life, in the Paterian manner, in the spirit of art. Both Lamb and WP combine a melancholy sense of mortality with an Epicurean attention to immediate experience, multifarious and sometimes trivial; the aesthetic accomodation to such experience WP sees as the triumph of Lamb's prose. WP sees Lamb's criticism fulfilling the critical ideal outlined in the "Preface" to *The Renaissance* and his profound sympathy strengthening the kind of incidental but "enduring moral effect" which in the essay on "Measure for Measure" he said art was capable of producing. While their aesthetic outlook gives both Lamb and WP peculiar awareness and heightened sympathy, it sometimes leads them into moral ambiguity and brings them, WP in the "Conclusion" and Lamb in "The Praise of Chimney Sweepers," to sacrifice human concerns to strictly aesthetic ends.

1006 Kenner, Hugh. "The Muse in Tatters," AGENDA (Lond), VI (Spring 1968), 43–61.
"The art of attending to radioactive moments, 'simply,' " in WP's phrase, " 'for those moments' sake' had preoccupied two English generations." Ezra Pound echoes WP and Symons on the need to "seize moments in our writing, seize gllmpses. . . . "

1007 Keynes, Geoffrey (ed). THE LETTERS OF RUPERT BROOKE (NY: Harcourt, 1968), pp. 53, 55, 57, 161.
[In a letter to St. John Lucas, dated ca. 4 June 1906, Brooke comments that reading WP's *Miscellaneous Studies*, particularly "The Child in the House," filled him with great "happiness." In another letter to Lucas, dated Sunday, July 1906, Brooke notes that his paper on "Modern Poetry," which he is to read to the Rugby Sixth, is "a rhapsody in prose modelled on Pater's 'Leonardo.' "]

1008 Langford, Thomas A. "The Ethical and Religious Thought of Walter Pater." Unpublished dissertation, Texas Christian University, 1968.
[Listed in Lawrence F. McNamee, DISSERTATIONS IN ENGLISH AND AMERICAN LITERATURE, SUPP I (NY & Lond: Bowker, 1968).]

1009 Lester, John A., Jr. JOURNEY THROUGH DESPAIR, 1880–1914: TRANSFORMATIONS IN BRITISH LITERARY CULTURE (Princeton: Princeton UP, 1968), pp. xvii, xviii, 3, 9, 18, 32, 35, 36, 50, 56, 64, 65, 71, 72, 76, 104, 106, 107, 109, 115, 122–23, 132, 133, 137, 141, 165, 166, 173–74, 182, 183, 185–86.
The "Conclusion" to *The Renaissance* denied the two main axioms of Victorian belief: that there existed "an eternal and credible truth" behind the phenomenal

world and that man was capable of perceiving that truth. But the withdrawal of the "Conclusion" from the second edition of *The Renaissance* is evidence of WP's own uncertainty concerning his solipsistic view of human consciousness. It was nevertheless accepted by his disciples as a basis for aestheticism. WP's "carefully prepared mask against the world" reflected a Schopenhauerian "withdrawal from life"; he also shared Schopenhauer's belief in salvation through art, the supreme position of music among the arts, and man's ability to create his own world. WP, like the French Parnassians, used precious gems as emblems of the purity and endurance of the ideal work of art. Yeats seems to have feared the influence of WP's hedonism and felt him perhaps responsible for the fate of "the tragic generation." [Numerous quotations from *Marius the Epicurean* and the "Conclusion" to *The Renaissance* aid in illustrating the dominant literary themes and motifs of the period.]

> **1010** Levine, George, and William Madden. "Introduction," THE ART
> OF VICTORIAN PROSE, ed by George Levine and William Madden (NY,
> Lond & Toronto: Oxford UP, 1968), pp. vii–xxi.

Although the effort of writers in English to produce consciously artistic nonfictional prose dates back to Malory, it did not gain great momentum until the nineteenth century, when it was fully realized in WP, who maintained that the prose essay was the mode of expression proper to modern literature. It was WP's example that produced the dilettantism of Saintsbury and others against which Eliot and the New Critics reacted, calling into question "the aesthetic attitude toward non-fiction." WP's attempts to describe not the aesthetic object itself but his impression of the object evidences, as does Ruskin's description of St. Mark's, the consciousness of self that is characteristic of nonfiction that attains toward art. WP's prose "is on the verge of becoming pure fiction in the technical sense, pure theory—the imitation of an action which is inward, spiritual, and profound." [In correlating the essays in the collection, Levine and Madden sketch a "poetics of non-fiction" in which WP holds a central position.]

> **1011** Merritt, Travis R. "Taste, Opinion, and Theory in the Rise of
> Victorian Prose Stylism," THE ART OF VICTORIAN PROSE, ed by George
> Levine and William Madden (NY, Lond & Toronto: Oxford UP, 1968),
> pp. 3–38.

The late-Victorian cult of prose stylism, which found its fullest expression in Saintsbury, Stevenson, and, in particular, WP, was a function of the aesthetic movement and represented an attempt to restrain both the didactic and the expressive tendencies of the prose stylists of the mid-century, concerning itself primarily with the formal perfection of the prose surface. In "Style" WP argues for the recognition of imaginative prose, De Quincey's "literature of power," as a fine art; and he stresses the need for discriminating those qualities which define its unique position in the aesthetic order. Reviewing Saintsbury's SPECIMENS OF ENGLISH PROSE STYLE, he advocates a scholarly *ascesis* in composition as a necessary balance to the prevailing eclecticism, natural to a complex and relativistic age, thus clearing the way for the achieving of a more perfect continuity between the various parts of the verbal structure and between that structure and the author's controlling "sense of the world." Saintsbury and Stevenson were concerned more exclusively with the prose surface and were less careful than WP of making distinctions between style and matter. Each, however, was responding to the same central stylistic problem of late-Victorian prose: how to achieve the aesthetic ideal of "lightness of touch" without sacrificing stylistic individuality.

1012 Miller, Eugene E. "Walter Pater and the Reality of Language," DISSERTATION ABSTRACTS INTERNATIONAL, XXVIII (1968), 5025A. Unpublished dissertation, University of Illinois (Urbana), 1967.

1013 Nunnally, Joseph C. "The Victorian *Femme Fatale:* Mirror of the Decadent Temperament," DISSERTATION ABSTRACTS INTERNATIONAL, XXXIX (1968), 1875A. Unpublished dissertation, Texas Tech University, 1968.
[Discusses WP, Wilde, and Beardsley.]

1014 Pinion, F. B. A HARDY COMPANION (Lond: Macmillan; NY: St. Martin's P, 1968), p. 33.
WP's description of the *Mona Lisa* may have influenced Hardy's description of Eustacia Vye in the "Queen of the Night" chapter in THE RETURN OF THE NATIVE.

1015 Sewell, Brocard. FOOTNOTE TO THE NINETIES: A MEMOIR OF JOHN GRAY AND ANDRÉ RAFFALOVICH (Lond: Cecil & Amelia Woolf, 1968), pp. 25, 38, 111.
Raffalovich had an interview with WP when planning to enter Balliol. Sidney Colvin later warned him against involvement with WP and John Addington Symonds, calling into question their morality; Raffalovich, however, felt the personalities of the two hardly comparable. Raffalovich and Wilde dined at WP's and talked afterward about Shakespeare and Mr. W. H.

1016 Shmiefsky, Marvel. "A Study in Aesthetic Relativism: Pater's Poetics," VICTORIAN POETRY, VI (Summer 1968), 105–24.
WP's views on the close relationship between art and morality conflict with his statements supporting art for art's sake; his most characteristic stance emphasizes the aesthetic end of art. His views on truth in art, the relationship between nature and art, and the end of poetry all point to an aesthetic that departs from the main line of Victorian critics represented by Ruskin, Carlyle, Arnold, and Newman. Truth in art consists in the correlation between the poet's vision and his language, not, as in Wordsworth, in a correlation between the mind of the poet and nature. Art consists in the beautiful formulation of a subjective vision. His argument in "Style" that the end of poetry is redemptive is not characteristic of a more prevailing view. As the end of his life is contemplation, so the end of art and poetry is ethically sterile and without moral significance.

1017 Stanford, Derek. "Introduction," "Fr. Rolfe," "Richard Le Gallienne," "Arthur Symons," SHORT STORIES OF THE 'NINETIES: A BIOGRAPHICAL ANTHOLOGY, ed by Derek Stanford (Lond: John Baker, 1968), pp. 13, 15, 16, 17–20, 21, 22, 23, 42, 135, 172, 188.

The high-toned dismissal of Philistine literary taste in the "Postscript" to *Appreciations* typifies the elitist attitude of the Nineties aesthetes; WP argued there and in *Marius the Epicurean* for the acclimatization of literature to the complexities of modern life. Though WP's fictional technique was static, the visual acuity demonstrated in *Marius* and *Imaginary Portraits* set the standard for much of the memorable descriptive writing of the period. WP and Henry James were primarily responsible for applying the standards of *belles-lettres* to fiction. Despite his advocacy of the higher sensuousness, WP modestly evaded the issue of the place of more explicit sensuality, such as that of Maupassant, in literature. Symons's SPIRITUAL ADVENTURES are modelled after *Imaginary Portraits*. Rolfe and Le Gallienne exhibit elements of the Paterian temperament.

1018 Stange, G. Robert. "Art Criticism as a Prose Genre," THE ART OF VICTORIAN PROSE, ed by George Levine and William Madden (NY, Lond & Toronto: Oxford UP, 1968), pp. 39–52.

Art criticism as an independent prose genre, prefigured in Friedrich Schlegel's theories on the criticism of poetry, was first practiced by Lamb and Hazlitt, whose method of verbal re-creation of personal responses to the graphic arts was later developed more fully by Ruskin and WP. Compared to Ruskin's treatment of Tintoretto's *Massacre of the Innocents* in MODERN PAINTERS, WP's passage on *The Birth of Venus* in "Botticelli," attempting as it does to evoke a mixture of melancholy and subtle eroticism, is both more restrained and more "poetic," though both Ruskin and WP work toward the same end: the creation, primarily through the synaesthetic effects of rhythm and tone, of *"expressive imitations"* of the aesthetic experience rather than descriptions of the art objects themselves. [Stange presents a diagram of "the process of response to the prose of art criticism," emphasizing the rich complexity of the relationship between the writer, the text, the reader, the art work, and the writer's response to the art work, which is the true reference of the criticism.]

1019 Svaglic, Martin J. "Classical Rhetoric and Victorian Prose," THE ART OF VICTORIAN PROSE, ed by George Levine and William Madden (NY, Lond & Toronto: Oxford UP, 1968), pp. 268–88.

[Svaglic points to the "Conclusion" to *The Renaissance* as an example of rhetorical peroration and lists "Coleridge," along with Carlyle's SARTOR RESARTUS, Newman's APOLOGIA PRO VITA SUA, Ruskin's UNTO THIS LAST, and Huxley's "Science and Culture," as an example of the predominantly hortatory rhetoric characteristic of all great Victorian prose, which aimed to persuade the reader to adopt a course of action or temper of mind with which to face the problems of the age. Svaglic maintains that since Aristotle's RHETORIC was a basic text of the *litterae humaniores* program at Oxford, Newman, Arnold, and WP were all grounded in the elements of classical rhetoric.]

> **1020** Tillotson, Geoffrey. "Matthew Arnold's Prose: Theory and Practice," THE ART OF VICTORIAN PROSE, ed by George Levine and William Madden (NY, Lond & Toronto: Oxford UP, 1968), pp. 73–100.

While WP approved of the "atmosphere of mind" in Wordsworth's poetry, that quality most expressive of the writer's individuality, George Eliot found the atmosphere of *The Renaissance* "poisonous." In condemning Newman's prose as overly conversational, Hopkins may have been guided by WP, who argued in his review of THE PICTURE OF DORIAN GRAY for a more learned, and in his essay "Style" for a less profuse English prose.

> **1021** Trilling, Lionel. "James Joyce in His Letters," COMMENTARY, XLV (Feb 1968), 53–64.

T. S. Eliot's remark that in writing ULYSSES Joyce had "killed the 19th century" may be interpreted to mean that he had destroyed the nineteenth-century novel by undermining the central moral assumption on which it was founded, that it was possible to achieve what WP in the "Conclusion" to *The Renaissance* called "success in life." [Partly a review of Joyce's LETTERS.]

> **1022** Weintraub, Stanley. "Introduction: The Critic in Spite of Himself," LITERARY CRITICISM OF OSCAR WILDE, ed by Stanley Weintraub (Lincoln: University of Nebraska P, 1968), pp. xvii, xxxi.

In approaching art from the aesthetic rather than the moral viewpoint Wilde "was diverging (but for Pater) from nine previous decades of nineteenth-century thought." WP was one of the few contemporary writers whom Wilde praised highly.

> **1023** Winner, Viola Hopkins. "The Artist and the Man in 'The Author of Beltraffio,' " PUBLICATIONS OF THE MODERN LANGUAGE ASSOCIATION, LXXXIII (March 1968), 102–8.

Mark Ambient, the hero in Henry James's story, is not a pagan sensualist but a figure partly modelled after many writers, one of whom is WP. He is not a Wildean aesthete.

1969

> **1024** Bagchi, J. "Walter Pater's Criticism and its Contemporary Relations." Unpublished dissertation, University of Cambridge, 1969.

[Listed in Lawrence F. McNamee, DISSERTATIONS IN ENGLISH AND AMERICAN LITERATURE, SUPP II (NY & Lond: Bowker, 1974).]

1025 Converse, William R. M. "Walter Pater: Abstraction and Abstractionism." Unpublished dissertation, University of Adelaide (Australia), 1969.
[Listed in Lawrence F. McNamee, DISSERTATIONS IN ENGLISH AND AMERICAN LITERATURE, SUPP II (NY & Lond: Bowker, 1974).]

1026 Daiches, David. SOME LATE VICTORIAN ATTITUDES (Lond: André Deutsch; NY: Norton, 1969), pp. 39–41.
In advocating the pursuit of experience for its own sake, the "Conclusion" to *The Renaissance* looks forward to the relishing of despair by Ernest Dowson and other late nineteenth-century aesthetes. Though Wilde preached "the Paterian creed" in "The Soul of Man Under Socialism" and THE PICTURE OF DORIAN GRAY, he could not avoid injecting a traditional moral into the latter.

1027 DeLaura, David J. HEBREW AND HELLENE IN VICTORIAN ENGLAND: NEWMAN, ARNOLD, AND PATER (Austin: University of Texas P, 1969); absorbs "Pater and Newman: The Road to the 'Nineties," VICTORIAN STUDIES (1966).
WP and Arnold adapted Newman's traditional religious culture to the needs of the later nineteenth century and transformed the substance of dogmatic Christianity into the fabric of aestheticism. Newman worked out a "personalist" theory of literature embodying WP's idea of the special function of literature in modern times. Newman's attractiveness for Arnold and WP is found in the "theological humanism" of the Oxford movement. WP experienced an exhaustion of thought similar to Arnold's after the careful irresolution of *Marius the Epicurean* failed to define the "mixed culture" he aspired to or the nature of the "third condition" of man, transcending dualism. The antithesis and proposed reconciliations of German Hellenism are central to the continuity from Arnold through WP to the Nineties; and the chief problem involved in the dialectic is of transcending, through rejection or synthesis, the dualisms with which Western tradition had burdened man. But whatever the mode of transcendence attempted, the norm for Arnold and WP is increasingly aesthetic. WP's Hellenism differs from Arnold's because WP accepts contemporary science. In "Winckelmann" the central problem is creating an art that preserves a sense of Hellenic freedom and an awareness that natural law extends to the moral order. In his "Preface" to *The Renaissance,* WP effects a marriage of aestheticism and scientific observation. He adds Dionysian tradition to Arnold's Apollonian to make his own Hellenism more complex and to advance an "enriched" view of Greek religion as a conscious alternative to a played-out Christianity. In his attempt to integrate Christianity into a higher synthesis, WP's development from paganism in the 1860s to an approximation of historic Christianity in the 1880s seems clearer than Arnold's. The deeper unifying pattern of WP's career appears in his repeated attempts at synthesis; but his failure at synthesis and transcendence stems from underemphasizing the social functions of the arts and criticism and from the specialness of his *morality,* which proceeds

from a special conception of the perfected life. In *Marius* WP realizes that self-cultivation is incomplete in isolation from others.

WP's career began without sympathy for Catholicism and Christianity. In "Winckelmann" he rejects and corrects Arnold's views of Christian and classical culture. In the William Morris essay WP emphasizes critical self-definition and applies to morals and his special vision of "life" what Arnold confined to the literary and critical sphere. *The Renaissance* contains WP's search for a more adequate formula of human wholeness and completeness through diverse but related visions of human nature, the Greek temper, Hebraism and Hellenism, medieval Catholicism, and Renaissance humanism. The ideal aesthetic observer in "Wordsworth" lives by the higher ethic of "impassioned contemplation" in which means and ends are identified and life is lived "in the spirit of art." In *Greek Studies* Greek religion has a holism that is at the base of humanism; and WP asserts the contemporary viability of a "pagan" religious ideal. "Romanticism" reconciles the Greek and medieval Christian aspects of the romantic temper. *Marius* recapitulates many stages in WP's development and the crucial struggles of Arnold's career. As WP borrowed the essential structures of his dilemmas from Arnold's work, so he responds in *Marius* to the pressures urging Arnold to reshape his own dilemmas. *Marius* becomes an epitome of the successive attempts by Arnold and WP to shore up the assailable basis of culture. *Gaston de Latour* is significant for its inconclusiveness and for its further exploration of a "third condition" of humanity. *Marius* and the later essays represent a realignment of the dialectically struggling forces in WP's synthesis; *Plato and Platonism* does not mark a retreat from the final adjustment in *Marius,* although it indicates that the calculated skeptical pose and double-consciousness of WP's later religious period were tipped further toward orthodoxy during his last decade of life. The central argument of Marius's conversion is taken from Newman's GRAMMAR OF ASSENT and THE IDEA OF A UNIVERSITY, the latter of which is also essential to a full understanding of WP's essay on "Style."

> **1028** Gordon, Jan B. "The Dialogue of Life and Art in Arthur Symons's SPIRITUAL ADVENTURES," ENGLISH LITERATURE IN TRANSITION, XII (1969), 105–17.

Symons's autobiographical "A Prelude to Life" suggests an attempt to elevate life to the condition of music, which Symons, like WP, regarded as the supreme art form. In its mythic dimension "Peter Waydelin" represents the self-mutilation and death of Dionysus and his rebirth as Apollo and recalls the life patterns of WP's Florian Deleal, Emerald Uthwart, and Sebastian van Storck, who sacrifice personal identity for the sake of a higher, aestheticized existence, and of the artist-heroes of *The Renaissance,* "who sacrifice themselves for the rebirth of the summertime, effete mood of Apollonian culture." The title character of "The Journal of Henry Luxulyan," lapsing into insanity, experiences a similar loss of self—burns with a "gem-like flame" and is transformed into a diaphanous,

Paterian figure. SPIRITUAL ADVENTURES belongs to the same *fin-de-siècle* literary genre as the *Imaginary Portraits* and the short stories of Ernest Dowson: all are concerned primarily with the aesthete who develops an aesthetic of the "moment" that eventually threatens the integrity of the self and provokes a crisis of consciousness resolvable only by a ritual self-martyrdom and the dying of the self into art.

1029 Gordon, Jan B. "The Imaginary Portrait: Fin-de-Siècle Icon," UNIVERSITY OF WINDSOR REVIEW, V (Fall 1969), 81–104.
As a literary genre of the *fin-de-siècle*, the imaginary portrait deals characteristically with "the reversal of roles between art and life" and is in part a reaction to such polarizations of moral and purely aesthetic concerns in art as that promoted by Ruskin in MODERN PAINTERS. It is related to the *bildungsroman* but is reflexive rather than linear in development, being based on the principle that all art is necessarily a reflection of the artist's self. WP's *Imaginary Portraits* deal with the sacrifice of self to art and are outgrowths of his conceptions of Leonardo da Vinci, Winckelmann, and other "artist-pilgrims" treated in *The Renaissance*. In attempting to grasp life in all its diversity, WP's "culture heroes" end either by imprisoning themselves epistemologically in a world of their own creating or by abandoning themselves to "the anarchy of random aesthetic moments." The only means of escape is "to will the disappearance of the ego that so fragments the world," to transform, as in the emblematic martyrdom of Sebastian van Storck, being into art and thereby transcend "both the maelstrom of sensation and a bifurcated existence." The self-sacrifice of Sebastian van Storck recalls, in its aesthetic dimension, that of St. Sebastian and anticipates the "stylized suffering" of the Wilde of DE PROFUNDIS, alias Sebastian Melmoth. WP's characters resemble in their development those of Yeats who multiply to a certain point aspects of their being and then enter self-consumed into "the artifice of eternity." The gesture of self-sacrifice also represents an aesthetic resolution of the Dionysian-Apollonian conflict prevalent in the literature of the period, the attainment of a "silent undifferentiation" of personality related to the neutralization of the masculine ego by which personality could be stylized into the ideal type described in "Diaphaneitè" and the individual enabled to proceed toward the full, aestheticized life outlined in the "Conclusion" to *The Renaissance*. Each of WP's "portraits" employs a structural device that both frames the narrative and bridges "the subject/object distinctions that promoted aesthetic alienation." Thus the second "pilgrim" in "The Child in the House" in receiving Florian's story assumes the mediating function of confessor; the theological treatise of the monk in "Apollo in Picardy" gives access to the writer's life and at the same time transcends it; and the diary of "A Prince of Court Painters" "constructs the 'life' from the art," merging the artist and his work. WP's diaphanous characters are more highly stylized versions of the luminous figures in the paintings of the Pre-Raphaelites. [Gordon finds other examples of the hazily defined genre in Rossetti's "Hand and Soul," Symons's SPIRITUAL ADVENTURES, Wilde's THE PICTURE OF DORIAN GRAY,

Synge's "Étude Morbide," Dowson's Dilemmas, and Joyce's A Portrait of the Artist as a Young Man.]

1030 Gordon, Jan B. "Pater's Gioconda Smile: A Reading of 'Emerald Uthwart,' " Studies in Short Fiction, VI (Winter 1969), 136–43.
Taken as a whole, "Emerald Uthwart" is an elaboration on the motif of the epitaph used to initiate the story and is meant to be read in a vein different from that of other incidental essays in *Miscellaneous Studies*. Like Marius (*Marius the Epicurean*) and Florian Deleal, Emerald is bound by a deep sense of home, yet he is aware of a certain freedom within the geographical and intellectual limits of the characteristic Uthwart domesticity. He is contrasted to the rest of his family by means of botanical metaphors; while his brothers cultivate their gardens and remain tied to their ancestral domain, Emerald enters the larger world as a "wild-growth" and becomes one with the flux of nature. His pilgrimage, like that of Marius, includes three stages: his homelife as a child, his schooldays, and his life in the army. Though Emerald, yielding always to the sense of place, first submits to the half-religious, half-martial atmosphere of school and then is broken by the discipline and monotony of military life, he is never completely dissociated from the sense of home, something of his native green being carried with him to his residence at school in Green Court and later projected onto the "gangrened places" of the battlefield. Through his idealization of the masculine beauty of Stokes, Emerald is able momentarily to harmonize the physical and ethical aspects of his divided nature much as WP's Winckelmann "harmonizes a monastic temperament with the hellenic fascination of beauty." There follows a mid-journey pause in his career which recalls that of Marius on his meeting Cornelius; but tiring of academic life and still hoping to emulate his one soldierly ancestor, Emerald is carried forward into the field where the domestic pull reasserts itself and finally overcomes him. The epilogue in the form of the physician's post mortem report, dated the same month as Emerald's birth, completes the circle temporally as the return home does spatially. Yet the conclusion is ambiguous, the unnatural preservation of Emerald's body suggesting an ultimate refusal to return to his native earth. "Emerald Uthwart" looks back to *Marius* in its being structured as a pilgrimage and forward to *Plato and Platonism* in its effort to reconcile the metaphysical concepts of permanence and flux. The "artificial confusion between Emerald's life and Pater's art" is related to Wilde's theory of nature's imitating art. There are certain thematic and structural parallels between "Emerald Uthwart" and The Picture of Dorian Gray.

1031 Gross, Beverly. "Walter Pater and the Aesthetic Fallacy," South Atlantic Quarterly, LXVIII (Spring 1969), 220–30.
Although in his successive roles as aesthete, humanist, and "converted Christian," WP held contradictory views on the relationship between form and matter in art, there is an underlying consistency in his aesthetics based on his sense of the relationship between art and life. The progression of Marius (*Marius the Epicurean*) from an indiscriminately sensational Epicureanism toward the moral refine-

ments of Cyrenaicism and, finally, Christianity parallels the movement of WP's own thought from the critical position held in the "Conclusion" to *The Renaissance* to a higher aestheticism which elevated culture to the level of religion. WP's criticism is concerned not with the art object itself, as was Arnold's, nor with the creative process, but with the appreciative response to the object. The critical impressionism outlined in the "Preface" to *The Renaissance,* with its emphasis on delineation of the particular response and avoidance of abstraction, makes the formulation of an aesthetic system impossible. The true aim of WP's critic is to justify his impression by analyzing it and disengaging the unique imaginative vision embodied in the work which produced it, thus making the impression one with the expression and so achieving a final communion with the artist. WP's concept of the fusion of form and matter as presented in "The School of Giorgione" applied also to the synthesizing effect of his criticism, which "glosses over objects, blurring distinctions" in an attempt to achieve the same unified effect produced by art itself. While the ideal of the fusion of form and matter presented in "Giorgione" appears to conflict with WP's statement in "Winckelmann" that form is the distinct source of pleasure in poetry and with his later argument in "Style" that the quality of matter determines the ultimate greatness of the work of art, the contradictions themselves evidence the most basic precept of WP's impressionism: that views of art must change to adapt to the changing demands of living. Thus in the "Conclusion" to *The Renaissance* WP first conceived of art as a means of escape; later, in "Giorgione" and "Wordsworth," he conceded that "art may have something to say to life"; finally, in "Style," he accepted art as a moral force, proclaiming, in effect, "the inherent self-defeat of the Aesthetic ideal." By playing down the value of the object in favor of the aesthetic response, WP ended by devaluing art. His placing form above matter and then matter above form are indications of his attempts first to evade the moral concerns of life and later to escape the psychological vacuity resulting from that evasion.

1032 Gross, John. THE RISE AND FALL OF THE MAN OF LETTERS: A STUDY OF THE IDIOSYNCRATIC AND THE HUMANE IN MODERN LITERATURE (NY: Macmillan; Lond: Weidenfeld & Nicolson, 1969), pp. 58, 101, 103, 131, 145, 177.
WP's criticism, as Eliot remarked, followed out of the Arnoldian tradition, which led eventually to the anemic aestheticism of the end of the century. The appreciative critics of the period from the late 1870s until the First World War "had taken to heart the lessons of Pater." [Includes references to attitudes toward WP of Morley and, incidentally, Saintsbury and Le Gallienne.]

1033 Heffernan, James. "Centripetal Vision in Pater's *Marius,*" VICTORIAN NEWSLETTER, No. 35 (Spring 1969), pp. 13–17.
Although WP cannot be *identified* with Marius, *Marius the Epicurean* seems to embody WP's dedication to the aesthetic ideal and may be a fictionalized defense of his own centripetal vision in which every experience yields both sensuous and

intellectual beauty. But in fact *Marius* ironically reveals the crucial weakness of the centripetal approach to all experience, especially in relation to the problem of evil and to ethical economy. Marius makes moral inferences from aesthetic facts: the ugly is evil. But since the ugly comes to exemplify the inescapable suffering of the human condition, it is a source of his sympathy. Ironically, Marius consistently compromises and confuses "real good and real evil," so that while he can commiserate the ugly sufferings of animals, he has no compassion for the poverty and wretchedness of working people because he considers them "picturesque." Human suffering is dissipated by aesthetic charm. Marius's "martyrdom" is the triumph of the centripetal vision, the supreme irony of the book, and a hoax. We are confronted with a comic and pathetic spectacle of one obsessed with centripetal vision who will not choose between earth and heaven but must have both—and not to choose is to violate one's ethical economy.

1034 Herendeen, Warren. "Three Unpublished Letters of Walter Pater," REVIEW OF ENGLISH STUDIES, XX (Feb 1969), 63–65.
[Herendeen's notes on one letter of WP to John Chapman, editor of WESTMINSTER REVIEW, and two to Richard Le Gallienne concern WP's WESTMINSTER REVIEW publications, his relationship with Sidney Colvin, a meeting with Le Gallienne, Le Gallienne's writings on WP, and WP's London addresses. Copies of letters are included in LETTERS, ed by Lawrence Evans (1970).]

1035 Hidden, Norman. "Walter Pater—A Victorian View on Hedonism," UNISA ENGLISH STUDIES, III (March 1969), 22–31.
The hedonism of the "Conclusion" to *The Renaissance*, which aroused much moral concern among WP's early critics, was given clearer and broader definition in *Marius the Epicurean*, allowing for the richness of experience available within the established moral and religious order. While John Morley in his review of *The Renaissance* granted genuine credence to WP's aesthetic "theory of life," such critics as Mallock put a vulgar construction upon his notion of hedonism. WP was thus brought to reformulate his position, *Marius* becoming, as most contemporary reviewers recognized, a species of *apologia pro vita sua*. Certain critics, however, found his new stand ambiguous. Whereas WP had failed to qualify clearly the nature of the "exquisite passion," the pursuit of which he advocated in the "Conclusion," in *Marius* he attempted to bring his Epicureanism more closely into line with conventional morality, emphasizing its value primarily for select personalities and insisting on the necessary strenuousness of the Cyrenaic life. The new Cyrenaics, WP believed, must not, as did those of the old school, reject the contemporary moral-religious order totally, but while striving to maintain liberty of the intellect and spirit, they must remain sensitive to its "venerable system of sentiment and idea." WP ended by identifying "the saint, and the Cyrenaic lover of beauty" in the character of Marius as martyr. [Refers to the treatment of WP's hedonism in Morley's review of *The Renaissance* in the FORTNIGHTLY REVIEW and reviews of *Marius* in MACMILLAN'S MAGAZINE (June 1885), ATHENAEUM (28 Feb 1885), ANDOVER REVIEW (Aug 1888), and THE CATHOLIC WORLD (May 1886).]

1036 Johnson, R. V. AESTHETICISM (NY: Barnes and Noble; Lond: Methuen [The Critical Idiom 3], 1969), pp. 3, 11, 14, 16, 17, 18, 19–23, 31–32, 33, 34, 35, 40, 41, 42, 46, 53, 55, 63–66, 68–71, 72–77, 81–82, 83, 85.

WP was "the foremost exponent of the aesthetic view of life." He defined beauty not in abstract terms but as something immediate to the experience both of art and of the natural world. The inconsistencies in the critical terminology used by WP and the "aesthetic" critics generally make it difficult to define aestheticism precisely. WP appears to hold that "form is the total unity into which matter is absorbed," while Swinburne represents a second branch of aesthetic criticism that sees form as distinct from matter. The "Conclusion" to *The Renaissance* is the classic formulation of "contemplative aestheticism," which proposes approaching life "in the spirit of art." Although WP's aestheticism runs counter to puritan morality, it does not advocate "unreflecting self-abandonment" but rather "cultivation of varied sensibility"; it is concerned with the value of the immediate impression rather than any "hypothetical after-effects." He agrees with Arnold in refusing to view life merely in terms of means and ends, but he lacks Arnold's social consciousness. To some extent the "Conclusion" encourages the kind of "retreat from life" which found its "supreme exemplar" in Huysmans's Des Esseintes; yet the appreciation of life includes the appreciation of people, and WP argues elsewhere for "a morality of sympathy" based on sensitivity to individual temperaments. In the "Preface" to *The Renaissance* WP defines the aim of aesthetic or appreciative criticism as the re-creation for the reader of the impression made by an artwork on the critic himself. Thus WP's criticism approaches the condition of art and provides the model for the critical theory of Wilde's "The Critic as Artist." According to WP the critic's task is to interpret, not to judge, but in the essay on "Style" he backs down from strict aestheticism and admits a distinction between good art and great art, assigning a higher value to that art which presents matter of significant human import. In spite of caricaturing WP in THE NEW REPUBLIC, Mallock was not entirely antagonistic to "self-culture," a concept which Dallas had attacked earlier in THE GAY SCIENCE as vain and effeminate, but which WP gave positive value in *The Renaissance*. Moore's idea of pure poetry derives in part from WP's aestheticism, but Moore empties art of its personal vision. Wilde too, though his criticism is basically impressionistic, diverges from WP's critical theory in adopting the Parnassian belief that perfection of form, not expression, is the ideal of art. Instead of stressing awareness of the splendor of experience, Wilde uses the banality of life as an argument for the superiority of art.

1037 L'Homme, Charles E. "The Influence of Walter Pater: A Study in the Making of the Modern Literary Mind," DISSERTATION ABSTRACTS INTERNATIONAL, XXIX (1969), 2517A. Unpublished dissertation, Columbia University, 1965.

1038 Masheck, J. D. C. "Art by a Poet: Notes on Published Drawings by Gerard Manley Hopkins," HERMATHENA, CVIII (Spring 1969), 24–37.

Hopkins's drawing entitled, "Waves. Study from the cliff above, Freshwater Gate. July 23" (1863) reveals his concern with nature in flux. His interest in Heraclitus' philosophy of flux, expressed in the poem, "That Nature is a Heraclitean fire and of the comfort of the Resurrection" may have been suggested to him by WP's "Conclusion" to *The Renaissance*. It is "a key document for any consideration of Hopkins' aesthetics." It may also be "the source of Hopkins' abundant gem imagery."

1039 Milic, Louis T. STYLISTS ON STYLE: A HANDBOOK WITH SELECTIONS FOR ANALYSIS (NY: Scribner's Sons, 1969), pp. 337, 341, 363, 364–67, 442, 506.

[Annotation of a selection from "Sir Thomas Browne," dealing mainly with WP's sense of what Morris W. Croll was later to define as Browne's Senecan style. Other notes point briefly to relationships between WP and such stylists as Wilde, Ruskin, and Cyril Connolly.]

1040 Miyoshi, Masao. THE DIVIDED SELF. A PERSPECTIVE ON THE LITERATURE OF THE VICTORIANS (NY: New York UP; Lond: University of London P, 1969), pp. 278, 279, 285n, 313, 318, 321, 329, 338n.

WP's "gentle and weary intoning of division as the condition of modern life" is expressed in terms of Heraclitean atomism. His impressionism, an outgrowth of Arnold's "disinterested" criticism, is not concerned with apprehending the continuity of life nor with the need the earlier Victorians felt for rooting man in time and society. He is a hedonist, but he is also a moralist. Though his philosophy may provide intensity of experience, it also results in the inability to act and interact with the contemporary world.

1041 Munro, John M. ARTHUR SYMONS (NY: Twayne [TEAS,76] 1969), pp. viii, ix, 17–23, 25–26, 32, 37, 38, 42, 72, 82–84, 92, 98, 105, 133, 136, 137.

When WP makes a plea for "the primacy of art," he reaffirms "Plato's belief in the inseparableness of beauty and goodness." Art becomes the true morality. Wilde either misunderstood or ignored WP's ethical stance. Symons did not. WP offered him a faith to replace the religious faith he had lost. WP inspired his thoughts and his style. But it is doubtful if the young Symons understood the complexities of WP's aesthetics. Symons did not discover an "ethical code" in WP's works at this time. Symons believed that both WP and Browning desired to isolate the "moment" in their works. In his review of DAYS AND NIGHTS, WP calls attention to Symons's clarity of expression, a distinguishing mark of Symons's craft. After 1900, in the new spirit of symbolism, Symons reread WP and discovered his ethical system, his " 'stoic sense of duty.' " He also discovered how WP's prose reflected moods. Symons believed that WP's most significant contribution to aesthetics was "the theory of the autonomous image."

1042 Pierle, Robert C. "Walter Pater and Epicureanism," SOUTHERN QUARTERLY, VII (Jan 1969), 131–40.

According to Bernard Duffey (TEXAS STUDIES IN LANGUAGE AND LITERATURE, 1960) WP has come to occupy an "unhonored place in the history of Victorian thought," but judgments made against him are typically philosophical rather than literary. The evaluation of WP's Epicureanism is "one of the most difficult problems in the whole area of Pater criticism." Critics of WP's Epicureanism fall into three groups: those who hold, approvingly or disapprovingly, that Epicureanism does constitute the philosophical basis of WP's work; those who maintain that though the early work is based on Epicurean thought, the later work represents a repudiation of it and an acceptance of Christian ideology; and those who attempt to avoid making literary judgments about WP on the basis of his philosophical stance. Much of the critical confusion is the result of misconceptions concerning the philosophy of Epicurus, which far from advocating sensual self-indulgence, valued "only those pleasures consistent with intelligence and modera-tion." Epicureanism differed from classical skepticism in insisting on man's ability to ascertain the truth through the operation of innate ideas, feelings, and sensations and from both Platonism and Christianity in abjuring metaphysics and relying on the evidence of the material world in defining its ethical system. While the first phase of WP's writing includes an attack on the idealism of Coleridge that recalls Epicurus' own impatience with the metaphysics of Platonism, praise for Winckel-mann's high-minded materialism, and the refined Epicurean strains of "Aesthetic Poetry" and "Two Early French Stories," it ends with the "Conclusion" to *The Renaissance,* which indicates a movement away from a purer Epicureanism toward a creed "totally self-regarding and completely sensational" and lacking in ethical import. The second phase is dominated by the semi-autobiographical "The Child in the House" and *Marius the Epicurean,* in both of which certain critics claim to find evidence of WP's movement toward Christian orthodoxy. But despite Florian's "appetite for sacred things" he is never able to accept the existence of the nonmaterial world. Similarly, Marius is drawn to Christianity primarily by the same sensual lures that drew him to the pagan religion of his ancestors, to the hedonism of Flavian, and to Cyrenaicism. In the final phase of his writing WP's philosophical attitudes are apparent only in "Sebastian van Storck" and *Plato and Platonism,* both of which hark back to "Coleridge" in the positions they take against mysticism and philosophical abstraction. Though WP was not a strict adherent to formal Epicureanism, he maintained throughout his career many views consistent with the philosophy.

1043 Pope-Hennessy, John. "Writing on Art," ESSAYS BY DIVERS HANDS, XXXV (1969), 101–14.

Though incontestably "great writing," WP's description of the *Mona Lisa* is extraneous to the painting itself. Berenson, on the other hand, despite his indebtedness to WP, is more balanced in his approach to Renaissance art, combining the role of critic with that of art historian. Reacting in his essay on Giorgione to the starkly factual method of the "new Vasari," Crowe and Cavalcaselle's HISTORY OF PAINTING IN NORTH ITALY, WP proceeded from the basis of his own more limited data to define Giorgione's artistic personality with unsurpassed "subtlety and sympathy and justice." Crowe's treatment of Titian and Giorgione's *Concert* is stylistically drab but more comprehensive and pointed finally than WP's description of the same work. In his last writings, Crowe becomes more eloquent, while WP in his last essay on Italian art, collected in *Miscellaneous Studies,* becomes "less unhistorical."

1044 Runcie, C. A. "The Relationship of Life and Art in the Thought of Matthew Arnold and Walter Pater." Unpublished dissertation, University of London, 1969.

[Listed in Lawrence F. McNamee, DISSERTATIONS IN ENGLISH AND AMERICAN LITERATURE, SUPP II (NY & Lond: Bowker, 1974).]

1045 Stock, Noel. "Fragmentation and Uncertainty," POETRY AUSTRALIA, XXXI (Dec 1969), 41–44.

The tendency of modern artists to wallow in the uncertainty engendered by social dislocation rather than to transcend it in their art is the result of a Romantic heresy that became manifest in Coleridge, who shrouded his thought in vague terminology rather than clear definition. WP describes this situation from a positive viewpoint in his discussion in "Coleridge" of the intellectual subtlety of the "relative" spirit. This and his attempt in "The School of Giorgione" to situate art beyond the pale of "mere intelligence" reveal "beyond any shadow of doubt that he was the precursor who prepared the English-speaking world for 'modern art.' " The idea that all the arts aspire toward the condition of music, however, significant as it is, is pushed too far without being given the qualification necessary for clear definition. WP's intense concern with the creative consciousness led to the placing of art and "intelligence" in opposition to the claims of society by such writers as Pound, Wyndham Lewis, and D. H. Lawrence.

1046 Sullivan, William Howard. "Walter Pater: Toward a New Literary Form," DISSERTATION ABSTRACTS INTERNATIONAL, XXXI (1969), 404A. Unpublished dissertation, University of Wisconsin, 1969.

1047 Titlebaum, Richard Theodore. "Three Victorian Views of the Italian Renaissance: John Ruskin, Walter Pater, John Addington Symonds." Unpublished dissertation, Harvard University, 1969.

[Listed in Lawrence F. McNamee, DISSERTATIONS IN ENGLISH AND AMERICAN LITERATURE, SUPP II (NY & Lond: Bowker, 1974).]

1048 Ward, Hayden Wightman, Jr., "The Religious Aesthetic of Walter Pater," DISSERTATION ABSTRACTS INTERNATIONAL, XXX (1969), 2503A. Unpublished dissertation, Columbia University, 1969.

1970

1049 Acton, Harold. MORE MEMOIRS OF AN AESTHETE (Lond: Methuen, 1970); pub in the U.S. as MEMOIRS OF AN AESTHETE, 1939–1969 (NY: Viking, 1971), pp. 227, 230, 334, 366.

[Acton compares his own sensibility, his interest in "the personality of bygone periods and phases of culture," to that of WP and Sacheverell Sitwell, refers briefly to WP's influence on the prose style of Max Beerbohm, and describes Bernard Berenson as the heir to Ruskin and WP.]

1050 Beckson, Karl. "Introduction," OSCAR WILDE: THE CRITICAL HERITAGE, ed by Karl Beckson (Lond: Routledge & Kegan Paul; NY: Barnes & Noble, 1970), pp. 6, 10.

WP's letter to Wilde concerning THE HAPPY PRINCE AND OTHER TALES would perhaps have been less filled with praise had WP been committing himself to print. His review of THE PICTURE OF DORIAN GRAY contained the most perceptive contemporary insights into the novel. Wilde probably considered the favorable responses of WP and Mallarmé to DORIAN GRAY "the ultimate accolades."

1051 Beckson, Karl, and John M. Munro. "Symons, Browning, and the Development of the Modern Aesthetic," STUDIES IN ENGLISH LITERATURE, X (Autumn 1970), 687–99.

Though the influence of Robert Browning on Arthur Symons has been largely ignored, it was as important to the development of his aesthetic as that of WP and the French Symbolists. In AN INTRODUCTION TO THE STUDY OF BROWNING Symons establishes a correlation between Browning's attempts at sudden revelation of soul and WP's desire to be "present always at the focus where the greatest number of vital forces unite in their purest energy" and finds that the central aesthetic principle of both Browning and WP is the capturing of the significant moment. The same principle operates in Symons's own DAYS AND NIGHTS, a collection of predominantly Browningesque poems, which WP, to whom the collection is dedicated, praised as superior in purity to those of Browning. Symons's aesthetic, in its turn, had profound effect on Yeats, Joyce, Eliot, Pound, and others of their generation.

1052 Bergonzi, Bernard. "Aspects of the Fin de Siècle," THE VICTORIANS, ed by Arthur Pollard. Vol. VI: HISTORY OF LITERATURE IN THE ENGLISH LANGUAGE (Lond: Barrie & Jenkins, 1970), pp. 366–71; rptd in Bernard Bergonzi, THE TURN OF A CENTURY: ESSAYS ON VICTORIAN AND MODERN ENGLISH LITERATURE (Lond: Macmillan; NY: Barnes & Noble, 1973), pp. 17–39.

WP's appeal grows with familiarity. He was one of the first English writers to deal analytically with some of the major artists of the Italian Renaissance. His historical relativism—his skepticism of absolutes and of final truth—marks him as a representative *fin de siècle* writer. WP's mistrust of system and his attraction for the brief, concentrated lyric are also characteristic of the *fin de siècle* frame of mind. *Marius the Epicurean* is a nominal novel with little sense of character or dramatic intensity.

1053 Bloom, Harold. "Introduction," *Marius the Epicurean: His Sensations and Ideas* (NY: New American Library, 1970), pp. ix–xix; rptd as "The Place of Pater: *Marius the Epicurean*," in Harold Bloom, THE RINGERS IN THE TOWER: STUDIES IN ROMANTIC TRADITION (Chicago & Lond: University of Chicago P, 1971), pp. 185–94.

English aestheticism, usually traced back to its French sources in Gautier and Baudelaire, may derive more directly from Hallam, who in a review of Tennyson's poetry is concerned, as Marshall McLuhan observed, with the same historical shift from objective to subjective aesthetic standards often treated by WP and T. S. Eliot. WP's popular reputation is built largely upon his personal eccentricities, but from the standpoint of literary history he "is one of the central figures in the continuity between Romanticism and Modernism," linking, as in the character of Marius, "the sensibility of Keats and that of the late Yeats or late Stevens." The surface diversity of *Marius the Epicurean* is the result of WP's belief in the importance of freely courting sensations and ideas and of the confusion of purposes, decried by Eliot, which caused him to write simultaneously as critic, creative artist, and moralist. Nevertheless, owing to his overriding skepticism and the limitations imposed by his naturalism, WP succeeds in producing in *Marius* "a unified reverie or aesthetic meditation upon history." He approaches the theme of decadent civilization with the same passionate desperation articulated in the "Conclusion." For him, as for Keats and Stevens, "Death is the mother of beauty"; yet there is a morbidity in "The Child in the House," *Imaginary Portraits,* and *Marius* not found in those poets. WP's Romantic vision, in contradistinction to Wordsworth's, remained concentrated in "outward sense." *Marius* pits the isolated aesthetic consciousness against the evanescent beauty of the natural world, welcoming the excessive self-consciousness earlier resisted by Wordsworth, Keats, Mill, and Arnold and thus inaugurating the decadent phase of Romanticism, characterized by keenness of apprehension but loss of faith in salvation through the synthesizing force of the imagination. *Marius* belongs to the same stylistic tradition as the mannered, confessional essays of Sir Thomas Browne and De Quincey; WP, in his turn, influenced all the prose of Yeats. The "marmoreal reverie" of *Marius,* like that of PER AMICA SILENTIA LUNAE and A VISION, is an example of the modernist attempt to unify artistic form and content. WP rejected the organic aesthetics of Coleridge and like Stevens was at pains to preserve the value of the individual sensibility, which, like art itself as described in "The School of Giorgione," strives always toward "pure perception." *Marius* is "a series of rituals" embodying various attitudes toward life, each giving way in succession to another, always evading any final truth, and remaining open to the experience of all forms of life. Thus while

Marius, having abandoned his childhood faith, seeks spiritual satisfaction first in a formal Epicureanism, then in Stoicism, and finally in Christianity, the informing vision of the novel is always essentially Epicurean. In Marius's death WP represents "the loss, not of a person, but of a major sensibility," such as received its ideal formulation in the "Conclusion."

> **1054** Bloom, Harold. "The Internalization of Quest Romance," ROMANTICISM AND CONSCIOUSNESS, ed by Harold Bloom (NY: Norton, 1970), pp. 3–24; rptd in Harold Bloom, THE RINGERS IN THE TOWER: STUDIES IN ROMANTIC TRADITION (Chicago & Lond: University of Chicago P, 1971), pp. 13–35.

[Bloom compares in passing Northop Frye as "romance theorist" to Ruskin, WP, and Yeats.]

> **1055** Bloom, Harold. "Late Victorian Poetry and Pater," YEATS (NY: Oxford UP, 1970), pp. 23–37.

WP is still "out of fashion, having been dismissed by T. S. Eliot to the large limbo inhabited by those who did not keep literature in its proper relation to Christian belief." But WP's vision had a highly individualistic quality of "aesthetic humanism." Yeats misrepresented WP when he accused him of having caused the disaster of "the Tragic Generation" (Johnson, Dowson, Wilde, and Yeats himself). Actually, the greatest threat posed by WP's aesthetic vision is the titanic effort that one must exert in order to sustain it. No poet of WP's time managed to maintain that level of "a quickened, multiplied consciousness" for very long, including Yeats himself.

The revolt of Yeats's generation of poets against Victorianism was a carry-over from the Pre-Raphaelites but with the added example of Baudelaire providing a picture of the stance of the poet quite different from that conceived by Rossetti or Morris.

WP, Lionel Johnson, and the young Yeats shared the belief that if the "ecstasy" could not be somehow sustained (e.g., in one sense, the loss of primal vision, "the 'sober coloring' given by the mature mind that has kept watch over human mortality"), life had failed. Johnson, Symons, Dowson quested for the privileged moment under WP's influence, just as Joyce, also under WP's influence, sought his early epiphanies. The young poets, along with Yeats, sought to achieve "pure poetry." The quest for the "privileged moment" was an attack on the Victorian obsession with recollections, reminiscences, instead of present "moments" and ecstasies. WP "had no myth of memory."

Yeats did WP a disservice by printing the *Mona Lisa* passage at the beginning of THE OXFORD BOOK OF MODERN VERSE. To Yeats, the passage suggested flux, the individual was nothing; WP, on the contrary, was interested "in the assertion of personality against the flux of sensations" in the passage. *Mona Lisa,* for WP, was "radiance" that "dazzles us amidst the flux."

WP is "the central link between nineteenth- and twentieth-century Romanticism in Britain and America," standing "mid-way between Wordsworth and his followers, and such major modernists as Yeats, Joyce, Pound, and Wallace Stevens." He bequeathed specifically to the "Tragic Generation" of poets, "first, an impossible aesthetic ideal; second, a stance against belief and against recollective spiritual nostalgia, whether personal or societal; third, a desperate trust in the flux of experience itself;. . .fourth, the final conviction that the fruit of experience is an intense consciousness or passion that cannot accomodate itself to experience again, that must seek its fulfillment in a dream that knows itself to be only a dream."

WP's vision is prolonged in the works of Stevens and the later Yeats.

1056 Bloom, Harold. "To Reason with a Later Reason: Romanticism and the Rational," MIDWAY, XI (Summer 1970), 97–112; rptd in Harold Bloom, THE RINGERS IN THE TOWER: STUDIES IN ROMANTIC TRADITION (Chicago: University of Chicago P, 1971), pp. 323–37.

WP's "privileged moment" is more "comprehensive" than those versions of the romantic epiphany conceived by Wordsworth, Joyce, Blake, Yeats, Stevens, Lawrence, and Hart Crane.

1057 Chapman, Raymond. FAITH AND REVOLT: STUDIES IN THE LITERARY INFLUENCE OF THE OXFORD MOVEMENT (Lond: Weidenfield & Nicolson, 1970), pp. 165, 166, 241, 277.

Marius the Epicurean was written partly about WP's own experience but also under the influence of Newman's CALLISTA. Later, WP steered his course far away from the great English Catholic. WP and his heroes always seem to come to wisdom through testing types of faith and also by using the evidence of their perceptions to define experience. WP evoked the sensory impressions of a past age and used them to teach his own age how to evaluate itself.

1058 Chapple, J. A. V. DOCUMENTARY AND IMAGINATIVE LITERATURE 1880–1920 (Lond: Blandford P; NY: Barnes & Noble, 1970), pp. 232–34, 238, 370.

In *Marius the Epicurean,* WP writes of the cost demanded of one who wishes to live the aesthetic existence in its fullness: " 'the sacrifice of a thousand possible sympathies.' " WP wanted his aestheticism to include ethics. On this matter, his position is similar to that of Henry James.

1059 Colby, Vineta. THE SINGULAR ANOMALY: WOMEN NOVELISTS OF THE NINETEENTH CENTURY (NY: New York UP; Lond: University of London P, 1970), pp. 131, 150, 239, 240, 247–48, 254, 257, 287, 293, 294.

Vernon Lee's description of WP's growth from aesthete to moralist and her criticism of his "carrying too much mental luggage" into his writing might be applied to herself as well. In his review of her JUVENILIA WP recognized both her social and her aesthetic consciousness. It is unlikely that the aesthete Walter Hamlin in her MISS BROWN was modelled after WP. [Also refers in passing to Mrs. Humphry Ward's friendship with WP and his finding her DAVID GRIEVE "mellower" than ROBERT ELSMERE.]

> **1060** Court, Franklin Edward. "Symmetry and Semantics: An Analysis of Walter Pater's Historical and Fictional Portraits," DISSERTATION ABSTRACTS INTERNATIONAL, XXX (1970), 4404A. Unpublished dissertation, Kent State University, 1969.

> **1061** Crinkley, Richmond. WALTER PATER: HUMANIST (Lexington: University of Kentucky P, 1970); rvd dissertation, "The Humanism of Walter Pater," University of Virginia, 1966.

Humanism is a modern idea suggesting "a combination of classical and Christian motifs." The humanist, like the Renaissance artists that WP admired, is forced to look beyond the Christian tradition to "an idealized time in which the soul lived in perfect harmony with the body." WP is himself a humanist because he reveals a "comprehensive sympathy," a "historical catholicity" that looks beyond any given period toward a synthesis of the Christian and the classical that includes in it the preservation of the best that has ever inspired mankind. WP's *Renaissance* begins in medieval-Christian France with overtones of paganism and ends with Winckelmann, who goes to Rome to see the pagan artifacts; *Marius the Epicurean* begins in a pagan world with Christian overtones and ends with a quasi-Christian death heavy with pagan suggestion. The circular journey is WP's also; he flirted equally throughout his life with the pagan-Christian synthesis. *Marius* is better viewed as WP's continuing effort to elucidate his "comprehensive sympathy" with both Christianity and paganism. *Marius,* accordingly, redefines WP's position in more understandable terms, an objective that was prompted in lieu of the initial misreading of *The Renaissance*. The philosophical argument of *The Renaissance* is continued and made fictionally explicit in *Marius*.

WP was a relativist influenced by Mill. WP was also obviously familiar with Renaissance mythology, and he dealt frequently with dualities of persons envisioned in terms of "creator" and "transmitter." One of his transmitter figures is appropriately characterized in "Diaphaneitè" as a "crystal man." The lives of the creators—saints, artists, and speculative thinkers—are crossed by the transmitters who, like crystals, assimilate, interpret, and redefine through the ages the works of the creators, the real culture-makers. The process can be termed the "great chain of transmission." WP used an "associative method" of writing: i.e., the ritualistic repetition of certain words and themes in the essays. The recurring theme of life and death, for example, is illustrative of WP's preoccupation with the human form and of an overriding awareness of physical beauty. Consequently, for WP the human form is viewed as an artifact through which the metaphysical or the divine becomes visible. This preoccupation explains WP's concern with detailed physical descriptions. Physical beauty is consonant with continuing life; hence, a beautiful corpse somehow symbolizes a continuing life in death. WP was, of course, extremely interested in beautiful, usually young, corpses. Other motifs that WP frequently used are the myth of Dionysus, the beauty of the dying form, and the sensual and harmonizing nature of religion as realized in ecclesiastical structures—the cathedrals of Chartres and Amiens, for example. The cathedral as symbol somehow parallels WP's own aesthetic humanism and is "relativistic." *Marius* incorporates the entire content of WP's final philosophical vision.

1062 Evans, Lawrence. "Introduction," LETTERS OF WALTER PATER, ed by Lawrence Evans (Oxford: Oxford UP, 1970), pp. xv–xliv; rvd dissertation, "Some Letters of Walter Pater," Harvard University, 1961.
Continued control of copyrights by the Pater sisters during the period of WP's greatest prestige discouraged efforts toward preserving his letters for publication. Aside from a group of letters to the editors of the CONTEMPORARY REVIEW, and a number of early letters to Alexander Macmillan, little remains of his literary business correspondence. The number of letters dating from 1885 to 1893 is out of proportion to the number covering the entire period from 1859 to 1885. Long personal letters occupied WP most frequently in the early 1880s; most later correspondence is comparatively insubstantial. WP seems to have been freely communicative only in conversation and only with younger, admiring friends such as Violet Paget [Vernon Lee], Mrs. Mark Pattison, William Sharp, F. W. Bussell, Lionel Johnson, and Arthur Symons. His letters also indicate that the section of the "Preface" to *The Renaissance* dealing with his aesthetic and critical theory may have been drawn from an early version of "The School of Giorgione" (1877). They also reveal that between the time of the publication of *The Renaissance* and the publication of *Marius the Epicurean,* WP made plans for a book of essays on Shakespeare and a collection of diverse essays to be entitled "Dionysus and Other Studies." Following publication of *Imaginary Portraits* in 1887, he projected a second such collection, to be called "Three Short Stories," continued work on *Gaston de Latour,* the second book of a proposed trilogy of which *Marius* was the first, and considered writing a work on religion analogous to Arnold's CULTURE AND ANARCHY. [A section of the "Introduction" is devoted to brief accounts of the lives of WP's more notable correspondents. The editorial problem of dating certain letters from the evidence of postmarks, internal information, handwriting characteristics, and letter paper and correspondence cards used by WP is also discussed.]

1063 Fish, Stanley. "Literature in the Reader: Affective Stylistics," NEW LITERARY HISTORY, II (1970), [123]–61.
WP's sentence from the "Conclusion" to *The Renaissance* (" 'that clear perpetual outline of face and limb is but an image of ours' ") initially leads the reader to some defined meaning until the meaning is suddenly impeded by the word *but.* WP intentionally frustrates the reader's desire to organize the particulars of many of his sentences.

1064 Fletcher, Ian. "Furtive Aesthete," NEW STATESMAN, nsLXXX (31 July 1970), 126–27.

Though always unwilling to give of himself, in his criticism WP's words and rhythms "enact his own, too private, visual" experience. His letters, feline and feminine, give nothing away and threaten to "mar" his "survival" as a critic and myth-maker. [Review of LETTERS, ed by Lawrence Evans (1970).]

1065 Fletcher, Ian. "Herbert Horne: The Earlier Phase," ENGLISH MISCELLANY, XXI (1970), 117–57.

Horne probably acquired his interest in the Renaissance through reading WP, but in his criticism he exchanged WP's subjective, intuitive approach for a close analysis of the aesthetic object within its historical context. Horne's introduction to NERO, like WP's essays on the Renaissance, is marked by "tension between the framework of fact and the individual response." WP resolved that tension "by turning away from history to fantasy in *Imaginary Portraits* and to the novel in *Marius the Epicurean*"; Horne, in LETTERS AND PAPERS OF ADAM LEGENDRE, "mythicized autobiography" in the manner of *Imaginary Portraits,* turned to "fantasy of a severer form" and finally "retreated into pure scholarship."

1066 Flora, Joseph M. WILLIAM ERNEST HENLEY (NY: Twayne [TEAS, 107], 1970), pp. 20, 21, 66, 79, 80, 90, 93, 95, 116, 117, 118.

Henley admired WP, referring to him as the "imperishable Mr. Pater," but his own prose was influenced mainly by Hazlitt. As an art critic he was opposed to the rhetorical criticism of WP and his confusion of the visual arts with literature.

1067 Frayne, John P. "Introduction," UNCOLLECTED PROSE BY W. B. YEATS, VOLUME I: FIRST REVIEWS AND ARTICLES, 1886–1896 (NY: Columbia UP, 1970), pp. 63–64.

Yeats found in WP's work "Platonic support for a belief in the Irish fairies." WP left his mark on THE SECRET ROSE. WP may also have influenced Yeats's own disdain for didactic art. But Yeats was too dogmatic to follow WP's plea for impressionism in criticism.

1068 Frazier, Sloane. "Two Pagan Studies: Pater's 'Denys l'Auxerrois' and 'Apollo in Picardy,' " FOLKLORE (Lond), LXXXI (1970), 280–85.

In "Denys l'Auxerrois" and "Apollo in Picardy" WP focuses attention on the irresolvable conflict between the pagan and Christian aspects of the life of the community and of the individual soul. Rather than limiting the extent of their influence, the spiritual isolation of Denys and Apollyon, which recalls that of Marius and of the heroes of *The Renaissance* and the other *Imaginary Portraits,* is what lends them their peculiar power to affect those about them; further, it contributes to the sense of timelessness in the two tales, the creation of which is WP's special achievement as a mythologist. Denys and Apollo fail to integrate their Christianity with the pagan impulses, in this case the Apollonian in its demonic aspect, that they have sought to hold at bay through the monastic life.

Both tales deal with the destruction of an "untenable stasis," the failure of a "monastic attempt to regularize nature" and of a "feudal attempt to regularize society"; WP seems to suggest that too complete an order has disorder as its necessary complement.

1069 Goff, Penrith. "Hugo von Hofmannsthal and Walter Pater," COMPARATIVE LITERATURE STUDIES, VII (1970), 1–11.

Hofmannsthal was influenced in his early career by various English aesthetes but was drawn most strongly to WP, sharing his views on the creative process and the psychology of the artist and his predominantly visual orientation toward the arts. He is closest to espousing WP's aesthetics in "Über moderne englische Malerei," in which he quotes WP's passage on the *Mona Lisa* and relates it to the attempts of the Pre-Raphaelites to capture the essence of beauty. In "Walter Pater" (DIE ZEIT, 1894) Hofmannsthal reviewed *The Renaissance, Marius the Epicurean,* and *Imaginary Portraits,* maintaining that WP's greatness as a critic was due to his imaginative insight into the mind of the artist and his appreciation of the aesthetic personality; yet he found WP's world view overly subjective and inadequate to the totality of life. Hofmannsthal was concerned with preserving a positive relationship between art and the public; his "Theodor von Hörmann," modelled after the *Imaginary Portraits,* presents the artist as removed from society not by disdain, as is WP's Watteau, but by a higher perception that allows him to achieve a true sincerity. "Shakespeares Könige und grosse Herren" is apparently an answer to "Shakespeare's English Kings," Hofmannsthal emphasizing the genuine nobility of Shakespeare's kings, where WP is most concerned with their eloquence. In "Unterhaltung über den Tasso von Goethe" Hofmannsthal's description of the princess of Goethe's play clearly recalls the sexless perfection of the Greek statues of "Winckelmann" and the transparent personality idealized in "Diaphaneitè"; Hofmannsthal's ideal personality, however, strives actively for perfection while WP's remains passive.

1070 Gordon, Jan B. "Wilde and Newman: The Confessional Mode," RENASCENCE, XXII:4 (Summer 1970), 183–91.

While influenced primarily by Newman, Wilde's DE PROFUNDIS derives from his reading of other writers in the confessional mode as well, including the WP of *The Renaissance* and *Imaginary Portraits,* the latter representing stylized versions of the Victorian religious crisis. Wilde's "parody" of the APOLOGIA PRO VITA SUA presages the modern tendency to value form above content in art, as does the typically *fin-de-siècle* religious conversion of WP's Marius (*Marius the Epicurean*), which "is as much 'aesthetic' as 'sincere.' "

1071 Hyde, H. Montgomery. THE OTHER LOVE: A HISTORICAL AND CONTEMPORARY SURVEY OF HOMOSEXUALITY IN BRITAIN (Lond: Heinemann, 1970); pub in the U.S. as THE LOVE THAT DARED NOT SPEAK ITS NAME: A CANDID HISTORY OF HOMOSEXUALITY IN BRITAIN (Bost: Little, Brown, 1970), p. 109.

[Classifies WP with the "allegedly homosexual Victorians": General Gordon, Cardinal Newman, and Frederic Leighton; and refers to A. C. Benson's discreet suggestions concerning "the secret of his life."]

1072 Jullian, Philippe. ESTHÈTES ET MAGICIENS: L'ART FIN DE SIÈCLE (Aesthetes and Magicians: The Art of the *Fin de siècle*) (Paris: Librairie académique Perrin, 1970), trans by Robert Baldick as DREAMERS OF DECADENCE: SYMBOLIST PAINTERS OF THE 1890'S (NY, Washington, Lond: Praeger, 1970), pp. 27, 40–41, 47, 71, 140, 142, 186, 187, 254, 255.

[Brief mention of the relative unimportance to the English aesthetic movement of the ideas of Ruskin, WP, and Wilde as compared to the visual images of the Pre-Raphaelites and Aubrey Beardsley, of the influence of WP's description of the *Mona Lisa* on the decadent conception of female beauty, and of Simeon Solomon's executing for WP some "frankly lascivious" drawings of boys.] [In French.]

1073 Monsman, Gerald C. "Old Mortality at Oxford," STUDIES IN PHILOLOGY, LXVII (July 1970), 359–89.

Information about WP's participation in the Old Mortality Society is scanty. While a member, he was quietly shaping the philosophy of beauty that startled the University in 1873. He carried the spirit of rationalism, characteristic of Old Mortality, to its logical conclusion regarding religion. His turning to art was, as in the cases of Ruskin and Arnold, an almost subconscious realization that reason alone was helpless to serve the cause of religion. For WP in 1864 the criterion of right conduct was not an external standard of morality but the comeliness of the individual life. He also posited a "subjective immortality" as the alternative to annihilation. Perhaps S. R. Brooke's objections to WP's idea of "subjective immortality" made WP wonder whether some better doctrine were not still possible and led to the explorations in *Marius the Epicurean*. WP's lecture at Old Mortality, "Diaphaneitè," is "an idealization of what is quintessentially human," whose hero is the "regenerative principle, the creative spark" in human culture.

1074 Munro, John M. THE DECADENT POETRY OF THE EIGHTEEN NINETIES (Beirut: American University of Beirut, 1970), pp. 16, 19–21, 23–24, 25, 30, 33, 59–60, 61, 72.

Arnold's insistence on the moral purpose of literature marked him as basically conservative, but in maintaining that literature could provide moral enlightenment without being didactic he prepared the way for the Epicureanism of WP. WP was the primary exponent of art for art's sake in England, arguing in the "Conclusion" to *The Renaissance* not, as it appears, for an irresponsible hedonism but for a higher morality based on widened sensibility and an aesthetic appreciation of "the fullness of the world." Wilde and others "either misunderstood or willfully ignored the fact that his theories were based on traditional ethics," but this misreading of WP was at least partly due to the lush quality of his prose, "which activates the libido rather than stimulates the brain." Furthermore, WP gave tacit sanction to sexual inversion by accepting Winckelmann's homosexual attachments as necessary to his realization of the Hellenic ideal, though he was later compelled to strengthen his moral stance by withdrawing the "Conclusion" from the second edition of *The Renaissance* and by redefining his own Epicureanism in his review of THE PICTURE OF DORIAN GRAY. The English Decadents generally failed to appreciate the importance of music to contemporary French aesthetics. They produced successful imitations of Verlaine's rhythms but were unable to grasp Mallarmé's subtler conception of music, which was close to that of WP as he described it in "The School of Giorgione."

> **1075** Peckham, Morse. VICTORIAN REVOLUTIONARIES: SPECULATIONS ON SOME HEROES OF A CULTURE CRISIS (NY: George Braziller, 1970), pp. 26, 217.

[Peckham refers to WP's dictum concerning the supreme position of music among the arts in discussing the Romantic view of music as productive of the most intense self-awareness and sees in WP's fiction examples of the Romantic use of illness as an occasion for "cognitive resynthesis."]

> **1076** Reade, Brian. "Introduction," SEXUAL HERETICS: MALE HOMO-SEXUALITY IN ENGLISH LITERATURE FROM 1850 TO 1900, ed by Brian Reade (Lond: Routledge & Kegan Paul, 1970; NY: Coward-McCann, 1971), pp. 18–20, 32, 35, 36.

Two initial influences behind *The Renaissance* were Otto Jahn's life of Winckelmann and the writing of Swinburne—its style and eroticism. Through Swinburne WP met Simeon Solomon, whose arrest in 1873 for homosexual activities may have been partly responsible for WP's withdrawing the "Conclusion" in the second edition of *The Renaissance*. The linking of the themes of male friendship and religious crisis in *Marius the Epicurean* is typical of the homosexual literature of the period, in which frustrated sexuality was sublimated and projected onto the spiritual plane. WP, however, found an outlet in aestheticism rather than religion. WP was probably influenced by the homoerotic poetry of William Cory's IONICA; he himself helped foster the same erotic strain in the writing of his apostles Mark André Raffalovich, A. C. Benson, and Richard Jackson.

> **1077** Ryals, Clyde de L. "Being and Doing in MANSFIELD PARK," ARCHIV FÜR DAS STUDIUM DER NEUEREN SPRACHEN UND LITERATUREN, CCVI (March 1970), 345–60.

In MANSFIELD PARK Jane Austen sets her heroine, Fanny Price, in opposition to the superficial values of nineteenth-century life, embodying in her the same virtues WP ascribed to Wordsworth, granting her an understanding of "those *manners* which are, in the deepest as in the simplest sense, *morals*," and making her one "whose ideal is rather in *being* than in *doing*."

> **1078** Scotto, Robert Michael. "Self-Portraits of the Apprentice Artist: Walter Pater's *Marius*, George Moore's CONFESSIONS, and James Joyce's

A PORTRAIT OF THE ARTIST," DISSERTATION ABSTRACTS INTERNA-
TIONAL, XXXI (1970), 2939A. Unpublished dissertation, City University of New York, 1970.

1079 Smith, Julia Amelia. "Narrative Art in Victorian Nonfiction:
Theory and Practice in Carlyle, Newman, and Pater," DISSERTATION
ABSTRACTS INTERNATIONAL, XXX (1970), 5421A. Unpublished disser-
tation, University of Texas (Austin), 1969.

1080 Stanford, Derek. "Introduction," "Walter Pater," "Oscar
Wilde," "John Addington Symonds," "Arthur Symons," "Havelock
Ellis," "Lionel Pigot Johnson," "Frederick Wedmore," CRITICS OF THE
'NINETIES, ed by Derek Stanford (Lond: John Baker; NY: Roy Pub-
lishers, 1970), pp. 11, 12, 15, 21, 37, 39–40, 41, 43, 62; 65–72; 79, 80–81,
82; 89, 93; 112, 114; 136; 194, 195; 231 respectively.
WP's "stringent over-writing" was the model for the prose style of the Nineties.
The Baudelairean and Pre-Raphaelite currents that converged in Swinburne run
through WP and Wilde to form the cultural staple of the period. WP's portrait of
Watteau indicates the same dandiacal concern with artifice as Beardsley's illustrations for "The Rape of the Lock" and Beerbohm's essay on George IV. The
"Conclusion" to *The Renaissance* was largely responsible for establishing the *fin
de siècle* "cult of mutability"; but though WP "talked about 'the living moment,' it
was generally the living moment in the past." Thus the chapter titled "Modernity"
from *Gaston de Latour* deals with the cultural milieu of sixteenth-century France,
and "Aesthetic Poetry" concentrates on the archaic aspect of Pre-Raphaelitism.
WP treats the contemporary moment only in "The Child in the House" and
"Emerald Uthwart." He attempted to evade comment on the questionable moral
stands of his disciples and was cautious in his praise of Symons's DAYS AND
NIGHTS and Moore's CONFESSIONS OF A YOUNG MAN. The heightened sense of
style and consciousness of sex that characterized the Nineties are combined in the
"Conclusion" in WP's formulation of "passion" as the key to "success in life."

WP's life was outwardly uneventful. He was often sketched by his contemporaries
and appears variously in Moore's CONFESSIONS, Frederick Wedmore's "The Vicar
of Pimlico," and Mallock's THE NEW REPUBLIC. Because of his presence at
Oxford, the continuing influence of *The Renaissance,* and the greatness of his
intellect relative to that of other writers of the period, "Pater *was* the 'nineties in a
way no other figure (save Beardsley) can lay claim to." His view of the human
condition, a projection of his own isolation, set the tone for the "largely elegiac
art" of his followers. With the Wilde scandal WP's reputation began the same
decline as those of the aesthetes in general; the progress of his eclipse is reflected in
Robert Ross's flippant review of A. C. Benson's WALTER PATER and Havelock
Ellis's assessment of him as "exquisite" but "scarcely great." T. S. Eliot's
"Arnold and Pater" (1930) marks the nadir of his reputation, which, however, has
grown again since the Second World War.

WP's thought is based on two main principles: "the relativity of all things, and the subjectivity of the artist and the receiver of his art." In insisting on the primacy of temperament in the determining of values, WP established for criticism a principle parallel to that which Kierkegaard established for philosophy; "Coleridge" may be compared with Kierkegaard's THE POINT OF VIEW IN MY WORK AS AN AUTHOR. WP aimed "to create incarnate points of view" in both his criticism and his fiction, as is evident in the narrator's personal slant on Watteau in "A Prince of Court Painters" and Gaston's impressions of Ronsard, Montaigne, and Giordano Bruno. The visual orientation of WP's imagination made possible a criticism by creation of images, and his notion that "all art constantly aspires towards the condition of music" fostered the development of a greater sensuousness in literary diction. Symons inherited something of the informing tone of WP's decadent sexuality, while Johnson carried on his decorous devotion to style. Wilde's "The Rise of Historical Criticism" may derive in part from WP's discussion of the relative spirit in "Coleridge"; but WP disassociated himself from Wilde's ethics in his review of THE PICTURE OF DORIAN GRAY. John Addington Symonds challenged WP's belief in the supremacy of formal over intellectual or spiritual values in art. Ellis's preface to AFFIRMATIONS echoes the subjectivism of WP's "Conclusion." Johnson worshipped WP's style and scholarship but balanced his critical skepticism with the logic of Newman. WP regarded appreciatively Wedmore's PASTORALS OF FRANCE. ["Walter Pater" includes a short summary of biographical material and the more significant critical studies appearing since 1945.]

1081 Stein, Richard L. "The Private Themes of Pater's *Renaissance*," in PSYCHOANALYSIS AND LITERARY PROCESS, ed by Frederick Crews (Cambridge: Winthrop Publishers, 1970), pp. 163–218.

"*The Renaissance* reads like a novel." Impressionism is the book's main topic. Impressionism also enables WP, in spite of historical accuracy, to depict the lives of the figures in *The Renaissance* as impressions. He seems to assert that impressionistic criticism has a degree of historical truth. The Giorgione essay is half theoretical, half historical. WP cannot seem to make up his mind about what the aesthetic critic is supposed to do. The Giorgione essay, added in the third edition, "alters the impact of the entire book." The essay is too defensive. WP treats history as a metaphor that "mirrors" man's growth; he attempts to personalize history. "Two Early French Stories" and "Joachim du Bellay," for example, "give the analogy of growth from 'ascesis' to 'decadence.' " The du Bellay essay reveals an oedipal conflict, with the son, du Bellay, revolting against the father over the favors of the "mother-tongue." Du Bellay, the "child of the times," has an infantile fear of castration. And he is sexually rebuffed by his parents for having lost control of his sphincter muscle. Here WP's "psychological retreat from genital ambition to a more primitive level of sexual pleasure"—anal eroticism—is dramatized. For he writes in the essay, " 'that the great whole—*le grand tout*—into which all other things pass and lose themselves, ought itself sometimes to perish and pass away.' " "Amis and Amile" is a homosexual romance that added to the book's lurid appearance when it appeared in 1877. For WP, heterosexual love was concomitant with failure. He consistently sought a return "to a world of self-gratification," that isolated state in which " 'experience is ringed round for each one of us by [a] thick wall of personality.' " History and criticism are for him symbolic of this retreat into the self. WP's interest in necrophilia, found in the Leonardo da Vinci essay, reappears in "The Child in the House." As a critic, WP sees himself as a woman administering maternal care and bestowing unrestrained love on historical father figures. The Michelangelo essay is a "rhetorical device for defining" WP's own image. Because maternal smiles " 'had *touched* his brain in childhood,' " da Vinci is to WP a symbol of masturbation; he represents "an attempt to recover the sense of being fondled" in childhood. Leonardo's treatment of art for art's sake stems from his "homosexual devotion to the youthful image of himself." Winckelmann, through his interest in Greek art, becomes in the essay on him an image of WP himself. He represents both father and son to WP; his contact with the past is described in sexual terms—the past " 'penetrates him.' "

1082 Thatcher, David S. NIETZSCHE IN ENGLAND, 1890–1914: THE GROWTH OF A REPUTATION (Toronto: University of Toronto P, 1970), pp. 4, 88, 127, 128–29, 131–168, 266, 271, 272, 273, 274.

Between 1905 and 1914 the introverted quietism of WP's influence in England was replaced by the hardness, extroversion, energy, and stridency of Nietzsche's influence. Yeats and Havelock Ellis understood, as Symons did not, how greatly WP and Nietzsche differed, their remarkable similarities notwithstanding. WP had not, for example, shaken himself free of Christianity—Nietzsche had. The cult of personality and artistic impressionism which his generation had inherited from WP, Yeats came to suspect, was too passive and feminine and resulted in instability and disaster. It was in opposition to WP that Nietzsche was seen as a "mighty liberating force, a force making for sincerity and valour, for a clean hard way of thinking." WP's aesthetics assumed an inevitable opposition between art and the way society was organized. Nietzsche, working in the tradition of Arnold, Ruskin, and Morris, broadened aesthetic enquiry, releasing it from the oppressively narrow confines which WP, and later Wilde, had imposed on it.

1083 Thornton, R. K. R. "Introduction," POETRY OF THE 'NINETIES, ed by R. K. R. Thornton (Harmondsworth, Middlesex: Penguin Books, 1970), pp. 27–31. [WP also mentioned in introductions to various sections of the anthology: "All the Arts," p. 38; "Poems and Ballads," pp. 185, 186; "The Roses Fall," p. 226.]

Despite his personal reserve, WP was, as Yeats attested in his introduction to THE OXFORD BOOK OF MODERN VERSE, a prime inspiration to the writers of the Nineties. His criticism was a source for three major features of English Decadent poetics: "the demand for freedom of choice in subject matter, the impressionistic style, and the notion of the musicality of verse." WP's statement that "nothing that has interested mankind can ever lose that interest," is consistent with the intellectual hedonism of the "Conclusion" to *The Renaissance,* which writers of the

Nineties construed as an argument for broadening the range of the subject matter of poetry, in the areas of both the "physical life" and the "inward world of thought and feeling," in WP's terms, the latter being the province of symbolism and of emergent psychoanalysis. WP agreed with Arnold that the aim of criticism was "to see the object as in itself it really is" but maintained in *The Renaissance* that this required knowing "one's own impression as it really is"; this and his statement that "the first condition of the poetic way of seeing and presenting things is particularization" were early formulations of the theory of literary impressionism. WP's belief that "all art constantly aspires towards the condition of music" was an important source for "the idea of the musicality of verse." [Thornton uses WP as a reference point for his discussion of the dominant aesthetics of the Nineties, pointing to echoes of WP's critical theories in the prose of Yeats, Symons, Le Gallienne, Dowson, and Pound and relating those theories to the work of various poets of the period.]

1084 Tirumalai, Candadai Krishnadesikan. "Continuity and Development in the Thought of Walter Pater," DISSERTATION ABSTRACTS INTERNATIONAL, XXX (1970), 3027A. Unpublished dissertation, University of Pennsylvania, 1969.

1085 Wellek, René. DISCRIMINATIONS: FURTHER CONCEPTS OF CRITICISM (New Haven & Lond: Yale UP, 1970), pp. 59, 158, 160, 166, 167, 172, 178, 180, 185, 253, 256, 258.

WP does not use the term *classicism* even when discussing Goethe and Winckelmann. WP recognized dialectical evolution as the essence of the historical method of criticism, even though he was not himself much of an historical critic. Vernon Lee's early writings are in the tradition of WP. For her, the work of art is an " 'existing, definite form,' " to be viewed as something quite different from the "fancy" or "association" it might attract. She too rejects the Ruskinian morality of art.

1971

1086 Abrams, M. H. NATURAL SUPERNATURALISM: TRADITION AND REVOLUTION IN ROMANTIC LITERATURE (NY: Norton, 1971), pp. 312, 419, 420.

The Victorian sense of alienation, which Carlyle views in PAST AND PRESENT as a result of economics supplanting human values, is equally evident in the "sensationalist solipsism" of the "Conclusion" to WP's *The Renaissance* and in the recurrent figure of the homeless traveler in the poetry of Arnold. Hopkins and Eliot reestablish a religious frame of reference for "the modern moment," the moment of intense consciousness, which for WP was purely sensational and secular.

1087 Albi, A. T. "The Aesthetic Experiment in the Work of Some Nineteenth-Century Writers: Tennyson, Gautier, Baudelaire, Pater, Huysmans, George Moore, Wilde." Unpublished dissertation, University of London, 1971.

[Listed in Lawrence F. McNamee, DISSERTATIONS IN ENGLISH AND AMERICAN LITERATURE, SUPP II (NY & Lond: Bowker, 1974).]

1088 "The Art of the High Wire: Pater in Letters," TIMES LITERARY SUPPLEMENT (Lond), 26 Feb 1971, pp. 229–31.

WP's letters are mainly examples of the formal, mannered response, typical of the nineteenth century, of a literary master to the homage of his admirers. His approach, however, though always guarded, varies with the recipients of the letters, ranging in character from Oscar Wilde and George Moore to Mrs. Humphry Ward. While much critical attention has been given to the dropping of the "Conclusion" from the second edition of *The Renaissance* and the supposed conversion of Marius (*Marius the Epicurean*) to Christianity, other indications, perhaps equally significant, of changes in WP's outlook have gone largely unnoticed owing to the unavailability of many of his early texts. Aside from the textual problems posed by WP's own endless revisions of his work, there is the problem too of Shadwell's handling of WP's literary remains and of his possibly being responsible for such revisions as those made in "Diaphaneitè" and "Emerald Uthwart" before their publication in *Miscellaneous Studies*. There are noticeable already, in his treatment of Wordsworth in the "Preface" to *The Renaissance* as well as in the "Wordsworth" essay itself, signs of resistance to an aesthetic credo that reduced man to the condition of a lonely witness of a passing spectacle. What he found very early in Wordsworth was, most importantly, that sense of community the development of which became so large a motive in *Marius* and which continued to preoccupy him in a work as late as "Emerald Uthwart." [Review of LETTERS, ed by Lawrence Evans (1970) and of the reprint of the 1910 edition of WP's works. See TIMES LITERARY SUPPLEMENT (Lond), 2 April 1971, for a response to this review from M. McCausland.]

1089 Beckson, Karl. "Yeats and the Rhymers' Club," YEATS STUDIES, I (1971), 20–41.

Yeats's friendships with Johnson and Symons led him to recognize WP's importance as one who could provide him with a philosophy of composition and of life. Yeats saw the asceticism beneath WP's aestheticism and looked to WP and Mallarmé as writers congenial to his own conviction that the burden art must carry is quasi-religious. As he attempted a Paterian fusion of form and feeling from his nationalist and occult interests, he remained ambivalent toward *l'art pour l'art* that others in the Rhymers' Club categorically rejected.

1090 Bloom, Harold. "Emerson: The Glory and the Sorrows of American Romanticism," VIRGINIA QUARTERLY REVIEW, XLVII (Autumn

1971), 546–63; rptd in ROMANTICISM: VISTAS, INSTANCES, CON-
TINUITIES, ed by David Thorburn and Geoffrey Hartman (Ithaca: Cornell
UP, 1973), pp. 155–73.
Emerson's prose is "as evasive and vacillating as Pater's or Yeats's," but it is
rhapsodic rather than hesitative. His Romanticism is characterized by a never-
resolved tension between "imaginative autonomy" and the force of "Necessity,"
unlike that of Blake, Shelley, Nietzsche, WP, Yeats, Thoreau, and Whitman,
which gives more positive emphasis to the realization of individual freedom.

1091 Bloom, Harold. "Epilogue: A New Romanticism? Another Decadence?" THE RINGERS IN THE TOWER: STUDIES IN ROMANTIC TRADI-
TION (Chicago: University of Chicago P, 1971), pp. 340, 345.
WP's definition of Romanticism as "the addition of strangeness to beauty,"
particularly as regards the quality of strangeness, may be applied to contemporary
mass culture, which recalls the decadence of the late nineteenth century. The
implied comparison in *Marius the Epicurean* between late Victorian England and
the Rome of Marcus Aurelius evidenced a sense of cultural decline analogous to
that felt by some late eighteenth-century Romantics and seemingly current again
today.

1092 Bloom, Harold. "Tennyson, Hallam, and Romantic Tradition,"
THE RINGERS IN THE TOWER: STUDIES IN ROMANTIC TRADITION
(Chicago: University of Chicago P, 1971), pp. 145–54.
WP was the only one of Tennyson's contemporaries to maintain an intense
Romantic faith in the autonomy of the imagination, a faith he helped foster in Yeats
and Wallace Stevens.

1093 Brake, L. R. "The Early Work of Walter Pater." Unpublished
dissertation, University of London, 1971.
[Listed in Lawrence F. McNamee, DISSERTATIONS IN ENGLISH AND AMERICAN
LITERATURE, SUPP II (NY & Lond: Bowker, 1974).]

1094 Bush, Douglas. MATTHEW ARNOLD: A SURVEY OF HIS POETRY
AND PROSE (NY: Collier; Lond: Collier-Macmillan, 1971), pp. 130–31.
WP and Oscar Wilde and their followers represent the first conspicuous perversion
of Arnold's influence. "Arnold's plea for disinterestedness, his warnings against
direct action, and his antipathy for Philistinism became a sanction for withdrawal
from the bourgeois world into the ivory tower of aestheticism," an attitude that
Arnold's concept of Hellenism reinforced.

1095 Dahlberg, Edward. THE CONFESSIONS OF EDWARD DAHLBERG
(NY: George Braziller, 1971), pp. 29, 58, 62, 113.
[Brief but extravagant praises of *Marius the Epicurean* and *Plato and Platonism*. Dahlberg claims to have turned to *Marius* to counteract his shock at
discovering a studied nakedness in LES FLEURS DU MAL.]

1096 Draffan, Robert A. " 'Without Taking Sides against Poetry': RICHARD II," ENGLISH (Lond), XX (Summer 1971), 39–44.
WP was an early promoter of the fallacy that Shakespeare's Richard II is the portrait of a hypersensitive poet-king.

1097 Fleishman, Avrom. THE ENGLISH HISTORICAL NOVEL: WALTER SCOTT TO VIRGINIA WOOLF (Baltimore: Johns Hopkins P, 1971), pp. 149–50, 164, 169–76.
Marius the Epicurean belongs to the class of late Victorian historical novel including Reade's THE CLOISTER AND THE HEARTH, Eliot's ROMOLA, and Shorthouse's JOHN INGLESANT, all of which take the form of the religious identity quest, are set in Italy, and evidence the Victorian interest in Italian culture. The characters in these novels, however, never fully enter into the historical setting but simply pass through it in pursuit of their identities. It is generally agreed that WP's skepticism made it impossible for him to find any final satisfaction in any one religious doctrine, but *Marius* is not merely a record of his sampling of various spiritual experiences for their own sake. Marius's personal quest represents a larger historical pattern and draws perhaps upon Hegel, but more upon the popular late Victorian notion that the development of the individual mind could be seen as reflecting the evolution of the race. WP's difficulty as historical novelist results from his attempting, as he did earlier in "Pico della Mirandola," to present alternately two contradictory concepts of history: the uniqueness of the particular age and the subordination of the age to the cyclical pattern of history. WP is most interested in tracing the growth of the individual mind; in presenting Marius as a universalized "man thinking," broadening out toward myth and the cyclical view of history, he destroys the concreteness and specificity necessary to successful historical fiction.

1098 Frean, R. G. "Pater and Martial," NOTES AND QUERIES, XVIII (Nov 1971), 418–19.
WP's description in *Marius the Epicurean* of the slaughter of the animals at the festival of Diana and the reference to the staging of the fall of Icarus are derived from Martial's DE SPECTACULIS and the description of the bejeweled Empress Faustina from his epigram to Mancinus. The depiction of Diana herself as "a famous courtesan" may have been influenced by a similar festival scene in Kingsley's HYPATIA. The treatment of Marius's fear of snakes is based partly on a personal aversion felt, according to Wright, by WP himself and partly on passages from Martial and W. A. Becker's GALLUS.

1099 Frean, R. G. "The Text of Pater's *Marius*—Some Problems (Synopsis)," AUSTRALASIAN UNIVERSITIES LANGUAGE AND LITERATURE ASSOCIATION: PROCEEDINGS AND PAPERS OF THE THIRTEENTH CONGRESS HELD AT MONASH UNIVERSITY 12–18 AUGUST 1970, ed by J. R. Ellis (Melbourne: AULLA and Monash University, 1971), pp. 150–51.

Phrases from such books as Boissier's LA RELIGION ROMAINE, Tylor's PRIMITIVE CULTURE, Beeker's GALLUS, Smith's various dictionaries of antiquities, and Northcote and Brownlow's ROMA SOTTEREANA appear in *Marius the Epicurean*. WP also used Jebb's Latin translation of Aristeides, Gataker's Latin translation of Marcus Aurelius, and the Bohn Classical Library's translation of Apuleius. The presence of Martial is evident in Chapter 14. The phrase "the defects of its qualities" (derived from Sir Joshua Reynolds) recurs in *Marius* and in other of WP's writings. Echoes of his reading for the essay on Rossetti also appear at several points in *Marius*. The posthumous fourth edition of *Marius* is the one that is most frequently reprinted. It differs from the earlier three that WP saw through the press. [A synopsis of an unpublished paper.]

1100 Harris, Wendell V. "Arnold, Pater, Wilde, and the Object as in Themselves They See It," STUDIES IN ENGLISH LITERATURE, XI (1971), 733–47.

Although it is generally recognized that the critical theories of WP and Wilde are, in their broadest outlines, variations on Arnold's doctrine of seeing "the object as in itself it really is," the underlying metaphysical grounds for WP's divergence from Arnold and for Wilde's divergence from both Arnold and WP are usually overlooked, as they are in T. S. Eliot's "Arnold and Pater," by scholars more often concerned with more obvious questions of aesthetics, morality, and religion. While arguing in "The Function of Criticism at the Present Time" the need of the critic to endeavor "to see the object as in itself it really is," Arnold fails to establish the possibility of so seeing it. The touchstones that he represents as objective standards by which the critic's vision is to be rectified are reflections of Arnold's own subjective preferences or, at best, a set of objects that the critic can know only mediatively by way of the effect they produce upon him. Arnold stops short of addressing the problem of how the critic can move beyond the limits of his individual impressions. In the "Preface" to *The Renaissance* WP recognizes the implications of Arnold's position when he points to the necessity of the critic's knowing his "impression as it really is," since, as he establishes in the "Conclusion," the object itself is discernible only through the medium of the individual personality. It being impossible thus for WP's critic to arrive at any totally objective, unqualified truth, he must confine himself instead to the delineation of the particular beauty of the given work of art. "Style" applies the same metaphysic to the act of creation, though here WP tends to identify truth with the artist's individual vision as derived from his unique "sense of fact" and beauty with the just accomodation of language to that individual vision. Just as the artist can come no closer to the object than the impression it makes upon him, so the critic has only his own impression of the artist's work to deal with and no means of comparing either the artist's work with the artist's impression or that impression with "the object as in itself it really is." Strongly informed by the currents of scientific empiricism, as Helen W. Young (WRITINGS OF WALTER PATER, 1933) has demonstrated, and uncompromising as it is in its separation of objective and subjective realities, WP's critical relativism prepares the ground for Wilde's complete reversal of Arnold's central critical doctrine. Insisting in "The Critic as Artist" on the necessary subjectivity of criticism, the critic's being limited, like the artist, to the knowledge of his own impressions, Wilde defines as the true aim of criticism seeing "the object as in itself it really is not." By reversing, in the larger context, Plato's theory of art as mere imitation and valuing art and criticism both according to the degree of their removal from primary experience, Wilde carries to its conclusion the relativism implied by Arnold and made explicit by WP. Though Wilde rejects the possibility of knowing the objects of experience, he sees the impressions conveyed by both artist and critic as an indication of the potential of the individual to move beyond individual consciousness and enter the larger consciousness of the race and thus returns to Arnold's position regarding the final importance of culture.

1101 Johnson, Lee McKay. "Art Criticism as a Genre of Literature: Baudelaire, Ruskin, and Pater," DISSERTATION ABSTRACTS INTERNATIONAL, XXXI (1971), 4123A. Unpublished dissertation, Stanford University, 1970.

1102 Kenner, Hugh. THE POUND ERA (Berkeley & Los Angeles: University of California P, 1971), pp. 28, 31–32, 51, 60, 69, 71–72, 74, 182, 365, 387, 388.

The post-Romantic literature of the solidly created object defined from a single point of view, which may be seen as culminating in WP's impenetrable passage on the *Mona Lisa,* gives way in Pound's CANTOS to the extra-temporal transparency of the vortex. WP's "aesthetic of glimpses" provided the formula for the minor impressionistic poetry of Symons and others of his generation, but it also helped prepare Pound and the Imagists for an appreciation of the fragmentary in art. The expatriate artists living in Paris during the 1920s were "the last Paterians"; Hemingway proposed to "be present always at the focus where the greatest number of vital forces unite in their purest energy." [Kenner echoes WP's description of the *Mona Lisa* in his own description of the Aphrodite of the CANTOS.]

1103 Mason, Mary. "Wordsworth and Pater's First Imaginary Portrait," HARVARD LIBRARY BULLETIN, XIX (April 1971), 194–203.

WP's feeling for the child in "The Child in the House" can be traced to Wordsworth. WP utilizes the Wordsworthian doctrine of metempsychosis in the portrait, and Florian's memories of childhood are similar to Wordsworth's "shadowy recollections." The major differences between WP's and Wordsworth's treatment of the child are to be found in Florian's awareness of his ability to cause pain; Wordsworth's child is a child of nature, but WP's Florian is born civilized. Art and not nature is Florian's only means of escape from the brutal realities of the universe, for art is the great humanizing force.

1104 McCausland, M. "Walter Pater," TIMES LITERARY SUPPLEMENT (Lond), 2 April 1971, pp. 396–97.

344

WP did not use scientific terms with narrow precision and did not vulgarize his scientific knowledge to instruct readers. Rather, he used scientific metaphors to relate terms in modern technical use to their previously less specific meaning. [Letter to the editor in answer to "The Art of the High Wire: Pater in Letters," a review of LETTERS, ed by Lawrence Evans (1970) in TIMES LITERARY SUPPLEMENT (Lond), 26 Feb 1971. The TIMES reviewer responds, noting WP's concern with wholeness of body and mind as encompassing not only the emotional but also the physical history of man and WP's uses of newer scientific terms as attempts to vulgarize them, since "vulgarization was one of the duties of the Victorian sage."]

1105 Milner, John. SYMBOLISTS AND DECADENTS (Lond: Studio Vista; NY: Dutton, 1971), pp. 10, 20.

WP's description of the *Mona Lisa* is a projection of his own personality and reflects the interest of the Symbolists and Decadents in capturing "the mental and spiritual experience of the individual." *The Renaissance* was influential in producing the decadent aestheticism of the 1890s.

1106 Monsman, Gerald. "Pater, Hopkins, and Fichte's Ideal Student," SOUTH ATLANTIC QUARTERLY, LXX (Summer 1971), 365–76.

The theological atmosphere at Oxford during the early 1860s is reflected in the rivalry between two Oxford essay societies, the Old Mortality and the Hexameron, representing respectively a liberal German idealism and a conservative Anglo-Catholicism. Evidence in the diaries and letters of members of the two groups, particularly of S. R. Brooke, a conservative member of the Old Mortality, and Henry Liddon, president of the Hexameron, indicates that the latter society was established in reaction to the former, its founders, including Hopkins, taking exception specifically to WP's reading of an essay on Fichte's ideal student before the Old Mortality on 20 Feb 1864. Judging from Brooke's comments on the reading and the text of Fichte's lecture THE NATURE OF THE SCHOLAR, WP's essay seems to have advocated a species of self-culture leading toward a progressive etherealization of the personality and ending in a "Subjective Immortality" which in effect denied belief in a future existence. Thus the essay was probably the original of "Diaphaneitè," dated July 1864, as actually presented to the Old Mortality, references to the sensitive issue of immortality being suppressed in the later version. "Since 'Diaphaneitè' can be regarded as the germination of Pater's critical, historical, and imaginary 'portraits' . . . we can now give 20 February 1864, as the date when Pater initiated the Aesthetic Movement." The controversy over WP's Old Mortality essay antedates by nine years the furor over *The Renaissance,* but WP's ideas of 1864 are substantially the same as those of the 1873 "Conclusion." Brooke's suggestion that self-culture implied hedonism anticipates Mallock's treatment of WP in THE NEW REPUBLIC, but both misconceive "the true aesthetic personality," which, as represented in the "portrait" of Michelangelo, assumes the character of a work of art, expanding into the *Zeitgeist* to embrace "all the interests and effects of a long history." WP's concept of the transmutation of personality belongs to the same tradition as Keat's doctrine of negative capability

WALTER PATER

and looks forward to Yeats's aspiration toward a depersonalized, aestheticized existence. Although Hopkins's initial reaction to WP and his conception of immortality were probably similar to and influenced by Brooke's, his own interests while at Oxford were perhaps more aesthetic than theological.

1107 Monsman, Gerald C. "Pater's Aesthetic Hero," UNIVERSITY OF TORONTO QUARTERLY, XL (Winter 1971), 136–51.

WP posited the aesthetic hero in "Diaphaneitè," gave self-culture a moral dimension, justified the contemplation of the beautiful, and laid the groundwork for his future development of religious hope in the hero who makes of his life a work of art. The creation of the aesthetic hero is an attempt to define the moral temperament possible in a rationalistic age, a postulation of a new variety of rationalistic unbelief, a new sort of religious phase which, minimally stated, is a form of hopeful agnosticism. In "Winckelmann" WP developed the aesthetic hero into a reconciler of opposites, a harmonizer. His most famous aesthete, Marius the Epicurean, is clearly an answer to religious skepticism: all of WP's heroes, historical and imaginary, are symbols of religious hope in skeptical ages. WP wrote *Marius the Epicurean* because the aesthetic life he sketched in his "Conclusion" to *The Renaissance* gave many, especially Wilde, the mistaken impression that he was sanctioning hedonism. The essential difference between Wilde's dandy, Dorian Gray, and WP's hero is in their characteristic temperamental variations: the emotional control of WP's aesthetic hero produces a balanced approach to self-culture; Wilde's hero is an emotionally uncontrolled decadent.

1108 Nelson, James G. THE EARLY NINETIES: A VIEW FROM THE BODLEY HEAD (Cambridge: Harvard UP, 1971), pp. 16, 20–21, 23, 49–50, 53, 56–57, 113–14, 123, 153, 170–74, 184, 188, 190, 210, 215, 236, 242, 243, 250, 260–61, 292–93, 339, 354.

Richard LeGallienne's reading of WP involved him in the aesthetic movement and influenced the critical principles he practiced as an author, critic, and reader for the Bodley Head. WP's recommendations of editions produced by Bibliothèque Elzévirienne may have helped prepare the way for the success of the Bodley Head books. With Wilde, Whistler, Rossetti, and the poets of the Nineties, WP was concerned with the total book as a work of art in which matter and form blended. WP's "Cupid and Psyche" in *Marius the Epicurean,* as well as the studies of Amis and Amile, Heloise and Abelard, and Aucassin and Nicolette, led to a vogue for that sort of story among the Bodley Head's writers.

1109 Reed, John R. "Mixing Memory and Desire in Late Victorian Literature," ENGLISH LITERATURE IN TRANSITION, XIV:1 (1971), 1–15.

Richard Le Gallienne and others wished to live in and by memory and to transform their arranged memories into hope, but few succeeded in converting past into future. To WP, for whom the Dionysian/Apollonian relationship was both historical and private, both privately and culturally memorable, an outcome, if not a solution, was in the deaths of his heroes. As the artist might die into art, the singer

346

become the song, so might each individual emulate Christ and WP's heroes, cancelled in the present between the forces of past pain and anticipated joy so that the permanent, timeless aesthetic work of art might live. WP offers an ambiguously personal and historical hope and an aesthetic for the future by commenting not on the present but on the past. The rebirth of aesthetic responsiveness, though cultural and historical, was contained within the world of the individual imagination. WP presents the designing power of memory as Le Gallienne's "impressionist of divine moments," a force blending the elegance of the past with the dream of the future through the medium of imagination. In contrast to Le Gallienne, WP offers not silent withdrawal but elegantly whispered participation, offers his own "interpretations" or "impressions" of existence through the medium of earlier interpreters who were already a part of the cultural memory that WP strove to enrich.

1110 Shuter, William. "History as Palingenesis in Pater and Hegel," PUBLICATIONS OF THE MODERN LANGUAGE ASSOCIATION, LXXXVI (May 1971), 411–21.

Despite the growing evidence of the influence of Hegel on WP, the dual nature of WP's mind, "hovering somewhere between theoretical criticism and imaginative creation," has made the extent and quality of that influence difficult to appreciate. Anthony Ward (WALTER PATER: THE IDEA IN NATURE, 1966) errs in concluding that this very ambivalence of temperament prevented WP's ever giving full imaginative assent to the Hegelian principle of order underlying the flux of experience; in truth, it was Hegel's own powerfully imaginative embodiments of his dialectical theory that allowed WP to resolve the conflict between his critical and his creative intelligence. In attempting to give form to his multidimensional sense of history, WP drew heavily upon Hegel's conception of the process of historical development, particularly as expressed imaginatively in his "imagery of cultural palingenesis." Hegel's influence is thus most clearly traceable in WP's own repeated use of images of rebirth. The first of these to appear in WP's work is the image of metempsychosis, the "fancy of the reminiscence of a forgotten knowledge" touched on in "Diaphaneitè" and apparently reflecting Hegel's view of the reembodiment of the spirit in recollection in THE PHENOMENOLOGY OF MIND. In *Plato and Platonism* again he treats Pythagoras' doctrine of the transmigration of souls in language strongly suggestive of Hegel. But metempsychosis figures most frequently in *The Renaissance*, where it serves in the essays on Winckelmann and Michelangelo, and most notably in the passage on the *Mona Lisa* in the essay on Leonardo, as a metaphor for historical recurrence. WP's conception of the Renaissance as a whole, as he presents it most succinctly in "Winckelmann," is developed upon the framework of Hegel's ÄSTHETIK. WP is much more directly indebted to Hegel in his repeated treatment of the death and rebirth of the pagan gods. In a note to the original version of "Winckelmann" WP quotes Hegel's description of the Greek gods of classical art. WP too sees in them "a premonition of the fleshless, consumptive

347

refinements" of the art of the Middle Ages, in which they are, as it were, reborn. This theme recurs in the essays on Pico della Mirandola and Raphael and is treated most fully in "Denys l'Auxerrois" and "Apollo in Picardy." For WP the revival of the pagan gods in the Middle Ages is both symbolic of the earliest stirrings of the Renaissance and, most characteristic of WP, of the idea that the Greeks themselves anticipated the medieval Christian sensibility. Thus, in "The Myth of Demeter and Persephone" he sees Demeter as a *mater dolorosa* and the death and resurrection of Persephone as prefiguring the death and resurrection of Christ; the entire myth serves to indicate that the Christian-romantic "worship of sorrow" was already present as an element of the Greek spirit. On the theoretical level the myth parallels Hegel's view of the Christian doctrine of the Resurrection. WP's use of the Demeter myth as an illustration of the dialectical process of history is an indication that he had fully assimilated Hegel's thought and no longer needed to draw upon his imagery. WP's principal source for the myth was the DEMETER UND Persephone of Ludwig Preller, who believed that in its earliest form it symbolized to the pre-Hellenic Greeks the wholly benign cycle of the vegetative life. This dialectical view of death became for WP emblematic of the entire Hegelian historical process as he treats it, most ambitiously, in *Marius the Epicurean*. The religion of Numa, treated in the opening chapter, is represented sentimentally and morally, in its feeling for nature and its reverence of the dead, as an anticipation of Christianity.

> **1111** Singh, Brijraj. "A Study of the Concepts of Art, Life and Morality in the Criticism of Five Writers from Pater to Yeats," DISSERTATION ABSTRACTS INTERNATIONAL, XXXII (1971), 3331A. Unpublished dissertation, Yale University, 1971.

> **1112** Small, I. C. "The Reputation of Walter Pater." Unpublished dissertation, University of Reading, 1971.

[Listed in Lawrence F. McNamee, DISSERTATIONS IN ENGLISH AND AMERICAN LITERATURE, SUPP II (NY & Lond: Bowker, 1974).]

> **1113** Stein, Richard Louis. "Art and Literature: Studies in John Ruskin, Dante Gabriel Rossetti, and Walter Pater," DISSERTATION ABSTRACTS INTERNATIONAL, XXXII (1971), 6634A. Unpublished dissertation, University of California (Berkeley), 1970.

> **1114** Sullivan, William H. "Four Early Studies from Pater's *The Renaissance:* The Aesthetics for a Humanist Myth," VICTORIAN NEWSLETTER, No. 40 (Fall 1971), pp. 1–7.

The true subject of all of WP's work is "the condition of modern man," which WP sees primarily in terms of the artist and, since he believes all modern art to be biographical, specifically in terms of himself. *The Renaissance* "defines the modern condition as existential freedom in a natural world of unceasing change," while *Marius the Epicurean* is an attempt to create an art form sufficient to that condition. WP believes the artist can prevail over the "conflict between metaphysical Christian myth and modern scientific epistemology" by the self-assertion of style, bringing, through the methods of impressionism, objective data into accord with his own subjectivity. Taken together "Winckelmann," "Poems by William Morris," "Leonardo da Vinci," and "Botticelli" comprise a statement on the need for "a humanist myth" and reveal the aesthetics of WP's humanism. "Winckelmann" treats the problem of the disunity of experience and the artist's role in resolving it by legitimatizing the subjective vision of outward reality and formulating a "humanist myth of the self." In the essay on Morris, the closing passage of which is the germ of the "Conclusion" to *The Renaissance,* WP aligns his aesthetics more closely with his world view by conceiving the forces of time and change as under the control of subjectivity. The "gemlike flame" is the supreme symbol of WP's aesthetics, relating the pyrophysical fusion of chemical elements to the production of an aesthetic unity, which is, however, transitory in a world where in time "each thing may become a symbol of every other thing." This idea is expanded in the passage on the *Mona Lisa,* in which all the diverse elements of "Leonardo" are transformed rhetorically into a symbol of "auto-salvation," encompassing all possible recombinations of physical reality and thus, like art itself, embodying all values. WP saw the Botticellian woman as representing, similarly, the generation of new value out of old myth, the rejection by Botticelli of Christian convention in favor of a subjective and more humane vision. For WP the melancholy of the Botticelli madonna indicates a half-realized desire to be free of "the myth that binds her to whatever is not human and of this world," while the Botticelli Venus, like the Mona Lisa, has become her own myth and is suddened by the burden of freedom that entails. Botticelli's humanism, the analogue of WP's own, reveals itself in the personalization of old myth, whereby the artist establishes unity of self, and the infusion of it with a new sympathy capable of answering to the awesome freedom of existential man.

1115 Wright, Samuel. "Richard Charles Jackson," ANTIGONISH REVIEW (Antigonish, Nova Scotia), I:iv (1971), 81–92.
Jackson met Thomas Wright in 1905, at the time the latter was preparing THE LIFE OF WALTER PATER. In the biography Wright represented as true Jackson's claim that he had been a close friend of WP and the model for Marius and reaffirmed his belief in Jackson's veracity in a 6 April 1907 letter to THE ACADEMY. Jackson may have met WP at St. Austin's Priory in New Kent Road, London, where Jackson was known and WP was supposed to have attended highly ritualistic Anglican services; but WP's known and intimate friends, such as Gosse, Shadwell, and F. W. Bussell, apparently had no knowledge of him, and Wright was chastised for his credulity by contemporary critics of the LIFE. Jackson himself complained in a 4 May 1907 letter to THE ACADEMY of not having been allowed to read the proofs of the book before its publication.

1972

1116 Bassett, Sharon. "Visionary Will: The Diaphanous Heroics of Walter Pater," DISSERTATION ABSTRACTS INTERNATIONAL, XXXIII (1972), 3630A. Unpublished dissertation, University of Rochester, 1972.

1117 Bergonzi, Bernard. T. S. ELIOT (NY: Macmillan [Masters of World Literature], 1972), pp. 59, 75.

In THE SACRED WOOD, writing under the influence of Remy de Gourmont, Eliot maintains that criticism must begin, as it does for WP and Symons, with personal impressions, but further that it must move beyond impressionism toward a final objectivity. Eliot's description of music hall comedienne Ethel Levey in a 1921 review in THE DIAL recalls WP's description of the *Mona Lisa* and is written from a similar aesthetic viewpoint.

1118 Bizot, Richard. "Pater's 'The Child in the House' in Perspective," in TOWARD THE MODERN: SOME PORTENTS OF THE "MOVEMENT," 1880–1920, ed by Nicholas Joost and Alvin Sullivan, pub as supplement to PAPERS ON LANGUAGE AND LITERATURE, VIII (Fall 1972), 79–95.

Critical interest in "The Child in the House" has centered variously on its form, its particular intrinsic literary merits, and its biographical implications. While most of WP's writings are to a degree autobiographical and when viewed chronologically may be seen to reflect successive stages of his intellectual development, the imaginary portraits are also, in a measure, retrospective and themselves survey the course of WP's thought leading up to the time of their composition. "The Child in the House" (1878) is the result of WP's reconsideration of the course of his "mental journey" from childhood to the late 1870s, and it seems to have been occasioned specifically by the adverse reaction to the publication of *The Renaissance*. Though the earliest reviews were generally favorable, later ones took WP to task for his stylistic excesses, his critical principles, and ultimately his moral stance, which within the Oxford community itself drew the disapprobation of John Wordsworth, the bishop of Oxford, and Benjamin Jowett. Despite his qualifying his metaphysical and ethical positions in "Wordsworth" and a number of other essays of the mid-1870s, the opposition continued and began to evidence a plainly sexual strain. WP's concern with such attacks as those of W. H. Mallock and W. J. Courthope on his sexual ambivalence was probably intensified by the earlier arrest for homosexuality of his friend Simeon Solomon. Though the changes in WP's thought following 1873 are neither insincere nor inconsistent with the overall evolution of his mind, his reexamination of his thinking was partly a response, nonetheless, to the pressure of public opinion. In "The Child in the House," less important for what it reveals of WP's childhood than of his mind at the time he wrote it, Florian's dominant sentiments of "beauty and pain" are reflections of the sentiment of beauty which produced the "Conclusion" to *The Renaissance* and of the sentiment of pain which brought WP after 1873 to stress the value of pity and sympathy. The superseding of the love of "visible beauty" by the "instinct of pity" is more clearly indicated in "An English Poet." As a corrective to Florian's, and his own, wearying "wanderings of spirit" in pursuit of intense experience, WP puts forward the principle of home and the "yearning toward home," which is the yearning, finally, toward the intellectual security of a past mental state. WP's account of Florian's efforts to reconcile the ideal with its sensible embodiment and his consequent turning back toward the comfort of Christianity can be identified with his own situation in the mid-1860s. Jan B. Gordon and Gerald C. Monsman assign a negative value to WP's homesickness as something to be overcome, but it is only by carefully and deliberately cultivating his sense of the past that WP is able to make the present understandable. The "Conclusion" to *The Renaissance* marked the most distant point of WP's spiritual wandering; having dropped the "Conclusion" from the second edition (1877), he was able to restore it to the third (1888) only after restoring to his own life, through the examination of his past that began with "The Child in the House" and ended with *Marius the Epicurean* (1885), the salutary principle of stability.

1119 Bridgewater, Patrick. NIETZSCHE IN ANGLOSAXONY: A STUDY OF NIETZSCHE'S IMPACT ON ENGLISH AND AMERICAN LITERATURE (Leicester: Leicester UP, 1972), pp. 21–29, 30, 36, 39, 41, 47, 175.
Because of close parallels between WP's "A Study of Dionysus" and Nietzsche's THE BIRTH OF TRAGEDY (1872), WP has frequently been seen "as a kind of proto-Nietzschean." Arthur Ransome ["Walter Pater," PORTRAITS AND SPECULATIONS (1913), q.v.] was the first critic to describe at length the affinities between them. Ransome's observations are particularly interesting because they deal mostly with *Plato and Platonism*, a work not normally seen as linking WP and Nietzsche. Though there are many parallels between them, neither should be viewed as an "influence" on the other. "It must be stressed. . .that there is no evidence that Pater was influenced by Nietzsche's analysis of the 'Apollonian-Dionysiac duality,' or indeed that he ever read THE BIRTH OF TRAGEDY." But both writers probably drew upon Karl Gottfried Müller's DIE DORIER (1824) for their conception of ancient Greece. [Remainder of study consists of an examination of the parallels and significant differences in their thought and their treatment of character types. There are also observations on similarities accounting for a mutual debt between WP's and Hopkins's aesthetics.]

1120 Court, Franklin E. "Pater and the Subject of Duality," ENGLISH LITERATURE IN TRANSITION, XV:1 (1972), 21–35.
WP's historical and imaginary portraits reflect his prolonged interest in dualities. The basis for his treatment of the idea is the contention that the individual acquires knowledge necessary to attain the "Ideal" from a companion figure—a double. WP states in *Plato and Platonism* that "true knowledge will be like the knowledge of a person." From *The Renaissance* (1873) to *Plato* (1893), he experiments with

four principal dualities: the gods in exile, the love duality, the teacher-student duality, and the great friendship. An examination of each of these dualities and some of the psychological, philosophical, and ethical implications behind them suggests that WP's world vision is hardly unique: Psychologically, his interest in dualities reflects his personal desire, one long recognized, for unity or the "higher synthesis"; philosophically, his interest reveals a debt to Renaissance Humanism; and ethically, his interest in dualities places him in a position of alliance with those Victorians who advocated the need for good example—"instruction in action—wisdom at work."

> **1121** Croft-Cooke, Rupert. THE UNRECORDED LIFE OF OSCAR WILDE (Lond & NY: W. H. Allen; David McKay, 1972), pp. 21–22, 50–52, 75, 110–11, 123, 128, 278.

Wilde had a "lifelong respect" for WP as "the greatest living prose-writer" and cared deeply for his prose. He could laugh at WP with Lionel Johnson but would not have been unkind to him. WP took more of an interest in the young Oscar Wilde than Ruskin did, but Wilde, as an undergraduate, was too much an extrovert to try to probe behind WP's nervous facade. WP wrote admiringly to Wilde about his reviews and short fiction, and Wilde wrote of the strange influence WP's *The Renaissance* had over his life. Despite the intense emotions "writing out of sight" necessary to the author of *Marius the Epicurean*, WP was a "dull stick, a shifty-eyed reticent scholar who had no words to waste on mere conversation."

> **1122** Downes, David Anthony. THE TEMPER OF VICTORIAN BELIEF: STUDIES IN THE RELIGIOUS NOVELS OF PATER, KINGSLEY, AND NEWMAN (NY: Twayne, 1972), pp. 1–47, 121, 125–32.

WP was one of many Victorians who tried to establish a new, viable view of Christianity. WP believed that the real import of metaphysical systems lay not in their professed relationship to any objective reality but rather in the "temper" of the historical period and of the particular mind that formulated them. This "relative spirit," which he defines in "Coleridge's Writings" and applies in his analysis of Coleridge's attempts to rationalize theology, WP applies as well in his attempt to clarify the relationship between theology and philosophy. Newman addressed the same question of the relationship between liberal knowledge and revealed religion in THE IDEA OF A UNIVERSITY, seeing the problem in a larger and truer perspective than WP. Seeing religions as the "natural products" of cultural evolution, WP valued them for what they reflected of the changing condition of humanity and maintained that from this humanistic standpoint pagan religion must be valued equally with Christianity. This is the basis for the argument of *Plato and Platonism*, the attempt to give new definition to Christianity by relating Christian to Greek humanism. WP looks on Plato as a forerunner of Christianity. WP sees the social organization prescribed in THE REPUBLIC as similar to a Christian monastic order and Platonic philosophy, like Christian spirituality, as aiming to satisfy man's whole nature, not merely his intellect. While he thus makes possible the reinfusion of Christianity with Greek humanism, it brings him no closer to a Christian belief in God.

WP's spiritual predicament, as it is most completely set forth in *Marius the Epicurean,* is better approached from the point of view of Newman and his formulation of the problem of belief in THE GRAMMAR OF ASSENT as a problem of reconciling notional assent to abstract theological truth and real assent to the separate order of religious truth. The significance of the pagan religion of Numa lies in its fostering the growth of conscience and in its intimation of immortality through its emphasis on the bonds between the living and the dead; all this is heightened in Marius's mind by an acute sense of evil, which intensifies his aspiration toward the priesthood. Marius's piety is overbalanced, however, by his susceptibility to the beauty of the physical world; yet brought to the verge of assenting to the Epicurean life that he finds idealized in Flavian and in Apuleius' story of Cupid and Psyche, he finds he cannot embrace it owing to the death of Flavian. Marius turns from Epicurus back toward Heraclitus, retracing the historic course of human thought in an attempt to provide a notional basis for a meaningful assent to what ultimately becomes a higher reality. But unable to give credence to his sense of "one universal life," he turns to Cyrenaicism, which allows in its theory of conduct for the incertitude of human knowledge on the notional level. Affirming as it does the supreme value of the real experience of the moment, WP's view of the Cyrenaic philosophy is in agreement with Newman's view of religion: for both WP and Newman, intuitive assent resulting from real experience precedes the notional acceptance of, in WP's case, abstract metaphysical formulae and, in Newman's, theology. While "New Cyrenaicism" represents WP's own intellectual position at the time of his writing the "Conclusion" to *The Renaissance,* he seeks now to spiritualize his former hedonism, tempering it by confronting it with the ethical concerns of Stoicism. By the end of Part Three Marius has virtually come to a Newmanian assent to the existence of the "unseen father" as inferred from both the real experience of the friendship of Flavian and Cornelius and from his abiding sense of "an unfailing companion, ever at his side." Part Three, then, culminates in Marius's making an act of faith. Marius having discovered God, Part Four deals with his discovery of the ideal spiritual society in what WP conceives to be the true Church, the Christian Church in the age of the Antonines, informed by "pagan charity" and "truer perhaps than she would ever be again." While WP sees two spiritual strains in Christianity, deriving from the ideas of both the suffering and the serene Christ, he prefers the humanism bred of the latter idea and ascendant in the Church at the time of the Antonines to the asceticism bred of the former, which dominated Christianity in earlier and later ages.

Marius's intellectual career is recapitulated in his graveyard conversation with the skeptical Lucian and in his reflecting in his diary on the inability of his old pagan religion to deal satisfactorily with death. He is brought thus to an overpowering sense of "the tears in things," and in the face of Marcus Aurelius's renewed persecution of the Christians he recognizes the necessity of meeting it with compassion and so is prepared for his final achievement of peace through martyrdom. Those who have found Marius's conversion incomplete have failed to consider properly the historical context, the particular humanistic Christian milieu within which it takes place, a supra-theological, existential phenomenon. WP was attempting to establish a religious belief within an historical, empirical context acceptable to the Victorian intellect. WP's great achievement is the combining of a never-abandoned skepticism and historical relativism with faith, seeing in the limited nature of the intellect itself a "pledge" of an ultra-rational dimension or order. Although the minds of Newman and WP are finally of two different orders, both men base their arguments for religious assent on the value of the individual consciousness in confronting the complexities of the world, making the will of God prevail by establishing the dignity of the human mind and will.

1123 Edel, Leon. HENRY JAMES, THE MASTER: 1901–1916 (Philadelphia: Lippincott, 1972), pp. 32, 115, 563.
[Edel refers to the reading of WP by Susan Shepherd Stringham in THE WINGS OF THE DOVE and compares briefly the statures of James and WP as literary figures.]

1124 Ellis, P. G. "The Development of T. S. Eliot's Historical Sense," REVIEW OF ENGLISH STUDIES, XXIII (1972), 291–301.
"Tradition and the Individual Talent" is generally seen as marking T. S. Eliot's break with the "imperfect critics" of the Eighties and Nineties; nevertheless the concept of tradition formulated in the first part of the essay, described as it is in terms of biological evolution and the Platonic process of becoming, looks back to the critical theories of WP, Wilde, and Yeats. In his rejection of the canons of late Victorian criticism Eliot follows the lead of Paul Elmer More, who in his essay "Criticism" describes the critics of the Nineties, the heirs of Arnold's theories of cultural "touchstones" and critical "disinterestedness," as languishing in a "sterile dream of the past." More may have had in mind something in the nature of the pastoral tableaux with which Wilde embellishes "The Critic as Artist" or WP's advocating, as in "Pico della Mirandola" and *Plato and Platonism,* the cultivation of an apparently static "historical sense." In working to establish a more dynamic theory of tradition More stands shy of WP and overlooks his more encompassing idea of "the secular process of the eternal mind," yet he accepts and adapts to his own purpose Wilde's view of "the collective life of the race," which he combines with Bergson's evolutionism to arrive at his own concept of the organic process by which present and future are created out of the operation of criticism upon the experience of the past. For More, as for Eliot, the past thus comes to represent an ever-evolving standard of taste rather than a collection of Arnoldian touchstones. WP too in "Winckelmann" goes beyond Arnold in viewing tradition as a series of cultural peaks, but as a series of such peaks "taking each from each the reflexion of a strange light," that light becoming the standard of orthodoxy against which the new work is judged. This same concern for the reconciling of the sense of cultural

permanence with the force of cultural change is central to the first part of "Tradition and the Individual Talent." Brought, apparently, by his reading of More to a reconsideration of Arnold and his critical heirs, even Eliot's touchings on tradition prior to the final formulation of "Tradition and the Individual Talent" contain phrases and ideas reminiscent of WP, Wilde, Yeats, and More himself: the terminology of biological evolution, which recalls WP's treatment of the theory of "development" in *Plato,* and the idea of the "general mind," which may owe something to Yeats's theory of the Great Memory but is more closely related to the belief in the "primitive power" or transhistorical value of words that WP attributes to Flavian in *Marius the Epicurean.* But Eliot's final concern is with the problem of standards necessary to relate the individual work to the tradition, the individual writer to a larger "comprehensive mind," such as that WP found symbolized in the *Mona Lisa.* In seeking to create, by the operation of criticism, an orderly tradition out of the flux of history, Eliot is closer in spirit to WP than to Arnold.

1125 Felstiner, John. THE LIES OF ART: MAX BEERBOHM'S PARODY AND CARICATURE (NY: Knopf, 1972), pp. 4, 19, 26, 58–59, 62, 66–71, 107.

The Renaissance "obscured the border between painting and prose"; though the art criticism of Beerbohm's WORDS FOR PICTURES was influenced by WP, Beerbohm kept that border clear. His essay on Hokusai's "Ho-Tei" parodies the "egotistic impressionism" of WP, Wilde, and Moore. In THE MIRROR OF THE PAST he makes satire of the contradiction between WP's professed hedonism and his retiring life.

1126 Fox, Steven James. "Art and Personality: Browning, Rossetti, Pater, Wilde and Yeats," DISSERTATION ABSTRACTS INTERNATIONAL, XXXIII (1972), 7510A. Unpublished dissertation, Yale University, 1972.

1127 Grant, Allan. A PREFACE TO COLERIDGE (NY: Scribner's Sons, 1972), pp. 180, 184.

WP's "Coleridge" faults the poet for pursuing an outmoded religious ideal rather than progressing toward the critical relativism and aesthetic detachment that form the basis of WP's own thought. "Coleridge, that is, failed to be Pater."

1128 Hill, John E. "Dialectical Aestheticism: Essays on the Criticism of Swinburne, Pater, Wilde, James, Shaw, and Yeats," DISSERTATION ABSTRACTS INTERNATIONAL, XXXIII (1972), 3648A. Unpublished dissertation, University of Virginia, 1972.

1129 Jeske, Robert Allen. "The Metal Honeysuckle: Walter Pater and the Spatial Dialectic," DISSERTATION ABSTRACTS INTERNATIONAL, XXXII (1972), 6980A. Unpublished dissertation, University of Wisconsin, 1972.

1130 Loeppert, Theodore Walter. "The Felt Perception of Order: Musicality in the Works of Carlyle, Tennyson, and Walter Pater," DISSERTA-

TION ABSTRACTS INTERNATIONAL, XXXII (1972), 4618A. Unpublished dissertation, Northwestern University, 1971.

1131 Lyons, Richard S. "The 'Complex, Many-Sided' Unity of *The Renaissance*," STUDIES IN ENGLISH LITERATURE, XII (1972), 765–81.
"The Renaissance is a work of aesthetics, based upon a concept of culture and animated by a moral idea. The unifying concept of *The Renaissance* is Pater's idea of *expression."* Expression can be defined as "the unique and untranslatable character of art that gives the critic his special function and art its privileged role in human life." As WP defines them in *The Renaissance,* the characteristics of "expression" are "uniqueness, unity, reduction to the moment." The work emphasizes the need for "being" rather than "doing," for the personality and freedom of the individual without appeals to things metaphysical, theological, and even moral. WP's most successful pages are those in which he accepts the contradictions and tensions of life, such as in the theme of the exile and the theme of childhood.

1132 McCraw, Harry Wells. "Walter Pater's 'Religious Phase': The Riddle of *Marius the Epicurean,"* SOUTHERN QUARTERLY, X (1972), 245–73.
WP hoped in writing *Marius the Epicurean* to capitalize on the vogue of religious fiction, as Newman had in LOSS AND GAIN. His audience was nonetheless limited to certain cognoscenti, *Marius* being weak as fiction and stylistically unsuited to popular consumption. Like Newman in APOLOGIA PRO VITA SUA, WP stood at the center of a moral-religious controversy and was working to revise popular opinion concerning the credo presented in the "Conclusion" to *The Renaissance.* WP may have had hidden revolutionary motives, but whatever his purpose in writing it, the "Conclusion" does have the ring of a manifesto. Though the "carpe diem" theme had fairly recently been sounded by Edward Fitzgerald in "The Rubaiyat of Omar Khayyam," WP's Epicureanism was couched in more solid philosophy and demanded a more serious hearing. Similarly, though Arnold had argued too for a return to the Hellenic spirit, WP's Hellenism was more thoroughgoing, not ballasted by the moral concerns of Arnold's Hebraism. *Marius* is a fictionalized autobiography designed to portray an intellectual progression via various inadequate philosophical positions toward what WP called in a letter to Vernon Lee the "sort of religious phase possible for the modern mind." In *Marius* WP succeeds in redefining the quality of his Epicureanism, but the success of his attempt to show that "religious phase" remains doubtful. Though WP shadows in ambiguity Marius's final spiritual state, the very failure of Cornelius, exemplar of Christianity, as a fictional creation, is itself an indication that WP was never able to reach beyond Epicureanism.

1133 McElderry, Bruce R., Jr. MAX BEERBOHM (NY: Twayne [TEAS, 111], 1972), pp. 21, 23, 26, 47, 73, 83–84, 123, 156.
Beerbohm admired the soundness of Symons's criticism but rejected his Pater-

ian belief that "Art matters more than life, and form in art more than meaning."
[Many incidental references to Beerbohm's fondness for WP.]

1134 Mittnight, Jeanne P. "Structural Methods in Walter Pater's *Marius the Epicurean.*" Unpublished dissertation, University of Chicago, 1972.
[Listed in Lawrence F. McNamee, DISSERTATIONS IN ENGLISH AND AMERICAN LITERATURE, SUPP II (NY & Lond: Bowker, 1974).]

1135 Monsman, Gerald C., and Samuel Wright. "Walter Pater: Style and Text," SOUTH ATLANTIC QUARTERLY, LXXI (Winter 1972), 106–23.
The textual history of the four versions of WP's "Conclusion" to *The Renaissance* gives us not merely a static view of WP's temperament but a "perspective" upon it. The steady increase in the length of WP's sentences during the first dozen years of his literary career may reflect a desire to tone down vivid images and startling ideas through circumlocution. His strategy of indirection provides him with a style expressive of feelings and attitudes difficult to suggest otherwise. At its best, the style has an atmospheric softness, a blending of forms and colors, characteristic of French impressionist painting. In the third edition of *The Renaissance* (1888) WP did not abandon his earlier iconoclasm but had learned discretion; the desire to avoid offense became one of WP's "touchstones" of moral conduct. His timidity in the revised "Conclusion" was born not from moral cowardice but from the moral conviction that violation of traditional standards is an offense against the mystical body of humanity. For WP's entire mature life the harmonizing of words and ideas increased and the dissonance was refined, absorbed through the distance of the years.

1136 Nye, Francis Leonard. "Walter Pater's Early Hellenism," DISSERTATION ABSTRACTS INTERNATIONAL, XXXII (1972), 6994A. Unpublished dissertation, University of North Carolina, 1971.

1137 Pine, Richard. "The Personality of Wilde," DUBLIN MAGAZINE, IX (Winter/Spring 1971–2), 52–59.
At Oxford Wilde sat, quite literally, at the feet of WP, whose great masterpieces of idolatry, his passion for the pagan and medieval ways of life, brought the Greek ideas already in Wilde's mind, due to the influence of Mahaffy, to a new state in which he steadily and unhesitatingly sought "the palpitating centre of romance."

1138 Schuetz, Lawrence F. "Pater's *Marius:* The Temple of God and the Palace of Art," ENGLISH LITERATURE IN TRANSITION, XV (1972), 1–19.
The Dionysius/Apollo myth established the broad cultural-historical background of *Marius the Epicurean,* but the novel's basic structural pattern lies in Marius's reenactment of the Cupid/Psyche myth, which WP treats as a moral and aesthetic allegory. The development of the aesthetic *anima,* which "treats life in the spirit of art," is WP's central concern in the novel. Psyche's quest for Cupid illustrates the

357

distinction not between spirit and matter but between their perfect organic functioning and human imperfection: it is the quest of the finite for the infinite ideal. Marius sees in Christianity and its ideal a transformation of the Palace of Art into the Temple of God and in "the touching image of Jesus" the essential unifying principle of a total *anima* capable of union with the Ideal. His death is thus the "sleep" of Psyche, the culmination of the quest of the individual soul.

1139 Small, I. C. "Plato and Pater: Fin-de-siècle Aesthetics, BRITISH JOURNAL OF AESTHETICS, XII (1972), 369–83.
Plato and Platonism is important both as a focus for the major trends in later Victorian Platonic criticism and as a final light on WP's continuing effort to define the relationship between ethics and aesthetics. It represents too an attempt by WP to retrieve his Oxford reputation by clarifying once more his position with regard to aestheticism; further, it seems to evidence something of the antagonism rumored to have existed between himself and Jowett during the Seventies and Eighties. The basis for such a conflict, at the philosophical level, is apparent in the comparison of WP's *Plato* with Jowett's introduction to his THE REPUBLIC OF PLATO. For Jowett Plato provided a substitute for Christian orthodoxy, and he tended to see Plato's aesthetics in orthodox terms: while arguing, along aesthetic lines, that THE DIALOGUES should be approached as literature, that they discriminated, as all art, only particular manifestations of beauty in life, he went on to maintain that absolute values could nevertheless be drawn from them. Jowett's emphasis on the importance of dialectic, the "poetic" and never fully formulated quality of Platonic ideas, determined the course of English Platonic criticism in the Eighties and early Nineties, though the work of German critics to place Plato in more solidly historical context in relationship to Heraclitus and other pre-Socratic philosophers gained recognition in England in the Nineties. WP turned both critical currents to his own purposes in *Plato,* using his own concept of historical recurrence in arguing Plato's modernity and going on in the last chapter to transform Plato as artist into Plato as spokesman for art for art's sake. While aware of the importance of seeing THE DIALOGUES in historical context, he was concerned mainly with relating the efforts of Plato and some pre-Socratics to the efforts of certain nineteenth-century thinkers toward establishing the value of the finite world, implying form and thus implying art, as against the formlessness of the infinite. Where Jowett maintained that language was ultimately inadequate to the expression of "ideal truth," WP held that any apparent inadequacy of language was merely a failure in style. WP's view of Plato as stylist parallels his earlier view of Rossetti. For WP the Platonic ideas represent finally an artist's formulation of his own relationship to a world of relative knowledge. "The Genius of Plato" and "The Doctrine of Plato" comprise an account of a solution to the problem of the relativity of knowledge corresponding to that presented in *Marius the Epicurean* and *Gaston de Latour.* WP approached Plato, then, primarily from the viewpoint of Heraclitus, examining the effects of Heraclitean thought in THE DIALOGUES but determining finally that Plato's triumph was the result of his reconciling the

Parmenidean idea of the Absolute with the evidence of the senses. *Plato* is in part a veiled account of a conflict of late Victorian moral values, but more specifically an account of WP's own reconciliation of aesthetics, and aestheticism itself, with ethics.

1140 Stavros, George. "Pater, Wilde, and the Victorian Critics of the Romantics," DISSERTATION ABSTRACTS INTERNATIONAL, XXXIII (1972), 2344A. Unpublished dissertation, University of Wisconsin, 1972.

1141 Stone, Donald David. NOVELISTS IN A CHANGING WORLD: MEREDITH, JAMES, AND THE TRANSFORMATION OF ENGLISH FICTION IN THE 1880's (Cambridge: Harvard UP, 1972), pp. 4, 17–19, 20–24, 28, 36–48, 50, 57–60, 62–63, 80–82, 94, 176, 187, 192, 201, 207, 222, 238–39, 243, 292–93, 298, 309, 311, 320, 327, 333, 334, 350n 47.

In the last two decades of the nineteenth century Nietzsche and WP testify to the presence of powerful and subversive elements in European thought: the death of God, the relativist spirit, and the preeminence of the individual. The change in intellectual climate is radical: Newman's "tradition" and Mill's "liberty" became, for WP, merely aesthetic and subjective attitudes. Nietzsche and WP emphasized perfecting one's self rather than one's world and saw in art the one redeeming quality of history. For Nietzsche, art is a tonic; for WP, it is an opiate. Both proclaim freedom of the will, Nietzsche stressing the will as creative agent, WP stressing the will as vision.

The aesthetic disturbance of the Nineties might be attributed to some Americans and Irishmen under the influence of Emerson and WP: Wilde, Moore, Shaw, Whistler, and James. Although James parodies WP's characters, there are sufficient affinities between the two. James argued against theorizing as WP did: neither the artist nor the philosopher should be hemmed in by absolutes. In the manner of WP James was a Romantic who argued the need for liberating the will from all external claims for the sake of feeling aesthetic sensations. James's major difference from WP lay in his ability to convert subjective impressions into literature, to relate his aesthetic consciousness of "life" to the enduring realm of "art." James's importance for the modern novel lies in the way he successfully transformed the message of the "Conclusion" to *The Renaissance* from an injunction to passive observers to an appeal for the active production of fiction. He transformed WP's dictum that the world exists at best as an aesthetic spectacle, not something the individual can or should actively exert himself in, into a formula for both the author of novels and the hero of fiction. And it is ironic that WP's appeal to court as many impressions as possible in order to keep from ending up the prisoner of one's dream of a world should have been transformed into the limiting and singular possibility that James made of it.

1142 Walsh, John J. "The Pattern of the Renaissance in the Works of Walter Pater and John Addington Symonds," DISSERTATION ABSTRACTS

INTERNATIONAL, XXXIII (1972), 7700A. Unpublished dissertation, New York University, 1972.

1143 Wollheim, Richard. "Introduction," THE IMAGE IN FORM: SELECTED WRITINGS OF ADRIAN STOKES (Lond: Penguin, 1972); rptd as "Adrian Stokes," in ON ART AND THE MIND: ESSAYS AND LECTURES, by Richard Wollheim (Lond: Allen Lane, 1973), pp. 315–35.

In INSIDE OUT, Adrian Stokes gives us a description of his childhood in which he retains throughout the perspective of the child. His passages describing his childhood are the equal of WP's "The Child in the House." Stokes has much in common with WP and Ruskin. Stokes read WP when he first began to visit Italy. He was " 'bowled over' " by WP's works. His prose style reveals the influence of WP: the same cadences, the same "certain precision in the use of language."

1144 Woolf, James D. SIR EDMUND GOSSE (NY: Twayne [TEAS, 117], 1972), pp. 23, 27, 30, 35, 44, 95, 114, 125, 128–30, 138, 140, 144, 147.

WP found in Gosse's poetry an Epicurean appreciation of man in relationship to nature. Gosse believed WP's "elevated hedonism" represented the culmination of the philosophy and critical spirit of English romanticism. [Refers to mutual criticism of Gosse and WP and includes a summary of Gosse's essay on WP in CRITICAL KIT-KATS (orig pub 1894).]

1145 Yeats, William Butler. MEMOIRS, ed by Denis Donoghue (Lond: Macmillan, 1972), pp. 22, 35, 36, 38, 42, 86, 95, 96, 97, 159.

Wilde imitated WP's manner of speech as well as his prose style; he praised *The Renaissance* as "the golden book." Lionel Johnson subscribed to WP's view of life as ritual, but in his absolute devotion to books took too literally "the Epilogue" to *The Renaissance* and the chapter of *Marius the Epicurean* entitled, "Animula Vagula"; like Sebastian van Storck, he refused to have his portrait made. Diana Vernon [Olivia Shakespeare] was a Paterian and an admirer of Watteau. Henley "never spoke of Pater and probably disliked him." Symons's literary impressionism perhaps derived from "Animula Vagula"; of WP's disciples he was closest to realizing the ideal of temperance. [A portion orig pub as section twenty-seven of ESTRANGEMENT (1926)].

1973

1146 Altick, Richard D. VICTORIAN PEOPLE AND IDEAS: A COMPANION FOR THE MODERN READER OF VICTORIAN LITERATURE (NY: Norton, 1973), pp. 105, 292–93, 295, 297.

With many Victorians, the "psychic need for . . . resting places in the past over-ruled their realism." WP and Symonds, for instance, found their refuge in the

Italian Renaissance. WP's "hedonism" was almost puritanical; he consistently "stressed the necessity of unremitting discrimination in one's choice of pleasures." But few understood what he meant. To his disciples, the only reality worth pursuing was individual human experience—"the detached 'spots of time.' " To some, it was a " 'fascination with corruption.' "

1147 Aubert, Jacques. INTRODUCTION A L'ESTHETIQUE DE JAMES JOYCE (Introduction to the Aesthetics of James Joyce) (Paris, Montreal, Brussels: Didier, 1973), pp. 20, 21, 25, 102, 176.
The chivalric nature of some of WP's heroes and the exotic atmosphere of his settings had a slight influence on Joyce. [In French.]

1148 Bassett, Sharon. "Pater and Freud on Leonardo DaVinci: Two Views of the Hero of Art," LITERATURE AND PSYCHOLOGY, XXIII:1 (1973), 21–26.
Both WP and Freud see Leonardo in terms of the mythical hero. WP assimilated Burckhardt's Renaissance historiography and converted his "idea that temperaments shape history" into the "idea that temperaments replace history." Freud adopts a less aesthetic approach, but both emphasize the importance of Leonardo's childhood and see in his life an example of "the struggle against aggression." Because he saw all knowledge as having its origin in perception, "Leonardo may be taken as the type upon which the attentive and unjudging critic of art and the comprehendingly dispassionate analyst rest." The treatments of Leonardo by WP and Freud, based on the legend established by Vasari, offer an alternative to the aggressive ideals of "striving, seeking, finding and not yielding" popularly endorsed in the late nineteenth century, reducing the anxieties of the quest for personal identity through an "understanding of the possibilities of the androgynous self" as expressed in Leonardo's portraits of women. To WP and Freud Leonardo represents "the hero of art," who is also the "archetypally fatherless man" and whose heroism consists in meeting the problem of his orphanhood by transforming artistically "the longing for childhood consolations" into "the enigma and ambiguity of the Mona Lisa's smile," in contrast to the attempts of Carlyle, Newman, and Hardy, for example, to maintain a more traditional anthropomorphic world view by creating emotionally satisfying substitutes for "fatherly authority." WP prefigures the approach of Freudian psychology in treating "the Mona Lisa as an emblem for the textured dream of childhood" and as a symbol for the gaining of "mastery over conventional anthropocentric panic" felt by most Victorians in face of Darwinian nature. He also shares the view of Freudian aesthetics that art lends value to fleeting and fragmentary life and provides, as he suggests in "Winckelmann," a sense of freedom capable of counteracting the pressures of necessity.

1149 Bizot, Richard. "Pater in Transition," PHILOLOGICAL QUARTERLY, LII (Jan 1973), 129–41.
WP borrows for use in *Plato and Platonism* (1893) a passage from the earlier "The Marbles of Aegina" (1880), and the character of the revisions the passage under-

goes indicates changes in his basic attitudes and beliefs. The passage deals with the conflict between the "centrifugal" and the "centripetal" tendencies at work in the Greek mind, as in the mind of WP himself throughout his career. These may be identified roughly with the aesthetic and the religious approaches to life, the rivalry between which he had treated variously in "Coleridge's Writings," "Winckelmann," "Notes on Leonardo da Vinci," "The Poetry of Michelangelo," "Pico della Mirandola," "Romanticism," *Marius the Epicurean,* and *Gaston da Latour.* In the 1893 version WP treats the centrifugal tendency more and the centripetal tendency less critically than he had in 1880, and in the course of his work as a whole there is a gradual shift in direction away from a predominantly aesthetic toward a more ascetic position. This change is reflected ultimately in WP's critics. From the time of "Coleridge's Writings" (1866) to the publication of *The Renaissance* (1873), WP's "application of the relative spirit to moral and religious questions" reduced ethics to a matter of taste and absorbed it into aesthetics. In "On Wordsworth" (1874), however, he allows art a role in the development of the moral sense and grants it power to promote sympathy, thus removing it from a purely subjective context. Charles Lamb's "boundless sympathy" comes to indicate a broader perfection than that Winckelmann attained by means of his "supreme, artistic view of life." The recognition of objective aesthetic standards in "The School of Giorgione" likewise signalled a movement toward the acknowledgement of objective ethical standards in *Marius.* To the end WP remained committed to an aesthetic ethic, but as his attitude toward art had gained in breadth so had his ethics. A more accurate appreciation of the stages of WP's development is necessary to correct the distorted images of him rendered by such critics as T. S. Eliot and Graham Hough.

1150 Brown, Terence. "Walter Pater, Louis MacNeice and the Privileged Moment," HERMATHENA, CXIV (1973), 31–42.

Though long dismissed as dated and irrelevant to the study of modern literature, the work of WP evidences a distinctly modern sensibility, which is apparent when WP's basic philosophical attitudes are compared with those of the "quintessentially twentieth-century" Louis MacNeice. Many of MacNeice's poems, placing the passive self amidst a swarm of unrelated sense impressions, represent the same solipsism in the face of a world in flux as the "Conclusion" to *The Renaissance.* Both WP and MacNeice reject the stability offered by belief in the absolute: WP attacks Platonic idealism in "Coleridge" and, most forcefully, in *Plato and Platonism,* censuring Plato and Parmenides in light of the dynamic metaphysics of Heraclitus; MacNeice denies static monism in various poems, while "verbs of vigorous action" throughout his poetry convey his sense of the Heraclitean flux. For MacNeice in "The trolls" and "Troll's courtship" as for WP in "Sebastian van Storck," the desire for the absolute is the negation of life. Yet both understand that the flux threatens finally to annihilate personal identity, and both affirm the redemptive potential of the "privileged moment," reinforcing personality by confirming its vital relationship to the material world, WP in *Marius the Epicurean* and the "Conclusion" and MacNeice in such poems as "Snow" and "Vistas" and passages from THE STRINGS ARE FALSE. For both, the "privileged moment" fulfills the desire of the intellect to feel itself fully alive and allows the individual to escape from solitude by entering into the life of the cosmos.

1151 Burstein, Janet. "The Journey Beyond Myth in JUDE THE OBSCURE," TEXAS STUDIES IN LITERATURE AND LANGUAGE, XV (Fall 1973), 499–515.

Hardy represents Jude as WP represents the isolated self in his "Conclusion" to *The Renaissance*. While some celebrated "one's own dream of a world," WP and others associated development of consciousness and personal vision with the isolation and imprisonment of self. Regretting that modern man had outgrown the Hellenic ideal of unity with self, physical nature, and the outward world, WP stressed the need to recover a mythic mode of perception. Although WP's reflection on "sympathy" between outward nature and the moods of men beguiled many Victorians, Hardy was ambivalent about myth. The wistfulness of WP's work may derive from his regret that such imaginative power was lost to modern man. In TESS OF THE D'URBERVILLES and THE MAYOR OF CASTERBRIDGE Hardy also appears to betray authorial regret for the loss of myth as a satisfactory way of knowing; but in JUDE THE OBSCURE the loss is faced and accepted. Jude, like Marius (*Marius the Epicurean*), cannot "act, mingle, read his time right or guide it"; he moves beyond Marius by asserting that the inadequacy of "social formulas" affects him and that "insight" must relate those formulas to the facts of personal experience.

1152 Caserio, Robert L., Jr. "Plot, Story and the Novel: Problematic Aspects of English and American Narrative from Dickens to Gertrude Stein," DISSERTATION ABSTRACTS INTERNATIONAL, XXXIV (1973), 2613A. Unpublished dissertation, Yale University, 1973.

[Section on WP's *The Renaissance*.]

1153 Cavaliero, Glen. JOHN COWPER POWYS: NOVELIST (Lond: Oxford UP, 1973), pp. vii, 91.

WP was one of many diverse influences on Powys. Powys resembles WP in his blending of natural observation with its aesthetic distillate.

1154 Court, Franklin E. "Virtue Sought 'As a Hunter His Sustenance': Pater's 'Amoral Aesthetic,' " JOURNAL OF ENGLISH LITERARY HISTORY, XL (Winter 1973), 549–63.

WP's concept of virtue serves as a central theme unifying his early essays— "Diaphaneitè" and "Wordsworth" particularly—with *The Renaissance,* his critical defense of that age, his imaginary portraits, including *Marius the Epicurean,* and the late volume on Plato. In *Plato and Platonism* (1893), WP discusses at length the relationship between virtue and the "relative spirit," cautioning that virtue must be understood as a force that is at all times expressly " 'relative' " to

" 'every several act, and to each period of life, in regard to each thing we have to do, in each one of us.' " A virtuous man is one who knows "who he is," who realizes what he does best, and then does it as completely and as intensely as possible. The system of discipline and obedience advocated by the Spartans possesses the quality of ascetic contentment. The measure of a Spartan's virtue then depended on how well he fulfilled this ascetic ideal. In "Diaphaneitè" (1864), WP refers to a pattern of life that he terms the "Imitatio Christi"; to live this way is to have the fair-mindedness to see a thing as it really is and to judge it according to that which it, in its own unique context, does best. The "eternal worth" of a man, he argues again in "Wordsworth" (1874), must be judged with such forbearance. For WP, Wordsworth's life is characterized by " 'inborn religious placidity.' " Wordsworth is a man of virtue because he realizes and admits the need for "simplicity" in his life and is able to communicate that feeling to others. Coleridge denied the " 'critical spirit' " that was an inherent part of his personality to cling stubbornly to outdated notions of the "absolute." He sacrificed the continuity of character congruent with a virtuous life. WP's concept of virtue reappears in *Marius* (1885) and "Emerald Uthwart" (1892) and is an aesthetic axiom by which the magnitude of his fictional and historical characters can be measured. It is also integrally related to his role as a critic of the arts, to his lifelong evaluation of Renaissance aesthetics, and to his "amoral" ethical stance: his critical vision refuses to admit absolutes; his concept of virtue is devoid of any considerations of a presupposed knowledge of or force for evil in this life, a stance that accounts largely for the noticeable absence of villains and intentional villainy in his fiction.

1155 Dahl, Curtis. "Pater's *Marius* and Historical Novels on Early Christian Times," NINETEENTH-CENTURY FICTION, XXVIII (June 1973), 1–24.

WP's *Marius the Epicurean* is an historical novel that seems to deal with ancient materials but actually deals with nineteenth-century issues. Both the Victorian age and Antonine Rome were times of religious confusion. *Marius*, stylistically and structurally, is superior to most other historical novels. Three images recur throughout *Marius:* the rose, the heavenly city, and the vistas from Roman houses. But the greatest achievement of *Marius* is the softening of the distinctions between paganism and Christianity.

1156 Dos Passos, John. THE FOURTEENTH CHRONICLE: LETTERS AND DIARIES OF JOHN DOS PASSOS, ed by Townsend Ludington (Bost: Gambit, 1973), pp. 181, 252, 253.

[Brief, ambivalent comments on WP's style, *Marius the Epicurean,* and *Greek Studies* in two letters to Rumsey Marvin. Describes *Marius* as the "sort of rot that is at times beneficial."]

1157 Françon, Marcel. "Pascal et Rousseau chez Walter Pater" (Pascal and Rousseau as Viewed by Walter Pater), ROMANCE NOTES, XIV (1973), 514–16.

In the "Conclusion" to *The Renaissance,* both in its final form and in its original form as the conclusion to "Poems by William Morris," WP makes reference to a statement by Victor Hugo that all men are "condamnés"; later he associates the same statement with Pascal. The statement was apparently drawn from Hugo's LE DERNIER JOUR D'UN CONDAMNÉ and was used in "Pascal" impressionistically to serve WP's own particular ends. WP's reference to Rousseau in the "Conclusion" takes a similar liberty with the substance of the CONFESSIONS. [In French.]

> **1158** Holland, P. H. "Aestheticism as Strategy: An Estimation of the Part Played by Walter Pater and Oscar Wilde in the Formation of a New Literary Consciousness." Unpublished dissertation, University of Manchester, 1973.

[Listed in Lawrence F. McNamee, DISSERTATIONS IN ENGLISH AND AMERICAN LITERATURE, SUPP II (NY & Lond: Bowker, 1974).]

> **1159** Inman, Billie Andrew. "Pater's Appeal to His Readers: A Study of Two of Pater's Prose Styles," TEXAS STUDIES IN LITERATURE AND LANGUAGE, XIV (Winter 1973), 643–65.

The most valuable stylistic studies of WP to date, those of Richard Ohmann, Edmund Chandler, and Zilpha Chandler, all assume a technical uniformity in WP's style which in fact does not exist. Comparison of the "Conclusion" to *The Renaissance* with passages of parallel meaning from the chapter "Animula Vagula" of *Marius the Epicurean* reveals a change in WP's stylistic technique, which suggests in turn a change in his attitude toward his readers. Aside from the distancing effect produced by the fictional context, the restatement of the Epicurean ethic in "Animula Vagula" is marked by an increase in sentence length and complexity and in frequency of syntactic interruption owing to a growing tendency toward qualification, an increase in overall degree of abstraction, and a movement away from engaging the reader rhetorically in the Epicurean argument. The change in style cannot be accounted for by a change in matter, WP advancing in both cases the same skepticism attended by the same hedonism, nor by a change in attitude toward the Epicurean doctrine; for though Marius attains a more "hopeful" skepticism and "enlightened" Epicureanism, this broader humanistic vision was already evident in large measure in "Diaphaneitè," "Coleridge's Writings," and "Winckelmann." Thus, although WP must have recognized the "Conclusion" as representing only one aspect of a larger "vision of truth," he seems purposely to have overemphasized the aesthetic viewpoint in order to enforce it upon the typically earnest Victorian readers of the WESTMINSTER REVIEW, in which it first appeared as the conclusion to "Poems by William Morris." Whatever his reasons for appending it to the collected essays of *The Renaissance,* to which it bears no clear relationship, the adverse reaction it occasioned from the Oxford community and the general public, John Wordsworth's high-minded denunciation of him, Mallock's caricature, and Wilde's embarrassing discipleship caused him, after withdrawing it from the second edition of *The Renaissance,* to begin a lifelong apology for his position, which culminates in "Animula Vagula." In contrast to the

"Conclusion," "Animula Vagula" and *Marius* as a whole appear to be aimed at the scholarly, critical reader whom WP envisioned later in "Style," and its ponderous, highly involuted prose is calculated to reassure that reader of the gravity and intricacy of his ideas. [Includes syntactical and dictional analyses of the passages in question. Draws frequently on Richard Ohmann, "Methods in the Study of Victorian Style," VICTORIAN NEWSLETTER (1965), and Edmund Chandler, PATER ON STYLE (1958), and concludes with several brief recommendations of methods for the further study of WP's style.]

1160 Ludwigson, Kathryn R. EDWARD DOWDEN (NY: Twayne [TEAS, 148], 1973), pp. 46, 51.

Dowden and WP were among those selected to give the Taylorian Lectures at Oxford in 1889. Dowden's essay on WP in ESSAYS MODERN AND ELIZABETHAN (orig pub 1902) is one of the best in the collection.

1161 McMullen, Roy. VICTORIAN OUTSIDER: A BIOGRAPHY OF J. A. M. WHISTLER (NY: Dutton; Toronto & Vancouver: Clarke, Irwin & Co., 1973), pp. 150, 232.

Whistler's likening of all art to music in his "Ten O'Clock" lecture echoes WP.

1162 Paterson, Gary H. "The Religious Thought of Lionel Johnson," ANTIGONISH REVIEW (Antigonish, Nova Scotia), No. 13 (Spring 1973), pp. 95–109.

Johnson praised WP's didacticism in *Marius the Epicurean*. He also shared WP's fondness for the pictorial and sensory aspects of Catholic ritual: it was Pateresque "ritual" that gave Johnson a compass to direct the needs of his own temperament; and though ritual, to the master, meant a system of thought, to the disciple it was a way of life. Johnson was quick to notice WP's *ascesis,* and by combining its discipline with the moral certainties of Newman's faith and Arnold's humanism he sought to give his life some ordering element. Johnson also sought in the realm of literature and his imagination a kind of idealized companionship with Arnold, Newman, WP, and others that he could not find in his own environment.

1163 Quennell, Peter. A HISTORY OF ENGLISH LITERATURE (Springfield, Mass: G. & C. Merriam, 1973), pp. 397–98, 433, 435.

Secluded at Brasenose much of his adult life, WP admired the masculine beauty of the athletes of the college. Jowett thought him possibly subversive, and Oxford as a whole distrusted him. In spite of his taste for Christian ritual, he remained temperamentally a pagan. His hunger for sensuous beauty was probably intensified by "the fact that he was himself an extremely ugly man." *The Renaissance* alarmed many contemporary readers, who felt that WP placed undue emphasis on the pleasure derived from the aesthetic experience; they preferred Ruskin's moral approach to art. In his aesthetic appreciation of the "fantastic" crimes of the Renaissance, WP anticipated Wilde. *The Renaissance* is "often brilliantly perceptive"; *Marius the Epicurean,* though "laborious" and "slow-moving," evidences "a genuine sensibility." While his style now seems "over-elaborate and otiose," WP "throws some gleam of light upon every subject that he touches."

1164 Scotto, Robert M. " 'Visions' and 'Epiphanies': Fictional Technique in Pater's *Marius* and Joyce's PORTRAIT," JAMES JOYCE QUARTERLY, XI:1 (Fall 1973), 41–50.

Joyce's use of the "epiphany" as a fictional technique in A PORTRAIT OF THE ARTIST AS A YOUNG MAN was probably suggested by WP's use of the "vision" in *Marius the Epicurean.* The "visions" of Marius, a further refinement on the moments of heightened aesthetic awareness described in the "Conclusion" to *The Renaissance,* are flashes of insight brought about by apparently inconsequential apprehensions, usually visual, of concrete realities or natural events that lead to a new self-knowledge. Each "vision" marks the completion of a phase of Marius's life and defines a distinct point in the progress of the *bildungsroman.* The most crucial occurs in the chapter "The Will as Vision," in which, during his solitary walk in the Sabine hills, Marius becomes aware that the active inquiry into the nature of things he has pursued thus far cannot provide full self-realization and that he must surrender to forces beyond himself. His sensibility thus broadened, and conscious as he is now of a certain insufficiency in the most fondly remembered moments of his past, of their inability to answer to man's "capacity for suffering" as he considers it in the chapter "Sunt Lacrimae Rerum," Marius is prepared to yield to the "power of sympathy" he recognizes in Christianity. Numerous critics have noted the influence of WP on Joyce's prose style; Scholes and Kain in THE WORKSHOP OF DEDALUS (1965) suggest that the influence was more than superficial by illustrating how Joyce's definition of "epiphany" was borrowed in part from *The Renaissance.* Many of the early "epiphanies" collected in THE WORKSHOP, the "gestures," "dreams," and "phases of mind," are distinctly Paterian in style and strive to achieve the same aesthetic distance between himself and the events of his own life as presented in *Marius.* Stephen's "epiphanies" in PORTRAIT, like Marius's "visions," are instances of sight leading to insight, and further, in some cases, to a sudden awareness of "tears in things." Stephen's profound shock at seeing the word *foetus* carved on a classroom desk recalls the "vision" of physical evil that comes to Marius as he approaches Rome. Like Marius, Stephen is drawn to religion by its sensuous appeal, but too proud finally to submit to Christian servitude, he goes "beyond" Marius to become a "high priest of art." Stephen's final "epiphany," occasioned by the sight of the girl on the beach, marks "the seminal moment of his life," the beginning of his career as an artist, and recalls in its "absolute assurance of insight" Marius's own great "vision" and the dawning moment of his own aesthetic career as it occurred on the road to Rome.

1165 Stanford, Derek. "Introduction," "Biographical and Critical Notes" ("Gabriel Charles Dante Rossetti" and "Robert Baldwin Ross"), PRE-RAPHAELITE WRITING: AN ANTHOLOGY, ed by Derek Stanford

(Lond: Dent; Totowa, NJ: Rowman & Littlefield, 1973), pp. xxiv, xxv, xxvii; 200, 201; respectively.

The overall success of the Pre-Raphaelite movement was due in part to the critical support of Ruskin, WP, Wilde, and Arthur Symons. The "definiteness of sensible imagery" that WP found in the poetry of D. G. Rossetti is one of the primary characteristics of Pre-Raphaelite poetry generally. Pre-Raphaelitism helped foster the development of the visual sensibility in such writers on art as WP and Symons. Robert Ross's essays on Swinburne and WP in MASQUES AND PHASES (1909) show the lack of respect of a "second generation Aesthete" for the great literary figures of the Sixties and Seventies.

1166 Uglow, Jennifer. "Introduction" and "Notes," WALTER PATER: ESSAYS ON LITERATURE AND ART, ed by Jennifer Uglow (Lond: Dent; Totowa, NJ: Rowman & Littlefield, 1973), pp. vii–xxiii, 147–53.

Though WP's early essays shocked the more traditional Oxford academics, the aesthetic movement, with which he was associated, belonged itself to a distinct Oxford tradition; like Arnold and Newman before him, WP looked to the broad European, and Catholic, past as a guide to establishing an ideal of refined temperament and perfected culture. WP's aesthetic theories are fully in line with the later Romanticism of Ruskin and the Pre-Raphaelites; but they also echo the anti-rationalism of the earlier English Romantics and reveal the influence as well of the French Romantics, with their sense of the bizarre and their concern for precision of style, and of the German Hellenists, with their grand ideal of harmony. Rejecting in "Coleridge" the limitations imposed on experience by idealism, he insisted on direct, personal observation as the first step toward attaining an Arnoldian perfection through culture. In the "Conclusion" to *The Renaissance* he is concerned with intense perception as a means, more particularly, of rescuing from the flux of experience the consciousness of a unified self, comparable to the larger Hegelian concept of the "Geist." Although WP later recognized the danger in his advocacy of living intensely for the sake of the moment, he was never really an adherent of an amoral, Swinburnean art for art's sake but always remained aware of the relationship of art to life. In "Winckelmann" WP follows Arnold in stressing the need for fostering an Hellenic desire of beauty, moral disinterested-ness, and clarity of mind as a counterbalance to a soul-numbing Hebraism; but while Arnold's aim was largely social, WP was concerned at this point solely with the edification of the individual. Furthermore, WP's Hellenism is less serene and, with its admixture of romanticism, more complex than Arnold's and arises rather from the careful apprehension of concrete experience than from the operation of the intellect. WP's view of history is related to his view that art gives continuity to the flow of experience. A basically dialectical view deriving variously from Darwin, Hegel, Heraclitus, and Comte, it allows him to discover traces of "the modern spirit" in earlier historical periods and in their art. The energies of art, as WP describes them in "The School of Giorgione," are based again in dialectic: the dialectic between reality and the subjective vision and between artistic matter and the formal exigencies of the particular medium. In "Giorgione" WP makes his highest claim for the ability of art to transcend time by arresting the significant moment while at the same time implying the force of the flux before and after. WP saw the struggle between the opposing principles of motion and rest as basic to the human condition. The striving for balance is central to his conception of good literary style, which he sees as the result of an exact correspondence between the writer's "sense of fact" and the manner of its expression. Ever aware of the struggle involved in the creative process, WP advanced a theory of art much more strenuous than that of the languid aesthetes with whom he is often identified. In the closing paragraph of "Style," WP's maintaining that greatness in art is dependent finally on a broad human significance of subject matter is not really inconsistent with the rest of his aesthetic theory, his concern here being merely the allying of the same extreme care of expression with a higher artistic vision. WP's critical method from the "Preface" to *The Renaissance* to *Plato and Platonism* is based on the rejection of absolute standards and the viewing of the art work in relationship to the age and the personality which produced it. In "Joachim du Bellay" he identifies the innate virtues of du Bellay's poetry as well as considering it in relationship to its own temporal milieu and to the poetry of the nineteenth century. In contrast, "Aesthetic Poetry" looks backward to the past from the vantage point of WP's own century; the essay is somewhat extravagant in its language, and this and its anti-Christian bias probably led to WP's dropping it eventually from *Appreciations*. In "Wordsworth" he is concerned more specifically with defining the "essence" of the poet's genius, the achievement of the sense of unity through "impassioned contemplation." "Measure for Measure" again stresses the quest for unity, here the dramatic unity of patterned human activity. While "Measure for Measure" demonstrates well the viability of WP's critical method, its weakness is revealed in "Charles Lamb," where WP's close identification with his subject destroys his critical detachment. WP was more careful, because more timid and polite, in his approach to his contemporaries: his review of ROBERT ELSMERE seems to reflect his own religious doubt and skepticism; in his review of THE PICTURE OF DORIAN GRAY he was intent on disassociating himself from Wilde's brand of Epicureanism. Though his criticism does not always display a strict adherence to the critical precepts of the "Preface," WP nevertheless remains true to his aesthetic theory. He is guided constantly by his ideal of education through culture and ever preoccupied with the need of achieving harmony through the reconciling of opposites. The final strength of his criticism lies not in any force of judgment but in its supple suggestiveness.

1167 Weiss, Winfried F. "Ruskin, Pater, and Hofmannsthal," COL-LOQUIA GERMANICA, INTERNATIONALE ZEITSCHRIFT FÜR GERMANISCHE SPRACH UND LITERATURWISSENSCHAFT, VII (1973), 162–70.
Hugo von Hofmannsthal found much of his philosophy expressed in the works of Ruskin and WP. He borrowed directly from WP. His "elaboration on the Pre-Raphaelites' symbolic representation of Psyche is essentially a rephrasing of

Walter Pater's description of the Mona Lisa." From WP's essay on Rossetti, Hofmannsthal borrowed the theory that Dante's imagery reveals the influence of contemporary artists. In his discussion of Rossetti, Hofmannsthal transfers WP's observations in his own essay on Rossetti's poetry to Rossetti's paintings. In a letter dated 6 Aug 1894, Hofmannsthal alludes to WP's comment on music and the arts in "The School of Giorgione." But Hofmannsthal's mind was not as analytical as WP's. Hofmannsthal also borrowed from WP's "Giorgione" essay for his Shakespeare essay.

> **1168** Wollheim, Richard. "Walter Pater as a Critic of the Arts," in On
> ART AND THE MIND: ESSAYS AND LECTURES (Lond: Allen Lane, 1973),
> pp. [155]–76.

It is wrong to think of WP as a " 'low-spirited hedonist.' " His writings on art fall into two broad categories: the critical and the theoretical. WP reveals a sense of the futility of metaphysical speculation. He never abandoned what he called " 'the wholesome scepticism of Hume and Mill.' " Solipsism is for WP "primarily an attack upon the common-sense view of the world, according to which the world consists in solid objects, impenetrable and enduring." And WP advocates that criticism should concentrate on surface qualities—but not on surface qualities *as such*. He suggests instead that criticism should concentrate on surface qualities as "expressive." [Essay contains an analysis of "A Prince of Court Painters" as an example of WP's finest "criticism."]

Index

AUTHORS

Included here are authors of articles and books on Pater, editors and compilers of works in which criticism on Pater appears. Editors and translators are identified parenthetically: (ed), (trans). Numbers after each name refer to the item(s) in the bibliography where the name occurs.

Index

TITLES OF SECONDARY WORKS

Titles of articles in periodicals and chapters in books are in quotation marks; book titles are in upper case; translations of article titles originally appearing in a foreign language are in parentheses, without quotation marks, and in lower case; translations of book titles originally appearing in a foreign language are in parentheses and in upper case. Numbers after each title refer to the item(s) in the bibliography where the title appears.

Index

PERIODICALS AND NEWSPAPERS

Included here are periodicals and newspapers for which entries occur in the bibliography. Numbers after each title refer to the number(s) of the item in the bibliography where the title appears.

Index

FOREIGN LANGUAGES

Included here are the languages in which articles and books listed in the bibliography originally appeared. Numbers under each language refer to items in the bibliography where the foreign-language title is given. English language items are not listed.

Index

PRIMARY TITLES

Included here are all titles by Pater which occur in titles of articles or books or in the abstracts. Numbers after each title refer to the item(s) in the bibliography where the title appears.

The Annotated Secondary Bibliography Series on English Literature in Transition 1880–1920 *was designed by John B. Goetz of Chicago, Illinois. This volume was typeset by Weimer Typesetting Co. of Indianapolis, Indiana. The text is set in Times Roman; the display face is Perpetua. The book was printed by Kingsport Press of Kingsport, Tennessee, on Warren #50 Olde Style wove paper.*